"Spellbinding in a revolting yet masterful way."

Chip Berlet, *co-author of Right-Wing Populism in America:*
Too Close for Comfort

"Spencer Sunshine's new book *Neo-Nazi Terrorism and Countercultural Fascism* is a tour de force for understanding America's contemporary white supremacist and neo-Nazi movements. It teases out the largely unexplored history of this movement's last 50 years, and provides the definitive account of how James Mason's *Siege* became the leading tome for today's far right extremists. The book is filled with details from the movement's major and minor players, much of which has never been documented. This is a must read for those who want to understand our country's history of white supremacy and the nature of the movement today."

Heidi Beirich, *co-founder, Global Project Against*
Hate and Extremism

"Sunshine has written the definitive book that exposes and links the old guard of American neo-Nazism to the modern day (and beyond) wave of white-power terrorism. A fascinating read!"

Christian Picciolini, *author of White American Youth:*
My Descent Into America's Most Violent Hate
Movement—and How I Got Out

"It is rare to find a study that combines grassroots anti-fascist research with the tools of scholarly analysis. Spencer Sunshine's detailed and discerning book examines neo-Nazism as a social movement and takes seemingly obscure ideas seriously, bringing critical attention to the history of counter-cultural crossover with the radical right. Anybody concerned with the incongruous resurgence of supposedly fringe political phenomena will learn sobering lessons from this book."

Peter Staudenmaier, *Marquette University, USA*

"The deepest dive yet into the godfather of modern neo-Nazi terrorism, told through the rare lens of James Mason's own writings. This book is essential reading to those hoping to understand the origins and nuances of violent right-wing extremism today."

Jared Holt, *Senior Research Analyst, Institute for*
Strategic Dialogue

NEO-NAZI TERRORISM AND COUNTERCULTURAL FASCISM

A new wave of aspiring neo-Nazi terrorists has arisen—including the infamous Atomwaffen Division. And they have a bible: James Mason's *Siege*, which praises terrorism, serial killers, and Charles Manson. *Neo-Nazi Terrorism and Countercultural Fascism*, based on years of archival work and interviews, documents for the first time the origins of *Siege*.

First, it shows how Mason's vision arose from debates by 1970s neo-Nazis who splintered off the American Nazi Party/National Socialist White People's Party and spun off a terrorist faction. Second, it unveils how four 1980s countercultural figures—musicians Boyd Rice and Michael Moynihan, Feral House publisher Adam Parfrey, and Satanist Nikolas Schreck—discovered, promoted, and published Mason. *Neo-Nazi Terrorism and Countercultural Fascism* explores a previously overlooked period and unearths the hidden connections between a countercultural clique and violent neo-Nazis—which together have set the template for today's Neo-Nazi terrorist underground.

It is obligatory reading for those interested in contemporary terrorism, postwar countercultures, and the history of the U.S. Far Right and neo-Nazism.

Spencer Sunshine holds a PhD in Sociology and has written extensively on the U.S. Far Right. He is the co-editor—with Pam Chamberlain, Matthew N. Lyons, and Abby Scher—of the Chip Berlet festschrift *Exposing the Right and Fighting for Democracy* (Routledge, 2022). Sunshine has also written for the Southern Poverty Law Center, *Daily Beast*, *The Forward*, and *Truthout* and has been translated into numerous languages.

Routledge Studies in Fascism and the Far Right

Series editors: Nigel Copsey, *Teesside University, UK* and Graham Macklin, *Center for Research on Extremism (C-REX), University of Oslo, Norway*

This book series focuses upon national, transnational and global manifestations of fascist, far right and right-wing politics primarily within a historical context but also drawing on insights and approaches from other disciplinary perspectives. Its scope also includes anti-fascism, radical-right populism, extreme-right violence and terrorism, cultural manifestations of the far right, and points of convergence and exchange with the mainstream and traditional right.

Fascist Italy in the Age of Corporatism
Searching for a Third Way
Alessio Gagliardi

Christian Nationalism and Anticommunism in Twentieth-Century South Africa
Ruhan Fourie

Far-Right Newspeak and the Future of Liberal Democracy
Edited by A. James McAdams and Samuel Piccolo

Neo-Nazi Terrorism and Countercultural Fascism
The Origins and Afterlife of James Mason's *Siege*
Spencer Sunshine

For more information about this series, please visit: www.routledge.com/Routledge-Studies-in-Fascism-and-the-Far-Right/book-series/FFR

NEO-NAZI TERRORISM AND COUNTERCULTURAL FASCISM

The Origins and Afterlife of James Mason's *Siege*

Spencer Sunshine

Routledge
Taylor & Francis Group

LONDON AND NEW YORK

First published 2024
by Routledge
4 Park Square, Milton Park, Abingdon, Oxon OX14 4RN

and by Routledge
605 Third Avenue, New York, NY 10158

Routledge is an imprint of the Taylor & Francis Group, an informa business

British Library Cataloguing-in-Publication Data
A catalogue record for this book is available from the British Library

Library of Congress Cataloging-in-Publication Data
Names: Sunshine, Spencer, author.
Title: Neo-nazi terrorism and countercultural fascism : the origins and afterlife of James Mason's siege / Spencer Sunshine.
Description: Abingdon, Oxon ; New York, NY : Routledge, 2024. | Series: Routledge studies in fascism and the far right | Includes bibliographical references and index.
Identifiers: LCCN 2023055849 (print) | LCCN 2023055850 (ebook) | ISBN 9780367190552 (hardback) | ISBN 9780367190606 (paperback) | ISBN 9780429200090 (ebook)
Subjects: LCSH: Mason, James, 1952---Influence. | Fascism--United States. | Neo-Nazism--United States--History. | Right-wing extremists--United States. | Political culture--United States. | Counterculture--United States.
Classification: LCC JC481 .S84 2024 (print) | LCC JC481 (ebook) | DDC 320.53/30973--dc23/eng/20240207
LC record available at https://lccn.loc.gov/2023055849
LC ebook record available at https://lccn.loc.gov/2023055850

ISBN: 978-0-367-19055-2 (hbk)
ISBN: 978-0-367-19060-6 (pbk)
ISBN: 978-0-429-20009-0 (ebk)

DOI: 10.4324/9780429200090

Typeset in Sabon
by SPi Technologies India Pvt Ltd (Straive)

To Kevin Coogan and Heather Heyer

CONTENTS

THANK YOU!

Innumerable people have helped me with this book during the over six plus years it took to write and edit it. Special thanks are in order to several of them. Craig Fowlie at Routledge acted as a true antifascist godfather in helping this project move to fruition, while Graham Macklin aided my investigations in many different ways. Joshua Fisher-Birch fielded innumerable inquiries and allowed me to have someone to gab with about James Mason minutiae. Peter Staudenmaier acted as my NSDAP guru; George Matiasz was endlessly supportive; Casandra Johns designed the book's charts; and the late Kevin Coogan helped me get the whole project off the ground. I would also like to thank all of my Patreon supporters, without whom this would not have been possible. And, of course, my parents, who supported me in this project even though I'm pretty sure they didn't understand why it was something worth obsessing over for so many years.

Many others deserve thanks as well, including Heidi Beirich, Chip Berlet, Karl B., Ana Bochicchio, Shane Burley, Ailed Cold, Anatole Dolgoff, Morgan Feralchilde, Jessica Fink, Andy Fleming, Leva Francisco, Brian Jackson, Joe Keady, Ernie Lazar (RIP), Shannon Foley Martinez, Julianna Neuhouser, Travis McAdams, Ben Meyers, NBD, Sylvia Nowak, MH, Rodney O, Angela P, Christian Picciolini, Betsy Pisik, the heretics of Queer Satanic, Julie Ruben, Christine Sarteschi, Tiffany Satan, Ryan Smith, Ken Stern, A.C. Thompson, Hardcore Tom, Alex Weiser and the staff at YIVO, Kristian Williams, Ali Winston, Kenyon Zimmer, and K. and S. for housing help. I really appreciate what everyone did for me.

For their help with fact-checking, I would like to thank the Bible Advocate, Buzz McCoy, Bobby BeauSoleil, William Harder, Lt. John Hill, Jesper Aagaard Petersen, Mark Pitcavage, and Laura Whitehorn.

Many archivists assisted in this project as well. The staff at the Kenneth Spencer Research Library at the University of Kansas in Lawrence, where the James Mason papers are housed, were invaluable; I would like to thank Becky Schulte and Kathy Lafferty in particular. Thanks are also due to Julie Herrada at the Labadie Collection at the University of Ann Arbor, Michigan; Deborah Schranz at the Jewish Theological Seminary Library in New York City; legions of librarians at the New York Public Library and Portland, Oregon's Multnomah County Library; and especially the comrades at the IWW Materials Preservation Project.

Many people graciously did interviews about events now receding into a distant past. I would especially like to thank James Mason for answering a battery of 50 questions. The numerous letters David Rust and I exchanged are of special note, as are the thoughts and research that Martin Kerr shared. Brian King not only agreed to talk about the interviews he did but went above and beyond by sharing previously unreleased footage. Karl Hand, Jeff Schoep, Gerhard Lauck, Shane Bugbee, Lucien Greaves, Luma from the United Front Against Fascism, Carl Raschke, Leigh Kendall, and Joseph A. Gervasi graciously found time to speak with me. And while Clifford Herrington refused to be interviewed without monetary compensation, he was willing to answer one question.

Jello Biafra and Michael A. Hoffman II declined to be interviewed. Attempts to contact Boyd Rice, Michael Moynihan, Greg Johnson, Peter Gilmore and the Church of Satan, and Mute Records were unsuccessful.

PREFACE

Books have often been compared to babies. Part of this is because some are planned and others accidents. This one is definitely the latter. Its origins are in what was to be an article I started in early 2018 for a think tank where I was a Fellow at the time. James Mason's *Siege* was being talked about a lot by Far Right monitors and journalists but little read. My plan was to write an overview of the book along with a backgrounder documenting Mason's political history, but the details of the few existing secondary sources wouldn't add up. Since I was missing a handful of primary texts that I thought would easily clear this up, I went to look at Mason's papers at the Kenneth Spencer Research Library, housed at the University of Kansas in Lawrence.

Once there, I found that Mason had apparently saved almost every letter, including copies of his outgoing ones, during his many decades in neo-Nazi circles. It was a unique window into the lives and internal politics of twentieth-century neo-Nazis in the United States. Reading the correspondence, I had hooked the proverbial whale. I realized my details hadn't added up because the secondary sources were often inaccurate. But it was his later period, when he worked with a group of (in)famous counterculturalists, that really fascinated me. I immediately grasped the importance of both of them.

And so one article became two and then, as soon as I sat down to write them, obviously a book. What I hadn't realized was that it would take over five years to write it. (My academic training as a sociologist, and not a historian, did nothing to help this.) During this time, the initial moment that inspired it—the rise of White Supremacist violence under the Far Right presidency of Donald Trump—soon passed. The Atomwaffen Division, the notorious Mason-inspired neo-Nazi group that advocated terrorism and spurred the revival of interest in *Siege*, disbanded. This was followed by the Trump administration itself leaving the stage of history, Joseph Biden taking power, and then continuing into their 2024 campaigns. Nonetheless—and happily for me, although not the world at large—*Siege* became the canon for budding racist terrorists, and it doesn't seem to be anywhere near the end of its popularity.

On a personal level, one of the most fascinating things was how much my own life was intertwined with this book. In 1978, neo-Nazi sniper Joseph Paul Franklin had attempted to assassinate *Hustler* publisher Larry Flynt outside the courthouse in my hometown, Lawrenceville, Georgia, about a mile from my house. Franklin wasn't publicly acknowledged as the shooter until later, so I grew up hearing much speculation about who did it, the general consensus settling on a Christian fundamentalist. In fact, my father played a bit role in the drama, helping deal with the media that swarmed the local hospital that Flynt was initially taken to. He has told me many times about how much he liked Flynt's wife, Althea.

In fact, Lawrenceville's picturesque courthouse was a favorite location for Klan rallies, some of which I witnessed when I was young. And the leaders of the National States Rights Party, a White Supremacist party that Mason considered a rival, lived close to where I spent my teenage years.

I also had a family connection that ran parallel with Mason's friend Ed Reynolds; an aunt taught in the same public school system where he got his start as a high school racist organizer. It's certainly in the realm of possibility that she had been his teacher.

Of greater impact was being in high school in 1988, the year of the Nazi skinhead explosion, which Mason embraced. One could not participate in the Georgia punk scene and not be exposed to their constant presence. And anyone familiar with the movement wouldn't fail to recognize its most prominent ideological leader, Tom Metzger—one of Mason's closest allies.

But I had an even more concrete connection to the second half. I was directly involved in both the publishing and music circles where the Abraxas Clique was based, which was also where they spread Mason's works. (The Abraxas Clique was a name given to four countercultural musicians and publishers: Boyd Rice, Adam Parfrey, Nikolas Schreck, and Michael Moynihan.) When *Siege* came out in 1993, it piggybacked on a revival of interest in Charles Manson—a trend I was intimately aware of as my girlfriend at the time partook in this morbid obsession. I was also a fan of industrial and neofolk music, and around 1996, I saw Boyd Rice and the Electric Hellfire Club play in Albuquerque. I thought it was an odd pairing, although now I understand the bill. I even remember a big Latino guy going up to Rice afterward and ask him, "I heard you were a Nazi?!" Rice weaselly denied everything.

Later, I lived in Portland, Oregon in the late 1990s at the same time as Michael Moynihan and Adam Parfrey; the former even spoke at my friend's fanzine store. In the course of my research, I was disappointed to find that the initial edition of *Siege* had been carried by a small book distro there, run by another friend. As I was finishing this book, I had lunch in Portland with some old friends, and they brought another writer along; it turned out she had been Parfrey's cat sitter. And she was only one of numerous people that Parfrey and I knew in common. Most, like her, had harmonious relationships, but not all; Parfrey once disrupted the talk of a fellow writer who covered the Far Right. As I was finishing this book, I found out that a former member of Moynihan's band Blood Axis was staying at a collective house another friend lived in. And I also found I had a number of mutual acquaintances with Third Position fascist Gary/John Jewell, dating from his days when he was still an IWW member. The walls between this crowd and mine where not just paper thin; the truth is, we were all in the same room together—sometimes quite literally.

Of course, Parfrey's Amok Press and Feral House books were always around my social circles; even now, I have a few of the less-odious Feral House titles on my shelf. I was not a fan of Parfrey's *Apocalypse Culture* anthology (the Nazi stuff was too reactionary for those of us who had seen the real thing in the wild), but I loved the RE/Search books. I bought a second-hand copy of the first book Parfrey published, the novel *Michael* by Nazi minister Paul Joseph Goebbels—something I distinctly remember because it sparked a discussion with a friend who was a guide at a former concentration camp. (I asked if it was legal to bring the book into Germany. She said technically it wasn't, but because of her job she could get a special exemption.)

However, mere book ownership did not stop me from crossing swords, at least digitally, with some of these figures. The most memorable incident was when Parfrey and James Porrazzo, a former Nazi skinhead leader and *Siege* fan, went to town on an article of mine that called on left-leaning projects to kick out white separatists, antisemites, and the like. Obviously, this would have included them, as they both sought out the Left as an audience and recruitment pool. I saved the screenshots.

Readers will notice a change in the different halves of the book. Whereas the first is more of a straight-up history and analysis of U.S. neo-Nazism in the 1970s, in tune with many academic histories of radical movements, the second contains much more of a more critical assessment regarding these figures' associations with the first—a relationship which they always tried to obscure.

I had continual doubts while writing this book. As the Far Right roiled in the United States, I was looking at the past, even if the goal was to help understand the present. Concurrent with this, I withdrew from direct activism, although I still tried to get things done, including writing the occasional article about the Far Right's twists and turns.

Written outside of the academy, this book comes from an antifascist perspective, in the sense that its goal is to seek to document the ideology, actions, and networks of the neo-Nazi milieu. Intent aside, I have tried hard to make it as objective as possible. From my viewpoint, accurate knowledge of the structure and ideas of this movement is crucial to antifascist work, and leftist propaganda and ideologically loaded readings are only harmful. (That does not mean I omitted analysis about the events I documented, however.)

Some of the individuals in the book died while I was writing this—including Parfrey, Manson, and Metzger. But those who are still living need to be held accountable for their actions, which they have almost all attempted to obfuscate and obscure.

I would like to be forthright about the problems with this book, as I see them. Although it hopes to correct past errors in scholarship, it too will have some, regardless of how attentive I have been and no matter how much it pains me. Some of the chapters are uneven, especially in terms of the time period covered. The research was based primarily on Mason's correspondence and periodicals held at the Spencer Research Library. I did my best to supplement those holdings with documents from other archives, secondary sources, documentaries, and interviews with a number of current and former neo-Nazis as well as those who interacted with them. Nonetheless, as a rule, this work follows the narrative arch that Mason set and generally remains within the limitations of the material from the archive.

From my view, the following avenues call out for more investigation. In terms of specific details, how were Mason's actions viewed by his friend-turned-enemy George Dietz as well as Matthias Koehl, Mason's former leader in the National Socialist White People's Party (NSWPP)? The role of Nick Bougas in both White Supremacist and countercultural circles needs more eyes on it. Regarding the Abraxas Clique, what's documented is obviously only a slice of their interactions with White Supremacists, although I am dubious that more information will come out, especially from the living members. If a biography of Parfrey is completed, perhaps it—and/or his papers, if made available—will have content of interest.

There are many more general topics that can profitably be expanded upon. First and foremost is the role of misogyny in these connections. Its importance to the Abraxas Clique was of obvious importance and directly or indirectly was an influence on the Alt Right and related contemporary movements like MRAs (men's rights activists) and incels (involuntary celibates). The use of eugenics, particularly because it is a discredited science, was also important as a glue for the countercultural fascists and is generally ignored in the analysis of contemporary White Supremacists. The role of Gnosticism in both Manson's ideas and how Mason incorporated them into the idea of the Universal Order, as well as the more general interest in this spiritual tradition by the Abraxas Clique, raises questions. And the political function of heterosexual fascist men sharing extreme pornography is a rich avenue for exploration.

Additionally, far more work needs to be done on the connections between modern Satanism and neo-Nazism. Mason's later spiritual beliefs may deserve a closer look, although their interest is probably limited to scholars studying the intersection between White Supremacists and Christianity and/or UFOs. Gary/John Jewell's influence should be investigated, as he took his impeccable leftist pedigree and turned it around to influence both British and U.S. Third Positionists. And *Siege*'s relationship to *The Turner Diaries* deserves a close look; it was first serialized in William Pierce's paper, which Mason was reading at the same time he created his core arguments. I will do my best to make myself, and the research materials I have collected, available to serious scholars who wish to pursue these areas.

Last, a note on the book's dedications. Parts of the second half of the book are a direct continuation of Kevin Coogan's essay "How 'Black' is Black Metal?," while the book as a whole continues the approach of his 1999 opus *Dreamer of the Day: Francis Parker Yockey and the Postwar Fascist International*. Kevin and I would go to political talks together in New York City. I had long admired his work, and it was particularly meaningful to me when we saw the *Lords of Chaos* film together. (Neither of us liked it.) As this project slogged on, I did take some comfort in the fact that he spent ten years working on *Dreamer of the Day*. Kevin was also very generous with his research, and one afternoon we sat down in Queens for several hours and went over the documents he had collected for the black metal essay, which I have used for this book. (For some reason, one thing that sticks out in my mind from that conversation was his contempt for Satanists, even though I disagreed with him on this.) His death in 2020 especially pained me, and I thought about him often as I worked on the book.

The other dedication is to Heather Heyer. Although she was not the first person killed by the Alt Right, her murder at the 2017 fascist-led "Unite the Right" rally in Charlottesville, Virginia was certainly most dramatic. A martyr in every sense of the word, Heyer's death was not in vain; outrage over it halted the advance of the Alt Right, thereby saving the lives of numerous others. I was down the block from her during the car attack, and only by raw chance was standing on the sidewalk and not the street. So, although I never met her, her death has also affected me greatly. As I wrote this book, sometimes I would find myself sympathizing with the characters; after all, they were just other humans, going through life and experiencing its successes, annoyances, and failures. Remembering her would always bring me back to why I was doing this.

May their memories be for a blessing.

GUIDE TO ORGANIZATIONS AND PEOPLE

Organizational Acronyms

ANP. American Nazi Party
Founded 1959 by George Lincoln Rockwell, he changed its name in 1967 to the National Socialist White People's Party (NSWPP). The American Nazi Party had small numbers but garnered significant media attention. Introduced to the postwar United States the idea of a public, organized neo-Nazi political current.

KKKK. Knights of the Ku Klux Klan
Founded by David Duke in 1973 after leaving the orbit of the NSWPP. Its media-friendly approach attracted significant attention. Included a number of former American Nazi Party/NSWPP members.

NSDAP. Nationalsozialistische Deutsche Arbeiterpartei (National Socialist German Workers' Party)
Founded in 1919, the German Workers Party attracted Adolf Hitler as a recruit. He became the party's leader in 1921 and changed its name to the National Socialist German Workers' Party (NSDAP). The party was dissolved in 1945 after its defeat in World War Two. Since then, numerous groups have claimed to be its continuation.

NSLF. National Socialist Liberation Front (student group)
The student group of the NSWPP from 1969 to 1970. Started by William Pierce and aimed at college students, its most famous member was David Duke.

NSLF. National Socialist Liberation Front
Founded 1974 as a split from the NSWPP, the NSLF adopted countercultural norms and advocated guerilla warfare. Initially based in El Monte, California, it went through four leaders: Joseph Tommasi, David Rust, John Duffy, and Karl Hand. James Mason was a member from 1976 to 1982. The group folded in 1986.

NSM. National Socialist Movement
Southern Ohio–based group founded 1975 by current and former NSWPP members James Mason, Greg Hurles, and Robert Brannen. Led first by Brannen, then Clifford Herrington and Jeff Schoep. In 2019, Burt Colucci became its fourth leader.

NSPA. National Socialist Party of America
Chicago group founded 1970 as a split from the NSWPP. Initially led by Frank Collin, the NSPA led mass pro-segregation marches in Marquette Park. Rose to national attention because of their lawsuit to allow them to march in the heavily Jewish suburb of Skokie, Illinois. Collin was replaced by Harold Covington and then Michael Allen.

NSRP. National States Rights Party
The NSRP was founded in 1958 by J.B. Stoner and Ed Fields in Georgia. It acted as a kind of rival and foil to the smaller American Nazi Party/NSWPP. The NSRP did not openly use Nazi imagery and was close to the Klan. By the 1980s, it had fallen apart.

NSWPP. National Socialist White People's Party
In 1967, the American Nazi Party changed its name to the NSWPP, just before George Lincoln Rockwell's assassination. Unhappiness with the new leader, Matthias Koehl, led to many splinter groups, especially in 1973 and 1974. In 1983, the NSWPP became the New Order. (Some other, unaffiliated groups also used the NSWPP name.)

NSWWP. National Socialist White Workers' Party
Allen Vincent founded this group in California 1975 after splitting from the NSWPP, and it was briefly a national party. James Mason was a member and the editor of two party periodicals between 1978 and 1980.

NSYM. National Socialist Youth Movement
The youth group of the American Nazi Party. Led by Allen Vincent. James Mason joined the group at age 14.

UWPP. United White People's Party
Cleveland group founded 1974 as a split from the NSWPP and led by Casey Kalemba.

WAR. White Aryan Resistance
In 1983, this became the name of Tom Metzger's organization; previously, it had been the White American Political Association and then White American Resistance.

Selected Individuals

Nick Bougas. White Supremacist artist who published in Tom Metzger's *WAR* newspaper. An associate of Adam Parfrey, he made documentaries about Anton LaVey and Charles Manson.

Robert Brannen. NSWPP supporter, NSM founder and chairman from 1975 to 1983. Died in 2004.

Joshua Buckley. Nazi skinhead and associate of Michael Moynihan, his co-editor at *TYR*.

Willis Carto. Gained a mainstream audience for White Supremacist and National Socialist ideas by disguising them as right-wing populism. Founder of the Liberty Lobby, *The Spotlight* newspaper, and the pseudo-academic organization The Institute for Historical Review, which popularized Holocaust denial in the United States. Associate of Keith Stimely. Died in 2015.

Raymond Chaney. Louisville NSLF leader.

Frank Collin. NSWPP member who founded the National Socialist Party of America (NSPA) in 1970. Central figure in the National Socialist Congress and the Skokie lawsuit. Deposed as NSPA leader in 1980 after a scandal involving underage boys.

Harold Covington. NSWPP member. In 1974, he formed the National Socialist Party of North Carolina (NSPNC), which fused with the NSPA. He became its leader in 1980, the same year he won 40 percent in the primary for North Carolina attorney general. A life-long White Supremacist activist, he led the Northwest Front until his death in 2018.

Fred Cowan. Perpetrator of the first U.S. neo-Nazi mass murder in 1977. Killed six at his job in New Rochelle, New York before committing suicide.

John Cameron Denton. One-time leader of the Atomwaffen Division. Associate of Mason who republished his works, including the fourth edition of *Siege*. Sentenced to over three years in prison in 2021.

George Dietz. Hitler Youth member who later moved to the United States and founded Liberty Bell Publications. Funded the Mason-edited *National Socialist* in 1976 before feuding with him in the "Dietz Affair." Died in 2007.

John Duffy. Third NSLF leader, from 1977 to 1981, which included its underground period.

David Duke. Member of the original NSLF, the NSWPP student organization, and its successor groups. In the mid-1970s, achieved fame as the leader of the media-friendly KKKK. Elected Louisiana state representative in 1989.

Eva. Mason's teenage girlfriend in early 1994. After their break-up, Mason was arrested for threatening her and her new boyfriend.

Larry Flynt. Publisher of the sexually explicit magazine *Hustler* and free speech advocate. Shot and paralyzed by Joseph Paul Franklin while on trial for obscenity in 1978. Died in 2021.

Joseph Paul Franklin. NSWPP member. Between 1977 and 1980, killed up to 22 people, including black men and mixed-race couples. Shot and wounded *Hustler* publisher Larry Flynt in 1978 and civil rights activist Vernon Jordan in 1980. Executed in 2013.

Lynette "Squeaky" Fromme. Manson Family member, also known as "Red." Arrested in 1975 for attempting to assassinate President Gerald Ford. In 1980, she was contacted by James Mason, whom she helped introduce to Charles Manson.

Aaron Garland. Editor of the pro-fascist *Ohm Clock* music fanzine; played with Blood Axis.

Peter Gilmore. Editor of the Church of Satan's *Black Flame* and the group's leader since 2001. Welcomed neo-Nazis into the Church and helped promote *Siege*.

Sandra Good. Manson Family member whom James Mason contacted in 1980. Also known as "Blue," she helped introduce him to Charles Manson.

William Grimstad. NSWPP and KKKK member. Author of *The Six Million Reconsidered* and associate of Adam Parfrey.

Karl Hand. NSWPP, KKKK, and NSPA member. Led the NSLF from 1981 until his arrest for attempted murder in 1986.

Bob Heick. Founder of the American Front, the first national racist skinhead gang in the United States. Associate of Boyd Rice, Tom Metzger, and James Mason.

Clifford D. (C.D.) Herrington. NSWPP member, Local Group Rockwell leader, and the second NSM chairman from 1983 to 1994.

John Hinckley, Jr. Attempted to assassinate President Ronald Reagan in 1981. Afterward was falsely accused of being a neo-Nazi.

Greg Hurles. NSWPP and NSLF member and co-founder of the NSM. Long-time collaborator of James Mason in Chillicothe, Ohio.

Gary/John Jewell. Member of the General Executive Board of the radical labor union IWW (Industrial Workers of the World) in the 1970s. Later a Third Position fascist and *White Aryan Resistance* writer.

Casey Kalemba. NSWPP member, founded the Cleveland splinter group United White People's Party.

Martin Kerr. Briefly a member of the American Nazi Party in 1966; from 1969 to 1971, he was in the National Renaissance Party and then the NSWPP/ New Order from 1971 to 1983. Resigned from New Order in 1983 but rejoined in 2007, becoming its leader after Matthias Koehl's death in 2014.

Matthias Koehl. American Nazi Party/NSWPP member and, after Rockwell's 1967 death, its leader. In the mid-1970s, his unpopularity caused numerous splits, which included James Mason's departure. Renamed the organization the New Order in 1983. Died in 2014.

Bob Larson. Christian evangelist and host of *Talk Back*. His guests included James Mason, Michael Moynihan, Boyd Rice, and Nikolas Schreck.

Gerhard Lauck. Prolific neo-Nazi propagandist since the 1970s working under the auspicious of the NSDAP/AO. In the late 1970s, was closely allied with Frank Collin's NSPA.

Anton LaVey. Founder and leader of the Church of Satan until his death in 1997. LaVey welcomed neo-Nazis into the Church.

Zeena LaVey. Daughter of Anton LaVey and, during the Satanic Panic, the Church of Satan spokesperson. Participated in the 8/8/88 performance and married Nikolas Schreck.

Steven Love. Cincinnati NSWPP member in early 1970s and editor of the *Southern Ohio Activity Report*. Briefly, NSM Vice Chairman in 1977.

Charles Manson. Leader of the cult "The Family" and mastermind behind the 1969 Tate–LaBianca murders. During the court proceedings, he carved a swastika in his forehead. His death sentence was changed to life in prison after California abolished the death penalty. Associate of James Mason, who promoted him in SIEGE as the new National Socialist leader. Died in prison in 2017.

James Mason. Member of the American Nazi Party/NSWPP from 1966 to 1976; co-founder of the NSM in 1975; NSLF member from 1976 to 1982; editor of two NSWWP periodicals between 1978 and 1980. Published the newsletter SIEGE from 1980 to 1982 for the NSLF and then until 1986 as Universal Order, which advocated an array of violent acts and promoted Charles Manson as the new neo-Nazi leader. An abridged anthology of the newsletter, *Siege*, was published in 1993. A second edition appeared in 2003 and additional ones in 2015, 2017, 2021, and 2023. Imprisoned between

1995 and 1999; afterward, Mason self-published a number of books, including *The Theocrat* and *Revisiting Revelation*. After a revival of interest in *Siege* in 2015, Mason became a cult figure and mentor to younger neo-Nazis who embraced his ideas.

Michael Merritt. Published spiritual National Socialist periodicals, including *New Dawn*. Inherited SIEGE's subscription list when it ended.

Tom Metzger. Christian Identity minister, member of David Duke's KKKK, and leader of the California Knights, which became the White American Political Association (WAPA). Won the 1980 California Democratic primary for U.S. Congress. WAPA eventually became White Aryan Resistance and published the *WAR* newspaper. Interviewed James Mason, Boyd Rice, Nikolas Schreck, and Karl Hand on his cable access TV show *Race and Reason*. Died in 2020.

Bob Miles. Christian Identity minister and Klan leader who was convicted of planning to bomb school buses in opposition to desegregation. Founder of the Mountain Church of Jesus Christ the Savior, he held non-sectarian White Supremacist gatherings at his Michigan farm in the 1980s. Died in 1992.

Michael Moynihan. Industrial and neofolk musician; worked under the name Coup de Grace starting in 1984 and as Blood Axis after 1991. Founder of the press and record label Storm, he edited and published Mason's *Siege* anthology in 1993. Co-author of *Lords of Chaos*, which documented the Norwegian neo-Nazi black metal scene. Later co-publisher of *TYR* journal.

Adam Parfrey. Publisher and Abraxas Clique member. Co-founded the periodical *EXIT* in 1984 and then Amok Press in 1986. Founded his own press, Feral House, in 1988. Published Moynihan's *Lords of Chaos* as well as a number of White Supremacists and Far Right conspiracy theorists. Died in 2018.

George Petros. Co-founder of *EXIT* with Parfrey. Later co-edited the music magazine *Seconds*, which included coverage of White Supremacist bands.

William Pierce. Professor who worked with Rockwell's American Nazi Party. Rescued a teenaged Mason and sheltered him at party headquarters. Part of the NSWPP's triumvirate until 1970, he later took over a faction of the National Youth Alliance, which became his National Alliance in 1974. His novel the *Turner Diaries*, which described a coming race war sparked by terrorism, inspired the 1995 Oklahoma City bombing. Died in 2002.

Ed Reynolds. Member of Ku Klux Klan groups and the NSLF. One of Mason's closest comrades and one of the only other people to work under the name Universal Order. Died in 1998.

Boyd Rice. Industrial noise musician who contacted Mason in 1986 and introduced him to the Abraxas Clique. A neo-Nazi collaborator, he was an associate of Mason, Parfrey, Moynihan, Heick, and Anton LaVey.

George Lincoln Rockwell. Founded the American Nazi Party in 1959, the first significant openly National Socialist group in the postwar United States. It launched the movement's revival and spun off numerous splinter groups. In 1967, Rockwell rebranded his organization the National Socialist White People's Party (NSWPP) but was assassinated later that year.

Bill Russell. In the mid-1970s, founded the NSM's Detroit chapter.

David Rust. Second NSLF leader from 1975 to 1977. After his arrest, he allowed Mason to merge the group with the NSM.

Nikolas Schreck. Satanist, Radio Werewolf singer, Abraxas Clique member, editor of *The Manson File*, 8/8/88 participant, and husband of Zeena LaVey.

Ryan Schuster. Publisher of the second edition of *Siege*. Wrote its introduction, which became the standard account of Mason's history.

Frank Spisak Jr. NSWPP member who killed three in Cleveland in 1982. Executed in 2011.

Keith Stimely. Staff member of Carto's Institute for Historical Review and editor of its journal, *The Journal of Historical Review* from 1983 to 1985. Associate of Rice and Parfrey. Died in 1992.

Robert N. Taylor. White Supremacist folk musician. National Spokesman for the Minutemen in the 1960s. An early figure in the Heathen movement, he later published in *Exit* and edited *Vor Tru*. Associate of Moynihan.

Thomas Thorn. Electric Hellfire Club founder. Also played with Slave State, Sleep Chamber, My Life With the Thrill Kill Kult, and Blood Axis. A Church of Satan priest, associate of Mason, and long-time friend and collaborator of Moynihan.

Joseph Tommasi. Charismatic NSWPP organizer in El Monte, California. His NSLF emerged as a split from the NSWPP in 1974, advocated guerilla actions, and engaged in several bombings. Killed by an NSWPP member in 1975.

Russell Vey. Second leader of the openly gay NSL (National Socialist League), which existed from 1974 to 1985.

Varg Vikernes. Norwegian black metal musician who recorded as Burzum. Member of the pioneering black metal band Mayhem; arrested in 1994 for murdering the singer and served 15 years. Admirer of Mason and lifelong White Supremacist.

Allen Vincent. American Nazi Party/NSWPP leader in California. Subject of the documentary *The California Reich*, he left the party in 1975 and founded the NSWWP. Died in 1999.

Robert Ward. Editor of *Fifth Path* music fanzine and *Siege* typesetter.

James K. Warner. American Nazi Party member. Later founded the New Christian Crusade Church and worked with Duke's KKKK.

Perry "Red" Warthan. In succession, a pyromaniac, teenage murderer, biker, Woodstock Anarchist Party founder, IWW member, neo-Nazi, go-between with Charles Manson, murderer of a teenager, and Christian convert. Died in prison in 1999.

NSWPP SPLINTER GROUPS

1968   JAMES K. WARNER AND ALLEN VINCENT (AMERICAN NAZI PARTY)

1970   WILLIAM PIERCE (NATIONAL YOUTH ALLIANCE, BECOMES NATIONAL ALLIANCE)
FRANK COLLIN (NSPA)

1971   DAVID DUKE (NATIONAL PARTY, LATER KKKK)

1974   JOSEPH TOMMASI (NSLF)
CASEY KALEMBA (UWPP)

1975   ROBERT BRANNEN AND JAMES MASON (NSM)
KARL HAND (NGP)

1976   ALLEN VINCENT (NSWWP)

1981   PERRY WARTHAN (CANS)

1983   RICK COOPER (NSV)

ACRONYMS   DATES NOTE WHEN EACH THE SPLINTER GROUP FORMED. IN SOME CASES, INDIVIDUALS LEFT THE NSWPP BEFORE OR AFTER THAT DATE

CANS	CHICO AREA NATIONAL SOCIALISTS
KKKK	KNIGHTS OF THE KU KLUX KLAN
NGP	NATIONAL GUARD PARTY
NSLF	NATIONAL SOCIALIST LIBERATION FRONT
NSM	NATIONAL SOCIALIST MOVEMENT
NSPA	NATIONAL SOCIALIST PARTY OF AMERICA
NYA	NATIONAL YOUTH ALLIANCE
NSWPP	NATIONAL SOCIALIST WHITE PEOPLE'S PARTY
NSWWP	NATIONAL SOCIALIST WHITE WORKERS' PARTY
NSV	NATIONAL SOCIALIST VANGUARD
UWPP	UNITED WHITE PEOPLE'S PARTY

FIGURE 0.1   NSWPP Splinter Groups

Source: Casandra Johns.

ABRAXAS CIRCLE

ABRAXAS CIRCLE (SELECTED OUTER MEMBERS)

ABRAXAS CIRCLE (INNER)

ABRAXAS CLIQUE

KATJA LANE

JIM GOAD

MICHAEL A. HOFFMAN II

GEORGE PETROS

GEORGE HAWTHORNE/BURDI

NICK BOUGAS

VARG VIKERNES

WILLIAM GRIMSTAD

TOM METZGER

BOYD RICE

THOMAS THORN

BOB HEICK

NIKOLAS SCHRECK

JAMES MASON

CHARLES MANSON

ANTON LAVEY

ADAM PARFREY

JOSHUA BUCKLEY

MARILYN MANSON

JAMES PORRAZZO

KEITH STIMELY

ZEENA LAVEY

SHANE BUGBEE

DOUGLAS PEARCE

MICHAEL MOYNIHAN

PETER GILMORE

PETER SOTOS

ROBERT WARD

R.N. TAYLOR

BOB FERBRACHE

SHAUN PARTRIDGE

PEGGY NADRAMIA

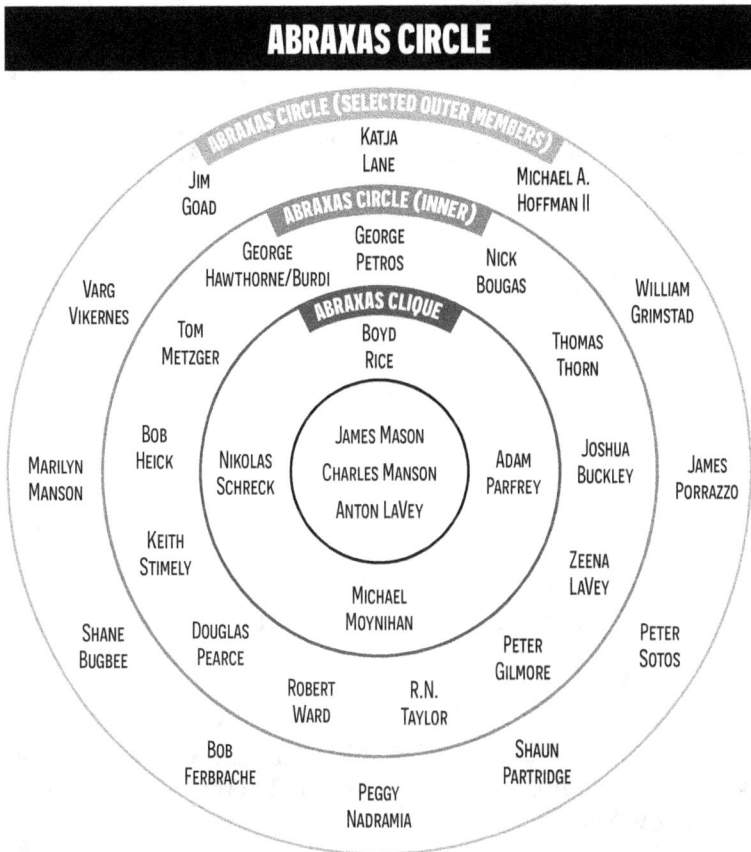

FIGURE 0.2   Abraxas Circle

Source: Casandra Johns.

CITATION AND ARCHIVE NOTES

1 Correspondence Dates

In a number of cases, the dates of letters sent to James Mason were taken from handwritten notes he made on them, sometimes prefaced with "TKO," the meaning of which was a mystery to both myself and the archivists in charge of his papers. In a written interview in 2023, after the manuscript was almost completed, Mason clarified that the acronym stood for "technical knock-out" and referred to the date he replied to the letter—not when he received it.

2 *Siege* / SIEGE / *Siege*

"Siege" refers to multiple periodicals and books; where possible they have been rendered distinctly. *Siege* #1 and #2 were periodicals published in 1974 by Joseph Tommasi. SIEGE was James Mason's periodical from 1980 to 1986. *Siege* also refers to Mason's anthology; unless otherwise specified, all references are to the third edition published in 2015. URL's for *Siege* have been removed to comply with various countries' laws.

Additionally, because the newsletters are difficult to access, in cases where this was possible, citations to the anthology are given as a supplement; for example: SIEGE 9(5) September 1980, p.1 (*Siege*, p.159). Note that in the original newsletter, the numbering was given in Roman numerals; for ease in reading, they have been rendered into the Arabic form.

3 *Articles and Interviews* and *.45 Dangerous Minds*

Two anthologies are cited repeatedly. James Mason's *Articles and Interviews* (cited simply as *Articles*) reprinted clippings from many extremely difficult-to-find newspapers, fanzines, flyers, CDs, and other sources. Items reprinted in the collection are cited both in the original and to the book; for example, Dominic Hampshire, "Siege Mentality,"

Scorpion #18, p.35 (*Articles*, p.62). However, please note that there is additional material in the anthology which was not previously published.

Similarly, a number of interviews from *Seconds* magazine appear in the Steven Blush and George Petros edited anthology, *.45 Dangerous Minds: The Most Intense Interviews from* Seconds *Magazine*, published by Creation in 2005. Interviews reprinted in it are also given a secondary citation to the book.

4 Archive Locations

Unless otherwise noted, all correspondence and other non-periodical material is located in the James N. Mason Papers at the Kenneth Spencer Research Library at the University of Kansas in Lawrence. This specifically includes all notations with just a [Folder/Box] locator. Citations for materials in other archives (Bridges, CDR, Labadie, and Stimely collection) correspond to the list below. All letters and emails to the author are in my possession.

Unless noted, all URLs were accessible as of October 1, 2023. Please note that while URLs for *Newspapers.com*, which is an online collection of digitized newspapers, have been provided for ease of location, the website itself is paywalled.

Archives

- Tyler Bridges Papers, Louisiana Research Collection, Tulane University Library, New Orleans, Louisiana [Bridges]
- Center for Democratic Renewal Records, Auburn Avenue Research Library on African American Culture and History, Fulton County Library, Atlanta, Georgia [CDR]
- The IWW Materials Preservation Project. Contact the IWW (iww.org) to request access to this online collection
- Jewish Theological Seminary Library, New York City, New York
- Joseph A. Labadie Collection, University of Michigan Library, Ann Arbor, Michigan [Labadie]
- James N. Mason Papers, Kenneth Spencer Research Library, University of Kansas, Lawrence, Kansas
- Multnomah County Public Library, Portland, Oregon
- New York Public Library, New York City, New York
- Keith Stimely collection on revisionist history and neo-Fascist movements, University of Oregon, Eugene, Oregon [Stimely collection]

INTRODUCTION

James Mason's *Siege* is the bible of the most extreme wing of the new generation of neo-Nazis. The influence of the book, and the groups it has inspired, has been well documented in media articles and monitoring group reports. In contrast, how the book came to be has received scant attention. This history seeks to correct that.

This detailed excavation of *Siege* is important for three reasons. *Siege* is a strange book, mixing National Socialism with serial killers and a veneration of Charles Manson. But like all ideas, it doesn't come out of a vacuum and there is a long backstory. While it is popular today to analyze "extremism" through an individual, psychological lens, a close look at this ideology of violence shows its emergence from a tendency from inside a larger political movement. In fact, in this case it came out of a wing of the American Nazi Party/National Socialist White People's Party that wanted to start a campaign of revolutionary violence. The most infamous figure from this faction was William Pierce, who would later pen the other well-known neo-Nazi book advocating terrorism, *The Turner Diaries*.

Second, this book investigates a little-known, but important, corner of U.S. political history: neo-Nazism in the 1970s. It is during this period that the groundwork was laid for the movement in decades to come. Additionally, in the United States in particular, neo-Nazism is almost always subsumed under the broader category of the White Supremacist movement. But neo-Nazism has its own distinct ideology, trajectory, organizing structures, and relationships to competing trends on the Right. Even in the scarce existing histories of this period, wrong information is legion, including in scholarly accounts. And

DOI: 10.4324/9780429200090-1

this is particularly true of two neo-Nazi groups that Mason was involved with, the National Socialist Liberation Front and National Socialist Movement, but also David Duke's early relationship with the movement.

Third, the book examines the role of a circle of publishers and musicians in the 1980s and '90s, who in turn were intertwined with the Church of Satan. Within countercultural circles, especially the industrial music scene, there have been decades of speculation about the involvement of Boyd Rice, Adam Parfrey, and Michael Moynihan with neo-Nazism. But all of them consistently put up a wall of denials and evasions, many of which were repeated by various writers and journalists. The detailed look at the nature and extent of these connections is necessary to illuminate the actual nature of their involvement as well as show the key role they played in the creation and dissemination of *Siege*.

These three, part of what is called the Abraxas Clique, were direct precursors to the Alt Right. One of the important things that linked them was an explicit misogyny, which would later be crucial to the Alt Right. But other elements include their "edgelord" approach of trying to shock and antagonize while immediately hiding their politics by saying it was "just a joke"; their desire to create a reactionary counterculture as an alternative to the dominant left-leaning one; forging relationships with outright neo-Nazis while not quite embracing all their politics (or at least not all the time); and combining their cultural and political work with Satanism.

As the book was written, what emerged, quite unintentionally, was a structure based around profiles of the various groups and individuals that Mason crossed paths with over the years. In almost all these cases, their relationship to Mason wasn't well documented, and more than a few weren't documented at all. And, in the second half much more so than the first, the profiles are as much or more about the various figures' relationship to neo-Nazism in general than to Mason himself.

This has made for an oddly shaped book, which is not just a history of certain parts of these political and cultural movements but also a reconstruction of Mason's intellectual and organizational trajectory. And so this book can profitably be read either cover to cover or by just looking at the people and groups of interest; it can also merely be a reference guide. But please don't be shy about how you engage with it; every word of mine is not sacred.

Some will like the first half about neo-Nazi history more, while others the second about the Abraxas Clique. For some, this will be a laborious trek through the minutiae of a repulsive political movement, with a focus on some of its more irrelevant doctrinal disputes. (Chip Berlet, who spent decades writing about the Far Right, once told me that my interest in the details of the movement's ideology was far more generous to them than they deserved.) For other readers, these detailed investigations will be a fascinating journey. Personally, I recommend reading both parts as a kind of soap opera. In the end, this book is mostly testament to my obsessive perfectionism—not necessarily a good thing. Regardless, I hope that it adds at least a little to readers' understanding of this movement and how it functions, and that it is, as academics like to say, a contribution to the literature.

PART I
#ReadSiege

1

A TWENTY-FIRST CENTURY *SIEGE*

How the Rediscovery of an Obscure Neo-Nazi
Book Helped Inspire a New Generation of White
Supremacist Terrorism

On May 19, 2017, a bizarre local story in Tampa, Florida ended up heralding a new era in neo-Nazi terrorism. An 18-year-old man was arrested after taking hostages in a shop. After surrendering to police, he led them to his apartment, where the bodies of two of his roommates lay. Local news ran with the headline that the murders were over a religious dispute, although further down it mentioned they were neo-Nazis.[1] The story broke on a Friday, but it didn't make national news until Monday, when a fourth roommate, Brandon Russell, was arrested. Despite finding materials for a radioactive dirty bomb in the apartment, he had been let go at first, only to be arrested shortly thereafter while fleeing in a car with two guns, cases of ammunition, and four loaded 30-round magazines.[2]

It was only then that the incident was linked to the Atomwaffen Division, a new neo-Nazi group that had previously escaped attention. All four roommates were members, and Russell the leader. But there was a reason this group wasn't on the radar of Far Right monitors.

For all quarters of the Far Right, Donald Trump's presidential election campaign and subsequent victory had been a match thrown on gasoline. This was especially true for the Alt Right. This new Far Right movement exploded in popularity starting in 2015; it was a huge break from what had come before, including in demographics, aesthetics, and digital strategies.

The Alt Right had double Janus-faced features. There was, for the first time in the United States, a new generation of fascist intellectuals, including Richard Spencer and Greg Johnson. The other, arguably more important, side was an online troll army, which congregated on the 4chan and 8chan message boards. Catalyzed by Gamergate, a 2014 online anti-feminist

DOI: 10.4324/9780429200090-3

harassment campaign, it featured the extensive uses of memes, an "edgelord" flaunting of extremes for their own sake and relying on claims of ironic play to both mask and avoid responsibility for its political views.

The other Janus face was the two political wings of the Alt Right. One, openly racist and antisemitic, was the first new wave of White Supremacists since the last in the mid-1980s to 1990s. The other, the slightly more moderate Alt Lite, allowed in people of color, Jews, and gay men. One of the largest and most violent groups to emerge out of this was the Proud Boys, who would play an important role in the Far Right for many years to come. Otherwise, both shared a general approach, including a strong element of misogyny.

In 2015 and 2016, the two wings worked in tandem. During his first presidential campaign, Trump even tweeted an image of himself as the movement's mascot, Pepe the Frog.[3] New Alt Right groups and adherents sprang up all over.

However, a new wave of neo-Nazis or not, internecine racist murders had long been a fact of life among White Supremacists, and that hadn't changed. So, even to those taking notes, while news of a double murder inside of an obscure new group did stand out for its sheer drama, it did not signify any greater importance. Yet.

The murders were also three months before the "Unite the Right" demonstration in Charlottesville, the largest fascist-led rally in the United States since the 1970s. The high point of the Alt Right, the day was marked by street-fighting between fascists and anti-fascists and ended with a neo-Nazi car attack on an antifascist march. One antifascist, Heather Heyer, was killed and around 30 others were injured. It was only with this event that the murderous implications of a revived White Supremacist movement became clear to the country at large.

While Charlottesville was a failure for Alt Right, to Atomwaffen it was a boon and allowed it to take a position as the most extreme group of a new generation of fascists. The group openly advocated terrorism and race war, and venerated racist murderers as "saints." And Atomwaffen had a bible: James Mason's *Siege*.[4]

Siege: The Collected Writings of James Mason itself was an unusual book; certainly there is no comparable text. Its contents were originally published in the monthly newsletter SIEGE between 1980 and 1986, which had a circulation of less than 100 copies. Selections of it were edited into a 1993 anthology, and a second edition came out in 2003. Despite its relative obscurity, the book was rediscovered in the 2010s by members of *Iron March*, an international online forum that attracted the most militant neo-Nazis under the slogan "Gas The Kikes! Race War Now! 1488! Boots on the ground!"[5] In 2015, *Iron March* published a third edition of *Siege*, jumpstarting its rediscovery.

Siege provided a coherent ideological justification for abandoning traditional neo-Nazi politics. Its length—over 400 pages long in the first edition (later ones were even longer)—gave it the authority of a serious tome. The book contained Mason's reflections on what would be his 20 years in the neo-Nazi movement by the end of the newsletter's publication. And these reflections came to a conclusion that Atomwaffen was in thrall to.

Mason had joined the American Nazi Party in the mid-1960s but within a decade rejected its law-abiding approach in favor of armed struggle. As he moved through neo-Nazi groups he became increasing frustrated with them, and SIEGE became his personal vehicle where he developed his tactical and philosophical views. Taking a page from the 1960s counterculture, he claimed that "the System" was completely corrupt. Approaches like grassroots organizing, public marches and rallies, member-based organizations, and political work that hide their true politics, were all dead-ends for neo-Nazis. Mason also proclaimed that the movement should reject traditional conservative themes such as opposition to immigration and support for police: what was needed was a new revolutionary approach which made a complete break from the right-wing.

Even guerilla warfare, which he originally espoused, would be insufficient on its own. Mason decided the only thing to do was to try to either speed up or wait out the System's collapse. He summed up his approach as "TOTAL ATTACK or TOTAL DROP-OUT."[6] As part of this, he now embraced serial killers and mass murderers—inspired in no small part by a number of neo-Nazis who took this approach, some of whom he had known personally. He also advised that neo-Nazis who planned on committing dramatic acts of violence should gear them for maximum impact. If they died in the act, all the better. And he embraced terrorist acts by other political factions too, especially those New Leftists who continued armed actions in the 1980s.

Obviously, Mason's approach broke dramatically with his neo-Nazi contemporaries. He rejected not just traditional conservative politics but also its cultural orientation, and he accepted countercultural fashion, drug use, and even Satanism. He also made extensive use of collaborators who were not neo-Nazis but were either sympathizers, free speech advocates, or useful idiots—even working with Jews and gay men to achieve his goal.

Perhaps most bizarrely, SIEGE also venerated Charles Manson, the cult leader whose followers committed a number of gruesome murders in 1969, for which he was serving a life sentence. After starting a correspondence with him, Mason quickly decided that Manson should become the new neo-Nazi guru. He was inspired by the Manson Family's attempt to start a race war which they would wait out in the desert; their leader's racism, antisemitism, and female following; and his popularity among rebellious young people, whom Mason hoped to recruit. Mason even developed what he called Universal Order, a new messianic and crypto-spiritual philosophy inspired by Manson.

Needless to say, Mason's new ideas were not popular among his contemporaries. But it was for just these reasons that decades later, in a new political and social context, *Siege* would finally find its moment.

In late March 2017, in between the Florida murders and Charlottesville, Atomwaffen made contact with Mason himself. A month before Charlottesville, *Iron March* published the first interview with Mason in well over a decade.[7] Atomwaffen now started to work directly with him, reprinting his books and disseminating new videos and writings. Mason would become the group's self-described advisor, meeting and taking pictures with members in his Denver apartment and occasionally acting as their spokesman.[8]

By then, the new edition of *Siege* had gained velocity; in July 2017, it had been downloaded 16,000 times from *Iron March*.[9] When Charlottesville happened, it neatly illustrated *Siege*'s argument about why neo-Nazis should not hold public, legal rallies. In fact, the actual rally part of the Unite the Right never happened. Police simply stood aside as fighting broke out between the fascists and antifascists, and then dispersed the rally before any speakers took the stage. Afterward, a wave of public revulsion spread against the Alt Right, destroying the inroads it had made in terms of popular support, and made open White Supremacists no longer welcome in the larger conservative movement. This also split the wings of the Alt Right, the White Supremacist faction and the Alt Lite, from each other. Back to political isolation, it certainly was true that, at for least for that moment in time, legal and public White Supremacist politics were a road to nowhere—just as Mason said.

The hashtag #ReadSiege spread after Charlottesville, too. On *Iron March*, references to "Siege" spiked between 2015 and 2017.[10] On the 4Chan message board, posts which included "Siege" and "Atomwaffen Division" rose sharply in the months after Charlottesville. One Atomwaffen member said membership peaked around November and December 2017.[11]

Siege and Atomwaffen were now linked together in the public mind. According to the group's *Siege Culture* website, "What we are creating here is something that James Mason attempted to put into form himself, but due to circumstance, he never implemented it."[12]

Atomwaffen's notoriety grew after even more murders were attributed to them. In December 2017, a 17-year-old, often described as an Atomwaffen "associate," was arrested for murdering his girlfriend's parents. In January 2018, Atomwaffen member Samuel Woodward was arrested for killing Blaze Bernstein, a gay Jewish man. Woodward previously had his picture taken with Mason in his apartment.[13]

Atomwaffen embraced these crimes.[14]

Aided by a refusal of social media to crack down on the group, a whole online lexicon grew up around *Siege*. #ReadSiege was now joined by phrases like "Siege Culture" (an obsession with the book), "Siege Pilling" (convincing others to adopt its outlook), and even "Siege Fags" (a derogatory term used by others on the Far Right to describe the book's fans). Numerous memes—some based on edgy humor, others just threats—appeared as well.

Undoubtedly, all those who clamored for others to "Read Siege" did not. The original edition clocked in at 434 pages, and later versions were even longer. Many of the nuances of *Siege* would not have been understood by readers unfamiliar with the internal debates of 1970s neo-Nazism, and one of the book's two strategies—to drop out of society—was mostly ignored. Instead, "Read Siege" became shorthand for militant, illegal action, and this found plenty of receptive ears around the world.

Atomwaffen itself had come out of *Iron March* but was not the only group that did. They included Reaction America, which later became Vanguard America. One of the men who marched with the group in Charlottesville became a murderer that afternoon after he rammed his car into the antifascist march. Another group that came out of the platform was National Action, whose members would be jailed for crimes like attempted murder before being proscribed by the British government. Russell had even travelled to England to meet the group prior to founding Atomwaffen.[15]

But it was Atomwaffen that would become the central node in a global network of neo-Nazi groups which promoted terrorism. (Terrorism here refers to attempts by non-state actors to further a political goal by either intentionally attempting to kill people or engaging in acts in which this is a direct possibility, such as plane hijackings and other hostage situations.) Those in other countries, including Germany, used the Atomwaffen brand. A number of groups, from Estonia to Australia, either had a relationship with Atomwaffen or were inspired by it or by Siege Culture more generally. These included Feuerkrieg Division, Sonnenkreig Division, System Resistance Network, Antipodean Resistance, and The Base.[16]

After his arrest, Russell was sentenced to five years in prison. (While on probation in 2023, he was arrested again, this time for plotting to attack the Baltimore power grid.[17]) The leadership was passed to John Cameron Denton, also known as "Rape" and "Vincent Snyder." Denton, who said he owned the rights to Mason's books, put out a fourth edition of *Siege* and new editions of others.[18]

Denton added his own essay, "Movementarian Menace," to his edition of *Siege*. It applied Mason's ideas to the age of the Alt Right. Denton said that White Supremacist leaders held their rallies as money-making opportunities. Attending them was just doing the System's work, which would never allow their movement to succeed anyway. He also attacked David Duke and the National Socialist Movement, two of Mason's old targets who were still around. To this was added Alt Right leader Richard Spencer, the planned keynote speaker at Charlottesville. Even with its murderous ending, Denton dismissed the rally itself as passé. The task at hand for Aryans was to embrace Mason's Universal Order philosophy.[19]

Even under Russell, *Siege* was required reading for new Atomwaffen members.[20] But Denton turned the group toward an even stronger fixation on Mason, while also becoming more involved with Satanism. The publication and dissemination of the original edition of *Siege* had been deeply connected to Church of Satan members, including the book's editor and publisher, Michael Moynihan. Atomwaffen replicated this association with Satanists, only it was entangled with the much more radical Order of Nine Angles, which had been founded by neo-Nazi David Myatt. This version of Satanism expected followers to participate in extreme movements, such as neo-Nazism and radical Islamism—at one point, even embracing human sacrifice. In a disturbing number of cases, murderers have been connected to Order of Nine Angles philosophy.[21]

Despite promoting terrorism, Atomwaffen expanded into a sizeable organization. At its height, Atomwaffen had up to 27 chapters and 80 members. And its members were young; the three arrested for murder were all under 21, while Denton himself was 24 when he met Mason. As of April 2020, every Atomwaffen member arrested has been under 30.[22]

It wasn't long before the rather hands-off approach of federal authorities changed. This was undoubtedly driven by a series of White Supremacist massacres, which included 11 killed in October 2018 at the Tree of Life synagogue in Pittsburgh, Pennsylvania and 51 at two mosques in Christchurch, New Zealand in March 2019. The last straw was apparently the murder of 23 at a Walmart in El Paso, Texas in August 2019, in an incident which targeted Latino immigrants.

After that, arrests of Atomwaffen members escalated; charges included child pornography, illegal weapons possession, and vandalizing a synagogue. These culminated in February 2020, when Denton and four others were arrested for threatening and swatting numerous people they deemed enemies. ("Swatting" is making a false report to law enforcement in order to trigger raids on a target's residence by a heavily armed SWAT team.)[23]

Although the United States doesn't have a designated list of domestic terrorist groups, it does for foreign ones. Because of Atomwaffen's overseas affiliates, in early March 2020 it was reported that the State Department pushed to have it designated as a Foreign Terrorist Organization. Less than a week after the report, Mason announced the dissolution of the organization—whose very existence had violated his dictum against organizing membership-based groups.[24] A few months later, Mason himself was banned from Canada as a "terrorist entity." Some members immediately reconstituted themselves as the National Socialist Order, although in September 2022 it split again.[25]

Nonetheless, the cat was out of the bag. *Siege* itself became known around the world as the premier neo-Nazi terrorist book; for the younger generation, it eclipsed even William Pierce's bloody race war fantasy *The Turner Diaries*. With the fading of Atomwaffen and the other *Iron March* groups, a second generation of similar neo-Nazi groups has sprung up as well.[26]

Siege has been translated into numerous languages, including Russian, Italian, and Spanish—even Mason said he does not know how many. If the tome is too long for you to get through, you can listen to the audiobook, read the 100-page pocket version, or just glance through *The Twenty Tenets of Learned Elder SIEGE*.[27]

Having been removed from social media platforms, the remnants of Atomwaffen—joined by others who espouse Siege Culture—now propagate their ideas on the Telegram. There, memes about, and references to, the book are common coin.

Post-Atomwaffen members who have remained loyal to Mason have also established a new website, *Siege Culture*, in cooperation with him. New editions continue to appear as well. In 2021, a fifth came out with a new preface by Mason. And in 2023, a sixth edition was issued by one of the splinter groups from Atomwaffen, the National Socialist Order of Nine Angles; it had the dubious distinction of being denounced by Mason.[28]

Siege—with its very contemporary advocacy of leaderless resistance, rejection of political organizing, goal of overthrowing the System, and promotion of extremes like serial killers and Satanism—looks like it is here to stay and will undoubtedly influence neo-Nazis and other White Supremacists for years to come.

What follows is the story of how James Mason developed the ideas in *Siege*, how his writings were turned into a book by an unlikely set of collaborators, and how this book was disseminated outside the cloistered world of neo-Nazism.

Notes

1 "Tampa PD: Double Homicide Suspect Killed Roommates because They 'Disrespected' His Muslim Faith," *ABC Action News*, May 19, 2017 (updated May 23, 2017), www.abcactionnews.com/news/crime/tampa-police-armed-man-admits-to-killing-2-leads-officers-to-victims-inside-apartment

2 "Roommate of Alleged Tampa Palms Shooter Charged Federal Explosives Violations," *Department of Justice*, May 22, 2017, www.justice.gov/usao-mdfl/pr/roommate-alleged-tampa-palms-shooter-charged-federal-explosives-violations; David Goodhue, "Neo-Nazi Guardsman Bought Rifles and Lots of Ammo, Cops Say. He May Go Free for Now," *Miami Herald*, June 13, 2017, https://web.archive.org/web/20170613153251/, https://www.miamiherald.com/news/local/community/florida-keys/article155849209.html

3 Libby Nelson, "Why the Anti-Defamation League Just Put the Pepe the Frog Meme on Its Hate Symbols," *Vox*, September 28, 2016, www.vox.com/2016/9/21/12893656/pepe-frog-donald-trump

4 "Transcript—Documenting Hate: New American Nazis," *Frontline*, Episode 21, aired November 20, 2018, www.pbs.org/wgbh/frontline/film/documenting-hate-new-american-nazis/transcript, www.pbs.org/video/documenting-hate-new-american-nazis-vrbezk

5 James Mason to author, November 6, 2022; "Atomwaffen Division," *Southern Poverty Law Center*, www.splcenter.org/fighting-hate/extremist-files/group/atom waffen-division [Hereafter *SPLC*].

6 Mason, *Siege*, 3rd. ed. (Iron March, 2015), p.493 [Hereafter *Siege*].

7 The 14-year date given was slightly miscalculated, however, as in 2004 Mason was interviewed on Denver community access cable TV show. Nate Thayer, "Treasure Trove of User Data Released by Anti-Fascist Hackers Lead to Identities of Scores of Clandestine Domestic Terrorists," *Nate Thayer - Journalist*, December 5, 2019, https://web.archive.org/web/20200601173634, https://www.nate-thayer.com/secret-identities-of-u-s-nazi-terror-group-revealed; "James Mason Is Back!—James Mason, Exclusive Interview after 14 Years," *Iron March*, July 25, 2017, reprinted in Mason, *Articles and Interviews*, 3rd ed., 2018, p.253 [Hereafter *Articles*].

8 Alex Newhouse, "The Threat Is the Network: The Multi-Node Structure of Neo-Fascist Accelerationism," *CTC Sentinel* 14(5) June 2021, https://ctc.usma.edu/the-threat-is-the-network-the-multi-node-structure-of-neo-fascist-accelerationism

9 Mason interview in *Iron March* (*Articles*, p.254).

10 Michael Edison Hayden, "Visions of Chaos: Weighing the Violent Legacy of Iron March," *SPLC*, February 15, 2019, www.splcenter.org/hatewatch/2019/02/15/visions-chaos-weighing-violent-legacy-iron-march

11 Andrew Thompson, "The Measure of Hate on 4Chan," *Rolling Stone*, May 10, 2018,www.rollingstone.com/politics/politics-news/the-measure-of-hate-on-4chan-627922; Mason, *Siege*, 5th ed., 2021, p.616.

12 "Worldview," *Siegeculture*, https://web.archive.org/web/20180607224851, http://siegeculture.biz/worldview

13 Buckley Kuhn-Fricker and Scott Fricker were murdered by Nicholas Giampa on December 22, 2017. But Giampa's exact relationship to Atomwaffen is unclear. His Twitter bio said "Read Siege," he interacted with an Atomwaffen account, and a former member said he was in direct contact with the group. The exact nature of the relationship aside, his double murder is almost always attributed to the group. Blaze Bernstein's murder, as well, appears to be more complicated than it might seem at first glance.

   Jessica Schulberg and Luke O'Brien, "We Found the Neo-Nazi Twitter Account Tied to a Virginia Double Homicide," *HuffPost*, January 4, 2018 (updated January 5, 2018), www.huffpost.com/entry/nicholas-giampa-neo-nazi-teenager-murder-girlfriends-parents-virginia_n_5a4d0797e4b0b0e5a7aa4780; AC Thompson, Ali Winston, and Jake Hanrahan, "California Murder Suspect Said to Have Trained With Extremist Hate Group," *ProPublica*, January 26, 2018, www.propublica.org/article/california-murder-suspect-atomwaffen-division-extremist-hate-group; "'Ryan' and James Mason: An Atomwaffen Affair," *Eugene Antifa*, February 2, 2019, https://eugeneantifa.noblogs.org/post/2019/02/02/ryan-atomwaffen-james-mason; Jonathan Krohn, "How a Gay Teen, an Internet Nazi, and a Late-Night Rendezvous Turned to Tragedy," *Mother Jones*,March/April2019,www.motherjones.com/crime-justice/2019/03/how-a-gay-teen-an-internet-nazi-and-a-late-night-rendezvous-turned-to-tragedy

14 AC Thompson, Ali Winston, and Jake Hanrahan, "Inside Atomwaffen as It Celebrates a Member for Allegedly Killing a Gay Jewish College Student," *ProPublica*, February 23, 2018, www.propublica.org/article/atomwaffen-division-inside-white-hate-group; "California Murder Suspect Said to Have Trained with Extremist Hate Group," *ProPublica*, January 26, 2018, www.propublica.org/article/california-murder-suspect-atomwaffen-division-extremist-hate-group

15 "Atomwaffen Division," *SPLC*; Hatewatch Staff, "Alleged Charlottesville Driver Who Killed One Rallied with Alt-Right Vanguard America Group," *SPLC*, August 13,2017, www.splcenter.org/hatewatch/2017/08/12/alleged-charlottesville-driver-who-killed-one-rallied-alt-right-vanguard-america-group

16 Newhouse, "The Threat Is the Network".

17 Ali Winston, "How Neo-Nazi Leader Brandon Russell Came to Be Accused of Targeting Baltimore Substations," *Baltimore Banner*, March 6, 2023, www. thebaltimorebanner.com/community/criminal-justice/brandon-russell-neo-nazi-sarah-clendaniel-power-substation-CH6ZNB2FVVDYREOUJEMGTOD DCM

18 Von Alexander Epp und Roman Höfner, "Atomwaffen Division Is a Militant Neo-Nazi Group in the U.S. Who Is Behind It?," *Der Spiegel*, September 7, 2018, www.spiegel.de/international/the-hate-network-an-inside-look-at-a-global-extremist-group-a-1226861.html

Mason's books reissued by Denton have included *Siege*, 4th ed., 2018; *The Theocrat*, 4th ed., April 2018, https://archive.org/details/TheTheocrat4thEdition; *One Verse Charlies*, 4th ed., May 2018, https://archive.org/details/OneVerse Charlies4thEdition; *Revisiting Revelation*, 3rd ed., May 2018, https://archive.org/ details/RevisitingRevelation3rdEdition; *Articles and Interviews*, 3rd ed., 2018. In 2022, the double volume *Out of the Dust* was also released, although without publication information, while scans of Mason's other books were put online without changes; *Out of the Dust, Vols. 1 & 2*, [2022], *Siege Kultur*, http:// siegeculture.org/documents/james/books/OofD1.pdf, http://siegeculture.org/doc uments/james/books/OofD2.pdf

19 Mason, *Siege*, 4th ed., pp.35, 621, 625–26, 629, 632–33.

20 Newhouse, "The Threat is the Network".

21 Nicholas Goodrick-Clarke, *Black Sun: Aryan Cults, Esoteric Nazism and the Politics of Identity* (New York: NYU Press, 2002), pp.216–24; Ali Winston, "The Satanist Neo-Nazi Plot to Murder U.S. Soldiers," *Rolling Stone*, June 5, 2022, www.rollingstone.com/culture/culture-features/the-satanist-neo-nazi-plot-to-murder-u-s-soldiers-1352629

For more on O9A, see Jacob C. Senholt, "Secret Identities in the Sinister Tradition: Political Esotericism and the Convergence of Radical Islam, Satanism, and National Socialism in the Order of Nine Angles," in Per Faxneld and Jesper Aa. Petersen, eds., *The Devil's Party: Satanism in Modernity* (New York: Oxford University Press, 2013), pp.250–74; Ariel Koch, "The ONA Network and the Transnationalization of Neo-Nazi-Satanism," *Studies in Conflict & Terrorism*, January 12, 2022, https://doi.org/10.1080/1057610X.2021.2024944; Daveed Gartenstein-Ross and Emelie Chace-Donahue, "The Order of Nine Angles: Cosmology, Practice & Movement," *Studies in Conflict & Terrorism*, March 7, 2003, https://doi.org/10.1080/1057610X.2023.2186737

22 "Atomwaffen Division," *SPLC*; Thompson, Winston, and Hanrahan, "Inside Atomwaffen as It Celebrates a Member for Allegedly Killing a Gay Jewish College Student"; Jacob Ware, "Fighting Back: The Atomwaffen Division, Countering Violent Extremism, and the Evolving Crackdown on Far-Right Terrorism in America," *Journal for Deradicalization* #25, Winter 2020/21, published December 25, 2020, https://journals.sfu.ca/jd/index.php/jd/article/view/411/0

23 "Atomwaffen Division," *SPLC*; "White Supremacists Targeted Journalists and a Trump Official, F.B.I. Says," *New York Times*, February 26, 2020 (updated May 4, 2021), www.nytimes.com/2020/02/26/us/atomwaffen-division-arrests.html [Hereafter *NYT*].

24 Natasha Bertrand, Nahal Toosi, and Daniel Lippman, "State Pushes to List White Supremacist Group as Terrorist Org," *Politico*, March 9, 2020, www.politico.com/news/2020/03/09/state-department-white-supremacist-group-124500. A former member said Mason pressured the group to disband; Ryan AW, "The Decline and Fall of the Atomwaffen Division," *Siege*, 5th ed., 2021, p.619.

25 Mason was listed June 25, 2021. "Currently Listed Entities—James Mason," *Public Safety Canada*, www.publicsafety.gc.ca/cnt/ntnl-scrt/cntr-trrrsm/lstd-ntts/

crrnt-lstd-ntts-en.aspx; Ben Makuch, "Neo-Nazi Terror Group Atomwaffen Division Re-Emerges Under New Name," *Vice*, August 5, 2020, www.vice.com/en/article/wxq7jy/neo-nazi-terror-group-atomwaffen-division-re-emerges-under-new-name; Gartenstein-Ross and Chace-Donahue, "The Order of Nine Angles," pp.13, 15.

26 Deeba Shadnia, Alex Newhouse, Matt Kriner, and Arthur Bradley, *Militant Accelerationism Coalitions: A Case Study in Neo-Fascist Accelerationist Coalition Building Online*, CTEC, June 7, 2022, www.middlebury.edu/institute/academics/centers-initiatives/ctec/ctec-publications/militant-accelerationism-coalitions-case-study; Miro Dittrich, Jan Rathje, Thilo Manemann, and Frank Müller, *Militant Accelerationism: Origins and Developments in Germany*, CEMAS, September 15, 2022, https://cemas.io/en/publications/militant-accelerationism

27 James Mason, "Preface to the Fifth Edition," *Siege*, 5th ed., 2021; "James Mason - Siege AudioBook"; *SIEGE: Pocket Edition*; *20 Tenets of Learned Elder SIEGE*.

28 *Siege Kultur: A New Level of Awareness*, www.siegeculture.org (note that a different website was previously at the same URL); Mack Lamoureux, "The Grandfather of Modern Neo-Nazism Is Fighting with Satanic Neo-Nazis Now," *Vice*, July 28, 2023, www.vice.com/en/article/3akvj9/neo-nazis-james-mason-fighting

PART II

Life among the Sects (1959–1986)

2

THE PARTY OF ROCKWELL

The American Nazi Party and NSWPP

The history and ideas of James Nolan Mason are inseparable from the origins of neo-Nazism in the United States. And central to both was George Lincoln Rockwell, founder of the American Nazi Party, which Mason joined as a young teenager. But just as important to Mason, if not more so, were the events of the 1970s which involved the party under a new name, the National Socialist White People's Party (NSWPP), which itself spun off numerous splinter groups during the first half of the decade. It was the ensuing soul-searching by those who left that led Mason to formulate the ideas he became known for.

Owing to his membership in the original American Nazi Party, Mason had an impeccable neo-Nazi pedigree. And since he joined the party in 1966 at the age of 14, he remained comparatively young as opposed to the already small number of his contemporaries who were also "Rockwell's men." Along with his ironclad commitment to National Socialism, Mason was able to outlast many who have this rarified background.

Rockwell always remained Mason's idol, but his ideas were not derivative of his former leader. *Siege* was Mason's answer to the practical questions that all neo-Nazis faced after Rockwell's death. What direction should their movement go in? Should they remain in the parent party, led by Rockwell's unpopular successor, Matthias Koehl? And if they left, how should they be organized, and what strategy and tactics should they adopt?

In the 1960s, Rockwell was often laughed off as a joke, and in the 1970s, this laughter at his followers continued. It was easy enough, as their rallies were still small, and they were still aping their German predecessors. Members sported brown uniforms with swastika armbands while guarding blustering leaders of micro-parties. In the late 1970s in the United States, there were

DOI: 10.4324/9780429200090-5

probably between 1,500 and 2,000 neo-Nazis, scattered into many small groups.[1] While the NSWPP never folded, the locus of neo-Nazi activism moved to these new groupings who gained notoriety first—and deep concern later, as their movement morphed from comic relief to violence.

Numerous incidents started to appear on the radar of average Americans; these were almost always the products of the splintering, through the direct involvement of either former members or those who engaged in acts inspired by them. Events included the Skokie incident of 1977 and 1978, when neo-Nazis successfully sued under free speech laws to hold a rally in a community with many Holocaust survivors; a serial killer's attempted assassination of Larry Flynt in 1978, which left the publisher paralyzed; the election of David Duke as a Louisiana state representative in 1989; and the mass casualty 1995 Oklahoma City bombing, which was inspired by a book written by former NSWPP member William Pierce. These are all in addition to Mason's *Siege* and its progeny.

What follows is the winding story of how a small group of marginal, squabbling political discontents started off essentially doing street theatre promoting racism and antisemitism but in less than two decades moved on to murder and terrorism.

Getting the Party Started

George Lincoln Rockwell was a World War Two veteran who, like many other White Supremacists, eventually decided he had been fighting for the wrong side. After the war, he worked as a commercial illustrator and in the mid-1950s became politically active in Far Right groups. Rockwell quickly moved to the most extreme end, though, after reading Adolf Hitler and embracing antisemitism. He concluded that existing right-wing approaches were dead ends, held back by moderation rather than excess, and something new was needed to overcome their limitations. Building off his background in public relations, Rockwell's new approach was to "Raise the Swastika" and organize as an open neo-Nazi. This would attract media attention and bring in recruits since "No one can ignore Nazis marching in the street."[2]

At age 40, Rockwell found a collaborator, Harold Arrowsmith, who previously ran the paper organization the National Committee to Free America From Jewish Domination. They revived the name, and in July 1958 Rockwell held a small picket outside the White House in Washington, D.C. Under the slogan "Save Ike From the Kikes," it opposed U.S. relations with Israel during the Lebanese conflict. (While antisemitic, Rockwell's group did not use swastikas or other outward symbolism of Hitler's regime.) But the two fell out that same year, after which Rockwell started recruiting for a new, openly neo-Nazi project. In March 1959, he launched his group, originally called the

American Party but soon rechristened the American Nazi Party.[3] With it started the neo-Nazi movement in the United States as we know it.

Rockwell was certainly not the first National Socialist in the country, however. Before World War Two, it was not taboo to hold these views, and figures as prominent as Henry Ford were sympathizers. Adherents grouped around two main organizations. The German American Bund, based in the German community in the United States, became best known for their 1939 rally in New York City's Madison Square Garden. The other was the Silver Shirts, whose leader William Dudley Pelley espoused a mystical fascism. These groups disbanded after the war drastically changed the country's opinions about fascism and antisemitism, and it took a number of years for these doctrines to regain a public face.

Postwar, there were two important National Socialist groups that Rockwell distinguished his from. The earlier and smaller National Renaissance Party was founded in 1949. Led by James Madole, it was politically not an orthodox National Socialist group, incorporating mystical and occult elements and advocating untraditional alliances for U.S. fascists.[4]

Later more groups emerged. In the early 1950s, the Far Right had found a national figure in Senator Joseph McCarthy, a conspiratorial anti-Communist. And white Southerners founded a new and violent movement to preserve Jim Crow segregation in the face of the Civil Rights Movement, which gained traction in 1954—the same year McCarthy was disgraced.

But it would be several more years before the watershed year for the U.S. Far Right, when three important groups were launched. The first group founded in 1958 was Rockwell's precursor to the American Nazi Party. The second was the John Birch Society, which followed McCarthy's lead and espoused a virulent but coded antisemitism. (Because it was the most popular group of the Far Right, many White Supremacist leaders would pass through the John Birch Society as they moved further right.) The third important group which was founded in 1958 was the National States Rights Party (NSRP), led by Ed Fields and J.B. Stoner. Much larger than Madole's outfit and extremely antisemitic, it had close ties to the Ku Klux Klan. Stoner would be convicted of a 1958 church bombing and suspected of many others.[5] Despite its difference of approach, numerous activists would go between the NSRP and American Nazi Party/NSWPP (ANP/NSWPP), including key figures.

Ideology aside, neither the National Renaissance Party nor the NSRP used the swastika as their symbol, and the NSRP in particular did not publicly promote themselves as National Socialists. Deriding them as "sneaky Nazis," Rockwell did the opposite, using swastikas, rhetoric, and imagery that were as vulgar as they were incendiary. The party's publicity stunts included picketing both left- and right-wing groups as well as various films and plays, disrupting Congress, and, on two occasions, assaulting Civil Rights Movement leader Martin Luther King, Jr.[6]

"An Americanized Version of National Socialism"

Rockwell was a much more successful showman and speaker than a recruiter or organizer, and estimates for American Nazi Party membership have varied from the dozens to 200. For example, one of its biggest mobilizations was a counter-protest at Martin Luther King, Jr.'s 1963 March on Washington, where his "I Have a Dream" speech was delivered. Rockwell drew fewer than ninety people—including the undercover law enforcement who joined their rally.[7]

He was far more successful in Chicago, however. A housing desegregation march led by King on August 5, 1966, was opposed by a crowd of over 4,000 which had gathered at Marquette Park, Chicago. The march was attacked, King was knocked down by a rock, and a riot ensued. Afterward, he said, "I have seen many demonstrations in the south, but I have never seen anything so hostile and so hateful as I've seen here today."[8] Before another civil rights march on August 14, American Nazi Party members distributed signs bearing swastikas and the slogan "White Power"; the angry crowd obligingly held another riot. Rockwell flew in for the August 21 rally. Standing on a camper and giving a barn-burning speech, he was cheered by a crowd of 2,000. It was his greatest success.[9]

The Chicago rallies convinced Rockwell that he had found a popular formula—although ironically it turned his party in the same direction he initially was reacting against. Rockwell had already started to tone down his approach, eschewing the swastika for the Confederate flag during his 1965 run for Virginia governor. But it was the next year that was the real beginning of "the de-Nazification of the party," in the words of Rockwell biographer William Schmaltz.[10] It was this more traditional racism—and not the anti-semitism which ideologically distinguished the American Nazi Party from similar groups—that finally drew him grassroots support. The slogan "White Power!," which struck a chord in the Chicago crowds and Rockwell popularized, would remain an important rallying cry for White Supremacists for decades to come. Starting on January 1, 1967, the party's catchy, high-impact name was changed to the unwieldy National Socialist White People's Party (NSWPP); soon after, its newspaper was also changed, becoming *White Power*.[11] Rockwell was to have no further victories, however, as he was assassinated six months later by a disgruntled former party member.

Rockwell was not just the first visible neo-Nazi leader in the postwar United States, he also adapted its National Socialist ideology to fit his own time and place, creating what Schmaltz called the beginning of "an Americanized version of National Socialism."[12] These innovations, which have indelibly influenced neo-Nazism, included changing the Hitler's conception of the master race from "Aryan" to being "white" to fit U.S. racial conceptions. Second, he embraced Holocaust denial early in its spread in the

United States and made it central to neo-Nazism. And third, he encouraged the link between neo-Nazism and Christian Identity, a racist version of Christianity.[13]

A spiritual element also could be found in Rockwell. His initial attraction to National Socialism was based in part on a mystical experience he had after reading *Mein Kampf*, when he conceived of Hitler's politics as a religion.[14] Much later, this spiritual element of neo-Nazism would profoundly influence Mason.

Rockwell also created a strategic plan, consisting of four "phases," which became part of the standard neo-Nazi organizing toolkit in the following years. Phase One was the creation of an outrageous public image to gain media attention. Phase Two was spreading National Socialist doctrine. Phase Three was organizing and building party "units." And Phase Four was taking power.[15]

But Rockwell's break with conservatism was only half complete. Rockwell sought an authoritarian government with free enterprise and no income tax—not a dictatorship with a state-run economy. He promoted Christianity and U.S. nationalism using the cross, flag, and swastika and sought a "White, Christian, Constitutional Republic."[16]

Unsurprisingly, Mason retrospectively saw the party as National Socialist "only in theory," and "without the swastika" it would be "indiscernible from a dozen other right-wing groups." Martin Kerr, who would take over the party—by then on its third name, the New Order—after Koehl died in 2014, largely agreed. According to Kerr, the original party's beliefs were "a mélange of basic NS radicalism, common sense, and traditional American rightwing politics."[17]

Nonetheless, Rockwell was able to make himself into the uncontested neo-Nazi leader in the country, the first—and only—one to achieve that. After his passing, a void opened for his cultish followers. As Mason put it, "We were lost when we lost him." The party "carried on in his absence as though we expected his eventual return. As it turned out, no one had the vaguest idea of what to do or how to do it."[18]

Mason Joins the Party

Rockwell used media attention as bait for recruits, and Mason was one of those who bit. Growing up in Chillicothe, Ohio, Mason became interested in National Socialism as a young teenager. "For a period of many months," Mason said, "the image of Hitler, the Swastika and the Third Reich were leaping out at me from newsstands, television, at school, everywhere." He also saw news reports about the release of Nuremberg prisoners and Rockwell's success in Chicago in the summer of 1966.[19]

A classmate of his, Hugh Marshall Black, had contacted the party and received literature. He shared with Mason the book *Extremism U.S.A.*, which included a picture of an American Nazi Party truck with a banner bearing the local group's address. (The picture would turn out to be of his future collaborator, Allen Vincent.) Mason wrote them, and in December 1966, at age 14, Mason applied for membership in the National Socialist Youth Movement (NSYM), the youth section of the American Nazi Party.[20]

Rockwell would always remain Mason's idol. Even after he struck out on his own political path, he said Rockwell was "My greatest source of education, though we never met. The greatest example of courage and devotion, resourcefulness and even humor that I can imagine."[21]

Mason was in constant trouble at his high school and was threatened with being sent to a juvenile prison. In a story he would retell many times, in December 1968 he decided to kill his principal and several of the school staff. First, however, Mason contacted party headquarters, and one of the leaders, William Pierce, suggested instead he come there, to Arlington, Virginia. He did and the crisis was averted; Mason credited Pierce as saving both his and others lives. Mason earned $15 a week at the squalid headquarters where he learned how to use a printing press—a skill that later would serve him well. Mason stayed in Arlington intermittently for the next two years.[22] During that time, he attended the First Party Congress in September 1969 along with two other young men in particular who would go on to be of note: Joseph Tommasi and Joseph Paul Franklin. Later that month, along with Franklin, Mason took part in an attack on the organizing office of a leftist anti-war demonstration.

On July 25, 1970, Mason's 18th birthday, he was sworn in as a full-fledged, adult party member.[23] He returned to Ohio, where he stayed for the next two decades.

The Swastika Splinters

Rockwell had been a charismatic leader, and although a number of members had broken with him over the years, none formed a lasting rival organization. The same was not true for his successor. Matthias "Matt" Koehl, who was 32 when he took over, had a good command of National Socialist doctrine but lacked the leadership abilities of his predecessor.

Although poorly documented by scholars, the post-Rockwell period of U.S. neo-Nazism is when it developed the basic form it would look like far into the future. The decentralization of neo-Nazism helped lay the groundwork for how the movement's structure unfolded. If Rockwell had lived, or been succeeded by a popular leader, a single major neo-Nazi party may have existed for much longer.

From the founding of the party into the early 1970s, different organizational forms and tactical directions were created by former members. The original group had dues-paying members, official supporters, and a youth section. Uniforms were worn at public events, and there was a main head-quarters building. There was also a set of tactics, including publicity stunts, public rallies, grassroots organizing, and electoral runs. Phone hotlines were set up with propaganda messages, and where there was enough money and staff, "bookstores" opened.[24]

Different ideological tendencies, which had been present although not always acted on, were later teased out and elaborated on, sometimes leading to new tactical and organizational approaches. There was an ever-present seesaw between a more traditional White Supremacist politic (albeit with a strong element of antisemitism) and a more ideologically pure National Socialism. In addition to that, one extreme was an inward turning to religious cultism and private Hitler worship ceremonies, which became the path taken by the NSWPP as it metamorphosed into the New Order. The other end was advocating violent action and race war, which included guerilla armed struggle and leaderless resistance. Mason would eventually advocate the most extreme form of that approach.

While some California members had formed a new group in 1967, the most important early rupture in the NSWPP was William Pierce's departure in 1970. Pierce went on to important things in the world of National Socialism and became one of the most important influences in Mason's life.

In the 1960s, Pierce was a physics professor in Oregon and member of the John Birch Society. Like many others, he moved from the group's coded anti-semitism and barely constrained racism into explicitly White Supremacist politics. He moved east to work with Rockwell and in 1966 started the *National Socialist World*, a magazine geared toward intellectuals and pub-lished under the auspices of the World Union of National Socialists. Despite their closeness, Pierce was not a card-holding party member until it became the NSWPP in January 1967.[25] After Rockwell's death, Pierce, Koehl, and Robert Lloyd formed a triumvirate that ran the party. But Pierce did not see Koehl as someone who filled Rockwell's shoes, and formally asked him to share power with himself and Lloyd. Koehl was not amused by this challenge to his authority and launched a counterattack; Pierce lost out in the struggle and soon left.[26]

In an August 1970 open letter describing his side of the events, Pierce said he would "not be at all surprised to see the Party retrench into a sort of Matt Koehl Nazi Fan Club consisting of a few dozen members and supporters within the next few months." Mason would later say he had "lost his faith" in Koehl after Pierce was elbowed out, but stayed because, "I didn't know what else to do."[27]

But obviously not everyone hated Koehl. Despite Pierce's biting dismissal, the party continued to be healthy for a number of years. (Nonetheless, Pierce was correct about the centrality of Koehl.) For example, Jim Saleam had a very different view, albeit in hindsight. Saleam, himself an Australian Far

Right politician with a background in neo-Nazism, wrote a master's thesis that is one of the few overviews of the postwar U.S. neo-Nazi milieu. He saw Koehl as not just a good manager but a leader who "stood above his contemporaries" as a neo-Nazi theorist. Koehl's ideas "appear to be the basis of American Nazi thinking and even rival groups echo his postulates. An examination of Koehl's major writings unravel the essence of American Nazism in the Post-Rockwell period." Saleam also estimated that there had been at least 1,000 NSWPP members and supporters (and possibly even twice that)—at least if these were defined in a "broad way."[28]

After his leave-taking, Pierce figured out fairly quickly what he was going to do. The new group he formed, the National Alliance, was the largest U.S. neo-Nazi organization for many years, thereby making it the most important one to come out of the NSWPP. In 1978, he also published his race-war novel *The Turner Diaries*, which became a classic of its genre, selling hundreds of thousands of copies. Its notoriety went ballistic after it inspired militia movement members to commit the 1995 Oklahoma City bombing, which killed 168 people.

The other important figure to leave the NSWPP that year was Chicago organizer Frank Collin. He had been energized by Rockwell's successes in Marquette Park but disillusioned by Koehl, who withdrew from local organizing and pulled resources back to Arlington, Virginia. (Koehl's NSWPP was often referred to as "Arlington" as well as "Franklin Road," where the headquarters building was located.) In particular, his insistence that buildings owned by local units had to be sold or the title transferred to him was a source of great tension.[29]

Collin formed the National Socialist Party of America (NSPA), which combined electoral campaigns, high-profile rallies and lawsuits, and grassroots organizing. Although their later Skokie lawsuit would bring them fame, it was an outgrowth of the NSPA's longer-term organizing. They were the only neo-Nazi group to establish an actual grassroots base after they positioned themselves as Marquette Park's symbol of resistance to desegregation.

Pierce and Collin aside, a few more years would pass before the NSWPP's dam broke in 1973 and 1974. The Fifth Party Congress, held in Cleveland in September 1973, was one of its greatest successes. One hundred uniformed neo-Nazis marched unopposed by counter-protestors and unhampered by police, making it the biggest uniformed march the party ever held. The event had a strong impact on Mason, and he would refer to it numerous times. At the Congress, Mason also met Allen Vincent in person for the first time, who would later play an important role in Mason's political journey.[30]

But behind closed doors, things were different. Koehl suspended the southern California-based Joseph Tommasi, one of the party's most talented organizers. By the end of the year, Cleveland organizer Casey Kalemba had also left the party. Both would take their followers and form new groups.

After the Fifth Congress, the party launched into a new period of activism. An American Jewish Committee report said that, starting in mid-October 1973, the NSWPP was hoping that war in the Middle East, coupled with the oil embargo, would provide "fertile ground" for antisemitism and recruitment. According to the report,

> Since the Yom Kippur War, units of the NSWPP have flamboyantly picketed foreign embassies, the White House, book stores, theatres, and Jewish houses of worship; appeared in full Nazi storm trooper regalia before Boards of Education and City Councils; distributed literature and defaced public buildings with propaganda stickers in downtown business areas; conducted "Free Rudolph Hess" vigils in a dozen cities and publicly announced the opening of "new" national headquarters in at least three cities. After a long lapse, its national and local leadership have been featured as news makers on television and radio broadcasts, as panelists on talk shows, and profiled in local newspapers. Unprecedented exposure and hitherto unobtainable publicity as Rockwell predicted, has seemingly come at last.[31]

Despite the loss of so many members by the end of 1974, the NSWPP changed its strategy and continued on. The Cleveland march had been the high point of its public rallies, and in 1975 they started contesting local political races. That year, Wolfgang Schrodt ran for Baltimore city council and received 12 percent of the white vote (1,200 votes). In 1976, Richard Johanson received over 5 percent in a San Francisco school board election (almost 8,800 votes). Three candidates also ran in Milwaukee. In 1976, Art Jones received 8 percent in the first round of voting for mayor. (It took a while, but Jones would briefly achieve national attention in 2018, when he won an uncontested Republican congressional primary in Chicago before going on to win 25 percent in the general election—56,000 votes.) In 1978, two women in the NSWPP's women's section ran in the Milwaukee school board primaries, and each received about 20 percent of the vote. Sandra Osvatic received 6,300 and Sandra Enders 7,700—the latter losing by only 300 votes.[32]

NSWPP members also tried their hand at more grassroots approaches, such as raising money for flood victims and painting over graffiti. Nevertheless, by 1978, the party clearly was in decline.[33]

The NSWPP in Southern Ohio

Mason was silent as he saw Pierce, his savior and mentor, and Tommasi, whom he had great respect for, pushed out of the party. But he bided his time before his own leave-taking.

A number of southern Ohio NSWPP members were active. These included Mason and Greg Hurles in Chillicothe, Robert Brannen in South Lebanon, and Steven Love in Cincinnati. They sometimes were joined at events by two Kentucky members, Clifford Herrington of Radcliff and Raymond Chaney of Louisville. In April 1970, the NSWPP opened a bookstore in Cincinnati, primarily through the work of Sanders "Sandy" Pierce, the brother of William Pierce. But by the end of the summer, William Pierce had been expelled and Sandy closed the space.[34] In 1972, the Cincinnati NSWPP started a small newsletter, the *Local Activity Report*, which in 1973 became the *Southern Ohio Activity Report*. Love edited it when he was not busy working as an astrologist who "specialized in predictions."[35]

In January 1972, the NSWPP/Ohio was founded as an entity separate from the Cincinnati unit[36]—although this appeared to be little more than a name for Mason and Hurles to work under. (Hurles, 21, was Mason's comrade in Chillicothe and remained close to him into the 1980s.) It allowed them to have more influence at movement meetings, as Hurles and Mason claimed they were representing different groups and therefore received two separate votes.

From 1972 to 1974, the southern Ohio NSWPP members were active in a number of local publicity efforts. They screened the 1930s Nazi propaganda film *Triumph of the Will* several times, on at least two of which Koehl spoke. They held literature distributions; flyered both right- and left-wing events, including an anti-abortion march (which they supported) and a Vietnam Veterans Against the War rally (which they opposed); and threw an Adolf Hitler birthday party.[37]

For years, the Cincinnati NSWPP also held "Free Hess" rallies. A rare popular issue for neo-Nazis to organize around—even President Richard Nixon was sympathetic to him—the campaign to free former NSDAP minister Rudolf Hess started in the late 1960s and gained traction around his 80th birthday in 1974. (Hess had been arrested after he made a secret flight to Britain in 1941 to negotiate a peace agreement. Convicted at Nuremberg, he was the only inmate of Berlin's Spandau Prison when he committed suicide in 1987.)[38]

That August was also the highpoint of Mason's grassroots organizing career as an Ohio neo-Nazi when he helped run a table at the Ross County Fair. Predictably, their application was met with an outcry, and the fair tried to prevent them from attending. The American Civil Liberties Union (ACLU) stepped in to back them, and in July, Koehl provided support by coming to Chillicothe for a talk. Mason reported that they successfully held the booth for five days in early August, although at one point there was what he called a "near riot," necessitating them to call for backup.[39]

Trouble with Teenagers

At the time, Mason and Hurles also had other matters on their mind, as before the fair they had been arrested for a particularly vile racial assault in Chillicothe. In October 1973, they went to a Lincoln-Mercury dealership and took a car out on a test drive. As one paper later reported, "The prosecution charged that Mason was the driver of a car from which a passenger sprayed a can of mace at several black teen-agers in a Dairy Queen parking lot"—including a 14-year-old girl. (In court, Mason was accused of being the mace-wielding passenger.)[40]

The next day, the duo was asked to report to the local police station. As they were arriving, the victims—having been positioned by the police—got a good look at them. They identified the neo-Nazis as their assailants, and Mason and Hurles were duly arrested. This unusual identification process led to the ACLU watching the case as an instance of political profiling.[41]

Mason went to trial in November 1973 and Hurles in July 1974. Both were convicted and sentenced to six months plus a $200 fine, and both appealed. While they were ultimately unsuccessful, they remained free during the county fair and so were able to staff the booth at the Ross County Fair. Mason started his sentence in October 1974 and spent it working as a hospital clerk at the Cincinnati Work House. Hurles did three months but was granted an early release in May 1975 due to his wife's pregnancy.[42]

When Mason was released in March 1975, his political life started a new course. He had long been disenchanted with Koehl. While many others continued to stick with him, Mason described Koehl as an "orthodox, cultist conservative" with "no talents" and "no charisma," who was mostly "concerned with your mode of dress and regulation-style haircut" and who sought to develop "a Nazi cult of personality around himself."[43]

Still, Mason remained an NSWPP member for a time, even after forming his own group. When he resigned in April 1976, the National Socialist Movement (NSM) issued a booklet which accused Koehl of being gay.[44] (This rumor would long follow Koehl around.) But while Mason could fling accusations, neither he nor anyone else produced evidence that would make them stick. But it didn't matter; by then, Mason was already off and running in a different direction entirely.

Notes

1 Milton Ellerin, *American Nazis -- Myth or Menace?* (New York: American Jewish Committee, 1977), p.11, https://ajcarchives.org/ajcarchive/DigitalArchive.aspx
2 Frederick J. Simonelli, *American Fuehrer: George Lincoln Rockwell and the American Nazi Party* (Urbana: University of Illinois Press, 1999), pp.26, 31.
3 Ibid, pp.27–28; William H. Schmaltz, *Hate: George Lincoln Rockwell and the American Nazi Party* (Washington, DC: Brassey's, 1999), pp.31–34.
   Sources give differing accounts of what happened after the split with Arrowsmith, including the party's original name and date of founding. Pierce's biography of Rockwell gave the March 1959 date and American Party name. James K. Warner identified it as part of another Rockwell creation, The World Union of Free Enterprise National Socialists. Later, Martin Kerr said it was both: the "American Party of the World Union of Free Enterprise National Socialists." In 1979, Mason

wrote that, "Two 'official' dates stand as the birthdate of the American Nazi Party: October, 1958, and March, 1959." The NSWWP recognized the former one, being the year Rockwell was first publicly identified as an antisemite after it was reported in the media that he was a suspect in the bombing of an Atlanta synagogue. More generally, it was common for neo-Nazis to date their organizations prior to their actual foundation. They were typically backdated to when the founding members either split with their prior group or started the political trajectory that ended up in the formation of the group in question; James Mason, "It Began with a Big Blast!," *Stormer* 2(1) Winter 1979, p.3; William L. Pierce, "George Lincoln Rockwell: A National Socialist Life," *National Socialist World*, Winter 1967, p.28, https://archive.org/details/glr-ansl-wlp; James K. Warner, *Swastika Smearbund* (Cincinnati: NSM, 1977), p.4 (originally released 1960); Martin Kerr, "The History of American National Socialism Part 6: The Rockwell Years (1959–1967)," *New Order*, www.theneworder.org/history---6.html

4 Jeffrey Kaplan, "The Post-War Paths of Occult National Socialism: From Rockwell and Madole to Manson," *Patterns of Prejudice* 35(3) 2001, pp.45–52, published online December 7, 2010, www.tandfonline.com/doi/abs/10.1080/003132201128811214

5 Michael Newton, *The National States Rights Party: A History* (Jefferson, North Carolina: McFarland, 2017), pp.25, 45, 46; Douglas Martin, "J. B. Stoner, 81, Fervent Racist and Benchmark for Extremism, Dies," *NYT*, April 29, 2005, www.nytimes.com/2005/04/29/us/j-b-stoner-81-fervent-racist-and-benchmark-for-extremism-dies.html

6 George Lincoln Rockwell, *This Time the World* (Ironmarch, 2017), chapter XII, p.182 (originally published 1969); Simonelli, *American Fuehrer*, pp.75–76.

7 Simonelli put it at 200 at the maximum, but with a "few thousand" supporters; *American Fuehrer*, pp.34–37, 51.

8 "Dr. King Felled by Rock," *Chicago Tribune*, August 6, 1966, pp.1, 2, www.newspapers.com/image/376510146, www.newspapers.com/image/376510155. The 1960 Census found that the area of Gage Park–Chicago Lawn–Marquette Park had over 100,000 residents—only seven of whom were not white; Gene Roberts, "Rock Hits Dr. King as Whites Attack March in Chicago," *NYT*, August 6, 1966, pp.1, 52, www.nytimes.com/1966/08/06/archives/rock-hits-dr-king-as-whites-attack-march-in-chicago-felled-rights.html

9 Schmaltz, *Hate*, pp.287–91. For the ANP/NSWPP version of the story, see Martin Kerr, "Forgotten History: The Chicago White People's Uprising of 1966 – Part One," September 17, 2017 (originally October 25, 2016), *New Order*, https://web.archive.org/web/20190508185742, https://neworderorg.wordpress.com/2017/09/17/forgotten-history-the-chicago-white-peoples-uprising-of-1966-part-one, https://web.archive.org/web/20190508134954, https://neworderorg.wordpress.com/2018/09/13/forgotten-history-the-chicago-white-peoples-uprising-of-1966-conclusion

10 Simonelli, *American Fuehrer*, p.97; Schmaltz, *Hate*, pp.254, 271.

11 Simonelli, *American Fuehrer*, p.100; Schmaltz, *Hate*, pp.304, 322.

12 Schmaltz, *Hate*, p.xvii.

13 Simonelli, *American Fuehrer*, pp.3, 4, 100–2, 104–22. For Christian Identity in general, see Michael Barkun, *Religion and the Racist Right: The Origins of the Christian Identity Movement* (Chapel Hill: University of North Carolina Press, 1994).

14 Rockwell, *This Time the World*, chapter VII, pp.115–17.

15 Ibid, chapter XX, pp.301–13.

16 Mason attributed this phrase to Rockwell; *Siege*, p.497.

17 Mason's interview with Tom Metzger on *Race and Reason*, July 31, 1993, online as "James Mason's Interview with Tom Metzger" (video), uploaded by SiegeKultur, September 15, 2022, https://odysee.com/@siegekultur:b/Metzgers-Interview:2;

Martin Kerr, "History of American National Socialism; Part 7: The National Socialist White People's Party (1967–1982)," *New Order*, www.theneworder.org/history---7-1.html

18 SIEGE 15(5) May 1986, p.4 (*Siege*, p.429); SIEGE August 1983 12(8), p.2 (*Siege*, p.43).

19 "James Mason: An Interview," *Regal Scroll* #1, March 1995 (*Articles*, p.86).

20 Ryan Schuster, "Introduction to the First Edition," *Siege*, pp.21–22. (Despite the title, this was originally the introduction to the second, 2003 edition that Schuster himself published); Mason to Moynihan, October 22, 1992 [Box 11, Folder 2]. The photos are in Mason, *Siege*, 1st ed., M.M. Jenkins (Michael Moynihan), ed. (Denver: Storm Books, 1992), pp.xv, xvi (actual print date is 1993); Mason interview in *Regal Scroll* (*Articles*, p.86).

21 SIEGE 15(5) May 1986, p.4 (*Siege*, p.429).

22 Schuster, "Introduction," *Siege*, pp.22–23.

23 "Universal Order: Where Manson Means Survival," *Compulsion* #3, 1998, p.49 (*Articles*, p.170).

24 These storefronts often had little more than propaganda leaflets. They served as a place for the group to meet, an opportunity for sympathizers to make contact, and a visible public presence. There would be few, if any, books for sale. For example, see Gerald Volgenau, "Religious Groups, Pickets Protest Nazi Bookstore," *Detroit Free Press*, December 29, 1977, p.3, www.newspapers.com/image/99062077

25 Leonard Zeskind, *Blood and Politics: The History of the White Nationalist Movement from the Margins to the Mainstream* (New York: Farrar Straus Giroux, 2009), p.19.

26 For an account of the 1970 split, see Jim Saleam, "American Nazism in the Context of the American Extreme Right: 1960–1978," Chapter 3: "The Post-Rockwell Period" (M.A. thesis, University of Sydney, 1985), https://archive.li/YYhX

27 William Pierce, "To My National Socialist Friends and Co-Workers and All Other Interested National Socialists" (open letter), August 5, 1970 [Box 47, Folder 20]. For the May 31, 2002 interview with Mason by Ryan Schuster, see "James Mason Interviewed in 2002" (video), uploaded by SiegeKultur, September 15, 2022, https://odysee.com/@siegekultur:b/jminterview2002:e

28 Saleam, "American Nazism," chapter 3.

29 Despite numerous former NSWPP activists attributing their leave-taking partly or primarily to this, Kerr has denied that this was the reason the bookstores were shut down, saying "Blaming any of this on Matt Koehl is puerile and dishonest." Instead Kerr said the closures were due to local organizers who were unable to retain their leases in face of opposition, or to make their payments; Kerr to author, email, October 1, 2023.

30 Mason frequently referred to this event as the party's last success before what he saw as its irrelevancy. SIEGE 9(5) September 1980, p.1 (*Siege*, p.159); Mason to Steven D. Love, January 9, 1974 [Box 7, Folder 12].

31 Milton Ellerin, *The American Nazis: Some Recent Developments* (New York: American Jewish Committee, 1974), http://ajcarchives.org/ajcarchive/Digital Archive.aspx

32 Ibid; Kerr, "History of American National Socialism, Part 7: The National Socialist White People's Party (1967-1982)"; Mitch Dudek, "Holocaust-Denier Gets Nearly 40 Percent of Vote in 2 Mount Greenwood Precincts," *Chicago Sun Times*, November 7, 2018, https://chicago.suntimes.com/2018/11/7/18449701/holocaust-denier-gets-nearly-40-percent-of-vote-in-2-mount-greenwood-precincts

33 Martin Kerr to author, email, August 17, 2023.

34 Love to Mason, April 9, 1970; Love, "Special Release to All Members, Supporters and Friends," September 1970 [both Box 7, Folder 12]. Sanders Pierce was involved in the National Alliance and after his brother's death was a member of NARRG, the National Alliance Reform and Restoration Group; Keegan Hanks, "Soundcloud Bans Recordings from the National Alliance Reform and Restoration Group," *SPLC*, October 7, 2014, www.splcenter.org/hatewatch/2014/10/07/soundcloud-bans-recordings-national-alliance-reform-and-restoration-group
35 Steven D. Love, business card [1974]; see issues of *Local Activity Report* in 1972 and *Southern Ohio Activity Report* in 1973 [Box 7, Folder 12].
36 "General Secretary's Notes," *National Socialist Bulletin* 7(11) January 1978, p.2.
37 "Street Action in Cincinnati," *Southern Ohio Activity Report* #9, April 1973, p.3; "Abortion Rally," *Southern Ohio Activity Report* #11, June 1973, p.1; "Hitler's Birthday Celebration," *Southern Ohio Activity Report* #10, May 1973, p.1; "Triumph of the Will," *Local Activity Report* #5–6, June & July 1972, p.1; "Nazi Chief Foresees 'White Revolution'," *Cincinnati Enquirer*, February 19, 1973, www.newspapers.com/image/100967903
38 "Calls Rising to Free Rudolf Hess, Near 80," *NYT*, April 21, 1974, www.nytimes.com/1974/04/21/archives/calls-rising-to-free-rudolf-hess-near-80-appeals-for-release.html; *National Socialist Bulletin*, 8(6) June 1979, back cover.
39 Jack McFarren, "Local Radical Group Gets Visit from National Commander," *Chillicothe Gazette* (Ohio), July 5, 1974, www.newspapers.com/image/292702295; Mason, "Report on N.W.P.P. Activity at 1974 Ross County Fair (Ohio)," August 11, 1974 (internal NSWPP report) [Box 15, Folder 11].
40 "Jury's Verdict Guilty in Assault," *Chillicothe Gazette*, November 3, 1973, www.newspapers.com/image/292429722
41 Ibid; "Mace Spray Conviction Appealed," *Chillicothe Gazette*, November 9, 1973, www.newspapers.com/image/292435013
42 "Mace sentence," *Chillicothe Gazette*, November 6, 1973, www.newspapers.com/image/292433130; "Appeals Court upholds ruling," *Chillicothe Gazette*, June 13, 1974, www.newspapers.com/image/292417334; SIEGE 9(12) December 1980, p.4; Mason, "Report on N.S.W.P.P. Activity at 1974 Ross County Fair (Ohio)"; "Man Convicted in Macing Released from Jail," *Chillicothe Gazette*, May 15, 1976, www.newspapers.com/image/292333440
43 Mason interview with Schuster (video).
44 NSM, *Anatomy of a Smear* (pamphlet), April 1976 [Box 47, Folder 21].

3

JOSEPH TOMMASI'S NSLF

The story of Joseph Tommasi's National Socialist Liberation Front (NSLF) is pivotal to the development of James Mason's projects. And more generally, the group played an important role in prying open neo-Nazism from the approach that had been in place for the 15 years since the founding of the American Nazi Party.

Mason had met Tommasi several times before his suspension from the party in 1973. As Mason became increasingly disenchanted with the National Socialist White People's Party (NSWPP), he closely followed the development of Tommasi's new NSLF. While Rockwell had inspired Mason as a leader and moral figure, it was Tommasi who had the greatest political influence. More than anyone else, he showed Mason the path that could be taken out of the wilderness of Matthias Koehl's party—an opening which Mason extended much further.

Before the falling out, Tommasi was a very successful organizer and charismatic leader in the California NSWPP. Like many others, he ended up taking his followers when he left and founded a new group, the NSLF. They were best known for openly advocating guerilla warfare, and members carried out at least the beginning stages of this. Politically, he emphasized that his was a revolutionary perspective that was not part of right-wing conservatism.

He also rejected the cultural and social norms of neo-Nazism and absorbed many elements of the 1960s and early '70s counterculture. This kind of openness was an important predecessor to those neo-Nazi groups who were able to embrace the Nazi skinhead movement early on. The influence of Tommasi can also be seen in Mason's collaboration with the circle of musicians and artists who became close to him.

DOI: 10.4324/9780429200090-6

Before that happened, however, Tommasi was killed in a fight with NSWPP members a little more than a year after the NSLF was founded. Afterward, Mason and others turned him into a martyr and built a cult around him, while the NSLF itself continued for more than a decade under various leaders. The Anti-Defamation League (ADL), a Jewish monitoring group, would dub the NSLF "the most violent of the Nazi splinter groups."[1]

NSWPP Days

Joseph Charles Tommasi lived in El Monte, California, just east of Los Angeles. The FBI noted his attendance at a December 1966 American Nazi Party meeting, when he was just 15, and the next year a teacher alerted the agency that he was passing out party propaganda at his high school.[2] At 17, he joined the party's local branch and rapidly advanced up the ranks. By October 1969, he was made a regional leader and, in September 1970, became one of seven members of the NSWPP National Council, which was formed to advise Koehl. He first met Mason at the 1969 Congress, and they saw each other at every party conference through 1973.[3]

Tommasi was no pale-skinned, blonde-haired Aryan warrior, however. His dark complexion earned him the nickname "Tomato Joe," while police called him the "Tomato Head Fuhrer."[4] He was, by all accounts, charismatic, reckless, and violent. The third NSLF leader, John Duffy, described Tommasi's lifestyle "as flamboyant and out-going as possible." Martin Kerr described Tommasi as "intelligent, charismatic, brave and committed to the cause"— but also "narcissistic, hot-headed and undisciplined."[5] In short, Tommasi absorbed the California counterculture of his era—even as he hitched its influence to a vehicle which intended to destroy the very ideals that culture espoused.

In 1969, Tommasi encouraged NSWPP members to work on military maneuvers and learn how to use Molotov cocktails. This embrace of violence was not a quirk of his, however. According to Mason, advocacy of violence was "never spoken, never printed and was, in fact, taboo in official party dealings." But he also described how rank-and-file members at the Arlington headquarters believed they needed to strike at the System "so that blood could be splashed from one end of the country to the other.... It was Right Wingism at its darkest."[6] William Pierce was the foremost party leader who gave voice to those dark urges. According to Mason, out of all the NSWPP leaders, Pierce "was the only one hot on revolution, and toying around with illegality as part of policy." (Nonetheless, it should be noted that despite these "dark urges," NSWPP members were prohibited from acting on them and so had to wait until their leave-taking for their opportunity to do so.)

In March 1969, a NSWPP phone line run by Tommasi was shut down after playing a recording of Pierce saying, "Let's clearly understand that there is only one effective way to deal with the rampaging blacks on our campuses and in our cities, and that is to kill them." This was by no means an isolated call for violence. In another phone message, Pierce called for killing senators.[7]

At the First Party Congress in September 1969, Pierce was asked what would happen to "White race traitors." Mason said he "spoke not a word but, gesturing with thumb and index finger forming the barrel and hammer of a pistol being fired, brought the entire assembly to its feet" in wild enthusiasm. At the next year's Congress, Tommasi made an impassioned speech calling for revolutionary action.[8]

That year he told a reporter, "We're not right-wingers...We're revolutionaries." But Tommasi "intensely hated" Pierce, and so when the party's highest pro-violence figure was forced out, Tommasi sided with Koehl.[9] Soon the same fate would befall Tommasi, however.

Clashes with Leftists

Tommasi led his followers into battle with their enemies and, in 1967 and 1968, took part in many Los Angeles counter-protests and clashes with leftist anti-Vietnam War demonstrators. And some of these clashes were with the Jewish Defense League (JDL), a scenario that would be repeated around the country with different neo-Nazi groups. The JDL didn't just brawl in the streets with neo-Nazis, though; it conducted a series of attacks and bombings against Nazi war criminals, Palestinian activists, and Soviet officials.

Tommasi purchased a house in El Monte and turned it into a swastika-festooned headquarters. On January 30, 1972, 1,000 people demonstrated outside, ending in a six-hour standoff during which protestors pelted police with rocks and bottles. The next day, the JDL and NSWPP fought outside the latter's headquarters. Tommasi claimed that shots were fired at him, and the Los Angeles JDL leader, Irvin D. Rubin, was arrested for attempted murder, although the charges were soon dropped.[10]

Kerr, part of the Los Angeles chapter under Tommasi, was one of several NSWPP members who came away with strong impressions about him. Like Mason, he had joined the National Socialist Youth Movement in 1966 when he was 14 years old, but stayed for less than a year. After a stint in the National Renaissance Party, he was in the NSWPP from 1971 through the end of 1983. However, he rejoined the New Order in 2007 and took over their leadership when Koehl died in 2014.[11] Kerr described Tommasi as "the most impressive and successful of the NSWPP's local leaders" and said that "At a time when many NSWPP units struggled to raise a dozen men for local demonstrations, Tommasi could put 40 to 50 troopers in the street." The NSLF claimed that the 67 Stormtroopers which Tommasi brought to a protest against the inauguration of Los Angeles's first black mayor, Thomas Bradley, was "the largest single demonstration for a local Unit of the Party in

Party History."[12] But also in contradiction to the NSWPP's strict rules, Tommasi allowed members to smoke pot and for members' girlfriends to stay at the headquarters.

CREEPy Deals

Tommasi also made an unusual political deal which ended up in the papers. In November 1971, he was hired by an associate of the Committee to Re-elect the President (CREEP), Richard Nixon's 1972 election fundraising vehicle which was implicated in the Watergate scandal. Tommasi and his followers were paid to go out and convince registered voters of George Wallace's American Independent Party to re-register as Republicans—thereby making the small party lose state ballot status.[13] (Wallace had been a segregationist Alabama governor who ran for president in 1968 and carried five southern states; Mason supported this run. Wallace ran again in 1972, during which he was paralyzed in an assassination attempt.)

The drive was unsuccessful, but a dispute over money caused the neo-Nazis to go public with the story. (Tommasi was to be paid $5,000 but received only $1,200—although apparently he also promised to provide 20 men but came up with only four.) The incident made the local press in November 1972 and, as the Watergate scandal boiled, the *New York Times* in June 1973.[14]

Conflict with Koehl

Tommasi's flamboyant lifestyle, lack of discipline, personal charisma, and organizing prowess were on a collision course with Koehl, who was tightening his control over the party. Mason said that Tommasi had signed the over ownership of the El Monte headquarters as a "testament of his loyalty to Koehl."[15] Tommasi's later actions showed how this remained a particularly bitter taste in his mouth.

Things came to a head at what the NSLF later described as an "insane kangaroo court" the evening before the September 1973 NSWPP congress in Cleveland. Tommasi was removed from his position and suspended from the party for six months, although not expelled—yet.[16]

A number of different reasons were given for his punishment. These included allowing drug use, having women stay at the headquarters, misusing funds, and the Nixon campaign deal. Mason said it was probably marijuana use and Tommasi's girlfriends staying overnight at the headquarters, although at the end of the day the real reason was Koehl's jealousy.[17]

Kerr claimed that in early 1973, Tommasi signed over the headquarters because he couldn't keep up the mortgage payments. Already unhappy with Tommasi, Koehl forced him to sign an agreement limiting his actions.

The suspension was set off by Tommasi violating the agreement by holding military trainings.[18]

The Los Angeles NSWPP would continue on without him, but the NSLF claimed that the unit lost over 45 members, with only close to 20 remaining. Furthermore, the NSLF claimed that NSWPP members were threatened with being expelled if they talked with Tommasi—or even his associates.[19]

The local NSWPP continued to stay in the news. In 1975, it was barred from a local school system for taking part in a racially driven conflict at a high school. In June 1976, the local unit of the party gave up their building because they could not make their mortgage payments, announcing they would give the city government of El Monte what it wanted and leave town for Pasadena.[20] But the intervening time had not passed without serious conflict between the unit and Tommasi's new NSLF.

Enter the NSLF

After it was clear that the rift was irreparable, Tommasi started his own organization, the NSLF. He took the name from a previous NSWPP student group which existed in 1969 and 1970 and which—under Pierce's guidance—had aped the New Left. There was no real connection between the groups, especially since Pierce and Tommasi did not like each other. Tommasi did get hold of some old membership cards from the initial group and reuse them, however.[21]

It was the new NSLF that would be the first to graft two important elements together: breaking from the social conservatism that had marked U.S. neo-Nazism to date and openly calling for violence. Tommasi's new organization also raised hopes in certain anti-Koehl quarters. One insider account observed that

> many people secretly hoped Tommasi would challenge Arlington's control of the NS Movement a la mass strategy and believe that, if he had not rejected Rockwellian concepts, he may have united a majority of the active NSWPP units in a successful mutiny and won enough financial support to build a propaganda machine capable of rivaling Arlington's.[22]

Forty-three people attended the NSLF's founding meeting on March 2, 1974 in El Monte.[23] (According to Kerr, Tommasi had refused to renew his NSWPP membership in February but was "only expelled" after the NSLF was founded.[24]) During the 15 months that Tommasi led the group, they took credit for several bombings, published two periodicals, and opened a bookstore. Rather than hiding underground, Tommasi gave TV and newspaper interviews.[25]

New Left Names

One of the most prominent aspects of the NSLF was how it borrowed from the New Left hook, line, and sinker. This included aesthetics, slogans, and strategic and tactical approaches. In fact, the group's name itself was taken from the Vietnamese Communists' National Liberation Front, which had inspired numerous militant leftist groups around the world to also dub themselves "Liberation Fronts."[26]

Tommasi's NSLF had two periodicals: *Siege*, which put out two issues in the second half of 1974, and the *National Socialist Review*, which debuted in January 1975. The name *Siege* came from the New Left, but its exact origin is shrouded in mystery. According to Mason, Tommasi "took the name SIEGE from an L.A. County Library book by that title which was devoted to the Weather Underground faction of the SDS," the Students for a Democratic Society. Later, Mason wrote that it came directly from the Weather Underground, the armed struggle group that emerged from the SDS leadership.[27]

However, there does not appear to be a book on the Weather Underground titled "Siege." The most likely candidate for the name is Norman Mailer's *Miami and the Siege of Chicago*. Long passages in the book described clashes during the 1968 Democratic convention in Chicago between police and protestors, including the SDS—but not the Weather Underground, as it had not formed yet.[28] However, this demonstration is often confused with the Days of Rage, the inaugural event of the Weather Underground, which was also in Chicago—but the next year.

Tommasi adopted the countercultural New Left's lifestyle, which was clearly an attraction (and probably a relief) for many of the younger people who wished to take part in the popular fashions and lifestyles of their day. Gone were the short haircut and brown uniform; Tommasi grew his hair long and wore a military field uniform. He specifically relaxed the prohibition on drugs, although some were still off-limits, like heroin.[29]

Last, Tommasi lifted his political approach directly from the most militant wing of the New Left. By the early 1970s, urban guerilla groups conducted bombings, plane hijackings, and other attacks in hopes of sparking revolutionary uprisings. The two groups most frequently referred to in the NSLF orbit were the Symbionese Liberation Army and the Weather Underground. Tommasi simply swapped out a National Socialist revolution for a Marxist-Leninist one, complete with image, strategies, and tactics. It was a simple but effective substitution.

Structure

Tommasi constructed a fusion aboveground/underground group. According to David Rust, the second NSLF leader, Tommasi had envisioned an organization with two separate organs. First - the underground. Believing that the legal struggle for control of the country (and our own destiny) has been lost, NSLF sees the development of an underground resistance movement as the only alternative to submission. Secondly the above-board or legal political machine - The job of which is to educate, propagandize, and recruit.[30]

Mason would later say Tommasi's "mistake was....trying to mix underground with overground"—a common criticism of similar groups, especially the Black Panther Party.[31]

In 1974, the NSLF listed three locations in Southern California, plus members in Cleveland, Ohio and Louisville, Kentucky. The next year, Frank Braswell's North Carolina NSWPP group switched allegiance to them, although shortly thereafter he was involved in a shootout. There was an affiliate in New Mexico, Unit 14, which dissolved because of the suspected presence of an FBI informer.[32] The NSLF also briefly ran the New Order Bookstore in El Monte, billed as "The Most Revolutionary Bookstore in California"—although in 1974 there would have been stiff competition for that title.[33]

Ideology

Tommasi appeared to have spent 1974 formulating the ideology of the NSLF and 1975 putting it into action.

The NSLF program outlined four rather typical political goals: running a bookstore and phone line, spreading propaganda, and hosting ideological workshops with the goal of fomenting "street action." But the program also promised far more.

> The crack of gunfire is the only reality the masses care to pay any attention to. The Revolution belongs only to those who are prepared to suffer the consequences of disrupting the silence of darkness. We must prepare to seize the time.

In the same breath, perspective members were asked to send $5 with their application and make a monthly pledge of at least the same amount. Dishonest applicants were threatened with lawsuits.[34]

The two-page "Strategy for Revolution" appeared in *Siege* #1 in 1974. Declaring that "The White Man has lost! We are an occupied people in our own land," the NSLF offered a five-point program. One, eschewing elections. Two, rejecting the mass strategy and recruiting "only the best movement people." Three, abandoning "petty bourgeois, bureaucratic hang-ups...the end justifies the means. What works is good!" Four, involving women "in every aspect of the NSLF." And five, embracing "armed struggle as the only effective means of forcing political change."[35]

Tommasi's ideological evolution toward a revolutionary opposition to conservatism was also evident. Mason would later make a flyer out of Tommasi's proclamation that

> We DO NOT wish for "Law and Order", for law and order means continued existence of this rotten rip-off Capitalist Jew System. We wish for anarchy and chaos which will enable us to ATTACK the system while her Big Brother Pigs are trying to keep the pieces from falling apart.[36]

"Building the Revolutionary Party"

Siege #2, published in November 1974, included Tommasi's major political statement, "Building the Revolutionary Party." Mason reprinted this as a standalone pamphlet, and it appeared in the *Siege* anthology.[37]

Tommasi argued that in the United States the existing methods used by neo-Nazis were insufficient to get the masses to overcome their apathy and join them. Neo-Nazis had held publicity stunts but had "never produced one significant political result." Tommasi laid particular blame on the NSWPP for failing to take advantage of the Boston bus riots against school desegregation, being particularly angry at the failure to arm students or burn buses.[38]

"Building the Revolutionary Party" borrowed liberally from theories used by the armed wing of the New Left. It argued that neo-Nazis needed "to go underground and build their own armed struggle to wage war against the State." A single violent act, emanating from an armed struggle group, could be the spark that ignited a revolution. Violence was "key to heightening contradictions," which would facilitate "revolutionary consciousness" and help "build our outside power bases from which to operate while building a popular base of support." Tommasi grandiosely proclaimed, "We will not make our most eloquent statement in courtrooms and at press conferences, but in the streets of Jew-Capitalist America!"[39]

Action

Tommasi tried to make these more than idle statements. Members were required to assemble a small arsenal: a 7-shot shotgun, .45 automatic pistol, semi-automatic assault rifle, and gas masks—in addition to the all-important swastika armband. The group also claimed, undoubtedly with some exaggeration, to be conducting extensive military training, including in guerilla war tactics, explosives, gas weapons, electronic surveillance, and escape techniques.[40]

While Tommasi's rhetoric and claims were white hot, the introductory nature of his direct action pedagogy showed how inexperienced the NSLF members were. They had to start with rocks and "trashing," before moving on to Molotov cocktails and bombs, and then finally guns.[41]

The NSLF claimed to have two "combat units" of four people each. Mason said that, in reality, there were only "four persons who carried out the illegal activities," while the rest were just regular neo-Nazis in practice, only "a lot more forward thinking."[42]

That first year, the NSLF claimed responsibility for several incidents. In Los Angeles, they said they found a white sex worker with a black man and handcuffed her to a streetlamp with a sign saying "I screw niggers, I deserve to die." They also claimed two arsons: the airplane of a Jewish NAACP official in Albuquerque and a business executive's car in Hollywood.[43] But in January 1975, the NSLF announced that the next month they were going to initiate "nationwide street confrontations with the enemy." NSLF members were told that "A violent year lay ahead" and that "You must not fail in your obligations to the Armed Struggle."[44]

In 1974, the NSLF said it had already infiltrated the Socialist Workers Party (a Trotskyist group) and the Communist Party USA as well as youth groups affiliated with them.[45] The NSLF also claimed credit for four actions in February 1975. At the beginning of that month, a tear gas grenade was set off during a Santa Monica meeting about reopening the case of Julius and Ethel Rosenberg. (The Rosenbergs were Jewish Communists who were convicted on espionage charges for giving U.S. atomic secrets to the Soviet Union and executed in 1953.) Three Communist offices in Los Angeles were also bombed: the Socialist Workers Party, UNIDOS Bookstore (affiliated with the October League, a Maoist party), and the East L.A. Instituto del Pueblo, a Chicano Marxist-Leninist community school.[46]

Two of the actions were claimed by the "Provisional Wing" of the NSLF, which Tommasi portrayed as separate from the main group. While this may have been misinformation to throw off law enforcement, it was possibly true. Kerr said that because Tommasi lacked adequate fighters, "he formed an alliance with an anti-Castro Cuban group based in South El Monte. The Cubans would commit small acts of violence against local marxist organizations, and by mutual agreement the NSLF would publicly take credit for them."[47] Tommasi did say he had contact with Commandos Libres Nacionalistas, a split from Alpha 66, an armed anti-Communist group of Cuban exiles. David Rust, who took over as NSLF leader after Tommasi's death, denied this. While acknowledging that there may have been minimal contact with the Cuban groups, regarding the bombings Rust said, "We never made any false claims." In any event, after Tommasi's passing, contact with these groups ended.[48]

The NSLF's "Political Terror" flyer was left at the Socialist Workers Party headquarters the day after the bombing. This striking flyer, made by Tommasi, was the group's greatest aesthetic triumph and legacy. At the top it said, "The Future Belongs to the Few Of Us Still Willing to Get Our Hands Dirty." Below and to the right, the words "Political Terror" lined up over a gun pointing at the phrase, "It's the Only Thing They Understand." At the bottom were a swastika and the slogan "Build the National Socialist Revolution through Armed Struggle."[49]

It was, by any standards, a high-impact image—as well as a message that was not easily forgotten. Neo-Nazis and sympathizers would recycle it for decades. For Mason, the flyer was "The thing that sold me the most on NSLF." He made it his signature image, and different incarnations of the NSLF used it. Later, groups like the American Front would recycle and rebrand it, and it even appeared in the 1999 Hollywood film *Arlington Road*.[50]

Death and the Party

The NSLF's violence was directed at not just the Left but also Tommasi's former NSWPP unit, who now occupied the same headquarters he had bought and signed over to Koehl.

In March 1975, the NSLF bragged about beating members of the NSWPP in retaliation for stealing literature and claimed to have firebombed their rivals' headquarters. After that, Tommasi claimed to have returned with 15 followers—which included John Duffy and Raymond Chaney, who would both play important roles in the NSLF—and "beat the daylights" out of Kerr and another member. (Asked about the incident, Kerr said that the six NSLF members who came mostly hit each other by mistake and then were quickly chased off.) Regardless, the stage was set for August.[51]

Bizarrely, beforehand Tommasi had reached out to Koehl and offered to work as the NSWPP's underground arm. Even after the attacks, less than two months before his death, Tommasi told Mason that "We have made some overtures to Commander Koehl to work together. I hope something comes out of it." Mason wished him luck but counseled that it would be better to "break all established patterns to date if you so much as receive a civil rebuff."[52]

Tommasi's aggressive actions were his undoing. Along with Rust, Tommasi drove up to the NSWPP headquarters in El Monte on August 15, 1975. After NSWPP guard Clyde Bingham made obscene gestures at them, Tommasi got out and yelled profanity at Bingham and the other guard, Jerry Keith Jones. In the ensuing confrontation, Jones shot Tommasi in the head, and the 24-year-old firebrand died instantly. Mason would receive his account of the incident directly from Rust.[53]

Both Bingham, 19, and Jones, 18, were arrested. Bingham was charged with assault with a deadly weapon, but it was dismissed. Jones pled guilty to second-degree murder and was given probation and released for time served.[54] Meanwhile, Koehl gloated over Tommasi's death, writing in the party's paper,

> Let the recent death of a certain individual who chose to wage war on the Party serve as a powerful warning that in the future the Party will actively defend itself against all those who seek to undermine and destroy it—whoever they may be or whatever they may call themselves.[55]

But Tommasi was not forgotten by his comrades; instead, he was made a martyr. The NSLF sold black and white lithographs of him for $3.50, and National Socialist Movement and NSLF units took his name.[56] Mason put him on the cover of several periodicals, frequently reprinted his last interview, and talked about him numerous times in SIEGE. In the anthology, Tommasi was referred to on over 40 pages, and the first edition included around 20 images related to Tommasi and his NSLF.[57]

Notes

1 Anti-Defamation League of B'nai B'rith, *Extremism on the Right: A Handbook* (New York: ADL, 1988), p.43.
2 FBI field report of April 13, 1970, in "TOMMASI, Joseph C. -- Los Angeles 157-1599," uploaded by ernie1241 on October 28, 2018, pp.82, 87, 88, https://archive. org/details/TOMMASIJosephC.LosAngeles1571599 [Hereafter "Tommasi FBI report"]. Elsewhere he is identified as having joined the party at age 14; Jeanne Cordova, "Local Nazis Admit to Rosenberg, Socialist Bombings," *Los Angeles Free Press* 12(12) #557, March 21, 1975, p.7, www.jstor.org/stable/community.28040134
3 Tommasi FBI report, pp.82, 103; Cordova, "Joseph Tommasi: His Last Interview—A Grim Prediction: 'I'll Never Reach My 30th Birthday'," *Los Angeles Free Press* 12(34) #579 August 22–28, 1975, p.18, www.jstor.org/stable/community.28040156; "National Council Named," *NS Bulletin* #70, September 15, 1970; Mason interview with Schuster (video).
4 Tommasi FBI report, p.17; Kaplan, "Post-War Paths," p.56n56.
5 Duffy to Mason, [December 1976] [Box 13, Folder 18]; Kerr to author, email, August 13, 2023.
6 Tommasi FBI report, pp.95, 98; SIEGE 12(8) August 1983, p.2 (*Siege*, pp.42–43).
7 Cited in Jenkins/Moynihan, "Introduction," *Siege*, 1st. ed., p.xvii; Lee Dye, "Court Ban Sets Stage for Hate Message Test," *Los Angeles Times*, March 23, 1969, pp.1, 26, www.newspapers.com/image/383095052, www.newspapers. com/image/383095295
8 SIEGE 12(8) August 1983, p.2 (*Siege*, p.43); "Joseph Tommasi," in Jeffrey Kaplan, ed., *Encyclopedia of White Power: A Sourcebook on the Radical Racist Right* (Walnut Creek, California: Altamira Press/Roman & Littlefield, 2000), p.302 [Hereafter *Encyclopedia*].

9 Robert Ballenger, "Nazi Emblem Lives on in El Monte," *Post-Advocate* (Alhambra, California), October 27, 1970, reprinted in Tommasi FBI report, p.130; Mason to Duffy, December 13, 1976 [Box 13, Folder 18]; SIEGE 12(5) May 1983, p.5.

10 Tommasi FBI report, pp.11, 86, 93, 94; Scott Harrison, "From the Archives: A Protest at Nazi Headquarters in El Monte," *Los Angeles Times*, February 16, 2018, www.latimes.com/visuals/photography/la-me-fw-archives-protest-at-nazi-headquarters-in-el-monte-20171005-story.html; "Jewish Militant Charged on Coast in Attack on Nazi," *NYT*, February 13, 1972, www.nytimes.com/1972/02/13/archives/jewish-militant-charged-on-coast-in-attack-on-nazi.html; "J.D.L. Aide Freed of Charge," *NYT*, February 24, 1972, www.nytimes.com/1972/02/24/archives/jdl-aide-freed-of-charge.html

11 Kerr to author, email, August 13, 2023.

12 Kerr, "The History of American National Socialism—Part 8"; *Siege* #1, Third Quarter 1974, p.1; Mason interview with Schuster (video).

13 SIEGE 15(1) January 1986, p.1.

14 Allen Zak and Mary Bess, "Local American Nazis Claims Republicans Paid Them," *Los Angeles Free Press* 9(44) #433, November 3–12, 1972, p.3, www.jstor.org/stable/pdf/community.28040021; Steven V. Roberts, "Nazi Party Linked to G.O.P. Anti-Wallace Move," *NYT*, June 8, 1973, www.nytimes.com/1973/06/08/archives/nazi-party-linked-to-gop-antiwallace-move-nofzigers-account-report.html. For the American Independent Party's response, see "Nazis Hired by GOP to Fight AIP," *California Statesman*, July 1972; *Siege*, 4th ed., pp.600–601.

Tommasi would be mentioned in the *New York Times* on three other occasions: "Jewish Militant Charged on Coast in Attack on Nazi"; "J.D.L. Aide Freed of Charge"; "Ex-Coast Nazi Leader Slain," *NYT*, August 17, 1975, www.nytimes.com/1975/08/17/archives/excoast-nazi-leader-slair.html

15 *Siege* #1, p.2; Mason, "Facts in Regard to the Matt Koehl Question," March 17, 1976 (insert in Mason to Koehl, April 28, 1976, p.4) [Box 47, Folder 21].

16 *Siege* #1, p.2; "Interview with James Mason, Part 2," *NS Worldview* #4, Winter 1995/106, p.13, https://web.archive.org/web/20130721041347, www.resist.com/Instauration/OtherPubs-20120723/NSWorldview-1995-Winter.pdf

17 Rust to Mason, June 25, 1976 [Box 15, Folder 13]; Mason interview with Schuster (video); CD Herrington, *The Events of 30th June 2006 & Its Aftermath: The Thirty Year War against the NSM*, uploaded by Lucius Montague on March 22, 2017, p.2, https://archive.org/details/THETHIRTYYEARWARAGAINSTTHENSM

18 Kerr to author, email, August 30, 2023.

19 As with many of the other details, Kerr has disputed these numbers, saying that out of 18 to 20 official dues-paying NSWPP members, Tommasi took four or five. However, Kerr did not dispute the larger numbers given, as long as they referred to a much looser definition of who was a member, such as those who only attended meetings or made donations. *Siege* #1, pp.2–3; Kerr to author, email, August 13, 2023.

20 Kerr to author, email, October 1, 2023; Mayerene Barker, "Nazis Leaving El Monte, May Try Pasadena," *Los Angeles Times*, June 17, 1976, www.newspapers.com/image/165932718, www.newspapers.com/image/165932776

21 Mason to author, November 26, 2022. For the NSLF student group, see Appendix 2 "The Original NSLF and David Duke".

22 Rex Springfield, *Power Struggle: Today for the Movement, Tomorrow for the World* (Liverpool, West Virginia: White Power Publications, 1976), pp.14–15.

23 Tommasi, "Strategy for Revolution," *Siege*, p.508. Rust's count was forty-eight; "Profile: David Rust, Leader N.S.L.F.," *National Socialist* #19, August 1976, p.7.

24 Kerr to author, email, August 30, 2023.

25 *Siege* #1, p.6; *National Socialist Review* #1, January 1975, p.2.

26 SIEGE 12(7) July 1983, p.3 (*Siege*, p.41).

27 Ibid; Mason, "National Socialist Liberation Front," *Encyclopedia*, p.222. Kaplan himself repeats this claim in two places: *Encyclopedia*, p.303 and "Post-War Paths," p.57.

28 Norman Mailer, *Miami and the Siege of Chicago: An Informal History of the Republican and Democratic Conventions of 1968* (New York: Signet Books, 1968), pp.131–74.

29 SIEGE 12(7) July 1983, p.3 (*Siege*, p.41). Duffy told Mason that, "Tommasi never allowed hard drugs (Acid, Coke, Smack) around his people. Marijuana, Amphedimines [sic] and Hashish were allowed were permitted. Maybe even partaken of. But never in the open"; Duffy to Mason, December 8, 1976 [Box 13, Folder 18].

30 Mason to Rust, September 26, 1975 [Box 15, Folder 13].

31 Mason to Moynihan, February 13, 1992 [Box 11, Folder 2].

32 Braswell would later pop up again as adjacent to the Greensboro massacre. *Siege* #1, pp.4, 7; *Siege* #2, pp.2, 15; "North Carolina Shootout," *National Socialist Review* #1, p.1; "Armed Struggle in N.C.," *National Socialist Review* #2, February 1975, pp.1, 4.

33 *Siege* #1, p.7; Cordova, "Joseph Tommasi: His Last Interview," p.6.

34 "The National Socialist Liberation Front," *Siege*, pp.505–8.

35 "Strategy for Revolution," *Siege* #1 (*Siege*, pp.508–10). Like a number of the texts reprinted in *Siege*, some of the lines were changed, although most were fairly minor.

36 "Some Facts to Consider," *Siege* #2, p.5; *Siege*, 1st ed., p.24.

37 [Tommasi], "Building the Revolutionary Party: The Road to Boreno," *Siege* #2, Fourth Quarter, 1974, pp.12–14 (*Siege*, pp.510–15).

38 Tommasi, "Building the Revolutionary Party," *Siege*, pp.510–11.

39 Ibid, pp.510–14. See Appendix 7, "Against Capitalism and the Liberal State," for the use of New Left slogans.

40 "Real Battle Ahead," *Siege* #2, p.8. They also sold books about bombs, boo-by-traps, and field fortifications; "New Guerilla Publications Available," *National Socialist Review* #1, p.4.

41 Tommasi, "Building the Revolutionary Party," *Siege*, pp.509, 513.

42 Ibid, p.510; Mason, December 16, 1996 letter, cited in Kaplan, "Post-War Paths," p.58.

43 "NSLF Scorecard," *Siege* #2, p.16.

44 "A Special Message," *National Socialist Review* #1, p.4.

45 The youth groups were the Young Socialist Alliance and the Young Workers Liberation League. The NSLF claimed the NAACP was also "under investigation." (Note that this passage does not appear in the book version.) Tommasi, "Building the Revolutionary Party," *Siege* #1, p.5.

46 "East L.A. Marxist H.Q. Bombed – Feb. 14" and "Local Bombings Increase," clippings reprinted in *National Socialist Review* #3, March 1975. p.1.

47 Cordova, "Local Nazis Admit to Rosenberg, Socialist Bombings," p.28; Kerr, "The History of American National Socialism, Part 8".

48 Cordova, "Joseph Tommasi: His Last Interview," p.18; Rust to author, January 8, 2021 (postmarked) and July 13, 2022.

49 Cordova, "Socialist Workers Party Bombed," clipping reprinted in *National Socialist Review* #2, p.3. Rust confirmed that Tommasi made the flyer; Rust to author, July 13, 2022.

50 Rust pointed out to the author that the flyer appeared in *Arlington Road*. Mason put copies in the first SIEGE, and it also was included in the anthology. Others who used it included the American Front, while the Abraxas Clique also reprinted it. Troy Southgate used the slogan "The Future Belongs to Those Still Willing to

Get Their Hands Dirty" in his "Declaration of Revolutionary Strategy." Mason to Rust, January 18, 1976 [Box 15, Folder 13]; SIEGE 9(4) September 1980, p.5 (*Siege*, 1st ed., p.19); John Brown Anti-Klan Committee, "Nazi Skinheads Active in San Francisco" (press release), May 25, 1988, p.9, https://freedomarchives.org/Documents/Finder/DOC37_scans/37.NaziSkinPressPkt1988.pdf.pdf; Adam Parfrey, ed., *Apocalypse Culture* (New York: Amok Press, 1987), p.192; Robert Luther 267, "We Can Kill You," *EXIT* #4, 1987, https://exitmagazine.net/toc.php?issue=4; Southgate cited in *Satanism and Its Allies: The Nationalist Movement Under Attack* (London: Final Conflict, 1998), p.89.

51 "NSWPP Reactionaries Attack Two NSLFers – Retaliation Issued – March 16," *National Socialist Review* #3, p.3; Kerr to author, email, August 13, 2023.

52 Tommasi to Mason, June 20, 1975; Mason to Tommasi, June 27, 1975 [both Box 21, Folder 30].

53 Greg Waskul, "Former Nazi Party Official Dies in El Monte Shooting," *Los Angeles Times*, August 16, 1975, p.8, www.newspapers.com/image/382814416; Rust to Mason, August 26, 1975 [Box 15, Folder 13].

54 "Shooting Incident in El Monte: Charges Dropped against Bingham," *Progress Bulletin* (Pomona, California), March 21, 1976, p.5, www.newspapers.com/image/74496485; "Accused Slayer to Be Arraigned," *Los Angeles Times*, October 12, 1975, p.1, www.newspapers.com/image/382851597

55 "Security Men Stop Attack on LA HQ," *White Power*, August–September 1975, clipping [Box 21, Folder 30].

56 *Ohio National Socialist* #15, Winter 1975/76; *National Socialist* #19, August 1976; *Stormer* 1(4) Summer 1978; *National Socialist Review* #6, April 1976, p.4; *The Storm* 1(7) June 1977; Joseph Tommasi Unit, NSWWP, application form 1979 [Box 33, Folder 10].

57 Tommasi's pictures and funeral card are in *Siege*, 1st ed., pp.289, 319, 385.

4

A TANGLED WEB OF NEO-NAZIS

David Rust's NSLF, the NSM, the White
Confederacy, and the National Socialist
Congress

The mid-1970s attrition from the National Socialist White People's Party
(NSWPP) did not mean that the neo-Nazi movement was dissipating—if anything, it was increasing. Matthias Koehl was trying to funnel this new pool of
neo-Nazis into his increasingly constrictive party rather than taking advantage of the mood to build it outward. Instead, their energy overflowed the
banks and spilled out into new forms and directions.

Excepting William Pierce's National Alliance, the continuing activism of
many former NSWPP members during the 1970s and beyond has been largely
overlooked by scholars. Until recently, James Mason has been almost entirely
ignored. There is no book on the NSWPP, despite its key importance to the
development of U.S. neo-Nazism. This is true of the party's various splinter
groups which Mason crossed paths with one way or another and were important to his own political development. Therefore, this study will focus attention on these smaller groups.[1]

After the breaks of the first half of the 1970s, these newly independent
neo-Nazis were now looking for political direction. While they were not in
short supply, if organized they were mostly in unaffiliated local groups and
this hyper-decentralization was a weakness. In an effort to overcome this,
the period of 1975 to 1978 was marked by experimental approaches by,
and alliances of, these small groups. While this pushed neo-Nazism in the
United States to quickly evolve, it also meant there was no shortage of feuds,
splits, and fusions. And Mason—at 22, filled with the bursting energy of a
young man thoroughly committed to a political movement which he saw as
self-evidently right, but also in possession of almost a decade of political
experience—was directly in the center of it.

DOI: 10.4324/9780429200090-7

While serving his time, he rejected acts like the hate crime he had committed as being politically fruitless, while mulling on the future of the movement and his role in shaping that. Joseph Tommasi's National Socialist Liberation Front (NSLF) excited him, and while incarcerated he developed a plan to launch a new project with his Ohio comrades who also were at odds with Koehl. The purpose of the National Socialist Movement (NSM) was not to be a new party but to promote militancy among the rudderless, local neo-Nazi groups.[2]

What NSM was proposing—of course, along with the NSLF and National Alliance—was actually quite new. While the Klan were well known for their violence, especially during the Civil Rights Movement, U.S. neo-Nazis were not. Some fisticuffs aside, the American Nazi Party always had more theater than organizing, and the profusion of single-actor murderers had not started, either: all of this was yet to come. But Mason was one of its first prophets.

The period was a whirl of activity for Mason and those around him. He published almost 30 issues of different neo-Nazi periodicals. Although Tommasi died soon after Mason's release, an extremely close connection was forged between the NSM and NSLF.

In the mid-1970s, the two groups also became part of two umbrella groups, where they unsuccessfully fought for control and influence. The White Confederacy was the more ecumenical of the two and contained both Klan and neo-Nazis, although it was mostly a paper organization. Mason spent a short but very intense time with the second group, the National Socialist Congress, which specifically sought to reunite the various neo-Nazi splinters. It was dominated by Frank Collin's National Socialist Party of America (NSPA), whose reputation soon became sky-high because of their legal case to march in Skokie, Illinois which eventually reached the Supreme Court. But before that, Mason's feud with another White Supremacist cut short the NSM's time in the National Socialist Congress and with it the majority of their hopes of influencing the various small groups.

After Tommasi's death, the NSLF dove into even greater violence, attacking leftists as well as the local NSWPP, which shortly led to the arrest of their second leader, David Rust. Rather than disband the NSLF, Mason convinced him to merge it with the NSM. Shortly thereafter, however, Mason became disenchanted with the more moderate direction the NSM was taking. Together with the NSLF, Mason's NSM faction bolted for yet another group, the National Socialist White Workers' Party (NSWWP), led by their comrade Allen Vincent. There Mason would bide his time while waiting for another opening.

Because during this period the NSM and NSLF were so closely related, both to each other and in relationship to the two umbrella organizations, these stories will be told together.

—1975—

National Socialist Movement

Mason spent his six-month sentence in the six-story Cincinnati Work House, a "dungeon" built in the late 1860s. Before Mason went inside, fellow Ohio neo-Nazi Robert Brannen showed him the first issue of the original *Siege*. Mason liked it, but "fell in love with the next issue." Mason said he "was deeply affected by Tommasi's ideas and pondered them all the six months I was in jail."[3] Inspired, Mason

completely outlined what I would like to see emerge as a serious and workable new front for a fresh revolutionary type of National Socialism.... Every detail was set in my mind by the time of my release right down to the name of the new propaganda front. I chose the most generic and the least pretentious label possible: National Socialist Movement.[4]

The project was called a "movement" in order "to avoid the term party at all costs." With typical dramatic flourish, Mason said this new "three-man partnership known as NSM" started the moment Greg Hurles and Brannen met him as he walked out of the dungeon on March 18, 1975.[5]

At 48, Robert F. Brannen was easily the eldest of the three, and he supported his large family by working in a Frigidaire factory in Dayton. A former Klansman, Brannen told a reporter that he joined the NSWPP in 1968, although Mason said his name popped up on the radar only when he was part of the brief-lived Cincinnati bookstore.[6] Brannen had been kicked out of the Cincinnati NSWPP in June 1974 and then expelled from the national party in August—making him available for a new project. From the very beginning, he was the NSM's chairman and paid for its publications.[7]

The third co-founder, Hurles, was soon given the title of NSM "Organizer."[8] Hurles had long been close to Mason, working with him in the NSWPP and committing the hate crime they both spent jail time for.

The NSM was openly National Socialist and used a swastika on their periodicals. According to Mason, it was a vehicle for promoting militancy among the party's many splinter groups. (A 1977 American Jewish Committee report agreed: "the NSM acts more as a goad and nettle to other neo-Nazi groups than as an operational entity."[9]) One of Mason's future publishers described the NSM as a "propaganda experiment" which hoped to

kindle a conglomerate federation between heretofore uncooperative National Socialist and KKK leadership pools, while subtly injecting this pan-Aryan echelon with profuse N.S.M. militancy. The N.S.M.'s aggressive ideological proclivities ranged from engendering outright overthrow—a la Tommasi, to a gentler mass strategy approach.[10]

Indeed, the NSM bragged they "had a specific plan and nothing whatsoever to lose by its implementation." In 1978, they proclaimed that "The N.S.M. is not a cult, debating society, educational institution, publishing house, personality fan club, money-making racket or anything of the kind. We are an organization of revolutionaries with one thing in mind: Power."[11] However, they were to fall short of their ambitious goals.

Influence of Tommasi and the NSLF

Mason cast the NSM as "a continuation of Tommasi's work." Like the NSLF, it promoted a different kind of internal neo-Nazi culture which rejected the numerous requirements and prohibitions of the NSWPP. There were "No activity reports, literature sale requirements, tithing of wages, no 'regulation haircut', no swearing off booze or broads." Not just that, but "Marching, uniforms, regimentation, even oratory are all out."[12] The NSLF's Rust summed up this change as "the revolutionary nature of National Socialism as opposed to the archaic philosophy of the right-wing."[13]

In April 1975, a month after the NSM was founded, Mason started writing Tommasi, although they exchanged fewer than a dozen letters before he was killed in August. Brannen, who had also been in contact with him, flew out to the funeral.[14]

Only details separated the NSM from the NSLF. In April 1975, Tommasi wrote Mason to offer that, if he was done with "Mass Movement politics and can identify with the Guerrilla [sic] concept," he should apply to be a member. Although Mason passed up the opportunity at that time, he later said, "But for a tiny, little bit, we'd have thrown in with the NSLF."[15] For example, the NSM did not have an underground component. The NSLF was focused on armed struggle, but the NSM—while inclusive of that approach—also embraced traditional activism like public rallies. In short, the NSM was designed to be a visible, public organization that collaborated with others in order to influence them. The NSLF sought to spark the revolution with dramatic acts of violence.

It was not just in ideology but also in practical organizational terms that the NSM was extremely close to the NSLF. When the NSLF was unable to attend conferences, the NSM would represent them. In 1976, the NSM said they "maintain the very closest relations in both ideology and activity" with the NSLF, even encouraging neo-Nazis in the Louisville area to join that NSLF unit.[16]

Ideas and Actions

One of the first things the NSM did was take over the *Southern Ohio Activity Report*, change its name to the *Ohio National Socialist*, and make it their official periodical. The first issue in winter 1975 listed the NSM's affiliates as the

NSLF and the NSWPP/Ohio, as well as two "affiliated ad hoc groups," Freedom for Rudolf Hess and Palestinian Liberation. While these were, in Mason's words, "pure invention," they showed the group's interests at the time.[17]

From the start, Mason used his new vehicle to develop his ideas about violence. The introductory statement of this was "Heroes of the Revolution," also in the first *Ohio National Socialist*, which praised two attempted and two successful assassinations: Sara Jane Moore and Lynette "Squeaky" Fromme, both of whom had tried to kill President Gerald Ford, dubbed a "Jew-Capitalist stooge"; Neal Bradley Long, who killed "Jew integrationist" Charles Glatt, a school desegregation busing planner; and Michael Edward Pearch, who shot seven black people, killing two in Maryland. The mention of Fromme was the first of a Manson Family member, and Mason noted that "It is significant that two of these heroes are women"—a thought he would develop later.[18]

The conflict over busing issues was important to White Supremacists in the 1970s. In an attempt to desegregate public schools, compulsory busing programs were implemented, with white and black students brought to different schools to change the racial composition. It was an unpopular policy, and in Boston in particular, but also Louisville, there were riots in opposition to it. In 1974, Klan leader David Duke went to Boston to take advantage of the situation.[19]

Writings aside, the NSM acted in many ways like a typical local neo-Nazi group, and they were active in the street. For the nine months left in the year, they held 14 activities, including literature distributions and the annual Hess rally.[20] And that year they also helped found the White Confederacy.

Rust's NSLF

In an autobiographical sketch, Rust described himself as a hippie teenager in Los Angeles who went to bohemian coffee houses and protests—including the 1966 Sunset Strip Riot. "But we were cannon fodder for the Reds and didn't even know it!"[21] He also said the participation of Communists and openly gay men in these circles disgusted him.

Against a background of bombings, kidnappings, and even murder from armed leftist groups like the Symbionese Liberation Army (SLA) and Weather Underground, Rust was sure the Left would stage a revolutionary uprising. Encountering Tommasi's outreach efforts, he attended neo-Nazi meetings and came under the charismatic leader's influence. Rust said, "There I was a bearded long-hair in the midst of a Nazi meeting- but hell what he said made sense!" and joined the NSWPP.[22] But before he did so, he went to Beirut and visited Palestinian refugee camps; the NSLF's neo-Nazi version of anti-Zionism reflected these experiences.[23]

Rust was in the NSWPP for a year, leaving two weeks after Tommasi's dismissal. As Tommasi drove past the NSWPP headquarters one day, Rust flagged him down to hear his side of the story. Deciding to throw his lot in with the then-forming NSLF, Rust helped run security at its founding meeting and on the group's behalf infiltrated the Socialist Workers Party. He was made NSLF second-in-command weeks before Tommasi's killing and was by his side when it happened.[24] At 26, Rust took command of the organization.

Like the NSM, Rust stressed that the NSLF was "not a Party, it's an organization with specific aims." And he laid claim to making it *more* militant than it was under Tommasi. "Because I was not NSWPP indoctrinated for so many years, as was Capt. Tommasi- The direction of the NSLF has become more singularized according to my own inclinations toward the Political Guerilla aspect." Still, Rust hoped to act in concert with, and receive support from, groups like the National Alliance. Its advantage, in particular, was that an "unswastika bedecked organization does fit nicely into a movement that in the end is going to have to attract the masses," while the NSLF engaged in "direct operations against the enemies of the race."[25]

Ideologically, Rust continued the course Tommasi set. The main exception was the focus on anti-Zionism, including a *National Socialist Review* double-issue. As Rust wrote Mason, "our leaflets are issue oriented – Black Terrorism – Red Terrorism – The solution WHITE TERROR. Zionist Capitalism and the U.S. devotion to Israel-Red Jews and the insanity of Marxism etc."[26]

The NSLF put these words into action. According to Rust, "The loss of Tommasi did not touch our strike apparatus, just our public presentation and Joe's connections with other political groups. That which was least affected was our ability to disrupt others through the use of violence." Targets included "both zionist and marxist gatherings."[27] In September 1975, the NSLF tear-gassed the opening of *The Hiding Place*, a film about a Dutch family that hid Jews during the Holocaust. In December, the NSLF claimed to have both fired upon and firebombed the El Monte NSWPP headquarters. The local media did not have much interest in the internecine battles between neo-Nazis, and Rust complained more than once that the NSLF's attacks on fellow Nazis went relatively unnoticed compared with those on leftists.[28]

White Confederacy

After preliminary talks in May 1975, that October the White Confederacy held its founding conference in Cleveland. The 11 groups present included the NSM, NSLF, and NSWPP/Ohio, plus another NSWPP splinter group, the United White People's Party (UWPP), which was led by Casey Kalemba and based in Cleveland. There were also ten groups that were either part of the original discussions or had agreed to join but did not attend the conference; they retained the option to join.[29] The White Confederacy was notable because it contained both neo-Nazi and Klan groups four years before the 1979 Greensboro massacre—usually considered the starting point of the collaboration between the two movements. Mason took great pleasure when the conference censured Koehl at its first meeting. The group also held a press conference where the UWPP's Kalemba announced that they intended to fight busing programs.[30]

Louisville NSLF

In addition to organizing local demonstrations, 18-year-old Raymond L. Chaney drove from Kentucky to Ohio in 1974 to attend NSWPP events, including helping staff the Ross County Fair booth.[31] Like the others, he soon broke from the party and spent time with Tommasi in California, and in March 1975, he took part in one of the attacks on NSWPP members.[32]

The next month, Chaney was back home and met Mason for the first time. Soon after, busing riots rocked Louisville as the 1975 school year started, and Chaney made the most of this opportunity. Chaney established the Louisville NSLF, and in July they started publishing the *White Liberator*; it claimed the group also had an underground "Provisional Wing." Prone to grandiose names and promising armed struggle, they announced, "Our slogan will be DEATH! NOT DIALOGUE."[33]

The August issue was no less dramatic. "There WILL be school buses going up in smoke! There WILL be shotgun blasts to the guts (if they have any) of mixmaster principals and superintendents!" The Louisville NSLF sold publications like "How to Blow Up a Car" and its hit list of local figures included left-wing anti-racist activist Anne Braden. In early August, they claimed responsibility for burning a Jewish-owned factory; firebombing a brothel; vandalizing a multi-racial church; and harassing a mixed-race couple until they moved from their home.[34] As the demonstrations went on, U.S. Attorney General George Long announced in mid-September that the FBI was investigating a hit list of 106 names that appeared on an NSLF poster titled "Death to the Bourgeois of Louisville." By that time—in addition to cross-burnings, Klan rallies, and a business boycott—in Louisville there were over 600 arrests, and Chaney was convicted at least twice for disorderly conduct that fall.[35]

National Alliance

Pierce's trajectory ran parallel to the other NSWPP splinter groups but rarely crossed over with them, Mason excepting. In September 1975, just after Mason finished his jail sentence, Pierce offered him a job working on the National Alliance's newspaper. However, Mason declined, saying he no longer wished to work under anyone—and of course, by this time the NSM was also off the ground. But Mason but stayed close to Pierce, visiting that December.[36]

Pierce's departure from the NSWPP had not slowed down his political work. In 1968, segregationist George Wallace ran as a third-party candidate in the presidential election, picking up widespread support on the Far Right. Wallace was popular among young people, and Willis Carto took advantage of this by setting up the Youth for Wallace front group.[37] (For decades, Carto was an important White Supremacist and Holocaust denier who formed a number of important groups and publications, including the Liberty Lobby and the Institute for Historical Review.) After the November election, the group was "reorganized" as the National Youth Alliance. But the members were divided over neo-Nazism, which was absent on the public-facing side but openly expressed internally. Pierce had joined the National Youth Alliance in 1970 after he left the NSWPP, but the same year he fell out with Carto and when Pierce's faction split, he ended up with the name. (Carto's faction became Youth Action.)[38] In 1974, the National Youth Alliance organization turned into the National Alliance.

Attack! had started as the National Youth Alliance newspaper in 1969, but Pierce also inherited it in the divorce and used it to continue his calls for violence. He recommended firearms and discussed the pros and cons of bombing movie theaters. (At the same time, Pierce was stockpiling dangerous chemicals in his family's home.)[39] One account put the circulation of *Attack!* at 15,000.[40] In January 1975, the paper (retitled that year the *National Vanguard*) started to serialize Pierce's infamous *Turner Diaries*, which was published as a book in the spring of 1978, under the pseudonym Andrew Macdonald.[41]

Mason especially admired the paper and was obviously reading the serialization at the exact time he was honing his own ideology and strategy of violence. This was so much so that in July 1976, Pierce's newspaper was the only one the NSM recommended. The NSM also issued a flyer, recycled by the NSLF, with a Pierce quote about being prepared to unleash violence when the time was right.[42]

Mason was very clear about how much he looked up to Pierce and in December 1975 told Rust that the older National Socialist was "my benefactor and my teacher. I owe the man much."[43] Rust, however, thought his comrade too enamored of Pierce and pointed out that the National Alliance, unlike the NSLF, refused to use the swastika—a bedrock of their approach. However, in February 1976, Rust did concede that

Pierce's National Alliance could play a very important role in the movement. The unswastika bedecked organization does fit nicely into a movement that in the end is going to have to attract the masses. The NSLF was realistically designed to carry out direct operations against the enemies of the race while maintaining a propaganda capacity of its own. We are not a movement![44]

—1976—

NSM

In January 1976, Mason joined the NSLF, meaning that for a short time he held memberships in four groups: the NSLF, NSM, and NSWPP, in addition to being a National Alliance official supporter.[45] Additionally, he was NSM's representative to, and engaged in the internal workings of, both the White Confederacy and National Socialist Congress.

But as for the NSWPP, Mason could not put off the inevitable forever. In February 1976, their newsletter attacked Brannen as an "agent provocateur"—even though he had been expelled two years prior.[46] (No doubt, this kind of approach did little to stop the party's attrition.) Citing the Brannen broadside as the last straw, after a decade in the party Mason finally quit the NSWPP on April 1, and a few weeks later the NSM issued their rebuttal, *Anatomy of a Smear*.[47] The last barrier to Mason's publicly acting against Koehl had been removed.

The Monkey's Paw

In May, Hurles was released from jail and jumped back into NSM work. Just the month before, Mason received the proverbial monkey's paw, when George Dietz offered to fund a new, monthly magazine. Dietz was an immigrant who grew up in Germany and had been in Hitler Youth. Settling in West Virginia, he ran Liberty Bell Publications and White Power Publications, making him one of the country's main publishers of neo-Nazi literature.[48] Mason was apparently too excited by the opportunity to consider the implications of Dietz's plans. The same day, he wrote Rust,

> what would you say if I told you that Santa Claus was a Nazi? Seriously, the dream connection has been made after ten years of groping around. The opportunities are so vast that I falter as I try to think of ways to take advantage of them.[49]

For Mason, such a publication could play a big role in helping bring together neo-Nazis to compete with the NSWPP. But Dietz had other plans—which he had been clear enough about. At the start, he explained his plan to start his own group, the White Power Movement, which he would lead, and the NSM would provide the personnel. They countered that there was already an existing movement, and Dietz said they would come back after realizing the error of their ways. Putting disagreements aside for the moment, Dietz and Mason struck a deal: Mason had his new magazine, with the only apparent requirement being a back cover ad for Dietz's White Power Publications.[50]

With Dietz's money, the NSM's *Ohio National Socialist* and the Louisville NSLF *White Liberator* combined to become the *National Socialist*, and three issues were published in summer 1976.[51] Although the cover said it was the NSM's magazine, it looked like the mouthpiece of the White Confederacy and included profiles of member groups. Mason also used to it spread the Tommasi cult, including publishing his correspondence with Brannen. The latter included Tommasi's admonition that "The underground is the only way to go now."[52] It was Dietz's money but Mason's content.

The Dietz Affair

In September 1976, the funding was gone and the so-called "Dietz Affair" was under way. The pamphlet *Power Struggle*, an insider's take on the state of neo-Nazism, portrayed it as "split into two hostile camps"—the NSWPP and the "independents."[53] But rather than forming a stable coalition, the independents quickly began circling each other like sharks.

The trouble started in August 1976 when, according to the NSM, Dietz ordered a completely new approach. "All calls for attacks upon the enemy, all calls for radical street activity, all specific instruction, all praise for Rockwell and Tommasi, and all exposure of Franklin Road would have to be dropped." The NSM accused Dietz of not being a National Socialist but, more shockingly, of attacking their hallowed icons. Tommasi was deemed an "agent," while Rockwell was a "pipe-smoking fool." Last, Dietz took the magazine's mailing list—in those days, a White Supremacist publisher's most precious asset.[54]

None too pleased, Brannen, Mason, and Hurles went to see Dietz in Reedy, West Virginia in late September. Mason said, "within the first five minutes of entering our place, Dietz pulled his gun on me," forced him and Hurles out, and unsuccessfully tried to win Brannen over. (This, at least, is Mason's version of events.) In October, Dietz fueled the conflict by issuing what Mason described as a 50-page broadside.[55]

That year, the NSM also did some traditional activism, including holding their annual Free Hess rally and a memorial for Tommasi. With the West Virginia money gone, Mason started a new NSM publication, the *National Socialist Bulletin*. While the Dietz Affair took up a lot of pages, Mason continued to develop his new obsession with violence.[56] Publishing it from September 1976 to April 1978, Mason also honed the ability to turn out a monthly publication. Some numbers could be mistaken for issues of SIEGE—so much so that Brannen later accused Mason of plagiarism, even though Mason had clearly written the anonymous pieces in question.[57]

NSLF

Under Rust's leadership, the NSLF was also busy in 1976. Like many militant radical groups that are unable to get traction for their ideas, they turned their attention to prisoners. And there the NSLF did find some success.

In December 1975, Rust put gears into motion which would run through the next year. Under Tommasi, *Siege* had been the NSLF's public periodical, whereas the *National Socialist Review* was for members. Rust abandoned the former and restarted the latter, this time as the outward-facing publication, and it was published through July 1976.[58]

Rust also moved to Reseda, on the edge of Los Angeles in the San Fernando Valley, as did Tommasi's pregnant widow, Rose.[59] He also restarted the weapons trainings and would be accused of running a "commando training camp." (Years later, Rust said "we were just going shooting but there was the idea that at some point it would develop beyond that.")[60]

The Louisville NSLF also maintained their militant posture. In spring 1976, it claimed it had seen rapid growth and, continuing the group's penchant for fanciful names, was now part of the "National Socialist Liberation Front—Liberation Front Underground United Forces of Ky." That year, the California NSLF would imply the Louisville group's responsibility for anti-busing bombings and attacks on leftists as well as for an unusual action—throwing a "gas grenade" during the 102nd Kentucky Derby. "Although this didn't stop the race, a message was left with the local government: 'Stop forced busing or the next time it will be TNT!'"[61]

Political violence frequently devolves into personal violence, and the NSLF was no exception. In Delaware, two NSLF members took part in a gun battle with unknown assailants in May 1976. Later that year in the same state, another NSLF member, Richard H. Robinson, was arrested after police ran his car off the road as he was trying to escape. Out in California, Bill Gould, 24, was arrested in August along with three others for a shotgun slaying over a drug deal. A friend of Tommasi since the NSWPP days and a pallbearer at his funeral, Gould was convicted of second-degree murder and sentenced to five-to-life.[62]

NSLF Gains a Mason and, Briefly, a Hand

In December 1975, Rust invited Mason, for a second time, to officially join the NSLF. This time, Mason had no compunctions and applied the next month—although he kept this a secret for the moment. Mason also said he was going to start rebranding NSM propaganda with the NSLF label, something he would do for years to come. As the NSM was not accepting new memberships at the time, potential recruits could join the NSLF instead, which was.[63]

Karl Hand, who would become the last NSLF leader, also briefly joined the organization. In January 1976, Hand's old NSWPP unit had joined the NSLF—at least for a few weeks. Rust complained that "One of the first things it's leader Mr. Karl Hand Jr. wanted to know was.... What rank shall I hold? It was a 'necessity for organizing'."[64] The NSLF would have to wait until later for Hand.

Rust and Mason spent a fair amount of time plotting against Koehl, hoping to out him as being gay and hence destroy his reputation in the movement. Privately, Mason admitted that "I am not prejudiced in any way against homosexuals," but this did not stop him from hoping they would be able to have their own personal Night of the Long Knives.[65]

Prisoners

Tommasi had already started the NSLF's prisoner support work. The original *Siege* included listings for Jim Long, who was serving nine months in California for a bombing, and Paul Mooney, arrested after he bit off the ear of an FBI agent during a raid on his home. Now Rust paid even more attention to prisoners, hoping to recruit them as soldiers and assassins. As opposed to relying on what he disparaged as the "little rats...weaklings and mental defectives" in the NSWPP, Rust put his "faith and efforts" in "a newer and stronger N.S. movement...on the rise from within the prison system."[66]

Rust focused on the American National Socialist Brotherhood (ANSB), a neo-Nazi prison gang in California that had already been in dialogue with Tommasi. The ANSB was involved in deadly racial violence on the inside; in 1974, two members were killed in a fight with black prisoners, and they claimed to have retaliated with two murders of their own.[67] The NSLF started sending literature inside, partly to counteract the influence of the leftist SLA. The NSLF pledged "to aid our imprisoned comrades in <u>every</u> way!" and in early 1976 announced a formal alliance with the ANSB.[68] Rust wrote that he was having "<u>much success</u> translating National Socialism into terms that the total violence types understand.... Start expecting National Socialist squads to dismember the red opposition with their BARE hands."[69] He also sought help from both the White Confederacy and National Socialist Congress in establishing educational programs for both prisoners and those newly released.[70]

White Confederacy and National Socialist Congress

The NSPA, another NSWPP splinter group, played the main role in the National Socialist Congress. The Chicago group, led by Frank Collin, concentrated on local organizing, trying—with a fair amount of success—to repeat Rockwell's 1966 success in the Marquette Park neighborhood, which almost a decade later had still prevented people of color from moving in.[71] In 1975, Collin ran for city alderman in a district that included the area and received 16 percent of the vote, assuring him that being an open neo-Nazi would not be an impediment to public support. NSPA members had taken part in raucous demonstrations in the park, often opposing anti-racist housing marches. In July 1976, 200 young people pelted police with rocks, and an off-duty corrections officer was shot.[72] The city retaliated by requiring that expensive insurance be taken out before the NSPA could hold rallies in the park.

Collin deftly out maneuvered them, scoring a massive publicity coup in the process, by applying for a permit to march in Skokie, a heavily Jewish suburb where many Holocaust survivors lived. This created a massive outcry. Residents were furious, and additional attention came as the well-respected American Civil Liberties Union (ACLU) took the case on. This legal group, committed to a far-reaching interpretation of the free speech guarantees in the U.S. Constitution's First Amendment, fought the case on behalf of the NSPA. The legal organization had previously represented White Supremacists, including Mason, and would continue to do so in the future. For example, the ACLU successfully sued to ensure that the 2017 Charlottesville Unite the Right rally could go ahead in its chosen location.[73]

Early 1976 had been marked by a rare period of friendly collaboration by the independent Nazis. Mason told Rust that the White Confederacy was "an encouraging step in the right direction." The NSM did a rare joint flyering with the NSPA. Kalemba's UWPP came down from Cleveland to join the annual Hess rally in Cincinnati and also published *The Eagle News* for the White Confederacy. Overseas groups, like the British Movement, joined the Confederacy as well.[74]

As *Power Struggle* put it in September, "The White Confederacy is a wonderful tool for promoting co-operation among racialists, but it is too broad to be regarded as an exclusive NS organization and could not fulfill its role if it attempted to be one." The pamphlet was written under a pseudonym by Gerhard Lauck, who also worked under the name the NSDAP/AO.[75] Lauck was primarily an editor and publisher specializing in producing neo-Nazi literature and sending it overseas, particularly to Germany, where it was banned.

In pursuance of this, several neo-Nazi groups, some of which had been involved in the White Confederacy, formed the National Socialist Congress in early fall 1976. The NSM was not part of its conception; Mason told Rust it was a "surprise (even to us)." The NSLF and NSM both kept dual membership in the two larger groups, although the NSPA would not.[76]

Under his own name, Lauck said the National Socialist Congress was "a vehicle for national re-unification" in the absence of a strong national leader. He hoped it would reverse "the long, unfortunate trend toward endless fragmentation and the appearance of numerous miniscule 'NS parties'."[77] The first Congress was held at the end of October 1976 in Chicago. Hosted by Collin's group, it was attended by 35 representatives, who came from groups including the NSM, Rust's NSLF, Vincent's NSWWP, Kalemba's UWPP, and Lauck's NSDAP/AO. The Congress designated three official periodicals. Lauck's *NS Report* was the "mass-organ," the *Newsletter of the National Socialist Congress* was for internal matters, and Mason's *National Socialist* was designated the "internal magazine" of the Congress—although no issue was published during the period of the affiliation.[78]

The meeting changed Mason's priorities. Afterward, "The White Confederacy immediately took the back seat (or even the trunk)...in my concerns."[79] The NSM was enthusiastic, proclaiming that the Congress—and not the NSWPP—was the true successor to Rockwell's party. (Numerous splinter groups would say the same thing.) The NSM wrote,

> from the period of 1970 to 1976, there emerged the nucleus of what today is known as the National Socialist Congress. It is the Party. It is the Rockwell tradition. It is Rockwell's very people. It is the movement transformed, reborn.[80]

That November, the NSM screened a film about the first meeting of the National Socialist Congress. To bolster their position, the NSM printed a chart showing the ratio of "independent" neo-Nazi groups to NSWPP chapters: it claimed that, in October 1976, the parent party had only "One Active Unit & Dwindling."[81] (In fact, as Martin Kerr pointed out, there were five units in California, plus headquarters or bookstores in Arlington, El Monte, Chicago, and Baltimore.)

Regardless of whether it was luggage in the trunk, the NSM and NSLF still attended the White Confederacy meeting in Cleveland in December 1976. Mason and Brannen met separately with the NSLF's John Duffy before and after the conference to hammer out the next steps for the NSM and NSLF.[82]

The complication was that, as Lauck wrote, the Dietz Affair had cast a "shadow on the first N.S. Congress and continues to be a potential disruptive factor in the future." Most of December's internal newsletter was devoted to it. Some said Mason's involvement stopped them from being Congress affiliates; additionally, the advocacy of violence by the NSM and NSLF was an issue. Mason was also ignoring requests to stop attacking Dietz. (Mason bragged about answering the 50-page attack on Dietz in a mere seven pages.) In response, a council made up of Collin, Kalemba, and Vincent was set up to adjudicate the issue at the next gathering of the Congress. Mason, sure of his victory, also took to behind-the-scenes politicking by encouraging then-allies like Clifford Herrington to come.[83]

NSM

The NSM declared 1977 the "Year of the Nazis." Although not the case, it was a busy year for them. In January, NSM members attended a "free speech" (and free beer) event in Cincinnati to support the legal battles of Larry Flynt, publisher of the pornographic magazine *Hustler*, who was about to be tried for "pandering obscenity and engaging in organized crime." Mason was quoted in a local paper as saying, "I support the free press. Without a free press I'd be out of business." (This did not stop Mason from later praising Flynt's would-be assassin, Joseph Paul Franklin.)[84] In March 1977, NSM started taking memberships and collecting dues, clearly signaling an organizational move away from their initial approach.[85]

A few months later, there was a brief reconciliation with neo-Nazi Steven Love, who became the NSM Vice Chair but resigned a month later.[86] The NSM also started working with prisoners. In December 1976, Brannen met with a representative of the National Socialist Pioneer Prisoners in West Virginia. The NSM became their affiliate on the outside and, in May 1977, created their own Bureau of Inmate Affairs.[87] But most of the year was taken up with the NSM maneuvering among fellow neo-Nazis and White Supremacists.

The 1975 article "Heroes of the Revolution" was no one-off. Having already congratulated Long and Pearch on their racist killings, during the next two years the NSM praised two explicitly neo-Nazi murderers, Frederick Cowan and Raymond Schultz.[88]

Cowan is notable for committing the first neo-Nazi massacre in the United States, in February 1977. A supporter of the NSRP, Cowan, after being suspended from his job by a Jewish supervisor, went back to his workplace to kill him; failing that, he murdered four people of color before committing suicide. Three months later, Schultz, a former member of both the American Nazi Party and NSRP, murdered a Jewish man in his suburban home with cyanide. Found unconscious by police, he committed suicide immediately afterward. In July 1977, Mason wrote

> ONE of the things we're up to is providing a beacon for those like Cowan in New Rochelle and Schultz in Chicago. The N.S.M. had had contact with NEITHER of these men. These men were indicators of what's out there and what can happen if the right moves are made.[89]

Around the same time, Mason made a flyer, which he would often refer to and reprint, declaring Charles Manson an "independent genius"; this showed his increasing interest in the Manson Family.[90] At the same time, Brannen boasted to a local paper that he was recruiting people willing to commit violence, which was plausible considering the NSM's prison outreach; somewhat less likely was his claim that they also had a branch of trained assassins.[91]

"A Case of the Heebie Jeebies"

Mason's seminal essay "A Case of the Heebie Jeebies" appeared in the October 1977 *National Socialist Bulletin*. It was Mason's first full-length exposition of what would become SIEGE's celebration of racist mass murderers. The article's catalyst was an attack by Kenneth Wilson in Charlotte, North Carolina. Wearing a swastika armband, he shot a group of black picnickers, killing one and injuring three, before committing suicide.[92]

Mason said Cowan's murders "will probably be remembered as the man who fired the Second Shot Heard Round the World" and that his actions were "history's jumping-off point" because he was the first one to be identified—albeit incorrectly—with the American Nazi Party. More importantly was that "TWO MORE KILLINGS HAVE TAKEN PLACE IN RAPID SUCCESSION by men having been identified or dubbed as Nazis," Schultz and Wilson.[93]

The fate of the perpetrators was also noted. Long was arrested and imprisoned, but Pearch, Cowan, Schultz, and Wilson all died in the course of their crimes—a point Mason would stress.

> This has never happened before! It is a basis for a REAL case of the "heebie-jeebies" for the Jews, niggers, liberals and Pig System! John Ross Taylor[94] has assured us that the Jews can not withstand opposition by those unafraid to die. Dr. Pierce told us that what is needed is an assault on the Enemy without thought of return. What we are seeing is prophesy come to life.
>
> The sick times are only just now beginning to pay off. A revolution has got to be a natural thing and that which is natural is also uncontrollable. (Were it under anyone's control the chances of human error, sabotage and giving pretext to the Pig Government to lock us all up would exist.) There is no defense from it! It can't be stopped! These killers cannot be detected! There is no pattern that can be traced. AND IT WILL CONTINUE AND BUILD!!! The Establishment Creeps will feel a chill up their spines at each new incident; The Jews will experience psychosomatic constrictions in their throats at each new killing; The niggers will be driven to greater fury until they meet with a bullet; We will be invigorated and inspired in our task.
>
> And the task must be to coincide with these killings. We must act in a manner to not only inspire these killings but to complement them! We must work in a duet with those forces we cannot control or anticipate. They're watching and they're watching you. BUT THEY CAN'T WATCH EVERYBODY! They weren't watching Cowan, Schultz, Wilson, or Long,

or Pearch. An American field commander once commented on war that all the noise of the big guns didn't mean a damn: Only the HIT counted. Let us make MORE NOISE and run interference while these unknown heroes continue to make more hits!

Nazi killers are on the loose and striking at will! Police can't learn what's behind them because the killers prefer to die! No prisoners, no stories, just dead niggers and Jews. Perfect. Where will it happen next? When? It's happened in Maryland, New York, Illinois, Ohio and North Carolina. Looks like California might be a good spot, doesn't it??[95]

This was Mason's greatest strategic innovation. The neo-Nazi movement was plagued by marginal characters. In SIEGE, Mason described neo-Nazi groups as "totally out-of-touch, cultist, hobbyist, fetishist Nazi organizations" consisting of "weirdoes, freaks and geeks." But in addition to them were legitimate psychopaths and murderers. In the "Year of the Nazis," these murders were a publicity nightmare for the public-facing tendencies of the movement.[96]

NSLF: Rust and Duffy

The NSLF started to attract a following elsewhere. In addition to Mason, Chaney, and Duffy, the group had affiliates in Detroit, Michigan, and Omaha, Nebraska. (The Detroit group was led by Seth Kliphoth, who was also involved in Nazi-Satanism.[97]) It grew inside the prisons as well. The ANSB was declared the "NSLF West coast convict group." The NSLF started recruiting prisoners in other parts of the country as the NSLF/CEC (Convict Enforcement Corps). The NSLF also praised two more "martyrs," one ANSB and one NSLF, who were killed in 1977.[98]

The NSLF's prisoner work didn't go unnoticed, though, gaining them a place in the *Congressional Record*. U.S. Congressman, and later chairman of the John Birch Society, Larry McDonald told Congress that the ANSB came from a complicated intersection of the Aryan Brotherhood prison gang, the Venceremos Organization (a Marxist-Leninist group), and the SLA. Having already accused the NSLF in 1975 of being a marxist group, he now claimed— genealogically wrong, but ideologically not without some truth—that they had "a strong Marxist-Leninist and Maoist coloration." Being on the Far Right himself, McDonald was not worried about the NSLF's racism and anti-semitism, though. He only invoked the neo-Nazis as part of his call to reconstitute the House Committee on Internal Security.[99]

Rust Arrest

The NSLF's plans came to a halt when Rust was arrested for conspiracy to commit murder in January 1977, as he was allegedly preparing to avenge Tommasi's death by dispatching Jerry Keith Jones. In June 1977, a newspaper reported that Rust had "recently" started his sentence after pleading guilty to possessing an unlicensed silencer, and he was sentenced to two years.[100] And the next month, Chaney was also arrested for attempted murder, but he was apparently free in a relatively short period of time.[101]

In August 1977, Rust circulated a letter to unit leaders ordering the NSLF to disband. The official reason was a lack of funds, although later Rust would admit this was also a requirement of his probation. Members were told they were free to join any new group they wanted. But Mason hadn't seen the letter and the NSLF had not disbanded. Instead, he pled his case to Rust for a "formal merger" of the NSM and NSLF, which Chaney and Duffy were on board with.[102] In December 1977, Rust said "Sorry the NSLF must fade from the scene call it a merger if you will," but "If you need it...I ~~advise~~ order all NSLF units and individuals to co-ordinate with you."[103]

Duffy and the "Shadow NSLF"

Before Rust's letter was circulated, he had already been replaced as the NSLF's leader. John Harry Duffy would oversee the NSLF at its low point, from 1977 to March 1981, although he spent much of his tenure either avoiding arrest or awaiting trial.

Like the others, Duffy had been an NSWPP member; he went from Delaware to California to spend time with Tommasi and then went back east. In March 1975, he was back in El Monte, where he, Chaney, and Rust took part in a beating of NSWPP members. Duffy became the NSLF second-in-command when Rust became leader. And so upon his arrest, in spring 1977, Duffy became the third NSLF leader.[104]

In a July 1977 letter, Duffy wrote

> the only way that we can ever hope to contest the Jew terror grip on America and ergo the White Race is through superior terror and violence...we of the NSLF not only condone violence but encourage and participate in striking blows against Jew power.[105]

At the beginning of 1977, Duffy published an east-coast NSLF periodical, appropriately named *Eastern Front*. But it did not fill the NSLF's national needs. In April 1977, he wrote Mason that "it would be good if we could have the new *Siege* as a continuance of the *National Socialist*." Mason liked the idea and suggested it become the main NSLF publication. Later, Duffy said he was preparing the issue and would make 250 copies which were to be ready in mid-August, but he ran out of money.[106] Other events in Duffy's life might have contributed to the failure of *Siege* to appear. Mason said that in October 1977 Duffy was on the lam, from an "old murder indictment," a situation that went on for a while. In any event, Mason put out, in its place, two issues of the now-Dietz-less *National Socialist*.[107]

White Confederacy and the National Socialist Congress

The showdown at the National Socialist Congress happened at the February 1977 meeting in Cleveland. Mason was convinced he would triumph—probably assuming that his factional allies, Vincent and Kalemba, would rule in his favor. In December 1976, Mason swore out an affidavit against Dietz and it was printed in the Congress's internal newsletter.[108]

In one letter to Rust, however, Mason was unusually honest about the situation. It was not about mailing lists or even money. Dietz and those around him "had concocted the SAME plan to capture the movement for [their] own ends"—just as the NSM had.[109] However, it would be Lauck and Collin who ended up the champions, although it was something of a pyrrhic victory.

Even before the Congress met, Lauck had out-maneuvered Mason with a new leadership proposal, which designated three leaders—Collin, Vincent, and Kalemba—with the power to make almost all decisions. This included the power to expel groups, and furthermore Lauck proposed that each state have a single representative. For Ohio this would be Kalemba—thereby nullifying the NSM's vote. (Lauck later said his interest was not in purging Mason but in making his own publication the Congress's main one.[110])

The organizations involved did not give public accounts about what transpired. Dietz did not show up. The NSM stressed that it "voluntarily withdrew" because of Lauck.[111] An undercover newspaper reporter, J. Ross Baughman, who infiltrated the NSPA and attended the National Socialist Congress as their official photographer, described the outcome thusly.

> A feud and professional rivalry between a Cincinnati propagandist and a Virginia pamphleteer had succeeded in confusing and embarrassing Nazis everywhere. Collin convinced one of the feuding Nazis to resign. Then, to the rest of the congress, he denounced the man for battling a fellow white man.[112]

Baughman published a syndicated four-part series for the *Lorain Journal*, which ran in newspapers around the country that summer. According to him, participants ranged in age from 10 to 60 and came from "all walks of life." He also reported seeing footage of a Collin speech in October 1976, when the NSPA leader said, "National Socialism will go forward—smash, kill, exterminate its enemies until the white race is the only race on the planet Earth!" Baughman also claimed they were planning a "Nazi youth olympics." Mason liked the coverage so much he reprinted some of it.[113]

Mason, having lost the internal struggle in the National Socialist Congress, helped assemble yet another group that debuted in February 1977, the Council of Revolution. Like the White Confederacy, it contained both neo-Nazi and Klan groups.[114] In May, four of the member groups—the NSM, NSLF, Hand's Knights of the Ku Klux Klan (KKKK) chapter, and the Western Guard Party—met in Buffalo, New York. Mason described the new group as "a very loose and informal alliance of radical, racist groups." Its purpose was to act outside of the White Confederacy without needing to adhere to its rules, although it saw itself as "a wing of the most radical members and friends" of the parent group.[115] However, the Council of Revolution also quickly disappeared without making an impact.

By March, the papers were already reporting that Collin's NSPA sought to march in Skokie. Coverage only heated up from there as the legal issues bounced between local, state, and federal courts and were heard at the Supreme Court in 1977. The media covered every twist and turn, and a few years later the affair would be turned into a made-for-TV movie.[116]

The July 1977, the National Socialist Congress in Chicago opened with a bloody street battle with 200 leftist protestors. With the backdrop of the Skokie controversy, the clash received national news coverage. Interest in the National Socialist Congress was dropping, and a third was held that year in Houston, Texas. Mason tried to talk Duffy out of attending (because of Lauck), but the meeting failed to revive the project anyway.[117]

This was followed by a third White Confederacy conference, which included Vincent's NSWWP, in late November in Columbus. Kalemba's UWPP did not come, having apparently disintegrated in July. The conference ended with a press release calling for the "disruption of forced busing by every legal means available."[118] Although Mason signed this on behalf of the NSM, he never showed any interest in this issue and assumedly signed it out of solidarity. Intervening in the bussing issue is likely what he would have thought of when he accused fellow neo-Nazis of "right-wingism."[119]

—1978—

The NSM, NSLF, and NSWWP

Around this time, the NSM drew closer to Vincent. It also appeared to have given up its project as a non-party with the goal of influencing others, codifying as a traditional group. They had some success, and in 1977 and 1978 there were eight affiliates in four states, two of which were of particular importance. The Oklahoma City unit was led by Herrington, who would later take over the NSM, and Bill Russell's Detroit chapter opened a series of bookstores and spun off another group that was initially affiliated with the NSM, the SS Action Group.[120]

The NSM also grew by absorption. Because of Rust's directive, in January 1978 it was announced that the NSLF "temporarily" became part of the NSM, which would control its literature and direction "until such time as a general reorganization can be effected and quasi-legal System attacks have abated," clearly referring to the legal problems of NSLF leadership. At the same time, the NSWPP/Ohio also merged into the NSM, with the note that the former "was an early attempt at doing what the N.S.M. is doing today."[121]

In January 1978, the NSWWP quit the National Socialist Congress, and Mason and Vincent became more closely aligned. Mason's group now announced that he had the power to command the NSM in street demonstrations and that members were to send reports to the NSWWP. (A bureaucratic tradition carried on from Rockwell's party, some of the splinter groups had chapters send military-style reports to the national leadership detailing their activities.[122])

At the end of April 1978, another White Confederacy conference was held, this time in Cincinnati. Taking advantage of the out-of-town support, on the first day Brannen led the usual Hess rally; the NSM was joined by Hand's KKKK, Vincent's NSWWP, and the Western Guard Party. Brannen claimed that Mason did not attend—which Mason contested.[123]

It was quickly revealed why. What appeared in place of the NSM's May 1978 *National Socialist Bulletin* was the *Special Bulletin—To All Members of the NSM, NSLF, & NSWPP—Announcement of Merger*, informing readers that both the NSM and NSLF had joined Vincent's NSWWP. The paper exuberantly declared, "We have just chosen ourselves as the winners-to-be of the future conflict with the World Enemy." The competition between the NSWPP and the National Socialist Congress had now widened into a three-cornered faction fight: Koehl's NSWPP versus Collin's NSPA versus Vincent's NSWWP.[124]

It's Not Your Party, So You Can't Give it Away—Only Splinter and Merge

The unauthorized announcement unsurprisingly made Brannen furious and initiated a long-running feud between the two. He quickly wrote to Vincent that "WE HAVE NOT AND NEVER HAVE DISCUSSED DETAILS OF A MERGER BETWEEN US. Mr. Mason has done this strictly on his own without my consent or even telling me about it." Brannen also claimed that Mason had suffered a nervous breakdown a week before the White Confederacy meeting. Brannen took over the *National Socialist Bulletin* and wrote, "It is with regret that we accept the resignation of the National Party Secretary due to ill health."[125]

Mason said his resignation was a forgery, and both he and Brannen laid claim to the NSM name and retained lawyers. In 1978, the feud got even stranger as Mason tried to get the postal authorities involved, claiming it was fraud for Brannen to get mail under the NSM name, but they declined to intervene.[126] In the December 1980 SIEGE, Mason called Brannen a "kook and faker." In return, his former chairman claimed that Mason was plagiarizing old content of his from the NSM paper—and furthermore that the NSLF itself was still part of the NSM.[127]

The feud went on even after SIEGE folded in 1986. Mason wrote to postal inspectors and police requesting an investigation against Brannen for the crime of filling out magazine subscriptions in his name. One officer who looked into the matter perceptively summed the situation up: "Mr. Mason and Mr. Brannen used to be good friends and someplace along the way parted."[128]

Brannen was just one of many National Socialist colleagues that Mason fell out with during his life. But all of them didn't visit him regularly in jail, nor believe that, together, they could lead the National Socialist movement in a new, revolutionary direction. The split was so deep that Mason refused to utter Brannen's name—for example, purposely excluding him from being mentioned in *Siege*.[129]

The White Confederacy had also been dragged into this new feud. A mid-November 1978 meeting in Columbus was so tense that according to Mason, "Brannen's Bruisers showed up with knives, chains and at least one gun," and that only the presence of armed security prevented bloodshed. At the conference, Brannen presented a lengthy document attacking Mason, and unsuccessfully tried to expel Vincent.[130]

Mason summed up the period of the National Socialist Congress as such:

> A great turmoil began in 1976-77 during a series of alliances and fallings-out amongst the various independent Nazi groups. Great energies were spent on infighting and self-searching. The principal thing which prevented unity was then the very thing which destroyed it while we had it from 1967 through 1973: Egotistical and childish personalities hung up on the "Führer" concept when no Führer actually is about.[131]

After Mason

The NSM continued long after Mason's departure in 1978, into the present day, while the White Confederacy only hung out for a shorter time. In early 1980, the NSM considered hosting a meeting, and soon it was renamed the White Confederacy United Patriotic Front.[132] But after that it disappeared, becoming yet another failed White Supremacist umbrella group.

The NSPA started its trajectory to national fame almost immediately after the NSM left the National Socialist Congress in February 1977. It was soon deep into its legal battle to march in Skokie, which intensified in the summer. The rallies in Marquette Park were not cooling down, either. In July 1977, 1,500 locals, "spurred on" by the NSPA, fought police and injured 16.[133]

But the NSPA also retained great interest in dominating the small neo-Nazi milieu it was part of. In January 1978, Lauck had called for a vote on the "total reunification" of the remaining groups, which happened at the last meeting in March in St. Louis, Missouri. Lauck was already working closely with the NSPA, and so after all the time and effort put into maneuvering, the only real prize was Harold Covington's group, the NSPNC (National Socialist Party of North Carolina). The NSPA now had 15 local groups.[134]

Like the others Covington had been in Koehl's NSWPP, and he would go on to become a notorious neo-Nazi insider. Aside from the usual hopping between neo-Nazi sects, he ran for office, went to Rhodesia, authored several bad novels, and spent decades making wild personal attacks against his fellow White Supremacists. Over the years, Covington would continue to cross Mason's path numerous times, both as friend and foe.

The Skokie controversy also reached its peak. An Illinois magazine wrote that in one week in June 1978, "there was a story about the Nazis on the front page of the *Chicago Tribune* every day." It has received extensive coverage on both local and national television.[135] When the courts finally allowed the NSPA to march, free speech advocates held up the victory as their gold medal. Meanwhile, it removed some of the remaining legal barriers to neo-Nazi organizing just as their movement was growing and becoming significantly more violent.

The threat to march in Skokie had been a feint all along. The NSPA, now free to hold rallies in Chicago without onerous restrictions, held a victory rally in Marquette Park on July 9, 1978. An estimated 2,000 people came. Two thirds were against it, while one-third supported the 25 uniformed neo-Nazis.[136] At that moment, NSPA were easily the most famous neo-Nazi group in the United States.

But it was to be their high point. In the February 1979 alderman election, Collin's vote declined to 10 percent. For him, the worst was yet to come, however. Collin had long been accused of being both Jewish and gay, but this was a typical accusation flung by neo-Nazis against opponents. For Collin, it turned out to be true: his father was Jewish and had been interned in Dachau.[137] Even worse, Covington and Lauck went through Collin's living space and found nude photos of boys and young teens, some taken in the headquarters, which they gave to police. Collin pled guilty in March 1980 to "taking indecent liberties with a number of boys aged eleven to fifteen" and received a seven-year sentence.[138]

Covington, then 27, took over the NSPA leadership. In May 1980, he received almost 43 percent of the vote in the in Republican Party primary for North Carolina attorney general—unheard of for a neo-Nazi leader.[139] But at the tail-end of March 1981, under murky circumstances, he stepped down and handed the party's leadership to Michael Allen. Allen, who had gone to visit Mason in June, was the next to go when he was revealed to be a federal informant with the Bureau of Alcohol, Tobacco, and Firearms. James Burford briefly replaced him, although he was also a convicted sex offender, having pled guilty to charges involving his 12-year-old daughter. The NSPA finally collapsed in 1982.[140]

Notes

1 For example, there is no book on the NSWPP, despite its key importance to the development of U.S. neo-Nazism. While Tommasi has received some mention, the NSLF of almost all periods gets short (or non-existent) shrift. This has also included the long career of Karl Hand; when he is mentioned it is usually in relation to David Duke. Allen Vincent played roles of note at various times but has rarely warranted a footnote. Books and articles on the Skokie incident usually include accounts of the NSPA from that period, although not the National Socialist Congress and much less the White Confederacy. Last, the first 20 years of the NSM are curiously overlooked. While its small size at the time makes this understandable for contemporaneous accounts, its importance starting in the '00s is a notable oversight in later ones. This problem is compounded by the overwhelming tendency to lump neo-Nazis in with other White Supremacists. Additionally, differences between decades are often ignored, leaving one to pick out the relevant pieces.

Local newspapers are an invaluable resource for this period, especially since most groups eagerly sought out coverage. Three reports from monitoring groups also stand out. Two were by Milton Ellerin for the American Jewish Committee, *The American Nazis: Some Recent Developments* (1974) and *American Nazis -- Myth or Menace?* (1977). The other is the Anti-Defamation League of B'nai B'rith's *Hate Groups in America: A Record of Bigotry and Violence* (New York: ADL, 1982).

Two studies written by fascists are also of importance. Martin Kerr's eight-part study, *The History of American National Socialism* (www.theneworder. org/NS-History.html), runs from 1924 to 1985. Jim Saleam's master's thesis, "American Nazism in the Context of the American Extreme Right: 1960–1978," has even more emphasis on this specific period.

For scholarly books written from outside the movement, there are some individual studies whose coverage includes this period, but no thorough overview. Betty A. Dobratz and Stephanie L. Shanks-Meile's *"White Power, White Pride!" The White Separatist Movement in the United States* (New York: Twayne Publishers, 1997) includes some of this time period and is notable for being based on primary sources and interviews. Kaplan's *Encyclopedia of White Power* is uneven but contains significant information on a variety of these otherwise under-documented groups. Jerry Bornstein's *The Neo-Nazis: The Threat of the Hitler Cult* (New York: Julian Messner, 1986) summarizes the 1970s quickly and proficiently. More specifically focused on Pierce, who is counterposed to Willis Carto, is Leonard Zeskind's *Blood and Politics*.

2 The NSM would later go on to become a major neo-Nazi group that was part of the Charlottesville rally and still exists today, even though it has done so by taking a position at odds with how it was founded. However, the NSM's origins are almost always recounted incorrectly. For more on this, see Appendix 1, "The NSM after Mason."

3 SIEGE 11(8) August 1982, p.2 (*Siege*, p.263); Mason to Rust, December 19, 1975 [Box 15, Folder 13]; Mason to Pierce, October 3, 1976 [Box 27, Folders 11 and 33].

4 SIEGE 9(8) December 1980, p.4.

5 "Politics Beyond the Pale—James Mason Forays the 90's with a New Breed of National Socialism" (interview by Aaron Garland), *Ohm Clock* #3, Spring 1995, p.6 (*Articles*, p.94); SIEGE 9(12) December 1980, p.4.

6 Ellerin, *American Nazis -- Myth or Menace?*, p.6; Dave Lyon, "South Lebanon Man Marches to Free Rudolf Hess, Nazi War Criminal," *Western Star*, May 12, 1976, p.10A, reprinted in *National Socialist* #17, June 1976, p.6; NSM, *Anatomy of a Smear*, p.2.

7 NSWPP-Cincinnati Unit, "Internal Bulletin" June 1974 (wrongly dated 1975) [Box 7, Folder 12]; Joseph Bishop to Steven Love, August 12, 1974 [Box 7, Folder 12]; *Ohio National Socialist* #14, Autumn 1975, p.6; Mason interview in *Ohm Clock* (*Articles*, p.94).

8 *Ohio National Socialist* #16, Spring 1976, p.3.

9 Mason interview with Metzger/*Race and Reason* (video); Ellerin, *American Nazis -- Myth or Menace?*, p.5.

10 Schuster, "Introduction," *Siege*, pp.26–27.

11 "On Your Guard," *National Socialist* #20, September–October 1976, p.1; "New Year's Greeting: The Strength of the N.S.M.," *National Socialist Bulletin* 7(1) January 1978, p.1.

12 Mason to Rust, January 4, 1977 [Box 15, Folder 13]; "It's Time... for YOU to join a WINNER!," *National Socialist Bulletin* 6(3) March 1977, p.2; Mason to Pierce, October 3, 1976 [Box 27, Folders 11 and 33].

13 Rust to Mason, June 25, 1976 [Box 15, Folder 13].

14 The first letter is Mason to Tommasi, April 2, 1975 [Box 21, Folder 30]; "Southern Ohio Activity Report," *Ohio National Socialist* #15, Winter 1975/76, p.5.

15 Tommasi to Mason, April 10, 1975 [Box 21, Folder 30]; Mason to Pierce, October 3, 1976 [Box 27, Folders 11 and 33].

16 *Ohio National Socialist* #16, p.12. For an example of the NSM representing the NSLF, see Mason to Pierce, October 31, 1975 [Box 27, Folders 11 and 33].

17 Brannen to Mason, June 5, 1975 [Box 4, Folder 4]; *Ohio National Socialist* #14, p.6; Mason to author, January 1, 2023.

18 "Heroes of the Revolution," *Ohio National Socialist* #15, p.4. It was later discovered that Long was a serial killer and there were many more victims. For more on the murderers Mason would venerate, see Appendix 4, "In Praise of Murder Men."

19 Michael Zatarain, *David Duke: Evolution of a Klansman: An Unauthorized Biography* (Gretna, Louisiana: Pelican, 1990), pp.202–4; Jane M. Hornburger, "Deep Are the Roots: Busing in Boston," *Journal of Negro Education* 45(3) Summer 1976, p.240.

20 "Southern Ohio Activity Report," p.4; *Ohio National Socialist* #15, p.4.

21 "Profile: David Rust, Leader N.S.L.F.," *National Socialist* #19, August 1976, p.6.

22 Rust to author, January 8, 2021; Rust to Mason, June 25, 1976 [Box 15, Folder 13]. This is also in *National Socialist* #19, August 1976, pp.6–7.

23 Rust went to Lebanon in late 1972 or early 1973 with the organization Americans for Justice in the Middle East. "Profile: David Rust, Leader N.S.L.F.," p.6; Rust to Mason, June 25, 1976 [Box 15, Folder 13].

24 Rust to Mason, September 26, 1975; Rust to Mason, December 16, 1975; Rust to Mason, August 26, 1975 [all three Box 15, Folder 13]; "Profile: David Rust, Leader N.S.L.F.," p.7.

25 Rust to Mason, [December 16, 1975]; Rust to Mason, June 25, 1976; Rust to Mason, February 12, 1976 [all three Box 15, Folder 13].

26 *National Socialist Review* #7, July 1976; Rust to Mason, January 16, 1976 [Box 15, Folder 13].

27 Rust to Mason, February 2, 1976; Rust to Mason, June 25, 1976 [both Box 15, Folder 13]. The "other groups" Rust referred to are possibly the prisoners and anti-Communist Cubans.

28 "Notes of Thanks" and "Bomb Halts Film Premier," clippings reprinted in *National Socialist Review* #4, [December 1975], pp.1, 2; Rust to Mason, February 23, 1976 [Box 15, Folder 13].

29 Originally "The White Nationalist Confederacy of Understanding," its name was shortened at the first conference. The other founding groups were the American White Nationalist Party, Christian Vikings of America, Minutemen of Indiana, Marion County Sheriff's Posse Comitatus, and Adamic Knights of the KKK, plus two Canadian groups, the Western Guard Party and Social Credit Association of Ontario. Other groups which had expressed interest, but had not joined by the October 1975 meeting, included Collin's NSPA and Lauck's NSDAP/AO; "Rules and Regulations –and in Effect Statute– of the White Confederacy," October 25, 1975, pp.2–3 [Box 10, Folders 22–25].
    The White Confederacy remained largely a paper organization. Of the 11 founding groups, Mason privately said that (assumedly other than the NSLF and NSM) only three had "any meat and muscle to them locally"—the UWPP, Western Guard Party, and American White Nationalist Party; Mason to Rust, November 4, 1975 [Box 15, Folder 13].

30 Mason to Rust, February 7, 1976 [Box 15, Folder 13]; "Group Will Fight Busing," *News-Journal* (Mansfield, Ohio), November 3, 1975, p.7, www. newspapers.com/image/295754348

31 Clifford Herrington to Mason, June 12, 1974 [Box 25, Folder 35]; "Oklahoma!," *National Socialist Bulletin* 6(1) January 1977, p.18; "Report on N.S.W.P.P. Activity at 1974 Ross County Fair (Ohio)," August 11, 1974, p.3 [Box 15, Folder 11].

32 *White Liberator* #5 [May 1975], p.4 [all issues in Box 11, Folder 24]; "NSWPP Reactionaries Attack Two NSLFers – Retaliation Issued – March 16," *National Socialist Review* #3, March 1975.

33 Mason to Tommasi, May 8, 1975 [Box 21, Folder 30]; *White Liberator* #1, July 25, 1976, p.2.

34 *White Liberator* #2, August 1, 1975, p.4; "N.S.L.F. Training Material" and "The Only Justice Is White Justice! In Memoriam," *White Liberator* #2, pp.10–11; "N.S.L.F. Louisville Notes," *White Liberator* #3, August 8, 1975, p.3.

35 AP, "Coalition Backs Business Boycott: Louisville Prepares for 2nd Week of School," *Messenger-Inquirer* (Owensboro, Kentucky), September 15, 1975, www.newspapers.com/image/378757644; Bruce Hadley, "Two Protest Cases Dismissed; Judge, County Official Argue," *Courier-Journal* (Louisville, Kentucky), September 20, 1975, www.newspapers.com/image/107842875; "Busing-Protest Cases in Area Courts," *Courier-Journal*, October 2, 1975, www.newspapers.com/image/108092993

36 Pierce to Mason, September 17, 1975; Mason to Pierce, January 12, 1976 [both Box 27, Folders 11 and 33].

37 George Michael, *Willis Carto and the American Far Right* (Gainesville: University Press of Florida, 2008), pp.94–95.

38 Ibid, pp.98–99.

39 Zeskind, *Blood and Politics*, p.24; *Attack* #1, Fall 1969, in "FOIA: National Alliance aka NYA-NYC-1," uploaded by Jason Scott, June 13, 2013, pp.18–26, https://archive.org/details/foia_National_Alliance_aka_NYA-NYC-1; Kelvin Pierce with Carole Donoghue, *Sins of My Father: Growing Up with America's Most Dangerous White Supremacist*, 2020, ebook, chapter 14.

40 Saleam, "American Nazism," chapter 3.

41 Zeskind, *Blood and Politics*, p.29.
42 *National Socialist* #18, July 1976, p.9; "Revolution and Legality"(flyer with Pierce quote), NSLF version, *Siege*, 1st ed., p.17.
43 Mason to Rust, December 26, 1975 [Box 15, Folder 13].
44 Rust to Mason, February 12, 1976 [Box 15, Folder 13].
45 In 1979 Mason told the National Alliance secretary that he had been a supporting member since the National Youth Alliance days, and it was the only group that he sent money to. He also invoked his personal relationship in a request that his dues be reduced from $2 to $1, and Pierce personally approved it. Mason remained a supporter until around 1982; Mason to Rosemary M. Rickey, April 14, 1979; Rickey to Mason, May 1, 1979; "Membership Dues Status Report" for James Mason, 1980–81 [all in Box 27, Folder 11].
46 According to Mason, "The Face of an Agent Provocateur" was in the February 15, 1976 NSWPP's *NS Bulletin*, and a clipping was reprinted in the NSM's *Anatomy of a Smear*.
47 Mason to Koehl (resignation letter), April 1, 1976 [Box 47, Folder 21]; "Action Report," *National Socialist* #17, June 1976, p.5.
48 "On Your Guard," p.1; ADL, *Extremism on the Right*, p.80.
49 Mason to Rust, May 3, 1976 [Box 15, Folder 13].
50 "On Your Guard," pp.2–3.
51 Mason to Rust, May 27, 1976 [Box 15, Folder 13]; *National Socialist* #17–19, June–August, 1976.
52 *The National Socialist* #19, August 1976, pp.6–7, 11.
53 Springfield, *Power Struggle*; *National Socialist Bulletin* 6(10) March 1977, p.4.
54 "On Your Guard," pp.2, 5.
55 "Everybody Loves a SMEAR," *National Socialist Bulletin* #21, October/November 1976, p.2; "The Big Blast," *National Socialist Bulletin* #23, December 1976, p.2.
56 Lyon, "South Lebanon Man"; Brannen, "Dear Friend" (Tommasi memorial invitation), [July–August] 1976 [Box 4, Folder 4].
57 Two years after leaving the NSM, Mason claimed he wrote "every word plus the masthead" of their periodicals, in addition to rewriting Brannen's editorials. Indeed, the style of almost all the pieces is consistent with SIEGE's; SIEGE 9(8) December 1980, p.4.
58 *National Socialist Review* #4–7, December 1975 to July 1976.
59 Rust to Mason, December 24, 1975; Rust to Mason, November 1, 1975 [both Box 15, Folder 13]; *National Socialist Review* #6, April 1976, p.4; Arnie Friedman, "Nazi Leader Says Valley Is Party's Main Training Base," *Valley News* (Van Nuys, California), June 19, 1977.
60 Rust to author, postmarked January 8, 2021. Frank Collin told the press it had existed for "about two years now," and was being run by a "council of officers" until Rust returned or was replaced; Friedman, "Nazi Leader Says".
61 "Louisville," *National Socialist Review* #5, February 1976, p.1; "NOTICE - Kentucky," *National Socialist Review* #7, July 1976, p.13.
62 "NSLF Shoot-Out in Delaware," *National Socialist Review* #7, p.8; "5 to Life for Sgt. Gould," *Jailbreak*, 1977, p.3 [Box 13, Folder 18]; "Convict in Shotgun Slaying Gets 5-to-Life Prison Term," *Sacramento Bee* (California), May 15, 1977, p.33, www.newspapers.com/image/620910253; "Officer Robinson Busted!," *Eastern Front* #1, [January 1977?], p.2 [Box 13, Folder 18].
63 Rust to Mason, December 24, 1975; "National Socialist Liberation Front" (membership application), filled out January 7, 1976 [Box 32, Folder 19]; Rust to Mason, February 23, 1976; Mason to Duffy, December 13, 1976 [Box 13, Folder 18]; Mason to Rust, December 26, 1975 [all Rust letters are in Box 15, Folder 13].

64 Rust to Mason, January 5, 1976; Rust to Mason, January 16, 1976 [both Box 15, Folder 13].

65 During the Night of the Long Knives in June 1934, Hitler purged the SA (Brownshirts) and executed its leaders, including Ernst Röhm, who was gay. Mason to Rust, September 2, 1975; Mason to Rust, March 5, 1976 [both Box 15, Folder 13]. For more on Mason and others views on gay men, see Appendix 6, "Women, Gay Men, and Extreme Pornography."

66 "Imprisoned Comrades," *Siege* #2, p.14; Rust to Mason, December 10, 1976 [Box 15, Folder 13].

67 "Brothers Behind Bars," *National Socialist Review* #7, July 1976, pp.15–17.

68 "From Dyle Bitner, San Quentin, CA," *National Socialist Review* #4 [December 1975], pp.3, 4.

69 Rust to Mason, June 14, 1976 [Box 15, Folder 13].

70 Rust, "To Whom It May Concern"; Rust to Mason, December 10, 1976 [both Box 15, Folder 13].

71 For the story of NSPA's organizing in Marquette from their perspective, see Leon Dilios, *White Revolt! An American National Socialist History*. (The author said he was as a former NSPA member, although it appears to be written from Collin's perspective.) For an antifascist counter-organizer's account, see Chip Berlet, "Hate Groups, Racial Tension and Ethnoviolence in an Integrating Chicago Neighborhood, 1976–1988," in Betty A. Dobratz, Lisa K. Walder, and Timothy Buzzell, eds., *Research in Political Sociology* (9) 2001, pp.117–63.

72 ADL, *Hate Groups in America*, pp.35–36.

73 Charles Ventura, "Federal Judge Allows 'Alt-Right' Rally to Go Ahead as Planned," *USA Today*, August 11 (updated August 12), 2017, www.usatoday. com/story/news/2017/08/11/charlottesville-braces-itself-yet-another-white-nationalist-rally-saturday/560829001

74 Mason to Rust, May 30, 1976, p.3; Mason to Rust, April 7, 1976 [both Box 15, Folder 13]; "Action Report," *National Socialist* #17, June 1976, p.7; *The Eagle News* #1, [January?] 1976 [Box 5, Folder 16]; Mason to Kalemba, February 18, 1976 [Box 5, Folder 16]; "Welcome: British Movement," *National Socialist* #18, July 1976, p.2. According to Saleam, an Australian party, the National Democratic Front, also became involved; Saleam, "American Nazism," chapter 3.

75 Springfield, *Power Struggle*, p.20. Mason surmised Lauck wrote it, which he later confirmed; Gerhard Lauck to author, email, February 1, 2021.

76 Mason to Rust, December 5, 1976 [Box 15, Folder 13].

77 "Lauck on Leadership," *Newsletter of the National Socialist Congress*, February 1977, p.8 [hereafter *Newsletter of the NSC*].

78 The other two were the Local Group Rockwell in Oklahoma City, Oklahoma and George Schwegler's St. Louis group, another one which called itself the American Nazi Party; "NS Congress Meets in Chicago," *NS Report* #7, Winter 1976/1977, pp.1, 3.

79 Mason to Rust, December 5, 1976 [Box 15, Folder 13].

80 *National Socialist Bulletin* 6(2) February 1977, p.3.

81 Brannen, "Dear Friend & Comrade," November 13, 1976 [Eph 373]; "Message from the N.S.M. Chairman: Year-End Report," *National Socialist Bulletin* #23, December 1976, p.15; Martin Kerr, email to author, July 6, 2023.

82 "White Confederacy Congress, Cleveland, December 4 and 5, 1976. Agenda" [Box 10, Folders 22–25]; "Duffy Meets with National Socialist Leadership," *Eastern Front* #1, p.3.

83 Schwegler's group quit the Congress over both Mason's "squabbling" and the NSM's advocacy of violence—and joined up with Dietz, instead. Lauck, "The Dietz

Affair" and "Schwegler Leaves Congress," *Newsletter of the NSC*, December 1976, pp.1, 2; Mason to Herrington, December 17, 1976 [Box 25, Folder 35].

84 Brannen, "The Year of the Nazis," *National Socialist* 2(2) Winter 1978, p.6; "N.S.M. Gets 'HUSTLED'," *National Socialist Bulletin* 6(2) February 1977, p.12; Dennis Cusick, "Vocal Flynt Forces Gather to Show Support to Publisher," *Cincinnati Enquirer*, January 7, 1977, www.newspapers.com/image/103080869. Mason was fully cognizant of the situation's irony in his description of it in "National Pornographic," *Out of the Dust*, vol. 1, pp.227–28.

85 Especially considering his future actions, it is worth considering whether Brannen was ever committed to Mason's hyper-militancy. "It's Time... for YOU to join a WINNER!," *National Socialist Bulletin* 6(3) March 1977, pp.1–2.

86 Steven Love became NSM vice chair on May 20 and resigned June 2; Love to Brannen, notarized resignation, June 2, 1977 [Box 7, Folder 12].

87 "Brannen Behind Bars," *National Socialist Bulletin* 6(1) January 1977, p.17; "Third N.S.M. Commission," *National Socialist Bulletin* 6(5) May 1977, p.17.

88 "Heroes of the Revolution," *Ohio National Socialist* #14, Autumn 1975, p.4.

89 "N.S.M. Shuffles the Deck" *National Socialist Bulletin* 6(7) July 1977, p.5.

90 See Chapter 8, "Charles Manson as Neo-Nazi 'Holy Man'".

91 Cited in Ellerin, *American Nazis -- Myth or Menace?*, p.12, original is *Cincinnati Post*, July 6, 1977.

92 His father later said that his son was dating a black girl, something his family disapproved of; James A Aho, *Politics of Righteousness: Idaho Christian Patriotism* (Seattle: University of Washington Press, 1990), p.72, https://archive.org/details/politicsofrighte0000ahoj

93 [Mason], "A Case of the Heebie-Jeebies," *National Socialist Bulletin* 6(10) October 1977, p.2.

94 Taylor was a longtime Canadian fascist activist who became leader of the Western Guard Party in 1976; Stanley R. Barrett, *Is God a Racist? The Right Wing in Canada* (Toronto: University of Toronto Press, 1989), p.14, https://archive.org/details/isgodracistright0000barr

95 Mason, "A Case of the Heebie-Jeebies," pp.2–3.

96 *Siege*, p.443; SIEGE 7(4) April 1983, p.2 (*Siege*, p.166).

97 *National Socialist* 2(1) Fall 1977, p.40.

98 Duffy, application to be an NSLF Prison Enforcement Officer, [1977]; Duffy to Mason, July 13, 1977; *Jailbreak*, 1977, p.4 [all three Box 13, Folder 18].

99 Larry McDonald, "The National Socialist Liberation Front—The New Marxist Terrorist Group," *Congressional Record (Bound)*, March 13, 1975, pp.6672–73, www.govinfo.gov/content/pkg/GPO-CRECB-1975-pt5/pdf/GPO-CRECB-1975-pt5-7-3.pdf; McDonald, "California Nazis Expand Contacts," *Congressional Record (Bound)*, January 6, 1977, p.400, www.govinfo.gov/content/pkg/GPO-CRECB-1977-pt1/pdf/GPO-CRECB-1977-pt1-2-3.pdf

See also McDonald, "National Socialist Liberation Front's New Alliances," from June 8, 1976, *Congressional Record (Bound)*, vol.122, part 14 (June 4, 1976 to June 11, 1976), issued June 11, 1976, p.17044, www.govinfo.gov/content/pkg/GPO-CRECB-1976-pt14/pdf/GPO-CRECB-1976-pt14-3-3.pdf

100 Friedman, "Nazi Leader Says Valley Is Party's Main Training Base," p.6. Rust said he received two years in prison and two on probation, and ended up serving 18 months; Rust to author, February 2, 2021 and July 13, 2022.

101 He was out of prison by December 1977 because at that time he was starting to close down his Louisville NSLF post office boxes. Chaney would pop up briefly in 1980 when Mason and Duffy were re-starting the NSLF, saying he was "getting active again in his area." Ultimately, however, that did not seem to be the case.

Duffy to Mason, July 28, 1977; Mason to Duffy and Candy, June 30, 1980 [both Box 13, Folder 18]; Mason to Rust, December 20, 1977 [Box 15, Folder 13].

102 Rust (letter disbanding the NSLF), [August] 1977; Mason to Rust, November 13, 1977 [both Box 15, Folder 13].

103 Rust to Mason, December 27, 1977; Rust to Mason, January 8, 1977 [both Box 15, Folder 13]; "General Secretary's Notes," *National Socialist Bulletin* 7(11) January 1978, p.2.

104 Cordova, "Joseph Tommasi: His Last Interview," p.18; "NSWPP Reactionaries Attack Two NSLFers," p.3; Duffy to Mason, April 25, 1977 [Box 13, Folder 18].

105 Cited in Ellerin, *American Nazis -- Myth of Menace?*, 1977, p.12.

106 *Eastern Front* #1, [1977]; Mason to Duffy, April 29, 1977; Duffy to Mason, April 25, 1977; Duffy to Mason, August 2, 1977; Duffy to Mason, [August 1979] [all Box 13, Folder 18].

107 Mason to Karl Hand, October 5, 1977 [Box 25, Folder 23]. This arrest was in addition to Duffy's January 1975 arrest for taking weapons across state lines; for that one, he was bailed out by August of that year. In March 1978, Mason said Duffy had been underground for "several months." Mason to Kathy Canavan, March 24, 1978 [Box 13, Folder 18]; Cordova, "Joseph Tommasi: His Last Interview," p.6; *National Socialist* 2(1) Fall 1977 and 2(2) Winter 1977/78.

108 "Mason's Affidavit," *Newsletter of the NSC*, February 1977, pp.3, 6.

109 Mason to Rust, December 5, 1976 [Box 15, Folder 13].

110 "Lauck on Leadership," pp.7–8; Lauck, email to author, February 1, 2021.

111 "Have It Your Way," *National Socialist Bulletin* 6(4) April 1977, p.7.

112 J. Ross Baughman, "Part 1: Viewing the Nazis: Suspicions; Dangers," *El Paso Times*, July 17, 1977, p.1, www.newspapers.com/image/435352877, www.newspapers.com/image/435354231; "We Were THERE!," *National Socialist Bulletin* 6(3) March 1977, p.13.

113 Baughman, "Part 2: Nazi Meeting Resembled Social Club," *Great Falls Tribune*, June 14, 1977, p.2, www.newspapers.com/image/240737138; Baughman, "Part 3: 'Ruthless Little Barbarians' Are Youth Trained as Nazis," *El Paso Times*, July 19, 1977, www.newspapers.com/image/435261734, www.newspapers.com/image/435261847; *National Socialist* 2(1) Fall 1977, pp.28, 29.

114 Mason to Herrington, February 28, 1977 [Box 25, Folder 35]. In April 1977, the NSM listed the Council of Revolution groups as: American White Nationalist Brotherhood, NSWWP, National Socialist Pioneer Prisoners, Western Guard Party of Canada, Social Credit Association of Ontario, Alpha Circle, New Order Party (KKKK), National Revolutionary Army, and Hand's KKKK. "Movement Directory," *National Socialist Bulletin* 6(4) April 1977, p.9.

115 "Forging New Solidarity: Meeting of the K.K.K.K., W.G.P., N.S.L.F, & N.S.M," *National Socialist Bulletin* 6(7) July 1977, pp.10–11 is two-page photo spread on the meeting, although does not identify it with the Council of Revolution. The Buffalo meeting was retroactively referred to as a Council of Revolution meeting; "First Address...Council of Revolution," 1977 [Box 10, Folders 22–25].

116 Ed McManus, "Nazi March: What's It All About?" *Illinois Issues*, November 12, 1978, www.lib.niu.edu/1978/ii781111.html; *Skokie*, dir. Herbert Wise, 1981, www.imdb.com/title/tt0083090, www.youtube.com/watch?v=35G28qXerFc

117 *Newsletter of the NSC*, July 1977, p.1; "The Fighting Congress," *NS Report* #10, Fall 1977, pp.3, 8; Mason to Duffy, August 4, 1977 [Box 13, Folder 18].

118 American White Nationalist Party on behalf of member organizations of the White Confederacy (press release), November 26–27, 1977 [Box 10, Folders 22-25]; "Congress Meets in Texas," *Newsletter of the NSC*, November 1977; *National Socialist Bulletin* 6(12) December 1977, p.2.

119 In fact, the NSM had previously claimed busing was "A FAKE ISSUE" to distract people from "Economic Slavery." Message from the NSM Chairman, "Keep Your Eye on the Culprits: Don't Be Misled by the Forced Bussing Issue," *National Socialist* #17, June 1976, p.1.

120 These were Cincinnati and Chillicothe, Ohio; Brandenton and Tampa, Florida; Detroit, Michigan; Mineola, New York; and Oklahoma City and Tulsa, Oklahoma. *National Socialist* 2(1) Fall 1977, p.40; *National Socialist Bulletin* 6(4) April 1977, p.9; *Stormer* 1(2) January 1978, p.29. For more, see Appendix 1, "The NSM After Mason".

121 "General Secretary's Notes," *National Socialist Bulletin* (7)11 January 1978, p.2. According to Mason, at that time there were "a lot" of NSWPP's which were not actually affiliated with the party, including one led by the Canadian John Beattie; Mason to author, November 26, 2022.

122 "Vincent Withdraws from Congress," *Newsletter of the NSC*, January 1978, p.1; "The 'Power Struggle' Is Over," *National Socialist Bulletin* 7(3) March 1978, p.6.

123 Brannen to Allen Vincent, May 24, 1978 [Box 4, Folder 4]; *National Socialist Bulletin* 7(5) April 1978, pp.1–5; Mason to author, November 26, 2022.

124 *Special Bulletin—To All Members of the NSM, NSLF, & NSWPP— Announcement of Merger*, May–June 1978, p.1 [D2247]; Saleam, "American Nazism," chapter 3. The last Mason-edited issue before the *Special Bulletin* was *National Socialist Bulletin* 7(4) April 1978.

125 Brannen to Allen Vincent, May 24, 1978; Brannen to Rich, June 11, 1978; Brannen to John Beattie, August 14, 1978 [all three in Box 4, Folder 4]; "Ill Health Forces Resignation," *National Socialist Bulletin*, 7(5) April 1978, p.5 (While the issue was dated April on the cover, it was printed later as it includes clippings from May.)

126 William B Moore to John C Quinn, September 15, 1978; Biggers to Mason, August 24, 1978; Mason to Biggers, September 12, 1978 [all in Box 4, Folder 4].

127 SIEGE 9(8) December 1980, p.4. In theory, since the NSLF had merged with the NSM, and if its subsequent merger into the NSWWP was invalid—as Brannen had always claimed—then he was correct, at least in the abstract.

128 Mason to USPS Inspector in Charge, August 1, 1986; Mason to Lee Kilburn, December 2, 1987; Lt. E. W. Butterbaugh to Ross Co. Sheriff, [1986–1987] [all in Box 4, Folder 4].

129 Herrington's name does not appear, either; Moynihan to Mason, October 6, 1989 [Box 5, Folder 9].

130 Mason to Hand, November 13, 1978 [Box 25, Folder 25].

131 Mason to Saleam, June 29, 1979 [Box 21, Folder 17].

132 "Unit Leaders Meeting," *National Socialist Bulletin* 9(2) February 1980, p.5; "Klan Says Former Leader Can't Resign," *Daily World* (Opelousas, Louisiana), April 9, 1980, p.23, www.newspapers.com/image/227907429

133 ADL, *Hate Groups in America*, p.36.

134 "Lauck Proposes Reunification Immediately," *Newsletter of the NSC*, January 1978, pp.1–2; *The New Order* #13, April/May, 1978, p.1, cited in Saleam, "American Nazism." Lauck later said the NSDAP/AO remained independent and that he never formally joined the NSPA, even though he became its "head of Publishing and Administration, in effect the #3 position in the NSPA" and was in charge of collecting dues; Lauck to author, email, February 1, 2021.

135 McManus, "Nazi March".

136 Douglas E Kneeland, "72 Seized at Rally of Nazis in Chicago," *NYT*, July 10, 1978, www.nytimes.com/1978/07/10/archives/72-seized-at-rally-of-nazis-in-chicago-police-keep-2000-under.html. A documentary was filmed of the July 9, 1978 rally and counter-protest; *Marquette Park II*, dir. Tom Palazzolo and Mark

Rance, 1980, *Chicago Film Archive*, www.chicagofilmarchives.org/collections/index.php/Detail/Object/Show/object_id/23710

137 "Ward-by-Ward Vote Totals for Alderman," *Chicago Tribune*, February 28, 1979, p.10, www.newspapers.com/image/386669537; ADL, *Hate Groups in America*, p.29.

138 "Frank Collin," *Encyclopedia*, p.62; ADL, *Extremism on the Right*, p.118.

139 ADL, *Hate Groups in America*, pp.29, 37.

140 Ibid, p.31; "James Burford," *Encyclopedia*, pp.32–33; *Articles*, pp.8, 41; John O'Brien, "Sex Offender Heads Neo-Nazi group," *Chicago Tribune*, October 31, 1982, www.newspapers.com/image/387995407; ADL, *Extremism on the Right*, p.1.

5

ALLEN VINCENT'S NSWWP AND JOHN DUFFY'S SHADOW NSLF

James Mason spent the next two years biding his time by editing publications for Allen Vincent's National Socialist White Workers' Party (NSWWP). The two had crossed paths many times since 1966, and Mason had long seen Vincent as an ally. Most of the other neo-Nazis that Mason worked with had joined Koehl's National Socialist White People's Party (NSWPP) after Rockwell's passing, but Vincent's lineage went back to the American Nazi Party, just as Mason's did. And the fact that it was Vincent's picture in the book that led Mason to join the party in the first place undoubtedly gave the older man a special place in his heart.

Vincent gained significant publicity through a documentary made about his group, *The California Reich*. He soon split from Koehl's group, forming the NSWWP, which for a minute became a national organization. So, after leaving the National Socialist Movement (NSM), Mason went to work as the editor of two NSWWP periodicals. But the group was using the opposite approach Mason wanted: the "mass strategy" of holding uniformed rallies and opening storefronts.

At the same time Mason remained a National Socialist Liberation Front (NSLF) member. Although it was inert outside of Delaware and New Jersey, John Duffy and the energetic Ed Reynolds kept it running there, despite constant legal trouble. Restless and unhappy with Vincent's group, in 1980 Mason broke ties with Vincent as well.

ANP/NSWPP Days

Vincent was one of many neo-Nazis who had extreme backgrounds in their personal life. He served over a decade in prison as well as almost a year in a

DOI: 10.4324/9780429200090-8

mental hospital. According to Mason's account, Vincent adopted National Socialism in San Quentin prison, joined the American Nazi Party when he was released in 1962, went to Arlington to work with Rockwell, and became the leader of the party's youth wing, the National Socialist Youth Movement.[1]

In February 1966, Vincent helped restart an American Nazi Party unit in San Francisco, which distributed literature near University California, Berkeley and picketed a film about interracial romance. That October, Rockwell came to San Francisco for a rally, where 18 neo-Nazis faced off against 4,000 counter-protestors. Vincent "climbed atop the camper and addressed the boisterous crowd before being shouted down and pelted with eggs."[2] This was merely one of Vincent's many pugnacious public appearances, and he became well respected among neo-Nazis as a fearless street brawler.

In 1964, a picture of Vincent holding a sign with an American Nazi Party address appeared in *Extremism U.S.A.* Two years later, Mason's life in neo-Nazism started when he saw the picture and wrote Vincent a letter. However, Vincent was part of the first major post-Rockwell break from Koehl's NSWPP. There had been increasing discontent in the California section over local leader Ralph Forbes, whom Koehl backed. This resulted in a split, and Vincent joined up with another member of Rockwell's original party, James K. Warner. Their new group, which claimed to have formed on January 1, 1968, was the first of many to recycle the name of the American Nazi Party.[3]

This group did not last long, however. Vincent lived in Germany for a few years but in 1973 came back to the NSWPP and restarted his activism in San Francisco. Vincent's group was still in the party when *The California Reich* was filmed in 1974 and 1975. It documented, largely without narration, the group's confrontational demonstrations and private gatherings as well as one-on-one interviews. The children of neo-Nazis were filmed receiving gifts from a Santa with a swastika armband while a woman shows off the swastika cake she baked. It also caught a rare moment of the existential appeal of National Socialism when Vincent told the filmmakers that, in his future society, "there's not going to be any lonely people. They're only going to be harmonious, compatible relationships—where no loneliness is possible. Where there won't be any lonely people."[4] Released in 1975, it was loved by neo-Nazis, condemned by many in the public—some of whom tried to prevent it from being shown—and nominated for an Academy Award.[5]

A Party to Call His Own

In March of that year, Vincent—at 43, one of the older men in the movement—finally broke from Koehl. Vincent's group now became the National Socialist White Worker's Party. They apparently hoped to remain associated with Koehl's party in the public mind, with an added proletarian twist, as the name no longer referred to the "people" but rather the "workers." (Jim Saleam said the NSWWP "appealed to sub-proletarian elements" and had "maybe a few hundred members and sympathisers, mostly of low educational standard.") Eschewing grassroots organizing, "the party presented no plan of action—other than sensationalist activities—to win tactical successes."[6]

After Mason's faction left the National Socialist Congress, the NSLF and NSM drew closer to Vincent. But David Rust complained that Vincent was a "hard-line believer in the 'uniform and demonstrate' tactic." Nonetheless, as early as November 1977, Mason said, "We are as close to Vincent as it is possible to be."[7]

In April 1977, the NSWWP opened a new bookstore in San Francisco's Sunset neighborhood; it was across from a synagogue attended by a number of Holocaust survivors. After a week of "blaring recorded martial music" while "brown-shirted party members" stood out front, protestors set it on fire; Vincent had to escape by crawling out of a back window. Ultimately no one was prosecuted, and in February 1978, Vincent sued elected officials and Jewish organizational leaders for $28 million.[8]

By this time, the NSWWP had gone national; in spring 1977, there were eight affiliates, and 11 a year later.[9] The Texas unit ended up in the papers when two members ran for mayor of their respective cities. Michael Ange tried in Galveston, although he ran into problems getting on the ballot. Dana McNatt did better in the November 1977 Houston race, receiving over 1,000 votes and carrying one precinct. Reversing course, in December 1977, the Houston group's recorded message offered a $5,000 reward "for every non-white killed during an attack on a white person."[10]

The NSWWP also held high-profile rallies in California. In 1978, they went to San Jose, where they faced off with 2,000 protestors. In September 1978, the group wasn't so lucky in Santa Rosa; antifascists got the jump on the neo-Nazis, beating them so badly that they had to be rescued by police. And in 1979, 800 counter-protestors confronted the Vincent and his followers in Walnut Creek.[11]

The NSWWP had taken part in both the National Socialist Congress and the White Confederacy. In April 1978, Vincent also went to Chillicothe before the fateful Cincinnati meeting of the White Confederacy, directly after which Mason announced the merger with the NSWWP.[12]

Mason was appointed the NSWWP General Secretary and editor-in-chief of the party publication, *Stormer*. Under Mason, *Stormer* ran typical fare for a U.S. neo-Nazi publication. Much of the content consisted of news clippings about the NSWWP, especially its street battles, and allied groups. Its focus was not on race but on "Jewish Communism," with special attention to Holocaust denial. Ideologically, it was so derivative that the American Nazi Party platform was reprinted in several issues. In one issue, Mason printed several pages on Joseph Tommasi, and another focused on the controversy about *The California Reich*. *Stormer* differed mainly from other publications Mason was associated with by the visible presence of women, including associate editor Charlotte Reich.[13]

Mason also ran a second NSWWP periodical, the *White Worker's Bulletin*; its 13 issues appeared to function as his personal vehicle. It explicitly was a continuation of the NSM's *National Socialist Bulletin* and just like it could be mistaken for some issues of *Siege*.[14] The tone was much softer in some places—although not others. There were clippings about the NSWWP, adoration of Vincent, and appeals for donations. The occasional praise for murderers, including Fred Cowan and the Greensboro massacre, did slip in, however.

Ed Reynolds

Days after the merger of the NSLF, Mason's NSM faction, and the NSWWP, both Vincent and Mason travelled to Vineland, New Jersey to hold a joint press conference with Ed Reynolds, who had just been expelled from his Klan group and had embraced National Socialism.[15]

Edwin Lawrence Reynolds IV alternated between being a leader in the NSLF and the Klan. He was briefly a youthful rising star as a New Jersey Klan organizer in the late 1970s. But after scandals and fallings-out, he turned toward National Socialism and became one of Mason's closest comrades as the 1980s went on.

Reynolds said he originally sent money to the NSWPP in 1967 at age 12 to get flyers ("Uptight about school? Or just the Niggers?"). But his organizing career started in 1970 when he was 15 years old, as his Vineland high school became one of many in the area on fire with conflicts between black and white students.[16] At his school, he formed a student group, STAB ("Students Together Against Blacks or Ship Them All Back"), and then joined the National States Rights Party. At age 17, he was inducted into the Klan in March 1972 at what he called a "really large, classy ceremony in Upper Darby, Pennsylvania."[17]

The next year, at age 18, Reynolds joined the military. Upon returning to civilian life, he ran a successful Klan organizing campaign in New Jersey in July 1976 and made frequent media appearances. Reynolds specialized in recruiting youth; at 25, he was described in a local newspaper as having only one member older than him in his core circle.[18] Initially affiliated with Raymond Doerfler's Pennsylvania Klan, Reynolds had spun off his own group around June 1977. At the end of the year, estimates put his Klan at 55 people, at most, in three klaverns. (Reynolds claimed there were more of both.)[19]

However, Reynolds's blazing star soon cooled. He was as sexually voracious as he was injudicious. In April 1978, he was "banished" from the Invisible Empire by Doerfler for "illegal use of organization funds, morals charges involving other members' wives and association with Nazis."[20]

And he certainly was associating with Nazis. At the joint press conference with Vincent, Reynolds said eight of his Klan group—assumedly including himself—had also joined the NSWWP.[21] In July, he told Mason, "The police and media seem to think there is a large Klan group and a small Nazi group operating in Atlantic City, when in fact the two groups are one in the same... US!" In August, he said that he was back in touch with Duffy and that "we will be working closely together... I like him a lot and we see eye-to-eye on everything."[22]

In October 1978, Reynolds was still "considered by some to be a bright young man of the fringe right," and the new group he formed, the White Knights, New Jersey Ku Klux Klan was "considering several offers to join other national Klan organizations."[23] But his problems had just begun.

"Free the Circle Plaza Two!"

In early July 1979, Duffy and Reynolds, now working closely together, were both arrested for raping a woman who was allegedly spying on them for the Jewish Defense League (JDL). This grabbed headlines, giving the NSLF another appearance in the *New York Times*, but the story that came out afterward was even stranger.[24]

The 19-year-old woman, identified in the paper of record simply as Annette, said that at the end of June 1979, Duffy and Reynolds (then 23 and 25, respectively) lured her to the Circle Plaza Motel in Vineland. She said that while in a room there, they raped her while handcuffed, breaking her wrist in the process.[25] Another paper luridly reported that she said the two Nazis threatened "to get nine blacks to rape her," torture her with lit cigarettes, and then murder her. The neo-Nazi duo was arrested in the first week of July. Duffy wrote Mason from jail, saying he was charged with three felonies and a misdemeanor but proclaimed his innocence.[26]

Annette had a bizarre backstory. She approached the neo-Nazis in February 1979, wanting to join. (Labeled a "Jewess" in the press, her mother was Catholic and her father was Jewish.) In fact, she had previously done work with the JDL. But in her guise as a neo-Nazi, she got in with the NSLF by revealing that a racist rally they were planning to attend was a honeypot: it was actually organized by a former JDL member who planned to ambush them. As the NSLF was still part of Vincent's NSWWP and not taking new members, she became a member of the latter and attended local meetings.[27]

Annette started double-dealing, giving Philadelphia JDL leader Edward Rainov detailed information on 20 Nazi and Klan members—while giving information on the JDL to Doerfler, the Klan Grand Dragon. In addition to warning the NSLF about the rally, Rainov blamed Annette for giving his girlfriend's unlisted phone number to Reynolds, who subjected her to a stream of harassment.[28]

This occurred during a larger period of fighting between the JDL (and other radical Jewish militants) and both Nazi war criminals who were in the country as well as neo-Nazis. For example, the JDL offered a $500 bounty to anyone who killed or maimed a neo-Nazi. In 1979, bombs were sent to neo-Nazis in multiple states. Although they did not name the sender, the FBI contacted both Mason and Vincent in June to tell them they were suspected targets.[29]

Duffy and Reynolds's preliminary hearing in July did not go well for the prosecution; Annette changed her accusation, now saying only Duffy raped her. After the proceedings, a policeman said that, despite Annette's Jewish background and JDL affiliations, she was staying with Reynolds's mentor-turned-nemesis Doerfler. The Klan leader seemed to be the only one to speak with some sense about the situation, saying Annette was "obsessed with intrigue" but "didn't realize the danger of it."[30]

Despite still being the leader of the NSLF, despite a published picture of him sporting a swastika armband while posing in front of a swastika banner, and furthermore despite meeting Annette specifically because she sought to join a neo-Nazi organization, Duffy claimed he had not been a neo-Nazi "for a number of years."[31] A local paper bought it, writing that he had left the NSLF and obligingly referring to him as an "Ex-neo-Nazi." (This kind of public dishonestly is standard for U.S. neo-Nazis when they land in the hot seat; Mason has stood out as a rare exception who has consistently owned up to his politics.) The next month, Duffy was back to shouting neo-Nazi slogans at reporters.[32]

In February 1980, a grand jury declined to indict either neo-Nazi after Annette refused to testify. Duffy, who admitted he had sex with her, claimed he was the real victim: apparently before the incident, Annette had been sending "weird letters" to his girlfriend.[33]

In early 1979, Reynolds had been simultaneously organizing for the NSWWP and the White Knights. After their arrests, Reynolds and Duffy sought to have greater autonomy from the NSWWP, and Mason assured them that it was okay for the NSLF to operate inside of it. A few days later, Mason wrote Duffy that, "Nothing would make me happier than to see the NSLF return full-blast and I would love to lend a big hand," but money was needed to make that happen.[34] Reynolds and Duffy agreed to stay in the NSWWP, saying they would not form another group; but even if they had, there would not have been much to work with. In July 1979, the ADL said there were only two east-coast NSLF groups and that the Delaware one had no more than 15 members and only held private events.[35]

Mason knew he was on a sinking ship, though. That July, he admitted that in the three-way race among the neo-Nazi groups, the NSWWP was lagging in third. Nine days after Reynolds said they would not form a new group, Mason broke the news to him that he had been dismissed from the NSWWP over the rape allegation, adding that the NSLF should be "immediately reactivated." Unsurprisingly, Reynolds agreed, saying "things are too hot and we have too much potential and chance staring us in the face here in New Jersey. The NSLF is my only alternative as an active revolutionary." He also claimed to be turning down offers from both Frank Collin to join the National Socialist Party of America (NSPA) and Koehl to join the NSWPP.[36]

In August 1979, a David Duke rally was held at a teenager's house in Barnegat, New Jersey. Twenty came outside for the rally, while others stayed inside the house. Karl Hand, still in Duke's KKKK, attended, as did Reynolds, who wore Klan regalia for the occasion. According to Reynolds, only two members of Duke's Klan showed but there were eight from the NSLF.[37]

Mason had already been reprinting NSLF material. In 1979, he reissued the "Political Terror" flyer and soon after reprinted "Building the Revolutionary Party."[38] In October 1980, he made 2,000 copies of Tommasi's *Strategy for Revolution*.

While waiting on the grand jury, Duffy also attempted to revive the NSLF's *National Socialist Review*. Although still working for Vincent, Mason prepared an issue based on the rape case. It was mostly of newspaper clippings but included an article by Mason, in which he claimed "This incident provided the biggest single shot-in-the-arm for the NSLF in the East in years!"[39] Whether or not it actually helped the NSLF as an organization, it was certainly their greatest piece of publicity, especially considering that the group was practically defunct. In October 1979, Reynolds, Duffy, and others drove to see Mason in Ohio with the money to print the new issue, but their car broke down en route and their savings were spent on repairs instead.[40] A publication announcing that the NSLF was still alive would have to wait another year.

After returning east, Duffy and Reynolds got into legal trouble yet again as they prepared to attend a Klan rally in Vineland. It was especially contentious as it was to take place only weeks after the Greensboro massacre.

On November 3, 1979, in Greensboro, North Carolina, a "Death to Klan" march led by the Communist Workers Party was attacked by a joint group of Klansmen and neo-Nazis. They shot and killed five of the anti-racist marchers. Despite the murders being caught on film, none of the perpetrators were convicted at trial.[41] Greensboro has also been commonly viewed as marking the start of the "Nazification of the Klan," a period of greater cooperation between neo-Nazis and the Klan—although examples like the White Confederacy show that this started earlier. It does seem clear that, at this point, the former exerted an increased ideological influence on the latter. Greensboro also symbolized the beginning of a violent new wave of the White Supremacist movement.

The Vineland rally did not go ahead as planned, as about 20 neo-Nazis and Klan members, including Duffy, were arrested on weapons charges. None of the rally-goers made it to the site, leaving hundreds of counter-protestors to march without opposition.[42]

Despite the promises after Reynolds's expulsion, the NSLF was still moribund. An early 1980 flyer showed that they had three units: Vineland, Wilmington, and Reading, Pennsylvania. That June, Reynolds prodded Mason again, buttering him up by calling him the "top NS propagandist in the movement today" while asking if he really had a future with Vincent.[43] Mason finally came around. He said that, for the last year, things had already been "off-again, on-again" and Mason was tired of Vincent's drinking, interference with the publications, and general organizing approach. Right as June turned into July, he finally cut ties with the NSWWP.[44]

In August, Mason's SIEGE started.

Vincent after Mason

The NSWWP carried on a few more years without Mason. In mid-1981, Vincent opened another bookstore in Berkeley, California. (Local police put his followers at six.) Media came, but there was little coverage after a combination of Jewish organizations and police asked them not to cover the story. Two months later, the bookstore shut down. In 1983, the ADL said, "Vincent's organization has been in decline in recent years, and many members have joined other groups."[45] *The Stormer* continued to be published until 1984.

In the late 1990s, Vincent came out of retirement to advise the NSM, now led by Jeff Schoep, and went to St. Paul, Minneapolis in 1998 for an aborted meeting. Vincent told a newspaper, "Jeff is a young man we have great confidence in"—apparently because he had "great bloodlines." But Vincent's comeback was brief, and he died of throat cancer in July 1999 at age 67.[46]

Notes

1 Ellerin, *American Nazis -- Myth or Menace?*, p.8; Mason to Saleam, June 29, 1979 [Box 21, Folder 17].
2 Schmaltz, *Hate*, pp.278, 297–98.
3 "James Warner" and "James K. Warner Open Letter 1968," *Encyclopedia*, pp.326–31, 557–63.
4 Mason to Saleam, June 29, 1979 [Box 21, Folder 17]; *National Socialist Review* #7, July 1976, p.12; *The California Reich*, dir. Keith Critchlow and Walter F. Parkes, 1975, www.imdb.com/title/tt0072757, www.youtube.com/watch?v=owtC7BY3P7s
5 John J. O'Connor, "TV: 'California Reich' Visits West Coast Nazis," *NYT*, December 12, 1978, www.nytimes.com/1978/12/12/archives/tv-california-reich-visits-west-coast-nazis.html. Vincent's *Stormer* printed a five-page spread on the film. One clipping said that a "substantial number" of PBS stations refused to air it, quoting one TV station president as saying it was "almost a recruitment film." Another documented how protestors stormed a theater showing it and destroyed the projector; *Stormer* 2(1) Winter 1979, pp.20–25.
6 Rust to Mason, April 26, 1976 [Box 15, Folder 13]; Saleam, "American Nazism," chapter 3.

7 Rust to Mason, May 27, 1976, pp.91–92; Mason to Rust, November 13, 1977 [both Box 15, Folder 13].

8 *Stormer* 1(1), pp.1–5; "Pain and Anger Remain in San Francisco Jewish Neighborhood After Destruction of Nazi Bookstore," *NYT*, April 6, 1977, www.nytimes.com/1977/04/06/archives/pain-and-anger-remain-in-san-francisco-jewish-neighborhood-after.html; "Nazis File $28 Million Suit Against a Jewish Editor," *JTA*, February 27, 1978, www.jta.org/1978/02/27/archive/nazis-file-28-million-suit-against-a-jewish-editor

9 *Stormer* 1(1), p.14; *Stormer* 1(3) April 1978, p.30.

10 "A Real Nazi in the Real World: Michael Ange of the NSWWP," clipping reprinted in *Stormer* 1(1), pp.11–12; Rob Wood, "Houston Mayoral Candidates Face Runoff Contest," *Denton Record-Chronicle* (Texas), November 9, 1977, p.5A, www.newspapers.com/image/31067036; ADL, *Hate Groups in America*, p.34.

11 *Stormer* 2(1), pp.14–15; AP, "Silence Closes Nazis' Hitler Hall," *Odessa American* (Texas), September 17, 1981, p.10, www.newspapers.com/image/303145953

12 "Nazi leader: 'Holocaust' Part of Campaign," *Chillicothe Gazette*, April 28, 1978; Tom Brinkmoeller, "Nazis Strut on Square and Leave," *Cincinnati Enquirer*, April 30, 1978, www.newspapers.com/image/101411260

13 *Stormer* 1(4) Summer 1978, p.3; *Stormer* 1(4), pp.3–11; *Stormer* 2(1), pp.20–25.

14 *White Worker's Bulletin* 7(7) July 1978, p.7 [all issues in Box 47, Folder 29].

15 "Klan, Nazis Have Parley in Vineland," *Millville Daily* (New Jersey), May 3, 1978, pp.1, 2, www.newspapers.com/image/416234375, www.newspapers.com/image/416234377; Kay Rudderow, "Nazis, Klan Meet in Vineland," *Bridgetown Evening News*, May 3, 1978, clipping reprinted in *White Worker's Bulletin* 7(7) July 1978, pp.1–2.

16 Reynolds to Martin Kerr, August 15, 1992 [Box 10, Folder 7]; Untitled, unsigned biography of Reynolds for the court system, incomplete (pp.4–7), made after April 1986 [Box 33, Folder 8]; Doug Fuhrman, "Local History: Racial Tension Leads to Bridgeton Riots in 1971," *Daily Journal* (Vineland, New Jersey), April 14, 2015, https://amp.thedailyjournal.com/amp/25754919

17 Elizabeth Duff, "The Hooded Empire Rides Again," *Philadelphia Inquirer: Today, The Inquirer Magazine*, October 15, 1978, pp.37, 44, www.newspapers.com/image/178199546, www.newspapers.com/image/178199566; Reynolds to Mason, March 13, 1985 [Box 33, Folder 7].

18 Duff, "Hooded Empire," p.44; Untitled, unsigned biography of Reynolds for the court system.

19 Joe Weber, "The KKK in Jersey: Varied Roots in the Klan's Family Tree," *Central New Jersey Home News* (New Brunswick), December 6, 1977, www.newspapers.com/image/316810376

20 AP, "N.J. Klansman; Nazi, Charged in Rape," *Courier-News* (Bridgewater, New Jersey), July 7, 1979, p.7, www.newspapers.com/image/222926072

21 "Klan, Nazis Have Parley in Vineland," *Millville Daily*, May 3, 1978, p.2, www.newspapers.com/image/416234375, www.newspapers.com/image/416234377

22 Reynolds to Mason, [July] 1978; Reynolds to Vincent, Mason, and National Socialist Comrades, August 11, 1978 [both Box 33, Folder 10].

23 Duff, "Hooded Empire," p.32, www.newspapers.com/image/178199529

24 *Articles*, p.25.

25 Janson, "Leaders in Klan and Nazi Party Accused of Rape," *NYT*, July 7, 1979, www.nytimes.com/1979/07/07/archives/leaders-in-klan-and-nazi-party-accused-of-rape-alleged-victim-was-a.html

26 Jack Knarr, "Was Female Spy a Double Dealer?" *Philadelphia Journal*, July 7, 1979 (*Articles*, p.31); Mason to Duffy, July 11, 1979 [Box 13, Folder 18].

27 Janson, "Leaders in Klan and Nazi Party Accused of Rape"; Gunter David, "Nazis Raped Me," *The Bulletin*, July 6[?], 1979 (*Articles*, p.25); "Nazi, Klan Rape Jewess," *Philadelphia Journal*, July 7, 1979 (*Articles*, p.23).

28 Janson, "Leaders in Klan and Nazi Party Accused of Rape"; Knarr, "Was Female Spy a Double Dealer?" (*Articles*, p.31); Barbara Lempert, "JDL and the Klan Should Keep Their Fights in the Family," *Philadelphia Journal*, July 9, 1979 (*Articles*, p.26).

29 Jane Musgrave, "Local Man Target of 'Vigilante' Group," *Chillicothe Gazette*, June 14, 1979, pp.1–2, www.newspapers.com/image/289622752, www.newspapers.com/image/289622817; "Turd Is the Word," *White Worker's Bulletin* 8(4) July–August 1979, pp.5, 7; "The Jewish Defense League," *ADL*, February 6, 2017, www.adl.org/resources/profiles/jewish-defense-league

30 William P Barrett, "JDL Rape Case Goes to the Grand Jury," *The Bulletin* (South New Jersey), July 27, 1979 (*Articles*, p.31); Knarr, "Was Female Spy a Double Dealer?".

31 Mike Schaffer, "Nazi Skeleton Comes Home to Haunt Duffy," *Morning News* (Wilmington, Delaware), July 27, 1979, p.14, www.newspapers.com/image/160874596; David, "Nazis Raped Me".

32 Mike Schaffer, "Ex-Neo-Nazi Held on Charges by Member of JDL," *Morning News*, July 27, 1979, p.14, www.newspapers.com/image/160874596; Donald Janson, "Is Klan Role in the State Waning?," *NYT*, August 26, 1979, www.nytimes.com/1979/08/26/archives/new-jersey-weekly-is-klan-role-in-the-state-waning-is-klan-on-the.html

33 Mike Schaffer, "Dismissed Rape Charge Not Justice, Accused Says," *Morning News*, February 29, 1980, p.12, www.newspapers.com/image/160737239

34 Mason to Reynolds, July 26, 1979 [Box 33, Folder 10]; Mason to Duffy, July 30, 1979 [Box 13, Folder 18].

35 Reynolds to Mason, July 31, 1979 [Box 33, Folder 10]; Jeffrey R. Welsh, "Wilmington Man Arrested in Rape of JDL Member," *News Journal* (Wilmington, Delaware), July 6, 1979, p.3, www.newspapers.com/image/161472613

36 Mason to Reynolds, July 26, 1979; Mason to Reynolds and Duffy, August 9, 1979; Reynolds to Mason, August 15, 1979 [all three in Box 33, Folder 10].

37 William W. Sutton, Jr., "Far Right Seems United—Nazi Attends Klan Rally," *Courier-Post* (Camden, New Jersey), August 13, 1979, p.4A, www.newspapers.com/image/182803823; Reynolds to Karl and Craig, October 31, 1979 [Box 33, Folder 9].

38 SIEGE 9(8) December 1980, p.5; Mason to Rust, October 11, 1980 [Box 15, Folder 13].

39 Mason to Reynolds and Duffy, August 9, 1979; Mason to Reynolds and Duffy, August 19, 1979 [both Box 33, Folder 10]; Mason, "We Must Be Doing Something Right! Jews Go Way Out on Limb to Frame East Coast Nazi Leaders" (*Articles*, p.32). Years later Mason published the aborted issue's page mock-ups, which would have been *National Socialist Review* 2(1) Fall 1979 (*Articles*, pp.22–26, 29–33).

40 Mason, "Introduction," *Articles*, pp.6–7.

41 Elizabeth Wheaton, *Codename GREENKIL: The 1979 Greensboro Killings* (Athens: University of Georgia Press, 1987).

42 UPI, "Vineland Set for KKK Rally," *Philadelphia Daily News*, November 24, 1979, p.2, www.newspapers.com/image/185275359; "White Power Rally Defused," *Daily News* (New York City), November 25, 1979, p.16, www.newspapers.com/image/legacy/484748735

43 Mason to Reynolds and Duffy, March 9, 1980; East Coast NSLF version of "Political Terror" flyer, 1980; Reynolds to Mason, June 28, 1980 [all three Box 33, Folder 10].
44 Mason to Duffy and Candy, June 30, 1980 [Box 13, Folder 18]; Mason to Ed Reynolds and Rita, July 2, 1980 [Box 33, Folder 10].
45 AP, "Silence Closes Nazis' Hitler Hall," p.10.
46 Doug Grow, "Hatemonger's Life Ain't Always Easy," *Star Tribune* (Minneapolis), April 15, 1998, p.B2, www.newspapers.com/image/195357965

6

KARL HAND'S NSLF

Having broken with Allen Vincent's NSWWP, James Mason, John Duffy, and Ed Reynolds finally brought the NSLF out of mothballs. Mason took the name SIEGE, last used by Joseph Tommasi, for the monthly newsletter, which he published first for the NSLF and later on his own. But despite the group's relaunch, Duffy did not take on an active leadership role, and the torch soon passed to Karl Hand.

Another former National Socialist White People's Party (NSWPP) member, Hand had a penchant for violence and its accompanying legal trouble. In the 1970s, he had gone through a number of Klan and neo-Nazi groups with varying success. After working closely with David Duke (who he concluded was unprincipled) and Harold Covington (unsupportive), Hand came back to his longtime comrades in the NSLF, with whom he always had a good relationship. In 1981, he became the NSLF's new leader.

But rather than being a flashpoint for guerilla activity, the NSLF became a fairly standard neo-Nazi group with chapters, dues, and book sales—once again, exactly what Mason wanted to get away from. In 1982, after the inevitable tensions came to a head, especially over Charles Manson, in 1982 Hand and Mason negotiated a parting of the ways acceptable to both parties. Each followed their existing trajectories: Hand continued the NSLF on its course, while Mason, who had kept SIEGE in the divorce, delved deeper into Manson, pessimism, and violence.

With the NSWPP's name change in 1983, what was now the New Order stopped acting as a party of the kind it had been in 1970s. In the place of it, and its spin-off competition like the NSPA and NSWWP, a new wave of organizations arose. One of the spinoffs, William Pierce's National Alliance, became a major group alongside others influenced by National Socialism,

DOI: 10.4324/9780429200090-9

such as the White Aryan Resistance (WAR), Aryan Nations, and the White Patriot Party. Moderates like Duke were able to gain much larger audiences with electoral approaches, as did the Populist Party. On the more violent end, Nazi skinheads appeared in the United States starting in the mid-1980s, while the pan-White Supremacist terrorist group The Order represented the ultimate manifestation of this wing of the movement.[1]

Hand's organization remained an active competitor to and ally of these groups, at least until 1986 when, after a dozen years, the NSLF came to a close. Hand's temper caught up with him again, and he shot a neighbor over a minor dispute, landing him back in prison. Rather than passing the torch to a fifth leader, he closed up shop and told the remaining members to join Tom Metzger's WAR, one of the major forces in the 1980s White Supremacist movement.

The NSLF, Reborn

With Mason's connection to Vincent finally severed, the new SIEGE debuted in August 1980. In it Mason wrote, somewhat cryptically, "no opinion or consent was solicited in bringing out SIEGE and, thereby, reactivating the NSLF."[2] Duffy followed the next month with his *National Headquarters Bulletin.* By the end of the year, the NSLF had a staff of "National Officers": Duffy, Reynolds, Mason, and three others.[3]

Mason singled Reynolds out for praise, saying he had "been a strong part of the shadow NSLF these past years and who has played an invaluable part in keeping the flame alive." And Mason's partner-in-crime and NSM co-founder Greg Hurles was also involved in the relaunch, taking care of the group's mail.[4]

In late September 1980, the Delaware NSLF scored a major victory. After a judge ruled that the initial search warrant that led to the NSLF 22 arrests was invalid, the prosecutor dropped the case on the day the trial was to start. And so it was not without cause that Duffy's paper complained about constant police harassment, writing that "about 50 people have been the object of quasi-legal attacks for the State of New Jersey." This included numerous arrests of the group's leadership.[5]

In addition to Duffy in Delaware and Mason in Ohio, the NSLF had five units in New Jersey and one in Pennsylvania in the fall of 1980. Mason's hometown paper, the *Chillicothe Gazette,* which had given him plenty of coverage over the years, ran an article about his embrace of ex-NSWPP serial killer Joseph Paul Franklin. The piece was to become one of Mason's favorites. In December, with the east-coast legal problems now in the past, NSLF members received an updated list of armament requirements: a .45 automatic pistol, a .223 semi-auto rife, a 12-gauge shotgun, and a .357 handgun.[6] Last, the NSLF announced that on December 15, 1980, "the membership roles of the NSLF have opened up for the first time since 1977." The application fee remained $5.[7]

With the restarting of SIEGE, Mason was once again free to bang the drum of violence. The first issue was sent out with a copy of Tommasi's "Political Terror" flyer. Mason also started advocating lone wolf attacks.[8] The mood also turned dark in the *National Headquarters Bulletin* #3, reflecting sentiments which Mason would develop over the next years. When the NSLF was founded, "the order of the day was strike and run." But now it was not a question of shooting racial enemies or toppling the government,

> but of leading our people to survival in the hellish nightmare world to come. ... We could be well on the way to conventional "military" victory when H-bombs could come raining down. The future indeed does belong to those who are willing to get their hands dirty. The future will not be a question of who won or lost, but who SURVIVED?[9]

Soon after that dour statement, however, Duffy handed the reigns over to Hand, who gave the NSLF a new lease on life.

Handover to Hand

Karl Hand was a veteran of numerous White Supremacist groups before he took over the NSLF at age 30. In an autobiographical essay, Hand said his early life of drugs and gangs ended with the discovery of National Socialism. He had initially ordered an anti-Communist book from the NSWPP, which eventually led him to joining the party. In Buffalo in 1971, Hand, along with another NSWPP member, was able to find recruits, including some of his former gang members. His early outreach strategies were not always sophisticated. For example, he took a classified ad out in a local newspaper, offering "Anyone interested in seeing a real live NAZI" to write him.[10]

Hand was arrested at least twice during Buffalo literature distributions, including one in 1973 while supporting a local high school that was the site of racial tensions. At 22, he was already focused on recruiting teenagers into the White Supremacist movement, and later he would branch out to children.[11] In October, he was able to form a group, and in December 1974, while still in the NSWPP, he opened the White Power Bookstore in Buffalo.[12]

After leaving the NSWPP, he started his own group, the National Guard Party, which had a youth group, the White Youth Alliance, for those age 14 to 17. They published *Defiance*, which was a title Hand would take with him as he moved through different groups. In January 1975, about ten people attended a protest he organized on Martin Luther King, Jr.'s birthday. Hand had a group in Buffalo for three months. Soon after, there were protests against both his bookstore and his appearance on a local TV show.[13] Later that year, he tried for the Buffalo city council nomination of the Conservative Party, a party in New York state that had ballot status. In January 1976, Hand was in talks to join the NSLF but in the end decided not to at that time.[14]

Instead, Hand became part of Duke's KKKK. Taking the title Great Titan, he published a number of periodicals for the group, including *The Shield and Eagle* and *Nightrider*. He also started the Klan Youth Corps, making *Defiance* their New York state periodical; in March 1978, it claimed to have affiliates in nine schools. (The KKKK kept the Klan Youth Corps going even after Hand's departure.[15]) Hand also moved up the ranks of the organization, becoming the KKKK's National Organizer, Duke's second-in-command, and editor of both *The Crusader* newspaper and *KKK Action*, an internal publication. He was so committed to Duke that he even moved to Metairie, Louisiana in mid-1978 to work directly with him.[16]

Hand's activities did not go unnoticed by others who had also left the NSWPP. Mason tried to recruit him to the NSM, saying his reputation as an effective organizer preceded him and that "you really do belong with open, fighting National Socialism and nothing less," which he would "be happier and feel more satisfied with." Hand returned the compliment, saying he appreciated the NSM leaders but was already "committed." However, "should unforeseen events occur that would cause me to leave the Klan," he promised to keep them in mind.[17]

Hand did agree to collaborate with the White Confederacy spinoff the Council of Revolution. Mason and Hand discussed this in April 1977, and in late May, the KKKK, NSLF, NSM, Western Guard Party, and White Unity Party met in Buffalo. In December 1977, Mason floated the idea to Hand of asking Duke to get involved in the White Confederacy, but nothing came of it. When the infighting in the group came to a head in 1978 and a shootout was narrowly averted, Hand sent a letter to Mason, Robert Brannen, Vincent, and Bill Sickles, telling them to cool it—and showing how much respect he commanded. Hand said, "I would walk through Hades and back for any of you, but I will not choose between my friends."[18]

Starting in 1977, Hand's arrests escalated into charges for violence. In September, Michael Johnson, a black man, was shot after a group of men poured out of a house. It belonged to Wayne Whiteside, a Klansman who had run for Buffalo mayor on the White Unity Party ticket. The group's treasurer was Hand, who was arrested as a suspect in the shooting. But as there had been no warrant, he was let go a week later, although it cost him his job. Hand responded by suing the city for $4 million.[19]

Despite his move to Louisiana in mid-1978, Hand became involved in activism in New Jersey, crossing paths with his NSLF allies. In August 1979, he was part of a bizarre David Duke rally that 17-year-old Aaron Morrison held at his family's home in New Jersey after permits could not be secured for local venues.[20] That December, Hand left the KKKK with a five-page resignation letter addressed to Duke. Hand wrote, "I am tired of seeing you hurt, abuse, use and deceive good white people, in the name of the Klan." The accusations included that Duke betrayed the Klan's principles by dropping his opposition to mixed-race couples and downplaying antisemitism. His sexual behavior was also deemed "unklannish." Hand said, "I appealed to you a hundred times, for the movement's sake, to be discreet if you couldn't be moral." Hand would continue to denounce and berate Duke for years afterward.[21]

Hand's letter was similar to one another California KKKK leader, Metzger, had issued a few days before. Within a few years, Metzger would become a major White Supremacist leader as he, too, left the Klan and moved toward neo-Nazism with his WAR. But he was still a Klansman at the time, and he accused Duke of writing problematic books in order to make money (including a sex guide), infidelity, mistreating his wife, and embezzling money.[22]

In February 1980, Hand was in New Jersey at Aaron Morrison's house with him and his brother James. After a night of heavy drinking, a bullet was fired into the home of a black neighbor. The three fled the next day; Hand surfaced in March when he was taken to a Miami, Florida hospital after trying to commit suicide by drinking antifreeze. He soon returned to Buffalo and later had a kidney transplant but would remain plagued by health problems related to this. In late January 1981, Hand received a six-month sentence for the shooting, with three suspended, but he appealed.[23]

But between these events, Hand returned to the neo-Nazi milieu and by June 1980 was affiliated with the NSPA, now run by Harold Covington. Hand restarted *Defiance* a third time, publishing two NSPA issues. The second issue talked about four murders of black men, in and around Buffalo, by the so-called ".22 Caliber Killer." (Eventually the perpetrator, Joseph Christopher, was caught after several more killings.) Fingers pointed at Hand, the local racist leader, although it ended up that Christopher was not tied to organized White Supremacists. While Hand speculated wildly on who might be behind the murders—naming Israel, the FBI, and black leaders as potential puppet masters—he shrugged his shoulders about the slayings. "I for one do not feel any remorse for his 'victims,'" he wrote.[24]

In January 1981, Hand held an NSPA rally in Buffalo, again protesting Martin Luther King, Jr. Day. The flyer said it "WANTED: 100 WHITE MEN WITH GUTS!" But attendance fell short of the goal, drawing five supporters and 400 counter-protestors.[25]

In early February, he resigned from the NSPA, telling Covington he was "offered a position in the NSLF and [was] giving it a great deal of consideration." Hand complained about the lack of support for the demonstration but also said that his views had changed and he was abandoning mass-strategy work. He now held that the white masses will never "wake up.... White revolution must be built through armed struggle by an elite group of racial idealists."[26]

In the ensuing exchange of letters, Covington berated Hand, saying "how in the hell do you expect to be a guerrilla fighter when you are required to go on kidney dialysis at least twice a week?" He also attacked Mason, saying

"The editor of your alleged official organ <u>Siege</u> is a man whose mental imbalance is notorious throughout the Movement and who commands not the slightest jot of respect from any serious racialist." Nonetheless, Covington said Hand could return to the party if Hand changed his mind. (Ironically, the next month, it was Covington who left the NSPA to go underground.) Hand retorted,

> Joining the NSLF was not a 'Kick', contrary to what you believe. I originally planned on joining them before I joined Duke, but decided to give politics one last shot, well, I gave it two shots and now have had my fill. No more![27]

Mason, for his part, assured Hand that Hand was not expected to be an underground guerilla, telling him that

> the 'new' NSLF… doesn't even involve the old Tommasi concept of 'combat units.' Much less running out and starting shooting. Rather it is to get in step with the spirit of the times and act as a conductor of the lightening when it strikes.[28]
>
> *(And it is striking.)*

On March 29, 1981, Duffy officially made Hand "Commanding Officer" of the NSLF. Duffy said he had lost hope in their approach, and so "rather than impose my will on the organization I feel that the movement will be better served by my voluntary abdication." He assured Hand, "I know you will not fail to bring honor to this cause and I would not relinquish control unless I knew that Tommasi's torch will be held high." But the letter plastered over other tensions. According to Mason, Duffy said he was resigning because "he couldn't reconcile certain differences." (Mason approved, because he thought that forcing the issue would have caused a split.) That did not mean Mason was sad to see Duffy go, however. Mason blamed him for failing to revive the NSLF and instead letting it lapse into inactivity.[29]

Like so many others, Duffy dropped out of the movement soon after. A Christmas card that Mason sent in December 1983 came back marked "Box Closed." In May 1984, Reynolds ran into Duffy at a racetrack and relayed an account of the meeting to Mason. "It was like, strange. He was talking to me like I was just a old high-school classmate or something. Told me that everything was a 'lost cause'."[30]

Hand celebrated his new position by calling for two more rallies in Buffalo, on May 30 and 31, 1981, but this time under the auspices of the NSLF. Beforehand, he also pumped out two more issues of *Defiance* under the new affiliation; one of them included a letter of support from David Lane, who would later go underground with the armed group The Order. The flyer for the rallies included the NSLF's swastika-and-automatic rifle logo. However, the new, more militant look was no more successful than the NSPA's more moderate one. One of the more generous accounts said ten supporters came to the first rally, where Hand was arrested and given a $150 fine. No doubt, having glimpsed greener pastures in the South, Hand moved back to Metairie in December 1981.[31]

Settled in his new home, and in command of his own neo-Nazi party, Hand quickly changed it to a more traditional group. Although he took command at the tail end of March, by August the NSLF was already taking memberships.[32] Hand spent a solid four years doing what he did best: recruiting and collecting dues, publishing newspapers and selling books, networking and holding uniformed events, and running afoul of the law.

In the first half of 1982, Hand produced four issues of *Defiance*.[33] In September, a small NSLF Congress was held in New Orleans, featuring Canadian Don Andrews of the Nationalist Party. The NSLF also bragged of its domestic connections to the NSPA and the SS Action Group and internationally to the Nationalist Party, Western Guard Party, FNE, and League of St. George.[34]

Mason and SIEGE Leave over Charlie

Before Hand could grow his group, he and Mason had to part ways. After Hand took over, Mason remained effusive, proclaiming that the NSLF was the only truly revolutionary group, and if Rockwell was alive, he would be with them "FIGHTING IN THE STREET!" But differences arose almost immediately as Mason started praising, and then fetishizing, Manson. Mason was already in touch with two members of The Family, Lynette Fromme and Sandra Good, visiting them in prison the same month Hand took over. That September, however, Mason introduced Manson worship in SIEGE, putting him on a collision course with Hand.[35]

In addition to SIEGE's contents, an August 1982 letter circulated by Rick Cooper (another disgruntled ex-NSWPP member who would soon form the National Socialist Vanguard) contributed to this coming to a head; in it, Cooper referred to the NSLF as "including Charles Manson-like types."[36] The ensuing exchange with Hand showed how completely Mason had fallen under Manson's spell. Mason said that Manson possessed "The key [that] has been missing since the death of Rockwell....and it is up to us to 'grasp it' like it says in Mein Kampf."[37] Amidst the exchange, Hand wrote an angry letter to Perry "Red" Warthan.

A California neo-Nazi who was visiting Manson on Mason's behalf, Warthan had quite the backstory. As a young teenager, he was placed in a state hospital after being arrested for setting fires, and there he took part in the murder of a younger boy. Released as an adult, Warthan became well-known in the 1970s in left-wing anarchist circles for his Woodstock Anarchist Party and as a member of a radical union, the Industrial Workers of the World (IWW). But in 1978, he made a sudden turn and joined a Klan group first and then the NSWPP. In 1981, he left the party and formed his own group, the CANS (Chico Area National Socialists). Warthan was then contacted by Mason, who had been unable to visit Manson in person and was looking for a go-between. Warthan agreed to do this and made a number of visits to the prison to talk with Manson, starting in summer 1982. In another twist, the exchange between Hand and Warthan occurred just before he committed a second murder, this time of a teenager who had been involved in his group.

In his letter, Hand said that Manson was not a National Socialist. Hand also wrote a similar letter to Mason, saying "Manson is not officially connected with NSLF, nor will he ever be." The Manson Family's drug use particularly incensed Hand, who had quit taking them as part of joining the neo-Nazi movement. Manson's reputation for having sex with both men and women was also a problem. Mason dismissed these concerns and affirmed his autonomy in the NSLF as well his rejection of the "leadership principle" as it applied to Hand. Mason called Manson "an individual of historic magnitude" whom they should defer to.[38]

Hand replied, reiterating that Manson was the "anti-thesis of National Socialism" and telling Mason that "as long as you persist in you illusions of Manson, and trying to orient this movement around that illusion, then I see no alternative then to ask for your resignation." In an effort to avoid yet another acrimonious split, Hand offered to print Mason's resignation letter in the NSLF publication along with an ad for SIEGE as well as "a handshake, a warm farewell and $200."[39]

Mason wrote back, insisting on his points again, but ultimately accepting most of Hand's offer—including the money. Mason noted that the October issue was already being prepared, so it was the November 1982 SIEGE that announced it was no longer part of the NSLF and was now the organ of Universal Order.[40]

In retrospect, Mason said that what he gave up when he left the NSLF was "the pretense that we are something and we're going to do something." This did not stop Mason from remaining a supportive comrade, though, and he continued to plug the NSLF in SIEGE.[41]

NSLF Units, Prisoners, and Ideology

During their 1982 split, Mason derided Hand as editing "an infrequent tabloid that falls far short of sufficient to make an organization." But Hand was a skilled organizer, and he pushed to expand chapters, albeit with modest success. In September 1982, he bragged that 8,000 copies of the NSLF paper were printed in the previous year.[42] By early 1984, in addition to the Louisiana members, the NSLF had six "aboveground" units, including one in Ireland. In June 1986, the number of units outside of Louisiana rose to nine, including one for prisoners. Two in New York state also published their own newsletters: the *Combat Report* in Waverly and the *National Socialist Report* in Corning.[43]

Although Hand could not replicate Tommasi's prisoner alliances, the revamped NSLF's outreach attracted some interest. New York prisoner Jerry Mitchell wrote Hand in January 1982 to request NSLF membership. (Soon after he was released in January 1984, Mitchell committed suicide after a gun battle with police.) In November 1983, Hand wrote two brothers, William and James Demick, who had been arrested in Louisiana for conspiracy to commit arson and murder. William Demick was also arrested for a plot to kill then-presidential candidate Jesse Jackson, a black leftist, but was quickly released. The Demicks both joined the NSLF for a period of time before renouncing National Socialism.[44]

In 1985, Karl Hand's wife, Mary Sue Hand, was in charge the NSLF's prison work. In May 1986, Karl said they were sending subscriptions to 700 prisoners; interestingly, he also mentioned that Mary Sue had "taken over the mailing responsibilities for the [Irish nationalist party] Sinn Fein newsletter." And by the next month, there was an NSLF "Prison Unit" in Lovelady, Texas.[45]

Shortly after Hand's arrest in December 1986, Mason said, "Quite probably Karl Hand is or was the final, active representative of National Socialism of the Hitler-Rockwell variety. His sacrifice was to that idea." Mason would later reflect that "It is ironic that, under Hand's direction, the NSLF resumed the more traditional type of uniformed political demonstration and refrained from overt illegality."[46] But Hand did this while continuing to promote armed resistance.

For example, as advertised in *Defiance* in 1982, the NSLF bookstore sold *The Turner Diaries* as well as books about explosives. On the same page as this was a list of the various kinds of NSLF memberships, including the "National Socialist Junior Youth" for kids age 9 to 12. (For $6, they got a subscription to *Defiance*, a patch, and a membership card.) It was one of ten different member categories, including ones for senior citizens, prisoners, and a "paramilitary arm." Although by 1983 Hand said the NSLF was now "a proponent of 'graduated revolution'," he kept up what was by then clearly a pretense of having both under- and above-ground wings.[47]

Ideologically, the group remained a typical neo-Nazi organization, with a twin fixation of racism and antisemitism. A 1982 article on Oi! music made the NSLF one of the first U.S. groups to be interested in the Nazi skinhead movement—then only starting to reach the country from Britain. (Oi! is a stripped-down form of punk featuring chanted vocals; in the early 1980s, it emerged as the music of the new generation of skinheads.) In 1985, Hand published "Aryan Manifesto: A Program for Whites," which was his most programmatic statement. It outlined that the "NSLF seeks the establishment of an **Aryan Imperium** that will transcend all divisions of our race and create a truly united and creative society." While stating "our only nation is our race," their first step was the establishment of an agriculturally based "racial state." The NSLF also promised a **"Day of Cleansing,"** a **"Dictatorship of the Political Elite,"** and a **"Revolution in Thought"** (emphasis in the original).[48]

1983 to 1986

In April 1983, Hand finally started his 90-day sentence for the 1981 shooting. He tried to get people to move to Louisiana so he could open an office and barracks.[49] By 1984, the *National Socialist Observer* was also being published; originally, it was intended as a quarterly supplement to *Defiance* but largely replaced it. The Louisiana NSLF also held uniformed street demonstrations in 1984 and 1985. A spring 1985 fundraising letter boasted of pickets at Holocaust memorial events in Baton Rouge and uniformed marches in New Orleans.[50]

In 1984, the NSLF printed a list of members of the Jewish Defense League, the party's old nemesis. They also praised a number of violent White Supremacists, including Gordon Kahl, Perry Warthan, Joseph Tommasi, and the Greensboro massacre perpetrators. Swastikas and pictures of Hitler graced the cover of the NSLF's publication.[51]

Avoiding getting ideologically cornered, Hand also spent time networking with other White Supremacist leaders. He spoke at the 1984 Aryan Nations gathering in Hayden Lake, Idaho—one of several times NSLF members attended. In April 1985, Hand went to Rainbow, California to address Metzger's WAR, spoke at an Easter egg hunt that doubled as a "White Tribal Film Festival," and taped an interview for Metzger's cable TV show *Race and Reason*.[52] On November 9, 1985, Hand was married to Mary Sue King in the "formal wedding ceremony of the SS," conducted by Klan leader Robert Miles. Hand specifically pointed out that it was held on the anniversary of Hitler's failed Beer Hall Putsch.[53]

At this time, the White Supremacist movement—now in an unusual period of cross-ideological cooperation—had started a wave of violence. In 1981, a number of activists, including ex-KKKK member Don Black, formed a mercenary band that intended to overthrow the Dominica government. (They were arrested before they began.) In 1983, The Order started its robberies, and the next year knocked over a Brinks truck; they distributed the funds to movement leaders, but apparently not to Hand. That year, The Order also assassinated Denver talk show host Alan Berg. And in 1983, Louis Beam, by then working with Aryan Nations, issued his influential "Leaderless Resistance" essay.

But while the real action was elsewhere, the NSLF fulminated on paper and, even then, claimed precious few "underground" activities. One of the few was the vandalism of actor Ed Asner's Los Angeles home, which was spray-painted with a swastika and "Kill Jews"; a call claiming responsibility said attacks would continue if Asner kept acting "in the interest of international communism and Zionism." Newspapers also noted that Metairie was a hot spot of White Supremacist activity, with three groups based there: the NSLF, James K. Warner's New Christian Crusade Church, and Duke's post-KKKK vehicle the NAAWP (National Association for the Advancement of White People).[54]

The Neighbors End the NSLF

At the end of summer 1986, Hand's modest National Socialist empire finally came crashing down after a felony charge landed him in prison for a number of years. But just before that, in June 1986, Mason's SIEGE came to an end. In the spirit of their unusually amicable separation, Mason offered his subscription list to Hand. The NSLF leader wrote back, "I don't agree with some of your conclusions but on most issues you and I are in 100% agreement," and "I want you to remember one thing. You will always have a position with NSLF should you desire one."[55]

But that offer expired in August when Hand was arrested for attempted murder. As with his New Jersey charge, it was not the result of NSLF guerilla activity but rather problems with a neighbor. Hand was involved in an angry argument, allegedly after "drilling young people in his front yard." Witnesses said Mary Sue Hand got a .38 caliber revolver, after which everyone retreated indoors. But Karl came out and started smashing the windows of a neighbor's car, and when the man came outside, a fight ensued. As Karl was losing, Mary Sue handed him the gun. He shot his opponent twice in the stomach and "pointed the gun at [his] head before driving away." The Hands were quickly apprehended.[56]

Karl Hand was tried and convicted in early December 1986 for attempted murder. During the next week, instead of appointing a successor, he opted for one last NSLF merger. In his letter, published in Metzger's paper, Hand wrote that, rather than appoint a successor, he chose a merger with WAR. "I am encouraging all NSLF'ers to join and support Tom Metzger." In reply, Metzger praised both Tommasi ("light years ahead of most of us at that time") and Hand, saying he greeted the former NSLF members with "open arms."[57] This message did not get out quickly, however. Just as happened when David Rust resigned from the NSLF in 1977, Mason was initially confused about what was happening, and outside observers even more.[58]

Hand after the NSLF

In February 1987, Hand was sentenced to 15 years of hard labor. Mary Sue Hand made a deal with authorities to avoid prison time and left her husband.[59] But whereas she didn't stand by him, movement allies did. Mason wrote Hand in prison, while Metzger published his writings in *WAR*, where he was listed as a political prisoner.

In January 1991, supporters in Georgia published in booklet form an interview with Hand as well as an issue of *In Vinculis: The Voice of Aryan POWs* which he edited. Hand's essay on organizing appeared along with addresses for prisoners such as Martin Luther King, Jr.'s assassin James Earl Ray; various members of The Order; Posse Comitatus minister James Wickstrom; and Richard Snell, whose execution date coincided—some think not coincidentally—with the 1995 Oklahoma City bombing.[60]

In January 1991, Klansman Dennis Mahon issued a flyer calling on "Racists, Skinheads, Nazis and Klansmen!!" to join a rally supporting Hand's pardon request. It had no effect. In July 1991, Mahon came down from Oklahoma for a second rally, leading a five-person march from the Baton Rouge Department of Corrections to the prison where Hand was held. He was denied parole again but was released in 1994 after serving about half his sentence.[61]

Although his most infamous days were behind him, Hand's career as a White Supremacist was not over. Shortly after his arrest, he told Mason that National Socialism was a dead end.

> We must learn that we can not win using symbols and labels of the past. I was told a long time ago to wear the swastika in the heart, not on the arm. To do otherwise is to invite animosity, not support. ... I can no longer visualize Hitler choosing to wear the swastika in 1987, in America, if he were here and in our time element. It is only window dressing anyways and doesn't alter our iron clad principles of white self-determination and survival.[62]

In an autographical essay, Hand said he conceived of the Racial Nationalist Party of America while in prison and founded it in 1998.[63] Although no longer a National Socialist, Hand still runs his group today in Lockport, New York.[64] It was part of another umbrella group, the Aryan Nationalist Alliance (later the Nationalist Front); Hand spoke at its April 2016 gathering in Rome, Georgia.[65]

Using the old tactics, Hand has occasionally made the local news since. In 2016, he was mocked for being the only person to attend a White Lives Matter rally in Buffalo at Cazenovia Park, the same place he had held an NSLF rally in 1981.[66] And in 2019, Hand was yet again in trouble in nearby Cheektowaga, New York, where he was charged for throwing his group's propaganda onto people's property. He fought the charge and even distributed more literature in revenge but was still found guilty and fined $300 plus court fees. But he had made the local paper again.[67]

Reynolds after SIEGE

Reynolds, too, continued his political career. In 1985, he was arrested on a previous charge but fled before his court date. Caught the next May, he was released in 1987, by which time SIEGE had ended.[68] In 1989, he proclaimed himself Exalted Cyclops of the Wolverines, a Klavern based in Vineland. In April 1990, he made the local papers after being "spat upon and pelted with mud" at a Klan rally in Millville, New Jersey—the same town where he had attempted to hold the 1979 rally circumvented by the NSLF 22 arrests.[69] The next month, Reynolds snuck out of the state with his family—ducking his landlord and leaving no forwarding address—and moved to Memphis, Tennessee. There he organized as the Shelby County White Knights and, with his wife Beth Helen, even campaigned for David Duke.[70]

In summer 1992, the Reynolds family moved to Florence, Alabama and immediately became involved in the Nazi skinhead and Klan scene that was flourishing in Alabama and Georgia. In August, the couple and their three children were present during a major raid by federal and local law enforcement on the Birmingham, Alabama property of Bill Riccio, leader of the Aryan National Front. While the Reynolds family was not arrested, Riccio caught weapons charges and ended up serving 15 months.[71]

In 1992 and 1993, Reynolds attended numerous events, including the annual joint Klan–Nazi rallies in Pulaski, Tennessee, a popular event for White Supremacists. In spring 1993, Reynolds wrote his old friend Mason that "I know that you are no longer involved with 'extremist politics' … but things HAVE NEVER looked better in my 20 year career," assuring him that there was a revolutionary current even among the younger Klansmen. By 1993, Reynolds also joined the neo-Nazi SS Action Group, a former affiliate of the NSM.[72] Hurles, too, was on Reynolds's wavelength, joining a Klan group and attending the 1994 Pulaski march.

Reynolds came up with *Siege*'s tag line, "The Mein Kampf of the 1990s," and was quoted or mentioned numerous times in it. Mason also credited him with a phrase that appeared four times, "We don't want to rock the boat, we want to SINK it!"[73]

But Reynolds's years of hard living took its toll, and in 1996 he was diagnosed with liver cancer. In April 1998, he died at age 42 in Eliza Coffee Memorial Hospital in Florence, Alabama. In 2002, Mason said he would dedicate his never-completed Rockwell biography to Reynolds.[74]

Notes

1 There are a limited number of general overviews of U.S. White Supremacists which focus on or include the 1980s. These best are James Ridgeway, *Blood in the Face: The Ku Klux Klan, Aryan Nations, Nazi Skinheads, and the Rise of a New White Culture*, 2nd ed. (New York: Thunder Mouth Press, 1990/1995); Martin

Durham, *White Rage: The Extreme Right and American Politics* (Abingdon: Routledge, 2007); and Dobratz and Shanks-Meile, *"White Power, White Pride!" The White Separatist Movement in the United States*. Zeskind's *Blood and Politics* is more narrowly focused on Pierce and Carto but also includes this period. There are also individual studies of groups and individuals like Duke, Metzger, and The Order—but not, for example, Aryan Nations.

2   SIEGE 9(4) August 1980, p.6.

3   *National Headquarters Bulletin* [#1, September 1980?], p.4 [all issues in Box 13, Folder 18]. The positions listed were: Commanding Officer John Duffy, National Organizer Ed Reynolds, General Secretary James Mason, Eastern District Commander Phillip A. Maier, Central District Commander Greg Hurles, Western District Commander James Duncan, and Enforcement Officer Edward Marciano. "Join NSLF," *National Headquarters Bulletin* #3 [December 1980?], p.6.

4   SIEGE 9(5) September 1980, p.6; SIEGE 9(7) November 1980, p.6.

5   "Another Brick in the Wall!," *National Headquarters Bulletin* [#2?, October 1980?], p.2; "Takin' Care of Business......," *National Headquarters Bulletin* #2, p.1.

6   "Takin' Care of Business......"; Tom Frazier, "They Hail Those Who Hate," *Chillicothe Gazette*, November 17, 1980, p.27, www.newspapers.com/image/292607885; "Happiness Is a Warm Gun," *National Headquarters Bulletin* #3, 1980, p.3.

7   "Join NSLF," p.2.

8   SIEGE 9(5) September 1980, p.5.

9   "Happiness Is a Warm Gun," p.3.

10 Karl Hand, "Rebel with a Cause: The Life & Times of Karl Hand," *Racial Nationalist Party of America*, https://web.archive.org/web/20140701221940, https://www.rnpaheadquarters.org/id45.html [hereafter *RNPA*]; Carol Wright, "Nazi Party Alive and Well in Buffalo," *The Griffin* (Buffalo, New York), March 1, 1974, p.8, http://nyshistoricnewspapers.org/lccn/np00030005/1974-03-01/ed-1/seq-8; "Classified," *The Spectrum* (Buffalo, New York), February 23, 1973, p.23, https://nyshistoricnewspapers.org/lccn/np00130006/1973-02-23/ed-1/seq-23

11 Hand, "Rebel with a Cause"; "Racially Tense High School Shut for 2d Straight Day in Buffalo," *NYT*, March 15, 1973, www.nytimes.com/1973/03/15/archives/racially-tense-high-school-shut-for-2d-straight-day-in-buffalo.html

12 *Defiance*, January 1975, p.11 [Box 25, Folder 23]; "Marchers Honor King," *The Journal* (Ogdensburg, New York) January 16, 1975, p.17, image 17, https://nyshistoricnewspapers.org/lccn/sn84031170/1975-01-16/ed-1/seq-17; Hand to author, February 7, 2021.

13 "Activity Report," *Defiance*, January 1975, p.1; National Guard Party/White Youth Alliance, "He May Be Your Equal, but He Sure Isn't Ours" (flyer) [CDR, Box 265]; David Haitkin, "Local Protests Arise over Racist Bookstore," *The Spectrum*, January 22, 1975, p.2, http://nyshistoricnewspapers.org/lccn/np00130006/1975-01-22/ed-1/seq-2; "Students Demonstrate against White Power," *The Spectrum*, April 28, 1975, p.4, image 4, http://nyshistoricnewspapers.org/lccn/np00130006/1975-04-28/ed-1/seq-4

14 Mark Fleisher, "Neo-Nazi Leader Karl E. Hand Jr. Has Had Many Brushes with the Law," *Star-Gazette* (Elmira, New York), February 26, 1984, p.8, www.newspapers.com/image/278006016; Rust to Mason, January 5, 1976; Mason to Rust, January 18, 1976 [both Box 15, Folder 13].

15 *Nightrider* 2(3) December 1977; *The Shield and the Eagle* #9, July 1977; *Defiance* #6, March 1978 [all in Box 25, Folder 23]; ADL, *Hate Groups in America*, pp.19–20.

16 Hand, "Rebel with a Cause"; Tyler Bridges, *The Rise of David Duke* (Jackson: University Press of Mississippi, 1994), p.75.

17 Mason to Hand, August 16, 1976; Hand to Mason, September 1, 1976 [both Box 25, Folder 23].

18 Sickles was with the Adamic Knights of the Ku Klux Klan, who were in the White Confederacy. "Forging New Solidarity: Meeting of the K.K.K.K., W.G.P., N.S.L.F, & N.S.M.," *National Socialist Bulletin* 6(7) July 1977, pp.10–11; Mason to Hand, December 1, 1977 [Box 25, Folder 23]; Hand to Mason, June 23, 1978 [Box 25, Folder 25].

19 Andy Nathanson and Harvey Shapiro, "KKK Involved in Shooting," *The Spectrum*, September 23, 1977, p.1, http://nyshistoricnewspapers.org/lccn/np00130006/1977-09-23/ed-1/seq-1; AP, "KKK Leader to Sue Buffalo," *The Journal*, October 12, 1977, p.2, http://nyshistoricnewspapers.org/lccn/sn84031170/1977-10-12/ed-1/seq-2; "The KKK in Buffalo (part 2)," *Buffalo Workers Movement Newsletter*, December 1977, www.marxists.org/history/erol/periodicals/buffalo-workers-movement-newsletter/bwm-dec-77.pdf

20 Bridges, *The Rise of David Duke*, p.75.

21 Karl Hand, "Letter of Resignation from Karl Hand to David Duke", December 9, 1979 [Bridges; Box 2, Folder 4]; "David Duke for President?," *National Socialist Observer* #8–9 (September–December 1985).

22 Tom Metzger, untitled open letter to Klansmen, December 4, 1979 [Bridges; Box 1, Folder 12].

23 Ken Branson, "Ex-Klan Member Subpoenaed in Trial," *Asbury Park Press* (New Jersey), June 16, 1982, p.5, www.newspapers.com/image/145602168; Fleisher, "Neo-Nazi Leader Karl E. Hand Jr."; ADL, *Extremism on the Right*, p.101.

24 Hand to Mason, June 25, 1980 [Box 25, Folder 25]; *Defiance* #1, [1980]; *Defiance* #2 [September or October 1980]. For more on Christopher, see Appendix 4, "In Praise of Murder Men."

25 NSPA / Western New York Information Center, "Wanted! 100 White Men with Guts" (flyer), 1981 [Box 25, Folder 25]; Fleisher, "Neo-Nazi Leader Karl E. Hand Jr.".

26 Hand to Covington, February 4, 1981 [Box 25, Folder 25].

27 Covington to Hand, February 10, 1981; Hand to Covington, February 12, 1981 [both Box 25, Folder 25].

28 Mason to Hand, February 19, 1981 [Box 25, Folder 25].

29 Duffy to Hand, March 29, 1981 [Box 13, Folder 18]; Mason to Ed Reynolds and Rita, May 13, 1981 [Box 33, Folder 9]; Mason to Hand, September 12, 1982 [Box 25, Folder 22].

30 Mason to Duffy, December 1, 1983 [Box 13, Folder 18]; Ed Reynolds and Cindy to Mason, June 13, 1984 [Box 33, Folder 8].

31 *Defiance* #3; [February 1981?]; *Defiance* #4 [late February/early March 1981]; Fleisher, "Neo-Nazi Leader Karl E. Hand Jr.".

32 SIEGE 10(8) August 1981, p.5.

33 *Defiance* #5–8, 1982.

34 *Defiance* #8, 1982, pp.2, 6; "First NSLF Congress," *Defiance* #9, 1983, p.9; *Defiance* #6, 1982, p.1. Graham Macklin has suggested that FNE may refer to the Faisceaux Nationalistes Européens.

35 SIEGE 11(5) May 1982, p.5; Mason, "Universal Order," *Encyclopedia*, p.307; SIEGE 10(9) September 1981, pp.2–6.

36 Rickey E. Cooper to Karl Hand, August 21, 1982 [Box 25, Folder 22].

37 Hand to Mason, mid-August, 1982; Mason to Hand, August 30, 1982 [both Box 25, Folder 22].

38 Hand to Warthan, September 2, 1982; Hand to Mason, August 6, 1982; Mason to Hand, September 12, 1982 [all three Box 25, Folder 22].

39 Hand to Mason, September 16, 1982 [Box 25, Folder 22].

40 Mason to Hand, September 18, 1982 [Box 25, Folder 22]; SIEGE 11(11) November 1982.

41 Mason interview with Schuster (video).

42 Mason to Hand, September 18, 1982; Hand to Warthan, September 17, 1982 [both Box 25, Folder 22].

43 *Defiance* #10, [February 1984], p.18; *National Socialist Observer*, June 1986, p.3. For a profile of NSLF Unit 96 in Tampa-St Petersburg, Florida, see Steve Otto, "Neo-Nazi Group May Have Tough Time Recruiting," *Tampa Tribune* (Florida), March 14, 1984, p.151, www.newspapers.com/image/336294660

44 Mark Fleisher, "La. Nazi Group Seeks Inmate Members," *Star-Gazette*, February 19, 1984, p.3, www.newspapers.com/image/278001771

45 *National Socialist Observer* #8–9, 1985, p.2; Hand to Mason, May 18, 1986 [Box 25, Folder 24]; "Action Reports," *National Socialist Observer* #10, June 1986, p.3.

46 Mason, "It Seems to Me," *The New Dawn* 3(5) November 1986; Mason, "NSLF," *Encyclopedia*, p.223.

47 *Defiance* #7, back cover. The different types were: regular NSLF membership (ages 18–60), National Socialist Junior Youth (9–12), Youth Group (12–15), Advanced Youth (15–18), Student Union (college students), Senior Citizens Group (60+), Prison Reform Group, SS (the "paramilitary arm"), Official Supportership, and SS Sponsor. Regular memberships were $40, while the others varied; "NSLF Restructured," *Defiance* #9, 1983, p.6.

48 The article, apparently reprinted from the music press, mostly features Blitz— ironically not one of the Nazi bands in the genre; "Oi—Music to Riot By," *Defiance* #5, 1982; *Defiance*, sample issue, 1985, p.2

49 Fleisher, "Neo-Nazi Leader Karl E. Hand Jr."; Hand, "Dear NSLF Supporters," August, 1983 [Box 25, Folder 24].

50 Mike Rogers, "Dear NSLF Supporter," included with *National Socialist Observer* 2(4) April 1985; fundraising letter signed by Karl Hand, 1985 [Box 2, Folder 4].

51 *Defiance* #10, January 1984; *National Socialist Observer*, #8–9, 1985.

52 *National Socialist Observer* 2(4) April 1985, p.2; "Easter 'Race In'"—Easter Spring Picnic, April 7, [1985] (flyer) [CDR, Box 265]; Hand interview with Metzger and David Wiley/*Race and Reason* (video), recorded April 10, 1985, DVD in possession of author.

53 Hand, "Rebel with a Cause"; "You Are Invited," *National Socialist Observer* 2(2–3) 1985, p.12.

54 AP, "Swastika, 'Kill Jews' Slogan Painted on Actor's Home," June 17, 1985, https://apnews.com/article/af05ee265dc8ba359455ffab367bf439; Gustav Niebuhr, "Three Racist Groups Coalescing in Louisiana," *Boston Globe*, April 7, 1985, p.18, www.newspapers.com/image/437719727

55 Hand to Mason, May 5, 1986.

56 "Ku Klux Klan Plans Rally to Support Prisoner," *Morning Advocate* (Baton Rogue, Louisiana), December 28, 1990, p.2B, clipping; Bob Ross, "Metairie Man's Condition Fair after Street Dispute, Shooting," [no publication information], August 1, 1986, clipping [both in Bridges; Box 2, Folder 4].

57 "By Karl Hand" and "From Tom Metzger," *WAR* 6(1) 1987, p.3; Jack Carter with Tom Metzger, *In the Eye of the Storm: The True Story of Tom Metzger*, 1996 (the copyright on this as-to-told autobiography is 1992/1993), p.106.

58 Hand to Mason, January 30, 1987; Mason to Hand, February 2, 1987 [both Box 25, Folder 26]. Even within monitoring organizations the NSLF's fate wasn't clear. In 1988, one ADL publication said, "Only time will tell whether the NSLF will survive the incarceration of its leader." Another ADL publication the same year did refer to its dissolution into WAR. ADL, *Extremism on the Right*, p.43; *Young and Violent: The Growing Menace of Neo-Nazi Skinheads*, 1988, p.3.

59 Hand, appeal of sentence, August 5, 1987; Hand to Mason, February 23, 1987 [both Box 25, Folder 26].
60 *The White Beret*, April–May 1991, p.7; *In Vinculis: The Voice of Aryan POWs* #2, January 1991 [Bridges; Box 2, Folder 4].
61 Like Hand, Mahon was an ally of Metzger who moved between Klan and neo-Nazi groups. Mahon also published Hand in his *The White Beret*, where he— through ignorance or chutzpah—called on Duke to help get Hand released. "Attention All Racists, Skinheads, Nazis and Klansmen!!," flyer for January 15, 1991 demonstration; Risa Robert, James Minton, John Semien, and Andy Crawford, "Officers Outnumber Supremacist Pickets," *Morning Advocate*, pp.1B, 2B, clipping with no date visible; "Free Karl Hand," flyer for July 28, 1991 demonstration [above three in Bridges; Box 2, Folder 4]; Hand to Eva, February 2, 1994 [Box 2, Folder 40].
62 Hand to Mason, March 7, 1987 [Box 25, Folder 26].
63 "About the RNPA," *RNPA*, https://web.archive.org/web/20190705015008, www.rnpaheadquarters.org/about-us
64 Hand to author, February 7, 2021.
65 Hand, "A Racial Nationalist Viewpoint: Speech by Karl Hand, Rome, Georgia, April 23, 2016," *RNPA*, https://web.archive.org/web/20190705141923, www.rnpaheadquarters.org/speech-a-racial-nationalist-viewpoint; Sarah Viets, "Meet the Aryan Nationalist Alliance – A Racist Hodgepodge Doomed to Fail," *SPLC*, July 21, 2016, www.splcenter.org/hatewatch/2016/07/21/meet-aryan-nationalist-alliance---racist-hodgepodge-doomed-fail
66 Phil Fairbanks, "Neo-Nazi Sympathizer Confronted by 350 Counterdemonstrators," *Buffalo News* (New York), July 30, 2016, https://web.archive.org/web/201607 31184459, https://buffalonews.com/city-region/neo-nazi-sympathizer-confronted-by-350-counterdemonstrators-20160730
67 Lou Michel, "Leafleting among Uptick of White Supremacy Activities in Buffalo, Niagara," *Buffalo News*, February 6, 2020, https://web.archive.org/web/2020062 9200111, https://buffalonews.com/news/local/crime-and-courts/leafleting-among-uptick-of-white-supremacy-activities-in-buffalo-niagara/article_414fc99c-776e-59dd-ab5e-99399494c61e.html
68 Reynolds to Mason, July 2, 1985; Reynolds to Mason, May 10, 1986 [both Box 33, Folder 7]; H. Kemp Vye to Reynolds, October 9, 1986 [Box 33, Folder 8].
69 One Wolverine flyer has a man in a black ski mask with an automatic rifle. Wolverines, "On Earth Is an Idea Whose Time Has Come—WAR, White Power" (flyer), [1989] [Box 33, Folder 10]; David Lee Preston, "Mud and Insults Fly at N.J. Klan Rally," *Philadelphia Inquirer*, April 8, 1990, p.2B, www.newspapers.com/image/176703320; Lauri Rice, "Klan Calls on Youth to Maintain White Supremacy," *Morning Call* (Allentown, Pennsylvania), July 5, 1989, pp.B1, 10, www.newspapers.com/image/283427975, www.newspapers.com/image/283428630
70 Reynolds to Mason, May 25, 1990; Mason to Reynolds, July 12, 1990 [both Box 33, Folder 8]; Ed Reynolds, Shelby County White Knights (flyer); Beth Helen Reynolds to Mason, March 9, 1992 [both Box 33, Folder 6].
71 Ed and Beth Helen Reynolds to Mason, July 15, 1992; Reynolds, "Dear Comrades," August 11, 1992 [both Box 33, Folder 6]; "Former Klansmen Tom Metzger and Bill Riccio Encourage Skinheads to Cooperate," *SPLC Intelligence Report*, Fall 2006, online October 19, 2006, www.splcenter.org/fighting-hate/intelligence-report/2006/former-klansmen-tom-metzger-and-bill-riccio-encourage-skinheads-cooperate; Carol Robinson Warren, "Raids Net Top Aryan, Skinhead Leaders," *Birmingham Post-Herald* (Alabama), August 8, 1992, pp.1, 12, www.newspapers.com/image/795457015, www.newspapers.com/image/795457035

72 Reynolds to Mason, February 4, 1993; Reynolds to Mason, [March or April] 1993; Mason to Reynolds and Beth Helen, December 22, 1993; Mason to Reynolds and Beth Helen, January 21, 1994 [all Box 33, Folder 5]; Reynolds to Mason, September 5, 1992 [Box 33, Folder 6]. Reynolds was also interviewed for a scholarly book where he represented the group; Dobratz and Shanks-Meile, *"White Power, White Pride!,"* pp.27, 150, 260.
73 Mason to Moynihan, March 10, 1990 [Box 5, Folder 9]. The phrase "rock the boat," as well as direct references to Reynolds, appeared in *Siege* a number of times; pp.28, 54, 93, 202, 321, 326.
74 Reynolds funeral card, 1998 [Box 33, Folder 4]; Mason to Gene Sotelo, May 1, 1998 [Box 22, Folder 49]; Mason interview with Schuster (video).

PART III

SIEGE the Newsletter (1980–1986)

7

THE SIEGE ITSELF

Cult of the Extreme

The Cult of the Extreme

James Mason had already embraced violence, just as other former NSWPP members like Tommasi and Pierce had. Now he took it a step further. While in the NSM, Mason had already praised the new wave of murders committed by neo-Nazis and related loose cannons, encouraging others to do the same.

Theoretically, his justification was that they would help set off a revolutionary process since the previous strategies were obviously unable to motivate white people. Mason held that deep down they still *believed* in white supremacy, which was a view that many of those on the Left who are focused on race would agree with. And white Americans would be willing to act if the circumstances were right—such as in a civil war.

This praise of destabilizing violence was brought to its highest manifestation with Charles Manson, the cult leader imprisoned for directing numerous senseless murders. While Manson was a racist, misogynist, and antisemite, many of his other views and acts were deeply opposed to what neo-Nazis believed in; these included copious drug use, untraditional sexual mores, and religious views. Even Tommasi, politically active in California at the time of the murders, had not embraced him.

On a macro level, these developing views were two things. That they were an ideology of violence and death is obvious. But they were also an ideology of failure. Rockwell's phases had not panned out—whether that was media stunts, grassroots organizing, or membership organizations—and neither had Tommasi's attempts at guerilla warfare. Unlikely as success might seem for Mason's approach, in another way it made perfect sense: if everything else

DOI: 10.4324/9780429200090-11

has failed, ratchet up the pressure. This was a typical approach, if not one typically of success, of radical movements.

And as extreme as those acts were that Mason championed, conceptually they were consistent with his existing trajectory. And in taking this position, he followed the well-trodden path of the radical sectarian theorist. Starting off in a mass movement, he went through split after split, alienating former collaborators as his circles became both smaller and smaller as well as more theoretically refined. This approach is generally facilitated by accesses to a publication, and Mason's skill as a printer was perfect for the situation.

Although radicals like this may seem to have boxed themselves into a corner, in fact they can draw sustenance from holding unique theoretical positions—especially those which are the logical conclusion of conceptual trajectories existing in the larger movement as a whole. This gives them a clearly staked out position within an existing ideological framework, and now those movement members who are not on board ideologically can become potential recruits. Simultaneously, the very outlandishness of the claims can draw attention from those outside that political movement—in a way that perhaps the more typical beliefs would not.

This approach is typically perpetrated by long-time insiders of a wide variety of movements, and similar examples can be found in anarchist, Trotskyist, environmental, and radical feminist politics.[1] Those who utilize this approach need to possess detailed knowledge of their movement's internal ideological positions to justify their own as the logical conclusion of the larger principles that their comrades have already accepted. Additionally, in order to keep access to potential sympathizers and recruits, they need two other things as well: knowledge of the communication channels which can be used to reach them, and personal connections acquired by being one of a few long-time members of marginalized radical movements.

This is the path that Mason went down.

Re-Enter the NSLF

While this section presents a general history of the arc and themes of SIEGE, a number of them are explored in greater depth in separate chapters.

Mason restarted SIEGE as part of the resuscitation of the NSLF—or, rather, he started a newsletter which borrowed the name of the Tommasi-era periodical which had influenced him so strongly. Unlike the NSM and NSWWP titles he edited, though, this time it was Mason's personal vehicle. He still suffered some ideological limitations while SIEGE remained officially an NSLF publication from its founding in August 1980 until October 1982. Thereafter, it became his completely independent mouthpiece.

Each issue was six pages and appeared, without fail, each month from August 1980 to June 1986. Other than its red masthead made by a commercial printer, it was mimeographed in black and white by Mason himself.[2]

SIEGE's numbering system was unusual. Just as neo-Nazis would back-date when their organizations were founded, Mason did the same with the issue numbers in SIEGE. It continued a numbering system that ran through at a half dozen earlier publications. This sequence started with a periodical edited by Steven Love and published in 1972 by the Cincinnati NSWPP, the *Local Activity Report*. The numbering sequence follows periodicals later published by the NSWPP, NSM, NSWWP, and NSLF and ends with the last issue of Mason's SIEGE in 1986.[3]

Almost all of SIEGE was Mason's own writing. Sometimes there were reprints of news clippings, and on a handful of occasions he ran other writers. A few times subscribers also received enclosures, including pieces by Tommasi and two imprisoned neo-Nazi murderers, Perry "Red" Warthan and Frank Spisak.

SIEGE was published under three different leaders and labels. From its beginning in August 1980 through March 1981, it was part of the NSLF led by John Duffy. From April 1981 to October 1982, it was published as part of Karl Hand's NSLF. Last, from November 1982 to June 1986, it appeared as part of Universal Order. Mason also divided SIEGE into two different periods. The first four years covered his views about "the state of affairs, how they got that way and what to do about it." In the two remaining years, he offered only "greater clarification."[4]

Last, despite an influence that has spanned decades, the pool of SIEGE readers during its publication was miniscule. Mason has said the run "never exceeded one hundred." In 1982, Hand said it was less than 75. When Mason handed over the remaining subscriptions away in 1986, there were 66 names—which included those publications he was trading copies with.[5] Financially, it wasn't a success either, although it also wasn't a failure. SIEGE was started with the proceeds of an insurance settlement, and Mason said that "came close to paying for itself, even though I always put more money into it than I took out."[6]

From the very beginning, SIEGE was based around Mason's reflections on his past activism in the neo-Nazi movement.[7] Here, he drew in particular on his participation in the attempt by the "independent Nazis" to create an alternative to Matthias Koehl's NSWPP. During this time, Mason had outlined a number of SIEGE's main themes in the NSM's *National Socialist Bulletin*. Although he had to largely shelve his vision while editing Allen Vincent's *Stormer*, with SIEGE Mason was finally free to explore his own ideas.

One thing that SIEGE also marked was Mason's withdrawal from the neo-Nazi movement. He had never been much of a street activist, although with the NSWPP and NSM, he had attended public events and helped organize private ones. And of course, between 1975 and 1978, he was involved in an attempt to steer the neo-Nazi movement in a particular direction, and this required interacting with a wide variety of movement members and organizations. Now that was all over with, although he remained in contact with many movement members, including the most important one he influenced at the time, Tom Metzger.

This process of disengagement was already under way while he was the editor of Vincent's paper, although it was not complete, as at the time Mason was involved with bringing back the NSLF. With this achievement unlocked, he retreated to his theoretical labors—something only accelerated by his disappointment with Hand's direction.

Past Nazis

Although Mason is often seen as one of the more untraditional neo-Nazi thinkers, his end goal was quite orthodox: the establishment of a National Socialist state modeled directly on Hitler's Germany. In 1996, Mason said,

> National Socialism would have to best describe the most perfect and just form of government and societal values that humans can erect to live. Hitler of course first put this into application with miraculous results.[8]

Mason also was orthodox in taking his own vision of National Socialism directly from Rockwell's Americanized version, including the reinterpretation of Aryan as "white"[9] and promotion of Holocaust denial. (Accepting Christian Identity as a legitimate part of neo-Nazism took Mason a few years, although he got there before SIEGE was over.)

Mason also opposed what Rockwell called "sneaky Nazis"—those who refused to use the swastika and instead replaced it with other symbols or even denied being National Socialists altogether. (Mason referred to them as "krinklejammers."[10]) According to this approach, neo-Nazis should be loud and proud, for both psychological and recruiting purposes.

There was also Hitler worship, although not to the extent some other neo-Nazis took it. Mason said Hitler's life was the "Greatest Story Ever Told."[11] Also, just as with Rockwell, Mason perceived the NSDAP as a monolith around Hitler, thereby ignored its different periods and its other prominent figures. Among other things, this downplayed the parts of the party where there were more pronounced occult, environmental, and anti-capitalist characteristics.[12]

Rockwell's centrality to Mason's thought can be seen even in the ways he was rejected. Mason followed one of the primary structural types that schools of thought utilize, the text–exegesis approach. Here, he started with Rockwell's claims and entered into a critique of them, alternately accepting, rejecting, or building on them. In several places, Mason also took what were clearly departures from Rockwell's views, in regard to violence in particular, claiming that if he had lived, he would have come to hold those positions. In all of these, Rockwell remained central, and after his revival, Mason would constantly speak about him to a younger generation, for whom Rockwell must have been little more than a symbol. But to really understand why Mason took the positions he did in *Siege* requires understanding Rockwell.

In particular, Mason's project was based on a rejection of the "mass strategy" approach of public organizing. The first SIEGE immediately staked out its position by starting with "<u>PHASE ONE HAS PHASED OUT</u>."[13] And Mason went on to repeatedly condemn the associated components of the mass strategy groups as well. This included their reliance on leaders (the "'phony fuhrer' system"), memberships, uniforms, headquarters buildings, party congresses, restrictions on haircuts and drugs, mail-order books, internal courts, and incorporated legal structures.[14]

Some of these things Mason had to downplay or backtrack on while Hand was in charge and quickly had the NSLF embrace them. One of them was a source of continual discussion among neo-Nazis: uniforms. These were key elements in classical fascism, and Rockwell and Koehl emphasized classical-looking brownshirts. Mason opposed uniforms starting with the NSM, but in fact the NSLF had retained them, although not necessary in the same form. According to David Rust, when he worked under Tommasi the look was a "black shirt w/ military press, black pants bloused into combat boots and the standard armband"—although these were required only at meetings and photo-ops.[15] Under Hand, the more traditional brownshirt was brought back.

Perhaps the only element Mason retained was the need for publications and, for a time at least, the development of cadres. After he left the NSLF in 1982, Mason turned his back on above-ground organizations altogether. To make his point clear, he also attacked, although only sometimes by name, the proponents of mass strategy who he used to work with: Koehl, Brannen, and Vincent.[16] (He left Hand alone.)

Mason's alternative was to follow the path of Tommasi's NSLF and endorse violence—not one of Rockwell's four phases. At first, this meant guerilla armed struggle as well as attacks by lone wolves and serial killers. As SIEGE went on, he praised violence from leftists and black nationalists, and in the second half, he increasingly advocated dropping out.[17]

Last, in SIEGE, Mason referred to the works and thoughts of a relatively small number of figures. Other than Manson, the most frequent touchstones were Rockwell, Tommasi, and Hitler, and, earlier on, Pierce.

Against the System

Related to the rejection of the mass strategy approach was the denunciation of "Conservatism" and "Right-Wingism."[18] This included support for the police; reforms like controlling immigration, abortion, or drugs; and suppressing left-leaning social movements. Instead, Mason said the NSLF was the "radical wing of the lunatic fringe."[19]

As early as 1978, he was already developing this approach, calling for the removal of conservative ideas from the thinking of neo-Nazis. Six years later, his rhetoric had amped up so far that he proclaimed, "Conservatism and Pigism are the same: Enemies of Revolution."[20]

Mason saw nothing left to "conserve" because "the System" (a term used by the 1960s counterculture) had degenerated so far it was beyond salvaging. (In this worldview, Mason was in the company of revolutionaries of many different stripes.) Hitler still had "healthy" institutions to take over and use, but he was the "LAST CHANCE for the revival of Western Civilization."[21] Rockwell, too, still had the opportunity to take power and turn the clock back. The institutions of his day "were still usable and could be co-opted, or worked through" to seize state power, and he could also hope that "loyal elements within the established government" would hold a "fascist-style coup d'etat."[22] But sometime between Rockwell's death in 1967 and the 1973 Cleveland NSWPP march, this opportunity evaporated.[23] (Mason seemed unaware that his view might have been an artifact of the time that he, personally, had been most excited by the potential of the ANP/NSWPP (the American Nazi Party and the group under its second name).

With the hope of taking over the system gone, Mason now attacked the police and the federal government. In the first issue of SIEGE, he declared the U.S. Government "the most evil thing that has ever existed on earth." He also consistently described law enforcement using 1960s countercultural slang, which was especially favored by Manson as he called upon neo-Nazis "to forge a Movement with which to smash Pig Power." This, as Mason said later, was a significant break in perspective from the 1960s strategies that saw neo-Nazis as allies of the police.[24] All of this lent itself to an approach, used by some latter-day marxists about Marx, which held that Rockwell was "right in his time" but that new conditions called for new approaches.

Violence Is the Key

The kind of violence that Mason advocated both varied both in form and over time. He stressed that it was not merely the seizure of state power that was needed but a cleansing revolution, "a TOTAL WAR" against "the Jew-Capitalist System!!" SIEGE's readers were exhorted to take actions that would not merely be sparks to ignite the masses but that had an openly messianic aim of a uniquely "total and complete" revolution.[25] And as with so many other revolutionary ideologies seeking to transform humanity in one fell swoop, violence was key to this.

Mason started with two approaches to violence. During the period when SIEGE was part of the NSLF, he advocated a more straightforward armed struggle approach. However, in October 1981, he admitted "few of us in fact could qualify as guerrillas." As part of this, the newsletter promoted Pierce's

The Turner Diaries, for example. (Almost a dozen references to the book and Pierce would end up in the anthology.)[26]

Mason stressed the need to develop committed cadres, something he continued for a time even after he parted ways with the NSLF.[27] Additionally, from the beginning, Mason praised shootings and assassinations; seemingly random mass murders and poisonings; and coordinated attacks by White Supremacists. Mason supported racially based rioting, including in 1980 in Miami—wishing there were a dozen similar events to distract the "System's troops" and "allow us to go after Big Brother himself!"[28]

Mason was generally coy about mass political violence and genocide, but in the same issue with his fusillade against Big Brother was also one of the few moments that he was explicit about his vision of mass violence. After the revolution, he said, "there will be no need for concentration camps of any kind, for not a single transgressor will survive long enough to make it to that kind of haven." Another rare time was in 1983; after claiming there was a global plan to commit genocide against white people, he said "if we are able to defeat that plan, it will just as surely spell genocide for them."[29]

In November 1980, he became excited by what looked like three racist serial killers. The .22 Caliber Killer in Buffalo, New York, who, at that point, was thought to have killed six black men. Ex-NSWPP member Joseph Paul Franklin was thought to have killed ten people, including black men and mixed-race couples, when he was arrested, while the Atlanta child murders had then claimed eleven victims. (In all three, the death tolls ended up being significantly higher.) Just as with the Miami riots, Mason would later muse about the Atlanta killings, "What if there currently were six or a dozen 'Atlanta's? The power to break the System does exist." The next year, Mason praised John Hinckley, Jr.— initially thought to be a neo-Nazi—for attempting to assassinate President Ronald Reagan in 1981.[30]

Enter Charlie

But it was Mason's adoration of Manson that drew him the most infamy in the 1980s and '90s. SIEGE's focus on Manson was primarily from mid-1982 to mid-1984. But before that, in September 1981, was the pivotal "The Power to Blow Nazis Minds," which introduced his new view of Manson. Mason described his initial contact as one would a spiritual experience.[31]

SIEGE next addressed Manson in June 1982, resulting in Mason's fighting with Hand and their subsequent parting of ways. The November 1982 issue was the first published under Universal Order's auspices. (The year before, Manson had already suggested that the title be changed from SIEGE to Universal Order and the gun in the logo be replaced by the scales of justice.)[32] SIEGE also debuted the new logo Manson suggested: a left-facing swastika in the middle of a set of hanging scales. Ironically, the previous issues of SIEGE had violated Mason's own dictum of insisting that groups openly use the swastika. The entire issue was dedicated to Manson and the 1969 murders, praised as a White Supremacist attack on the corrupt Hollywood elite.[33]

Here, Mason started to develop his new, Universal Order philosophy, which melded his existing version of National Socialism with some of Manson's ideas. Some of these extended existing elements, like the idea of an internal, psychological revolution and an abandonment of a traditional association with the Right. Others came from Mason's translation of Manson's ideas into neo-Nazism. These included hiding out to form racial communities while waiting on society to collapse and the notion of a natural, underlying order that National Socialism was but one expression of.

In almost every issue through the spring of 1983, Manson's qualities were elaborated. These included his contemporary feel; grasp of "REALITY" in the face of the "Jewish-created illusion"; his honesty, selflessness, and fearlessness; and the very concrete fact that, unlike other National Socialist leaders, he was still alive.[34] In January 1983, the Manson Family was held up as an example for families to emulate: "people of the same Race, the same Spirit, coming together for mutual security." In August 1984, however, Mason reported that Manson told him there was no more to teach him.[35] Last, as SIEGE wound down in 1986, Mason returned to summarize the views he had developed earlier about Manson.[36]

Violence—But with Style

The break with the NSLF led to other changes in Mason's thinking, too. The National Socialist movement was neither large nor well organized enough to take power, leading Mason to two options: launching carefully planned individual attacks that were done with style or—his preferred option—to drop out.

Denouncing what he called a "national death sleep," Mason pinned his hopes on the System collapsing in a "general conflagration—which in this country would mean a Race War and a Civil War." In 1982, he claimed this has become the neo-Nazi consensus: "not only is the total destruction of the world-wide System and Establishment inevitable now, but it is our only best hope."[37]

After the break with Hand, Mason continued praising various murderers. Even though a number of them later did not turn out to be committed by racists at all, they provided grist for the mill at that time. Manson, of course, was heavily praised, starting in 1982, as was Mason's contact Warthan, who was arrested for murdering a teenager.[38]

By 1983, lacking new murders to promote, Mason's pessimism reached new heights, and he desired action "to break the boredom and the deadlock." And so, later that summer, Mason showed interest in the "general terror and panic" created by the rash of Tylenol bottle poisonings that killed seven in the Chicago area and copycat attacks that caused several more deaths. He also saluted Gordon Kahl, a Posse Comitatus member who died in a shootout with police.[39] (Typically, Mason generally avoided any relationship with those in the Patriot movement, which epitomized the right-wingism he despised, although he made some exceptions for those engaged in violence.[40]) Former NSWPP member Frank Spisak, who murdered three people in 1982, was consistently covered, starting in March 1984. The next month, Mason suggested that an ideal message would be sent by assassinating the celebrity couple Brooke Shields, a white actress, and black pop star Michael Jackson. The October 1984 issue covered James Huberty's massacre of 21 at a McDonald's in San Ysidro, California. Mason claimed, on the flimsiest of evidence, that Huberty was a neo-Nazi.[41]

At the end of the same issue, Mason printed the mailing addresses of five prisoners: Warthan, Spisak, Franklin, Manson, and Hess.[42] These five were symbols of Mason's interests: three ex-NSWPP murderers, his new guru, and a high-ranking member of the defeated regime he worshipped.

Violence was in the zeitgeist of the White Supremacist movement of the 1980s, and in that sense Mason was part of it. In another sense, it is very curious that his fixation on it was isolated from the violence being practiced by the larger movement. The 1981 attempted Dominica raid didn't seem to impact him. Mason made nary a mention of Louis Beam and his 1983 call for leaderless resistance. Aryan Nations barely registered. And so when The Order did finally make his ears perk up, it took him by surprise.

Starting in January 1985, SIEGE praised The Order, although they represented a return to the tactics of Tommasi, which Mason had since abandoned. After that, however, Mason was left with little to work with. In March, he begrudgingly talked about Bernard Goetz, a white man who shot four black teenagers who allegedly tried to mug him on a New York City subway. Mason nearly dismissed the action as right-wingism that was too little and too late; but his lack of enthusiasm was undoubtedly influenced by the fact that Goetz was Jewish. (Similarly, Mason dismissed apolitical serial killers like John Wayne Gacy, a gay man, and Charles Ng, a person of color.) Later that summer, Mason praised Muslim forces in the Middle East who kidnapped Westerners and looked for "Jewish-sounding names."[43]

For aspiring murderers, Mason stressed that if one chose to go ahead and launch an attack on the System, they should choose their fight in a way that would have maximum impact, and they should fight to the death. He chastised those arrested in the attempted 1981 Dominica raid for surrendering. In 1982, he wrote, "In revolution the price of failure generally is death.... don't sell yourself cheap. MAKE IT COUNT." Future Mason publisher Ryan Schuster summarized Mason's view as "if you are determined to unleash iron justice or make a valiant sacrifice with your life, then do so with finesse and style."[44]

There were also articles which were by-products of the emphasis on violence. One popular theme was how to deal with local police, federal agents, informants, and the press. Imprisoned White Supremacists received support in SIEGE. He often ran their prison addresses on the back page of each SIEGE, and one issue was dedicated to his reflections on working with prisoners.[45]

The Reds and the Blacks

In terms of violence, another recurring interest of Mason's was the potential of clashes with the System by underground Communist militants and black nationalists, whom he called "the Reds and Blacks"—among less charitable names.[46]

Two events inspired him to move past the usual neo-Nazi opposition to these traditional opponents. The first was the 1981 robbery of a Brinks armored truck, when two police were killed in a joint raid by the Black Liberation Army and a spin-off of the Weather Underground. The second was the 1985 bombing of the headquarters of black radical group MOVE in Philadelphia by police, which killed 11 and burned down an entire city block. Both times, Mason wished these groups well and in the latter case suggested a dialogue.[47]

The most comprehensive statement on this appeared in September 1985. Mason counseled neo-Nazis not to get involved in the first stage of a civil war, but let the "Blacks and the Reds," fight it out with the System and weaken it. Then neo-Nazis could mobilize the white masses and capture areas where they would have a base of support.[48]

Total Attack or Total Drop Out!

Mason's other option—ever-popular among radical movements after the high tide of their success has passed—was, again following his adaptation of 1960s slang, to "drop out." In October 1981, Mason outlined his plan, which he distinguished from the popularity of the survivalist current in the 1980s. In fact, what he advocated was not so different from it, telling neo-Nazis to leave the cities and be self-supportive in majority-white areas. He continued to emphasize this, saying in 1982 that "it will be the one who finishes LAST who will be the real winner."[49] As Manson came to the fore in SIEGE, he became an example of this: "Manson and those who follow his Idea LIVE IT by dropping out of the System and attacking the System." In 1984, again citing the Manson Family's example, Mason talked about the importance of women to this project and of creating racist family units, which could federate into a series of increasingly larger structures until they formed a new white nation.[50]

In 1984, Mason summed up the tactical approaches he advocated. One, "I simply say if comrades are going to sacrifice their lives and liberty, DO IT IN THE MOST EFFECTIVE MANNER POSSIBLE!" Second, one could engage in armed struggle and try to create a situation where white people will have to choose a side, as in *The Turner Diaries*. Third, "totally withdraw from it all and dig in as deeply as possible with the expectation of surviving once all the rest of it has been blown away and blown over." At the very end of SIEGE, he simplified this approach to "TOTAL ATTACK OR TOTAL DROP-OUT!"—although he recommended the latter.[51]

Philosophy and Christianity

SIEGE also addressed a number of other themes of a more personal and philosophical nature. Mason spent a significant amount of time musing about what the most important qualities were for neo-Nazis, both as individuals and for the movement as a whole. These included action, discipline, commitment, duty, intellect, instinct, morality, and loyalty—especially relevant because the movement was rife with marginal and unstable individuals. He also contemplated more philosophical questions, such as the meaning of "alone" and "the now." And he shared his disgust about how his beautiful hometown had been tarnished by modern architecture—a complaint familiar to many on both the Left and the Right.[52]

Last, Mason spent the arc of SIEGE grappling with Christianity. He started off claiming that the good parts of Christianity were merely those that were part of the white race that it had incorporated, but overall, it was a toxin. But as SIEGE progressed, Mason developed a growing respect in particular for Christian Identity, which in 1983 he affirmed was congruent with National Socialism—Rockwell's position. And in the last SIEGE, he started to grapple with specific Biblical passages and prayers.[53] All of this was the lead-up to Mason's prison Bible studies in the second half of the 1990s, which resulted in the creation of his own brand of Christianity.

Tom Metzger

SIEGE had a miniscule number of committed readers, but one of those had a very high profile among White Supremacists: Tom Metzger.

Metzger's politics had taken a far longer route than Mason's to a similar place. Metzger started his career on the Far Right with an eight-year stint in the John Birch Society and then, in a series of steps, moved to promoting revolutionary violence.[54] As he did, he became involved with numerous ANP/NSWPP veterans. In January 1974, Metzger was ordained a Christian Identity minister before joining the New Christian Crusade Church, run by James K. Warner, later in the year. In July 1975, while staying with Warner, David Duke initiated 30 men—including Metzger—into his Knights of the Ku Klux Klan (KKKK), making this the second former ANP/NSWPP member (after Warner) that Metzger worked under.[55] (Metzger would later become disillusioned by Christian Identity and became an atheist.[56])

In January 1976, Metzger was made the Grand Dragon of the California KKKK, but he broke with Duke in late 1979.[57] Metzger's new group organized as the California Klan. In March 1980, he announced his bid for the 43rd District's U.S. Congressional seat, running in the Democratic Party primary. The next month, his group became the White American Political Association (WAPA), to separate himself from the Klan's association with both Christianity and violence.[58]

To the surprise of many, Metzger won the Democratic primary with 33,000 votes (37 percent)—although by less than 400 votes over his closest opponent. While he did not win the general election, more than 46,000 voters (over 13 percent) chose him.[59] In 1980, despite Mason's disavowal of electoral politics, he sent Metzger a letter of congratulations on his win.[60]

Metzger ran again in spring 1982, this time in the Democratic primary for U.S. Senate. At 76,000 votes (2.8 percent), he came in sixth out of the 11 candidates.[61] Mason started corresponding regularly with him at this same time, and Metzger wrote, "I certainly enjoy your articles in SIEGE."[62] Metzger later told Mason that

> I was very much influenced by SIEGE. I picked up a lot of good ideas because I felt that you were being straight out, get all the nonsense out of the way. You were stepping on toes and you didn't care.[63]

In April 1983, Metzger's WAPA became White American Resistance, and in September 1984, it changed again to White Aryan Resistance (WAR). (The newspaper did not make the "Aryan" change until later, though.)[64] Metzger also became the most important U.S. White Supremacist to adopt Third Position politics. He stressed opposition to "monopoly capitalism"[65] and supported white separatism—like Rockwell, he met with the Nation of Islam—and environmentalism. Although not a traditional National Socialist, he was not averse to using Nazi imagery. He also openly identified with the Strasserite wing of the original NSDAP.[66] (The Strasser brothers, Otto and Gregor, emphasized the anti-capitalist elements in National Socialism.) And two former leftists helped run WAR: ex-IWW member Gary/John Jewell and ex-Trotskyist Wyatt Kaldenberg.[67]

In late 1983, in the midst of this transformation, Metzger circulated an open letter about the various foibles and failures of the White Supremacist movement.[68] It reached Mason, who replied to Metzger that "I find myself already in agreement with practically everything you outline" and recommended that he visit Manson in prison. In SIEGE, Mason gave his own take on the questions posed in the letter.[69]

In December 1985, he had been one of the few people to give Mason a platform to speak to younger movement members. Mason addressed a WAR meeting in San Diego, California via phone, and the audience listened to it over loudspeakers. In it he praised Metzger, saying he was "among the top half-dozen or so over the past twenty years in the area of reaching and leading and organizing people." Mason gave a quick overview of his history and the lessons he had learned in the neo-Nazi movement and summarized the perspective and conclusions he had developed in SIEGE.[70]

Metzger was "distressed" when he found out that SIEGE was shuttering in 1986, writing Mason that

> Your paper has been recommended by myself to as many people as possible. I was in hopes that you would have gotten a noticeable rise in subscriptions. Promise me this, that you will write a column for our WAR paper every month or every other month. I believe your thoughts have a much more far reaching effect on the right people than you realize.[71]

Mason took him up on the offer, and *WAR* would become his largest mouthpiece for the years to come, even listing him on the editorial staff.[72] Between 1986 and 1993, Mason published one or two articles a year in *WAR* and then many more after he was imprisoned—almost 20 in 1996 and 1997 alone.

Ending the SIEGE

Mason gave a number of reasons for ending SIEGE. Probably the most accurate was the admission that "I did feel I had said about all I needed to say at that time. But I was also undergoing a severe depression" at the time. Elsewhere, he said simply, "I'm just plain tired of it."[73] After all, it had now been a number of years after Mason was actively involved in the movement beyond self-publishing, and he had, by his own admission, taken SIEGE's ideological path to its end.

However, there was a more immediate reason, which involved Gene Laws, an undercover operative of a private agency whom Mason met in 1992. His act was strangely obvious—giving Mason "free dinners, free gifts, cash contributions and subscriptions," even taking him on flights on his private plane—but also quite professional and otherwise convincing. After The Order's attacks, Laws was eager to meet other movement leaders, including Metzger, the widely respected Robert Miles, and Aryan Nations leader Richard Butler. At the same time, Laws encouraged Mason to engage in illegal financial acts. Mason turned around and wrote the three White Supremacist leaders, saying he found an undercover agent who was seeking to contact them. Mason said he had talked to a lawyer who would take the case for free, but needed $500 to hire an investigator, and so Mason asked the three to help pay for it. **Only one even replied and none gave money; Mason was "disgusted but not surprised." A year later, the same three were among those subpoenaed in the Fort Smith case, a mass trial of White Supremacists. Laws was one of the witnesses.[74]

Finally, as Mason was wrapping things up, he offered his mailing list to two other publishers so that they could either complete his unfulfilled SIEGE subscriptions with their own periodicals, or send new subscription offers for their own wares. The first publisher was his old comrade Hand. The second was Michael Merritt, whose publications explored spiritual National Socialist issues in the same vein as Mason. Mason gave them "sixty-six of my best names"—with the caveat that many of these were publication trades or just free subscriptions he had given people. And so in June 1986, Mason announced that was the last issue of SIEGE. However, he did promise to continue work on other projects, the next of which would be a Manson pamphlet that ended up playing an important part in his future.[75]

Notes

1 Examples from other political tendencies of this include: anarcho-primitivist John Zerzan's call for the abolition of language and agriculture; among Trotskyists, the Spartacist League's position of military support for ISIS, as well as the Posadists' view that Communism will come after aliens visit Earth; Dworkinite radical feminist claims that all heterosexual intercourse is rape; the anti-Deutsche *Bahamas*'s support for Islamophobia and the U.S. invasion of Iraq; radical environmentalist Pentti Linkola's embrace of genocide; and NAMBLA's advocacy of the legalization of "Man-Boy" sex. Many more examples can be found among both political and religious groups.

2 Mason, "Introduction to the Third Edition," *Siege*, p.9.

3 Mason explained the numbering system in 1989 to Michael Moynihan, although he misremembered the name and year of the initial publication; Mason to Moynihan, June 20, 1989 [Box 11, Folders 1–2]. For more on the continuity question, including the skipped months, see Mason to author, November 26, 2022. For details of the exact progressive of the numbering sequence, see the "Periodical List".

4 SIEGE 13(6) June 1984, p.1.

5 Mason to author, November 6, 2022; Hand to Warthan, September 17, 1982 [Box 25, Folder 22]; Mason to M. Merritt, May 5, 1986 [Box 22, Folder 1].

6 Mason, "Introduction to the Third Edition," *Siege*, pp.8–9.

7 SIEGE 12(4) April 1983, p.1.

8 "James Mason the Path to Universal Order; an Interview Conducted August 1996 by Edmund Krolikowski," *Strength through Joy Productions*, 1997 (*Articles*, p.145).

9 Hitler's racial worldview did not include the category of "white," which was not used by to Europeans of his time. "Aryans" were distinct from various other groups that would be considered white today, such as Slavs.

10 Rockwell, *This Time the World!*, chapter X, p.182. For an example of "krinklejammer," see SIEGE 10(9) September 1981, p.2 (*Siege*, p.187).

11 SIEGE 13(6) June 1984, p.4.

12 NSDAP leaders looked to by contemporary fascists to establish a legitimizing predecessor for their specific theoretical take include Otto Strasser, Gregor Strasser, Heinrich Himmler, Richard Walther Darré, Alfred Rosenberg, Joseph Goebbels, and Gottfried Feder.

13 SIEGE 9(4) August 1980, p.1 (*Siege*, p.37).

14 SIEGE 10(3) March 1981, p.3; SIEGE 9(6) October 1980, p.3; Mason to Reynolds, June 1, 1980 [Box 33, Folder 10]; SIEGE 11(11) November 1982, p.6; SIEGE 11(5) May 1982, p.5; SIEGE 11(1) January 1982, pp.3–5.

15 Rust to author, July 13, 2022.

16 SIEGE 9(8) December 1980, p.5; SIEGE 11(2) February 1982, p.5. Mason explicitly rejected his past allies in the NSWPP, NSWWP, NSM, NSPA, and UWPP; SIEGE 11(5) May 1982, pp.4–5.

17 SIEGE 15(1) January 1986, p.5.

18 Also included were "provincialism," "States Rights," and "Reaction"; SIEGE 12(5) May 1983, p.1.

19 SIEGE 10(8) August 1981, p.1.

20 *Special Bulletin*, p.2; SIEGE 13(3) March 1984, p.5.

21 SIEGE 10(12) December 1981, pp.2–3; SIEGE 12(3) March 1983, p.3.

22 SIEGE 10(9) September 1981, p.2 (*Siege*, p.186); SIEGE 15(1) January 1986, p.2 (*Siege*, p.498).

23 Mason to Reynolds, July 21, 1978 [Box 33, Folder 10].

24 SIEGE 9(4) August 1980, p.2 (*Siege*, p.38); SIEGE 11(4) April 1982, p.2; SIEGE 14(9) September 1985, p.3 (*Siege*, p.83).

25 SIEGE 14(9) September 1985, p.3 (*Siege*, p.175); SIEGE 9(6) October 1980, p.4; SIEGE 10(12) December 1981, p.4.

26 SIEGE 9(4) August 1980, p.5; SIEGE 10(10) October 1981, p.2. There are almost a dozen Pierce and *Turner Diaries* references in *Siege*; pp.22–23, 43–44, 304, 318, 397, 444, 481, 557.

27 SIEGE 11(2) February 1982, p.4; SIEGE 12(4) April 1983, p.3.

28 SIEGE 9(4) August 1980, p.5; SIEGE 10(8) August 1981, p.4; SIEGE 9(6) October 1980, p.1.

29 SIEGE 9(6) October 1980, p.3 (*Siege*, p.101); SIEGE 12(5) May 1983, p.4. In case it was too abstract for readers, on the next page he wrote that Greensboro "was no 'massacre'. But we'll SHOW them massacres!".

30 SIEGE 9(7) November 1980, p.1; SIEGE 10(4) April 1981, p.2 (*Siege*, p.290); SIEGE 10(5) May 1981, p.2 (*Siege*, p.292).

31 SIEGE 10(9) September 1981, pp.4–5.

32 SIEGE 11(6) June 1982, pp.1–2; Mason to Ed and Rita Reynolds, September 10, 1981 [Box 33, Folder 9]; Mason to Hand, February 19, 1981 [Box 25, Folder 25].

33 SIEGE 11(11) November 1982, pp.1–6. For the swastika-bedecked scales of justice image, see "File: Universal Order.svg," https://web.archive.org/web/20230920 224547, https://en.m.wikipedia.org/wiki/File:Universal_Order.svg

34 SIEGE 12(2) February 1983, p.4 (*Siege*, pp.454–55); SIEGE 13(8) August 1984, p.3 (*Siege*, p.422); SIEGE 12(3) March 1983, p.3 (*Siege*, p.419).

35 SIEGE 12(1) January 1983, pp.4–5 (*Siege*, p.448); SIEGE 13(8) August 1984, p.4 (*Siege*, pp.422–23).

36 SIEGE 15(5) May 1986, pp.4–5 (*Siege*, pp.430–33); SIEGE 15(6) June 1986, pp.3–6 (*Siege*, pp.493–95).

37 SIEGE 9(4) August 1980, p.3 (*Siege*, p.56); SIEGE 10(4) April 1981, p.2; SIEGE 11(7) July 1982, p.2 (*Siege*, p.400).

38 SIEGE 11(12) December 1982, p.2.

39 SIEGE 12(1) January 1983, p.5; SIEGE 12(8) August 1983, pp.3, 4. The fact that Mason was driven in part by "boredom" is worth further exploration; SIEGE 12(6) June 1983, p.5.

40 The Patriot movement's postwar origins were in anti-Communist groups in the 1950s like the John Birch Society, which promoted an ultra-patriotism wrapped around a core of authoritarianism and crypto-antisemitic conspiracy theories. The influential Posse Comitatus emerged in the 1970s, which advocated armed politics, White Supremacy, and antisemitism. But in each proceeding decade, these politics became more washed out and coded within the Patriot movement. In the mid-1990s, what became dubbed the "militia movement" burst onto the scene, gaining infamy with the 1995 Oklahoma City bombing. The movement has continued through and beyond the Alt Right era, with armed groups like the Oath Keepers and the decentralized Three Percenters. Stewart Rhodes, the leader of the Oath Keepers, would later be convicted of seditious conspiracy and sentenced to 18 years for his role in the January 6, 2021 takeover of the U.S. Capitol.

For background on the Patriot and militia movement, see Kenneth Stern, *A Force Upon the Plain: The American Militia Movement and the Politics of Hate* (Norman: University of Oklahoma Press, 1997); David Neiwert, *In God's Country: The Patriot Movement and the Pacific Northwest* (Pullman, Washington: Washington State University Press, 1999); Chip Berlet and Matthew Lyons, *Right-Wing Populism in America: Too Close for Comfort* (New York: Guilford Press, 2000), pp.287–304; Daniel Levitas, *The Terrorist Next Door: The Militia Movement and the Radical Right* (New York: St. Martin's Press, 2002); Spencer Sunshine, et al., *Up in Arms: A Guide to Oregon's Patriot Movement* (Scappoose, Oregon: Rural Organizing Project, 2016), https://rop.org/up-in-arms; and Sam Jackson, *The Oath Keepers: Patriotism and the Edge of Violence in a Right-Wing Antigovernment Group* (New York: Columbia University Press, 2020).

41 SIEGE 13(3) March 1984, p.6; SIEGE 13(4) April 1984, p.1; SIEGE 13(10) October 1984, pp.1–2, 5.

42 SIEGE 13(10) October 1984, p.6.

43 SIEGE 14(1) January 1985, pp.1, 3; SIEGE 14(3) March 1985, pp.5–6; SIEGE 14(7) July 1985, p.4 (*Siege*, pp.234–35); SIEGE 14(8) August 1985, p.4.

44 SIEGE 11(8) August 1982, p.4 (*Siege*, p.266); SIEGE 13(4) April 1984, p.1; Schuster, "Introduction," *Siege*, p.18. Mason continued to advocate that White Supremacists should fight to the death throughout SIEGE. SIEGE 10(6) June 1981, p.2; SIEGE 14(6) June 1985, p.6.

45 SIEGE 15(4) April 1986, pp.1–2; SIEGE 13(7) July 1984, p.4; SIEGE 15(5) May 1986, pp.1–2; SIEGE 12(6) June 1983, pp.1–4. Mason was very cynical about this, saying that, at that time, there were less than ten legitimate political prisoners from his camp; ibid, p.2.

46 SIEGE 9(4) August 1980, p.4.

47 See Appendix 7, "Against Capitalism and the Liberal State".

48 SIEGE 14(9) September 1985, pp.3–4 (*Siege*, pp.83–84).

49 SIEGE 10(10) October 1981, p.3; SIEGE 11(2) February 1982, p.4.

50 SIEGE 11(12) December 1982, p.5 (*Siege*, p.445); SIEGE 13(3) March 1984, p.2.

51 SIEGE 13(4) April 1984, pp.1–2; SIEGE 15(6) June 1986, p.3 (*Siege*, p.493).

52 SIEGE 13(1) January 1984, pp.1–3; SIEGE 14(6) June 1985, pp.5–6; SIEGE 12(10) October 1983, pp.1–2 (*Siege*, pp.209–12).

53 SIEGE 10(7) July 1981, pp.2, 6; SIEGE 15(6) June 1986, pp.2–3. See also Appendix 5, "Christianity".

54 Carter and Metzger, *In the Eye of the Storm*, p.57.

55 Barkun, *Religion and the Racist Right*, p.209. Metzger was made a reverend not by Warner but by Rev. Bertrand Comparet, a well-known Christian Identity preacher. Carter and Metzger, *In the Eye of the Storm*, pp.70–71.

56 Durham, *White Rage*, p.78.

57 Metzger's autobiography gives September 1979 as the date of the break; Carter and Metzger, *In the Eye of the Storm*, pp.73, 118. Metzger sent an open letter about this a couple months later. Tom Metzger, untitled open letter to Klansmen, December 4, 1979 [Bridges; Box 1, Folder 12].

58 Carter and Metzger, *In the Eye of the Storm*, pp.121–22, 128.

59 March Fong Eu, compiler, *Statement of Vote, Primary Election, June 3, 1980*, p.18, https://archive.org/details/statementofvote31980cali; March Fong Eu, compiler, *Statement of Vote*, General Election, November 4, 1980, p.12, https://archive.org/details/statementofvote41980cali

60 Mason to Metzger, July 3, 1980 [Box 27, Folder 9].

61 March Fong Eu, compiler, *Statement of Vote*, Primary Election, June 8, 1982, p.17, https://archive.org/details/statementofvote81982cali

62 Metzger to Mason, March 2, 1982 [Box 27, Folder 9].

63 Mason interview with Metzger/*Race and Reason* (video).

64 Carter and Metzger, *In the Eye of the Storm*, pp.160, 183. During the *White American Resistance* period, Metzger would continue to use the WAPA name, which WAR was said to be an "arm" of; *White American Resistance* 4(10) 1985, p.2.

65 Chip Berlet, "What Is the Third Position?," *Political Research Associates*, December 19, 2016, www.politicalresearch.org/2016/12/19/what-third-position

66 This point is made by Durham, *White Rage*, p.31. Metzger is referred to as a "neo-Nazi" in this study following the convention of using the term to refer to any White Supremacist who utilizes National Socialist ideas and imagery, even if they only form part of their ideology.

67 Carter and Metzger, *In the Eye of the Storm*, p.166. For Third Position fascism, see Appendix 7, "Against Capitalism and the Liberal State."

68 White American Resistance, "Dear Movement Members" (open letter), [November] 1983 [Box 27, Folder 9].

69 Mason to Metzger, November 14, 1983 [Box 27, Folder 9]; SIEGE 12(12) December 1983, pp.2–3 (*Siege*, pp.198–99).

70 The talk was printed in *Siege* as "Appendix I: Address," pp.495–505. The quote is on pp.495–96, although the date was erroneously given as 1986.

71 Metzger to Mason, May 14, 1986 [Box 7, Folder 21].

72 Mason to Metzger, August 24, 1986 [Box 7, Folder 21]. Mason released a compilation of them in 2003, *Articles of WAR*; some are reprinted in *Out of the Dust*; and a folder of *WAR* clippings are in Box 35, Folder 14. All of them contain slightly different articles.

73 "James Mason" (interview by Joseph A Gervasi), *NO LONGER A FANzine* #5, summer 1994, p.14; Mason to Merritt, May 5, 1986 [Box 22, Folder 1].

74 SIEGE 15(4) April 1986, pp.1–3 (*Siege*, pp.253–59); Mason interview with Schuster (video).

75 Mason to M. Merritt, May 5, 1986 [Box 22, Folder 1]; Mason to Hand, May 29, 1986 [Box 25, Folder 24]; SIEGE 15(6) June 1986, p.6. See also Appendix 9, "Michael Merritt and Keith Stimely".

8

CHARLES MANSON AS NEO-NAZI "HOLY MAN"

Charles Manson was a late 1960s cult leader in California whose followers, mostly young women, were called "The Family." He became infamous after members committed multiple gruesome murders in the summer of 1969, together referred to as the Tate–LaBianca murders. On the night of August 8 and 9, 1969, Manson Family members entered a Los Angeles home in a wealthy neighborhood and butchered five people, including pregnant actress Sharon Tate, and wrote "pig" on a door in blood. The next night at another home, they killed Rosemary and Leno LaBianca and wrote "Helter Skelter" in blood on the refrigerator. Although Manson did not personally participate in the killings, he and several Family members were arrested, tried, and sentenced to death. However, California abolished the death penalty before their execution, leaving Manson to serve the rest of his life in prison. There, Manson—often known by his nickname "Charlie"—became another kind of cult figure, with books, TV interviews, and movies made about him and the Family. While the audience for these varied, it never lacked an appeal to those interested in extremes.

Manson carved a swastika in his forehead during his trial and held racist and antisemitic views. In the public's eye, however, the swastika was often seen as just another eccentricity in Manson's bag of extremes, while his antisemitism and racism were generally dismissed as products of his poor education. The result of this is that Manson is generally not associated with neo-Nazism.

But it was these very elements that drew Mason to him, leading to his attempt to create a neo-Nazi cult around Manson. Mason proclaimed him to be the new leader and under his inspiration made ideological and tactical changes.

DOI: 10.4324/9780429200090-12

Mason's interest in Manson also led him to his connection with the Abraxas Clique—a group of the musicians, publishers, and Satanists consisting of Boyd Rice, Adam Parfrey, Nikolas Schreck, and Michael Moynihan. They would be four of his main collaborators for the next decade after SIEGE, with Moynihan being the one who would edit and publish *Siege*.

Charlie's Appeal

There were some rather pragmatic reasons that Mason was attracted to Manson. Some of the more explicit draws of Manson included the swastika on his forehead; his racism, antisemitism, and praise of Hitler; ability to draw women followers but still within a misogynistic worldview; appeal to youth and acceptance of countercultural fashion and sexuality; and the fact that he was alive. Mason also worked his ideas into his political approach, including the notion of an underlying natural order, environmentalism, the role of families, and the use of dropping out of society.

Mason's encounter with Manson also had a religious quality. This was perhaps not surprising, considering how many people fell under Manson's spell over the years. As Gavin Baddeley put it, "Manson received his new disciples...in the same way that he'd learned to deal with everybody—reflecting back at them their own desires and preconceptions." A former Family member, Brooks Poston, said Manson "said the right words at the right time." Mason openly described his first encounter as a "revelation."[1]

Mason was again seeking a new path for the neo-Nazi movement, which he saw as having reached a dead end. Manson was "the threshold of alienation and a symbol of radicalism beyond the most extreme."[2] Mason described the feeling of his discovery as "a replay of 1966"—the year he fell under George Lincoln Rockwell's spell.

> It was all as intuitive as it was irresistible.... There had been Manson like a comet in the sky in 1969, only two years after Rockwell's assassination, and not one of us had seen it. We were too wrapped up in "Hollywooding" with uniforms, etc.[3]

Manson, he said, had "provided the missing parts."[4]

Swastikas, Right and Left

Immediately after the Tate–LaBianca murders, some leftists embraced Manson. This included Yippie leader Jerry Rubin and the armed June 2nd Movement in Germany.[5] But the most infamous one was at the last Students for a Democratic Society (SDS) conference, the Flint War Council, which was the founding event of the Weather Underground. Bernardine Dohrn, one of the group's leaders, gave a speech praising the Tate murders. "Dig it; first they killed those pigs, then they ate dinner in the room with them, then they even shoved a fork into pig Tate's stomach. Wild!" Attendees chanted "Charles Manson Power!" and saluted each other by holding up four fingers to represent the fork. (Dohrn later called this an "ironic joke.")[6] Combined with his position as a countercultural icon, Manson's association with a vaguely left-leaning ambience was never quite severed, despite his continued expressions of bigotry.

The symbol on Manson's forehead went through several changes. In late July 1970, Manson came to court with an "X" carved in his forehead with a razor, saying it symbolized that he had "X'ed" himself out of society. (Some committed Family members followed suit.) In March 1971, while proceedings were still ongoing, he turned the X into a left-facing swastika, now saying that society was corrupt—but that he could bring order to the "anarchy."[7] While he was in prison, but before their own sentences, Lynette "Squeaky" Fromme and Sandra Good—two of Manson's most dedicated followers—took to wearing capes embroidered with left-facing swastikas as well. (In the Family, Fromme was known as "Red" while Good was "Blue.")[8]

According to Mason, after the appearance of Manson's swastika, William Pierce said that "The Jewish/leftist Peanut gallery that had been cheering on Manson fell silent." Mason, for whom the open use of the swastikas was important, specifically noted this image as part of his argument for adopting Manson. Around the time that SIEGE ceased being an NSLF publication, Manson changed the swastika on his forehead, so it was right-facing. (The arms on the Nazi swastika were right-facing, whereas in other swastikas the arms frequently face left.)[9]

Racism, Antisemitism, Manson

The "Helter Skelter" idea was also an inspiration to Mason. Vincent Bugliosi, who prosecuted Manson, said this was his plan to start a race war. While it went on, the Family would hide out in the desert, and after it was over, they would emerge and take power. The argument was tied to the graffiti left at the Tate–LaBianca murder scenes, which sought to implicate black radicals in hopes of kicking off the race war.[10] Manson denied Bugliosi's version of his views. But regardless of its veracity, Mason embraced the idea and wove it into his ideology.

Bugliosi reported that although Manson avoided slurs in court, privately he "often referred to blacks as 'niggers'." Manson claimed he had no ill feelings toward black people, while also saying "I know they hate me." So it was not surprising that Manson promoted racial separatism. During his November 1970 testimony, he said, "my family is of the white family," which he distinguished from black, yellow, cow, and mule families. Elsewhere,

Manson denounced "blackie" for "balling the blond, blue eyed daughters and making mixed babies. It's all leading to bad shit."[11] At a 1986 parole hearing, he said black people were

> sub-underworld people for long over 700 years. This will be the fifth wave of negro babies your system has been bussing up your own children's ass. Negroes eat white people. Like wolves eat dogs.[12]

Just as with other White Supremacists, for whom racism and antisemitism are inseparable, Manson said Jews were "bloodsuckers" who "run everything."[13] (Apparently, he was not too dogmatic on this matter, however, and one Family member, Catherine "Gypsy" Share, was Jewish.) Manson also praised Hitler because he "started putting order into the world," and said "I see how the Second World War has made people racists" against Jews.[14] Manson Family member and future Mason friend Good espoused similar views. In one letter, reprinted in *The Manson File*, she said, "Would you cross a horse and a zebra and cause the zebra to lose its stripes? ... Mixing with whites would only destroy their race." Good also denounced the "American nigger type" for being "messed up in a phony Jews' culture."[15]

None of this was lost on Mason, of course. He was fond of Manson's statement denouncing society as "Dead in the Jews' Money." Mason was also sure to point out that Tate's husband, Roman Polanski, was Jewish. As for the fact that Tate was pregnant when she was murdered, Mason said he had no tears, as "it was, after all, a Jew."[16]

The Family and the Brotherhood

James Mason was not the first White Supremacist that Manson was allied with, however. In the early 1970s, the Manson Family had a chaotic relation-ship with the notorious White Supremacist prison gang the Aryan Brotherhood. Even among other prison gangs, the Aryan Brotherhood has stood out for their extreme violence, and different kinds of violence resulted during the two groups' short-lived relationship. But Manson's relationship to them may have paved the way intellectually to the later connection with Mason. (Despite his extensive prisoner contacts, Mason did not appear to have any more than a passing, at most, association with members of the Brotherhood.[17])

The Family-Brotherhood alliance started in 1971 when Manson—already known for his racist views—became worried about being attacked by black prisoners. Manson received protection from the Aryan Brotherhood, appar-ently "in return for Family women providing sex for AB members on the outside." Manson's Aryan Brotherhood contact was Kenneth Como.[18]

Como escaped from custody twice during a brief period. Along with five Family members, he took part in a failed robbery of a Hawthorne, California gun store that resulted in a shootout with police. Back inside, Como ended up in physical altercations with Manson over his romance with Share, a Jewish member of the Family. (They were later married.)[19]

An even more violent set of crimes came from a different Family–Brotherhood pairing. Members of both groups were arrested together for murdering a married couple in Sacramento, California, morbidly burying the woman in the basement of the house they were staying in.[20] A second marriage between a Brotherhood and Family member came out of this as well.[21]

Last, Bobby Beausoleil, the first Family member arrested for murder, was also identified as being in the Aryan Brotherhood, in both a newspaper article and an interview with author Truman Capote. Beausoleil later claimed the article quoted a prison spokesperson who was misinformed, and furthermore that Capote fabricated that part of the interview. Beausoleil also adamantly denied that he was ever in the Aryan Brotherhood, saying "It would have put my life at risk to even claim such an affiliation, especially when it was untrue. Moreover, I have never been an adherent to any racial supremist [sic] or racial separatist ideologies."[22] But regardless of Beausoleil's disavowal of white separatism, he was connected to Moynihan; the latter interviewed him for a 1999 *Seconds* issue, wrote about him for *Apocalypse Culture II*, and even played on a 2018 album Beausoleil made from prison.[23]

The Moon and the Sun

Mason had shown interest in the Manson Family while still in the National Socialist Movement, as early as 1975 praising Fromme's attempted presidential assassination.[24] In 1977, he made his "independent genius" flyer, which he reprinted numerous times. It was a picture of Manson with a quote from the playwright George Bernard Shaw: "Whilst we…the conventional…were wasting our time on education, agitation and organization, some independent genius has taken the matter in hand…"[25] (The original quote was no less outrageous, as it was about Jack the Ripper!) Mason would later say, "I did it almost as a gag, just to rock 'em and shock 'em"—although he also suspected there was something deeper behind it.[26]

Because of the old clipping, Mason knew where Good and Fromme were and he started writing them in September 1980.[27] According to Mason, they soon told him, "We only represent the moon. We only reflect the sun's light. You must go directly to the sun." And so, as an introduction him, they passed on to Manson the letters that Mason had sent them.[28]

On January 18, 1981, Mason wrote Manson for the first time, approaching him as if he was a spiritual seeker. Mason said that the neo-Nazi movement had "been in some trouble for the past several years," and during this time he has been searching for answers. While he said he'd done his best, "Red [Squeaky Fromme] tells me something I've always known: I've only got part of it. She says you have the rest of it."[29]

At the very beginning of their correspondence, Mason sent Manson a copy of the flyer he made of him. In their ensuing discussion, Manson made his recommendation to replace the existing logo with the scales of justice. In June 1981, Mason told Ed Reynolds that he had established a working relationship with Manson.[30]

Manson in SIEGE

In September 1981, Mason said in SIEGE that he had been looking for "truly a personality of extraordinary proportions," just as Hitler was.[31] After this nameless buildup, under the heading section "The Power to Blow Nazis Minds"—"We were supposed to be the ultimate mind-blow," but after Rockwell, "One man succeeded in doing this without so much as trying"—Mason reveals who this Hitler-caliber person is: Manson. One of the Manson Family women (undoubtedly either Good or Fromme) was cited as saying, "Where Rockwell stops, Manson begins." About his own relationship to them, Mason said "We have essentially arrived at the same place having come across widely divergent paths. We have a lot to offer one another."[32]

In March 1982, one of Mason's visitors suggested that a southern California neo-Nazi they knew, Perry "Red" Warthan, become a go-between with Manson. In July, Warthan made his first visit—the first of four he would make that year until his own arrest. Afterward, newspapers made note of this connection.[33]

After the August 1981 SIEGE, in order to placate Karl Hand, the Manson references were tamped down, but in June 1982, there were a few important paragraphs. With the abandonment of traditional right-wing politics, Manson's actions were described as being consistent with parts of *The Turner Diaries*.[34]

> It was once said of Hitler and the Swastika that they represented the "threshold of anger." At the very mention most will curse you, a few will join you, none will remain neutral. I have found the same is true of Manson and the Swastika, even within the Nazi Movement. Manson is the threshold of alienation.[35]

The July 1982 SIEGE also contains a similar short but explosive section, which said neo-Nazis needed a man who could "pick up where Hitler left off." People like fascist writer Frances Parker Yockey had implied that "a man would one day come to take all the loose, unexplained, incomprehensible ends into his hands and make something of them that we could use, that we could understand and follow." In fact, there had been a "historic pattern" of such a savior appearing amidst a crisis.[36]

Mason's description of this savior was tailored to Manson. The coming leader would be "be totally APART, right from birth, from this System." He would be a charismatic leader of "exceptional magnitude," and the System would deem him too dangerous to be free. Third, this coming figure, unlike most of the neo-Nazis of Mason's day, would not be "a pretentious lout all decked out in gaudy uniform and demanding fealty from a handful of pitiful defectives like some idiot."[37]

Mason waited to print more Manson material, but in September 1982, things finally melted down with Hand, who became livid. He told Warthan, "I consider any attempt to connect Manson and Hitler to be slander against the greatest white man to walk the face of this earth since Jesus Christ." To Mason he said that, since 1981, "I have kept quiet in the hope that you would funnel your talents for more constructive purposes, I sincerely hope that I was not wrong."[38]

He was wrong. Hand was essentially correct in his assessment that Mason hoped to turn the NSLF "into the political arm of the Manson family."[39] While Mason held that Manson was "the greatest National Socialist alive today," Hand saw him as "the anti-thesis of National Socialism," merely "a hippie with slight racial overtones."[40]

Mason told Hand they should approach Manson as "an individual of historical magnitude in hopes of just maybe learning something. Let's not make assholes of ourselves in front of this man." Befitting his role as a new acolyte, Mason said, "Manson is, after all, the leader" and the key to their problems. Apparently, this was something "all but the blind" could see.[41] The split became final, albeit cordial, leaving Mason finally free to openly evangelize.

SIEGE resumed its Manson content in October, proclaiming "The next big step forward has been found." The next month's issue, which was the first one published as Universal Order, was an analysis of the Tate murders. (One of its section heads, the "Night of the Buck Knives"—a riff on the "Night of the Long Knives"—would be recycled by others.) Mason said the murders were "prime examples of DIRECT ACTION, and in cases of revolution, or national liberation, direct action alone merits the highest respect."[42]

In January 1983, the Manson Family was held up as an example of how white families should withdraw from the system. "Manson had the right idea about Family. It involved people of the same Race, the same Spirit, coming together for mutual security."[43]

In March 1983, he noted the very usefulness of Manson as a hook. "From direct personal experience I tell you that the name of Manson can be used for the same purposes the name of Hitler can be used…MINUS 95% of the usual hassles which immediately follow." Neo-Nazis, however, did not understand Manson's appeal to "average people"—especially those who were "wild, American, anti-Establishment, and finally, yes, a criminal type."[44]

In 1984, Mason tried to visit Manson, but although his request was approved, by the summer the visit was off. According to Mason's future publisher, Ryan Schuster, it was because "Manson became irate at not being able to secure a private conference room."[45] It may also have been in part or whole a reflection of Manson losing interest in Universal Order. In the August 1984 SIEGE, Mason said he was told, "by this man whom I revere that there is little more of a building nature to be exchanged between us, that I am in a position to take it on my own." In the same breath, however, Mason continued to praise his guru.[46]

> I still consider this man as the only one who can teach or tell me anything. I can't foresee the day when this feeling will change. I can't foresee the day when I will no longer bow before this man as my own mentor and inspiration. The day will never come when this man will cease to be The Leader as long as he is alive.[47]

In December 1984, however, the Manson–Universal Order connection received an unexpected boost in the form of a short article in a supermarket tabloid, "Is Charles Manson the New Hitler?"[48] However, the end of the "building nature" was not the end of their correspondence, and they remained in touch for several more years.[49]

By 1986, SIEGE's praise of Manson had attracted the attention of another person in touch with Manson, Boyd Rice. Rice established a correspondence with Mason and then quickly introduced him to Adam Parfrey. Together with two other Manson fans, Schreck and Moynihan, the four of them would profoundly influence Mason's life.

As SIEGE wound up, Mason took stock of what he learned from Manson. The federal government was also interested; the undercover agent who cozied up to Mason was very interested in his relationship to Manson.[50] In the penultimate issue, he bemoaned the lack of acceptance from the movement. In the last SIEGE, Manson was praised as "the master" of the "total attack or total dropout" philosophy.[51]

In the end, like many spiritual seekers, Mason also expressed his frustration at not being able to grasp what he thought Manson had to offer—the "missing parts" he thought he had found. Manson remained a

> source from which I can still draw understanding and knowledge—from which I can still LEARN. For these past five or six years, I have had a sure feeling that when I could approach Manson's grasp and understanding, I'd have achieved something truly great.[52]

But that never happened. Like all good cult leaders, Manson had promised the key to revelation and wholeness, but did not—could not—deliver.

Initial Manson Worship Reception

Over its six years of publication, SIEGE's veneration of Manson did not gain traction among neo-Nazis. Mason's comrade Reynolds was definitely on board, as obviously was Warthan. Harold Covington made "FREE MANSON" stickers in 1982. Apparently independent of Mason, Joseph Paul Franklin said he was trying to copy Manson during his numerous murders. Some women who were members of the early Nazi skinhead group CASH (Chicago Area Skinheads) were "Manson girls" beforehand.[53]

In 1982, Mason said that others in his movement were calling him "insane" and Manson a "freak and a murderer"; even Mason's allies had "opted to bypass the issue with some embarrassment." Pierce, whom Mason said he had remained "in very close contact" with, got cold feet over this.[54] Tom Metzger was also in this camp; in 1984, he asked permission to reprint one of Mason's articles—but only if the Manson references were removed. (Metzger later said, "I got off the track with Mason when he supported Charlie Manson; that was just too much.")[55] Some neo-Nazi reactions to Manson were even stronger. A member of Detroit's SS Action Group told an interviewer that Manson was an example of someone he would execute without hesitation.[56]

But SIEGE's fusion of National Socialism and Manson would also attract a circle of musicians and publishers who were not traditional White Supremacists.

Environmentalism

Mason was not done promoting Manson yet, and Manson's philosophy continued to influence Mason.

After his imprisonment, Manson had developed a new environmental philosophy, A.T.W.A. (Air-Trees-Water-Animals and sometimes All the Way Alive). Manson Family members Fromme and Good were also both imprisoned for threats and acts of violence in the name of environmentalism. In September 1975, Fromme was arrested for trying to assassinate President Gerald Ford, whom she blamed for failing to stop tree-killing smog. Good threatened to kill more than 170 corporate executives she held accountable for environmental destruction and was arrested that December.[57]

In March 1987, Mason released the trifold pamphlet *Charles Manson: Drugs, Power & Sanity*, which consisted of two open letters from Manson about environmentalism. The first called on President Ronald Reagan to stop the "War on Drugs" because "Your war should be against pollution and for putting trees back before you lose the air, water and wildlife." In the pamphlet's other letter to a journalist, Manson ordered, "<u>Cars must stop. No more trees cut.</u>"[58]

This gave Mason at least a small environmental consciousness. In a 1995 interview, he said had hadn't considered environmental issues before his encounter with Manson. "I was concerned about racial purity to which he replied, 'If the planet is poisoned, there aren't going to be any races'." Nonetheless, by 2002, Mason reversed the argument to make race central again; a pure environment would be meaningless if white people were contaminated by racial mixing.[59]

Red Letters, Blue Letters

Even after they referred him to Manson, Mason stayed in touch with Fromme and Good. Mason got Reynolds to write all three, and in turn the east-coast neo-Nazi got his romantic partners to do the same.

At the start of 1981, Mason tried to procure copies of Rockwell's *This Time the World* and *White Power* to send them. At the time, Fromme was reading Pierce's short biography *George Lincoln Rockwell: A National Socialist Life*, while Good perused *Mein Kampf*.[60] In March, Mason was allowed to visit Good, spending 20 hours with her until the authorities wised up to who he was. Mason continued to write both of them for many years.[61]

Reynolds and Rita, his partner at the time, also wrote them. Mason passed on the women's address in February 1981 and soon after asked if Reynolds could fill a request from Good for a cassette of Pink Floyd's *The Wall*.[62] That summer, Rita was pregnant, and they asked Manson if he would name their baby.[63]

The Pop Cult of Manson

Moynihan's busy schedule, and the scope of the work, frustratingly delayed *Siege*'s release for years. But this turned out to be fortunate as the book's release came as a revival of interest in Manson was at its peak.

Like almost all media stars, Manson's popularity went up and down. The national attention following the murders was accompanied by numerous books, including Ed Sanders's *The Family* (1971), although it was Vincent Bugliosi's *Helter Skelter* (1974) that became a best-selling classic. In the 1980s, a series of TV interviews, including with Tom Snyder in 1981 and Charlie Rose in 1986, were aired.[64] These coincided with SIEGE's focus on Manson.

But it was interest from musicians that would be of crucial importance to *Siege*. Manson was one himself and, although his music never garnered much interest before the murders, the Beach Boys recorded a reworked version of one of his songs. (He did not receive publishing credit for it, as it was apparently payback for favors that band member Dennis Wilson gave the Family when they stayed at his house.)[65] However, after Manson's arrest, interest in his music spiked. His first and best-known record, *Lie: The Love and Terror Cult*, was released in 1970, but songs he recorded in prison would be issued as different albums starting in the 1980s.[66]

Attention also came from the underground music scene starting in the mid-1970s. In particular, the pioneering industrial band Throbbing Gristle was fascinated by him. Their interest spilled over into both later industrial bands as well as the genre's more commercial successor, industrial dance.[67] Punk bands like the Ramones referenced him, and in 1985, Sonic Youth and Lydia Lunch released the Family-inspired song "Death Valley '69".[68]

In the early 1990s, Manson reached his pop culture popularity peak. In 1990, an opera was made about him. In 1992, Trent Reznor, singer of the industrial dance band Nine Inch Nails, rented the house where the Tate murders had been committed; there he recorded both *The Downward Spiral* (which also featured Marilyn Manson) and the *Broken* EP.[69] In 1993, "Manson Can't Surf" t-shirts became a national fad, drawing public condemnation. But the peak of Manson's popularity was when hard rock band Guns N' Roses recorded his song "Look at Your Game, Girl" for their 1993 platinum album *The Spaghetti Incident*.[70] The timing with *Siege*'s release was perfect.

Manson's music also interested the musician Moynihan, who helped White Devil Records release *Commemoration: Sixty Years of Struggle Against Cowardice, Stupidity and Lies* in 1995. Based on tapes that had been given to Mason, it included liner notes from both him and Moynihan.[71] (The label later released a number of other Manson records, including *Manson Speaks*, where he expressed negative views about both Mason and Rice.) Moynihan built a song around Manson's voice for a Blood Axis album. Internationally, numerous bands played songs by or about him.[72]

There were films and videos, too. In 1989, artist Raymond Pettibon released a homemade documentary, *The Book of Manson*, and that year Schreck's *Charles Manson Superstar* also came out. In 1992, Abraxas Circle member Nick Bougas made a documentary about Manson.[73]

When *Siege* was finally released in 1993, it was dedicated to "The Son of Man"—Charles Manson. In addition to the text, it included almost a dozen images related to Manson.

Although 1993 was the second peak in Manson's popularity, the fascination with him has never abated, and new films and books continue to be released. While the Atomwaffen Division continued to venerate Manson, interest in this aspect of Mason's ideology was minor compared with the centrality that it had occupied in the 1980s and 90's. And even though it was certainly not what he was best known for, when Manson died in 2017 amid the height of the Alt Right's popularity, his influence on its neo-Nazi wing was not missed by the media.[74]

Notes

1 Gavin Baddeley, *Lucifer Rising: Sin, Devil Worship & Rock'n'Roll* (London: Plexus, 1999), p.152; *Manson*, dir. Robert Hendrickson and Laurence Merrick, 1973, www.youtube.com/watch?v=qUUtAAdx-XA&t=3981s; Mason interview with Metzger/*Race and Reason* (video).
2 George Petros, ed., *Art That Kills: A Panoramic Portrait of Aesthetic Terrorism, 1984–2001* (Creation Books, 2006), p.189 [Hereafter *Art That Kills*].
3 "Hollywood Nazis" is a derogative term for the "uniform and demonstrate" approach; Mason interview in *NO LONGER A FANzine*, p.13.
4 Ibid.
5 Vincent Bugliosi with Curt Gentry, *Helter Skelter: The True Story of the Manson Murders* (New York: W.W. Norton, 1974), ebook, "Part 4: The Search for the Motive"; Nikolas Schreck, ed., *The Manson File* (New York: Amok Press, 1988), pp.140–41.
6 Harold Jacobs, ed., *Weatherman* (Ramparts Press, 1970), pp.347, 481; "User Clip: Professor Bernardine Dohrn remarks on her Manson Family remarks," *C-Span*, June 7, 2009, www.c-span.org/video/?c4460430/professor-bernardine-dohrn-remarks-manson-family-remarks.
7 Douglas Robinson, "Manson Called a Megalomaniac By Prosecutor as Trial Begins," *NYT*, July 25, 1970, www.nytimes.com/1970/07/25/archives/manson-called-a-megalomaniac-by-prosecutor-as-trial-begins.html; Bugliosi, *Helter Skelter*, "Part 6: The Trial"; Theo Wilson, "Manson Girl's First Attorney Tells of Deal with DA," *Daily News* (New York City), March 6, 1971, www.newspapers.com/image/464036723; Mary Neiswender, "Manson tells why he has a swastika," *Independent* (Long Beach, California), March 12, 1971, p.A5, www.newspapers.com/image/720963953.
8 Jess Bravin, *Squeaky* (Buzz Books/St. Martin's, 1997), ebook, chapter 7.
9 Mason interview in *Iron March* (*Articles*, p.256); SIEGE 10(9) September 1981, p.3 (*Siege*, p.396); Mason to author, January 1, 2023.
10 Bugliosi, *Helter Skelter*, "Part 4: The Search for the Motive".
11 Ibid, "Epilogue: A Shared Madness"; Manson, "The Testimony of Charles Manson, November 19, 1970," in Schreck, ed., *The Manson File*, p.45; "Charles Manson," *Encyclopedia*, p.192.
12 Cited in Jeffrey Kaplan and Heléne Lööw, eds., *The Cultic Milieu: Oppositional Subcultures in an Age of Globalization* (Walnut Creek, California: AltaMira, 2002), p.249.
13 *Charles Manson Superstar*, dir. Nikolas Schreck, 1989, www.imdb.com/title/tt009704, www.youtube.com/watch?v=cI292IidG8M; Schreck, ed., *The Manson File*, p.194.
14 Bugliosi, *Helter Skelter*, "Part 8: Fires in Your Cities"; Kaplan and Lööw, eds., *The Cultic Milieu*, p.250; *Charles Manson Superstar* (video).
15 Sandra Good, "A Letter from Sandra Good," Schreck, ed., *The Manson File*, pp.155–56.
16 SIEGE 11(4) April 1982, p.2 (*Siege*, p.425); SIEGE 11(11) November 1982, p.3 (*Siege*, p.439); *Siege* p.437.
17 Mason said the father of Eva, Mason's teenage girlfriend in Colorado, "had been an A.B. member and loathed Manson"; Mason to author, November 26, 2022.
18 Jeff Guinn, *Manson: The Life and Times of Charles Manson* (New York: Simon & Schuster, 2013), p.386
19 Edward George with Dary Matera, *Taming the Beast: Charles Manson's Time Behind Bars* (New York: St. Martin's Press, 1998), ebook, chapter 4.
20 Ibid.

21 UPI, "Michael Monfort, a convicted double-murderer and onetime associate of...,"
www.upi.com/Archives/1984/05/04/Michael-Monfort-a-convicted-double-murderer-and-onetime-associate-of/7605452491200.

22 Robert Hollis, "3 Inmates Hurt In Wild Fight," *San Francisco Examiner*, April 25, 1973, p.13, www.newspapers.com/image/460220674; "Then It All Came Down" (interview with Beausoleil), in Truman Capote, *Portraits and Observations* (New York: Modern Library, 1993/2013), p.423; "The Farcical Capote Interview," *Bobby BeauSoleil Reference Archive*, https://bbreferencearchive.tumblr.com/post/154781012640/the-capote-interview (Originally written summer 2006. BeauSoleil confirmed that the quote was accurate; email to author, July 21, 2022).

23 "Bobby Beausoleil" (interview with Moynihan), *Seconds* #50, 1999, pp.14–23, reprinted in Steven Blush and George Petros, eds., *.45 Dangerous Minds: The Most Intense Interviews from* Seconds *Magazine* (Creation Books, 2005), p.28 [Hereafter Moynihan, *.45 Dangerous Minds*]; Moynihan, "Inaugurator of the Pleasure Dome: Bobby Beausoleil," in Parfrey, ed., *Apocalypse Culture II* (Venice, California: Feral House, 2000), pp.253–75; Bobby BeauSoleil, *Voodoo Shivaya* (Ajna Offensive, 2018), www.discogs.com/release/12160434-Bobby-Beausoleil-Voodoo-Shivaya; "Bobby BeauSoleil comments on this album release," *Bobby BeauSoleil*, www.bobbybeausoleil.com/voodoo-shivaya.html (written Summer Solstice, 2018).

24 "Heroes of the Revolution," *Ohio National Socialist* #14, p.4. Mason had written Rust that the was going to praise Squeaky "to fire things up a bit and to become operational as the communists have been doing with great success. Such types as the Fromme woman may be a far cry from National Socialists but anyone who would take a crack at Ford can't be all bad"; Mason to Rust, September 29, 1975 [Box 15, Folder 13].

25 The flyer is in *Siege*, 1st ed., p.xx; Schreck, ed., *The Manson File*, p.139.

26 Schuster, "Introduction," *Siege*, p.27; Alan Prendergast, "Beyond the Pale: On the fringe of the fringe, racist guru James Mason preaches a siege mentality," *Westword* 16(48) July 28–August 3, 1993, p.27 (*Articles*, p.55).

27 Mason interview with Schuster (video); SIEGE 11(11) November 1982, p.5.

28 *Art That Kills*, p.189; Schuster, "Introduction," *Siege*, p.29.

29 Mason to Manson, January 18, 1981 [Box 9, Folders 1-3].

30 Mason to Hand, February 19, 1981 [Box 25, Folder 25]; Mason to Reynolds, June 30, 1981 [Box 33, Folder 9].

31 SIEGE 10(9) September 1981, p.3 (*Siege*, p.395).

32 SIEGE 10(9) September 1981, pp.4–6 (*Siege*, pp.404, 406–8).

33 AP, "Manson refuses to help 'good friend' Warthan," *Stockton Record*, December 12, 1982. It was also incorporated into a Universal Order flyer "Lies, Distortions & Half-Truths," which Mason reprinted in both *Siege*, 1st ed., p.301 and *Articles*, p.28. The AP article was based on a longer piece in a local paper; Roger Aylsworth, "Manson: Warthan is on his own," *Chico Enterprise-Record* (California), December 10, 1982, pp.1, 18, www.newspapers.com/image/680270137, www.newspapers.com/image/680270235. See also Appendix 3, "Gary/John Jewell and Perry 'Red' Warthan".

34 SIEGE 11(6) June 1982, p.2 (*Siege*, p.325).

35 Ibid.

36 SIEGE 11(7) July 1982, pp.1–3 (*Siege*, pp.400–401).

37 SIEGE 11(7) July 1982, p.2 (*Siege*, pp.401–2).

38 Hand to Warthan, September 2, 1982; Hand to Mason, September 6, 1982 [both Box 25, Folder 22].

39 Hand to Mason, September 6, 1982; Hand to Warthan, September 17, 1982 [both Box 25, Folder 22].

40 Cited in Schuster, "Introduction," *Siege*, p.29; Hand to Mason, September 16, 1982; Hand to Warthan, September 17, 1982 [both Box 25, Folder 22].

41 Mason to Hand, September 12, 1982; Mason to Hand, September 18, 1982; Mason to Hand, August 30, 1982 [all three Box 25, Folder 22].

42 SIEGE 11(10) October 1982, p.5 (*Siege*, p.418); SIEGE 11(11) November 1982, p.4 (*Siege*, p.441).

43 SIEGE 12(1) January 1983, p.5 (*Siege*, p.448).

44 SIEGE 12(3) March 1983, p.2 (*Siege*, p.460–61).

45 Mason to Reynolds, January 8, 1984 [Box 33, Folder 9]; Mason to Reynolds and Cindy, June 30, 1984 [Box 33, Folder 8]; Schuster, "Introduction," *Siege*, p.29

46 SIEGE 13(8) August 1984, p.4 (*Siege*, pp.422–23).

47 Ibid. In 1987, Mason gave one reason for the cooling of relations was because when Manson received money he would donate it to organizations to "Save the Whales" instead of someone like himself, and "so we sort of parted"; Mason interview with Schuster (video).

48 "Is Charles Manson the New Hitler?," *National Enquirer*, December 25, 1984 (*Articles*, pp.39–40); *Siege*, 1st ed., p. xxvi.

49 The last letter Mason sent was in March 1989. [Box 9, Folder 9].

50 SIEGE 15(4) April 1986, p.2.

51 SIEGE 15(6) June 1986, p.3 (*Siege*, p.493).

52 SIEGE 15(5) May 1986, p.5 (*Siege*, p.431).

53 Mason to Warthan, April 22, 1982 [Box 29, Folder 10]; Tom Callahan, "Race Stalker" (interview with Franklin), *Gallery*, September 1997, p.63; Christian Picciolini, email to author, July 2, 2022.

54 SIEGE 11(6) June 1982, p.2 (*Siege*, pp.325–326); Mason interview with Schuster (video); Metzger to Mason, January 12, 1984.

55 "Radio Wehrwolf—Wolfman's Activism & Entertainment: Tom Metzger, 4/30/18," posted on May 1, 2018 by RWW, https://web.archive.org/web/20180922070515, https://radiowehrwolf.us/2018/05/01/wolfmans-activism-entertainment-tom-metzger. Mason was gracious in agreeing to Metzger's edits around this and other things; Mason to Metzger, January 16, 1984 [both Metzger letters Box 7, Folder 21].

56 Raphael S. Ezekiel, *The Racist Mind: Portraits of American Neo-Nazis and Klansmen* (New York: Viking, 1995), p.179.

57 "Fromme saw Ford as a symbol of government inaction on smog," *CBC*, August 27, 2017, www.cbc.ca/radio/asithappens/as-it-happens-friday-edition-1.4201433/as-it-happened-the-archive-edition-the-fightin-words-episode-part-i-1.4201435 (transcript of a 1976 interview with Barbara Frum); William Endicott, "Sandra Good Indicted in Death Threat Conspiracy," *Los Angeles Times*, December 23, 1975, p.1, www.newspapers.com/image/382807880.

58 He humbly added that, "Only a one-world government will redeem ATWA on earth…. You will do what I say or there will be nothing"; *Charles Manson: Drugs, Power & Sanity* (trifold pamphlet), Universal Order, 1987.

59 Mason interview in *Ohm Clock*, p.7 (*Articles*, p.95); Mason interview with Schuster (video).

60 Mason to Duffy, January 15, 1981 [Box 13, Folder 18].

61 Mason to Reynolds and Rita, March 13, 1981 [Box 33, Folder 9]; Mason to Parfrey, June 18, 1987 [Box 17, Folder 4].

62 Mason to Reynolds, February 26, 1981 [Box 33, Folder 10]; Mason to Reynolds and Rita, March 13, 1981 [Box 33, Folder 9].

63 Rita to Mason, [June-July] 1981 [Box 33, Folder 9].

64 Charles Manson interviewed by Tom Snyder, *The Tomorrow Show*, June 12, 1981, www.imdb.com/title/tt0726337, www.youtube.com/watch?v=T0BFZiKe4i0; Charles Manson interviewed by Charlie Rose, *Nightwatch*, March 7, 1986, www.cbsnews.com/news/charles-manson-defiant-in-1986-cbs-news-interview-happened-in-your-world-not-mine, www.youtube.com/watch?v=H4uT6ou_ZGw.

65 Manson's "Cease to Exist" became the Beach Boys, "Never Learn Not to Love," *20/20* (Capitol, 1969), www.discogs.com/master/78053-The-Beach-Boys-2020; Bugliosi, *Helter Skelter*, "Afterword," note 11.

66 Charles Manson, *LIE: The Love And Terror Cult* (Awareness, 1970), www. discogs.com/release/1506934-Charles-Manson-LIE-The-Love-And-Terror-Cult.

67 Industrial music is sometimes split between early "industrial noise," like Throbbing Gristle and Whitehouse, which played with atonal and no chord sounds. The later genre, "industrial dance," had more traditionally structured songs, and included acts like Ministry and Front 242. Some, like Clock DVA, transitioned from the first to the second.

68 Ramones, "Glad to See You Go," *Ramones Leave Home* (Sire, 1977), www.dis cogs.com/master/39289-Ramones-Leave-Home; "Death Valley '69" (with Lydia Lunch) on Sonic Youth, *Bad Moon Rising* (Blast First/Homestead, 1985), www. discogs.com/release/381545-Sonic-Youth-Bad-Moon-Risingfettinon.

69 Allan Kozinn, "Will the Manson Story Play As Myth, Operatically at That?," *NYT*, July 17, 1990, www.nytimes.com/1990/07/17/arts/will-the-manson-story-play-as-myth-operatically-at-that.html; "The Truth About Trent Reznor's Time in the Manson Murder House," *Grunge*, December 17, 2020, www.grunge. com/226761/the-truth-about-trent-reznors-time-in-the-manson-murder-house.

70 Susan Christian, "Manson Shirt Brings O.C. Firm Notoriety: Fashion: Some decry the garment, but the two brothers behind it capitalize on the attention," *Los Angeles Times*, December 14, 1993, www.latimes.com/archives/la-xpm-1993-12-14-mn-1845-story. html; Guns N' Roses, "Look At Your Game, Girl," *The Spaghetti Incident* (Geffen, 1993), www.discogs.com/master/9620-Guns-N-Roses-The-Spaghetti-Incident.

71 Charles Manson, *Commemoration* (White Devil, 1995), www.discogs.com/ master/1138588-Charles-Manson-Commemoration; "The Storm Before the Calm: An Interview with Blood Axis" (by Wulfing One), *EsoTerra #5*, 1995, https://web.archive.org/web/20010217112633, www.esoterra.org/moynihan.htm (*Articles*, pp.196–97, 199).

72 Charles Manson, *Manson Speaks* (White Devil Records, 1995), www.discogs. com/release/759982-Charles-Manson-Manson-Speaks; Blood Axis, "Herr, Nun Laß in Frieden," *The Gospel of Inhumanity* (Cthulhu/Storm, 1996), www.discogs. com/release/188151-Blood-Axis-The-Gospel-Of-Inhumanity.
    William Scanlan Murphy told Bugliosi that, as of 1994 and in Europe alone, there were at least seventy bands that had songs by or about Manson; Bugliosi, *Helter Skelter*, "Afterword".

73 *Charles Manson Superstar* (video); *The Book of Manson*, dir. Raymond Pettibon, 1989, www.imdb.com/title/tt0096967; *Charles Manson Then and Now 1992*, dir. Nick Bougas, 1992, www.imdb.com/title/tt2426948.

74 See, for example, Adam Lusher, "Charles Manson: Neo-Nazis hail serial killer a visionary and try to resurrect fascist movement created on his orders," *Independent*, November 20, 2017, www.independent.co.uk/news/world/americas/charles-manson-death-dead-serial-killer-neo-nazis-resurrect-fascist-movement-cult-family -universal-a8065781.html.

9
UNIVERSAL ORDER AS IDEA AND ORGANIZATION

Universal Order referred to two separate but overlapping things for James Mason. First, it was his new conception of National Socialism, influenced by Charles Manson. This had a much more spiritual, timeless, and universal approach than more traditional forms, and it also incorporated political strategies taken from Manson—although Mason only sketched it out in broad outlines. The second was the use of the actual name Universal Order. This was a publishing imprint, but at first it was also presented as—if not exactly an organization, then at least a name to use for political work. Mirroring Universal Order as a philosophy, its meaning was also opaque and amorphous.

Universal Order as Idea

In 1978, Mason had already advocated a complete transformation to create a new kind of revolutionary National Socialist consciousness.[1] Now he took this idea a step further.

In 1981, Manson had suggested the name Universal Order, which Mason used starting the next year. Having already been grasping for a way to move beyond the ANP/NSWPP approach, Mason said that "For me personally, Manson provided the missing parts" of his new ideology.[2]

This came out in the wash as a kind of National Socialism Plus, a revolutionary ideology that he claimed was neither Left nor Right.[3] (One could also call it Mason-Manson-National Socialism.) While obviously a neo-Nazi vision, it also reflected Mason's contention that his version of National Socialism was, could, or should be a clean break from the traditional Far Right. Nonetheless, as with other parts of Manson's influence, Mason talked

DOI: 10.4324/9780429200090-13

about Universal Order in broad outlines without ever developing it in depth. It often seemed like something he could see and experience but not quite put into words.

Mason introduced the idea even before his break with the NSLF. In the September 1981 SIEGE, he wrote that the ideas of Hitler and Manson were different expressions of the same thing. In the first post-NSLF issue in late 1982, Mason declared that Universal Order "is everything National Socialism is and much, much more," in particular because it had a living leader. He also described Universal Order's other elements as: being oriented to the present and "uniquely 'American'," having no ties to "Conservatism or the Right Wing (or the Left, for that matter)," and that youth were supposedly interested in it. Later, he would stress it was "a break with the past."[4] In March 1983, he emphasized that Universal Order was a broad notion

> as opposed to some kind of localized, specialized, exclusive "order." When order is truly universal—and only then—it will be right, proper and, most of all, everlasting. This will include National Socialism, of course, and by direct implication, it will provide no place anywhere in the universe for alien "order."[5]

Universal Order emerged out of National Socialism because, according to Mason, that's where "the complete Truth has resided for so long, where enough idealistic and altruistic individuals have rallied and fought." But it was only an elite vanguard of neo-Nazis who could understand it was "what they had been reaching and striving for" since the NSWPP's splintering. Elsewhere in SIEGE, Mason wrote that Universal Order was not a dogma to impose on people. Instead, it was going to help create "whole people, real people who can see, think and act independently, free of any artificial, phony input" created by a corrupt society.[6]

Mason would suggest to a Christian preacher that Universal Order's balance, represented by the swastika-bejeweled scales which graced SIEGE's cover, also included *both* hate and love. Mason pointed out that if there was only love, as Christianity has advocated, "the scales of justice would be awfully lopsided...ours are nice and even."[7] (This dualistic vision is a clear example of the undercurrent of Manson's gnostic thinking that permeated Mason's later thought.)

Mason continued to emphasize that Universal Order encompassed National Socialism. In a 1987 interview, he said, "The connection with Manson doesn't interrupt, or interfere with, or contradict in any way my National Socialist beliefs—it's an extension of them." In 2003, he said the primary reason he used a different term was "to give our certain line of thought a distinguishing title so as to at least attempt separate it from the more conservative takes on National Socialism."[8]

Especially post-SIEGE, he described Universal Order as encompassing Charles Manson, George Lincoln Rockwell, and Jesus, which in turn reflected Manson's philosophy that "The Truth is One." According to Mason, its name would change in different places and times. In the time of Jesus, it was Christianity; in Germany in the 1920s, National Socialism; and in 1982, it was Universal Order.[9]

In a 1994 article, Mason made a rare in-depth elaboration of what Universal Order was. He described it as inclusive of "widely divergent backgrounds: Left, Right, Communist, Nazi, Christian, Satanist." Although on their own each could grasp only partial answers, Manson's vision of an underlying truth "removed the artificial and divisive labels and barriers." (The next year, Mason specifically added that the Universal Order would be based on racial separatism and antisemitism. This would probably have come as a surprise to the Communists and non-Identity Christians whom Mason envisioned as part of it.)[10] This One Truth was not just an overarching philosophy, it also had an active component. It required

A basic change in thought and perception. We needed to get away from pretending "that which is" as that which is, is solely the dominion of the System, rotting and decaying as it is. Instead, we had to embrace and represent what was missing, what was called for, and what would ultimately come.[11]

In 1994, Mason showed both a profound pessimism and optimism. He now said that Universal Order wasn't a political program; instead, it was an imperative to wait until "Nature" would "reassert mastery over everything" with no regard to people, rights, or profit. After a "massive purging perhaps…a new humanity will emerge….but Universal Order will have been reestablished." Until that time, however, Mason was optimistic about what belief in Universal Order provided believers. "It removes doubt and fear. It installs courage and tranquility. It provides purpose and meaning."[12] Now that Mason had developed a spiritual outlook by any other name, the stage was set for his quickly approaching embrace of Christianity—albeit, like many of his views, a version of his own making.

Universal Order as Organization

Universal Order was also the name Mason used to put on his publications starting with SIEGE's severance from the NSLF. Occasionally, Universal Order also had some elements of an organization or political project—or, as Mason put it later, a "front."

This wasn't unusual. The annals of neo-Nazism are filled with "parties" consisting entirely of one man's post office box and a publication of dubious quality. At the same time as SIEGE, in the more general world of fanzine and underground publishing, there was a vogue for creating faux organizations; they were often just as small as their neo-Nazi counterparts.

On rare occasions, Universal Order was directly portrayed as a concrete political entity, especially by Ed Reynolds. He used the name for his local projects as if they were actually affiliates of a national organization, and this use was obviously okay with Mason.

What Universal Order unquestionably was the name Mason used for his publications. This included not just SIEGE but also flyers and pamphlets.

At the very beginning, Mason did seem open to the idea of Universal Order having some kind of organizational structure, possibly structured with different nodes for the dissemination of propaganda. In particular, in October 1982—before the first post-NSLF SIEGE was even out—Mason wrote Reynolds, "Can you drop me a line indicating whether you want to be given as a unit of Universal Order or not as I'd like to list a couple of addresses with the December issue." And so it was possible that, if there had been greater interest in the idea, Universal Order might have ended up with far more structure than it did. (In 2022, Mason denied this, although he said that "when folks offer their help in getting the word out, I accept.")[13]

That November, Mason certainly hoped to *portray* Universal Order as an organization to ABC News, which expressed interest in a feature story. Lacking an actual party, Mason proposed a charade with roles played by himself, Reynolds, and Manson. Mason told Reynolds that

> Charlie is leader; I'm the street-side chairman; We're basically underground at this point; Your particular cell consists of a few dozen current and former Nazi members, etc. If you want, you can call yourself East Coast Organizer.[14]

Of course, nothing of the sort existed. The next month, Mason's bluster grew even bolder when the Associated Press ran his claim that Universal Order had 200 members.[15] If Universal Order had no pretense of being an organization at that point, Mason certainly sought to give the impression that it already was.

It was Reynolds who would actually take the name on for activist work. In December 1983, he wrote Mason to say that although he still had "affections for Redneck, Inc. and U-Boat Reunions," he agreed that the old Klan and neo-Nazi politics were going nowhere.

> So please count on me as 100% UNIVERSAL ORDER. I'm not expecting (nor want) a drum roll, a uniform, a membership card and certificate. A mere roll of thunder and flash of lightning will suffice… smile.[16]

Reynolds used the Universal Order name on several flyers. A very crude one in 1983 gave typical White Supremacist talking points and used racial slurs; a later one advocated White Student Unions. While these were hardly Mason's politics, nonetheless SIEGE encouraged readers to write Reynolds—"A comrade we are proud to have active with us in Universal Order."[17]

In a few instances, Reynolds used Universal Order to refer to an actual activist group rather than just a contact point. In September 1984, he told Mason that a project he was working on with others, "The Heathen Brotherhood of the Universal Order," was going to become a church and establish a "home base" in Schuylkill County, Pennsylvania. A four-page manifesto, "Why We Are National Socialists," undoubtedly written by Reynolds, was attributed to the Delaware/Pennsylvania Unit of the Universal Order. Last, in 1991, one could write the Universal Order at Reynolds's Memphis, Tennessee post office box, which was doing double duty as the Shelby County White Knights' address.[18]

Despite these flashes of Universal Order taking a more tangible form (or at least pretending it did), Mason soon became more explicit that it had no structure. Parallel to this, as Mason noted, the NSWPP changed its name to New Order in January 1983—just months after Mason had started publishing as Universal Order. One reviewer noted that SIEGE's change from the NSLF to Universal Order also denoted Mason's move from advocating guerilla war to waiting for social collapse.[19]

The March 1983 SIEGE said, "Universal Order is more a concept than the name of any group or organization." Even as he was moving away from any suggestion of an organization, the "more" was perhaps the operative word and still left some wiggle room. Nearer to the end of SIEGE's run, Mason became more concrete about his rejection of organization. The July 1985 issue said,

> Universal Order is not the name of an organization. It is the name given by Charles Manson to the Idea. There is no membership, no provision for any membership, there is no corporation, there is no handstanding, no chest-thumping, no meetings of any kind…. There is no leader.[20]

In the 1990s and '00s, Mason repeated firmly that the Universal Order was not an organization and did not have a membership. But it was still *something*. During a 1991 appearance on a radio show alongside Mason, Michael Moynihan was referred to twice, without objection, as a representative of the "organization" Universal Order.[21]

In 1993, Mason said, regarding a potential classified ad, that he could "utilize the old Universal Order front again."[22] Perhaps "front" was the ideal way to refer to Universal Order as mostly-an-idea-but-also-something-with-a-nebulous-form. In 1994, the label was also used for an exhibit at an art show in Seattle.

Other Post-SIEGE Uses

After SIEGE stopped, other than references to Mason's philosophy and as a publishing imprint, the name would still be occasionally used. A playful example—by neo-Nazi standards, at least—was when Mason and Reynolds sent a proposal to Milton Bradley Company to add new rules to the board game Stratego. Coming a year after the 1995 Oklahoma City bombing, these included the option of using a Ryder Truck loaded with a bomb. The proposal was sent under the cover of the Universal Order Game Company.[23]

While Mason was in prison, his website was named *Universal Order*. The press that released the second edition of *Siege*, Black Sun, had a link on their website explaining the concept of Universal Order.[24] And when Mason was rediscovered in the 2010s, his new followers would continue to promote his philosophy under that name.

Notes

1 "New Year's Greeting: The Strength of the N.S.M.," *National Socialist Bulletin* 7(11) January 1978, p.1.
2 Mason interview in *NO LONGER A FANzine* #5, p.13.
3 In addition to Manson, Mason's philosophy was influenced by Savitri Devi's Hitler worship. It also had similarities to Julius Evola's vision of postwar fascist violence. However, any influence of the Italian fascist on Mason was either indirect or merely reacting to similar circumstances, as Mason first read Evola in 2021; Mason to author, November 26, 2022.
4 SIEGE 10(9) September 1981, p.5 (*Siege*, p.405); SIEGE 11(11) November 1982, p.5 (*Siege*, p.444); Mason interview in *Ohm Clock* (*Articles*, p.94).
5 This also appeared to be a swipe at his former comrades in the newly named New Order. SIEGE 12(3) March 1983, p.1 (*Siege* p.458).
6 SIEGE 12(3) March 1983, p.1 (*Siege* p.458); *Siege* pp.447–48.
7 Mason interview with Bob Larson on *Talk-Back* ("Neo-Nazi Satanism"), June 29, 1993; "James Mason on Talk-Back with Bob Larson" (video), uploaded by White Line, June 6, 2019, https://altcensored.com/watch?v=lpG8SFT0N4A
8 Mason interview with Ken Swezey and Brian King, February 19, 1987; "The AMOK Interview" (video), uploaded by SiegeKultur, January 22, 2023, https://odysee.com/$/embed/@siegekultur:b/AMOK-Interview:3?r=AwrpwTHb1zE3qBv ojv7zc62NuKuE8ySM (also cited in *Siege*, 559); "Universal Order: An Interview with James Mason" (by AAC), 2003 (*Articles*, p.238).
   See also Mason's 1995 description of Universal Order: "Well, it's National Socialism. It does have its differences over Adolf Hitler's National Socialism and Cmdr. Rockwell's National Socialism"; Mason interview in *NS Worldview*, p.16.
9 Mason interview with Schuster (video). For more on these relationships, see Appendix 5, "Christianity".
10 Mason, "Universal Order," *Rise* #II, Winter Solstice 1994 (*Articles*, p.84); Mason interview in *NS Worldview*, p.16.
11 Mason interview in *Strength Through Joy Productions* (*Articles*, p.145).
12 Mason, "Universal Order," *Rise* (*Articles*, p.84).
13 Mason to Reynolds, October 20, 1982 [Box 33, Folder 9]; Mason to author, November 26, 2022.
14 Mason to Reynolds and Rita, November 23, 1982 [Box 33, Folder 9].

15 AP, "Manson Refuses to Help 'Good Friend' Warthan".

16 Reynolds to Mason, March 10, 1983 [Box 33, Folder 9].

17 "The Problem in Willington Is…" (flyer), [1983] [Box 33, Folder 9]; SIEGE 13(5) May 1984, p.6; "White People! What Are You Waiting For? Now Is the Time to Work for a White Student Union on <u>Your</u> Campus" (flyer), [spring 1986] [Box 33, Folder 7].

18 Reynolds to Mason, September 26, 1984; "Why We Are National Socialists," [summer 1984], p.4 [both Box 33, Folder 8]; "Shelby County White Nights" (flyer) and Universal Order, Memphis Tennessee, "Public Service Announcement," [1992] [Box 33, Folder 6].

19 SIEGE 12(2) February 1983, p.1 (*Siege*, p.450); Dominic Hampshire, "Siege Mentality" (review of *Siege*), *Scorpion* #18, p.35 (*Articles*, p.62).

20 SIEGE 14(7) July 1985, p.3.

21 Moynihan, Rice, and Mason interview with Bob Larson/*Talk Back*, on July 8, 1991 ("Manson Maniacs"); "James Mason, Michael Moynihan, and Boyd Rice VS Bob Larson" (video), uploaded by EC, August 2, 2022, www.youtube.com/watch?v=UeI8WubQ4RM

22 Mason to Parfrey, December 15, 1993.

23 Universal Order Game Company to Milton Bradley Game Co., July 1996 [Box 33, Folder 4].

24 "What Is Universal Order?" (link leads to unarchived page), *Black Sun Productions*, https://web.archive.org/web/20030409225244, http://www.blacksunpublications.com/Manson.htm

10

LIFE AFTER SIEGE

Although SIEGE was ended in summer 1986, James Mason's activities did not. Between the end of the run and the release of the *Siege* anthology in 1993, three important things would happen to Mason.

The most important was his encounter with the Abraxas Clique, who took his work and disseminated it in their periodicals, books, and video—culminating in the creation of the book itself. Second, Mason would be arrested for child pornography involving a teenager, which would portend his later, more serious charges. Third, his criminal and financial problems led him to move to Colorado.

Mason also continued to write, now for Tom Metzger's *WAR* as well as Michael Merritt, who had inherited the SIEGE subscription list. And in the spring of 1987, Mason printed the last important piece of literature he would do for a number of years to come, the pamphlet *Charles Manson: Drugs, Power & Sanity*, which would eventually make its way to Michael Moynihan.

Pictures of Girls

Starting 1988, Mason was once again in legal trouble, something which would culminate in his spending the second half of the 1990s in prison. In 1973, Mason had served six months for assault, but he stayed out of law's arms during both his period of sectarian maneuvering as well as while publishing SIEGE. During this time, he saw many of his comrades arrested, was closely monitored by the FBI, and apparently became the target of an entrapment attempt. But when legal trouble finally caught up to him, it was not because of politics, but rather his predilection for 15- and 16-year-old girls.

DOI: 10.4324/9780429200090-14

In November 1988, Mason was raided by police for the first time; they were looking for child pornography. Mason claimed that he took the pictures by request for a 15-year-old girl and her husband. (However, the local newspaper said the pictures were of two sisters who were 15 and 17.) Mason was originally indicted for five counts ("one count of gross sexual imposition, three counts of child pornography and one count of child pornographic material") and faced ten years. In the end, he pled guilty to a single misdemeanor, "illegal use of a minor in nudity-oriented material," and in September 1989 was sentenced to 30 days.[1] Bizarrely, Mason spent 1990 and early 1991 in court trying to get his pictures back.[2]

Although he was working with the Abraxas Clique during this same period, Mason had practically dropped out of neo-Nazi circles. In early 1990, he told Reynolds that at that point he had fewer than six correspondents—a number that included his old comrade.[3]

In August 1991, however, he was arrested again for possessing the same pictures; he had not just made copies of them but bragged to a reporter about this. Now he was charged with a fourth-degree felony. Mason had been making his living by renting out properties he owned in Chillicothe, but he ran into financial trouble, which was compounded by an IRS audit.[4]

Colorado, Ho!

With the walls closing in around him, Mason packed up his belongings and, along with his girlfriend, bought a house sight-unseen in Colorado. In January 1992, they moved to Las Animas, a town of 2,500 which was three hours southeast of Denver—where two musicians who were Mason's allies, Boyd Rice and Michael Moynihan, were living.[5]

Coming back to Ohio, on April 20, 1992, he pled guilty in return for a $600 fine and a suspended six-month sentence "with the stipulation that Mason not return to Ohio without permission from his parole officer." The Ohio authorities, thrilled to have Mason out of their hair, reportedly gave their Colorado counterparts fair warning about what they had just inherited.[6] For the next few years, Mason dallied in Las Animas, receiving visitors, hanging out, collecting videos and furniture, and helping Moynihan put together *Siege* for publication.[7] Mason told him that

> I don't care if I die as a direct result of or during the course of the fall of the System. I just want to <u>see</u> it even if I can't be at least partially responsible for it.
>
> And the only thing holding me back is: (a) Being broke and; (b) Being isolated.[8]

But after the book came out, Mason had plenty to do.

Notes

1 Mason to Rice, December 12, 1988 [Box 9, Folder 20]; Lou Moliterno, "Convicted Nazi Wants Nude Photos Back," *Chillicothe Gazette*, February 8, 1991, p.3A, www.newspapers.com/image/292693046; Prendergast, "Beyond the Pale," p.30 (*Articles*, p.57).

2 Mason to Reynolds, February 2, 1990 [Box 33, Folder 8]; Moliterno, "Convicted Nazi".

3 Mason to Reynolds, February 11, 1990 [Box 33, Folder 8].

4 Moliterno, "Pictures Land Man in Trouble," *Chillicothe Gazette*, August 27, 1991, p.1, www.newspapers.com/image/292754399; Mason, "Jacob's Trouble," *Out of the Dust*, vol. 1, pp.209–10; Mason to "NS Comrade," March 25, 1986 [Box 25, Folder 24].

5 Mason interview with Schuster (video); Mason, "My Crime and My Time," *Out of the Dust*, vol. 1, p.168.

6 "Nude-Photo Case Settled with Guilty Plea," *Dayton Daily News* (Ohio), April 22, 1992, p.6, www.newspapers.com/image/408836167; Mason, *Out of the Dust*, vol. 1, p.167; Prendergast, "Double Exposure: Underage Girls, A Nazi with a Camera, and Partying Cops—What's Wrong with This Picture?," *Westword*, September 20, 1995, p.16, www.westword.com/news/double-expo sureunderage-girls-a-nazi-with-a-camera-and-partying-cops-whats-wrong-with-this-picture-5055531 (*Articles*, p.114).

7 Mason to Reynolds and Beth Helen, July 13, 1994 [Box 33, Folder 3].

8 Mason to Moynihan, September 21, 1992 [Box 11, Folder 2].

PART IV

Countercultural Fascism
(1986–1995)

11

THE ABRAXAS CLIQUE AND COUNTERCULTURAL FASCISM

The third section of this study consists primarily of profiles of four cultural figures who comprised the "Abraxas Clique": Boyd Rice, Adam Parfrey, Nikolas Schreck, and Michael Moynihan.[1] Rice, who acted as the key node in the network, was an industrial musician who performed as NON and collaborated with an array of other musicians. Parfrey was a publisher who co-edited *EXIT* magazine and later founded the well-known press Feral House. Schreck, a Satanist, created both a book and documentary on Charles Manson. And Moynihan was an industrial and neofolk musician as well as a publisher. All four were united by their membership in the Abraxas Foundation, a faux think tank. The name came from Rice, and Schreck shared Manson's interest in Abraxas, the Gnostic deity who embodied both good and evil; Rice even said that Manson bestowed the name on him.[2]

A detailed look at the Abraxas Clique illuminates their relationship both to James Mason and to neo-Nazism more generally. The latter was a relationship they sometimes flaunted but mostly denied—occasionally doing both simultaneously.

Four separate but overlapping terms will be used in this section. The Abraxas Foundation refers to projects which specially carried that label. The Abraxas Clique refers to the work of the four, including before and after the Foundation's existence, as well as projects not specifically done under that label. The Abraxas Circle is the name for both those in the Abraxas Clique and the people around them; it existed from the late 1980s through the mid-1990s. As the Abraxas Clique members joined up with *Seconds* magazine, their networks expanded even further into the extended Abraxas Circle, some of whose members had

DOI: 10.4324/9780429200090-16

little connection to the original four. Taken together, this expanding network made up a distinct scene of musicians, writers, publishers, and artists.

The Abraxas Clique encountered Mason within the framework of what has been referred to as the "underground" counterculture of the 1980s. It was through this milieu that word of Mason and SIEGE spread and where his writings and flyers were circulated for the first time outside neo-Nazi circles. The Abraxas Clique were able to openly disseminate Mason's work by playing on the political ambiguity of the particular cultural niche they were in, which was obsessed with extremes and among which there were others who shared their social and political views. And their work with him was part of a larger project they were engaged in which sought to create a countercultural fascist lineage.

The Underground Culture of the 1980s

The Abraxas Clique facilitated their modest fame, notoriety, and influence by engaging in a relentless reciprocal promotion of themselves. In addition to playing on and releasing each other's records and touring together, they reviewed, interviewed, and published each other.[3] And the Abraxas Circle which grew around them did the same.

The four were all based in a particular corner of the underground culture of the 1980s which had emerged primarily out of the British punk rock scene of the 1970s. In turn, punk was only one of a number of postwar subcultures and musical genres which developed mostly in both the United States and Britain, including mods, skinheads, and goths. Towering behind these was the hippie movement of the late 1960s, which had an explosive, global effect on cultural and politics—and which the later subcultures were all reacting to in different ways. At first, these subcultures were embraced mostly by teenagers and those in their early twenties, and the line between the different subcultural niches was often quite permeable.[4]

Rock bands had used Nazi imagery and references starting in the 1960s, and early punk had a definite obsession with it. This was generally used as an apolitical provocation—the most notorious example being the swastika t-shirt worn by Sex Pistols bassist Sid Vicious—but it was also used in critical and ironic ways. Intent aside, rock bands continued to use Nazi imagery throughout the 1980s. But it was the skinhead scene that played the most important role in the underground culture's crossover with the organized neo-Nazi movement.

The skinhead movement had its origins in Jamaica but, in the late 1960s, developed into a coherent subculture as a working-class youth movement in Britain. Skinheads sported a standardized and distinct look which included shaved heads, jeans, Fred Perry shirts, suspenders ("braces"), and Doc Martin boots. However, its members were primarily known for violence. Owing to its origins, it was originally a multiracial movement which included black members—although this did not mean it wasn't racist. One 1970 news article said, "Next to beating up hippies and soccer referees, skinheads enjoy picking fights with Britain's Pakistani population, a sport known as 'Paki bashing.'"[5]

By the 1970s, the fascist National Front had some success in recruiting skinheads, although it was only in the early 1980s that there arose a distinct faction committed to neo-Nazi politics, centered around the Oi! band Skrewdriver. (Only a minority of skinheads have ever been White Supremacists, however. While skinheads have always leaned rightward, especially toward patriotic nationalism, there have long been explicitly antifascist and leftist skinheads as well.)[6]

As the decade went on, the larger underground music scene included new influences which went beyond punk and its direct descendent hardcore (a faster and more stripped-down version). They all built off punk's "do it yourself" ethos of participants forming their own bands, publications, and record companies. There was a revival of older genres of guitar-based music like rockabilly, garage, and surf rock; these scenes, in particular, became known for more conservative social views. Alongside this was an experimental noise scene that included, but went beyond the scope of, industrial music.

Bands like Joy Division laid the groundwork for the goth (gothic) genre, which had come out of punk at the end of the 1970s. In the early 1980s, there became an offshoot genre called neofolk. This dark form of folk, mixed in with European medieval music, was played on acoustic instruments, frequently included references to Nazism and other kinds of fascism, and was connected to the industrial scene.

There were non-musical elements, too. The media of the 1980s—especially radio and TV—tended to be capital-heavy, top-down, and with a limited range of views. In contradiction to this, a whole array of independent media developed. There was a strong visual artists element, including painters, graphic designers, and filmmakers, often propelled by the new media technologies.

Independent publishing houses sprang up, with the most important being (from Right to Left politically) Amok Press and Feral House, Loompanics, RE/Search, and Autonomedia. But the underground's most important media were fanzines, which quickly became the primarily method of communication and would play a notable role in spreading Mason's work. These periodicals were self-published, typically in small runs and made on photocopiers. Most fanzines were focused on music, but others covered a wide range of interests, from fiction to art, spirituality to humor, and philosophy and lifestyle. A few fanzines, like Peter Sotos's *Pure* and Mike Diana's *Boiled Angel*, became embroiled in legal trouble.

One end of this music and publishing milieu, sometimes called simply "extreme culture," pushed the envelope of the existing fascination with extremes. It was less focused on music and more connected to avant-garde artistic and intellectual work. While its immediate origins were parallel and intersecting with the emergence of punk in Britain in the mid-1970s, like so many parts of the underground culture it only came to the United States later. In the mid-1980s, a scene based around this emerged in downtown New York City. A sympathetic description of this current said it encompassed the "transgressive, subversive, pornographic and forbidden." Influences included rock music, drugs, fringe philosophical and spiritual figures, and murderers. One assessment said that "Only in retrospect does the scene come into focus; at the time it seemed to be simply a super-alienated version of Punk."[7]

Other parts of extreme culture included body modification, Satanism and occult spirituality, pro-situ politics, conspiracy theories, UFOology, and an interest in National Socialism—of both the original and postwar variety. There was a special fascination with serial killers, and it was popular to write to them and collect their prison art. Simultaneously, in the broader culture, there was a revival of interest in Manson which would culminate in the early 1990s.

Two publishers in the New York City scene would become of special importance to Mason. Parfrey, who would go on to form Feral House press, was co-publisher of the art magazine *EXIT*. It would be the first place to give Mason exposure in this scene, which Parfrey dubbed "apocalypse culture." Although Parfrey had an on-again, off-again relationship with the publication's co-editor George Petros, the two would travel in the same publishing circles for decades. Parfrey also established a relationship with Mason.

In the United States in the 1980s, neo-Nazism was as popular as it had ever been in the postwar era, as a new generation followed the mostly fading remnants of the NSWPP and its splinters (with the exception of Pierce's National Alliance). A new wave of White Supremacists was rising. Neo-Nazis now worked more closely with others, and some fused National Socialism with other White Supremacist ideologies.

But this growth was in no small part because of the Nazi skinheads, who formed an adjacent scene to the punk/hardcore scene and underground culture. While skinheads were seen in the United States since at least 1980, it was only around 1985 that they started to form explicitly racist gangs. By 1987, the skinhead movement had grown significantly, and in 1988 it exploded.[8] This growth was fueled by a media frenzy, including coverage in national newspapers and magazines but most importantly on national TV talk shows. (Tom Metzger even said, "After *Oprah* and *Geraldo*, our recruiting went up at least 100 percent."[9])

According to the monitoring groups which tracked the White Supremacist movement (including the SPLC, ADL, and smaller groups), the numbers of Nazi skinheads went from the hundreds to the low thousands. According to the ADL's count, in October 1988 there were 2,000 Nazi skinheads—an increase of between 500 and 1,000 since that February alone. Other monitors gave even higher estimates.[10]

Parallel to this was the "Satanic Panic," a focus of the Christian Right and other conservatives. Two currents fed into this folk panic. The first consisted of accusations of ritual abuse and murder by Satanists. As part of the then-current vogue for repressed memories, people came forth with claims about having been victims of these rituals. At the same time, many heavy metal bands incorporated Satanic symbols and made references to Satanism in their lyrics, although relatively few took it to heart. Regardless, just as punk's use of anarchist symbolism helped spur more serious interest in that political movement, heavy metal helped spread Satanism—and in doing so fueled religious conservatives' reactions.

Because of this folk panic, attention turned to Anton LaVey's Church of Satan. Founded in the mid-1960s, it had been crucial to the spread of modern Satanism. The Church's popularity had faded in the 1970s, but it now took advantage of this new wave of interest. Its representatives now went on mainstream media to defend, and promote, their beliefs.

With this backdrop of the notoriety of a new wave of neo-Nazis and Satanists, it was not surprising that at least some in the underground would develop a relationship with both. And here stepped in the Abraxas Clique. They were deeply embedded in this culture of extremes, including being adjacent to the Nazi skinheads, and by the late 1980s had developed relationships with LaVey and the Church of Satan.

Social Darwinism

The Abraxas Clique was united by their interest in Manson, LaVey, and Mason. Especially in Mason's case, this was facilitated by a number of shared reactionary interests, which weren't explicitly racist or antisemitic but which created common intellectual ground with National Socialism. Many of these shared ideas were not typical talking points for Mason or his neo-Nazi contemporaries, but as they were influential in the creation of National Socialist ideology in the 1930s, they remained part of the ideological assumptions of neo-Nazism.

There was an explicitly and deeply misanthropic element. On several occasions, Abraxas Clique members expressed the need for a global reduction in population through mass murder. For example, on a radio show, Rice said that 75 percent of humanity should be killed. In the interviews for 8/8/88, Schreck said, "we would like to see most of the human race killed off" as part of their program of "forming an elite, a master race." On Metzger's TV show, he said, "I consider 'human' to be an ugly word. I think most of humanity is debased and deformed, and evolution[arily] unfit to continue."[11]

These views seamlessly slid into an interest in Social Darwinism by the Abraxas Clique and LaVey. Social Darwinist philosophies, which emerged in the late nineteenth century, hold that life is primarily defined by a struggle—"nature red in tooth and claw"—in which "only the strong survive." (Depending on the version, this struggle can be between either individuals or groups, including races.) Hitler was influenced by Social Darwinism, and correspondingly after World War Two it was largely considered a discredited science. This did not stop the Abraxas Clique; indeed, it may have been a selling point as one of many philosophies which Colin Campbell dubbed the "cultic milieu"—ideas that exist outside of mainstream acceptance and that form a pool where they cross-pollinate with other. Rice believed the "primal law" of humanity was that "The strong dominate the weak and the clever dominate the strong."[12]

The attitudes of Rice and LaVey were deeply influenced by Ragnar Redbeard's turn-of-the-century Social Darwinist book *Might is Right*, which propagandized a crude version of these views. Included in this was that power was necessarily expressed through violence—itself a positive attribute. Moynihan also emphasized how close the Social Darwinist views were to National Socialism.[13]

Parfrey would often express an interest in dysgenics, the study of how a particular population inherits undesirable traits, as well as the related field of eugenics, which seeks to either promote or curb inheritable traits. He was especially interested in the role dysgenics played in serious health issues among relatives, although he cast this in racial terms to Mason—just as Schreck did with Metzger. As part of this, Parfrey harbored a particular contempt for disabled people.

Their disdain for equality was the corollary to their belief in a hierarchical society. While Mason was interested in this at the racial level, Rice and LaVey were focused on individuals. The Abraxas Clique also rejected the Left because it sought social equality. (However, they did not take issue with the Left's opposition to capitalism. This they did not espouse any love for, and sometimes condemned parts of.)

Opposition to feminism permeated the group. Rice, who would be arrested for domestic violence, loudly embraced misogyny. Parfrey would blame "ultra-feminists" specifically for attempting to cancel a talk.[14] Manson was openly misogynistic, having used coercive techniques on his largely female followers. Even LaVey, whose Church of Satan had women in leading roles, expressed reactionary views about gender.

Obviously, racism was a component in the intersection of the Abraxas Clique and Mason. While each of the four had different attitudes toward the White Supremacist movement, only Moynihan embraced its ideology as part of their long-term belief system (as opposed to expressing more vulgar, everyday racist expressions). Fred Berger, editor of the popular goth magazine

Propaganda, was asked, "Who's the court philosopher of Nazi chic?" In a moment of unusual frankness about this milieu, he replied,

> In terms of racial philosophy, Michael Moynihan. In terms of ethical philosophy, Boyd Rice. He always shied away from the ethnocentric aspects of it and more toward the ethical aspects of fascist philosophy. You have to break it down. I'd say Moynihan was more ethno-centric. This is very dangerous stuff, if it gets into the hands of the wrong people.[15]

Abraxas Foundation

Rice, Parfrey, Schreck, and later Moynihan were all part of the Abraxas Foundation, which billed itself as an "occult-fascist think tank." With its clever name and description, it received a lot of attention, but its activities were quite minimal. Its main product was the one-off publication *WAKE*.

Rice started the supposed foundation in 1987, seeking to create "a new demographic of people who are into the occult, Fascism, and Social Darwinism. It's out there as an alternative for kids who are growing up and need that information."[16] Elsewhere, Rice described it as "a worldwide think tank" dedicated to spreading the doctrine of "Primal Law" and creating "a renaissance of resurgent atavism."[17]

Schreck, who claimed he was a co-founder, had a more racial take on things. In 1988, he said the Abraxas Foundation was "sort of a Thule Society for the '90s."[18] It was

> dedicated to bringing about the values which we consider true and determined by the Natural Order.... Humanity has moved away from nature. Race mixing, genetic suicide, the destruction of the gene pool—all of that is completely inimical to the Natural Order. We need to return to Order.[19]

Rice's 1991 account for a more mainstream audience omitted race-mixing and genetic pollution, however.

> We don't believe in a master race.... We think there are strong people who do what they want to do, and there are other people who just follow along. Race is an issue, but I don't think you can have a master race, because every race has a handful of people who are really intelligent, who are achievers, and a bunch of people who are what Lenin called "stuffing in the mattress."[20]

Parfrey, who also claimed membership in the Abraxas Foundation, said their belief was that the world was divided into more and less intelligent people and that the former should be ascendant. But he also called it a joke which sought to get people "upset and anxious" upon hearing about this "occult-Fascist think tank. There was no such thing!"[21]

Having made contact with Rice the year before, by March 1989 Moynihan also joined the Foundation,[22] publishing a poem/manifesto of sorts under its name that month. Besides *WAKE*, this would be the most coherent statement out of the Abraxas Foundation. It argued that "man is a destroyer" but his actions were now the product of a "life in dysfunction." It also called for a reorientation of destruction to be "an ally of creation," hailed "the Order" and "the Wheel of the Law," and ended with the prewar fascist slogan "Long live death!"[23]

WAKE would have to wait a few years to be released, although Parfrey published an excerpt from it in 1990. In the meantime, a few recordings came out under the Abraxas Foundation label.[24] In February 1991, Rice and Moynihan took a public access cable TV class for an Abraxas Foundation show they were planning.[25] However, the two fell out soon after, and so after *WAKE*'s 1992 publication, the Abraxas Foundation ghost was given up.

"Young, creative geniuses"

From the moment the Abraxas Clique first encountered Mason, they tried to figure out how to market him. Almost immediately after contact, they set about introducing Mason's work to the underground counterculture in bits and pieces; the *Siege* anthology was the culmination of years of work by Parfrey, Petros, Schreck, and others to do this.

The process started in February 1987, when two associates of Parfrey's, Brian King and Ken Swezey, visited Mason in Chillicothe, Ohio to videotape an interview. In spring 1987, the third issue of *EXIT* magazine, co-edited by Parfrey and George Petros, included Mason's "Independent Genius" flyer, and later that year he was thanked in Parfrey's *Apocalypse Culture* anthology, which included two more of his flyers. Mason also had his own section in Schreck's *The Manson File*, which was the first significant reprinting of his work. The book appeared in 1988, five years before *Siege* would come out.[26] The next year, parts of Mason's 1987 interview were included in Schreck's *Charles Manson Superstar* documentary, and more of his flyers appeared in the Petros-edited *EXIT* #4. In 1989, Moynihan agreed to make the *Siege* anthology, and in 1991 he appeared with Mason and Rice on Bob Larson's Christian radio show *Talk-Back*—which the Abraxas Foundation would sell copies of.[27] (Larson was a Christian preacher whose broadcasts would be important in fueling the folk panic around Satanism in the 1980s; Rice, Moynihan, Schreck, and Mason all appeared on his show.) Mason also contributed to *EXIT* #6, slated for 1992, although it did not appear until much later. All this preceded Moynihan's publication of *Siege* in 1993.

From the very beginning of this process, Mason was ecstatic about working with this new group. In the late 1980s, Mason told Moynihan that he, Parfrey, and a "damned few others are what I consider as young, creative geniuses" who would "carry on and in a superior fashion" to his own work.[28] Around the same time, Mason said that Moynihan, Parfrey, Petros, and Schreck were "very high on my list of priorities" versus the traditional White Supremacist "movement builders."[29] Mason believed that when the Abraxas Clique discovered him, they saw his views as "in line with their own view of politics in general... that the present society, all of its morals and values, its leadership etc., reflected only rottenness and decay."[30]

However, Mason would later deny they were National Socialists. At first, he downgraded them to mere "free thinkers." In 2022, he said that Rice, Parfrey, and Moynihan had "adhered to some idea other than the true faith." They were

"Nicht Nazi." I have several classifications for those who no longer wish to acknowledge their past. To have... added their services and then to have passed on out...is an alright thing. What puzzles me is that these people imagine that to do this will somehow clear them of any splash-back from the enemy who never forgets.[31]

When asked about the "Cult Rapture" art show that Parfrey curated in 1994, Mason said there was a "direct correlation" between his views and those of certain rock musicians and artists, especially in the Abraxas Circle.

It's a rough message but it's the same, which is DEATH TO THE SYSTEM. So, I think we can respect each other, even though we may not fully understand or appreciate each other. The priority is that we are aware that we're political allies.[32]

Mason also related to the Abraxas Clique on a cultural level, as he had spent years as a designer for print magazines and flyers and, not wrongly, considered his own work to be art.

Interestingly, music was probably the cultural form he least shared with them. Like many neo-Nazis of his generation, he listened to classical music, declaring "I hate rock." Nonetheless, it had long been a talking point of his about the necessity for his movement to embrace those in the counterculture who did have those tastes. After *Siege* came out, Mason said, "The book is popular amongst a lot of rock musicians—that's an audience I never targeted."[33]

Mason, Moynihan, and Parfrey were explicit about the effect of circulating Mason's work. On one hand, it had an appeal to those and others in the extreme culture as an object of fascination. On the other, they acknowledged that it was straight-up political propaganda. Trained in George Lincoln Rockwell's shock tactics, Mason understood that some people were titillated by the very extremity of neo-Nazism (as opposed to the contents of its beliefs), but this could be used draw in interested parties and convert them. But Mason also saw these collaborations as a different kind of dualism, too: as promoting his ideas using both cultural and political approaches. Both pairs were different paths to spread his message. Rightly or wrongly, he believed the Abraxas Clique was part of a serious project to facilitate this.

The use of Mason's work by Parfrey as content to sell the extreme culture was obvious. But the publisher's private letters expressed agreement with a number of Mason's ideas. Whether Parfrey was honest, partly honest (most likely), or simply lying, Mason obviously saw him as a comrade.

Irrespective of what his own thoughts were, Parfrey acknowledged that objectively he was spreading straight-up neo-Nazi propaganda. About the Universal Order's exhibit in the "Cult Rapture" art show, he said it "proved that all is context now." On the other hand, Mason saw the show not through a Duchampian lens but as a ruse to reach the public. He called it "a nice, safe cover" to promote neo-Nazism. As opposed to the old uniform and demonstrate events, which had little if any impact, "this accomplished a great deal because it was done very shrewdly, smoothly, and with a lot of intelligence and finesse. And we'll be getting ripples off this from now on."[34]

The Making of a Countercultural Fascist Lineage

Part of the goal of the Abraxas Clique's interest in 1960s figures like Manson, LaVey, and folk singer Robert N. Taylor was to help build a lineage of "countercultural fascism."[35] This functioned both as part of and an opposition to the hippie and punk countercultures. (Nonetheless, it did not encompass the Nazi skinhead movement per se; that was too crude, too artless, and too *obvious*.) This new lineage shared the parent counterculture's aesthetic tastes and definition of itself as a collective endeavor that was opposed to the dominant society, often using the darkest aesthetic approach it could find. But whereas the main current of the counterculture embraced a left-leaning critique of "the System" as a capitalist, hierarchical, and alienating structure, the countercultural fascists saw the System as imposing a totalitarianism based on a false belief in equality and wished to replace it with a hierarchical system with reactionary social goals in its place—whether those were based on race, gender, or individual ability.

In this new lineage, the handful of reactionary figures from the 1960s they picked out were followed in the 1980s by the right wing of the extreme culture and adjacent neofolk scene and then in the 1990s by fanzine writers like Jim Goad and, on occasion, the more articulate White Supremacists like George Eric Hawthorne. This vision of a reactionary cultural movement—

not based on traditional cultural forms, but rather avant-garde and icono-clastic approaches—was another way in which the Alt Right of the 2010s inherited the fruits of the Abraxas Clique's labors.

Deny Everything

Another common thread among the Abraxas Clique was their ambiguous public presentation about whether they were White Supremacists or not. In the pre-internet period, it was extremely difficult to access even basic infor-mation about many bands. Even purchasing their records was not always possible, much less gaining access to interviews in fanzines which interested parties may or may not have known even existed. The prolific use of Nazi and other totalitarian imagery by a variety of bands—more often than not deployed in an intentionally ambiguous manner—only obscured the situa-tion even more. Within this, neo-Nazis (and sympathizers) could easily hide simply by publicly denying their views. And Parfrey, Rice, and Moynihan would all spend years deploying this method.

Notes

1 The term "Feral House/Abraxas Clique" is taken from Chris Mathews, *Modern Satanism: Anatomy of a Radical Subculture* (Westport, Connecticut: Praeger, 2009), p.142.
2 Rice would often refer to Abraxas, which he described as a dualistic "ancient gnostic deity" which was the embodiment of "a pre-christian world view ... in which good and evil are reconciled and harnessed in the service of evolutionary imperative." Therefore, Abraxas represented two of Rice's interests: Social Darwinism and Gnostic philosophy. Rice credited Manson for his interest in the Gnostic deity, especially after he wrote a letter from prison which said, "Rice, I'll call you Abraxas, because you stand in two circles at once." Schreck described Abraxas somewhat differently, saying he was "a symbol of the eternal Now, a state of mind that exists beyond the false dichotomies of light and darkness, good and evil, right and wrong"; *WAKE* #1, 1992, p.2; Rice, "I'll Call You Abraxas: Conversations with Charles Manson," in Rice, Brian M Clark, ed., *Standing in Two Circles: The Collected Works of Boyd Rice* (Creation Books, 2008), p.100 (originally written 1997) [Hereafter *Standing*]; *Charles Manson Superstar* (video).
3 Knipfel emphasized this, noting Mason as a common connection; Jim Knipfel, "The Other Nazis," *Welcomat* 23(25) January 5, 1994, p.12 (*Articles*, p.69).
4 Sometimes a distinction is made between "subculture," which is more apolitical, and "counterculture," which is more politicized; however, at other times they are used interchangeably.
5 Tom Cullen (NEA), "British Hippies Come under Fire of Skinheads," *Poughkeepsie Journal* (New York), January 11, 1970, p.18, www.newspapers.com/image/legacy/114876727
6 George Marshall, *Spirit of '69: A Skinhead Bible* (Dunoon, Scotland: S.T. Publishing, 1991).
7 *Art That Kills*, p.7.

8 Tiffini A Travis and Perry Hardy, *Skinheads: A Guide to an American Subculture* (Santa Barbara, California: Greenwood, 2012), pp.xvi–xvii, xix, 56.

9 Cited in ibid, p.44.

10 ADL, *Young and Violent*, p.1. The Center for Democratic Renewal gave a slightly larger figure. According to them, Nazi skinheads went from 300 in 1986 to 3,500 by the end of 1988; figure is cited in Jeff Coplon, "Skinhead Nation," *Rolling Stone* #540, December 1, 1988, p.56.

11 Moynihan, Rice, and Mason interview with Larson/*Talk Back* (video); "8-8-88 Rally Plus Interviews" (video), uploaded by Kristian Day, May 21, 2017, www.youtube.com/watch?v=Y11mThIvGE8; Nikolas Schreck interview with Metzger/*Race and Reason* (video), 1988; "Race & Reason - Tom Metzger Interviews Nikolas Schreck" (video), uploaded by Nat-Sat, January 11, 2019, https://archive.org/details/NikolasSchreckInterviewedByTomMetzger

12 Colin Campbell, "The Cult, the Cultic Milieu and Secularization," *A Sociological Yearbook of Religion in Britain* (5), pp.119–36; Brian M. Clark, *Boyd Rice: A Biography* (Discriminate Media, 2015), p.25 (originally written 2007) [Hereafter *Biography*].

13 Moynihan to Mason, June 1, 1990 [Box 5, Folder 9].

14 "Adam Parfrey – The Force Behind Feral House Press" (interview by Robert Ward), *Fifth Path* #4, Winter 1992/1993, p.24.

15 *Art That Kills*, p.99.

16 Cited in Coogan, "How 'Black' Is Black Metal? Michael Moynihan, *Lords of Chaos* and the 'Countercultural Fascist' Underground," *Hit List* #1, February/March 1999, p.38; Clark, *Biography*, p.33. In one place, Rice gave a 1984 founding date, which Coogan repeated in "How Black" (p.38). However, no other information supports this date; "Boyd Rice Speaks: 'Do you Want a Total War?'" (interview by Robert Ward), *Fifth Path* #3, Spring 1992, p.7, https://web.archive.org/web/20160916235819, http://www.boydrice.com/interviews/fifthpath.html, Rice interview in *Fifth Path* #3, p.7.

17 *WAKE* #1, p.2.

18 Schreck interview with Metzger/*Race and Reason* (video). The Thule Society has traditionally been seen as an occult group that started the German Workers Party (DAP), which Hitler joined and renamed the NSDAP. However, the actual relationship between Thule and the DAP is "indeterminate" according to Nicholas Goodrick-Clarke, *The Occult Roots of Nazism: Secret Aryan Cults and Their Influence on Nazi Ideology* (New York: NYU Press, 1985/1992), p.150.

19 Schreck interview with Metzger/*Race and Reason* (video).

20 Alan Prendergast, "Family Ties: The Secret Service Freaks over Charles Manson's Pen Pals," *Westword* 14(41) June 12–18, 1991, p.30. Rice made a similar statement, affirming the desirability of domination while denouncing the idea of a master race, in "Boyd Rice, Media Monster: A Bobby Sherman Fan Speaks" (interview by Lisa Janssen), *Your Flesh*, [1991], pp.32–33, www.scribd.com/document/58280166/Boyd-Rice-Media-Monster

21 *Art That Kills*, p.157.

22 A business card, mailed in March 1989, listed Abraxas Foundation addresses for Moynihan in Belgium and Rice in San Francisco; Abraxas Foundation, business card, [1989], stapled to a letter, Moynihan to Mason, March 22, 1989 [Box 5, Folder 9].

23 Coup De Grace, "The Abraxas Foundation," *1988-1989 Report/Update*, March 1989, p.12 [Box 5, Folder 9].

24 Abraxas Foundation, "Long Live Death!," in Parfrey, ed., *Apocalypse Culture, Expanded & Revised* (Port Townsend, Washington: Feral House, 1990). One of the releases included NON, *Total War* videocassette (Soleilmoon, 1989), www.discogs.com/master/698352-NON-Total-War-Live-In-Japan

25 Moynihan to Mason, February 5, 1991 [Box 5, Folder 9]; *Fifth Path* #2, August 1991, pp.2, 34, https://archive.org/details/TheFifthPath02

26 Parfrey, ed., *Apocalypse Culture*, pp.6, 118, 192; Schreck, ed., *The Manson File*, pp.139–47.

27 Review in *Fifth Path* #2, p.34.

28 Mason had told Reynolds an almost identical thing in 1987: "Parfrey and Petros are two creative geniuses who are avidly following the Manson idea and who have the potential to form a new movement." Mason to Moynihan, September 1, 1989; Mason to Moynihan, March 2, 1989 [both Box 5, Folder 9]; Mason to Reynolds, December 25, 1987 [Box 33, Folder 8].

29 Mason to Moynihan, August 16, 1989. A few years later, he reiterated this, saying they were "people who were creative in their own right and not more dead-ass Right Wingers"; Mason interview in *NO LONGER A FANzine*, p.14 (*Articles*, p.141) [Box 5, Folder 9].

30 Mason interview with Swezey and King (video).

31 *Art That Kills*, p.189; Mason to author, November 26, 2022 and January 1, 2023.

32 Mason interview in *Ohm Clock* (*Articles*, p.98).

33 *Art That Kills*, p.189; Mason interview in *Ohm Clock*, p.9 (*Articles*, p.97).

34 Parfrey to Mason, [October or November 1994?] [Box 17, Folder 4]; Mason interview in *Ohm Clock*, p.10 (*Articles*, p.98).

35 This is taken from a term used by both Jeff Bale and Kevin Coogan in "How Black"; Bale, Introduction, p.34. and Coogan, p.40.

12

BOYD RICE

Neo-Nazi Collaborator

Boyd Rice has been a cult figure in the counterculture for over 40 years, starting as an industrial noise musician in the late 1970s and later branching out into other creative endeavors. He has an impressive record of positioning himself on the frontlines of emerging trends. For such a relatively obscure figure, his collaborations and connections with a wide variety of musicians, publishers, and artists—as well as Charles Manson and Anton LaVey—have given him an outsized influence.[1] And since the 1980s, Rice has been dogged by accusations of being a neo-Nazi.

For decades, he has sought to downplay, deflect, and deny these accusations. In this task, he has been enabled by many of his friends in the music industry, interviewers, and journalists as well as both a sycophantic biographer and a documentary filmmaker.

Documentation shows that for years Rice was directly connected to three prominent neo-Nazis: James Mason, Tom Metzger, and Bob Heick. Rice's association with the latter two, documented in pictures and video, is undeniable. But his connection to Mason has not played a significant role in the controversy, probably owing to the limited and hard-to-find evidence that has previously been available.[2]

Without Rice, Mason would never have been known outside of his tiny neo-Nazi world. The first member of the Abraxas Clique to contact Mason, Rice proceeded to introduce him to both Adam Parfrey and Michael Moynihan. In addition to portraying himself as a neo-Nazi in his correspondence with Mason, Rice was also the first to suggest that the SIEGE newsletter be turned into a book.

DOI: 10.4324/9780429200090-17

Early Industry

Rice grew up in Southern California, first attracting public attention in March 1976 when first lady Betty Ford visited a senior center in San Diego. Rice, then 19, welcomed her by holding up a skinned pig's head. Detained by Secret Service agents, he said during his interrogation that it was a Dada-esque art prank. He was released without charges.[3]

In 1977, Rice released an untitled album, recorded two years earlier and later given the name the *Black Album*, that easily fit in the burgeoning British industrial music scene. One record guide described it as "droning noise slices" which "seem to consist of short tape loops layered over one another to create repetitive but varying textures." Its judgment? "Unlistenable."[4]

NON was formed in 1978, originally as a duo, but it quickly became a name that Rice primarily used for his solo work—although on certain occasions it would also include his accompaniment.[5] He attached himself to the burgeoning punk scene, even though his approach was more influenced by a pop version of avant-garde art traditions than guitar-driven three-chord rock and roll. Going to Britain in 1978, he met Daniel Miller, the founder of Mute Records. This pioneering electronic label would release records by artists such as Depeche Mode, and Mute would release Rice's output for decades to come. But Miller wouldn't be the only person he met on the visit who greatly impacted on him.

Genesis of Hitler–Manson Interest

Rice also met Genesis P-Orridge of Throbbing Gristle, the band that was the touchstone for the new genre of industrial music.[6] Making harsh, chord-less music as part of a multi-media presentation—the band had emerged from the performance art group COUM Transmissions—they delved into a variety of transgressive acts and themes. But it was their injudicious interest in both Nazism and Manson that would apparently have the most impact on Rice and start his trajectory which ended in meeting the imprisoned cult leader and cavorting with actual National Socialists.

Throbbing Gristle was not political in the traditional sense. Instead, their interests lay in extreme sexual practices, sadism, occult mysticism, and psychological manipulation—including a fascination with cults. But the group trafficked in Nazi images and references which were deployed in a morally ambiguous way. Nazi imagery had been used by rock bands starting in the 1960s, and swastikas in particular were common among the very first wave of punk bands in 1976 and 1977. But in 1978, the fascist National Front had organized its Punk Front, although they were far more successful in recruiting skinheads.[7] With the entrance of organized fascist groups into the punk scene, the meaning of Nazi imagery suddenly took on a new gravity.

Throbbing Gristle's use of Nazi imagery was more unsettling than simply a swastika patch, though. They used a photo of an Auschwitz crematory chimney as their record company logo. Song titles included "Zyklon B Zombie," and one record cover was a band picture taken in front of the NSDAP's Propaganda Ministry. And these are just a few examples.[8] Throbbing Gristle's logo resembled Oswald Mosley's British Union of Fascists, and they wore paramilitary uniforms on stage. And they also worked with another industrial musician, Monte Cazazza, whom rock critic Simon Reynolds went so far as to dub the band's "unofficial fifth member," and who also used Nazi imagery.[9]

Manson was another fascination of theirs. COUM Transmissions named a series of performance pieces after a Manson song, while Throbbing Gristle wrote song lyrics about Sharon Tate's murder and included a quote from him on their album *Heathen Earth*.[10] The band's interest in the cult leader became widespread in the industrial music scene, a harbinger of later things.

Although an unreliable narrator, Rice claimed he initially sought out a meeting with P-Orridge because "he was very into Manson and Hitler. Back then, NO ONE was into that sort of thing." Whether true, or fabricated to buttress his own open Nazi influences, Rice claimed that at the time P-Orridge "still wore swastikas and would tell anyone who would listen (and many that wouldn't) what a great guy Hitler was. Uncle Adolf he called him." Rice also said that while Throbbing Gristle was in California, he brought them to Spahn Ranch, one of the places the Manson Family lived.[11]

From an outsider's view, it was decidedly unclear whether the band was criticizing or glamorizing the Nazis and what was a critique and what was a seemingly unhealthy fascination. Reynolds described it as having a "dark proto-fascist" angle.[12] Rice came to adopt not just Throbbing Gristle's interest in Nazis and Manson but also military-looking uniforms and a fascist-themed logo. Their relationship was so close that in February 1981 NON opened Throbbing Gristle's last show in Britain.[13]

Boyd in the Bay

Having recorded an industrial record even before the scene existed, Rice had already shown his ability to be on the very cutting edge of culturally marginal trends. He moved to San Francisco at the start of the 1980s and—always the charismatic chameleon—quickly integrated himself into the San Francisco punk and associated avant-garde scene.[14] He released more records like the NON album *Physical Evidence* in 1982 and *Easy Listening for the Hard of Hearing*, a collaboration with Frank Tovey of Fad Gadget, in 1984.

He also became close to RE/Search Publications, especially its co-publisher V. Vale. According to Parfrey, "Boyd considered Vale a close friend who knew 'everything' about him." Rice was interviewed for *Re/Search* #1 (the "issues" soon became books in terms of size, length, and binding) in 1980.[15] In 1983, he was also featured in RE/Search's classic *Industrial Culture Handbook*, which became the main source of information about this scene as it was just becoming known in the United States. The book reflected ideas swirling around in their circles; the editors wrote, "Hitler and Manson are amazing—their power came from other people believing in their words," while Rice expressed his awe of Hitler's ability to enact his fantasies.[16] Rice also contributed RE/Search's *Incredibly Strange Films* in 1986 and *Pranks* in 1987.

Making Contact with Mason

In 1986, even before SIEGE had stopped, Rice was the first of the Abraxas Clique to make contact with Mason, whose political circles had become smaller and smaller. Rice first learned about SIEGE from his trips to gun shows, where he met neo-Nazi Viktor Malik, who had been involved in Teutonic Order and then the National Socialist Party. Rice must have been fascinated to hear about an actual neo-Nazi who was not just in contact with Manson but who fused the two together. Malik—who had previously worked with Mason's comrade Michael Merritt—gave the address for SIEGE to Rice.[17]

On April 24, 1986, Rice wrote Mason for the first time, saying, "I am completely of the Manson-Hitler thought & do whatever I can to further it," adding that he had already passed on Mason's address to "key people." Rice also praised Manson as

> the perfect embodiment of Odinism as a way of life, a Hitlerian ideal! I find it difficult to breathe within the confines of more mainstream National Socialism which seems to be made up of people who lack any inner vision & are still thinking in terms as small as those who they oppose.[18]

(Rice, no doubt picking up on Mason's disinterest, did not mention Odinism again in his correspondence.) Mason, who probably had received numerous grandiose letters of this kind during his years as a publisher, sent Rice back a polite note and a couple copies of SIEGE.

Rice quickly replied, saying "Love the SIEGE!" and "I like your angle on things. Consciousness should be at the root of National Socialism, its very life blood, yet seems often conspicuously absent." With more than a little irony considering his own proclivities for uniforms, Rice added that most neo-Nazis "would rather play dress-up at the moment." He also noted he was not just writing Manson but trying to get on his visitors' list. "I feel closer to him than anyone I can think of. I feel as though I'm at one with his thought." Rice also talked about his plan to get a Manson album released in Europe and signed off with the Wolfsangel—a symbol of particular importance to Rice.[19]

Under separate cover, Rice also sent a photocopy of a collage centered on Manson as a Jesus figure. Rice wrote on the bottom, "James, a friend in Jew York did this. I gave him your address & if you haven't heard from him yet I'm sure you will." His "Jew York" friend was Parfrey. After receiving the letter, Mason wrote Manson, asking if he knew Rice.[20]

Quickly bonding over their mutual love of trading videos and music, Rice sent Mason a cassette of Manson's new music. Rice said, "This is the tape some Jew lawyer was hawking to the record companies for Manson. A Jew & a lawyer. Bad news!"[21] Rice also told Mason that he was sad SIEGE was ending, as "you present precisely the focus most needed by N.S. people." He then suggested what Moynihan would later make a reality:

> It would be nice even to consolidate some of the issues dealing with key topics & key concepts into a "Best of Siege" to at least take the seeds of that thought & situate it out amongst men, out in the world to take root, grow & become something with a life of its own. Just an idea…[22]

Mason countered that he wanted to anthologize all the issues, but to do so he needed a free printer. Rice signed off his letter with a Hitler quote. Mason's flyers started to circulate now outside of his direct circles. He had sent them to Parfrey, who passed them on to Rice, who in turn made copies to pass on to even more people.[23]

Visiting Charlie…Briefly

Rice's friendship with Manson is often portrayed as a lengthy and intimate affair. For example, the promotional material for *Iconoclast*, a four-hour documentary about Rice, said, "Boyd Rice may well be the only person alive who's been on a first name basis with both Charlie Manson and Marilyn Manson."[24]

In 1992, Rice said of Manson, "I still consider him a friend," even while admitting they hadn't been in touch for a number of years.[25] Indeed, previously, Rice had gushed about being able to visit Manson.

> Imagine having the chance to spend 4 or 5 hours with Hitler every week… Imagine how much you could learn. Thats how it feels being with Charlie. The truth of what Charlie actually is lies so far beyond most peoples realm of experience that it would be impossible for them to conceive such a person could exist.[26]

In fact, there was a period of only a month or two that Rice could have visited him. This started in June or July 1986 but ended in early August when Rice was arrested after he tried to enter San Quentin with a bullet in his pocket. He was initially charged with a felony, although the charges were dropped. Manson, however, was put into solitary confinement.[27] This ended not just their visits but their relationship. In 1997, Rice even said that after the incident, "My friendship with Charles Manson was over, and I haven't communicated with him since."[28] And Manson certainly had no kind words for Rice afterward. In one interview he said,

> Boyd dropped the ball. Boyd gave his whole generation of people up so he could be a rock'n'roll singer. He had the whole thing, man, if he wanted to move it—but he didn't. He talked to me more like a black pimp. I think somebody scared him, I think some Negro scared him or something. He sounded like he was afraid of Negros.[29]

In another interview, Manson called Rice an "idiot." Rice's problem was that he wanted to dress up in uniforms but not "abide by orders"—orders given by Manson, of course.[30]

In 1994, Rice, getting some critical distance, called Manson a "cranky, bitter old man." In 1997, Rice would have a more insightful perspective, describing him as "part con-man, part shaman and a total paradox." Whereas a decade prior, Rice had said, "The murders to me are the least important and interesting thing," now he flipped around, saying that if Manson hadn't masterminded them, "then the crimes aren't interesting and neither is Charles Manson."[31]

Regardless, Rice continued to champion Manson in the period directly after their break. In October 1986, Rice, Parfrey, and Nikolas Schreck decided to hold a series of concerts under the name Friends of Justice, to help Manson. These were planned for March 20, 1987 in Los Angeles, New York City, and London. The letterhead for the event included the three cities plus Chillicothe (Mason), Alderson (Sandra Good), Burlington ("Squeaky" Fromme), San Francisco (Rice), and Reykjavik. (However, Fromme soon asked to be removed, and apparently Good as well.)[32]

The London performance, which was to include Current 93 and Coil, and possibly Death in June, collapsed. Schreck claimed there was "support" for the idea from the band Sonic Youth (then still years away from their future stardom). But although they had "made much from the Manson mystique," they "withdrew very early from it," and Schreck denounced them as "dilettantes." The shows were also attacked because of Rice and Schreck's links to White Supremacists. Police in Los Angeles and New York City were also alleged to have pressured them, and so none of them came off.[33]

But this failure didn't dissuade Rice from publicly supporting of Manson. Taking part in a five-person rally outside San Quentin during Manson's February 1989 parole hearing and sporting what was by-then his trademark black paramilitary-esque uniform, Rice held a sign saying "Guilty of Witchcraft? Manson Killed No One."[34]

Tom Metzger TV

Rice's more recent attempts to dismiss his past involvement with neo-Nazism, the proof of which had mostly revolved around a photo from 1989, were further complicated in the '00s. It was then that a copy of his 1986 appearance on Metzger's *Race and Reason* was put online.

Late that year, Rice was asked to be on the show but was hesitant. In mid-December, Parfrey wrote to Mason,

> my friend Michael Hoffman who spoke on Nazi ecological policy at the last Aryan Nations and made documentaries on the Zundel trial, has offered to get Boyd Rice on Metzger's Race and Reason TV show to speak on Manson's racial policies. I'm trying to encourage Boyd to go on, but he's hedging. A letter of encouragement from you might work wonders, especially if they had pointers....[35]

Parfrey described both Schreck and Rice as having "good communications with Michael A. Hoffman II and Metzger." At the time, Metzger described Hoffman as a "WAR associate" and credited him with shooting video footage of White Power bands in Britain and meeting with Skrewdriver. Whether or not he was influenced by the Holocaust denier Hoffman[36] or Mason, Rice soon changed his mind and agreed to go on, in Parfrey's words, to "talk about Manson and Race, among other things." (Indeed, Rice did talk about race in the interview, something he usually took pains to avoid.) The show was taped December 30, 1986.[37]

Metzger and his co-host Tom Padgett mostly asked Rice about the industrial music scene. Metzger, who hadn't heard Rice's music, couldn't get his head around it—but Padgett, who had seen Rice play, was effusive. While Rice was not the one who brought up these questions and perspectives, Metzger offered a racist reading of both the music scene and Rice's politics. Rice in turn agreed to a number of his statements and sometimes elaborated on why they were true.

For example, when Metzger asked, "what's the evolution of this underground music into the more, say, white racially oriented music?" Rice replied that people in the punk scene started with dissatisfaction before going "back to something, something organic... a biological knowledge of what you are." Asked about "racialist-type singers and bands in Europe," he recommended Current 93 ("moving more and more towards racialist stuff"), Death in June ("very racialist oriented"), and Above the Ruins (explicitly part of the British fascist political milieu). Members of these groups would all later be part of Rice's 1989 Japanese tour.[38]

When Padgett offered that "electronic music is very white...by its very nature," Rice replied "Yeah, yeah, that's what I feel, too" and stressed the lack of black influence. When Metzger said, "modern music has been pretty much [a] propaganda instrument of Jewish interests...you see emerging a new propaganda art form for white Aryans," Rice affirmed it, saying, "Yeah, yeah, I think so." Similarly, when asked "Do you feel that the music that we're talking about here is sort of the beginning of an orchestration of an Aryan underclass movement?," Rice said, "I think so, I think it's engendering a new will, among people. That's, that's what, what I'm interested in." Metzger asked, "how do you feel about racial separation and tribalism...as opposed to national borders," and Rice replied, "it seems like the only intelligent way to go. It seems like the way people would go if they weren't forced to go another way."[39]

About Metzger, Rice told Mason that "I liked him a hell of a lot. Liked his attitude & his outlook. He's really <u>doing it</u>!" They continued to hang out after the show, with Rice spending New Year's Eve with Metzger almost immediately after the taping. In the middle of 1987, the neo-Nazi leader also went along with Rice to a local music performance.[40]

Metzger's association with Rice did not end there, however, and they were in touch, on a first-name basis, through at least 1996—a decade after the *Race and Reason* show. Whatever their relationship, Metzger sold videos of Rice's music as early as 1987. In the 1990s, Metzger continued to call Rice a "white racialist performance artist," and right up until Metzger's death, his mail-order service sold videos and then DVDs of Rice, including his *Race and Reason* appearance.[41]

Blood & Flame

In 1986, NON released the instrumental recording *Blood & Flame*; its cover had a Wolfsangel on it. This inaugurated Rice's public use of this image, which would continue for the rest of his career.[42] Also called a wolf's hook, the Wolfsangel was a medieval symbol often used as a heraldic design element. Like many other ancient symbols, the swastika foremost among them, it was adopted by the NSDAP. In the postwar period, the Wolfsangel has become a common neo-Nazi symbol, utilized as an alternative to the swastika for legal reasons, public relations, or simply to have aesthetic options. Rice claimed to have gotten a tattoo of it in 1980.[43]

Inside *Blood & Flame*'s sleeve was a quote from Alfred Rosenberg, the NSDAP's antisemitic theoretician—a usual reference point neither for neo-Nazis nor for those in cultural circles that traffic in Nazi references.[44] Rosenberg's turgid tome *The Myth of the Twentieth Century*, which Rice would later recommend, had been widely distributed in Nazi Germany. Rice's interest was no doubt based partly on the Nazi's Gnostic influences, which also gave Rice a convenient excuse to promote him.[45] (Moynihan shared an interest in Rosenberg.)

For good measure, the album also contained a quote from Arthur de Gobineau, a nineteenth-century advocate of scientific racism who influenced the NSDAP. He, too, would continue to pop up in the Abraxas Circle. Much later, Rice continued to promote him, saying in 2012 that "I love de Gobineau!"[46]

And so it was that *Blood & Flame*, his first album with Nazi themes, was released the year that Rice came into direct contact with prominent neo-Nazis Metzger and Mason. And it made an impact on at least one person in the record-buying public. Reflecting on it, Moynihan said, "I got 'Blood and Flame' when it came out and was amazed to see NON suddenly presenting more concrete (or blatant) ideas in the record and packaging—things which specifically related to my own interest."[47]

In the spring of 1987, Rice sent the CD cover to Mason (he didn't have a player for the disc), along with a "Wolfsangel patch, the insignia of our newly formed ABRAXAS FOUNDATION." Mason replied that the patch was "super-well-done and looks as if it might have come straight out of NS Germany."[48]

Just before that, in February 1987, Rice had sent Mason a photocopy of newspaper clipping involving a black man arrested for raping a white woman; next to it, Rice wrote "Happy 'Black "History" Month!'" His next letter to Mason had a swastika on top, and it was signed off with an "88!" (An alpha-numeric, "88" stood for "Heil Hitler!") In the letter, Rice relayed that he'd just read George Lincoln Rockwell's *White Power* and that it was "an awesome book."[49] He would use the "88" sign-off at least three more times in letters he wrote to Mason.[50]

That year, Parfrey also released his infamous *Apocalypse Culture* anthology. Rice, who was thanked, provided a selection of Hitler quotes for the book. And the third issue of Parfrey's other project, *EXIT*, included a two-page spread by Rice which consisted mostly of quotes from Manson and the antisemitic composer Richard Wagner.[51]

Might is Right

In the late 1980s, Rice started to refer to *Might is Right or The Survival of the Fittest*, an 1896 work written under the pseudonym Ragnar Redbeard. Some have seen it as an inspired, poetic revelation—but it is a turgid, bigoted rant to others. *Might is Right* praised an amoral individualism in a world ruled by "Natural Law" where "nature red in tooth and claw" is the truth of the world, and only the most ruthless succeed.

In part a vulgarization of German individualist philosophers Friedrich Nietzsche and Max Stirner, Redbeard's book added a number of ideas popular in his day: a crude Social Darwinism, White Supremacist racial ideas, antisemitic conspiracies about Jewish wealth and power, and intense misogyny. In his worldview, the strong Anglo-Saxon man—weakened and mislead by the false ideologies of religion, morality, and egalitarianism—had to realize the brutal truth of nature and exert his will to dominate others.

Like so many other Far Right bigots, Redbeard cast himself as an iconoclast as he denounced egalitarianism, morals and laws, Jews and Judaism, Christianity and religion in general, politicians, socialism, democracy and constitutions, miscegenation, and the masses. He championed a caricatured "he-man" who cared about nothing and no one and used brute force to get his way. This hero, he argued, was feminized by contemporary culture and philosophy and could express his true self only through conquest, violence, and war. People of color were clearly inferior. And women were singled out in particular and described in extremely disparaging terms; they were weak, stupid, and existed only to be dominated.

Rice was particularly taken by the book, which he discovered in the late 1980s and used as the basis of his philosophy.[52] A number of references to it worked their way into Rice's music. For example, the song "Might is Right" was played on the 1989 Japanese tour, and all the lyrics to his 1995 NON album *Might!* are taken from the book.[53] A 1992 publication from Rice also promoted *Might is Right*, both explaining its ideas and providing quotes.[54]

Mason himself recognized the book as common ground between neo-Nazis and the Satanists that Abraxas Clique allied with. According to him, "Ragnar Redbeard's 'Might Is Right', so 'Viking' in its nature, even provides a direct philosophical link between the two groups."[55] Metzger himself confirmed this. He sold his own spiral-bound copies of *Might Is Right* and said he read it "religiously, almost like a Bible. And every few days, I read some of it."[56]

Anton LaVey

In 1987, Rice also made an important connection when he befriended the Church of Satan founder Anton LaVey. They had shared opinions on misanthropy, eugenics, and *Might is Right* and remained friends until the latter's death in 1997. According to Rice, in February 1993, LaVey made him a Magister in the Church of Satan. He continued to quickly move up in rank, becoming a Grand Master of the Trapezoid and finally a member of the Council of Nine, the group just under LaVey himself.[57]

Always the matchmaker, Rice introduced LaVey to a number of his contacts, including Parfrey, Moynihan, and the latter's friend Thomas Thorn.[58] Rice also represented the Church of Satan in public; he appeared on the Bob Larson show several times and was featured on Geraldo Rivera's TV special on Satanism.[59]

Rice conducted the last traditional interview with LaVey in 1997.[60] Rice also claimed that as LaVey was dying, he was offered—and declined—the leadership of the Church of Satan. His warm relationship with the Church soured, though. In 2010, Rice claimed to retroactively accept LaVey's offer of leadership, denounced the current leadership as "sycophants and functionaries," and declared "my first official act...is to declare that the organization no longer exists."[61] Strangely, this did not seem to have much of an impact on the Church.

8/8/88

The Abraxas Foundation had brought together Rice, Parfrey, and Schreck—at least for a moment. Nikolas Schreck's anthology *The Manson File* appeared on Parfrey's Amok Press. Rice was listed as a contributing editor, and an image he made depicting Manson as an angel appeared alongside contributions by others in the Abraxas Clique, in addition to Mason.[62]

The Abraxas Clique had its greatest moment on August 8, 1988 with its 8/8/88 event, held at the Strand Theater in downtown San Francisco.

It included Rice, Parfrey, and Schreck, all of whom were to have taken part in the Friends of Justice shows the year before. (Moynihan was not yet embedded with them.) The three were joined by Zeena LaVey, the daughter of Anton LaVey. Officially billed as "An Evening of Apocalyptic Delight," it was the most blatant display of the Nazi–Satanist nexus they had been creating, even though it remained cloaked in the typical ambiguity of the underground.[63]

The 8/8/88 date referred to three things. According to Rice, Anton LaVey had done a destruction ritual at the same time, 19 years prior. And that very same night in 1969, the Manson Family murdered Sharon Tate and four others in Los Angeles.[64]

Of course, 8/8/88 was also a neo-Nazi reference that no one in those circles would have missed, even if they chose to believe it was extremism for its own sake. Parfrey even admitted the reference was intentional, though simultaneously carving an out by claiming that Rice did it "as a way of making people anxious."[65] And certainly the presence of neo-Nazis at the event itself might have caused some people anxiety.

The main act was billed as NON, which for this performance included Schreck and Evil Wilhelm from Radio Werewolf and Parfrey on oboe. Zeena LaVey also took part, reading from of the *Satanic Bible*.[66] Rice explained the billing to Mason this way: "James we'll use whatever label necessary to put out our thought."[67] And while undoubtedly this was an overstatement, and the event was not a straight-up, ideologically motivated neo-Nazi event, it was also not *not* an event without real neo-Nazi elements.

The most damning part was a picture taken to memorialize the event. It showed a group, which included Schreck, Rice, Zeena LaVey, and neo-Nazi Bob Heick, giving a collective sieg-heil salute to the camera. Another shot of the group, obviously taken at the same time, included Parfrey and Nick Bougas, a White Supremacist who published in Metzger's paper.[68] After the show, Rice and Schreck were interviewed sitting in front of Nazi flags. Both explained their extreme misanthropic views and expressed admiration for Hitler and the Nazis.[69]

The performance was taped for a Rivera two-hour TV special, "Devil Worship: Exposing Satan's Underground," which aired that October.[70] Afterward, Rice expressed his displeasure at how it went, saying "it fell way short of its potential." Although "the talent was there"—he included Parfrey, Evil Wilhelm, and Heick—Schreck was accused of having sunk the event.[71] Rice even complained that Rivera made him look bad.

> What ended up on *The Geraldo Show* was twenty seconds of me appearing to exhort the audience to murder, saying, "Murder is the predator's prerogative," and, "There is no Earth without blood." They took the most outlandish moment and put it on TV.[72]

A strange complaint from someone who spent his career espousing outlandish cultural and political positions—and who spoke those very words knowing full well he was being filmed for national television.

Bob Heick and the American Front

Summer 1988 was dubbed the "Summer of Hate" as a new wave of mostly White Supremacist, mostly teenage, skinheads exploded in popularity that year. (All White Supremacist skinheads are referred to as "Nazi skinheads" regardless of whether they actually hew to National Socialism.) TV talk shows and print media couldn't get enough of them. And this meant that Rice—already embedded in the milieu—was, once again, right on the cutting edge of the latest niche development in the underground. His closest tie was Bob Heick, leader of the Nazi skinhead gang American Front. Originally based in San Francisco, it would go on to be a national group.

Skinheads had been in the United States for many years but usually unorganized and, for lack of numbers, typically just an identity within the punk scene. That changed in the mid-1980s, especially as Nazi skinhead groups started to form. The American Front came out of an increasingly violent and racist scene in San Francisco's Haight neighborhood. In March 1985, a flyer, left at Bound Together, an anarchist bookstore in the neighborhood, said, "Punks, Communists, Anarchists, Hippys and Homosexuals... Your Days Are Numbered." Soon after, Heick reportedly kicked in the bookstore's window.[73] Rice was very taken with Heick.

> I was good friends with that guy Bob Heick from the American Front; he was a really funny, smart guy. He'd just come into a party and turn everything topsy-turvy. I really liked him and I really liked all his friends. I was never really a member of the American Front.[74]

Even if Rice was being truthful, the focus should be on the word "really." By 1987, Rice had already started referring to his views as "fascist," though not—in public at least—as a "Nazi."[75] (He would continue to do so for many years.)

In the spring of 1988, however, American Front held their most provocative act: holding a White Workers March down Haight Street on May Day, the annual left-wing holiday. Rice gushed to Mason, "We just staged a May Day march down Haight St. here in San Francisco & the results were great. 65 skinheads with signs & banners, but it looked more like a few hundred."[76]

Again, the "we" should be paid attention to. Two months later, in July, Rice wrote Mason that the American Front has "reissued your 'Political Terror' flyer (with their mailing address) & put them up all over the Bay Area. It's scared the hell out of the press around here!" He signed the letter with an "88!"[77] (Heick would later tell Mason, "I would like to personally thank you for all the propaganda that I have co-oped over the years."[78]) And the next month, Heick came to the 8/8/88 performance.

In 1988, there was a flurry of coverage on Nazi skinheads, which reflected its growth but significantly spurred on its explosion. That February, *The Oprah Winfrey Show* had on Nazi skinheads, including one who was thrown off the show for calling Winfrey a monkey.[79] In May, Rice told Mason that the TV show *Current Affair* has been in contact and that he would "love to see the lot of us on nationwide T.V. espousing Manson & National Socialism."[80] But it was Heick who was present for the Nazi skinheads' most notorious media moment in early November 1988 during a taping of an episode of Rivera's popular talk show. A brawl broke out on the show, featuring both Nazi and anti-racist skinheads, and in the fray Rivera's nose was broken by a flying chair.[81]

By this time, skinhead violence was ramping up. There had already been numerous hate crimes, including assaults against people of color, Jews, and LGBTQ+ people as well as attacks against synagogues and leftist spaces. A 1988 report identified California as the state with the most skinheads and documented numerous acts of violence there.[82] Now skinheads started turning into murderers, and these would come to include those affiliated with American Front.

During this period, the *USA Today* TV show ran a series called "Racist Youth." The third episode featured interviews with both Heick and Rice.[83] Heick, Rice, and others were shown walking through the streets and toasting in a bar. For his sit-down interview, Rice wore sunglasses and his paramilitary uniform, with an American Front patch on the breast. At a time when Nazi skinheads were starting to murder people in earnest, Rice told the interviewer,

Every single one of us in this room, we'd be prepared to kill if need be, we would be prepared to die for what we believe in. But what scares the people out there a thousand times more is that we're prepared to live for what we believe in.[84]

It was a strong statement for someone with his dress code. Another part of the segment showed Heick in front of a pulled-down rolling gate, with Rice standing behind him. Pointing to graffiti on the gate, Heick said, "Even amongst this entire street, even amongst all this multi-racial slime, it says 'Destroy Racism.' It's like, yeah right. Goodbye Destroy Racism." As he said this, Rice took a sharpie, marked the slogan out, and drew a swastika next to it.[85]

Around that time, an American Front publication, *Aryan Warrior*, included "The Abraxas Foundation on Evil," a puff piece for the supposed think tank. The article's placement in the ideological organ of a Nazi skinhead group shows how the Abraxas Foundation's politics were portrayed as consistent with neo-Nazism. According to the piece, the foundation was a "cadre of individuals…whose lives are dedicated" to the "Natural Order." (The piece does not directly mention race, although around the same time, Schreck said the Foundation was against "race-mixing" and "genetic suicide.") Next to the article was a cartoon of a Doc Martin–clad foot kicking caricatures of a black man and a Jew in the head, with the headline, "The Only Solution is White Revolution."[86] Both Parfrey and Moynihan would later refer positively to the *Aryan Warrior* article.[87]

Sassy Rice

By this time, the skinhead murders had begun; there were six between December 1987 and June 1990—but it rose rapidly. In 1993, the number was up to 22, and by early 1998 had reached at least 49.[88] In 1990, for example, one American Front–affiliated skinhead killed an anti-racist skinhead in Sacramento, California, while a Florida organizer took part in a group attack on a member who was left for dead. Those connected to the American Front would go on to commit other murders as well as numerous assaults, desecrations of synagogues and churches, and the bombing of an NAACP office and a gay bar.[89]

The organized White Supremacist movement, and especially neo-Nazis, had initially been wary of this new generation of violent youth and what they saw as a degenerate culture. But those leaders who did embrace them reaped a whirlwind. Metzger was among their earliest champions and probably the greatest beneficiary. He had an unusually wide media reach for a White

Supremacist; Metzger said his cable TV show *Race and Reason* reached 60 markets while in 1984 his *WAR* newspaper had a circulation of 4,000. His early recruitment of Nazi skinheads, and embrace of their violence, gave him a young, militant base—"I depend on skinheads."[90] But there was a downside, too. Metzger had a heavy hand in the most infamous of the early Nazi skinhead crimes, and he paid a price for it.

In November 1988, Ethiopian immigrant Mulugeta Seraw was killed in Portland, Oregon by a group of Nazi skinheads affiliated with WAR. The murder happened six months after the White Workers March that Rice was so enthralled by. On behalf of Seraw's family, the SPLC used an innovative legal strategy to sue Metzger and, in October 1990, won a judgment of $12.5 million against him and his associates.[91] This bankrupted Metzger, ended his on-the-ground organizing efforts, and spurred his advocacy of leaderless resistance.[92]

Before that happened, though, Metzger and Heick (who had made an alliance) tried to hold an outdoor Aryan Woodstock concert in northern California. Community opposition and the lack of a sound permit made the event a bust.[93]

This happened in March, only four months after Seraw's murder. And that same month, an article came out which would follow Rice around for the rest of his career. The popular magazine *Sassy*, whose audience was teenage girls, ran one of the many articles that year profiling Nazi skinheads. There was nothing of importance in it about Rice; indeed, he had said much more provocative things elsewhere. But accompanying it was a picture that made public, on a national level, the relationships he had been nurturing for years. In it, Rice and Heick held knives and wore matching uniforms with American Front patches sewn on the breast.[94] Rice's appeared to be the same as the one he wore for his previous TV appearance with Heick. As this picture would come up again and again in interviews and criticisms of Rice, he would try to squirm out of its obvious implications.[95]

Certainly during this period, observers could be forgiven if they thought Rice was in the American Front, especially as he appeared publicly with their leader at least twice while wearing the group's insignia. Even if one accepted the argument (which Rice claimed applied to himself) that in the postwar era one can be a non-racist fascist and legitimately distinguish those views from National Socialism, it was certainly another thing for him to describe himself this way in this context.

Rice wasn't the only one in the Abraxas Clique who was drawn to Heick, however. Heick was described in a 1989 *Hustler* article by Parfrey as "a top skinhead leader in the country" and "the matinee idol of skinheadom."[96] Moynihan also befriended Heick, and once they were even arrested together.

Völkisch Folk in Japan

In December 1988, Rice told Mason that "I have no doubt that '89 will see us all consolidating the advances that we gained in '88. TOWARD THE CROSS OF IRON!" He again signed off his letter with "88!" But before he did, Rice also made sure that Mason was in touch with Moynihan.[97]

A short tour of Japan in 1989 by an expanded version of NON was the highpoint of the Nazi influence on Rice's musical performances. This period also marked a shift in Rice's musical production from primarily atonal noise to collaborations which made Rice's output both more melodic and include more vocals. While Moynihan had been in contact with Rice by phone and mail, they did not meet in person until Moynihan was invited to take part in the tour and flew out to San Francisco beforehand.[98]

The musicians on the Japanese tour played neofolk and trafficked, to a greater or lesser degree, in fascist aesthetics—and sometimes politics. Playing in NON were Moynihan, Douglas Pearce (Death in June), Tony Wakeford (Sol Invictus), and Rose McDowall, while David Tibet (Current 93) was the opening act.

Pearce's Death in June was the pioneering neofolk band which launched the genre. They made a multi-decade career out of their heavy usage of Nazi symbols, songs titles, and lyrics while denying they were National Socialists. (By the time of the tour, "Death in June" had been reduced to a name used solely by Pearce.) Pearce has also been quite open about his views which might fall short of National Socialism but were still on the Far Right. For example, when asked about his "fans that are Eurocentric/Racialist," Pearce replied "Depending upon their 'version' of Eurocentric Racialism, then 9 times out of 10 I feel very comfortable with it. This is how it's supposed to be." Death in June's evocation of fascist themes in combination with expressed Far Right views showed an obvious sympathy with, and glorification of, National Socialism—at the least.[99]

There was no question about one Death in June member's involvement in fascist politics, however. This was given as one of the reasons that founding member Tony Wakeford was kicked out of the band in 1984. (Assumedly, he spoiled the "are-they-or-are-they-not" position that Pearce cultivated.) Wakeford then formed Above the Ruins, who were openly fascist. Although he had previously denied being a member of the National Front, in 1997 Wakeford admitted he had been—although adding he had had no connections to those politics since 1987, when he formed Sol Invictus. In fact, he had been associated with the National Front as early as 1982 while he was still in Death in June, and the connections continued well after his reputed break.[100]

Tibet had the least connection to fascist politics, although several Current 93 albums were significantly influenced by National Socialist themes and titles. For example, both Pearce and Rice played on the Current 93 album *Swastikas for Noddy*, released the year before the tour.[101]

Moynihan, meanwhile, had already made an agreement with Mason to work on turning SIEGE into an anthology. He started the work almost immediately upon returning from Japan.

The tour started a few months after the March *Sassy* issue. NON played only three concerts, although they stayed three weeks.[102] One, the early July 1989 Osaka show, was filmed. Musically, it was composed of droning martial songs with drums and keyboards, but the stage show was equal in importance. The musicians wore black uniforms with Wolfangel armbands, and the symbol also adorned their drums. The first song, "Total War," took its name from the famous 1943 speech by NSDAP propaganda minister Joseph Goebbels.[103]

The event built upon two from the last summer, the 8/8/88 performance and a comparable show Moynihan had played in Belgium. Rice later talked about the influence of a particularly striking picture he had seen of Oswald Mosley, the most prominent British fascist leader of the prewar and immediately postwar period. In the picture, Mosley is on a high podium with his lightning bolt symbol flanking his sides and towering above him. Rice said the Osaka show in particular was an attempt to replicate this "on a small scale," as part of a desire to turn his concerts into something "more like rituals or ceremonies or rallies."[104]

While the musicians were all still in Japan, they also made some recordings with each other. Four of the songs that ended up on Rice's next album were recorded there, as was a Current 93 single.[105] The NON Osaka show came out that year as a VHS tape, and in 1992, it was released again as one side of NON's *In the Shadow of the Sword* album. (The same year also saw the release the NON "best of" *Easy Listening for Iron Youth*, whose title and cover had a distinctly fascist aesthetic.[106])

Bay Area Left to Denver Right

According to his biographer Brian Clark, Rice's relationships with the Bay Area cultural radicals soon crumbled as his neo-Nazi ties became too obvious to ignore—especially as he was associating with those who had blood on their hands.

Clark said, "rancor toward him was steadily mounting" in San Francisco after the *Sassy* article. In March 1988, Rice mailed Mason a copy of the RE/Search book *Pranks*. In it was a picture from the year before of Rice on stage with Jello Biafra, the singer of the popular left-wing punk band the Dead Kennedys.[107] But according to Clark, Biafra was only one of a number of underground luminaries who broke ties with Rice.[108] Parfrey even claimed (truthfully or not) that avant-garde singer Diamanda Galás, Rice's label-mate on Mute, had "spent a lot of energy" in an unsuccessful attempt to get Rice dropped.[109]

Those who had made records with Rice broke with him, too, notably Fad Gadget's Tovey and Peter "Sleazy" Christopherson of Coil, who previously had been in Throbbing Gristle. Years after making a record with Rice, Sleazy said, "we fell out because of Boyd's increasingly racist public image. It wasn't because of political or social correctness" but because it was "simply moronic" to demonize people because of their identity.[110]

But undoubtedly the most personal falling out was with RE/Search. In Rice's accounting, RE/Search editors Vale and Andrea Juno said he "underwent some sort of Jekyll and Hyde transformation. Like I was this really nice guy who became an asshole overnight." Rice was particularly hurt over RE/Search's *Incredibly Strange Films*, which he had worked on since 1983.[111] In the early 1990s, Rice claimed he was owed thousands for his work on it, "but ever since they decided I was a crazed Nazi I haven't seen a penny." He threatened to sue.[112]

Returning that summer from Japan to find burning bridges, Rice moved to Denver before the end of the year.[113]

Music, Martinis, and Misogyny

He soon had company, though. In January 1990, Moynihan moved across country and became roommates with Rice in the basement of a remodeled girl's school dubbed "the bunker."[114] That March, Pearce came to Denver to finish recording the tracks for what was to become *Music, Martinis, and Misanthropy*, released as Boyd Rice Experience. It came out in August on Death in June's house label, New European Recordings. Like the tour, it was a change in music for Rice, reflected by the fact that it was not released as NON. Pearce went so far as to call it a "surrogate" Death in June album.[115] In their small cultural world, it was a successful record.

Rice had long expressed misanthropy, but in Denver he added blatantly misogynistic expressions. He contributed to a 1994 rape-themed issue of *ANSWER ME!*, a popular fanzine co-edited by Jim Goad. Rice's "Revolt Against Penis Envy" waxed nostalgic for a "a once-glorious past" when women were "without rights, a second-class citizen. In some places, she wasn't considered a citizen at all; she was property." This world of happiness needed to be restored through "a war *of* the sexes, against the pernicious doctrine of sexual equality. And if the chief weapon in this war is rape, then let there be rape."[116] When asked about this in 1997, Rice explained, "That was at least half serious. Because everything in it is basically true. It's obviously an idea taken to its logical extreme." Rice said he was a misogynist "more and more all the time" and that "I don't think women deserve the same rights as men."[117] Goad continued their misogynistic collaboration by contributing the track "Let's Hear it For Violence Against Women" to the 1995 Boyd Rice Experience album *Hatesville!*[118]

Rice would end up being arrested in 1995 for domestic violence. His former partner Lisa Crystal Carver wrote in her autobiography that "Boyd strangled me and threw me against walls and bashed my head against the futon frame." Rice said the charges were dropped just before the trial.[119] Goad did not get off so easily after he brutally beat his girlfriend in 1998, although he ended up serving only two and a half years.[120]

The President and the Preacher

For a while, Moynihan and Rice seemed to get along well and participated in each other's recordings. In the first half of the year, Moynihan was part of the *Music, Martinis, And Misanthropy* recordings, and in the second half, Rice played on two tracks by Moynihan's Blood Axis.[121]

In May 1991, Rice was home when the Secret Service came to question his roommate about an alleged plot to kill President George H. W. Bush.[122] The next month Rice, Moynihan, and Mason went on the "Manson Maniacs" episode of the radio show of Christian preacher Bob Larson. There they sparred with not just Larson but also Doris Tate, mother of Sharon Tate, the actress murdered by the Manson Family.

Flanked by the two firebrands, Rice came off as comparatively mild-mannered for most of the show—with some definite exceptions. He shared a Bible that had belonged to Manson with a horrified Larson. When Rice said there needed to be a return to a "pre-Christian way of life," Larson retorted "and people like me out of the way?" to which Rice replied, "people like you wouldn't exist in a world like that." Asked if he thought war and mass murder were good, Rice readily agreed. And he affirmed that "three-quarters of humanity" needed to die in order to restore balance to the world.[123]

His misanthropic views were not limited to outrageous appearances on Christian radio shows. That year, in a fanzine interview, he hoped for a catastrophe that would "kill off a huge segment of the population on the planet." On another occasion, he praised AIDS for killing Africans.[124]

But as with so many others, conditions between Rice and his partner-in-misanthropy slash roommate Moynihan deteriorated, and by the end of 1992, the latter moved out of their underground bunker.[125] Rice initially described the split in unfriendly terms, saying Moynihan "was younger and hadn't made his mark on the world" and that he had complained he didn't get enough credit for his work.[126] At the beginning, Moynihan said he would "never work with Boyd Rice again, due to personal differences,"[127] although later on, the bad feelings apparently dissipated enough that Moynihan blurbed one of Rice's books. "I'm glad I was able to spend a few years collaborating with him, and striking blows against prevailing idiocy in the ways we did."[128]

A *Wake* for Abraxas

Rice's most comprehensive ideological publication of this period was *WAKE*, although he published only one issue. A long time coming. Moynihan had started working on *WAKE* after joining the Foundation in March 1989.[129] In 1990, the two received a visit from Keith Stimely, a Holocaust denier who had worked for the Institute for Historical Review (IHR). (The organization was the primary vehicle responsible for the more widespread dissemination of Holocaust denial in the United States.) Stimely ended up working on the technical side of *WAKE*. Despite Moynihan's work, when *WAKE* finally appeared in early 1992, Rice was listed as the sole editor.[130]

Rice described *WAKE* as "the world's first newspaper dedicated to Barbarism and Social Darwinism," claiming it was part of the "public propaganda program" of the Abraxas Foundation.[131] It was an oversize newsprint publication illustrated with striking graphics—but it also showcased Rice's intellectual flimsiness. Despite its size, it was low on written content. (After all, in the counterculture, one just needed some kind of erudite-sounding philosophy to build an aesthetic around, ideally buttressed by quotes from known thinkers. Intellectual depth was optional—and often absent.)

The centerpiece essay, "Nature's Eternal Fascism," was based on the same talking points Rice had espoused for years. (It was originally written in 1989, during the highpoint of Rice's neo-Nazi involvement.) It bandied about phrases like the "New Barbarism," "Nature's Order," and "Primal Law."[132] Most of *WAKE*, including a significant amount of "Nature's Eternal Fascism," consisted of quotations from 18 people. On the cover was a quote attributed only to "H.H.," implying "Heil Hitler" (but actually from Herman Hesse). The centerfold, "Long Live Death!," was a series of quotations, of which five were from White Supremacists or fascists: Ragnar Redbeard, Italian fascists Gabriele D'Annunzio and Benito Mussolini, Robert Jay Mathews of The Order, and Lothrop Stoddard, author of the influential prewar racist book *The Rising Tide of Color Against White World-Supremacy*.[133]

When *WAKE* was finally out, Rice made sure to send a copy to Mason. His assessment was that "it looks great and reads great. This should generate a lot of interest and support."[134]

The Continuing Appeal of Savitri Devi

Additionally, Savitri Devi's *The Lightning and the Sun* was one of four books *WAKE* suggested as further reading, and she would be a reoccurring touchstone for the Abraxas Clique.

Born in France, Savitri Devi spent the 1930s and early '40s in India. Immersed in pro-Nazi Hindu nationalist circles, she created a new philosophy which combined National Socialism and Hindu religious teachings.

It held that the world was at the end of the cosmic cycle of the Kali Yuga, representing the depths of a dark age. But certain "Men against Time" could resist this and return the world to a flourishing state. Unsurprisingly, Hitler was the foremost among these, and she claimed he was a divine being. Arrested for spreading Nazi propaganda in Germany immediately following the war, Savitri Devi authored numerous books promoting her esoteric views. These would profoundly influence postwar National Socialist thought, including that of Rockwell and, even more, his successor Matthias Koehl.[135]

They also had a clear influence on Mason's adaption of Manson as a spiritual guru. Savitri Devi was mentioned at least three times in SIEGE, especially in a 1982 issue where Mason quoted a long passage from *The Lightning and the Sun* about the "divine cause" of Hitler, the "last Man Against Time."[136] In 1995, Mason said she had penned "some of the greatest monuments of prose to the glorification of the Adolph Hitler and the Third Reich" and deserved a wider readership.[137]

Rice also had an interest in Savitri Devi. Her works were adapted for his song "Paradise of Perfection," a collaboration with Death in June.[138] References to her also show up in Rice's associates Radio Werewolf and Current 93, and *Apocalypse Culture* contained an excerpt of Savitri Devi's *The Lightning and the Sun*.[139] Rice listed the book in his "Recommended Reading List" and in 2001 penned an essay discussing her theories.[140] While it avoided saying that she was of note because she advocated Hitler worship, Rice's own dictum on Manson was germane here: If Savitri Devi didn't promote Hitler's divinity, why would her writings be of interest?

Brown Rice: 1993 and After

The impact of neo-Nazism on the counterculture had been cutting edge in 1986 but by 1989 had peaked. During this time, Rice had incorporated many Nazi influences into his work, from *Blood & Flame* to the Japanese tour. And Rice had taken elements not just from books about the prewar fascist movement but from contact with contemporary neo-Nazis who were directly encouraging murder and race war. But soon after, Rice's interest faded precipitously. For what could be worse for a trend spotter than yesterday's fad?

Much of *Siege* had been put together while Moynihan and Rice were roommates in Denver, and after its release, Mason reported that Rice "commented that one can open it at any point 'and find something good.'"[141] But Rice's views weren't broadcast for public consumption.

After 1993, Rice kept some of the elements of Nazism that he had already picked up, including uniforms and Hitler iconography, even as he moved on. His attention turned towards tiki bars and Holy Grail mysticism, cultivating a relationship with actor Tiny Tim, and collecting Barbie dolls as well as writing and making art.

The Nazi imagery he used became blatant and—as he was no longer embedded in the neo-Nazi milieu—more ironic. He posed for a photo in *ANSWER ME!* fanzine, in a T-shirt with "RAPE" in large white letters, in additional to wearing a swastika necklace. One art piece spelled out "LOVE," with each letter in separate boxes and with a swastika in the middle of the "O."[142]

Rice continued to churn out records, including many collaborations. Rice appeared on *Calling Dr. Luv* by the Electric Hellfire Club, which was led by Moynihan's friend, and Mason associate, Thomas Thorn. Rice would also tour with them as the opener.[143] From 1996 to 2000, Rice published about a dozen pieces in *Seconds* magazine, which was co-edited by Parfrey's former collaborator, George Petros.[144]

Rice also influenced a young musician who was soon to become a major star, Marilyn Manson. According to Rice, Marilyn Manson—also known for using Nazi imagery—met the industrial pioneer before he had a record deal; Rice claims he called him a "mentor."[145] Marilyn Manson also submitted a piece to the unreleased 1992 issue of *EXIT* and was interviewed in *Seconds* three times between 1994 and 1996.[146] His first album, *Portrait of an American Family*, thanked Rice and LaVey. The latter was no surprise. When Marilyn Manson met LaVey, he was made a priest on the spot, and in turn the musician wrote the foreword to LaVey's posthumous *Satan Speaks!*[147]

Although he had moved on from this period of his work, Rice stayed in touch with both Metzger and Mason; after all, they were not about to break with him because he had moved too far to the right. Metzger remained in contact, and on a first-name basis, through at least 1996. Asking about a TV appearance by Rice that summer, Metzger wrote Mason, "Have Boyd let me know if he has a copy of the tape, if you talk to him before I do."[148]

Rice also met up with Mason in 1999 and again for beers in 2000.[149] In 2003, Rice promised to come to one of Mason's talks. Mason's new publisher in Montana, Ryan Schuster, said he was going to attend, although in the end neither made it. Schuster told Mason, "Give my best regards to Herr Rice." This was the last contact Mason and Rice had.[150]

The years of accusations of neo-Nazism against Rice have added to his radical chic. And for a while he flaunted this, using swastikas and putting up his infamous photo with Heick on his own website. But starting in 1994, Rice seemed to waver in his identification with these politics, saying "I find the extremist stuff of whatever bent stimulating and interesting" but specifying that "I don't necessarily adhere to it as a political agenda."[151] Even though he admitted in 1996 that his associations had hurt his career, he continued to call himself as a fascist at least through 1997. But in 1999, he seemed to tire of it all, and in 2003, he stated, "I'm not a fascist at all."[152]

Rice has retained his cult following. He published several books, and Brian Clark's introduction to Rice's anthology *Standing in Two Circles* was republished as a standalone biography. A four-hour biographical documentary, *Iconoclast*, was released in 2010.[153] Boycotts against his concerts and art exhibitions continued, some successful but others not. For example, a 2013 show opening for Cold Cave in New York City went on despite community pressure, while a planned 2018 solo art show in the city was sunk—although Rice gained a fair amount of press both times.[154]

Rice has continued to position himself on the Far Right. During the Trump administration, he posted pictures on the social media platform Instagram palling around with Diamond and Silk, two well-known Trumpist commentators—although, par for Rice's recent course, both were black.[155] The evening before the 2017 rally in Charlottesville, the neo-Nazis and other White Supremacists held a torch-light demonstration, which the media derisively but accurately dubbed a "tiki-torch march." In response, Rice posted a picture on Instagram of a backyard party he was at; the caption said, "Heard a guy on news radio reference a 'neo-nazi tiki torch rally'. So, we had one."[156]

Once again, Rice had positioned himself on the side of violent neo-Nazis, something that would be reciprocated. The first Atomwaffen Division leader, Brandon Russell, was released from prison in August 2021. The next month, on a Twitter account, Russell posted a picture of himself at the beach. He was wearing a NON T-shirt.[157]

Rice Replies and Denies

Despite the substantial amount of public evidence of Rice's involvement with neo-Nazism, he has consistently denied that this constituted anything meaningful. He has been repeatedly questioned about this, although those interviewing or writing about him almost never cite an expert on neo-Nazis. Meanwhile, Rice's supporters have regularly claimed that his associations with neo-Nazis, and especially his appearance with Heick, were provocations or pranks. Others simply dismiss them out of hand. Parfrey, for example, responded to one criticism by saying,

> If Boyd Rice is such a terminal Nazi, how is that he has long-term Jewish friends and girlfriends? How is that he collects Barbie dolls? Is Boyd Rice a neo-Nazi, or is he something else...?[158]

The "something else"—a self-proclaimed fascist who collaborated with neo-Nazis—is the correct answer. Interestingly, Rice himself has chosen to downplay rather than deny the situation. For example, in 2011, he said, "I wanted to be an irritant.... But this wasn't gratuitous reactionary contrarianism." And the next year, he said "That wasn't meant to wind anybody up."[159] But he used a number of other rhetorical tactics as well.

Projection

Rice had already started his campaign of denial while still deeply embedded in the neo-Nazi milieu. During the Ken Swezey and Brian King interview in March 1987, the same day the Friends of Justice shows were supposed to happen—but were cancelled partly because of accusations of White Supremacist involvement—Rice squirmed out of direct questions about that relationship. Less than three months after taping his interview with Metzger, Rice admitted nothing and instead claimed the criticisms were the work of others. Asked, "Is there any truth to the rumor that you guys are White Supremacists or are backed by White Supremacists?," Rice replied, "See if you use a term like 'supremacist,' that has an instant prejudice built into it. It's an emotional term," because "it implies somebody else is inferior and no one wants to be inferior."[160] When asked where the rumor came from, Rice said,

> I think it probably came from you, because you interviewed James Mason, and people knew Mason was connected with Manson. And they knew we were connected with Manson, and they knew that there was this whole network of people who were interested in Manson.[161]

Rice forgot to mention that he was both a key node in that network and in frequent contact with Mason. In fact, Rice sent Mason a letter directly after the cancelled events, gushing over the bomb, arson, and death threats they had received. The top of the page was festooned with a swastika.[162]

Social Darwinism and Fascism Are Not National Socialism

In 1991, Rice said he was called a Nazi on the basis of his Social Darwinist beliefs. However, at the same time (and unlike later), he acknowledged that the NSDAP members "were kind of Social Darwinists"—although he stressed that his version did not champion a "master race."[163] In 1993, he said "There's a new McCarthyism out there, and its agenda is to annihilate anything that doesn't march in lock step with its liberal humanist dogma."[164] (Elsewhere Rice said that "Liberal Humanists" labeled him a Nazi because that was their name for anyone who expressed the "intrinsic truth" that some people are stronger and smarter than others.) And much later, Rice accused some of those speaking against him of not being familiar with his work and instead merely reacting emotionally to third-party accusations.[165]

Riced Jews

Somewhat oddly, Rice vehemently denied he was an antisemite in particular. According to him, "I've never had anything bad going against Jewish people." He also claimed that he had a lawyer send a cease-and-desist letter to someone accusing him of being a neo-Nazi; according to Rice, it said "<u>my client doesn't have anything against Jews or Judaism</u>" and threatened legal action.[166] And, reversing accusations against one critic, Rice accused that person of making antisemitic statements themselves. Indeed, there is no evidence that Rice himself utilized antisemitic conspiracy theories or denied the Holocaust. While on Larson's show, Rice was asked if Jews were a problem; he explicitly said that they were not, because what was at play was a different process.[167]

In a 1996 interview, he talked about his view of Jews, once again denying that he was an antisemite, though in a curious way.

> I like Jews. I like what Jews have done. I only get pissed off at Jews when I hear them whining endlessly about anti-Semitism and talking about the Holocaust ad infinitum. Jesus fucking Christ, give it a break.

… Where have I said anything against Jews? I mean, love **Hitler**. I love a lot of what he did, and people throw out the baby with the bathwater.[168]

Rice's previous history casts some doubt on his love of the Jewish people. Putting aside his interest in Hitler and direct relationship with neo-Nazis such as Metzger, Mason, and Heick, he wrote to Mason about "Jew York" and denounced a lawyer for also being Jewish. During his interview with Metzger, he agreed with the statement that music had become a "propaganda instrument of Jewish interests." Rice's albums and publications uncritically quoted various antisemites (including Rosenberg, Savitri Devi, Redbeard, and a member of The Order), while a Holocaust denier helped him produce *WAKE*.

Not a Political Fascist

Especially in the 1990s, Rice held that his use of fascism wasn't meant as a political position.

In one statement, Rice said that while he was interested in fascism because it was an extreme belief, "I don't necessarily adhere to it as a political agenda." Here, he defined fascism as "just the corporate state, it's about economics and that sort of thing, and that doesn't interest me at all." He said he used the term only because "if fascism is just being anti-democratic and against the consensus-reality we live in, I might as well just say I'm a fascist." In 1994, he said, "For years I've been called a fascist—and I guess I am (laughs). Not in a political sense."[169] In 2003, he told Clark "I'm not a fascist at all. I have absolutely not a political bone in my body." Furthermore, "I'm the least fascistic person you will ever meet." And on at least one occasion, he used a time-worn argument that his use of the Wolfsangel was not a reference to National Socialism but simply an "ancient symbol."[170]

The Fifteen-Minute Friend

As the years grew further from the infamous 1989 photo, Rice has tried to distance himself from it—and Heick—more and more. Early on, Rice was quite open about his time hanging out with Nazi skinheads in San Francisco, saying he was attracted to their outlaw status, seeing it like the Hells Angels. He claimed that it was this socializing which made the "artists and intellectuals" he knew jealous, as Rice preferred the company of aggressive, hairless men to these "dilettantes."[171]

In 1997, he admitted that he was "good friends" with Heick but that he had gone to the *Sassy* photo shoot only because of a promise of free food and alcohol. It was just the two of them because none of the skinheads who were invited had shown up. (He did not mention the other time he was caught on camera with Heick in the same uniform.) Rice complained that after the photo appeared, people said he was a neo-Nazi. "I used to say, jeez, are people so damn stupid and one-dimensional that they think you're as much of a cartoon as they are?"[172]

By 2018, Rice had back-peddled significantly after the cancellation of his art show. By now Heick, the man who had been his "good friend," was now someone Rice knew for only "15 minutes."[173]

NO *Nazis*

Another technique was to deny he was a "Nazi," or had connections to Nazis, because they were limited "to a specific time and place; a specific historical moment."[174] (Moynihan would use this argument as well.)

In his 2009 book NO, Rice downplayed the existence of contemporary neo-Nazis altogether. In the present, he said, "There *are* no Nazis. Certainly there exist people who imagine they're Nazis, perhaps some who dress up as Nazis in uniforms." He also dismissed their danger, writing, "If you were to make a list of the 1000 things that constitute a threat to your personal well-being, the Nazis needn't be included."[175] It was a quite a statement from a man who associated with neo-Nazi leaders whose followers committed numerous acts of violence, including several murders. Rice's list of a thousand things appeared to be referring to himself.

Years later, Gavin McInnes, founder of the violent Alt Right group the Proud Boys, would similarly say, "Nazis don't exist"—although his own group had constant attrition to neo-Nazism.[176]

Born without Feelings

Rice has long hid in plain sight about his deep involvement with the neo-Nazi milieu. Asked about this numerous times over the years, he has done his best to refuse to own up to his actions, and he has always portrayed himself as the victim of unfair accusations. Beyond attempting to explain away what he is asked about, he has never volunteered anything about his extensive relationships—in particular with Mason.

In some places, Rice has described his own perspective and emotional state. This perhaps gives insight into his past behavior of associating with neo-Nazis and doing so with barely an acknowledgment and without any kind of apology. In his book *NO*, Rice directly described himself as "a sociopath of sorts."

> When you are born without the ordinary feelings and emotions shared by most other human beings, life looks different to you. It seems at times like a movie you're walking through, more a spectator than a participant. There is above all a lack of empathy with most of mankind, a sense of detachment.[177]

The director of the documentary about Rice ultimately agreed with this assessment. After their falling out, Larry Wessel called him "a lonely, cold-hearted, pretentious, hypocritical sociopath."[178]

If Rice were a sociopath, it would certainly be consistent with how he was closely connected to neo-Nazis for a time, but soon after moved on to different things—including working with people from the same identities that his neo-Nazi friends had promoted violence against. But consistency and diagnosis are not the same, and only a qualified professional could decide whether Rice was a sociopath. As for his own self-conception, there is only his word on it.

Notes

1 Although some of them broke with him later over his neo-Nazi affiliations, musicians who Rice has been connected to include Throbbing Gristle, Coil, Death in June, Current 93, Marilyn Manson, Marc Almond (Soft Cell), Frank Tovey (Fad Gadget), Matt Skiba (Alkaline Trio), Cold Cave, Michael Moynihan, Electric Hellfire Club, Der Blutharsch, Hirsute Pursuit, and Ze'ev. Other figures include Daniel Miller (Mute Records), Rodney Bingenheimer (KROQ), Adam Parfrey (Feral House), and V. Vale and Andrea Juno (RE/Search).

2 Rice appeared on Larson's show "Manson Maniacs" with Mason in 1991. A picture of Rice, Moynihan, and Shaun Partridge was taken with Mason at his home on April 30, 1993—less than two weeks after *Siege* was released; for the occasion Rice wore a black T-shirt with "RAPE" emblazoned on it. He was back in Larson's studio during Mason's June 1993 appearance, where a photo of all three of them was taken. In 1994, Rice admitted to a reporter that he had been the one who initially tracked down Mason. And in the 2006 *Art That Kills*, there is a brief reference to Rice having written Mason, as well as a group picture both are in. *Articles*, pp.8, 49, 183, 189; *Art That Kills*, pp.189, 191; Knipfel, "The Other Nazis," p.22 (*Articles*, p.71).

3 Dorothy Townsend, "Mrs. Ford Dances to Win California Votes," *Los Angeles Times*, March 11, 1976, pp.1, 27, www.newspapers.com/image/382859025, www.newspapers.com/image/382859158. Rice's re-telling of the story is in V Vale and Andrea Juno, eds., *Pranks* (San Francisco: RE/Search, 1987), pp.18–20.

4 "Boyd Rice," in Ira A Robbins, ed., *Trouser Press Record Guide*, 4th ed. (New York: Collier Books, 1991), p.552, https://trouserpress.com/reviews/boyd-rice

5 Both the 8/8/88 show and the later concerts in Japan were also billed as NON but included other musicians. V Vale and Andrea Juno, eds., *Industrial Culture Handbook* (San Francisco: RE/Search, 1983), p.54.

6 *Art That Kills*, p.127.

7 The most comprehensive examination of the band is Simon Ford, *Wreckers of Civilisation: The Story of COUM Transmissions and Throbbing Gristle* (London: Black Dog Publishing, 1999). Simon Reynolds, *Rip It Up and Start Again: Postpunk 1978–1984* (New York: Penguin, 2005), ebook, chapter 4. For Nazi skinheads and the National Front, see Nigel Copsey and Matthew Worley, "White Youth: The far right, punk and British youth culture, 1977–87," in Copsey and Worley, eds., *'Tomorrow Belongs to Us': The British Far Right since 1967* (London: Routledge, 2018), pp.113–31, and Graham Macklin, *Failed Führers: A History of Britain's Extreme Right* (London: Routledge, 2020).

8 Ford, *Wreckers of Civilisation*, pp.7.1–7.2, 8.15, 11.5. For more examples, and a far more critical assessment of their relationship to fascism, see the chapter on Throbbing Gristle in Benjamin Bland's PhD dissertation, "Extremism in the British Underground: Subcultural Fascism(s) and Their Reflections in Music Culture, c. 1975-1999," Department of History Royal Holloway, University of London, September 2019, pp.238–77.

9 Vale and Juno, eds., *Industrial Culture Handbook*, pp.68–81; Reynolds, *Rip It Up and Start Again*, chapter 8. The band pointed out the logo also resembled things as harmless as the danger sign for electricity and David Bowie's Ziggy Stardust flash; Ford, *Wreckers of Civilisation*, pp.7.1–7.2.

10 Ford, *Wreckers of Civilisation*, pp.6.30, 7.22, 10.5.

11 Rice interview in *Fifth Path*, pp.8–9; Rice, "I'll Call You Abraxas," *Standing*, p.95.

12 Reynolds, *Rip It Up and Start Again*, p.238, cited in Bland, "Extremism in the British Underground," p.252. On Throbbing Gristle's use of Nazi imagery, see Bland as well as Ford, *Wreckers of Civilisation*, pp.7.10–7.20; for their less critical relationship to fascism, see pp.8.15, 9.7, 9.18, 9.23, 10.22, 10.29.

13 Rice performed as NON at the Throbbing Gristle show in London on February 8, 1981; Ford, *Wreckers of Civilisation*, p.11.6.

14 Clark, *Biography*, p.11.

15 Parfrey, "If We're So Wrong, How Come Mr. Moynihan's so *Right*?" (letter to the editor), *Hit List* #3, June/July 1999, p.5; *RE/Search* #1, 1980.

16 Vale and Juno, eds., *Industrial Culture Handbook*, pp.50–67. This reflected the idea, popularized in the 1970s, held that Hitler was a magician who bamboozled the German people. In 1992, Rice said he was interested in the idea of Hitler as a Jungian archetype, and that he harnessed him during performances; *Art That Kills*, p.127; Rice interview in *Fifth Path* #3, p.11.

17 Knipfel, "The Other Nazis," p.22 (*Articles*, p.71); Rice to Mason, August 11, 1986; Mason to Rice, August 14, 1986 [both Box 9, Folder 20].

18 Rice to Mason, April 24, 1986 [Box 32, Folder 23].

19 Rice to Mason, May 12, 1986 [Box 9, Folder 20].

20 Ibid; Mason to Charles Manson, May 17, 1986 [Box 9, Folders 1–3].

21 Rice to Mason, [May] 1986 [Box 9, Folder 20].

22 Ibid.

23 Mason to Rice, May 29, 1986; Rice to Mason, June 24, 1986; Rice to Mason, [August 11], 1986 [all three Box 9, Folder 20].

24 "Iconoclast San Francisco Premiere Nov. 1, 2010 (ad by Tora Wessel)" [sic] (video), uploaded by Larry Wessel, [2010], https://vimeo.com/16041423

25 Rice interview in *Fifth Path* #3, p.12.
26 Rice to Mason, August 11, 1986 [Box 9, Folder 20].
27 A letter from Rice, either dated or postmarked August 11, was the first time he wrote Mason about his excitement at visiting Manson—but the P.S. to the same letter referred to his arrest. Rice's previous letter, marked June 24, 1986, did not refer to meeting Manson; Rice to Mason, August 11, 1986. [Box 9, Folder 20].
   An auctioneer of murder-related memorabilia sold a record of Rice's arrest record at San Quentin, dated August 6, 1986. The seller affirmed its authenticity with the author and said he discussed Rice in a visit to Manson. And in one place, Rice admitted that after his second visit, "I was only to see him a few more times" until the bullet incident. "Charles Manson/Boyd Rice San Quentin arrest report 8/6/1986," MurderAuction.com, https://web.archive.org/web/20210430210418, https://www.murderauction.com/auction/listing/charles-manson-boyd-rice-san-quentin-arrest-report-8-6-1986/220017; *Art That Kills*, p.127.
28 Rice's description of the incident, and admission that it ended their friendship, is in Rice, "I'll Call You Abraxas," *Standing*, pp.104–5.
29 Manson, *Manson Speaks*.
30 *Iconoclast* (video), dir. Larry Wessel, 2010, www.imdb.com/title/tt1827439, www.bitchute.com/video/HO8doYE7YZvz (part 2).
31 Knipfel, "The Other Nazis," p.22 (*Articles*, p.71); Schreck and Rice interview with Brian King and Ken Swezey (video), filmed March 20, 1987, unreleased (video in possession of author); Rice, "I'll Call You Abraxas," *Standing*, pp.104–5.
32 "Friends of Justice" letterhead, undated [1986/1987] [Box 17, Folder 4]; Parfrey to Mason, [January 1987?], Mason's handwritten notes on letter refer to February 16, 1987 [Box 17, Folder 4].
33 Schreck and Rice interview with King and Swezey (video); Parfrey to Mason, March 30, 1987 [Box 17, Folder 4].
34 UPI, "Manson Parole Rejected for Seventh Time," *San Francisco Examiner*, February 9, 1989, p.A10, www.newspapers.com/image/461379918
35 Parfrey to Mason, December 14, 1986 [Box 17, Folder 4].
36 Parfrey to Mason, April 15, 1987 [Box 17, Folder 4]. Among others, during his long career Hoffman worked with Metzger and the Institute for Historical Review. For more, see Mattias Gardell, *Gods of the Blood: The Pagan Revival and White Separatism* (Durham, North Carolina: Duke University Press, 2003), pp.98–100, 363n53.
37 Linda Blood, *The New Satanists* (Grand Central Publishing/Warner Books, 1994), chapter 8, https://archive.org/details/linda-osborne-blood-the-new-satanists-1994-warner-books-libgen.lc_202012. Although Blood is not always reliable, others point to a date that is, at the least, very close, as does the fact that Rice stayed with Metzger the next day. See, for example, Parfrey to Mason, December 28, 1986 [Box 17, Folder 4].
38 Copies of the video have been removed from multiple video sites, including YouTube; Rice interview with Metzger and Tom Padgett/*Race and Reason* on December 30, 1986 (video), DVD in possession of author. A transcript of the show is available at "Boyd Rice on Tom Metzger's 'Race and Reason' (1986)," *Radical Archives*, January 15, 2024, https://radicalarchives.org/2024/01/15/ricemetzger
39 Ibid.
40 Rice to Mason, [January 22], 1987 [Box 9, Folder 20]; Metzger to Mason, [August?] 1987 [Box 7, Folder 21].
41 Metzger to Mason, August 13, 1996 [Box 11, Folder 5]; *WAR* 6(2) 1987, p.12; Jack Carter and Metzger, *In the Eye of the Storm*, p.163. The author purchased a DVD of the interview directly from Tom Metzger immediately before his November 2020 death.

42 This point is made in Clark, *Biography*, p.18. The date on the release is 1986, although Discogs gives it as January 12, 1987; NON, *Blood & Flame* (Mute, 1996), www.discogs.com/release/4099594-NON-Blood-Flame

43 "Wolfangel," *ADL*, www.adl.org/education/references/hate-symbols/wolfsangel; Rice interview in *Fifth Path* #3, p.7.

44 The quote is given as, "It is the legacy of our age that we must sink...submerge to the deepest depths in order that the highest be elevated to light"; Rice, *Blood & Flame* (Mute, 1986), www.discogs.com/release/128828-NON-Blood-Flame. For the original version of the quote, see Alfred Rosenberg, *Selected Writings*, Robert A Pois, ed. (London: Cape, 1970), p.120. Rosenberg's *The Myth of the Twentieth Century* later showed up on Rice's recommended reading list; "BOYD RICE'S Recommended Reading List," *Boyd Rice*, http://web.archive.org/web/20041021025914, http://www.boydrice.com/readinglist.html

45 Amit Varshizky has argued that Rosenberg took the structure of Gnostic theology and Nazified it. The Gnostic vision is of a transcendent God which humanity contains a spark of, although it is trapped in a corrupt world. Therefore humans must make a spiritual journey inward (ie, not through acts or words) in order to find their way back to God. Rosenberg made this into a conflict between the "race-soul" and a world corrupted by liberalism, Judaism, and Catholicism—which the Nordic race had to find its way out of. Furthermore, he claimed the "spiritual vitality" of the race-soul was expressed in blood. (More generally, both Moynihan and Rice expressed their interest in blood as a carrier for concepts that intrigued them.) Amit Varshizky, "Alfred Rosenberg: The Nazi *Weltanschauung* as Modern Gnosis," *Politics, Religion & Ideology* 13(3), pp.314, 320, 325, online September 11, 2012, http://dx.doi.org/10.1080/21567 689.2012.698977

46 The quote inside the album is, "Not every beautiful thing is dead which has been swallowed up in silence...perhaps it is only sleeping." Arthur de Gobineau, *The Inequality of the Human Races* (London: William Heinmann, 1915), p.xiv (originally published 1854), https://archive.org/details/inequality-of-the-human-races; Robert Barry, "FACT Meets Boyd Rice," *FACT*, [2012], www.factmag. com/2012/10/03/i-always-felt-apart-from-everybody-else-fact-meets-boyd-rice-noise-pioneer-film-buff-leader-of-the-church-of-satan/3

47 "Blood Axis: >>Blood=Life=Death<<" (interview with Moynihan), *Fifth Path* #3, Spring 1992, p.27.

48 Rice to Mason, [February/March] 1988; Mason to Rice, March 4, 1988 [both Box 9, Folder 20].

49 Rice to Mason, February 20, 1987; Rice to Mason, [February or March] 1987 [both Box 9, Folder 20].

50 Rice to Mason, July 4, 1988; Rice to Mason, [early September] 1988; Rice to Mason, [end of December] 1988 [all three Box 9, Folder 20].

51 Adolf Hitler, "A New Dawn Has Come...," in Parfrey, ed., *Apocalypse Culture*, pp.61–62; Rice, "Love Opened My Eyes," *EXIT* #3, 1987, https://exitmagazine. net/page.php?id=26

52 Clark, *Biography*, pp.24–26.

53 NON, *Total War Live in Japan* (videocassette); NON, *Might!* (Mute, 1995), www.discogs.com/release/48216-NON-Might

54 *WAKE*'s main piece, "Nature's Eternal Fascism," was an exposition of *Might Is Right*. The publication also contained a selection of Redbeard quotes, and his book was first on Rice's reading list for those interested in "primal law"; "Nature's Eternal Fascism," *WAKE* #1, 1992, pp.3, 4–5, 7.

55 Redbeard, *Might Is Right*; Robert Burns/Mason, "Three Faces of Satanism," *Universal Order*, [1996 to 1998?], https://web.archive.org/web/19980526 141533, http://www.universalorder.com/satan.html.

56 A transcription is available at "Might Is Right 24-Hour Radio Special: Working Transcript of the Might Is Right 24-Hour Stream on September 11, 2003," https://the.satanic.wiki/index.php/Might_Is_Right_24-Hour_Radio_Special, accessed January 6, 2023. Audio is archived at https://archive.org/details/ MightIsRightSpecial. For more on the conceptual connections between Satanism and National Socialism, see Chris Mathews, *Modern Satanism: Anatomy of a Radical Subculture* (Westport, Connecticut: Praeger, 2009).

57 Clark, *Biography*, pp.19, 21; LaVey to Rice, February 27, 1993, reprinted in *Art That Kills*, p.128.

58 Parfrey interview in *Fifth Path* #4, p.24; Justin Norton, "Satan's Little Helpers: An Oral History of the Electric Hellfire Club," *Decibel*, October 31, 2016, www.decibelmagazine.com/2016/10/31/satan-s-little-helpers-an-oral-history-of-the-electric-hellfire-club; "An Interview with Michael Moynihan," *Hit List* #1, February/March 1999, p.51.

59 Clark claimed Rice was on thirteen episodes of Larson's TV show, and more of his radio show; however, this should be taken with a grain of salt. On a video, Larson said that although he hadn't counted how many, he generally agreed a Wikipedia entry, which said Rice was on the radio show only five times, was accurate. Clark, *Biography*, p.21; "BOB LARSON VS. AMERICA'S #1 SATANIST!" (video; with Boyd Rice), uploaded by "Bob Larson... The REAL Exorcist!," October 27, 2021, www.youtube.com/watch?v= VlZO84X5WGo

60 Rice gave the last traditionally conducted interview with LaVey in 2007; *Art That Kills*, p.129.

61 Clark, *Biography*, pp.22–23, 145; "To Whom It May Concern," *Boyd Rice*, https://web.archive.org/web/20110717090200; http://www.boydrice.com/news. html

62 Rice, *Manson as the Archangel Michael Slaying the Devil*, in Schreck, ed., *The Manson File*, p.125.

63 "San Francisco Movie Guide: Strand," *San Francisco Examiner*, August 8, 1988, p.24, www.newspapers.com/image/461357661

64 *Art That Kills*, p.197.

65 Ibid.

66 Ibid. The bill included another band, the Secret Chiefs, and two films: 1971's *The Other Side of Madness* about Manson, and one from local performance art group Survival Research Laboratories, *A Bitter Message of Hopeless Grief*.

67 Rice to Mason, September 19, 1988, handwritten note on enclosure [Box 9, Folder 20].

68 *Art That Kills*, p.196; "8-8-88 Rally 25th Anniversary: Love in the Summer of Hate," *Mistress Astarte's Gallery of Marvels*, August 15, 2013, https:// mistressastarte.tumblr.com/post/58362145473/8-8-88-rally-25th-anniversary-love-in-the-summer (originally on www.nikolasschreck.eu, but removed).

69 "Radio Werewolf: 8/8/88 Rally," uploaded by Haphaestus on July 22, 2011, https://archive.org/details/Radio-Werewolf-8-8-88-Rally

70 "Devil Worship: Exposing Satan's Underground," *Geraldo Rivera Show*, October 22, 1988, www.imdb.com/title/tt1136645

71 Rice interview in *Fifth Path* #3, p.11.

72 *Art That Kills*, p.196.

73 The exact starting date of the American Front is unclear. Sometimes 1984 has been named, including by later iterations of the group itself. The American Front emerged out of the earlier S.F. Skins, which included Heick, then known as Bob Blitz. According to Eric Anderson, the flyer posted in March 1985 was initially signed as "American Front," although that wasn't a group name until a little later

on; Marsha Ginsburg, "Thugs Terrorize the Haight," *San Francisco Examiner*, April 11, 1985, pp.A1, A20, www.newspapers.com/image/460691202; Eric Anderson, in Travis and Hardy, *Skinheads*, pp.136–37.

74 "'With Pity towards None' from *Tangents*" (interview), BoydRice.com, https:// web.archive.org/web/20160425004542; http://www.boydrice.com/interviews/ tangents.html (originally 1997).

75 In 1987, his Abraxas Foundation was already dubbed an "occult-fascist think tank."

76 Other sources give the number at fifty. Rice to Mason, [between May 4 and 7], 1988 [Box 9, Folder 20]; John Brown Anti-Klan Committee, "Nazi Skinheads Active in San Francisco" (press release), May 25, 1988, p.1, https://freedomarchives.org/ Documents/Finder/DOC37_scans/37.NaziSkinPressPkt1988.pdf.pdf. A brief clip of the march can be seen in "Behind the Burning Cross-John Brown Anti-Klan Committee" (video), uploaded by aralosangeles, February 28, 2017, www. youtube.com/watch?v=53W0fwxOa9s&t=843s

77 Rice to Mason, July 4, 1988 [Box 9, Folder 20].

78 Heick to Mason, [March or April], 1994 [Box 25, Folder 27].

79 UPI, "Racist Remarks: 'Oprah Winfrey Show' Ousts Neo-Nazi," *Los Angeles Times*, February 5, 1988, www.latimes.com/archives/la-xpm-1988-02-05-me-27455-story.html

80 Rice to Mason, [between May 2 and 7], 1988 [Box 9, Folder 20].

81 "Geraldo Rivera's Nose Broken in Scuffle on His Talk Show," *NYT*, November 4, 1988, www.nytimes.com/1988/11/04/nyregion/geraldo-rivera-s-nose-broken-in-scuffle-on-his-talk-show.html

82 ADL, *Young and Violent*, pp.11–14.

83 "Skinheads in the Media (Late 1980s, early 1990s)" (video), uploaded by SufferinSprings, November 26, 2015, www.youtube.com/watch?v=L1uHww WxCLU. While the video is not dated, the show ran from September 1988 to January 1990. The context implies that it was filmed around the same time as the *Sassy* photo shoot; John Carmody, "'USA Today on TV' Axed," *Washington Post*, November 23, 1989, https://web.archive.org/web/20130117083054, http://www.highbeam.com/doc/1P2-1224653.html

84 "Skinheads in the Media" (video).

85 Ibid.

86 "The Abraxas Foundation on Evil," *Aryan Warrior*, [1989], clipping [Box 9, Folder 20]. The exact date of release is unclear, but it had to be published before the end of February, 1989, when Moynihan refers to it; Moynihan to Mason, February 28, 1989 [Box 5, Folder 9].

87 Moynihan to Mason, February 28, 1989 [Box 5, Folder 9]; Parfrey, "Skinned Alive," *Hustler*, July 1989, p.90.

88 ADL, "The Skinhead International: The United States," excerpt from *The Skinhead International: A Worldwide Survey of Neo-Nazi Skinheads*, 1995, http://nizkor.com/hweb/orgs/american/adl/skinhead-international/skins-united-states.html; "Wave of Skinhead Violence Hits Denver," SPLC *Intelligence Report*, March 1998, online March 15, 1998, www.splcenter.org/fighting-hate/ intelligence-report/1998/wave-skinhead-violence-hits-denver

Not all these murders were by Nazi skinheads, as opposed to skinheads with other politics, but even those committed by the latter were sometimes hate crimes, particularly against LGBTQ+ people. One of the most notorious examples of the latter was the 1990 murder of Julio Rivera in New York City; Charlie Leduff, "Parole Is Denied Skinhead in 1990 Anti-Gay Murder," *NYT*, February 16, 1997, www.nytimes.com/1997/02/16/nyregion/parole-is-denied-skinhead-in-1990-anti-gay-murder.html

89 The violence turned inward towards members of the group, too; the third American Front leader, David Lynch, was murdered in 2011, although no one was ever convicted for it. American Front, *ADL*, https://web.archive.org/web/20130112013029, http://www.adl.org/learn/ext_us/american_front/criminal_activity.asp; "Racist Skinhead Leader David Lynch Slain in California Home Invasion," SPLC *Intelligence Report*, Summer 2011, online June17,2011,www.splcenter.org/fighting-hate/intelligence-report/2011/racist-skinhead-leader-david-lynch-slain-california-home-invasion

90 Carter and Metzger, *In the Eye of the Storm*, pp.165, 167, 188. For his general take on skinheads, see pp.186–89.

91 "Berhanu V. Metzger, Case Number A8911-07007," *SPLC*, www.splcenter.org/seeking-justice/case-docket/berhanu-v-metzger, accessed September 20, 2022; Darlene Himmelspach, "Metzger, 3 Others Lose Lawsuit, Must Pay $12.5 million," October 22, 1990, *San Diego Union*, pp.1, 3, www.sandiegouniontrib une.com/news/local-history/story/2020-10-23/from-the-archives-12-million-judgment-white-supremacist-tom-metzger-1990

92 "Tom Metzger," *SPLC*, www.splcenter.org/fighting-hate/extremist-files/individual/tom-metzger

93 Andrew Pollack, "Boredom and Rain End Racist Rally," *NYT*, March 6, 1989, www.nytimes.com/1989/03/06/us/boredom-and-rain-end-racist-rally.html

94 "Young White Racists: They're Violent, Angry and Dangerously Charismatic," *Sassy*, March 1989, p.47.

95 The picture has often been reproduced, by critics but also Rice himself. See Clark, *Biography*, p.92; *Boyd Rice*, https://web.archive.org/web/20071006061347, www.boydrice.com/gallery/friends_gallery/1980-08.html; Ridgeway, *Blood in the Face*, p.186; "Boyd Rice," *Wikipedia*, accessed August 11, 2023; "After Backlash, Greenspon Gallery Scraps Show by Alleged Neo-Nazi Boyd Rice," *ArtForum*, September6,2018,www.artforum.com/news/after-backlash-greenspon-gallery-scraps-show-alleged-neo-nazi-boyd-rice-76547

96 Parfrey, "Skinned Alive," p.80.

97 Rice to Mason, [late December] 1988; Mason to Rice, January 2, 1989; Mason to Rice, May 25, 1989 [all three Box 9, Folder 20].

98 "Blood Axis: Interview with Michael Moynihan," *Heretic* #10, October 1994, http://imperium.lenin.ru/EOWN/DIJ-politics.html, published online February 12, 1996; Moynihan to Mason, June 16, 1989 [Box 11, Folder 1].

99 Cited in "Queers to shut down Death in June in San Francisco on September 13th / DIJ exposed by queer anti-fascist," *Who Makes the Nazis*, September 13, 2013, https://whomakesthenazis.blogspot.com/2013/09/queers-to-shut-down-death-in-june-in.html
No small number of observers have felt no need to analyze Death in June as anything but simple fascists shielding themselves under a flimsy pretext, and Anton Shekhovtsov claimed they are part of an intentional fascist cultural strategy. Midwest Unrest, "Death in June: a Nazi band?," *LibCom*, November 19, 2006, https://libcom.org/article/death-june-nazi-band-midwest-unrest; Shekhovtsov, "Apoliteic Music: Neo-Folk, Martial Industrial and 'Metapolitical Fascism'," *Patterns of Prejudice* 43(5) December 2009, pp.431–57, www.shekhovtsov.org/articles/Anton_Shekhovtsov-Apoliteic_Music.html. For an analysis of Death in June, see chapter six ("'What Happens When Symbols Shatter?': Nazism, Metapolitical Fascism, and Neo-Folk") in Bland, "Extremism in the British Underground," pp.278–314.

100 Richard Lawson, a former leader in the National Front, was the best man at Wakeford's wedding in 1999. Robert Forbes, *Misery and Purity: A History and Personal Interpretation of Death in June* (Amersham, UK: Jara Press, 1995),

pp.29, 31; Tony Wakeford, "A Message from Tony," February 14, 2007, *Tursa*, https://web.archive.org/web/20070502130941, http://www.tursa.com/message. html; "Tony Wakeford on Manoeuvres," *Who Makes the Nazis*, September 16, 2010, https://whomakesthenazis.blogspot.com/2010/09/tony-wakeford-on-manoeuvres.html; "Danger! Neo-Folk 'Musician' Tony Wakeford of Sol Invictus Is Still a fascist Creep!," *Stewart Home*, www.stewarthomesociety.org/wakeford.html

101 Current 93, *Swastikas for Noddy* (L.A.Y.L.A.H. Antirecords, 1988), www.dis cogs.com/master/22216-Current-93-Swastikas-For-Noddy

102 Moynihan interview in *EsoTerra*; Forbes, *Misery and Purity*, p.137.

103 "NON / Boyd Rice - Live in Osaka, Japan (1989)" (video), uploaded by Pobednik1985 on January 19, 2014, www.youtube.com/watch?v=imksQuyh6-Q&t=577s; Clark, *Biography*, pp.93, 94; Forbes, *Misery and Purity*, p.127.

104 *Iconoclast* (video). For the Belgium show, see Chapter 14, "Michael Moynihan".

105 Forbes, *Misery and Purity*, p.135. In addition, Rice, Wakeford, McDowall, and Pearce played on a 1989 Current 93 release, and with Moynihan on a 1990 Rice album. Current 93, "She Is Dead and All Fall Down"/"God Has Three Faces and Wood Has No Name" 7 (Shock, 1989), www.discogs.com/master/212061-Current-93-She-Is-Dead-And-All-Fall-Down-God-Has-Three-Faces-And-Wood-Has-No-Name; Boyd Rice and Friends, *Music, Martinis, and Misanthropy* (New European Recordings, 1990), www.discogs.com/Boyd-Rice-And-Friends-Music-Martinis-And-Misanthropy/master/28565

106 NON, *Total War Live in Japan*; NON, *In the Shadow of the Sword* (Mute, 1992), www.discogs.com/release/6555585-NON-In-The-Shadow-Of-The-Sword; *Easy Listening for Iron Youth: The Best of NON* (Mute, 1989), www.discogs.com/master/21550-NON-Easy-Listening-For-Iron-Youth-The-Best-Of-NON

107 Vale and Juno, eds., *Pranks*, p.34.

108 Clark, *Biography*, pp.27, 31. However, in 1991 Rice claimed, "Jello Biafra is a good friend of mine"; Prendergast, "Family Ties," p.30.

109 Parfrey, "Introduction" to "Boyd Rice" (interview by George Petros and David Aaron Clark), *Seconds* #38, 1996, p.36; part of this also appeared in Clark, *Biography*, pp.63–64.

110 Clark, *Biography*, pp.27, 31; "Sleazy Peter Christopherson Unedited" (interview), *Wire*, www.thewire.co.uk/in-writing/interviews/sleazy-peter-christopherson-unedited (originally in *Wire* #306, August 2009).
    In 1981, Tovey and Rice had recorded *Easy Listening for the Hard of Hearing* (Mute, 1984), www.discogs.com/master/28541-Boyd-Rice-Frank-Tovey-Easy-Listening-For-The-Hard-Of-Hearing. In 1985, Rice played with Coil under the name Sickness of Snakes; 93 Current 93* / Sickness of Snakes, *Nightmare Culture* mini-LP (L.A.Y.L.A.H. Antirecords, 1985), www.discogs.com/release/104001-93-Current-93-Sickness-Of-Snakes-Nightmare-Culture

111 "Boyd Rice Interview from MISANTHROPE by Chris A. Masters," 1997, https://web.archive.org/web/20071004165738; http://www.boydrice.com/interviews/misanthrope.html; Vale and Juno, eds., *Industrial Culture Handbook*, p.53.

112 However, it should be emphasized that many people in the underground scene did not break with Rice; Rice interview in *Your Flesh*, p.32; "Boyd Still Loves Barbie" (interview by Suzy Rust), *Forced Exposure* #18, 1993, p.44.

113 Clark, *Biography*, p.31.

114 Moynihan to Mason, March 7, 1990 [Box 5, Folder 9]; Lisa Crystal Carver, *Drugs Are Nice* (London: Snowbooks, 2006), pp.207–8.

115 Moynihan to Mason, March 7, 1990 [Box 5, Folder 9]; Boyd Rice and Friends, *Music, Martinis and Misanthropy*; Forbes, *Misery and Purity*, p.136.

116 Rice, "Revolt against Penis Envy: Contributing to an Understanding of Male/Female Harmony," *Standing*, pp.82, 83 (originally in *ANSWER ME!* #4, 1994).

117 Rice interview in *Misanthrope*.

118 Parfrey and Shaun Partridge also contributed tracks; The Boyd Rice Experience, *Hatesville!* (Hierarchy, 1995), www.discogs.com/master/191762-The-Boyd-Rice-Experience-Hatesville

119 Rice's mugshot in in *Iconoclast* was dated December 28, 1995; Carver, *Drugs Are Nice*, p.309; "Have a Nice Day: An Interview with Boyd Rice" (by Arvo Zylo), *WFMU*, May 19, 2011, https://blog.wfmu.org/freeform/2011/05/a-con versation-with-boyd-rice.html

120 Matthew Korfhage, "Two Decades after Author Jim Goad Fell from Grace in Portland, He's Re-Emerged as an Icon of the Alt-Right," *Willamette Week*, October 17, 2017, www.wweek.com/arts/books/2017/10/17/two-decades-after-author-jim-goad-fell-from-grace-in-portland-hes-re-emerged-as-an-icon-of-the-alt-right

121 Moynihan to Mason, December 16, 1990 [Box 5, Folder 9]; Blood Axis, "Lord of Ages" and "Electricity," various artists compilation, *The Lamp of the Invisible Light* (Cthulhu Records, 1991), www.discogs.com/release/185734-Various-The-Lamp-Of-The-Invisible-Light

122 Prendergast, "Family Ties".

123 Moynihan, Rice, and Mason interview with Larson/*Talk Back* (video).

124 Rice interview in *Your Flesh*, p.29; "'The Black Pimp Speaks': Boyd Rice interviewed by Brian Clark via telephone, 2003" (edited version of interview in *Rated Rookie* #6, 2004), www.scribd.com/document/72879291/Interview-Manson-Related-the-Black-Pimp-Speaks

125 *Art That Kills*, p.213.

126 Ibid, p.125.

127 Cited in Coogan, "How Black," p.45.

128 Rice, *Standing*, p.1.

129 Moynihan to Mason, March 22, 1989 [Box 5, Folder 9].

130 Moynihan to Mason, June 1, 1990 [Box 5, Folder 9]; Mason to Rice, May 12, 1992 [Box 9, Folder 20].

131 Rice interview in *Your Flesh*, p.27; *WAKE* #1, p.2.

132 *WAKE* #1, pp.2, 7.

133 Several of the other figures quoted also had racist and related views although they are not readily known for them, including Gustav LeBon and Jack London. Stoddard also appears in Parfrey's article "Eugenics" in *Apocalypse Culture*, p.164.

134 Rice to Mason, May 12, 1992; Mason to Rice, May 12, 1992 [both Box 9, Folder 20].

135 Nicholas Goodrick-Clarke, *Hitler's Priestess: Savitri Devi, the Hindu-Aryan Myth, and Neo-Nazism* (New York: NYU Press, 1998).

136 SIEGE 11(10) October 1982, pp.4–5. There is a notice of her death in SIEGE 12(3) March 1983, p.6; a passing reference in SIEGE 12(6) June 1983, p.3; and a portrait of her in the first edition of *Siege*, p.305.

137 Mason interview in *Regal Scroll* (*Articles*, p.89).

138 The lyrics are in Rice, *Standing*, pp.255–56. The collaborative album the song was on, *Heaven Sent*, was originally released by Twilight Command in 1996 under the band name Scorpion Wind; www.discogs.com/Scorpion-Wind-Heaven-Sent/release/292681

139 Current 93, *Thunder Perfect Mind* (Durtro, 1992), www.discogs.com/master/22268-Current-93-Thunder-Perfect-Mind; *Hitler as Kalki* (Durtro, 1993), www.discogs.com/release/284691-Current-93-Hitler-As-Kalki; Radio Werewolf, *The Lightning and the Sun* (Unclean, 1989), www.discogs.com/Radio-Werewolf-The-Lightning-And-The-Sun/release/188982; Parfrey, ed., *Apocalypse Culture*, pp.40–41.

140 The list also includes the postwar fascist classic *Imperium* by Francis Parker Yockey as well as Rosenberg. Rice said Savitri Devi's works "are often strikingly profound, and explore a wide variety of intriguing themes and concepts" although they are, to different people, "fascinating and compelling or misguided and contemptible." "BOYD RICE'S Recommended Reading List," *Boyd Rice*, http://web.archive.org/web/20041021025914, http://www.boydrice.com/readinglist.html; Rice, "Savitri Devi, the Externsteine & the Pagan Ritualism of the Nazis," in *Standing*, pp.152, 155 (written in 2001).

141 Mason to Reynolds and Beth Helen, May 7, 1993 [Box 33, Folder 5].

142 Clark, *Biography*, pp.107, 114. The images are also available at https://web.archive.org/web/20071004170513, http://www.boydrice.com/gallery/boyd_gallery/boyd_unpopshow.html

143 Justin Norton, "Satan's Little Helpers".

144 These included interviews with LaVey, Thorn, and Daniel Miller; *Seconds*, https://secondsmagazine.com/pages/mags.php

145 "Marilyn Manson" (interview by Boyd Rice), *Seconds* #40, 1996, pp.16–29, https://secondsmagazine.com/pages/mags.php; Clark, *Biography*, p.49.

146 *EXIT* #6; *Seconds* interviews by Interviewed by Petros (#27, 1994), David Aaron Clark (#30, 1995), and Rice (#40, 1996), https://secondsmagazine.com/pages/mags.php

147 Manson also said about LaVey: "he's been a great influence on me philosophically over the years…. he shared with me a lot of very important things I've taken into effect in my life." Andrew Trendell, "The Church of Satan clarifies Marilyn Manson's Role," *NME*, August 23, 2018, www.nme.com/news/music/church-satan-clarifies-marilyn-mansons-role-2370035; Marilyn Manson, "Foreword," in LaVey, *Satan Speaks!*, pp.viii–ix; Marilyn Manson interview with David Aaron Clark, *Seconds* #30, 1995 (*45 Dangerous Minds*, p.217).

148 Metzger to Mason, August 13, 1996 [Box 11, Folder 5].

149 Both the meet-ups included Robert Ferbrache, who played on albums by both Rice and Moynihan; Mason to Reynolds and Beth, December 18, 1999 [Box 33, Folder 1]; Mason to Moynihan, October 7, 2000 [Box 32, Folder 14].

150 Mason to Schuster, May 13, 2003; Schuster to Mason, May 28, 2003; Mason to Schuster, June 7, 2003 [all three Box 32, Folder 27]; Mason to author, November 26, 2022.

151 Cited in Baddeley, *Lucifer Rising*, p.151.

152 Rice interview in *Misanthrope*; Rice interview with Petros and Clark in *Seconds*, p.38; "Beyond Good & Evil" (interview with Rice), in Baddeley, *Lucifer Rising*, pp.160–61, https://web.archive.org/web/20071004084445, http://www.boydrice.com/interviews/beyondgoodandevil.html; Rice interview with Clark ("The Black Pimp Speaks").

153 In addition to Rice's anthology *Standing in Two Circles* (2007), Clark's *Boyd Rice: A Biography* (2015), and the film *Iconoclast* (2010), Rice published *NO* in 2009 and *Twilight Man* in 2011, both on Heartworm Press.

154 Daniel Maurer, "Todd P: Boyd Rice Show Will Go on Even Though He 'Sucks as a Human Being'," *Bedford and Bowery*, June 28, 2013, https://bedfordandbowery.com/2013/06/todd-p-boyd-rice-show-will-go-on-even-though-he-sucks-as-a-human-being; Alex Greenberger, "Cancellation of Exhibition Featuring Alleged Neo-Nazi Divides New York Art World," *ARTnews*, September 10, 2018, www.artnews.com/art-news/news/cancellation-exhibition-featuring-alleged-neo-nazi-divides-new-york-art-world-10947

155 "With Diamond and Silk last weekend," @boydriceofficial, Instagram, www.instagram.com/p/B1fvFlMJ30A, August 23, 2019.

156 As with Diamond and Silk, one of the people in the photo was a person of color—just as were a number of those attended the fascist rally itself. "Heard a guy on news radio reference a "neo-nazi tiki torch rally". So we had one." [sic], @boydriceofficial, Instagram, August 22, 2017, www.instagram.com/p/ BYFylYwH0WW; Gabriela Resto-Montero, "With the Rise of the Alt-Right, Latino White Supremacy May Not Be a Contradiction in Terms," *Mic*, December 27, 2017, www.mic.com/articles/187062/with-the-rise-of-the-alt-right-latino-white-supremacy-may-not-be-a-contradiction-in-terms

157 @Brandon_Bahama, September 20, 2021, https://web.archive.org/web/2021 0921201516, https://twitter.com/Brandon_Bahama/status/1440129659413286 920

158 His collection of Barbie dolls often came up as "proof" that Rice was not a neo-Nazi; for example, see Parfrey, "If We're So Wrong," p.5.

159 Rice interview on WFMU; Barry, "FACT meets Boyd Rice," www.factmag. com/2012/10/03/i-always-felt-apart-from-everybody-else-fact-meets-boyd-rice-noise-pioneer-film-buff-leader-of-the-church-of-satan/4

160 Schreck and Rice interview with King and Swezey (video).

161 Ibid.

162 Rice to Mason, March 26, 1987 [Box 9, Folder 20].

163 Rice interview in *Your Flesh*, p.32.

164 Ibid; Rice interview in *Forced Exposure*, p.46.

165 *Art That Kills*, p.123; Alex Greenberger, "Greenspon Gallery Cancels Show with Artist Boyd Rice, Alleged Neo-Nazi," *ARTnews*, September 6, 2018, www.art news.com/art-news/market/greenspon-gallery-cancels-show-artist-boyd-rice-alleged-neo-nazi-10931

166 Rice interview in *Your Flesh*, p.32; *Iconoclast* (video).

167 Rice interview in *Your Flesh*, p.32; Moynihan, Rice, and Mason interview with Larson/*Talk Back* (video).

168 Rice interview with Petros and Clark in *Seconds*, p.39.

169 Rice interview in *Lucifer Rising*, pp.160–61; Knipfel, "The Other Nazis," p.13 (*Articles*, p.70).

170 Rice interview with Clark ("Black Pimp Speaks"); Baddeley, *Lucifer Rising*, p.160.

171 Rice interview in *Your Flesh*, p.33; see also Rice interview on WFMU.

172 Rice interview in *Tangents*; Rice interview in *Your Flesh*, p.33.

173 Greenberger, "Greenspon Gallery Cancels Show with Artist Boyd Rice, Alleged Neo-Nazi."

174 Knipfel, "The Other Nazis," p.13 (*Articles*, p.70).

175 Rice, *NO* (Heartworm Press, 2009), p.80.

176 Hatewatch Staff, "Do You Want Bigots, Gavin? Because This Is How You Get Bigots," *SPLC*, August 10, 2017, www.splcenter.org/hatewatch/2017/08/10/ do-you-want-bigots-gavin-because-how-you-get-bigots

177 Rice, *No*, pp.15, 99.

178 "Boyd Rice Biographer's Non-Disclosure: 'He Doesn't Seem to Give a Shit What Most People Think'" (interview with Brian M Clark), April 6, 2016, *Dangerous Minds*, https://dangerousminds.net/comments/boyd_rice_biographers_non_disclosure_ he_doesnt_seem_to_give_a_shit_what_mos

13

ADAM PARFREY

A Neo-Nazi's Best Friend

After Adam Parfrey's death in May 2018, numerous obituaries of the founder of Feral House press appeared, including in the *New York Times*. They lavished praise on this publisher who had championed fringe, outsider publications while testing the limits of morality and tolerance, although some did mention his more tasteless offerings. However, the paper of note forgot to mention his role in creating *Siege*—although this was not lost on the White Supremacist press.

Parfrey himself received significantly more attention for his creative endeavors than the others in the Abraxas Clique combined. Starting with a magazine in the downtown New York City underground scene, in the late 1980s as co-editor of Amok Press he published several well-received titles, including the cult classic *Apocalypse Culture*. He turned his next press, Feral House, into a major independent publishing house. Parfrey was just one of many publishers, musicians, and artists who promoted various kinds of extreme material under the cover of irony or morbid fascination. But starting in the mid-1980s with *EXIT*, he was already in touch with Holocaust deniers and publishing neo-Nazi and White Supremacist material—including being one of the first outside neo-Nazi circles to publish James Mason. He would go so far as to publish one of his own works in Tom Metzger's *WAR* newspaper and was thanked in, and privately praised, *Siege*. But as Parfrey's success grew—Feral House books were eventually made into Hollywood movies—he moved further away from the use of White Supremacist materials, which he had made a cornerstone of his early publications. And as people questioned his own politics, he engaged in verbal acrobatics that succeeded in keeping his own publishing boat afloat through the end of his life.

DOI: 10.4324/9780429200090-18

The typical approach writers have taken has to look at Parfrey in terms of his cultural impact during the 1980s and '90s, brushing off political questions by excusing them as a mere participation in a carnivalesque celebration of extremes. Sometimes, the articles mentioned his own bigoted publications, although usually they were contextualized away. When the question of his relationship with White Supremacists was broached, it typically focused on what it meant to *him* when he published them: Was he or wasn't he a believer in these doctrines?

What this approach has ignored, among a number of other things, is analyzing what it has meant to *them*. Parfrey was embedded in neo-Nazi and Holocaust denial networks, and he gave them a rare platform outside of their circles. And, many years before *Siege* came into existence, Parfrey championed Mason, breathing new life into his work, giving him a new audience that they otherwise would not have been able to reach, and reinvigorating his flagging spirits. These pre-*Siege* reprints of Mason's works are easily accessible in Parfrey's most famous early book, *Apocalypse Culture*, and in a magazine he helped edit whose issues are online. And so it is curious that after his death in 2018, Parfrey's role in helping disseminate terrorist ideology did not merit even a passing mention in the paper of record.[1]

Mason wasn't the only White Supremacist that Parfrey platformed, although he was the most important. Parfrey went through a period of involvement specifically with the neo-Nazi milieu that roughly paralleled Boyd Rice's: mostly from mid-1986 to early 1988. But also like Rice, he maintained his connections with them afterward, incorporated Nazi aesthetics into his works, obscured his previous (and sometimes ongoing) involvement, and vehemently attacked those who criticized him. He also kept up a crudely racist and antisemitic correspondence with Mason. And while Parfrey held Far Right views for the rest of his life, he was probably less authentically interested in neo-Nazism than Rice. But Parfrey's evasions, omissions, and denials tend to suggest that his sympathies were substantially stronger than what he said in public.

Living in the '80s

Parfrey's career in publishing began in 1975 when he started college at UCLA and wrote for its student paper, the *Daily Bruin*. He dropped out, enrolled at UC Santa Cruz, dropped out again, and moved to San Francisco. There he made his first stab at publishing, with a magazine called *IDEA*. Describing it as "a punk rag without coverage of punk music," it lasted two issues. The first, published in May 1981, included interviews with both RE/Search's V. Vale and a member of the Aryan Brotherhood prison gang.[2]

He later moved to New York City, where he met George Petros; together they started the "outlaw liberal Fascist Sci-Fi Pop Art magazine" EXIT. Its five published issues of collages, drawings, and text dwelt on themes of negativity and included portrayals of extreme sexuality, serial killers, and copious usage of Nazi imagery.[3] The first issue in 1984 included Parfrey's image of Hitler with a child as well as Jim Jones's final sermon.[4] The second issue, in 1985, dove much deeper into Nazi material; it included more Hitler images, a set of détourned photos named "Hiding from Heinrich Himmler" and "Hiding from Simon Wiesenthal," and the Petros and Parfrey image "What is Democracy?" (Answers included "Forced Integration," "Mandatory Miscegenation," and "Overpopulation.") Contributors included Genesis P-Orridge, formerly of Throbbing Gristle, and Mark Mothersbaugh from DEVO. (Petros and Parfrey would even design some of the interior images for the DEVO CD E-Z Listening Disc.[5]) EXIT fit right in with the nihilistic mood embraced by the Lower East Side's art and music scene.

In early May 1986, Rice sent Mason a copy of a Parfrey collage, *The Revelation of the Sacred Door*, which would play a notable role in the Abraxas Clique–neo-Nazi interaction. It portrayed Manson as Jesus, clinging to a left-facing swastika and in front of a door with "Helter Scelter" [sic] and "Love, Charlie" written on it. Rice added that he sent Mason's address on to Parfrey.[6] Mason wrote back that it was "absolutely GREAT!" and asked for a better-quality copy. He was so excited that he also wrote Manson himself about it.[7]

On May 27, 1986—while SIEGE was winding down but was still being published—Parfrey wrote Mason directly.

> My friend Boyd Rice informs me of your interest in Manson as an important figure in saving the white race from a dysgenic conclusion. Well, I happen to concur with your particular beliefs: I thought I was the only one who held them until I knew of Boyd.[8]

He described *EXIT*, which he co-published and where the piece would appear, as a magazine that "repudiates the kind of liberal humanism which is infecting this country like a plague." In an ensuing quick exchange of letters, Mason told Parfrey how much he liked the image, asking if he could turn it into a poster. Parfrey demurred, explaining that it was already slated for a forthcoming ten-page piece "titled Helter Skelter which details Race-War, Nuclear Detonation and the resultant conversion to an orderly, white society."[9] Parfrey's next letter elaborated that *EXIT* was

> aimed at cynical and lazy but "hip" young people. We feel it is a propaganda tool to legitimize a certain type of thought among race-mixing and otherwise polluted people. We've already had a number of conversions to our racialist stance. Now these once "liberal" types are gun owning Spenglerians.[10]

Parfrey admitted to Mason that while his father was "Nordic," his mother was Jewish—thereby making him a Jew, too, by the tradition of matrilineal descent. (His father was, in fact, actor Woodrow Parfrey, who played Dr. Maximus in *Planet of the Apes* and even had a part in *Dirty Harry*.) Nonetheless, he assured Mason that "I am sympathetic to all your stated ideals in Siege, and particularly your edict to Race Traitors." Mason replied with the characteristic practicality that he had already used to justify collaborating with gay neo-Nazi Russell Veh. "Things are so desperate," Mason said, "that no one can afford to get 'personal' with anyone else who is performing a service to the cause"— especially when it came to "top-notch, competent artists" whose "work electrified me." Mason included some of his old National Socialist Movement posters in his reply.[11]

In the summer of 1986, Parfrey teamed up with Ken Swezey, then living in Los Angeles, and started a new publishing house: Amok Press.[12] When their books appeared the next year, two of the press's earliest and most important (both of which would later be republished on Feral House) incorporated Mason's work.

In mid-July 1986, it was Parfrey's turn to gush over Mason's posters. "You are better than an 'artist'—your work is <u>effective</u>. I was quite taken w/ most the pieces, and particularly with the one of Manson w/ the Shaw quote." He asked to use it in the upcoming *EXIT* as part of the ten-page piece he had mentioned.[13]

A December 1986 letter from Parfrey showed that he was in touch with Holocaust deniers from the very beginning of his book publishing career. In it, he asked Mason, as he had before, for additional issues of SIEGE, as well as the writings of Perry Warthan and copies of any of Mason's correspondence with Manson, to use in Nikolas Schreck's upcoming *Manson File* book (then titled *Manson Apocrypha*). Parfrey pitched it to him by saying, "I really need your cooperation on this, so Manson's racial and action-oriented ideas get their exposure." He also shared the draft of the book cover, which again featured his Manson collage, as well as covers for two other forthcoming Amok Press titles, including the press's initial offering: a translation of *Michael*, Joseph Goebbels's novel.[14]

Life with the Holocaust Deniers

Parfrey also asked if Mason would share his mailing list to promote both *EXIT* and his forthcoming titles from Amok Press. He then name-dropped two of his "movement correspondents." The first was William Grimstad, who had edited the NSWPP newspaper *White Power* as well as David Duke's *Crusader* but was most famous for writing *The Six Million Reconsidered: Is the 'Nazi Holocaust' Story a Zionist Propaganda Ploy?*[15] In this December letter, Parfrey complained to Mason that "I seem to be getting some flak from movement correspondents concerning the Manson affiliation. Good people such as Bill Grimstad have really rode me about involving myself with the 'psychotic derelict.'"[16]

Grimstad would be involved in the Abraxas Clique. In September 1987, he put another Holocaust denier, Keith Stimely, in touch with Parfrey, and the two met in 1988. With a view to the situation quite like Mason's, Grimstad described Parfrey's circle to Stimely as "an apparently vital and by no means traditional 'right wing' reactionary group, of the type that we absolutely have to have if we are to get anywhere."[17] The three were soon in mutual contact; Michael Moynihan would later be added as well. In October 1988, Parfrey suggested that Grimstad write the introduction to a George Lincoln Rockwell book Mason was planning.[18]

Additionally, Parfrey mentioned "my friend" Michael A. Hoffman II, another prominent Holocaust denier, whose work would appear in both *Apocalypse Culture* and its follow-up.[19] Parfrey then again stepped over the line into actively encouraging the participation of others in the neo-Nazi milieu when he asked for Mason's help in encouraging Rice to go on the show.[20]

Mason wrote back in December 1986 with some more material and mailing list contacts, but now it was his turn to ask a favor: Would Parfrey make an image for him? He described it as the Norse god Thor superimposed on a nuclear mushroom cloud, overlooking a street filled with panicked New Yorkers trying to flee. "Contrast the anything-else-but-White faces in the mob with his Nordic countenance" as Thor swung his hammer to deliver a "completely devastating blow to the scum of the earth.... This would be a poster for OUR side to be massively reproduced and distributed. Can you imagine the effect?"[21]

This would not be the last time in his correspondence with Parfrey that Mason would refer to them as being part of the same movement. In 1988, Mason told Parfrey that Holocaust denier David Irving "is one of us." On his part, Parfrey would take quite an interest in Irving, whose assessment of Goebbels—"a tender, introspective patriot"—was used as a blurb for his edition of *Michael*.[22] Parfrey later said,

> I hear that politically correct forces are hounding Irving on all ends of the earth, making it very difficult for him to earn a living. You cannot express revisionist views in public, or else you're made a pariah. You're going against very powerful interests with big museums, big money, and a very dependent Zionist state.[23]

Parfrey did not elaborate on whom he thought the Zionist state was dependent *on*. (In a turnabout, Parfrey himself would gleefully say that "I get a thrill out of being a professional pariah."[24])

Although warning that it was a very time-consuming process to create the images, which he was doing on a computer, Parfrey told Mason that "Your idea for the propaganda poster sounds good.... effective. I'd like to collaborate with you on such a project." He asked Mason to help in finding appropriate images.[25]

1987

Despite their discussion, Parfrey does not appear to have created the collage. In January 1987, he told Mason that, "As for the scum I'm tempted to go out with a camera myself and document the most despicable varieties." In April, Parfrey promised that he hadn't forgotten about the image but in the same sentence also spoke about his increasing publishing obligations.[26]

Parfrey also sent a flyer for the upcoming concerts by the Friends of Justice, of which he was part and which listed both Chillicothe, Ohio and New York City as participating cities—illustrating the extent to which Parfrey and Mason were, at that moment, collaborators. (Parfrey was to be the emcee at the New York City event.[27]) Similar to how Rice portrayed 8/8/88 to Mason, Parfrey added,

> We wanted to soft-peddle the movement aspects in order to get a more receptive inroad into the press and potential musicians and filmmakers to back to the concerts. I have it in mind to invite some guys from the CT KKK to come and tell it like it is to the dysgenic crew who shows up at the proceeding.[28]

In February 1987, Parfrey asked Mason to do an on-camera interview with Ken Swezey and Brian King. (In an extremely confusing situation, King ran Amok Books in Los Angeles with Stuart Swezey. The latter's brother, Ken, had started Amok Press with Parfrey the year before.) At the time, King and Ken Swezey were working on a documentary about Satanists and neo-Nazis who were into Manson.

Parfrey's letter to Mason was probably his most hammy missive to the neo-Nazi: "From what I can tell of King and Swezey, they are a couple of armchair bourgeoisie [sic] however instilled with a curiosity for 'alternative' information." But, he stressed, it might expose "non-movement types" to Mason's ideas, even suggesting that it could "start a minor 'vogue' for subversive racialist views."[29] (After the interview, Mason had a very different assessment, saying "they've been around for some time and are more than loosely familiar with the movement."[30])

Later that month, the two travelled to Chillicothe to film the 50-minute interview. The only extensive video of him in the 1980s, Mason would make use of it repeatedly in the future. A transcript of part of it appeared in *Siege*, and Mason would make an edited version for community access television. In the Alt Right era, the interview would widely circulate in militant neo-Nazi circles.[31]

While the documentary was never completed (King said that, in addition to financial problems, he was "sick of racist freaks"), they also did a joint interview with Rice and Schreck the month after Mason's. More importantly, King would go to San Quentin to film Schreck's interview with Manson, which became the basis of *Charles Manson Superstar*.[32]

Soon after, Parfrey told Mason that, with *EXIT #3* done, he was no longer going to work with "my prima donna collaborator" Petros. (By the next year, Rice had also fallen out with Petros.) Instead, Parfrey was starting the new magazine, *Blood and Flame* with Schreck, and Mason was asked to contribute to the first issue.[33] The planned magazine, which never seemed to come out, appeared to have a racist and antisemitic thrust. In a late March letter, Parfrey blamed the shutdown of the Friends of Justice concerts on "The Jewish Press frothing + RANTING + DEMANDING OUR SEVERED HEADS on a platter." With it, he enclosed an ad reading "Above ground burial. The Jewish choice," which he said would appear in the magazine. In a similar vein, Parfrey later sent Mason a newspaper clipping reporting on Soviet accusations that the United States had "developed a lethal gas that kills black people but not whites." Parfrey wrote in red below it, "Let's keep our fingers crossed."[34]

Mason told Parfrey that "Working now with other creative and productive people has regenerated my own juices which is resulting in a stream of fresh printed material." In March 1987, Mason printed the pamphlet *Charles Manson: Drugs, Power & Sanity* under the Universal Order label. He asked Parfrey to help him out by buying half the run from him: $100 for 500 copies. At the time, he was planning on making two further Manson pamphlets, although they did not seem to ever appear.[35]

Parfrey pled relative poverty, although he still sent $20, for which Mason gave him 80 copies. But Parfrey also suggested several possibilities for getting the pamphlet out. A new mail-order distribution was being set up by Hoffman, whom he described as "more open-minded than most movement types," and said it "could be put across…quite forcefully…that Mansonism converts the heretofore unconverted, as it did with a few friends of mine." Parfrey also suggested people, stores, and magazines that might either carry or review the pamphlet. Last, he said he would ask Mike Kosmatka, whom Parfrey described as William Pierce's former "right-hand man" and known to help out a "good cause." Parfrey signed his letter with a left-facing swastika—the only time this appeared in his direct correspondence with Mason.[36]

The exchange occurred just as *EXIT #3*, Parfrey's last issue as an editor, was released—the one that trafficked most heavily in Nazi references. (Parfrey later called the look he created for *EXIT* "equal parts National Socialist and social realist.") Parfrey and Petros had jointly created the cover image of a swirling universe with Hitler at its center.[37] The inside cover included a quote from Goebbels. Two Parfrey collages, each featuring a slightly different picture of Hitler with a child, had in small text "Eugenics Now!" (Parfrey would often return to the themes of eugenics and dysgenics.) A collage by a different artist was based around a figure being stabbed, with the words "No Free Speech for Racists" superimposed on their body. Last was Parfrey's promised ten-page spread, now titled "The Book of Charlie." In addition to *The Revelation of the Sacred Door*, it included Mason's "Independent Genius" flyer, complete with the Universal Order logo.[38] If the correspondence with Parfrey hadn't already been convincing, surely *EXIT* #3 must have settled any doubts Mason had about whether Parfrey was playing on the same team.

With *The Manson File* in the works, Parfrey complained to Mason that "Manson and Lynette Fromme have inexplicably turned against me, Nikolas Schreck, and especially Boyd. Guess they think we're hustling them somehow."[39] Parfrey had previously shared with Mason a letter he sent to Manson but was returned. Again, in a clear exaggeration (although still reflecting ideas he expressed elsewhere in milder forms), Parfrey wrote,

> Yeah, the Jews got pissed at that magazine I sent you. None of them want to see my friend Hitler get his due…. [Hitler] lifted the pride of the white people up and tried to get rid of the commies and exile the Jews where they wouldn't hassle anyone but themselves…But of course "society" is making an "example" of Charles Manson in the same way they made an example of the Germans at Nuremburg.

Explaining that he was sick of living in "Jew York,"

> I was looking for a spot 3,000 miles away from California, and found it in spades and spics and Jews and rich assholes…I want to work with you, but more than that, I hail you with a stiff-armed salute from ground zero.[40]

Here Parfrey drew a left-facing swastika.

But Mason remained on good terms with Manson, who approved of his proposed series of pamphlets.[41] This must have made it even more important for the Abraxas Clique to keep Mason close, as they jockeyed for position and clout in a cultural milieu that fetishized Manson.

Things sped up for Parfrey as the Amok Press titles made a splash. In August 1987, the Goebbels novel was reviewed in the *New York Times*—an incredible achievement for a first book by a rookie publisher. Other reviews were not so kind, however; Parfrey complained that *The New Republic* said he was trying to start a "neo-Nazi revival."[42]

By October, Mason received his copy of the Parfrey-edited anthology *Apocalypse Culture*. Parfrey signed the copy, "To James Mason—Dragon slayer, propagandist extraordinaire!" The book became an underground classic. In the summer of 1988, Parfrey claimed it was already on its third printing on Amok Press. It was reissued on Feral House, went through multiple editions, spawned a sequel, and was reported to have sold 100,000 copies by 2010.[43]

Apocalypse Culture was like a less-illustrated *EXIT* but with similar Nazi and neo-Nazi content. Mason, Schreck, and Rice were all thanked in the acknowledgements. "The Importance of Killing" by Daniel Burros, a former American Nazi Party member who committed suicide after he was outed as a bar-mitzvahed Jew, came before a Savitri Devi excerpt, which in turn was followed by Rice's selection of Hitler quotes. Two of Mason's flyers, including "Political Terror," were included. Parfrey's friend Hoffman had a piece and was thanked in the beginning, as was Grimstad. And Parfrey's thoughts on eugenics came complete with quotes by prewar racists Arthur de Gobineau, Lothrop Stoddard, Houston Stewart Chamberlain, and Madison Grant, plus, of course, Hitler. If one wished to read White Supremacist and neo-Nazi literature, *Apocalypse Culture* had a sampling on offer. The revised edition also included contributions from the Abraxas Foundation and Robert N. Taylor. (Taylor was a 1960s White Supremacist folk singer, writer, and Heathen who established a close relationship with Moynihan.[44])

But there was plenty of other fringe material that was not related to racism or antisemitism: interviews with an "Unrepentant Necrophile" as well as Peter Sotos (who was arrested for child pornography and was part of the larger Abraxas Circle), anarchists Hakim Bey and John Zerzan, and a statement from the Red Brigades, an Italian armed Marxist-Leninist group.[45]

Mason told Parfrey that the book was "FABULOUS" and reminded him of Rockwell's *White Power*. Mason even requested that a copy be sent to his occasional ally Harold Covington.[46] On their part, the neo-Nazis who embraced the Abraxas Clique *did* seem to hope that Parfrey's work would be a vehicle for their movement's revival—or at least help it attract a new, young, hip audience.

Parfrey caught the attention of other neo-Nazis as well. Pierce picked up *Michael* for his mail-order bookstore. This caused Mason to write Parfrey, "Congratulations! He is very discerning about what he offers for sale under his heading." In September 1987, Metzger told Mason that he had "met Parfrey briefly in L.A. at a Radio Werewolf gig about a month ago. His 'Exit' magazine has some very interesting material." Parfrey sent him a copy of Goebbels's *Michael*, which Metzger said he would promote. Metzger also said, "We included a couple of Parfrey's pieces of art in our latest issue."[47]

It was perhaps one of the most flagrant instances of Parfrey's associations with neo-Nazis. Instead of him reprinting *their* material—something that could always be dismissed as part of his business of trafficking in extremes—now he was being reprinted by *them*. And indeed, the fall 1987 *WAR* issue that Metzger referred to included part of Parfrey's *The Revelation of the Sacred Door* collage. Curiously, the image was uncredited.[48] Afterward, publishing in *WAR* was not something that Parfrey bragged about.

In March 1988, Mason received his copy of the Schreck-edited *The Manson File*. Featuring contributions from numerous members of the Abraxas Circle, it included yet another reprint of Parfrey's Manson-as-Jesus collage. *The Manson File* was another underground hit for Parfrey.[49]

The Rockwell Book that Wasn't

Parfrey rung in the new year by writing Mason, "My very best to you in this year of 88."[50] At the end of January 1988, shortly before *The Manson File* was released, Mason made his big pitch to Parfrey: a book about Rockwell. Not only did Mason have access to rare Rockwell materials, but a decade before he had already made an outline for the book, then titled *The Swastika Bearers*.[51]

Parfrey was "very interested" in the proposal and also wanted a chapter on Rockwell for a "follow-up to *Apocalypse Culture*." (Parfrey also hoped to get a chapter on the unorthodox fascist Francis Parker Yockey.) In the same typewritten letter, next to this passage about Rockwell and Yockey—both of whom died under unusual circumstances—Parfrey wrote an asterisk and, in big letters, "OUR MARTYRS."[52]

Excited about its political potential, Mason wrote Rice that it "will be a super-sneaky way to get out GLR's [George Lincoln Rockwell's] propaganda message over twenty years after his death." Mason suggested to Parfrey that it look like *The Manson File* and sent a prospectus.[53]

However, Parfrey quickly took a step back. *The New Republic* was not the only magazine that had taken issue with his promotion of White Supremacist material. In 1994, Parfrey claimed that reviews of *Apocalypse Culture* were killed at both the *Village Voice* and *Artforum*, and he feared stores would refuse to carry his books.[54] Whereas in his private letters to Mason he had railed against the "Jewish publishing industry" (and later "ZOG," the supposed Zionist Occupied Government), Parfrey was now more circumspect. What happened in New York City, he said, was that

> the media there is really controlled by certain people and if they just don't like you...and they smell that you aren't part of the team you're not going to get anywhere.... So I thought of a way to publish something I like at the same time and try to appeal to that liberal sensibility.[55]

And, in fact, Amok Press titles would include titles like *Rants*—an anthology that Parfrey edited with anarchist Bob Black. But despite this willingness to collaborate, anarchists split over him. He published some of them and some of them published him in turn, while others denounced him as a reactionary. At least one, Hakim Bey (né Peter Lamborn Wilson) did both.[56]

Whether Parfrey was afraid of "ZOG," "certain people," or what he later called "oligarchic totalitarianism"[57]—or whether he just realized that this might be a bridge too far even for an edgy underground publisher—his ardor for the Rockwell book wavered. In April 1988, he wrote Mason that

> I'm tiptoeing the tightrope in between mass market and oblivion. I can sell this book to my business partner, my distributors, bookstores, and the media with just the right approach. It will take a lot of brainstorming and a few compromises. But the end result will be a media coup.[58]

He also asked Mason, "Are you aware of the fact that the little monkey Michael Jackson has Rockwell and Hitler on his video 'Man in the Mirror'?" (It included Rockwell's "Hate Bus.") Parfrey hoped that the Rockwell book could piggyback on the media attention on White Supremacists at the time, and he even offered to write the forward.[59] But soon after that, Parfrey fell out of touch and the project was dropped.

Mason didn't give up on the book idea, though, and over a decade later, he tried again with *Siege*'s second publisher. It ended with a very similar result.

A Big Fish in a Small Pond Doesn't Completely Forget Old Friends

Parfrey's attention was taken up with, among other things, the 8/8/88 event with Rice and Schreck. Two group pictures from the event (both of which included two White Supremacists, American Front leader Bob Heick and Metzger collaborator Nick Bougas), obviously taken one after the other, illustrated Parfrey's approach to and relationship with these politics. Parfrey is in the one where they are merely standing and posing. In the other, where the group is sieg-heiling, Parfrey is no longer in the visual frame.

No doubt of more importance to Parfrey's delay in writing Mason was the collapse of Amok Press. Out of its ashes came his new venture: Feral House. Its name was suggested by Rice.[60]

However, as Parfrey said in a Halloween 1988 letter, he needed to have some money-making books first, like his initial offering: Anton LaVey's *The Satanic Witch*.[61] (Parfrey had been introduced to LaVey by Rice in 1987 or 1988, and a later commentator described LaVey books "as cash cows for Feral House."[62]) Nonetheless, Parfrey said the Rockwell book was still on track for a spring 1990 release, but he had to be careful about possible blowback.

> I'm counting on heavy censorship, condemnation and subtle boycotts by ZOG when it appears. I'm trying to get together a book written by nigger and spic gang members on youth gangs for release at about the same time.

To me, letting these cocaine-addled nigger murderers prattle on about their miserable lives will be rope enough for them to hang themselves. But then I can always point to the book when the ADL gets on my case about racism, neo-Nazism, etc.[63]

Parfrey also appeared to have a particular bigotry against Latinos. He also asked Mason to send mail to his post office box rather than his home address because, "I live in a Mexican neighborhood, and their respect for mail parcels left outside the apartment complex is reputed to be quite small."[64] In 2002, he said,

Next spring I'm publishing a book version of a cholo gang magazine by one Reynaldo Berrios called "Mi Vida Loca." Reynaldo is all about "Aztlan"—the idea that brown-skinned people will retake North America from the honkies in any way possible. It occurred to me that this is not a good time to be light-skinned.[65]

Parfrey also thought that Rice's Social Darwinist views were too "optimistic" when it came to new arrivals in the country. Parfrey espoused a version of the racist "Great Replacement theory," which would become popular in the late 2010s and early '20s.[66] In an interview, he said that in another time period,

a country that is overcome by immigrants of racial difference would have been called an "invasion." I live in a Mexican gang neighborhood, gunfire every night. Many of the Mexicans who move here aren't aware that we have flush toilets, so many deposit their babies' shitty diapers in public places.[67]

Furthermore, he mused, "What might happen when these people cannot get food stamps or welfare? What about a simple drought, or severe economic situation?" Integrating his larger worldview, he said "I don't look forward to those times, but I do have front row seats to the apocalypse."[68]

Despite the fact that his father was an American soldier in World War Two who had been captured and interned in a Nazi prison camp, Parfrey described that war as "really a civil war between white people, and white people have been feeling guilty about themselves ever since." Instead of taking responsibility for the impact of White Supremacy, white people have "forgotten about themselves. They should listen to the words of Spengler."[69] (Oswald Spengler, an influence on but not a follower of National Socialism, was most famous for his work *The Decline of the West*, which portrayed Western civilization as being in a period of decay.)

Parfrey also floated the idea of pairing the book with a biography of Nation of Islam leader Louis Farrakhan. The black separatist leader had had discussions with Metzger, just as Farrakhan's predecessor Elijah Muhammad had a parley with Rockwell. Mason approved of both the idea of a Grimstad introduction and a Farrakhan book, but afterward Parfrey seemed to have moved on to more lucrative projects—or at least easier sells.[70]

In July 1989, *Hustler* ran Parfrey's "Skinned Alive," one of many pieces around that time about the Nazi skinhead movement. At least half of it consisted of verbatim quotes from neo-Nazis like Heick, Metzger, and his son John. The opposing view consisted of a two-sentence quotation from the Center for Democratic Renewal's Leonard Zeskind. It was basically a six-page advertisement with a mass audience that allowed neo-Nazis to elaborate their views and deliver recruiting pitches. In it, Parfrey described the typical Nazi skinhead as "a vessel of wrath, shaved for battle and at all times ready to bust heads."[71]

Parfrey's journalistic ethics showed here, as he did not divulge that he was personally acquainted with said neo-Nazis, had contributed to Metzger's publication, or had been publishing neo-Nazi content himself. He also specially mentioned that Heick's *Aryan Warrior* included "contributions from a Manson-inspired group called the Abraxas Foundation that preaches a doctrine of evil"—while conveniently omitting his own membership in said group. As in other dealings with White Supremacists, Parfrey had no vested business interest in writing this. Mason loved the article.[72]

Around this time, Parfrey floated away from Mason, and their correspondence petered off. Petros stayed in touch, however. In 1989, *EXIT #4* came out. In it was a quote from Goebbels, two of Mason's old flyers, and—despite the falling out—Parfrey's "Eugenics" piece that also appeared in *Apocalypse Culture*.[73] In 1991, the Petros-edited *EXIT #5* included another Goebbels quote and a long piece by Taylor. Also included were quarter-page images from Mason, Schreck, and Zeena LaVey.[74]

After *EXIT*, Petros went on to more popular publications but at first continued to work with many of the same people. The music magazine *Seconds*, which he helped put out between 1990 and 2000, became a regroupment vehicle for the Abraxas Circle. Its gravitational pull attracted even more musicians, writers, and fringe cultural figures, leading to the extended Abraxas Circle. Moynihan was a prolific contributor to the magazine, and Rice and Taylor also got into the show. Parfrey, having buried the hatchet with Petros, did at least eight interviews starting in 1996. Unsurprisingly, the Abraxas Circle's circular promotion migrated to this new platform. LaVey was interviewed twice, first by Moynihan and then by Rice; Thorn by Rice; Rice jointly by Parfrey and Petros; and Moynihan by Petros.[75]

In late 1992, Mason thanked Parfrey for being "primarily the one that first picked up my old leaflets from the mid-Seventies and breathed new life into my stuff" and sold him the mockups of his late 1970s flyers and magazines.[76] Parfrey was also thanked in *Siege* and after he got his copy, told Mason that,

"I'm bowled over by the SIEGE book" and that "it's better than good: it's definitive!" He told Moynihan he would offer the names of potential reviewers. Additionally, Parfrey had a book agent looking for a contract for his own book in which he wanted to include a Universal Order chapter, with *Siege* as "a prominent lynchpin for that section."[77]

Parfrey didn't just help out with advice. He had already bought pamphlets and publishing mockups from Mason in the past. In December 1993, Parfrey didn't just send a broke Mason money, he gave him pointers on how to place a classified ad in Willis Carto's White Supremacist newspaper *The Spotlight*—even offering to pay for it to run four times.[78]

However, Parfrey said one thing to Mason's face and another thing behind his back. Elsewhere, while the publisher complimented Mason's flyers, he called Mason's promotion of Manson as a neo-Nazi leader "remarkable but dumb." Parfrey's final judgment? Mason "had some ideas that didn't really go very far."[79]

Whatever his true feelings, Parfrey arranged an art show to promote his upcoming book *Cult Rapture*. In September, a show he curated, bearing the same name, opened at a Seattle gallery. Amid the usual Feral House extremes was a Universal Order booth as well as contributions from Taylor.[80]

Feral House would expand the range of political views it published, but when Parfrey's *Cult Rapture* came out in 1995, there wasn't much in it that represented "both sides." While most of the essays were Parfrey's, there were a few other contributors. They included neo-Nazi murderer Jonathan Haynes; Fritz Springmeier, a conspiracy theorist arrested for bombing an adult video store; and the militia leader Linda Thompson, whose "Ultimatum" threatened an armed march on Washington, DC. Hoffman and Grimstad were also thanked.[81]

While the book's last 100 pages consist mostly of slavish militia movement apologia, the most important was Parfrey's own essay, "Finding Our Way Out of Oklahoma," about the Oklahoma City bombing and its perpetrators, Timothy McVeigh and Terry Nichols. One of the more comprehensive and openly political pieces Parfrey authored, it echoed how his previous *Hustler* piece dealt with Nazi skinheads: by doing everything short of praising them. And even more so than the skinhead piece, Parfrey's new piece was more explicit about his own Far Right beliefs.

Published right after the Oklahoma City bombing, the essay attacked the major watchdog groups, denounced President Bill Clinton for giving a "hate rant" after the massacre, and compared him to Mussolini—while also telling readers to ignore the viciously racist and antisemitic Christian Identity groups which had a sizeable influence on the militias. Parfrey demanded that media outlets ask 19 conspiratorial questions, several of which contradicted each other, about the Oklahoma City bombing. He accused Jews of being "oversensitive" and waved away mass casualty terrorism altogether ("Does it really matter who blew up the Oklahoma City building?"). Last, he not only asked whether McVeigh's and Nichols's appearances at militia meetings were actually body doubles but also brought up the possibility that McVeigh had a microchip implanted in his buttocks.[82]

Parfrey's fact-free approach to the bombing would soon land him in trouble, though. After a lawsuit over a 1998 Feral House book about the bombing which made allegations against a former FBI official, Parfrey was forced to apologize and pulp the remaining copies.[83]

In another article, Parfrey quoted a Thompson supporter saying that even if some of the information she heard was wrong, 80 percent was true.[84] In light of Parfrey's own history, this perspective seems to represent his views quite well. In 1988, he made a related statement, claiming he was providing "pure information" (Manson's and LaVey's philosophies were named as examples) as opposed to the mainstream's "world of illusions," which could only create "automatons" and "good consumers."[85] Apparently, if a whole spectrum of fringe ideas—including contradictory extremes, blatantly false information, and rank bigotry—was provided to the public, this false veil could be broken through. (As with the Abraxas Clique members, Parfrey's notion of life as a pernicious illusion appeared to be influenced by Gnosticism.)

Another event of importance was Moynihan's 1995 move to Portland, where Parfrey was at the time. There, Moynihan worked with Feral House as managing editor and worked on his book about Norwegian black metal.[86]

Mason was to have one last direct influence on Parfrey. In late 1994, Mason sent him a Special Olympics medal he found in a thrift store. The next year, a drawing of it was used as the cover of a record by one of Parfrey's musical projects, the Tards.[87] It continued Parfrey's bigotry against those who held the least amount of power in a society as well as his interest in dysgenics. Parfrey also sent Mason a clipping of a book review of Richard Herrnstein and Charles Murray's *The Bell Curve*, a famous restatement of scientific racism; in the accompanying letter he wrote, "Americans aspire to the dysgenic idea." He added, "The Jews, of course, are the biggest racists of all," comparing them to "MTV (Miscegenation TV), who see great profit from preaching gangster rap to middle america."[88]

Post-1995

In 1996, there was an attempt to start a record label, Feral House Audio, but only one release came out of it, Burzum's *Filosofem*.[89] (Burzum was the one-man band Varg Vikernes, a neo-Nazi Satanist murderer-turned-racist pagan.) In 1998, the press published another underground classic, Moynihan and Didrik Søderlind's *Lords of Chaos*, which focused on the Norwegian black metal scene, of which Vikernes was the most famous figure.

However, Parfrey did not forget his old friend who had helped him get his start. When Ryan Schuster was working on reissuing *Siege* in 2003, Mason told him that "Adam Parfrey indicated that he would be most happy to talk to with you, offering any advice he may have that you might need," and included Parfrey's phone number.[90]

By this time, Feral House had not just become a fixture in underground circles; its influence permeated into the mainstream, including the film industry. These films included two directed by Tim Burton: *Ed Wood*, a 1994 Hollywood production starring Johnny Depp, and *Big Eyes* in 2014. Meanwhile, the 2018 *Lords of Chaos* was based on Moynihan's book.

And the press moved into publishing a more diverse range of authors and topics; even its critics owned its books. Authors included liberals, leftists, and assorted other radicals, such as Chicana feminist punk musician Alice Bag and anarcho-primitivist theorist John Zerzan. Other books ranged in subject matter from *American Advertising Cookbooks* to *Extreme Islam*.

But Feral House continued to publish other Far Right, including neo-Nazi, material. Like Parfrey's other edited collections, *Apocalypse Culture II*, released in 2000, contained politically unproblematic articles. Alongside them were essays by Hoffman, Moynihan, and Rice; the misanthropic racist Pentti Linkola; and pieces from Aryan Nations and the gay neo-Nazi group National Socialist League. And it also included former *ANSWER ME!* editor and convicted domestic abuser Jim Goad.[91]

ANSWER ME! ran the usual extreme content about serial killers, suicide, and pedophilia. Issues also included Bougas's racist cartoon of black politician Al Sharpton; a back page image of Hitler on a cross with a soldier praying to him; an interview with David Duke; and LaVey, Rice, and Parfrey. Feral House would do two of Goad's books in the '00s.[92]

In the fall of 1992, Moynihan was still figuring out his publicity strategy. He suggested four fanzines to target: Petros's *EXIT* as well as *Ungawa*, *Geek*, and *ANSWER ME!*[93] Mason agreed that the last one was good because of its anti-system approach but warned that because Goad had "A Jewess for a wife" and as the contents were "liberally laced with Blacks," it "might give some people of our stripe pause."[94]

Goad ended up as one of the direct lines from the extended Abraxas Circle to the Alt Right. After prison, Goad started writing for *Taki's Magazine*, which ran White Supremacist content; Gavin McInnes wrote for them as well. According to the Proud Boys founder, Goad was "The greatest writer of our generation," and he would attend the election night celebration of Donald Trump's 2016 victory with the group. In 2020, Goad became a columnist at Greg Johnson's openly White Supremacist website *Counter-Currents*.[95]

Feral House released other books about Nazis and neo-Nazis. In 2007 was a re-release of a book Moynihan worked on about SS occultist Karl Maria

Wiligut, and in 2015 was a book about Nazi skinhead music written by participants from inside the scene.[96]

Parfrey's private connections with neo-Nazis also remained intact. In the 2010s, he participated in the secret Facebook group of New Resistance, a fascist group led by James Porrazzo, the second leader of the American Front. Parfrey chimed in on conversations about Holocaust denial. Ever the salesman, he used this as an opportunity to promote his Nazi skinhead book to the group's members. (He also attacked an essay by the author which called on the Left to expel white separatists, antisemites, and Islamophobes—as well as their publishers.[97])

Near the end of his life, Parfrey gave up his practice of not associating with White Supremacists in public. In October 2015, he gloated on Feral House's website that Porrazzo came to an art show Parfrey curated and spoke at in Salem, Massachusetts; they took a picture together to mark the occasion.[98] (Porrazzo had called Feral House "the best publisher on Earth" and said, "*Apocalypse Culture* quite literally changed by life."[99]) Parfrey also made appearances in media that either were openly White Supremacist or would run such content, doing an interview with *Heathen Harvest* in 2016 and a podcast with *The Stark Truth* in 2017.[100] He passed away at age 61 in May 2018.

After his death, Michael Gault wrote in *Vice* that Parfrey's books "exposed white supremacists for what they are, then and now—ridiculous, intellectually bankrupt, racists."[101] This statement would come as a surprise to all the "ridiculous" White Supremacists who were eager to be published by Parfrey, considered him a friend and helped him out, and were helped out by him in turn. And so unsurprisingly, after his death, he received praise from a number of White Supremacists—and some of them, unlike *Vice* and the *New York Times*, remembered Parfrey's relationship to James Mason and *Siege*.[102]

Parfrey Is Always Innocent

Parfrey said that, regarding his own politics, "God help me, I'm a pot-smoking libertarian."[103] And while that might have been true to some extent, bigoted attitudes have long been common among libertarians. In the United States, they were pioneers of Holocaust denial, and during the Alt Right years, a whole "libertarian-to-fascist pipeline" emerged.[104] If Parfrey was a libertarian, he was in good company.

Parfrey had a lot to lose from being publicly branded a White Supremacist, something he was aware of from the very beginning of his book publishing career. And so, like the others, Parfrey denied being a White Supremacist or even admitting he might be a sympathizer.

Parfrey frequently invoked his Jewish background as a reason for this. His other rhetorical strategies included attacking the Left, feminists, and groups that monitored the Far Right; projecting his own claims and actions on opponents by accusing them of the very same things he did; defending, dismissing, and downplaying the Far Right's beliefs and crimes; and misrepresenting his own actions and statements. Last, he could always duck under the protection of the numerous writers and followers who belonged to his "apocalypse culture" cult.

It is true, at least to some extent, that his propagation of White Supremacist material was driven by his business model of flaunting a variety of extremes. But, especially in the eyes of his apologists, this excused practically anything he did. And, in fact, he occasionally admitted to enjoying being able to *épater le bourgeoisie*. The introduction to *Cult Rapture* said,

> How, why, did I sit with some of these characters long enough to not only obtain quotes, but glean their reptilian essence? Easy. My mind was on the payoff: thousands of people receiving an antidote to the Hallmark Card reality of America. Consider this book an emetic for the soul.[105]

Even if this could be taken at face value—his writings in the same book contradict that—there were numerous people in his cultural cohort who also mined a variety of extremes for content but avoided associating with the Far Right. And, of course, seeing Parfrey's actions as merely promoting "extremes for their own sake" obscured his own positive interactions with the White Supremacist milieu—even at the same time that he made no shortage of public statements which overlapped with their politics.

Parfrey's mother was Jewish, and he frequently trotted this out to deny claims to neo-Nazi and related associations or adherence or those of allies like Rice.[106] This would work on many journalists, though not those familiar with the Far Right. There is, of course, a long history of Jewish involvement in neo-Nazi political circles. This has included the NSPA's Frank Collin, Daniel Burros (one of Parfrey's interests), and even the Association of German National Jews, a prewar pro-Nazi group.

When he did invoke this, Parfrey would invariably forget to mention his own antisemitic statements, including about ZOG, and his associations with Holocaust deniers in particular. He also made a point of mocking and disparaging Jews—for example, blaming the Jewish community for Burros becoming a neo-Nazi.[107]

There was also a deep irony about Parfrey invoking his Jewish parentage as supposed proof that he couldn't have White Supremacist views. Actual neo-Nazis he dealt with, like Mason, were well aware of his background and didn't care.

Like Rice and Moynihan, Parfrey would claim he was the victim of persecution by feminists, liberals, and a totalitarian, politically correct police state. For example, when there was a 1992 protest against his appearance at a

Portland, Oregon bookstore, he blamed "ultra-feminists to want to silence anyone who doesn't hew to their views."[108] To those opposed to his association with Rice, he said, "To cull Boyd Rice out of a group of published friends and then do a guilt-by-association trip is sinister McCarthyism."[109]

Parfrey also accused his critics of what he himself was guilty of. In 1994, when asked if he's a racist, he said "I think the better way to approach this is to ask all these egalitarian-minded people if *they're* racist," criticizing white liberals for patronizing people of color and being unwilling to "start treating everyone the same."[110]

Parfrey would try to weasel out of accusations. For example, he said he would never publish Holocaust denial ("No, I'm not going to get into that world").[111] But he published writings on other subjects by Holocaust deniers and had extensive personal connections with a number of them.

He was careful to tailor his public image, such as when he made sure not to be photographed sieg-heiling at the 8/8/88 event. After all, a full disclosure of what was happening behind the scenes would only harm to his reputation. These techniques can be seen clearly in an exchange with antifascist researcher Kevin Coogan, after he published a deeply researched piece which focused on Moynihan but also addressed Rice and Parfrey. Parfrey claimed that it was "verifiably wrong. Incredibly wrong."[112] While he nitpicked facts—even picking a fight about a particular fact where he was verifiably wrong—and argued about interpretations, the dispute over RE/Search's Andrea Juno shows the intentionality of his strategies. In Coogan's article, one of endnotes said, "Feral House types hated women like Andrea Juno." Parfrey replied that "not one word has ever been printed in a Feral House book insulting or even discussing Andrea Juno." Coogan's reply was to quote an interview where Parfrey himself called Juno a "psychotic cunt."[113]

The exchange illuminated Parfrey's strategy. In his parry, Parfrey said nothing had been printed about Juno "in a Feral House book." Although Coogan accurately cited Parfrey's slander, Parfrey had been very careful to misdirect the claim being made. The quote was not from a Feral House *book* at all, as Parfrey himself had introduced into the argument; rather, it was from an interview with him in a *publication*. Parfrey never denied the insult happened somewhere else.[114]

So was Parfrey a White Supremacist or even a neo-Nazi, as some of his critics claim? At least some of the bigotry in his private correspondence with Mason was undoubtedly an act, although it certainly was not a necessary one. Mason never used this language in his own letters. To say that Parfrey merely availed himself of an opportunity to do so is a charitable reading— although one must wonder why a person would want to convince a neo-Nazi that they were of the same mind.

In 1994, in a rare moment in which Parfrey admitted anything, he said, "I never really considered myself (part of the Nazi movement)—I was just flirting around with the aesthetics."[115] Of course, he did more than just that. But this statement is unusual in that Parfrey appeared to agree that it was not completely unreasonable for an outside observer of his actions to conclude that he was a neo-Nazi.

National Socialism aside, Parfrey's public statements were readily identifiable as part of the Far Right. These included his wild conspiracy theories, bigotry toward disabled people and people of color, and support of the militias. He attacked his critics in other political movements—especially accusing feminists and leftists of being "totalitarian"[116]—and groups that monitored the Far Right; meanwhile, he let the Far Right itself slide. And his loud defense of "free speech for fascists" was something he made extensive use of—whether for business reasons, ideological sympathy, or both.

Whether or not Parfrey was a neo-Nazi sympathizer, especially during the second half of the 1980s, is something only he could know. Any statement he made about this could be contradicted by a different one. But what is clear is that Parfrey was connected to, promoted, shared ideological positions with, and financially assisted neo-Nazis and Holocaust deniers. Both his public record and private correspondence show this in abundance.

Notes

1 Sam Roberts, "Adam Parfrey, Publisher of the Provocative, Dies at 61," *NYT*, May 14, 2018, www.nytimes.com/2018/05/14/obituaries/adam-parfrey-publisher-of-the-provocative-dies-at-61.html

2 Scott Timberg, "Prince of Darkness: Adam Parfrey, publisher of the troublemaking press Feral House, has made it his life's work to propagate the apocalypse," *New Times L.A.*, August 26, 1999, https://web.archive.org/web/20001101070309, www.newtimesla.com/issues/1999-08-26/feature.html/index_html?qs=8; Parfrey, "Three Criminal Brotherhoods Exposed: Aryan Brotherhood" and "RE/Search Unveiled," *IDEA Magazine* #1, May 1981, pp.5, 7–9, 26 [Labadie, HM 647.I34].

3 *Art That Kills*, p.161. A sixth issue was unfinished, but its contents posthumously appeared online; *Exit* #6, https://exitmagazine.net/index.php

4 *EXIT* #1, 1984, www.exitmagazine.net/page.php?id=. As he did with a number of different images, Parfrey recycled the Hitler image, using it in Parfrey, ed., *Apocalypse Culture II*, p.235.

5 *EXIT* #2, 1985, https://exitmagazine.net/page.php?id=111; *Art That Kills*, p.163; see also Parfrey to Mason, [February 16] 1987 [Box 17, Folder 4].

6 Rice to Mason, May 12, 1986 [Box 9, Folder 20]. The collage was reprinted as part of a larger piece in *EXIT* #3, 1987, https://exitmagazine.net/page.php, as well as in Schreck, ed., *The Manson File*, p.32.

7 Mason to Rice, May 14, 1986 [Box 9, Folder 20]; Mason to Manson, May 17, 1986 [Box 9, Folders 1–3].

8 Parfrey to Universal Order, May 27, 1986 [Box 17, Folder 4].

9 Parfrey to Mason, May 27, 1986; Mason to Parfrey, May 30, 1986; Parfrey to Mason, June 30, 1986 [all three Box 17, Folder 4].

10 Parfrey to Mason, June 30, 1986 [Box 17, Folder 4].

11 Ibid; Mason to Parfrey, July 2, 1986 [Box 17, Folder 4].

12 Parfrey to Mason, July 14, 1986 [Box 17, Folder 4].

13 Ibid.

14 Parfrey to Mason, December 14, 1986 [Box 17, Folder 4].

15 Bridges, *The Rise of David Duke*, p.41.

16 Parfrey to Mason, December 14, 1986 [Box 17, Folder 4]. In the early '00s, Grimstad repeated his objection to Manson, expanding it to include LaVey; Grimstad to Mason, September 25, 2003 [Box 30, Folder 29].

17 Grimstad to Keith Stimely, September 7, 1987 [Stimely collection].

18 Linda Maizels, "The Universal Nature of Hatred: Keith Stimely and the Culture of Holocaust Denial," MA thesis, Portland State University, History Department (Dissertations and Theses, Paper 5836), 1999, p.64, https://doi.org/10.15760/etd.7707; Parfrey to Mason, October 31, 1988; Parfrey to Mason, [June?] 1989 [both Box 17, Folder 4].

19 Michael A Hoffman II, "Alchemical Conspiracy and the Death of the West," in Parfrey, ed., *Apocalypse Culture*, pp.233–38; "The Scapegoat: Ted Kaczynski, Ritual Murder and the Invocation of Catastrophe," in Parfrey, ed., *Apocalypse Culture II*, pp.64–88.

20 Parfrey to Mason, December 14, 1986 [Box 17, Folder 4].

21 Mason to Parfrey, December 17, 1986 [Box 17, Folder 4].

22 Mason to Parfrey, January 29, 1988 [Box 17, Folder 4]; James Joll, "The Nazi in the Rye" (review of Goebbels's *Michael*), *New Republic*, October 13, 1987, p.43.

23 Parfrey interview in *Fifth Path* #4, p.23.

24 Knipfel, "The Other Nazis," p.26 (*Articles*, p.75).

25 Parfrey to Mason, December 28, 1986 [Box 17, Folder 4].

26 Parfrey to Mason, [early January] 1987; Parfrey to Mason, [April 15] 1987 [both Box 17, Folder 4].

27 "Friends of Justice Benefit Concerts: March 21, 1987; Los Angeles, New York, London" (press release) [Box 17, Folder 4].

28 Parfrey to Mason, [early January] 1987 [Box 17, Folder 4].

29 Parfrey to Mason, [January] 1987 [Box 17, Folder 4].

30 Mason to Parfrey, February 28, 1987 [Box 17, Folder 4].

31 Mason interview with Swezey and King (video). Ken Swezey's name did not appear in *Siege*, only King's; "James Mason Interview with Brian King," *Siege*, pp.558–60.

32 Schreck and Rice interview with King and Swezey (video); Brian King, email to author, March 16, 2023.

33 Rice to Mason, July 4, 1988 [Box 9, Folder 20]; Parfrey to Mason, [February] 1987; Parfrey to Mason, [February 25] 1987 [both Box 17, Folder 4].

34 Parfrey to Mason, [March 30] 1987; Parfrey to Mason, June 14, 1987 [both Box 17, Folder 4]. The article was Bill Keller, "American Outraged by Soviet Article," *NYT*, June 6, 1987, www.nytimes.com/1987/06/06/world/american-outraged-by-soviet-article.html

The next year, Grimstad said Schreck and Parfrey "have recently completed issue 1 of their new ideological/political mag, BLOOD." It is unclear if it was ever printed, however; Grimstad to Stimely, April 16, 1988 [Stimely collection].

35 Mason to Parfrey, February 28, 1987; Mason to Parfrey, April 1, 1987 [both Box 17, Folder 4].

36 In addition to implying that Mason pressure Rice and Schreck to buy copies, Parfrey also suggested reaching out to small stores that carried fanzines, including See Hear in New York City, as well as trying to get reviews in *Forced Exposure* and *Factsheet Five*. Parfrey said he would ask that Amok Books list it in their next Amok Catalog. Parfrey to Mason, April 15, 1987; Mason to Parfrey, April 17, 1987 [both Box 17, Folder 4].

37 Timberg, "Prince of Darkness"; *EXIT* #3, https://exitmagazine.net/page. php?id=26. By April 11, Mason had received a copy, and asked Parfrey to send one to his comrade and fellow "Manson devotee" Ed Reynolds; Mason to Parfrey, April 11, 1987 [Box 17, Folder 4].

38 *EXIT* #3.

39 Parfrey to Mason, [early June] 1987 [Box 17, Folder 4].

40 Parfrey to Manson, December 16, 1986 (letter returned) [Box 17, Folder 4]. Parfrey forwarded it to Mason with a note that he would try again.

41 Mason to Parfrey, June 18, 1987 [Box 17, Folder 4].

42 John Gross, "Books of the Times," *NYT*, August 28, 1987, www.nytimes. com/1987/08/28/books/books-of-the-times-494887.html; Parfrey interview in *Fifth Path* #4, p.22.

43 "8-8-88 Rally Plus Interviews" (video); Mason interview with Swezey and King (video); Ellis E Conklin, "For Adam Parfrey, Publishing the Unabomber's Book Is All In a Day's Work: 'America's most dangerous publisher' lives in Port Townsend and enrages readers worldwide," *Seattle Weekly*, November 23, 2010,www.seattleweekly.com/news/for-adam-parfrey-publishing-the-unabombers-book-is-all-in-a-days-work

44 Parfrey, "Eugenics: The Orphaned Science," in *Apocalypse Culture*, pp.155–66; R N Taylor, "The Process: A Personal Reminiscence," in Parfrey, ed., *Apocalypse Culture, Expanded & Revised*.

45 Parfrey, ed., *Apocalypse Culture*, pp.27–34, 125–27, 63–66, 129–39, 205–6.

46 Mason to Parfrey, October 26, 1987 [Box 17, Folder 4].

47 Mason to Parfrey, April 11, 1988 [Box 17, Folder 4]; Metzger to Mason, September 2, 1987 [Box 7, Folder 21].

48 *WAR* 6(4) 1987, p.12.

49 Parfrey to Mason, [March 9] 1988 [Box 17, Folder 4]; Schreck, ed., *The Manson File*, p.32.

50 Parfrey to Mason, [January 1988] [Box 17, Folder 4].

51 Mason to Parfrey, January 29, 1988 [Box 17, Folder 4]; Mason to Schuster, October 24, 2001 [Box 32, Folder 33]; Mason to author, November 26, 2022.

52 Parfrey to Mason, [March 9] 1986 [Box 17, Folder 4].

53 Mason to Rice, May 8, 1988 [Box 9, Folder 20]; Mason to Parfrey, March 9, 1988; Parfrey to Mason, [mid-April] 1988 [both Box 17, Folder 4].

54 Parfrey interview in *Fifth Path* #4, p.22.

55 Ibid.

56 Whether from lack, tact, or opposition, *Rants* did not include the quotes from Rockwell and Tommasi that Parfrey had previously solicited from Mason; Bob Black and Parfrey, eds., *Rants and Incendiary Tracts: Voices of Desperate Illumination 1558 to Present* (New York: Amok Press / Loompanics Unlimited, 1989), https://archive.org/details/rantsincendiarytractsvoicesofdesperateillumi nation1558present; Parfrey to Mason, December 14, 1986 [Box 17, Folder 4].

Many of *Rants* authors were leftists and anarchists—including Hakim Bey, Emmett Grogan, Wilhelm Reich, and Louis Lingg. But the collection also included Redbeard, LaVey, former neo-Nazi Kurt Saxon, and antisemites Louis-Ferdinand Céline and Ezra Pound. Feral House would go on to publish Black's *Beneath the Underground* (Portland, Oregon: Feral House, 1994). But Black—also one with a long history of fallings out—would denounce Parfrey as "a pissant hustler, a liar, and a thief"; Black, introduction to "The Realization and Suppression of Situationism," *Spunk Library*, www.spunk.org/texts/writers/ black/sp001671.html; originally 1994.

In addition to Black, Parfrey's reception was warmest with those anarchists most influenced by a mix of pro-Situ ideas and Stirnerite individualism, and which sought to separate themselves from the more traditional socialist Left. Strongly overlapping with the freewheeling underground fanzine culture, these anarchists sometimes entertained other fringe ideas, including discredited science, conspiracy theories, and reactionary politics.

Hakim Bey, author of *T.A.Z.: The Temporary Autonomous Zone*, was originally co-editor of *Rants* with Parfrey until leaving over his "strangely reactionary mind-set." Bey denounced the publisher's crowd as fetishists for Manson, as well as "occult 3rd-Reich bricabrac & child murder." Whatever the motivation, Bey's denunciation itself appeared in *Rants*, and he also contributed to *Apocalypse Culture*; Bey, "Intellectual S&M Is the Fascism of the 80s," *Rants*, pp.214, 216; "Instructions for the Kali-Yuga," *Apocalypse Culture*, pp.63–66.

Jason McQuinn, the editor of *Anarchy: A Journal of Desire Armed*, reprinted Parfrey's conspiratorial rant "Finding Our Way Out of Oklahoma" in another magazine he ran; *Alternative Press Review*, Winter 1996, pp.60–67. John Zerzan, in particular, made Feral House his primary outlet, publishing seven books on the press starting in 2005. Moynihan would publish a sympathetic review of one of Zerzan's Feral House books, comparing him to Evola; see *TYR* #1, pp.212–13.

But Parfrey also drew harsh condemnation from anarchists positioned more firmly on the Left, such as Janet Biehl from Murray Bookchin's Institute for Social Ecology. She hazed Parfrey's Oklahoma City essay, advocacy of Left-Right alliances, and dismissal of antisemitism, concluding that "the left has nothing to learn from paranoid racists, no matter how psychedelic their conspiracies may be"; Janet Biehl, "The Fallacy of 'Neither Left nor Right': Militia Fever," *Left Green Perspectives* #37, April 1996, https://social-ecology.org/1995/10/the-fallacy-of-neither-left-nor-right-militia-fever

57 Knipfel, "The Other Nazis," p.13 (*Articles*, p.70).
58 Parfrey to Mason, [mid-April] 1988 [Box 17, Folder 4].
59 Ibid.
60 Parfrey, "Introduction" to Rice interview with Petros and Clark in *Seconds*, p.64.
61 Parfrey to Mason, October 31, 1988 [Box 17, Folder 4]. *The Satanic Witch* (Los Angeles, California: Feral House, 1989) was a reissue of LaVey's *The Compleat Witch* which first appeared in 1971. The introduction to the Feral House edition was by Zeena LaVey.
62 Parfrey interview in *Fifth Path* #4, p.24; Timberg, "Prince of Darkness."
63 Parfrey to Mason, October 31, 1988 [Box 17, Folder 4].
64 Ibid.
65 "Adam Parfrey – July 2002" (interview), *Mark's Record Reviews*, www.markprindle.com/parfrey-i.htm
66 Jason Wilson and Aaron Flanagan, "The Racist 'Great Replacement' Conspiracy Theory Explained," May 17, 2022, *SPLC*, www.splcenter.org/hatewatch/2022/05/17/racist-great-replacement-conspiracy-theory-explained
67 Parfrey interview in *Mark's Record Reviews*.
68 Ibid.
69 "8-8-88 Rally plus Interviews" (video).
70 Parfrey to Mason, [December 22?] 1989 [Box 17, Folder 4]. Mason tried one more time in May 1993, sending Parfrey a film script for a documentary about Rockwell. Parfrey passed, referring him to Bougas; but as before, the project didn't go anywhere. When Mason finally did make several Rockwell videos for community access TV, he wrote Parfrey to offer copies—but his letter came back undeliverable. Parfrey to Mason, [May?] 1993 [Box 17, Folder 4]; Mason to Parfrey, October 13, 2003, letter returned [Box 30, Folder 49].

71 Parfrey, "Skinned Alive," pp.78–80, 90, 92, 106, 114; quote on p.80.

72 Ibid, p.90; Mason to Rice, May 25, 1989 [Box 9, Folder 20].

73 Goebbels, "Manifesto," Robert Luther 267, "We Can Kill You," and Parfrey, "Eugenics," *EXIT* #4.

74 *EXIT* #5, 1991, www.exitmagazine.net/page.php?id=58. The unpublished *EXIT* #6 also had a Mason contribution; www.exitmagazine.net/page.php?id=198

75 Petros would go on to become a contributing editor at the art magazine *Juxtapoz* and a senior editor at the goth magazine *Propaganda*. *Seconds*, https://secondsmagazine.com/pages/mags.php; *Art That Kills*, p.302.

76 Mason to Parfrey, November 12, 1992; Mason to Parfrey, November 21, 1992 [both Box 17, Folder 4].

77 Parfrey to Mason, [late April or early May] 1993 [Box 17, Folder 4]; Moynihan to Mason, May 28, 1993 [Box 11, Folder 2].

78 Parfrey to Mason, December 13, 1993 [Box 17, Folder 4].

79 *Art That Kills*, p.155.

80 "Archives: 1990–1995," *Center on Contemporary Art*, https://cocaseattle.org/1990-1995

81 Parfrey, *Cult Rapture* (Portland, Oregon: Feral House, 1995), pp.99–111, 241–48, 217–20. Haynes had also appeared in the Petros-edited *EXIT* #5 in 1991.

82 Parfrey, "Finding Our Way Out of Oklahoma," *Cult Rapture*, pp.323–47.

83 The book was David Hoffman's *The Oklahoma City Bombing and the Politics of Terror* (Venice, California: Feral House, 1998); Nolan Clay, "Publisher to Destroy Bomb Book," *Oklahoman*, December 10, 1999, www.oklahoman.com/story/news/1999/12/10/publisher-to-destroy-bomb-book/62218121007

84 Parfrey, "Finding Our Way Out of Oklahoma," *Cult Rapture*, p.306.

85 "8-8-88 Rally plus Interviews" (video).

86 "INTERVIEW: Michael Moynihan of Blood Axis: conducted by Matt G. Paradise for Not Like Most #4," *Purging Talon*, https://web.archive.org/web/20040206154414, http://www.purgingtalon.com/nlm/moynihan.htm

87 Mason to Parfrey, October 22, 1994; Parfrey to Mason, [October/November] 1994 [both Box 17, Folder 4]; The Tards, "Pissed You in the River"/"Wind-up Doll" 7" (Sympathy for the Record Industry, 1995), www.discogs.com/master/1406213-The-Tards-Pissed-You-In-The-River

88 Parfrey to Mason, [October or November?] 1994 [Box 17, Folder 4].

89 Burzum, *Filosofem* (Misanthropy Records/Cymophane Productions/Feral House Audio, 1996), www.discogs.com/Burzum-Filosofem/release/1327160

90 Mason to Schuster, May 13, 2003 [Box 32, Folder 27].

91 Parfrey, ed., *Apocalypse Culture II*.

92 *ANSWER ME! The First Three* (Edinburgh: AK Press, 1994).

93 *Ungawa!* featured trash and exploitation films from the 1950s and '60s. Boyd Rice interviewed Martin Delany in #4, pp.36–39, https://archive.org/details/Ungawa_4/page/n35/mode/2up

94 Mason to Moynihan, September 30, 1992 [Box 11, Folders 1–4].

95 Adam Leith Gollner, "The Secret History of Gavin McInnes," *Vanity Fair*, July/August 2021, online June 29, 2021, www.vanityfair.com/news/2021/06/the-secret-history-of-gavin-mcinnes; "Jim Goad Joins White Nationalist Publishing House as a Biweekly Columnist," *Angry White Men*, October 30, 2020, https://angrywhitemen.org/2020/10/30/jim-goad-joins-white-nationalist-publishing-house-as-a-biweekly-columnist. See also https://counter-currents.com/tag/jim-goad

96 Moynihan and Stephen E Flowers, *The Secret King: The Myth and Reality of Nazi Occultism* (Los Angeles, California: Feral House, 2007); Robert Forbes and Eddie Stampton, *The White Nationalist Skinhead Movement: UK & USA 1979-1993* (Port Townsend, Washington: Feral House, 2015).

97 Screenshots from New Resistance Facebook group, March 2015, in possession of author. The offending essay was Sunshine, "Drawing Lines Against Racism and Fascism," *Political Research Associates*, March 5, 2015, www.politicalresearch. org/2015/03/05/drawing-lines-against-racism-and-fascis. The author was deeply wounded to be lumped in with other "wimpy White intellectuals."

98 Parfrey, "Against the Modern World," *Feral House*, October 16, 2015, https:// web.archive.org/web/20190815063657, https://feralhouse.com/against-the-modern-world; James Porrazzo, New Resistance group post, Facebook, October 12, 2015, screenshot in possession of author.

99 Porrazzo, comment on New Resistance group post, Facebook, October 7, 2012, and Porrazzo, New Resistance group post, Facebook, October 16, 2015, screenshots in possession of author.

100 Tenebrous Kate, "Fringe Culture and Fearlessness: An Interview with Adam Parfrey of Feral House," *Heathen Harvest*, March 11, 2016, https://web.archive. org/web/20160429034533, https://heathenharvest.org/2016/03/11/fringe-culture-and-fearlessness-an-interview-with-adam-parfrey-of-feral-house; "Robert Stark Interviews Adam Parfrey," *The Stark Truth with Robert Stark*, March 6, 2017, www.starktruthradio.com/?p=3948

101 Matthew Gault, "Adam Parfrey's Feral House Was the Forerunner to Reddit and 4chan," *Vice*, May 11, 2018, www.vice.com/en/article/ywez7w/adam-parfrey-dies-feral-house

102 Margot Metroland, "'Zine Master Adam: Remembering Adam Parfrey, April 12, 1957–May 10, 2018," *Counter-Currents*, May 11, 2018, https://counter-currents.com/2018/05/zine-master-adam

103 Mark Dery, *I Must Not Think Bad Thoughts: Drive-by Essays on American Dread, American Dreams* (Minneapolis: University of Minnesota Press, 2012), p.238.

104 John P Jackson, Jr., "The Pre-History of American Holocaust Denial," *American Jewish History* 105 (1–2), January/April 2021, https://muse.jhu.edu/article/804147; John Ganz, "Libertarians Have More in Common with the Alt-Right than They Want You to Think," *Washington Post*, September 19, 2017, www.washingtonpost. com/news/posteverything/wp/2017/09/19/libertarians-have-more-in-common-with-the-alt-right-than-they-want-you-to-think

105 Parfrey, "Introduction," *Cult Rapture*, p.9.

106 For examples of Parfrey's use of being Jewish as a defense against accusations of either being a White Supremacist or working with them, see *Iconoclast* and Coogan, "Kevin Coogan Responds" (response to Parfrey's letter to the editor), *Hit List* #3, June/July 1999, p.6.

107 "Annotated Bibliography," *Cult Rapture*, p.368.

108 Parfrey interview in *Fifth Path* #4, p.24.

109 Dery, *I Must Not Think Bad Thoughts*, p.238.

110 Knipfel, "The Other Nazis," p.13 (*Articles*, p.70).

111 Conklin, "For Adam Parfrey."

112 Parfrey, "If We're So Wrong," p.5.

113 Coogan, "How Black Is Black Metal," p.48n38; Parfrey, "If We're So Wrong," p.5. Coogan's rebuttal letter ("Kevin Coogan Responds," p.6) cited Parfrey's interview in *Fifth Path* #4, p.24.

114 The exchange also featured disputes over whether Stimely had ever been Parfrey's publicist and when *IDEA* #1 was published. In both, Parfrey made claims contradicted by the documentation Coogan had.

115 Knipfel, "The Other Nazis," p.13 (*Articles*, p.70).

116 Parfrey interview in *Fifth Path* #4, p.24.

14

MICHAEL MOYNIHAN

From Mason-Manson-National Socialism to
Decentralized Ethno-separatism

Michael Moynihan is a musician, writer, editor, book publisher, and record label owner. He also played a singularly important role in the dissemination of James Mason's terrorist ideology. Starting in 1989, Moynihan edited the book *Siege* by excerpting Mason's out-of-print newsletters before self-publishing it in 1993. *Siege* would never have existed without Moynihan.

Moynihan first met Boyd Rice, who, as he did with many others, introduced him to several figures who would affect his life, including Anton LaVey, Adam Parfrey, and Mason. (In turn, Moynihan introduced his occasional collaborator Thomas Thorn to the others.) Moynihan toured Japan with Rice in 1989, and the next year the two moved to Denver and became roommates during the bulk of the time that Moynihan edited *Siege*. Moynihan would move from playing industrial music under the name Coup De Grace to making neofolk as Blood Axis, something Rice would also do sometimes. Also like Rice, he is primarily known outside his small circle of admirers for being shrouded in controversy over accusations of neo-Nazism.

Although never openly admitting to being a neo-Nazi, Moynihan strongly implied that he was one during the years he worked on *Siege*. This included letters to Mason with swastikas, his connections with other neo-Nazis and Holocaust deniers, as well as publicly acting as a representative of Universal Order. Moynihan's relationship with the older neo-Nazi was so close that when Mason made his will before going to prison, he left everything to Moynihan.

As with the others in the Abraxas Clique, though, his more radical political positions tapered off when Mason was imprisoned and especially after Moynihan moved to Portland, Oregon to work for Feral House. After the 1998 release of his successful book on Norwegian black metal, *Lords of*

DOI: 10.4324/9780429200090-19

Chaos, Moynihan started to openly deny being a neo-Nazi, even denouncing those politics—to the dismay of actual neo-Nazis familiar with him. Each year, the distance between him and National Socialism grew, as he consistently attempted to mislead interviewers and readers. These deceptions were aided by a number of writers, who either took him at his word or aided him in what were apparently intentional moves. However, a close look at Moynihan's shifting positions illuminates the evolution of both his politics in the late 1980s and '90s and his attempts to obscure them.

Teenage Noise (1984–1988)

Moynihan has been known by various names, including Michael M. Jenkins, the name he used for *Siege*. Moynihan's winding story started in Cambridge, Massachusetts in 1984, when, at age 15, he started making music as Coup De Grace, a name he used until early 1989. He described the project as having "a violent sound, and could have been termed 'Power Electronics', whilst at other times it was of a more atmospheric nature."[1] In 1985, he self-released two cassettes under the auspices of Coup De Grace Productions, and he also released a series of print items under that name.[2]

During this time, the musician Thomas Thorn wrote Moynihan, and the two soon became friends and collaborators. While still a teenager, Moynihan also met Boston record store owner John Zewizz of the group Sleep Chamber. Moynihan played with them between 1985 and 1987,[3] appearing on the album *Submit to Desire* and a number of subsequent live releases. Thorn also played in the group, including a short overlap with Moynihan. But Thorn left after falling out with Zewizz, and Moynihan followed soon after.[4]

Moynihan dropped out of high school at 16 and started making trips to Belgium, where he worked with the space Club Moral.[5] Meanwhile, Thorn went to Wisconsin and formed the industrial band Slave State. (After a stint playing with the popular band My Life With The Thrill Kill Kult, he achieved minor success in the mid-1990s with his own band, the Electric Hellfire Club. Like the others, he joined the Church of Satan and befriended Mason.[6])

In 1988, Thorn spent a few weeks in Belgium with Moynihan, who was living in an old factory next to Club Moral, and together they did a special show as Slave State. It was held in a cellar room that had been discovered under the factory's basement floor. Moynihan said, "we were both skinheads at the time," and the audience of about 50 included "quite a few suspicious types…because the propaganda for the show looked incredibly fascist." The duo "wore black uniforms, had shaved heads, and played Wagner at volume for an hour before we went on." The performance "was extremely dangerous, totally illegal, and a death trap, to boot, with that many people in a place that had only a tiny metal ladder to get out of the hole." Moynihan described the performance, held on August 5, 1988, just days before the

8/8/88 San Francisco event, as "utilizing some similar ideas."[7] Both events would influence the next year's NON tour.

Moynihan soon returned to the United States and in late 1988 put out his last Coup De Grace Productions release, a pirated edition of philosopher Friedrich Nietzsche's *The Antichrist*.[8] The cover art featured what one fanzine described as "Christ superimposed on a swastika with truncated limbs."[9] Before *The Antichrist* was released, however, Moynihan had made contact with Rice and Mason.

Blood Rice (1988–1989)

Moynihan was impressed by Rice's *Blood & Flame* album and got hold of his contact information in 1987. However, he did not reach out until the next year, after which they developed their relationship through phone calls. In 1987, Moynihan also received a copy of the Universal Order pamphlet *Charles Manson: Drugs, Power & Sanity* from Jack Stevenson.[10] Parfrey had previously suggested him to Mason as a distributor for the publication; and like the others, Stevenson would be connected to LaVey.[11]

Mason was of obvious interest to Moynihan. "I'd already been intrigued by Manson for awhile, and I was also getting more and more interested in National Socialism (I read *Mein Kampf* around that time), so it was particularly exciting to see something which fused these elements together."[12] That this combination was done directly in conjunction with the cult leader, and not just in the abstract, could have only made it all the more interesting.

Moynihan first wrote Mason in June 1988, although Mason seemed to have quickly forgotten about this. Moynihan wrote again at the tail end of December, and in January 1989, they started their correspondence in earnest. (Rice had written Mason in December to make sure the two were in touch.[13]) One of the first things that Moynihan sent was a flyer with a Joseph Goebbels passage that appeared in Hitler's *Mein Kampf* as well as a snake intertwined with a swastika.[14] By then, Rice and Moynihan had drawn closer, and in January 1989, Moynihan said Axis Sanguinarius, the name he used on the flyer, was "closely related to Boyd's ABRAXAS Foundation, and is working hand-in-hand." By March, the two had formally joined forces.[15]

Moynihan was also involved in the early stages of the eventual Abraxas Foundation publication, *WAKE*. He solicited Mason to contribute but with the caveat that it wouldn't be a typical National Socialist publication but "something much more all-encompassing." Moynihan said, "I'm thinking along the lines of stuff that either most papers wouldn't DARE publish (as being too 'far-out' or whatever) or material that was even beyond the general tone of SIEGE as far as its extremity." The next year, still waiting for *WAKE* to be released, Moynihan told Mason, "[I]t isn't blatant NS, but rather 'social Darwinist' in outlook. Of course, it's only a short skip to NS from there!"[16]

From the time he joined the Abraxas Foundation to the end of 1990, Moynihan continually insisted *WAKE* was about to be released.[17] But when it did finally come out in 1992, his name was absent. "I did a lot of work on the initial one, most of which was unused at the last minute or went uncredited," he said; and in his opinion, the result was an inferior product.[18]

Moynihan also developed an obsession with blood. In 1989, he spoke to a reporter, who had taken out an ad looking to contact a vampire, about drinking blood. Three years later, an interview showed the biological and racial aspects of Moynihan's blood fetish. By then, "Axis Sanguinarius" had become "Blood Axis," which he would use for his musical output. The name represented "blood, violence, sex, heredity, and an undefinable mythic spiritual quality as well. Of course I was well aware of the fascist connotation of the word 'axis,' and accepted this willing."[19] Blood wasn't the only body part he was interested in, though. He put out a call looking for both human and animal remains.[20]

Mason, *Siege*, Swastikas (1989)

The question of a SIEGE anthology, already suggested by Rice, came up almost immediately in Moynihan's correspondence with Mason. Near the end of January 1989, Moynihan asked, almost as an aside, if Mason had considered "republishing selections from your past writings in another form? They deserve it." Mason quickly responded that the idea is "getting more attractive all the time. Whoever felt like the task might be worthwhile would have all my blessings to go straight forward with it."[21] At the end of February, Moynihan embraced the idea, saying

> It would be great to see a book of SIEGE writing & graphics ("THE BEST OF SIEGE"?). It would be a lasting document and exert a lot of influence... I would definitely be <u>keenly interested</u> to invest a lot of work into such a project.[22]

And it would end up being a lot of work. Mason accepted the proposal and said he was willing to provide the complete run of SEIGE. "You'd have all the rights, reap all the benefits (or take all the losses) and I'd take all the bows."[23]

At this point, Moynihan started drawing swastikas in his letters. He had already used them as part of illustrations on *The Antichrist* cover and the Axis Sanguinarius flyer. A right-facing swastika in a circle, the traditional Nazi swastika, graced the top of his letter of February 28, 1989, in which he expressed his interest in making SIEGE into a book. That same swastika, apparently made with a rubber stamp, was also used in the letters he sent to Mason in June and August.[24] Near the end of that month, Moynihan wished Mason "GOOD LUCK" in the text of a letter, and the well-wishes were bookended with two swastikas—the first right-facing and the second left-facing. Moynihan apparently stopped using them until July 1990, when, as he was working on *Siege*, he again signed a letter with both right- and left-facing swastikas. Furthermore, Moynihan publicly admitted to using left-facing swastikas in his letters to Manson around this time.[25]

In March 1989, Moynihan told Mason that he would be in Europe until the end of the year. He planned a "pilgrimage" to Hitler's birthplace in Braunau am Inn, where he promised to mail a postcard on April 20 (Hitler's birthday) if the timing worked out. His trip's itinerary also included visits to the former concentration camp Dachau, Wewelsburg castle, and the Externsteine.[26] Moynihan would later use a photograph of himself posing in the middle of the black sun mosaic at Wewelsburg and turn it into a holiday card.[27]

His trip was cut short, however, and by May 1989, he was back in the States. He had been asked to take part in the NON tour of Japan and so the next month flew San Francisco to meet Rice and work on the carefully designed stage show, which sought to summon the atmosphere of a Nazi rally. Moynihan also made sure to mail Mason a Wolfsangel armband he made.[28] While they were preparing for the tour, Rice introduced him to LaVey, and they met up again after returning to the United States. Of the meetings, Moynihan said, "We immediately hit it off and had a phenomenal, very special time there."[29]

He wasn't just catching up on Satanism, though. He was reading, and praising, Tom Metzger's *WAR* newspaper. In August 1989, he said Nick Bougas's cartoons in *WAR* were "unbelievable."[30]

Bougas was an artist, filmmaker, and omnipresent figure in the Abraxas Circle. His viciously bigoted cartoons for *WAR*, signed "A. Wyatt Man," were iconic in the White Supremacist milieu of the 1980s and '90s. Among other things, Bougas was also a *Manson File* contributing editor; was at 8/8/88; drew covers for Jim Goad's *ANSWER ME!* and *Black Flame*; and made documentaries about Manson and LaVey (the latter of which included Parfrey and Rice). He was also co-credited with artwork for Mason's 2000 book *When We Were All Jews*. Years later, Bougas's "Happy Merchant"—a crude drawing of a yarmulke-wearing, hook-nosed Jew, greedily rubbing his hands—became ubiquitous in the Alt Right.[31]

Moynihan, also befriended Bob Heick from the American Front. In the fall of 1989, Moynihan designed a poster to submit to *Aryan Warrior* and in 1990 stayed with him in San Francisco, during which time the two were arrested for putting up posters.[32] When Heick appeared in a 1992 *Village Voice* group photo, Moynihan bragged that he had made two of the T-shirts in it: an American Front shirt on an adult and a Totenkopf shirt on a baby.[33] (The Totenkopf was a skull-and-crossbones image used by the SS, which has long been popular with neo-Nazis.)

Starting Siege

Just before leaving for Japan, Moynihan discussed his plans for the book with Mason. When Moynihan returned in mid-July 1989, he set to work on it, quickly making progress.[34] At this point, he made no bones about where his political sympathies lay, telling Mason, "If this all comes together it could work out to be a VERY STRONG enlightenment of the THOUGHT (and the resultant ACTION which comes out of it...)." He also agreed to include the mailing addresses of White Supremacist organizations if they approved it. This detail was undoubtedly important to Mason since it was a picture in a book, which included the American Nazi Party's address, that led directly to his joining the party.[35]

In October, Moynihan mused about the need for a new project name to publish the book under, as he had retired the Coup De Grace moniker. He came up with Storm Books, complete with a lightning bolt logo. This reflected neo-Nazi imagery while remaining nicely ambiguous—being equally Nietzschean, for example. (In 1994, Moynihan said, "Storm was basically created to publish Siege."[36])

Through the fall of 1989, Mason and Moynihan discussed which passages should be in the book, with Mason providing background information. That October, Moynihan said he hoped that *Siege* would be released in the second part of 1990.[37] But the book's gestation period was much longer than expected.

Go West, Young Fascist (1990)

In December 1989, Moynihan told Mason, then still in Ohio, that he would be moving to Denver; after doing some events there, the Mile High City had made a favorable impression on him. He arrived in mid-January 1990 and moved in with Rice but did not get back in touch with Mason until March.[38]

Like the others, Moynihan started to correspond with the Manson Family. Moynihan would describe Manson as "a man of incredible insight, one of the few truly perceptive people I've encountered." In November 1989, Moynihan asked about the possibility of getting one of the Family members to write *Siege*'s introduction.[39] The next spring, Mason provided some of their addresses but later told Moynihan that he doubted (correctly) that they would be amenable. Although she wouldn't write one either, Moynihan started corresponding with Manson Family member Sandra Good in July.[40]

In March, Moynihan had finished the *Music, Martinis, and Misanthropy* recording with Rice. But all was not copacetic, and during that time, the Abraxas Foundation started unraveling. While Moynihan was still working on *WAKE*, he launched a blistering attack on Nikolas Schreck. In March 1990, Moynihan wrote Mason that we've <u>completely</u> disassociated ourselves from Shreck [sic]. This was a long time coming. Actually the break in ties occurred months ago. Nicholas has turned out to be a deceptive liar. All talk/<u>no</u> action. On top of all that he has been revealed and <u>lives</u> a complete lie. His real (Jewish) name is Barry Dubin.[41]

Despite what he told Bob Larson, this would not be his only antisemitic statement of the sort. Two years later, he called Jewish TV host Geraldo Rivera "Jewraldo."[42]

Ironically, Mason turned out to be more tolerant of Jews than Moynihan was—or at least those useful to him. Mason told Moynihan that the break with Schreck was unfortunate, as he had seen "these breaks destroy the old movement. I developed the philosophy that unless I'm attacked personally, I'll continue to cooperate." And it went without saying that he had no qualms with Parfrey.[43]

Moynihan spent the rest of 1990 working on *Siege*. Ever the optimist about publishing schedules, he said in August that he remained "totally committed" and the projected release date was January 1991. But as the end of the year rolled around, they were still finalizing the section order and working on the introduction.[44]

Although his relationship with Rice had not yet degenerated, Moynihan was not content to be a sideman. In 1990, his new project, Blood Axis, started to get off the ground; other than Moynihan himself, its members varied.[45] While the first Blood Axis album would not be released for a number of years, two songs were recorded in November 1989 and included Rice's participation. One, "Electricity," ended with Moynihan shouting "Hail Victory!"[46]

The Church and the State (1991)

In early 1991, *Siege* still was not near completion, and Moynihan was looking for both financing and typesetting help.[47] He also used his existing relationship with LaVey to get permission to use a quote in *Siege*.[48] Moynihan also stayed in touch with the Manson Family. He had hit it off with Good well enough that he visited her in Vermont,[49] although she was not pleased with the forthcoming book. Moynihan complained about "how unreasonable and difficult those folks can be,"[50] although, according to Mason, Manson was "not bent out of shape on the book." Mason added, "He'll like the thing when he sees it (If we can succeed in getting a copy to him.)" Later, Mason said Lynette "Squeaky" Fromme and Good saw it, "and they approved."[51]

Moynihan was also able to write Manson directly. In 1992, they were on good enough terms that Manson sent him some business cards for his new environmental project, ATWA (Air, Trees, Water, Animals).[52] But later, the ever-fickle Manson would denounce him in the same breath as Rice, saying "Moynihan's an idiot."[53]

Secret Service

However, Moynihan's correspondence did not go unnoticed, and in May 1991, the Secret Service showed up at his door. Alan Prendergast, a journalist for the local alternative weekly *Westword*, covered this—the first of a several stories he wrote about Moynihan, Rice, and/or Mason. Prendergast said the agents "were investigating a possible plot to assassinate President [George H. W.] Bush... during his upcoming visit to Colorado." Apparently Moynihan was supposed to be the gunman in a convoluted plot that also involved Manson and Good.[54]

Courtesy of his Boston lawyer father, Moynihan quickly retained representation and agreed to take a polygraph test to satiate the federal officers. They were satisfied, his legal problems were disposed of, and Moynihan netted some nice press—where he got practice in how to get journalists to aid him in dodging accusations of neo-Nazi involvement.

Siege *Introduction*

In fact, Moynihan wrote the introduction to *Siege* the same spring as his FBI visit. Here, he was very clear that the book was presenting Mason's National Socialist ideology in the hope that readers would adopt it.

> The SIEGE volume you hold in your hands is intended both as a guide and a tool. For the observer, or the curious, it serves as a guide through the netherworld of extremist political thought.... This book offers a unique and direct access-point to understanding the philosophy, tactics, and propaganda of an increasingly militant and uncompromising brand of National Socialism. ... Secondly, and more importantly, this book is meant to serve as a practical tool. A majority of readers will hopefully not be mere sociologists or researchers, but rather that small faction of people who may be already predisposed towards these ideas. This certainly does not only refer to National Socialists, but revolutionaries and fanatics of all stripes.[55]

The end of the introduction addressed some of the book's contradictions: the "conservative" George Lincoln Rockwell versus the "mind-blowing" Manson; committing murder versus ensuring your own safety; terrorism versus dropping out. Moynihan also hoped that *Siege* would "lead us closer to the revelation where the real balance of Truth and Order resides."[56] This was hardly a 'fascination with extremes' as later apologists argued but rather a clear advocacy of National Socialism, James Mason–style—terrorism and all.

"Manson Maniacs"

In July 1991, just after the Secret Service visit, the preacher Bob Larson had Mason, Moynihan, and Rice on his national radio show, an episode that was titled "Manson Maniacs." Moynihan was introduced as a representative of Universal Order and wore a T-shirt with a left-facing swastika. Despite this, when confronted by Larson, he denied being a National Socialist, claiming that the term was applicable only to the NSDAP. (Elsewhere, Mason himself directly contradicted this view, saying Universal Order "is National Socialism...just another name for it."[57])

However, Moynihan denied that Jews were a problem. "They're not a problem to me, personally." Asked again if he was concerned about them, Moynihan said, "I'm not. That's not my reality," adding that he wasn't interested in black people either. His honest views on these groups aside, Moynihan's primary interests lay elsewhere, and he used Larson's platform to convey them to a national audience. Ranting he said, "I'd like to see order! There's not any order!! What kind of order is out on the streets right now?!" But it wasn't just chaos that bothered him. Humans were "too far gone to even hope of changing." The apocalypse was coming. It would bring "violence, bloodshed, turmoil" which would lead "the System" to "self-destruct."

Having gotten going he said, "Our hearts are closed to pity" and "there's going to have to be a lot of murder to get rid of what's going on now." (Here, Rice jumped in to clarify this meant most humans needed to die.) Having repeated the schema Mason laid out in SIEGE, Moynihan said their plan was to "pull back and watch the sparks fly." He ended the show with "Hail victory!"[58]

While Moynihan obviously chose his words for their shock value, everything he said was consistent with the beliefs he expressed elsewhere. He was merely antagonistic in their presentation and unusually explicit in spelling out what putting them into practice would actually mean.

In June 1991, Moynihan started the process of typing in the pieces he chose for the book into a computer (something that was only starting to become common in households), but the next month, Moynihan begged for Mason's help cutting down the book's sprawling contents. In the fall, work on the passages was still ongoing.[59]

Writing Racist Rock (1992)

Siege's final corrections were entered only in January 1992. It was not, however, so easy to find a printer. The next month, one turned down the job, saying that it was difficult to reject a paying client but that management, unsurprisingly, "decided that the contents would be offensive to some of our employees." September found Moynihan still trying to get printing arrangements finalized.[60]

Mason was sympathetic to this struggle. He relayed a story about how the American Nazi Party made Rockwell's *This Time the World* by printing the actual pages on their own printing press, collating them by hand, and then binding them with clamps, glue, and even car jacks.[61] The time overrun was such that while *Siege* carried a 1992 publication date in the front matter, it still wouldn't actually be out until the next year.

After he moved to Denver, Moynihan started writing about rock music in earnest. The new death and black metal bands were of particular interest—especially if they had White Supremacist or misanthropic content. In the summer of 1991, he expressed interest in the band Carcass, stressing to Mason their popularity and noting that their "new and very intense and over-the-top ultra violent" music had fans with "presumably no moral considerations whatsoever." He even hoped to "join one of these bands myself and subtly influence it that way."[62]

In 1993, Moynihan sent Mason an interview with David Vincent, of the metal band Morbid Angel, where he expressed racist views; Moynihan said he was a friend and gleefully noted that Vincent's interview had "caused a huge stink!"[63] (In *Lords of Chaos*, the band's show in Oslo would be credited as "a meeting point for fans who would become integral to the inner core of the Black Metal scene," and Moynihan would later interview the band in *Seconds*.) In 1995, Mason said he went to a Type O Negative concert and was "enthusiastically welcomed."[64]

Moynihan also became involved in two fanzines: Robert Ward's *Fifth Path* and Aaron Garland's *Ohm Clock*. They covered similar cultural, political, and spiritual issues and were distributed through Tower Records, a major retail chain. Moynihan encouraged Garland to publish *Ohm Clock*, the more fascist of the two. Moynihan was a contributor, and the zine ran articles about the Italian fascist Julius Evola and an interview with the openly White Supremacist band RAHOWA. Garland later played bass with Blood Axis on their 1998 European tour.[65]

But Moynihan was more involved in *Fifth Path*. He started in 1992 as a guest reviewer and soon was associate editor. Continuing their incestuous tradition, *Fifth Path* interviewed Moynihan and Rice, Moynihan interviewed Electric Hellfire Club, and reviews of *WAKE* and *Siege* were printed. Moynihan also wrote two articles on "Odinism in Heavy Metal," which showed that by the winter of 1992 he was already exploring ideas that would be fully developed in *Lords of Chaos*—and at the same time he was still working on *Siege*.[66]

During his time in Denver, Moynihan's interest in Karl Maria Wiligut blossomed. Nicknamed "Himmler's Rasputin," Wiligut was a mystic who had a special interest in runes and worked for the SS. Although the project started in 1990, two years later Moynihan would work on translating a Wiligut poem, which had originally been dedicated to SS leader Heinrich Himmler.[67] Moynihan's interest in the rune mystic would continue for many years. In 1994 and 1995, Storm would release records based on Wiligut's works,[68] and in 2001, Moynihan edited a book that combined translations of, and commentary on, him.[69]

But Moynihan had not ignored making music. Although the project had been around for about two years at that point, Blood Axis played their first show on Halloween 1992 in Denver.[70] And at the end of 1992, Moynihan, after a falling out with Rice, moved out of their shared space.

The Next Holocaust (1993–1994)

It was only in 1993 that *Siege* finally came out. Mason was delighted that it arrived on April 20—an auspicious date for a National Socialist. That wasn't the end of Moynihan's work on the book, though, and he spent significant time publicizing *Siege*. He also stayed in Denver for a few years, taking classes at the University of Colorado Denver.[71] Moynihan also recorded more music, and one song would come out the next year as Blood Axis's half of a split 7". It was Storm's first music release.[72]

Lenient Entrance Requirements

Moyhihan was an able publicist and netted a number of *Siege* reviews and interviews with Mason and sometimes himself. The one that would haunt him most was an interview with both Mason and Moynihan which appeared in *NO LONGER A FANzine* #5, published in summer 1994 in the Philadelphia area. (This was probably the only time Mason was interviewed in a zine that was not already on board with his politics.) The popular fanzine's editor, Joseph A. Gervasi, came into contact with Moynihan after ordering an algiz rune T-shirt from Storm, which he saw in a *Fifth Path* advertisement; a flyer for *Siege* came with his package.[73]

Gervasi wrote, "Since I had grown bored with the radical Left, I figured it was time to give the radical Right a look" and so he bought *Siege* and asked for interviews. The fanzine editor wrote Mason that he was "very fascinating" and that his own publication was a "forum free of any form of censorship"—even though they strongly disagreed politically.

In his introduction to Mason's interview, Gervasi said he shared an interest in Mason's organizing strategies and anti-government views. While they disagreed about race—because Gervasi felt that the differences between races were a positive thing—still he held that "further scientific investigation of DNA...will reveal differences in the races that some would rather not be known." He also distanced himself from "reactionary anarcho-publications, who are better suited to pump out hollow anti-fascist slogans," while clearly denouncing "Holocaust revisionists who feign impartiality." (He later stressed that nothing else in the zine reflected Far Right attitudes and said that at the time he was booking all ages and explicitly inclusive shows; if

Nazi skinheads showed up, they were summarily kicked out.) But still, like so many others, Gervasi was fascinated by a variety of "extreme" perspectives and used his publication to explore them.[74]

Gervasi asked Moynihan several point-blank questions. First, in reply to his query, Moynihan denied being a White Supremacist. Second, did Moynihan, unlike Mason,[75] believe that 6 million Jews were killed in the Holocaust?

> This is a touchy question, because I have very mixed feelings about it. On the one hand, I think the Six Million number is just arbitrary and inaccurate, and probably a gross exaggeration. I have read revisionist books which make a good case against much of the Holocaust "canon," and even the Jewish historians are constantly changing their claims.[76]

The main problem, Moynihan said, is that the Holocaust revisionists thought that "killing millions of innocent people is inherently 'bad.'" He would have preferred if "the Nazis did commit every atrocity ascribed to them." The next question was "If you were given the opportunity to gas blacks, Jews, whomever, would you do it?," to which Moynihan answered, "If I were given the opportunity to start up the next Holocaust I would definitely have much more lenient entrance requirements than the Nazis did."[77]

Last, Moynihan was asked specifically about what Gervasi called the "pseudo-academic" Institute for Historical Review (IHR). After saying that the organization did not promote fascism as such, Moynihan called their authors a mix of "serious historians" and everyday people. He said,

> Do you believe that the mainstream or acceptable history books you find in Waldenbooks are written by impartial researchers who don't harbor their own agendas? Frankly I find the mainstream media and publish [sic] industry far more insidious and full of covert propaganda than people like the I.H.R.[78]

The rest of the interview was quite amiable. Moynihan thanked Gervasi for reading *Siege* and conducting the interviews, adding that he wished more people were like him. The zine editor also tacked on his own letter to another local alternative paper, *Welcomat*, which had also covered Mason and Moynihan. In it, Gervasi called for a "drastic reduction" in human population through abortion as well as using methods to "liquidate our current stock of the retarded and crippled," after which would come the "obese and stupid."[79]

Holocaust Deniers

During this period, Moynihan, like Parfrey, had direct contact with a number of Holocaust deniers, in addition to Mason. In 1994, Moynihan said, "I'm reading a lot of revisionist stuff. I have mixed feelings about it—but it really pisses people off, really drives all these Jewish Holocaust worshippers straight up the wall."[80]

Moynihan had met former IHR staffer Keith Stimely when he came to Denver in May 1990. Holocaust denier and ex-NSWPP member William Grimstad was thanked in a 1992 Moynihan publication. Moynihan even picked up some jargon from him, saying lost mail "Could just be the N.I.P.O., as Bill Grimstad would say ('Niggers in the Post Office')."[81]

Moynihan also made contact with James J. Martin, an important intellectual within the Holocaust denial set who was also affiliated with the IHR. In 1991, Moynihan said he was going to Colorado Springs, where Martin lived, and hoped to conduct a recorded interview with him.[82] In 1993, as part of their correspondence, Martin was sent a copy of *Siege*, and he wrote Moynihan back with his impressions.[83]

Last, he also seemed to be quite taken with one of his professors at University of Denver Colorado, Carsten Seecamp, whose former students have accused him of being a Holocaust denier. On the *Rate My Professors* website, four different entries between 2013 and 2017 claim that Seecamp was a "Holocaust denier/minimizer" or that he had similar views. One said he "quotes and defends David Irving in class." Indeed, a Seecamp syllabus from 2016 included two of Irving's books as "recommended" readings. The syllabus also promoted "a controversial but interesting website"—Irving's— and students were told how to sign up for his newsletter.[84]

A 1993 essay Moynihan wrote for Seecamp's class, "The Faustian Spirit of Fascism: From Oswald Spengler to Oswald Mosley," would be published in Satanist and neo-Nazi publications. Moynihan also told an interviewer that Seecamp was a "brilliant professor" whom he befriended and who in turn told him about his family's business, L.W. Seecamp Firearms. Moynihan acquired a special .32 caliber pistol they made; he was apparently so taken by it that he thanked the company in *The Gospel of Inhumanity*.[85]

In 1999, Moynihan made a turnabout on these views on the Holocaust, directly stating that "I'm not a historical revisionist."[86] His various forays into antisemitism aside, Moynihan never embraced classical antisemitic conspiracy theories. The introduction to the 2003 second edition of *Lords of Chaos* expounded on comments made about this in the first, now stating in no uncertain terms that "The notion of a 'Protocols of the Elders of Zion'-style Jewish cabal running the world is absurd."[87]

Heathenism

By 1993, Moynihan's interest in Heathenism had significantly increased. Already writing about music's relationship to this religious current, he now deepened his own personal involvement in Asatrú. (This is the name for a subset of Heathenism that focuses on Scandinavian and German pre-Christian religion.)

One important milestone occurred when he met Robert N. Taylor in 1993. Taylor had a colorful background. In the 1960s, he was a member of the Far Right paramilitary organization the Minutemen. In 1969, Taylor formed a folk duo called Changes, which retroactively was cast as a precursor to White Supremacist neofolk. In the mid-1970s, he became deeply involved in the emergence and spread of Asatrú, a type of northern European paganism, in the United States. When this new religious current split over questions of race, Taylor joined the more moderate White Supremacist wing. Moynihan would release recordings of Changes, and Taylor contributed to Petros and Parfrey's projects. Moynihan also joined his Asatrú group and became an associate editor at the Asatrú publication *Vor Trú*, which Taylor was also working with.[88]

In 1993, Moynihan also started what would become frequent contributions to *Seconds*, where he would eventually publish over 20 pieces. His coverage included others in his circles, like Manson, LaVey, Death in June, and Peter Sotos, but also racist bands like Burzum and RAHOWA.[89]

Mason was anything but ungrateful to Moynihan. After Mason's April 1994 arrest for brandishing a gun at his ex-girlfriend, and undoubtedly worried about what would happen to him in prison, Mason drew up a will. In it, he left everything—vehicles, several pieces of property, and all his personal belongings—to Moynihan. According to Ed Reynolds, Mason called him his "patron saint."[90]

COCA Cult Culture

In September 1994, Moynihan made his last major act to promote Mason and *Siege* when he represented Universal Order at Parfrey's "Cult Rapture" art show in Seattle. (Mason was on bond and could not leave the state.[91]) The booth, which Moynihan designed, was made to look like a bunker. Mason described it as

> set up like a shrine—all draped in black with the Universal Order scales and swastika. There was a copy of Siege under plastic. On the surrounding walls were illustrations of Hitler, Tommasi, Manson, some printed propaganda, and some handwritten letters from Manson.[92]

The *Seattle Times* covered the show but didn't even bother to mention the booth. However, the paper's art critic described most of the exhibition as "a bit like collecting flyers from politicians at the county fair. Neither illuminating nor, I'm afraid, very interesting." After all, it wasn't really art—just propaganda.[93]

Satan's Priest (1994)

While Moynihan was lukewarm about Satanism, LaVey clearly impressed him. After Rice introduced the two in 1989, Moynihan became a Church of Satan member. Although Satanism did not play as important a part in his life as other ideas did, he was made a High Priest in late 1994.[94] His ordination came during a continuing debate inside the Church about the relationship between Satanism and fascism.

Moynihan became a contributor to *Black Flame*, the Church of Satan's official magazine, which was edited by Peter Gilmore, who would go on to be its leader. In 1994, the periodical ran Moynihan's essay that had originated as a class paper, "The Faustian Spirit of Fascism." The introduction that Moynihan wrote said that the conjunction of Satanism, National Socialism, and fascism was "a perfectly natural evolution" and the answer to the question of if "Satanism is inherently Fascistic…seems quite obvious to me."[95] He continued,

> Given the preponderance of this victim culture—glorifying the lowest and holding no one accountable for his or her actions—a heroic Fascism in a *pure* form would be a welcome antidote. The same can be said for many of the tenets of National Socialism, including the dreaded "Holocaust" (which in the future will have far less stringent entrance requirements).[96]

The body of the article argued that Nietzsche, Spengler, the NSDAP, and Mosley were all driven by the "Faustian spirit." This was defined as the human attempt—consequences, literally, be damned—to take actions which sought to take down a degenerate, liberal society. Although Moynihan favored the approaches of Spengler and Mosley, he also had plenty of sympathy for the NSDAP; Abraxas Clique–favorite Alfred Rosenberg in particular was quoted favorably.[97] "The Faustian Spirit of Fascism" was also one of two Moynihan pieces that ran in *Plexus*, which called itself "A National Socialist Theoretical Journal."[98]

Seconds ran a Moynihan interview with LaVey in 1995. Pieces of that interview, which had ended up on the cutting room floor, also appeared in *Black Flame*. If Moynihan had any qualms about the post-LaVey trajectory of the Church of Satan, he kept his affiliation—unlike Rice.[99]

One of the bands that Moynihan interviewed in *Black Flame* was RAHOWA, an acronym for "racial holy war." Led by George Eric Hawthorne (né Burdi), they became one of the most popular White Supremacist bands in the 1990s as they moved from an Oi!-influenced rock into "goth metal with some elements of neo-classical metal."[100]

Hawthorne was one of the fairly small number of blatant White Supremacists associated with the Abraxas Circle. He was smarter than the average racist bear, which must have drawn their attention as a potential addition to the making and sustaining of a countercultural fascism. In 1995, Hawthorne's magazine *Resistance* ran Mason's controversial article arguing for Manson. In 1996, Moynihan interviewed Hawthorne for *Seconds* and the next year for *Black Flame*. (Garland also interviewed him in *Ohm Clock*.[101]) And in addition to Mason, Moynihan, and Garland, Hawthorne was connected to another member of the extended Abraxas Circle, Shane Bugbee, who was hired to do promotional work for the band and later published a Hawthorne piece.[102]

Puddletown (1995–1997)

In 1995, with Mason in prison, Moynihan moved to Portland, Oregon, where Parfrey was living, took a job as managing editor at Feral House, and continued his German studies at Portland State University.[103]

First, however, in the immediate aftermath of *Siege's* release and before his move out west, Moynihan started work on his Norwegian black metal book in 1994. Originally titled *Blood and Ashes*, it was later changed to *Lords of Chaos*.[104] In October 1995, he went to Norway for two weeks to conduct interviews and spent two days with White Supremacist black metal musician Varg Vikernes in prison. Additional interviews continued through 1997.[105]

This was also a fertile period for Storm. In 1995 and 1996, Moynihan's label released eight records, including ones by Blood Axis, Changes, and Allerseen.[106] And he also helped with some Manson releases by White Devil Records, including one with liner notes by Moynihan.[107]

The first Blood Axis album, *The Gospel of Inhumanity*, was formally released in 1996. It was one of the comparatively few full-length projects he was the unquestioned primary creator of; even his one proper book was co-authored. A reviewer in a politically sympathetic periodical wrote that *The Gospel of Inhumanity* had "a strong European sensibility." It stressed themes like "war, strength, power" and overall was "a musical articulation of the esoteric elements of fascism."[108] One song, "Herr, Nun Laß in Frieden," was built around a recording of Manson speaking from prison.[109]

During this time, Moynihan also revived Taylor's music career by releasing material by his Far Right folk group Changes, which had formed in 1969. The first full-length released was a compilation of old recordings, *Fire of Life*, in 1996.[110]

Lords of Chaos (1998)

Lords of Chaos: The Bloody Rise of the Satanic Metal Underground, co-written with Didrik Søderlind, drew from several of Moynihan's existing areas of interest. He had already been writing about Odinist metal bands since the early 1990s. And, of course, he was well versed in both Satanism and neo-Nazism.

In 1998, Feral House published the book; a number of the Abraxas Circle were thanked in it.[111] Members of the Norwegian black metal scene, many of whom were Satanists and heathens who identified with National Socialism, had initially attracted attention for burning old wooden churches, which were cherished in the country. The book was primarily focused on the most prominent of these, Vikernes, who at the time was still a Nazi Satanist. As a musician, he became popular for the recordings he made under the name Burzum. But he also played in the band Mayhem, and it was with them that he became best known—for murdering their guitarist. (Their original singer had already committed suicide.) If it was not enough to garner black metal sufficient notoriety, there were other murders attributed to the scene; this included a gay man in Norway and a 14-year-old in Germany. (Hendrik Möbus of the band Absurd, who was jailed for the latter murder, would violate his parole by illegally sieg-heiling. To avoid arrest, he fled the country and hid out at William Pierce's National Alliance compound.[112])

While Norwegian black metal's notoriety had reached the United States, very little information on it was available. So when *Lords of Chaos* was released, Moynihan and Søderlind's sympathetic account was lapped up. Reflecting how Moynihan suggested *Siege* could be read, *Lords of Chaos* also functioned on two levels: as a political guide to those interested in its ideas and as a sociological guide for those who were not.

For interested parties, there were four important angles. One, the book argued that the Norwegian events were the emergence of the archetype of Wotan, supposedly a buried, pre-Christian racial consciousness. Psychoanalyst Carl Jung developed this idea in his 1936 essay "Wotan," which has been often quoted by contemporary Asatrú practitioners. The end of *Lords of Chaos* proclaimed that "The forces of finance and materialism" were at war with this underground being, trying "to root it out and then stamp it out"— but they have not been able to.[113]

Second, the book interviewed, or explained the views of, a number of fascists. Among these were New Zealand writer Kerry Bolton and Gungnir, the editor of *Napalm Rock*, a Third Positionist music magazine published by Christian Bouchet's Nouvelle Résistance.[114]

Third, it showed a move that this political/religious movement was making. The Norwegian scene started off by intertwining Nazism, Satanism, and murder—just as Mason had championed. But the book also documented its turn away from these toward an ethno-nationalist Heathenism, the same change that Moynihan was making in his own outlook at the time.

Fourth, contact information for racists was included. Mason and Moynihan previously discussed including mailing addresses for White Supremacist groups in *Siege*. And *Lords of Chaos* would include several addresses for racist projects—sometimes embedded in the images.[115] But the book generously included their critics as well, making the racist content subtle and obscure enough that it could be overlooked by those mostly interested in reading about music history or the culture of extremes. Just as many people did with Feral House in general.

Lords of Chaos was a success. In 1999, Moynihan said it was Feral House's best-selling book; by 2000, it had reportedly sold 20,000 copies, and in 2003, a revised edition was released.[116] A film adaptation came out in 2018—although it was not nearly as popular. (Worldwide it grossed only $365,000, with the film review website *Rotten Tomatoes* giving it a 72 percent rating.[117])

Afterlord

After *Lords of Chaos*, Moynihan continued writing, playing music, publishing fascist authors, and pursuing academic studies. The occasional Blood Axis album, such as 1998's *Blót: Sacrifice in Sweden*, sometimes came out on other labels. Storm put out music infrequently, issuing only seven releases between 2003 and 2014.[118]

Moynihan's politics had now shifted into his last phase, which he would continue for the decades to come. By now, he had abandoned whatever prior interest he had in a National Socialist, or other kind of fascist, state. In its place, he embraced decentralized, homogenous communities. As early as 1999, Moynihan said he rejected an identification with the term "white" and in 2000 spurned an ethno-nationalism as well, turning to even smaller, sub-national groups. In this, he reflected the perspective of Stephen McNallen, a leading figure in Heathenism in the United States, as well as from the decentralized fascism of Alain de Benoist and the French New Right.[119] Moynihan would develop these ideas further in the '00s and 2010s in his publication *TYR*.

In 1999, a letter Moynihan sent to *Scorpion* magazine was printed; at the time, it was the premier English-language magazine promoting French New Right ideas. (Editor Michael Walker had been a member of the National Front in Britain and, like Moynihan, was looking for alternatives to traditional National Socialism while still stressing many of the same themes.) Moynihan's co-author Søderlind also wrote a review that appeared in the same issue.[120]

In 2000, Moynihan contributed to Parfrey's *Apocalypse Culture II* and in 2003 to Richard Metzger's *Book of Lies: The Disinformation Guide to Magick and the Occult*. That anthology had contributions from the Abraxas Circle, including Rice, LaVey, and Feral House artist Joe Coleman—as well as Julius Evola. Moynihan also started his own press, Dominion, with Annabel Lee. In 2001, they published the Wiligut book he did with Stephen E. Flowers, *The Secret King: Karl Maria Wiligut, Himmler's Lord of the Runes*[121]—the culmination of his interest in the SS member, which had started while Moynihan was working on *Siege*.

Despite his move away from National Socialism, Moynihan continued to uphold his duties as Mason's publisher. Through at least 2001, he continued to forward to Mason inquiries that he had received about *Siege* and Universal Order.[122]

At this time, Moynihan was also helping popularize Julius Evola to English-language audiences. Evola was an Italian fascist active from the prewar era through the 1970s. Well versed in art, philosophy, and esoteric and Eastern spirituality, he was the movement's most sophisticated theoretician and an inspiration to the most violent of Italy's postwar fascists. In 1995, Moynihan was already trying to arrange a translator so he could publish Evola's works.[123]

In 1998, Blood Axis contributed to an Evola-themed compilation. The next year, Moynihan was editing one of Evola's major political works, *Men Among the Ruins*, which would be released in 2002.[124] (Much later, an audiobook of Evola's *Revolt Against the Modern World*, read by Moynihan over a period of 17 hours, would be released and distributed by the mainstream press Simon & Schuster.[125])

Moynihan also turned to more serious scholarly writing. Despite—or because of—his politics, he contributed to two academic collections: Jeffrey Kaplan's *Encyclopedia of White Power* in 2000 and Bron Taylor's *Encyclopedia of Religion and Nature* in 2005.[126]

In 2002, he started the periodical he would become known for, *TYR: Myth–Culture–Tradition*. Five issues of the book-length journal came out between 2002 and 2018. Co-edited with former Nazi skinhead Joshua Buckley,[127] they espoused a pessimistic, volkisch, ethno-separatist worldview. Taking on the label "radical traditionalist," *TYR* promoted ecology, denounced modern society, and advocated "small, ethnically and culturally homogenous tribal societies" which were "in accord with tradition."[128] *TYR* ran articles by and about Evola, de Benoist, and McNallen.

Comparatively little attention has been paid to Moynihan's collaborator Buckley, who for decades has been active in White Supremacist politics in the Atlanta, Georgia metropolitan area. In September 1991, the first meeting was held of the SS of America Marietta Unit, led by Buckley, then a Nazi skinhead. Working with the National States Rights Party's Ed Fields, one local monitoring group described them as "the most sophisticated Nazi youth group to date in the Atlanta area." In 1992, Buckley was accused of making harassing phone calls and was spotted at a David Irving talk hosted by local White Supremacist lawyer Sam Dickson.[129]

Buckley soon encountered Moynihan, who in 1996 thanked him on *The Gospel of Inhumanity* as well as in 1998 in *Lords of Chaos*. Like Moynihan, he started writing for *Black Flame* and *Vor Trú*. In 1999 or 2000, Buckley helped convert Greg Johnson to White Supremacist politics. He also started Ultra!, a press and record label. It was the publisher of *TYR*, which he co-edited with Moynihan, but the project also released music by Markus Wolff's Waldteufel and published de Benoist's *On Being a Pagan* in 2004. That year, Dickson also introduced Buckley to John Tyndall, the former chairman of both the National Front and British National Party. Soon after, Buckley and Dickson went into business together.[130]

Despite some of his fringe ideas, Moynihan had a penchant for legitimate academic work and would go back to grad school. In 2017, he completed his doctorate at the Germanic Languages and Literature department at the University of Massachusetts Amherst.[131]

Evasive Measures

Especially after the success of *Lords of Chaos*, Moynihan's politics came under scrutiny. The book itself raised red flags, and even a brief look into Moynihan's background was sure to reveal even more extreme politics. When challenged about this, Moynihan would obfuscate, omit, accuse, lie, and generally create confusion. And in this he was aided by a number of journalists and academics.

Moynihan's politics—or at least his representation of them—went in phases. In the first, roughly from 1989 to 1993, he was explicit about his interest in and desire to promote Masonite National Socialism while embracing Social Darwinism. By 1994, in the second stage, his self-identification moved closer to "fascist." In the third, after *Lords of Chaos* came out in 1998, he became quite cagey and represented his views as being neither Left nor Right but also specified that they were neither National Socialist nor Social Darwinist. This was quickly followed by a fourth stage. Although still promoting Nazis and collaborators like Wiligut and Evola, Moynihan began expressing his allegiance to what could be called an ethno-separatism (although he did not use the term) based on sub-racial identities, à la de Benoist, and started using the description "radical traditionalist."

Moynihan's evasive strategies were visible, for example, in his choice to use the Kruchkenkreuz as the symbol for Blood Axis. It looked like a cross with equal length arms; at the end of each arm was a bar running across it. It was used historically in different permutations (just as many NSDAP symbols were). Moynihan mentioned this included a symbol used during the Crusades and by the Order of the New Templars,[132] a group led by German proto-fascist mystic Jörg Lanz von Liebenfels.

However, the Kruchkenkreuz is best known in Far Right circles as the symbol of the Vaterländische Front (Fatherland Front) of the 1930s, which scholar Peter Staudenmaier has described as "the Austrian variant of fascism."[133] (Moynihan was well aware of this use, as he had reproduced a Vaterländische Front poster in a publication.[134]) Moynihan also said, in two separate interviews, that the symbol could be viewed as two overlapping swastikas.[135] This approach was a common tactic of the Abraxas Circle: presenting something explicit and obvious, while also simultaneously denying it. The Kruchkenkreuz was a pair of swastikas if you wanted but a mere Christian symbol if you didn't—and, of course, Moynihan did not have a high opinion of Christianity.

According to a 1991 article covering Moynihan's Secret Service visit, agents quizzed him about why he sent letters to Manson signed with a swastika and asked him about the T-shirts he made with the Universal Order logo.[136] "Moynihan tried to argue that he used a backwards swastika, that it was a 'religious symbol' in use centuries before the Third Reich adopted it, found in Hinduism, Buddhism and other religions." He was quoted as saying "I don't belong to any neo-Nazi groups, I haven't had any contact with the skinheads."[137] (He omitted his relationship with Nazi skinhead leader Bob Heick despite having been arrested with him the year before. Moynihan also failed to mention his comment to Mason less than two months prior that a Denver Nazi skinhead rally was "Fun fun fun!") He also told the journalist that "I have no interest in politics whatsoever" and the idea that he might be a National Socialist "is just nuts"—even while at that the exact same time he was working on *Siege*.[138]

Just prior to the article, he appeared on Larson's radio show and was introduced as a Universal Order representative. When Larson asked if he was an "out and out Nazi," he replied, "Not necessarily." When Larson followed up by inquiring if it was "fair to say" Universal Order "is a Nazi organization," Moynihan's reply was "It's beyond Nazism. Nazism existed in a certain time and a certain place, in certain political conditions, and this is not referring to that."[139]

While he had stuck close to National Socialism, albeit with a strong Social Darwinist flavor, in 1994 he started moving towards accepting the "fascist" label, again just as Rice did. He elucidated this position in three interviews. In January, Moynihan said he didn't identify with being a "Nazi"—but as for being a fascist, "I wouldn't deny it."[140]

In the second interview, regarding the thought of Mason and Manson, Moynihan affirmed that "I'm committed to some of their ideas and others I can take or leave. I think the gist of their beliefs are valid and important." As opposed to National Socialism, which he now said was too fixated on the "Hitler cult," Moynihan said he preferred the term "fascism" because it was "more open-ended. I wouldn't say it encompasses my worldview, but it's a step in the right direction." He also affirmed a racial approach, saying "Any honest, thinking person will admit that race affects reality. I am certainly racially aware." And, of course, he denounced "equalitarianism and humanitarianism."[141]

In the NO LONGER A FANzine interview, he was asked if he was a fascist, White Supremacist, or neo-Nazi. Moynihan responded in the negative because he viewed those terms as outdated but specified that "of course I'm interested in a lot of these ideas." According to him, the United States was breaking apart and he wanted to "live in a place that reflects my heritage as opposed to some dysfunctional multi-cultural pressure cooker."[142]

In 1997, just before the release of *Lords of Chaos*, Moynihan's publicly stated political views were still in the same ballpark. "I have no problem," he said, "being called a fascist, and I obviously won't deny doing much to encourage such accusations" and repeated previous statements that "if fascism will restore some sense of order, then I am all for it." But he was now backing further away from *Siege*, saying "I don't agree with all of Mason's ideas by a long shot"[143]—whereas three years before, he held that the "gist" of Mason's beliefs were still "valid and important."

In *Gods of the Blood: The Pagan Revival and White Separatism*, scholar Mattias Gardell quoted Moynihan as saying he did not want fascism if it was a "totalitarianism, all-encompassing government," but he approved of the idea if it meant establishing a hierarchy where everyone has their place. (Assumedly, he would be part of this elite.) "I think that fascism has to function in a much smaller way, on a much more decentralized level" than a central government, ideally a "tribal society functioning in a fascist manner."[144]

Backing Away

With the release of *Lords of Chaos*, Moynihan's political reputation started to precede him, and Blood Axis shows drew protests and cancellations.[145] Although he had already been backing away from identifying with National Socialism, now he did a U-turn. By the end of 1998, he made a curious statement, which seemed to be aimed at Rice but which also obviously separating him from the "fascist" label.

> I'm sick of people saying they're 'not political,' as I think this is a cop-out...If you're going to espouse 'fascist' ideas, then I believe you have to accept some of the responsibility for their application in the real world... Terms which are bandied about like 'occult fascism' don't have any tangible meaning as far as I can tell, though they sound impressive.[146]

In 1998, American Front member Gene Sotelo wrote to Mason that Moynihan "stated he <u>was not</u> racial and only put out your book, cause 'you were out there.'" Mason replied, "I know Moynihan pretty well. He's playing it somewhat cagey now that he's getting mainstream media exposure. Not to worry. He's headed for big things."[147]

And Moynihan remained cagey even as he expressed some of the same ideas in a new, toned-down way. That same year, he told the politically aligned *Occidental Congress* that "most Europeans have lost any sense of themselves" and that "when one surrenders their identity and traditions, they enter the void…and most never return." Still, he expressed hope this identity would be reborn after a "winter of decay."[148]

Hitting the Bull's-eye

In February 1999, soon after the release of *Lords of Chaos*, Kevin Coogan's exposé of Moynihan and others around him, "How 'Black' is Black Metal?: Michael Moynihan, *Lords of Chaos* and the 'Countercultural Fascist' Underground," appeared in *Hit List*, a new music magazine run by Jeff Bale. (Bale had previously co-founded *Maximum Rocknroll*, which became the most popular punk fanzine of the 1980s and '90s.) Coogan's piece was the first, and most comprehensive, analysis of not just Moynihan's political involvements but the Abraxas Clique itself.[149]

Bale provided a long introduction to both the material and fascism in general. Coogan, despite having access only to public materials, probed into various aspects of the Abraxas Circle's views.[150] Tying the industrial music, and larger extreme culture scene, to the views of Evola, the French New Right, and the proto-Nazi Conservative Revolutionaries, Coogan profiled a number of figures. These included not just Moynihan but also Parfrey, Rice, Vikernes, Mason, Taylor, and the Church of Satan. The exposé hit its target and produced howls of pain and attempts to discredit it.

The issue included an interview with Moynihan himself. He said, "I don't consider myself a 'fascist' in any typical sense." Affirming that he was an elitist, he nonetheless now said, "I would like to stress that I am not a misanthrope" and that none of his beliefs is "an outgrowth of 'Social Darwinist' views, because I don't consider myself a Social Darwinist." He once again separated himself from both the Left and Right—in regard to both, "my opinion…is exceedingly low." He also said that he did not "characterize" himself with labels like "anarchist" or "Nazi."[151]

Moynihan had made similar claims in the past, and he would continue to do so in future. In 1994, he said both the Left and Right were failed approaches. In 1999, he said his views "do not fit into any strict political definition" and that Left and Right were "obsolete catchphrases."[152]

In 2006, he said his views were "a grey area of Nietzschean amorality and paradox; the inability of people to handle it, or even grasp it on these terms, only proves how successfully it embodies this." By that time, he made clear his separation from identifying with the concept of race, which he had earlier held onto. He said, "I don't share an affinity for Nordicist racialism" while affirming what he called "an abiding admiration for European culture."[153]

Moynihan also flung gratuitous insults and made unprovable claims against his critics. For example, his response to leftists having his concerts cancelled was that they believed in "retarded Marxist gibberish" and were "totalitarian thought police" that made him "nauseous." He claimed he didn't even know what terms like "fascist" meant when they were used as accusations. A year later, he would say that "to call me a 'Nazi' is to deliberately misrepresent my views" and that leftists use the term fascist for "ANYONE they disagree with."[154]

In one of the few interviews where the specifics of *Siege* were brought up, he was asked in *Hit List* about its veneration of murderers who sought to "disrupt" the current order. Moynihan's reply was that they didn't matter because "I don't think they've managed to disrupt anything in the slightest, so there's not much to have an opinion on."[155]

Fall 1999

Later that year, groups that monitored the Far Right also turned their attention to Moynihan. This was especially true after the Columbine massacre in Colorado, the first major modern school shooting in the United States and considered the inaugural event of a trend that would continue for decades. The perpetrators were counterculturalists who were accused of neo-Nazi ties, especially as the massacre occurred on Hitler's birthday.

After Coogan, the first follow-up was a 1999 Center for New Community report on White Supremacist music, which included several pages on Moynihan, Rice, and Thorn.[156] But the reach of these smaller profiles was dwarfed by the SPLC, which pointed their finger at Moynihan. Whereas Coogan's investigation was carefully documented and tightly argued, the SPLC pieces were not. Moynihan was labeled "a major purveyor of neo-Nazism, occult fascism and international industrial black metal music" and was included in a list of six up-and-coming leaders of the White Supremacist movement. The short piece was riddled with errors. (Ironically, Moynihan had previously said, "I would have no interest in being a political leader as the position seems inherently tainted with compromise."[157]) A second article in the same issue was better, but it still described Blood Axis, NON, and Electric Hellfire Club as "black metal."[158] (They were not.) Last, Blood Axis was also talked about on a National Public Radio (NPR) segment, which included a critical interview with Moynihan.

These mistakes gave Moynihan a wide opening to impeach criticisms of him as completely uninformed—and to draw attention away from his verbatim quotes about his relationship to fascism and thoughts on the leniency of the Holocaust. And he launched a campaign to counter these claims.

Eye *Denies*

The first major piece to do this was a sympathetic interview in *Eye* magazine, which denounced Coogan's article. Given a series of soft pitches, it gave Moynihan an open platform to spin out his various denials.[159] In *Eye*,

Moynihan did his best to impeach Coogan's article, saying "there are literally dozens of serious errors" and that Coogan made "sweeping but ill-informed judgments based on a smattering of erratic sources." One of these complaints was about Coogan writing that Moynihan drank blood; Moynihan tried to debunk this by saying the claim was based on two questionable sources. In fact, Coogan showed that the claim came from Moynihan himself in an interview in a different source.[160]

Moynihan also addressed his Holocaust statement in the 1994 *NO LONGER A FANzine* interview. In the course of the interview, Moynihan praised Gervasi for reading *Siege*, adding that "I would only hope more people follow your example."[161] Now, in *Eye*, Moynihan said it was an "incredibly silly" question that was "ludicrous" because he was not in any political organization. "My answer to this clearly inflammatory hypothetical question was simply another hypothetical statement."[162] In 2000, Moynihan claimed that the question was "in response to a question from a snotty 15-year-old punk rocker, and that's the spirit in which it was answered." In fact, Gervasi was 23 at the time; he called Moynihan's swipe "utterly disingenuous."[163] (In 2006, Moynihan would use a similar manipulation of dates to try to make quotes from him appear as if they were much further in the past than they were.[164])

But Moynihan's call for "more lenient entrance requirements" was no off-the-cuff remark. First, the interview was done by mail, and Moynihan had all the time he wanted to ponder his answer. Second, and more importantly, Moynihan repeated this same thing—practically word for word—in not just one but *two* pieces published the same year. In *Welcomat*, he said "The Holocaust should've been just the beginning. It should've continued, but with far less stringent requirements." In the introduction to the *Black Flame* publication of Moynihan's "The Faustian Spirit of Fascism," he said, "The same can be said for many of the tenets of National Socialism, including the dreaded 'Holocaust' (which in the future will have far less stringent entrance requirements)."[165] Moynihan did not mention any of these things in the latter interview.

In the same *Eye* interview, he also significantly backed away from the actual answer he gave about historical revisionism, now saying it "isn't of any particular interest to me (but for some unknown reason the interviewer cared about it), and in fact I clearly state I'm NOT a historical revisionist." (His actual response in the interview was that the "Six Million number is just arbitrary and inaccurate, and probably a gross exaggeration" and that the IHR was more trustworthy that mainstream media sources.[166])

He also put distance from the term "fascist" because of its "incessant misuse" and said that "most people...don't know what they mean." But he did not abandon Far Right views. Asked "In today's era of multi-culturalism, do you feel Blood Axis is a celebration of pan-European culture?," he answered, "I certainly hope it serves that purpose, and I make no apologies for it."[167]

Interference on the Flipside

In the fall of 1999, another major interview appeared in *Flipside*, one of the largest fanzines covering punk and related underground genres. Involving not just Moynihan but other Blood Axis members, it too was conducted by an openly sympathetic interviewer.[168]

Moynihan now said he published *Siege* only to help people smash "bourgeois" thought and explore "problematic" ideas. When asked about his political opinions "at this point in your life," his reply was that "I don't think National Socialism is a realistic answer to most people's problems." Moynihan again said "I've never classified myself as 'fascist'," but that he would not try to stop people from doing it either.[169]

The band members were asked if they were "racists" or "involved in a religion which is exclusively white, non-Jewish, and heterosexual. Are you Racial Odinists?" Moynihan did not answer directly but replied that "The worst form of racism in the world is that which is practiced by capitalist big business" which seeks to "wipe out" different cultures, whereas he "would like to see the unique multiplicity of cultures on the planet retain their traditions."[170] He later on again denounced any fidelity to the category of "white." Condemning mindless consumption, Moynihan said,

> I can't imagine why anyone in their right mind would be a "white supremacist." White people in general have devolved into such a sorry bunch at this point in history, I'm not sure how much lower they can sink. The so-called "white race" hardly seems like any kind of concept worth rallying around.[171]

White Lies

Moynihan would continue to separate himself from seeing his separatist views as based on either race or nation, as he continued his trajectory toward decentralization. While on this path, he was introduced to Bill White by Cletus Nelson of *Eye*. White was on his own trajectory, but headed in the opposite direction. He first received attention for his Utopian Anarchist Party, but by 1999 was involved in paleoconservative politics, and in 2005 joined Jeff Schoep's National Socialist Movement. But it was his penchant for wanton online threats that would land him in prison for several years.[172]

In the 2000 interview with White, Moynihan refused, as he did in *Flipside*, to embrace the "white" racial category. He said, "I certainly don't identify with any vague racial category like being 'white', and have never attempted to project such a notion"—a far cry from his statement only a few years before that he was "racially aware." But he went further, saying that "ethnic nationalism... holds little or no interest to me. I am certainly not a nationalist." Afterward, White credited Moynihan for introducing him to Evola, leading him into National Socialism.[173]

Dundas Diversion

Zach Dundas's 2000 article in Portland's alternative weekly *Willamette Week* also allowed Moynihan space to weave his tale. He denounced nation-states and endorsed what Dundas described as "a tight tribal mosaic of small, tightly bonded groups would better suit a human nature he views as largely unchanged from ancient times." Again channeling de Benoist, Moynihan said that the real threat is a "global corporate monoculture" which wanted to destroy different cultures, whereas he advocated for "a diversity of human groups surviving on earth."[174]

Now Moynihan tried to pivot away from fascists and instead toward anarchists. "The far right is a bunch of isolated losers, I probably have more in common with anarchists than I would with any right-wing person, and they would probably agree." Like Rice, Moynihan mocked people who were "worried about some skinhead takeover… It's not like the average black person in America…is really threatened by skinheads." Again, he did not mention his own history with skinheads.[175]

By 2002, Gene Sotelo's worries about Moynihan's racial politics had percolated to other National Socialists. As Ryan Schuster was preparing the second edition of *Siege*, he wrote Mason with his concerns. Although they had been in touch for a couple years, Moynihan had not replied to Schuster's inquiry about updating the first edition's introduction. Schuster said, "it does seem his gained reputation as a 'responsible' editor and publisher now precludes any overt association with National Socialism." Indeed, Moynihan asked that not just his introduction be removed, but any other mention of him as well. But that did not mean Moynihan was unwilling to help with the new edition, and he supplied the original plates for the reprint.[176] Taking the place of the original introduction was Schuster's much more extensive biography of Mason.

Enabling Writers

Moynihan could never have continued to function in the public sphere without numerous people praising him, obscuring his background, and providing him with public platforms which he used to spin disingenuous stories about himself. Four writers of note for facilitating this were Alan Prendergast in *Westword*, Cletus Nelson in *Eye*, Zach Dundas in *Willamette Week*, and Mattias Gardell in *Gods of the Blood*. Whether they were fully cognizant of what they were doing, hoodwinked by his smooth talk, lacking in critical judgment—or just too lazy to fact-check—they would repeat the stories Moynihan spun.

Prendergast

Moynihan described Alan Prendergast as a friend of a friend. The journalist wrote an extremely sympathetic *Westword* feature about the 1991 Secret Service raid, later writing about Mason, too. Prendergast portrayed Rice and Moynihan as artists with eccentric tastes who were unfairly targeted. Although both were closely connected to the neo-Nazi milieu at the time, Prendergast dismissed the swastikas and Nazi books, portraits, and memorabilia in their place as kitsch. He gave Moynihan airtime to offer different kinds of denials, and he even wrote that "Mason claims to have eschewed National Socialism for Mansonism."[177] (It is most likely that this claim wasn't fact-checked with the source.)

Mason was thrilled at the article, calling it "Just incredible…great press." He encouraged Moynihan to "exploit this…in anyway you can. If I can do anything to help out, let me know." And during Mason's time in and out of prison in the late 1990s, he said that Prendergast went to so far as to recommend a lawyer to him.[178]

Nelson

In addition to allowing him abundant space in the 1999 *Eye* interview, Cletus Nelson made sure to add his own spin on Moynihan. He wrote, "His independent thinking comes with a heavy price, though: Moynihan is now branded as a right-wing extremist," while what the musician and writer was actually doing was exploring "the heretical, the sublime, and the forbidden." Coogan's piece in particular was "incongruously written in the paranoid prose style common to conspiracy publications." The real problem with the controversy was the "oppressive streak within the radical Left," and Moynihan was portrayed as a martyr whose "ordeal" might be the beginning of a new "totalitarian state."[179]

Dundas

Zach Dundas's 2000 cover story in the Portland alternative paper *Willamette Week* was the strongest of the whitewash articles which came out soon after *Lords of Chaos*. He openly claimed Moynihan had been slandered, calling the largely accurate claims against Moynihan a "jihad." Dundas dismissed even verbatim quotes from Moynihan on the basis that they were "in old fanzines and outfield websites, and is thus built on quicksand." (He did not question their accuracy or explain how the popularity of a website changed the density of sand.) Regarding the Holocaust statements, Dundas attributed them to Moynihan's position in the extreme-culture scene. The article talked about Asatrú and specified that there were both racist and anti-racist forms, but omitted that Moynihan belonged to one of the *racist* factions! Dundas even stated that Moynihan's Storm distribution carried *Siege*—without mentioning that Moynihan was either its editor or publisher. And, again, Mason was said to be "an ex-Nazi." (Moynihan's own introduction to *Siege* said Mason was "a National Socialist, and will be one for life.") The article's sidebar helpfully included information about where to buy the latest Blood Axis album.[180]

Gardell

Gardell's 2003 *Gods of the Blood* was one of the most important scholarly books on its subject matter. However, he repeated a number of Moynihan's claims in it. Regarding the Holocaust entrance requirements, Gardell, in an echo of Moynihan's *Eye* interview, described Gervasi's questions as "silly and irrelevant" which was why "Moynihan took the ride." (Elsewhere, the book cited the same *Black Flame* piece where Moynihan repeated his Holocaust comment, although Gardell did not note the repetition.[181])

Even while quoting part of Moynihan's 1994 statement where he said the six million number was "probably a gross exaggeration," Gardell was content to not label this as revisionism, chalking it up to a "craving" for publicity, and printed Moynihan's denial that he was a "Holocaust Revisionist"—a statement he made several years later.[182] Moynihan's other public statements about similar matters were not cited.

The main section where Moynihan's politics were grappled with does not include his numerous earlier answers about whether he was a fascist (although in another part of the book, a pro-fascist statement by Moynihan was quoted). Instead, Gardell chose to cite the Dundas article where Moynihan dismissed fascism as not having anything to do with today's world.[183]

Gardell included one line about Moynihan's relationship to *Siege*, which said only that he *published* the book—not that he edited it. Answering criticisms, Gardell said Moynihan "has never styled Manson an avatar of Hitler, and there is nothing to substantiate the charge that he fancies lone-wolf assassinations," despite the fact that he personally created a section in *Siege* just to highlight the latter.[184] And nowhere in Gardell's book does he explain that these were the positions Mason espoused in *Siege*. Considering not just Moynihan's role as editor and publisher but also his introduction, critics certainly had plenty of grounds to assume that he, too, might hold these ideas.

By this time, Moynihan's political journey seemed to have reached its end. On one hand, many political people experience an arc in their politics over time; it is certainly understandable (perhaps even necessary) that one's teenage politics would not match theirs as an adult. On the other, this particular evolution from National Socialism to a decentralized ethno-separatism was of significant importance. While it mirrored the more sophisticated European fascist intellectuals, Moynihan was one of the first in the United States to adopt these positions and did so—to a greater or lesser extent—from a different set of influences. But regardless of the influence his later views around the *TYR* period have had, and his music writing aside, Moynihan's lasting contribution to politics will almost undoubtedly be the creation and dissemination of *Siege*. Whatever he thinks of this today, modern neo-Nazi terrorism owes him a huge debt of gratitude. It would not exist in the form it does without him.

Notes

1 Coogan, "How Black," p.37; Moynihan interview in *Fifth Path*, p.26.
2 The publications included annual reports, which started in 1984; "Coup De Grace Booklets & Writings," *Blood Axis Archives*, https://bloodaxisarchives.wordpress. com/coup-de-grace/coup-de-grace-booklets-writings. Two cassettes were released in 1985, under the label Coup De Grace Productions: Coup De Grace, *Commencement/ Corpse Education* and *Anthems For Doomed Youth*, www.discogs.com/ release/364839-Coup-De-Grace-Anthems-For-Doomed-Youth, www.discogs.com/ release/696597-Coup-De-Grace-Commencement-Corpse-Education. In 1986 a live recording was released in Belgium; Coup De Grace, *Over Europe* (Club Moral, 1986), www.discogs.com/release/83109-Coup-De-Grace-Over-Europe
3 Sleep Chamber was a trancey, atmospheric band focused on BDSM themes. Zewizz was also interested in Nazi aesthetics, albeit of the sexual fetish type. For example, one of his side projects was Women of the SS. Mason interview in *EsoTerra*; "The Gospel According to Blood Axis: An Interview with Michael Moynihan," *Compulsion* #3, 1998, p.43.
4 Moynihan was credited under the name Coup De Grace. Sleep Chamber, *Submit to Desire* (Inner-X-Musick, 1985), www.discogs.com/release/293184-Sleep-Chamber-Submit-To-Desire; Moynihan interview in *EsoTerra*; Moynihan to Mason, June 4, 1989 [Box 5, Folder 9].
5 Moynihan interview in *Hit List*, p.51.
6 See Appendix 8, "Robert N. Taylor and Thomas Thorn".
7 Moynihan interview in *Compulsion*, p.43; Moynihan interview in *EsoTerra*; Coup de Grace, *1988–1989 Report/Update*, March 1989, p.5.
8 Friedrich Nietzsche, *The Antichrist* (Antwerp: C.D.G. Publications, 1988); Moynihan interview in *EsoTerra*. According to the title page, it was a public domain translation by Thomas Common, but in fact Moynihan admitted it was Walter Kauffman's copywrited translation; Moynihan to Mason, January 29, 1989 [Box 5, Folder 9].
9 "Hear No... See No... Speak No... Evil! An Interview with Tokyo's Trevor Brown," *Ohm Clock* #4, Spring 1996, p.13.
10 Moynihan interview in *Fifth Path*, p.27; Moynihan interview in *Hit List*, p.52; "Michael Jenkins" (Moynihan interview with Gervasi), *NO LONGER A FANzine* #5, Summer 1994, p.17.
11 Parfrey to Mason, April 15, 1987 [Box 17, Folder 4]; Carl Abrahamsson, *Anton LaVey and the Church of Satan: Infernal Wisdom from the Devil's Den* (Rochester, Vermont: Inner Traditions, 2022), ebook, chapter 17.
12 Moynihan interview in *NO LONGER A FANzine*, p.7. Moynihan repeated his interest in Hitler and Manson in Lamar B. Graham, "Interview with a vampire...sort of," *Boston Phoenix*, October 20–26, 1989, Section 2, p.7. Elsewhere, Moynihan said he was partly inspired by *Helter Skelter*, "with all the Manson /

Hitler comparisons." Indeed, Bugliosi frequently mentioned Hitler in *Helter Skelter*. In one long passage, Bugliosi wrote about "parallels between Hitler and Mason." These included that were both: vegetarians, failed artists, racists who may have had a background in the same group they hated, influenced by Nietzsche, harbored a hatred of society, and had such tremendous personal charisma that their followers would kill on their orders. Knipfel, "The Other Nazis," p.24 (*Articles*, p.73); Bugliosi, *Helter Skelter*, "Epilogue: A Shared Madness".

13 Mason to Moynihan, June 6, 1988 [Box 25, Folder 8]; Rice to Mason, [late December] 1988 [Box 9, Folder 20]; Moynihan to Mason January 4, 1989; Mason to Moynihan, January 6, 1989 [both Box 5, Folder 9].

14 Moynihan to Mason, [January?] 1989 [Box 5, Folder 9]. The quote is, "We shall reach our goal, when we have the courage to laugh as we destroy, as we smash, whatever was sacred to us as tradition, as education, as friendship and as human affection." It also appeared in *Siege*, p.131, and Adolf Hitler, *Mein Kampf* (New York: Reynal and Hitchcock, 1940), p.233, https://archive.org/details/meinkampfcomplet00hitl. On the June 1991 "Manson Maniacs" show, Larson read a shorter version of this quote, which Moynihan had supplied him with; Moynihan, Rice, and Mason interview with Larson/*Talk Back* (video).

15 Moynihan to Mason, January 29, 1989; Moynihan to Mason, March 22, 1989 [both Box 5, Folder 9].

16 Moynihan to Mason, October 14, 1989; Moynihan to Mason, June 1, 1990 [both Box 5, Folder 9].

17 Moynihan to Mason, February 28, 1989; Moynihan to Mason, March 22, 1989; Moynihan to Mason, June 9, 1990 [all three Box 5, Folder 9].

18 Moynihan interview in *Heretic*.

19 Graham, "Interview with a vampire," section 2, p.7; Moynihan interview in *Heretic*.

20 *C.D.G. 1988-1989 Report/Update* [Box 5, Folder 9].

21 Moynihan to Mason, January 29, 1989; Mason to Moynihan, February 1, 1989 [both Box 5, Folder 9].

22 Moynihan to Mason, February 28, 1989 [Box 5, Folder 9].

23 Mason to Moynihan, March 2, 1989 [Box 5, Folder 9].

24 Moynihan to Mason, February 28, 1989; Moynihan to Mason, June 4, 1989; Moynihan to Mason, August 18, 1989 [all three Box 5, Folder 9].

25 Moynihan to Mason, August 29, 1989; Moynihan to Mason, July 19, 1990 [both Box 5, Folder 9]; Prendergast, "Family Ties," p.26.

26 Moynihan to Mason, March 22, 1989. Mason did say he received a card from "Brannau"—although did not specify if it was dated April 20; Mason to Moynihan, May 25, 1989 [both Box 5, Folder 9].
    Wewelsburg castle, controlled by Himmler, was the site of SS ceremonies. Today it is known in particular for the large black sun (sonnenrad) image inlaid in a floor, which has become a popular symbol among neo-Nazis. The Externsteine is an unusual sandstone rock formation that was supposedly the site of ancient pagan worship. Among others, Savitri Devi wrote about its importance to National Socialism; Goodrick-Clarke, *Hitler's Priestess*, pp.166–68.

27 "Seasons Greetings" card (from Moynihan), 1996 [Box 11, Folder 2].

28 Moynihan to Mason, May 23, 1989; Moynihan to Mason, June 16, 1989; Moynihan to Mason, June 4, 1989 [all three Box 5, Folder 9].

29 Interview with Moynihan in Abrahamsson, *Anton LaVey and the Church of Satan*, chapter 15.

30 Moynihan to Mason, August 18, 1989 [Box 5, Folder 9].

31 Joseph Bernstein, "The Surprisingly Mainstream History Of The Internet's Favorite Anti-Semitic Image," *Buzzfeed*, February 5, 2015, www.buzzfeednews.

com/article/josephbernstein/the-surprisingly-mainstream-history-of-the-internets-favorit; Mason, *When We Were All Jews*, April 2000, 1st ed., inside cover, https://archive.org/details/when-we-were-all-jews

32 Moynihan to Mason, October 14, 1989; Moynihan to Mason, March 7, 1990 [both Box 5, Folder 9].

33 Moynihan to Mason, May 16, 1992 [Box 11, Folder 2]; Kathy Dobie, "Long Day's Journey into White," *Village Voice*, April 28, 1992, p.25.

34 Moynihan to Mason, June 4, 1989; Mason to Moynihan, June 8, 1989. Within a month he had marked up half the newsletters received from Mason; Moynihan to Mason, August 11, 1989 [all three Box 5, Folder 9].

35 Moynihan to Mason, August 18, 1989 [Box 5, Folder 9].

36 Moynihan to Mason, October 14, 1989 [Box 5, Folder 9]; Knipfel, "The Other Nazis," p.24 (*Articles*, p.73).

37 Moynihan to Mason, October 14, 1989 [Box 5, Folder 9].

38 Moynihan to Mason, March 7, 1990 [Box 5, Folder 9].

39 Moynihan interview in *Compulsion*, p.44; Moynihan to Mason, November 5, 1989 [Box 5, Folder 9].

40 Mason had prompted her to do so. Mason to Moynihan, March 29, 1990; Mason to Moynihan, June 12, 1990; Mason to Moynihan, July 13, 1990 [all three Box 5, Folder 9].

41 Moynihan to Mason, March 7, 1990 [Box 5, Folder 9].

42 Moynihan to Mason, [between February and April], 1992 [Box 11, Folder 2].

43 Mason to Moynihan, March 10, 1990 [Box 5, Folder 9].

44 Moynihan to Mason, August 24, 1990; Moynihan to Mason, December 5, 1990 [both Box 5, Folder 9].

45 They would include Kelly Cowan, Robert Ferbrache, Markus Wolff (of Crash Worship), Aaron Garland (*Ohm Clock* editor) Thomas Thorn (under the pseudonym Alfred Thomas), and Annabel Lee (who Moynihan would marry). Blood Axis/In Gowan Ring/Witch-Hunt, *The Rites Of Samhain* CDr, (no label, 2001), www.discogs.com/master/67977-Blood-Axis-In-Gowan-Ring-Witch-Hunt-The-Rites-Of-Samhain; Moynihan interview in *Fifth Path*, p.26; *Art That Kills*, p.217.

46 Despite the obvious implications of using this slogan at the same time he was editing a neo-Nazi terrorist tome, Moynihan said that "The victory referred to is that of the spirit over materialistic/commercialistic tendencies. Such a victory would be worth hailing, in my opinion." "Bill White and Mike Moynihan: A Dialogue on Race and Hate in Music," *Overthrow.com*, https://web.archive.org/web/20000424101033, http://overthrow.com/moynihan.html; Moynihan to Mason, December 16, 1990 [Box 5, Folder 9]. The songs appeared on a 1991 compilation album; Blood Axis, "Lord of Ages" and "Electricity," various artists compilation, *The Lamp Of The Invisible Light* (Cthulhu Records, 1991), www.discogs.com/release/185734-Various-The-Lamp-Of-The-Invisible-Lightw

47 Moynihan to Mason, February 5, 1991 [Box 5, Folder 9].

48 Moynihan to Mason, March 8, 1991; Moynihan to Mason, May 1, 1991 [both Box 11, Folders 1–4].

49 Moynihan to Mason, July 11, 1990 [Box 11, Folder 2]; Prendergast, "Family Ties," p.26.

50 Moynihan to Mason, April 25, 1991 [Box 11, Folder 2–3]; Moynihan to Mason, May 1, 1991 [Box 11, Folders 1–4].

51 Mason to Moynihan, May 6, 1991 [Box 11, Folders 2–3]; Mason interview in *Ohm Clock*, p.8 (*Articles*, p.96).

52 Moynihan to Mason, August 25, 1992 [Box 11, Folder 2]; Moynihan to Mason, September 16, 1992 [Box 11, Folders 1–4]. While usually ATWA is given as an

acronym for "Air, Trees, Water, Animals," at others it is supposed to be "All the Way Alive." According to Moynihan, Manson started to use it in the early 1980s to represent his "ecological-spiritual worldview.... ATWA is a state of radical consciousness, a way of thought and action that seeks to completely redress not just worldwide industrial pollution and ecological imbalance, but also the perceived unnatural evils of media control, consumerism, feminism and matriarchy, overpopulation, and racial intermixing"; Moynihan, "ATWA," in Bron Taylor, ed., *Encyclopedia of Religion and Nature* (London: Continuum, 2005), p.128.

53 *Iconoclast* (video).

54 Prendergast, "Family Ties," pp.22, 24.

55 Jenkins/Moynihan, "Introduction," *Siege*, 1st. ed., pp.xii, xxvii.

56 Ibid, p.xxvi–xxvii.

57 Moynihan, Rice, and Mason interview with Larson/*Talk Back* (video); Mason interview in *Ohm Clock*, p.6 (*Articles*, p.94).

58 Moynihan, Rice, and Mason interview with Larson/*Talk Back* (video).

59 Moynihan to Mason, June 1, 1991; Moynihan to Mason, July 22, 1991; Moynihan to Mason, October 17, 1991 [all three Box 11, Folders 1–3].

60 Moynihan to Mason, January 21, 1992; Brent McPhie/Publishers Press [SLC] to Moynihan, February 24, 1992 [both Box 11, Folder 2]; Moynihan to Mason, September 16, 1992 [Box 11, Folders 1–4].

61 Mason to Moynihan, January 28, 1993 [Box 11, Folder 2].

62 By 1991 he was writing for local music publications; for example, Lance Barton and Moynihan, "The Manson Family Sings the Songs of Charles Manson," *Colorado Music Magazine* 2(13) August 1991, p.17; Moynihan to Mason, June 6, 1991 [Box 11, Folders 1–4].

63 Moynihan to Mason, [May] 1993 [Box 11, Folders 1–4], handwritten note on clipping of magazine cover containing "Morbid Curiosity" (interview with David Vincent), *Kerrang!* #440, April 24, 1993, pp.48–49. Among other things, Vincent said in the interview that, "I just believe in mingling with my own type...I wouldn't think of wanting to be a part of any other culture, so I think you should have the right of association. That's the whole point: any time you have people of different cultures forced to come together, there's conflict." Regarding famine in Africa, he said, "Mother Nature is doing her best to destroy that area—it's slop!" The interviewer said, "He appears to be wearing a British Movement badge on his lapel" and dryly noted that Vincent sounded "disturbingly like a Neo-Nazi spokesperson."

64 Michael Moynihan and Didrik Søderlind, *Lords of Chaos: The Bloody Rise of the Satanic Metal Underground* (Venice, California: Feral House, 1998), pp.28, 66, 69; "Morbid Angel" (interview with Moynihan), *Seconds* #26, 1994, pp.64–67, https://secondsmagazine.com/pages/mags.php; Mason to Hawthorne, March 25, 1995 [Box 9, Folder 41].

65 *Art That Kills*, p.257; Moynihan to Mason, [November 1992] [Box 11, Folder 2]; *Ohm Clock* #4, Spring 1996, pp.1, 2, 4–8, 29–31; "Drawing Lines: Waldteufel and Markus Wolff's Involvement in the New-Right Cultural Movement," *Rose City Antifa*, January 3, 2016, https://rosecityantifa.org/articles/waldteufel-and-markus-wolffs-involvement-in-the-new-right

66 Moynihan and Rice were interviewed in *Fifth Path* #3. *Fifth Path* #4, Winter 1992/93, included two Moynihan interviews, "The Electric Hellfire Club: Burn, Baby, Burn" and "Odinism in Heavy Metal—Part One: An Interview with Johnny Hedlund of Unleashed" plus reviews of *WAKE* and *Siege*, pp.32–37, 42–47, 72–73. *Fifth Path* #5 included "Odinism in Heavy Metal Pt. 2—Bathory, an exclusive interview by Michael Moynihan," pp.36–41.

67 Moynihan to Mason, June 1, 1990 [Box 5, Folder 9]; Goodrick-Clarke, *Black Sun*, pp.135–36, 208. Moynihan worked with Kadmon and Markus Wolff on the translation. For more on Wolff, see "Drawing Lines," *Rose City Antifa*; for more on Wiligut, see Goodrick-Clarke, *The Occult Roots of Nazism*, chapter 14.

68 Kadmon often recorded under the name Allerseelen. The lyrics on their side of the first Storm record were taken from a Wiligut poem, and their 1995 album was the entire poem set to music. Kadmon's essay "Oskorei" appeared in the appendix of *Lords of Chaos*. Blood Axis/Allerseelen, "Walked In Line"/"Ernting" 7" (Storm, 1994), www.discogs.com/master/362173-Blood-Axis-Allerseelen-Walked-In-Line-Ernting; Allerseelen, *Gotos=Kalanda* (Aorta/Storm, 1995), www.discogs.com/Allerseelen-GotosKalanda/release/182384. See also, "Allerseelen on Tour - Austrian Far-Right Musical Project on West Coast Tour, Playing Support to Northwest Heavy Metal Act," *Rose City Antifa*, December 13, 2010, https://rosecityantifa.org/articles/allerseelen-on-tour; Moynihan and Søderlind, *Lords of Chaos*, pp.336–43 (see also 173–74).

69 Wiligut, Stephen E. Flowers and Moynihan, *The Secret King: Karl Maria Wiligut, Himmler's Lord of the Runes* (Waterbury Center, Vermont: Dominion/Rûna-Raven, 2001). A revised edition of the book, *The Secret King: The Myth and Reality of Nazi Occultism*, was co-published by Feral House and Dominion in 2007.

70 *Art That Kills*, p.218.

71 Mason, "Introduction to the Third Edition," *Siege*, p.10; Gardell, *Gods of the Blood*, p.300.

72 Blood Axis/Allerseelen, split 7".

73 Joseph A. Gervasi, untitled introduction to Moynihan and Mason interviews, *NO LONGER A FANzine* #5, p.10.

74 Ibid; Gervasi to Mason, December 14, 1993; Gervasi, phone interview with author, August 25, 2021.

75 Mason, "George Lincoln Rockwell A Sketch Of His Life And Career," *Siege*, p.551.

76 Moynihan interview in *NO LONGER A FANzine*, p.18.

77 Ibid

78 Ibid

79 Gervasi, "To the editor" (of *Welcomat*), *NO LONGER A FANzine* #5, p.19. Gervasi later said that, although at the time he harbored misanthropic views, the letter was a prank to see if *Welcomat* would print something so extreme; Gervasi interview with author.

80 He denounced revisionists for valuing human life in their desire to show that the Nazis did not commit genocide. Meanwhile, Moynihan held that, "We should start lining people up and gunning them down. They're just dead weight"; Knipfel, "The Other Nazis," p.24 (*Articles*, p.73).

81 Moynihan to Mason, June 1, 1990 [Box 5, Folder 9]; *Blood Axis* (booklet) [1992], p.12 [Box 11, Folder 2]; Moynihan to Mason, April 25, 1991 [Box 11, Folder 2–3].

82 Jackson, "The Pre-History of American Holocaust Denial"; Moynihan to Mason, February 26, 1991 [Box 11, Folders 2–3].

83 James J. Martin to Moynihan, May 31, 1993 [Box 11, Folder 2].

84 "Carsten Seecamp," www.ratemyprofessors.com/ShowRatings.jsp?tid=896172, accessed January 5, 2022. The 2016 syllabus is Dr. Carsten Seecamp, "German 1000: Germany & the Germans," Department of Modern Languages, College of Liberal Arts & Sciences, University of Colorado Denver, Spring 2016, provided by the University Communications office at UC Denver, November 2022. For what was described as a 2011 version, see https://web.archive.org/

web/20210811223511, https://essaydocs.org/university-of-colorado-denver-department-of-modern-languages.html

85 The paper was for his German 3512 class in the Modern Languages Department, [1993]. Moynihan, "The Faustian Spirit of Fascism: From Oswald Spengler to Oswald Mosley" (class paper) [Box 11, Folder 2]; "Good Morning Europa! Interview with Michael Moynihan (Blood Axis)," *Occidental Congress*, Winter 1998/1999, www.occidentalcongress.com/interviews/OC3MM.html; "About Us," *L.W. Seecamp Co.*, http://seecamp.com/companyhistory.htm

86 "Michael Moynihan: From Abraxas to Nietzsche" (interview by Cletus Nelson), *Eye* #23, September/October 1999, p.33.

87 Moynihan and Søderlind, "Preface to the New Edition," *Lords of Chaos*, Revised and Expanded Edition (Los Angeles: Feral House, 2003).

88 Gardell, *Gods of the Blood*, p.300. See also Appendix 8, "Robert N. Taylor and Thomas Thorn.".

89 *Seconds*, https://secondsmagazine.com/pages/mags.php; some interviews are reprinted in the *.45 Dangerous Minds* anthology.

90 Mason, "Last Will and Testament," May 17, 1994 [Box 11, Folder 2]; Reynolds to Mason, June 9, 1994 [Box 33, Folder 3].

91 Although the authors and the artists were different, the themes were the same, and the show was obviously an advertisement for Parfrey's forthcoming anthology of the same name; Steve Schultz, "Mark of the Beast," *PDXS* 4(12) September 12, 1994, p.3 (*Articles*, p.77); *Articles*, p.9.

92 Interview in *Ohm Clock*, p.10 (*Articles*, p.9). Esoteric Hitlerists, including Mason, have often created shrines with National Socialist paraphernalia.

93 Fred Birchman, "Coca's 'Cult Rapture' Has Raw, Complex Art," *Seattle Times*, September 23, 1994, https://archive.seattletimes.com/archive/?date=19940923 &slug=1932098

94 Gardell, *Gods of the Blood*, p.300; Mason to Reynolds, Beth Helen, Bailey, Susie, January 31, 1995 [Box 33, Folder 3].

95 Moynihan, "The Faustian Spirit of Fascism," *Black Flame* 5 (1–2) 1994, p.13.

96 Ibid.

97 Ibid, pp.13–16.

98 Moynihan, "The Faustian Spirit of Fascism," *Plexus* #14, February 1994, pp.6–8. Rosenberg is also quoted favorably in Moynihan, "Where Light Becomes Darkness, and Evil is Good: An Esoteric Inquiry into Hesse's *Demian*, Gnosticism, Fascism, and the Indo-European World View," *Plexus* #19, July 1994, pp.6–8.
   A third publication of the "Faustian Spirit" was in *Filosofem*, which altogether published three articles by Moynihan in 1994 and 1995, including "Where the Light Becomes Darkness." Moynihan later claimed there were only two articles; Goodrick-Clarke, *Black Sun*, pp.208, 226, 340n44; "Blood Axis" (interview with Moynihan, Annabel Lee, and Markus Wolff by Kirin), *Flipside* #120, September/October 1999, third page of unnumbered interview pages.

99 "Anton LaVey" (interviewed by Moynihan), *Seconds* #27, 1994, pp.56–61, www.secondsmagazine.com/pages/mags.php (*.45 Dangerous Minds*, pp.178–83); "Anton Szander LaVey interviewed by Michael Moynihan," *Black Flame* 5(3–4) 1995, pp.4–7. Moynihan continued to publish in *Black Flame* and appeared in a 2019 documentary on LaVey, where he talked about his deep appreciation for the Satanist; *Anton LaVey: Into the Devil's Den*, dir. Carl Abrahamsson, 2019, www.imdb.com/title/tt13655214

100 "RAHOWA," www.discogs.com/artist/263142-RAHOWA

101 Moynihan, "George Eric Hawthorne of RAHOWA" (interview), *Seconds* #36, 1996 (*.45 Dangerous Minds*, pp.234–41); Moynihan, "RAHOWA" (interview with Hawthorne), *Black Flame* 6(1–2), 1997, pp.40–42; "RAHOWA: Heeding

the Call Of A Cultural Imperative" (interview with Garland), *Ohm Clock* #4, Spring 1996, pp.4–8.

102 Hawthorne said he wanted to work with Moynihan, who was noncommittal; Kaplan, "Postwar Paths," p.262n102. For Bugbee, see Appendix 11, "The Satanic Temple."

103 Moynihan interview in *Purging Talon*; Gardell, *Gods of the Blood*, p.300.

104 Moynihan and Søderlind, "Preface to the New Edition," *Lords of Chaos*, revised edition; Moynihan interview in *EsoTerra*.

105 Moynihan interview in *Hit List*, p.50; Moynihan, introduction to "Burzum" (interview by Moynihan and Søderlind), *Seconds* #41, 1997, https://secondsmagazine. com/articles/41-burzum.php; Moynihan and Søderlind, *Lords of Chaos*, p.vii. For Vikernes, see Appendix 10, "Varg Vikernes and the Heathen Front."

106 "Storm," www.discogs.com/label/18043-Storm

107 Moynihan was part of the Manson Work Group, "a loose network of people who were trying to expose others to Manson's ideas in a positive way," which spun off the label; Moynihan interview in *Compulsion*, p.45.

108 The album was "conceived" of in winter 1994. According to Discogs, an advance promotional cassette was released in 1995, but the formal release was 1996. Those thanked in it included Manson, Parfrey, Taylor, Thorn, Pearce, Sotos, Søderlind, Robert Ward, and Josh Buckley. Mason's name was conspicuously absent. Blood Axis, *The Gospel of Inhumanity* (Storm/Cthulu, 1996), www. discogs.com/release/188151-Blood-Axis-The-Gospel-Of-Inhumanity; Moynihan interview in *Compulsion*, p.42.

109 Blood Axis, "Herr, Nun Laß in Frieden," *The Gospel of Inhumanity*.

110 These included the "Fire of Life" 7" in 1995 and album of the same name in 1996, both co-released by Storm and Cthulu; www.discogs.com/release/188694-Changes-Fire-Of-Life, www.discogs.com/release/188162-Changes-Fire-Of-Life

111 The usual suspects thanked included Church of Satan members LaVey, Gilmore, and Peggy Nadramia, as well as Petros, Goad, Taylor, Buckley, and Thorn. LaVey and Thorn appeared in the book itself; Moynihan and Søderlind, *Lords of Chaos*, p.viii.

112 Ibid, pp.106–13, 241–66; "Arrest of German Neo-Nazi Reveals Growing Internationalization of 'White Power' Music Scene," SPLC *Intelligence Report*, Fall 2000, online December 6, 2000, www.splcenter.org/fighting-hate/ intelligence-report/2000/arrest-german-neo-nazi-reveals-growing-internationalization-white-power-music-scene

113 Goodrick-Clarke in *Black Sun* (p.387n18) said these included Moynihan, Ward, and Taylor; *Lords of Chaos*, p.332.

114 Moynihan and Søderlind, *Lords of Chaos*, pp.309–15.

115 Ibid, pp.286, 310, 313, 350.

116 Moynihan interview in *Hit List*, p.50; Zack Dundas, "Lord of Chaos: Activists Accuse Portland Writer and Musician Michael Moynihan of Spreading Extremist Propaganda, But They're Not Telling the Whole Story," *Willamette Week*, August 16, 2000, p.27, https://web.archive.org/web/20010301171407, http:// www.wweek.com/html/leada081600.html

117 *Lords of Chaos*, dir. Jonas Åkerlund, 2018, www.imdb.com/title/tt4669296; "Lords of Chaos," *Rotten Tomatoes*, www.rottentomatoes.com/m/lords_of_ chaos, accessed October 7, 2022.

118 Blood Axis, *Blót: Sacrifice In Sweden* (Cold Meat Industry, 1998), www.discogs. com/release/60652-Blood-Axis-Blót-Sacrifice-In-Sweden

119 De Benoist, the towering figure of the French New Right (Nouvelle Droite), proposed a system of extreme decentralization wherein groups tied by sub-national ethnicities would form their own enclaves, an approach sometimes called

the "Europe of One Hundred Flags." These new zones would be used as counterweights to liberal, internationalist, and capitalist political and economic forms. Similarly, McNallen was a supporter of ethnic and nationalist struggles—including the Tibetan freedom movement and the Zapatistas in Chiapas, Mexico—as well as a proponent of various other ethnic religions. Tamir Bar-On, *Where Have All the Fascists Gone?* (London: Routledge, 2007); Gardell, *Gods of the Blood*, p.280.

120 Moynihan, letter to the editor, *Scorpion* #20, Winter 1999/2000, pp.33–34; Didrik Søderlind, "Terrible Dialogues" (review of Andreas Winsnes, *Terror eller dialog?*), *Scorpion* #20, Winter 1999/2000, pp.44–45.

121 Richard Metzger, ed., *Book of Lies: The Disinformation Guide to Magick and the Occult* (New York: The Disinformation Company, 2003); *Dominion Press*, https://web.archive.org/web/20100601052019, http://dominionpress.net/titles/the-secret-king

122 Mason to Mr. Brown, March 23, 2001.

123 "Love is Blood Axis" (interview with Moynihan), *Warcom Gazette*, February 1995, p.2.

124 Blood Axis, "Herjafather," various artists compilation, *Cavalcare La Tigre - Julius Evola: Centenary* (Eis Und Licht, 1998), www.discogs.com/label/22308-Eis-Und-Licht; Moynihan interview in *Eye*, p.35; Evola, *Men Among the Ruins: Post-War Reflections of a Radical Traditionalist* (Rochester, Vermont: Inner Traditions, 2002). A second Evola book he edited came out in 2001; Evola and the UR Group, *Introduction to Magic: Rituals and Practical Techniques for the Magus* (Rochester, Vermont: Inner Traditions, 2001).

125 Evola, Revolt *Against the Modern World: Politics, Religion, and Social Order in the Kali Yuga* (Inner Traditions Audio, January 4, 2022), www.simonandschuster.com/books/Revolt-Against-the-Modern-World/Julius-Evola/9781644113486

126 Moynihan, "Bathory" and "Black Metal," *Encyclopedia*, pp.13–16, 24–31; Moynihan, "ATWA," "Walther Darré," "Julius Evola," and "Odinism," in Taylor, ed., *Encyclopedia of Religion and Nature*, pp.127–29, 450–51, 625–27, 1218–20.

127 The first issue had a third editor, Collin Cleary; *TYR* #1 (Atlanta: Ultra, 2002/2008), p.3.

128 *TYR* #1, pp.8, 9; "TYR Journal," *Ultra*, https://web.archive.org/web/20080308185318, http://www.radicaltraditionalist.com/tyr.htm

129 Patrick Kelly, et al., *Hatred in Georgia, 1991: A Chronology and Analysis of Hate Activity* (Atlanta, Georgia: Neighbors Network, 1992), p.40, https://radicalarchives.files.wordpress.com/2013/01/1991-hatred-in-georgia.pdf; Neighbors Network, *Hatred in Georgia, 1992 Report: A Chronology and Analysis of Hate Activity* (Atlanta, Georgia: Neighbors Network, 1993), pp.iii, 12, 26, https://radicalarchives.files.wordpress.com/2013/01/1992-hatred-in-georgia.pdf

130 "Satan's Little Helper" (Thorn interview with Buckley), *Black Flame* 6(1–2) 1997, pp.17–19; *TYR* #1, p.283; Graham Macklin, "Greg Johnson and Counter-Currents," in Mark Sedgwick, ed., *Key Thinkers of the Radical Right: Behind the New Threat to Liberal Democracy* (New York: Oxford University Press, 2019), p.205; "Tyndall in America," *Spearhead*, https://web.archive.org/web/20040803011131, www.spearhead.com/0407-jt2.html; Alexander Zaitchik, "How Klan Lawyer Sam Dickson Got Rich," *Intelligence Report*, Fall 2006, online October 19, 2006, www.splcenter.org/fighting-hate/intelligence-report/2006/how-klan-lawyer-sam-dickson-got-rich

131 Moynihan, "From Householder to War-Lord to Heavenly Hero: Naming God in the Early Continental Germanic Languages," PhD dissertation, Germanic Languages & Literatures, University of Massachusetts Amherst, May 2017, https://doi.org/10.7275/10010802.0

132 In one interview, he gives over a half dozen uses and interpretations; Moynihan interview in *Compulsion*, p.43.
133 Goodrick-Clarke, *Black Sun*, p.207; Peter Staudenmaier, email to author, October 18, 2021.
134 *Blood Axis* (booklet), back cover. The image was also used as an illustration for the Moynihan interview in *Compulsion*, p.47. For the original poster, see "Image / Klarer Kopf - reine Hande - offene Augen - Starke Faust," *Calisphere, University of California, Hoover Institution Digital Collections*, https://calisphere.org/item/acbe48e0961ab8e8acaa38c2544aca4f. It translated as "Clear head – pure hands – open eyes – strong fist."
135 Moynihan interview in *Compulsion*, p.43.
136 Prendergast, "Family Ties," p.30; *Siege* advertisement, *Black Flame* 3(12) Spring/Summer 1991, p.12.
137 Prendergast, "Family Ties," pp.26, 28.
138 Moynihan to Mason, April 25, 1991 [Box 11, Folder 2–3]; Prendergast, "Family Ties," pp.24, 28.
139 Moynihan, Rice, and Mason interview with Larson/*Talk Back* (video).
140 Knipfel, "The Other Nazis," p.23 (*Articles*, p.72).
141 Moynihan interview in *Heretic*.
142 Moynihan interview in *NO LONGER A FANzine*, p.17.
143 Moynihan interview in *Compulsion*, p.46.
144 Gardell, *Gods of the Blood*, p.304. He gives 1997, but some of his dates are slightly off.
145 Ibid, p.301.
146 Moynihan interview in *Momentum*, [1997 or 1998], cited in Coogan, "How Black," p.45.
147 Gene Sotelo to Mason, [October] 1998; Mason to Sotelo, October 27, 1998 [both Box 22, Folder 49].
148 Moynihan interview in *Occidental Congress*.
149 Much of this section is based on the article and in places follows its outline, although Coogan did not have access to many of the materials in this study—in particular, Moynihan's correspondence with Mason.
150 Coogan, "How Black," pp.33–49; Bale's introduction is pp.33–35.
151 Moynihan interview in *Hit List*, pp.51–52.
152 Moynihan interview in *Heretic*; Moynihan interview in *Eye*, p.31.
153 J. Bennett, "NSBM Special Report," *Decibel*, 2006, http://web.archive.org/web/20080208184453, http://www.decibelmagazine.com/features/may2006/nsbm.aspx; Moynihan interview in *Hit List*, p.53.
154 Moynihan interview in *Hit List*, p.53; "Heathen Harvest Interview with Michael Moynihan," *Heathen Harvest*, May 24, 2005, https://web.archive.org/web/20060219193021, http://www.heathenharvest.com/article.php?story=20050514073345369; White and Moynihan dialogue on *Overthrow.com*.
155 Moynihan interview in *Hit List*, p.52.
156 Devin Burghart, ed. *Soundtracks to the White Revolution: White Supremacist Assaults on Youth Music Subcultures* (Chicago: Center for New Community, 1999), especially pp.66–70, 77–79, www.irehr.org/2015/12/01/2079
157 "…And Another Springs Up," SPLC *Intelligence Report* #96, Fall 1999, p.19. Moynihan's profile was removed from the online version, "…And Another Springs Up," *SPLC*, December 15, 1999, www.splcenter.org/fighting-hate/intelligence-report/1999/and-another-springs; Moynihan interview in *Compulsion*, p.47.
158 Eric K. Ward, John Lunsford, and Justin Massa, "Sounds of Violence," SPLC *Intelligence Report* #96, Fall 1999, pp.28–32, online version is "Black Metal

Spreads Neo-Nazi Hate Message," *SPLC*, December 15, 1999, www.splcenter. org/fighting-hate/intelligence-report/1999/black-metal-spreads-neo-nazi-hate-message

159 The *Eye* interview would be responded to by Bale and Coogan in *Hit List*; Jeff Bale and Coogan, "Will That Be a Bloody Mary, Mr. Moynihan?," *Hit List* #4, September/October 1999, pp.9–12.

160 Moynihan interview in *Eye*, pp.29–31; Coogan, "Kevin Coogan Responds," pp.11–12.

161 Moynihan interview in *NO LONGER A FANzine*, p.19.

162 Moynihan interview in *Eye*, pp.32–33.

163 Ibid, p.32; Dundas, "Lord of Chaos," p.30; Gervasi interview with author.

164 In reference to the work of watchdog groups, in 2006 Moynihan said in the *Decibel* interview that the basis of their accusations were "on a few provocative statements selectively culled from interviews done nearly 15 years ago. These statements become far more ambiguous when contextualized into everything I've said and done over the years." The interviews quoted were from *Compulsion* in 1998, and *NO LONGER A FANzine* in 1994. When the monitoring groups' works appeared in 1999, one interview was two years old, and another five—making them relatively recent. Even counting from the *Decibel* interview's date, the distance would still only be eight and thirteen years; Bennett, "NSBM Special Report".

165 Knipfel, "The Other Nazis," p.24 (*Articles*, p.73); Moynihan, "The Faustian Spirit of Fascism," *Black Flame*, p.13.

166 Moynihan interview in *Eye*, p.33; Moynihan interview in *NO LONGER A FANzine*, p.18.

167 Moynihan interview in *Eye*, pp.29, 35

168 In the introduction, the interviewer said that, regarding *Siege*, "I never saw anything in your introduction which would suggest" an affinity for National Socialism; Moynihan, et al. interview in *Flipside*, first page of interview.

169 Ibid.

170 Ibid.

171 Ibid.

172 Dan Casey, "Nazi leader Bill White -- in his own words," December 17, 2009 (updated June 6, 2019), *Roanoke Times*, https://web.archive.org/web/2021 1015221624, https://roanoke.com/news/local/nazi-leader-bill-white----in-his-own-words/article_7e5c7e03-bdcf-5542-a6be-0433ba2d7aee.html; "Bill White," *SPLC*, www.splcenter.org/fighting-hate/extremist-files/individual/bill-white

173 White and Moynihan dialogue on *Overthrow.com*; Casey, "Nazi leader Bill White -- in his own words." White showed the influence of the Mason as well. In 2012, he threatened three officials who were involved in the arrests of a number of American Front members in Florida. His email claimed the threats were coming from "JOE TOMASSI, CHARLES MANSON AND SON OF SAM," and signed it as "NATIONAL SOCIALIST LIBERATION FRONT—HELTER SKELTER BRIGADE"; United States Court of Appeals, Eleventh Circuit, *UNITED STATES OF AMERICA, Plaintiff-Appellee, v. WILLIAM A. WHITE, Defendant-Appellant*, No. 14-15525, Decided: June 30, 2016, https://caselaw. findlaw.com/us-11th-circuit/1740622.html

174 Dundas, "Lord of Chaos," pp.27, 32.

175 Dundas, "Lord of Chaos," p.29. Other than what could not have been more than a small handful of exceptions—Moynihan never names who he is referring to—in fact most anarchists, including those in Portland's own Rose City Antifa, vehemently disagreed with him; "Drawing Lines," *Rose City Antifa*.

176 Schuster to Mason, March 4, 2002 [Box 32, Folders 27–33]; Mason to author, November 26, 2022.

177 Moynihan to Mason, June 1, 1991 [Box 11, Folders 2–3]; Prendergast, "Family Ties," pp.24, 30.
178 Mason to Moynihan, June 14, 1991 [Box 11, Folders 2–3]; Mason to author, November 26, 2022.
179 Moynihan interview in *Eye*, pp.28, 32–33.
180 Dundas, "Lord of Chaos," pp.25, 30; Moynihan, "Introduction," *Siege*, 1st. ed., p.xi. Dundas would later write more about Moynihan, while keeping essentially the same approach, and in a second interview with Moynihan repeats these talking points. Dundas also reviewed *TYR* in 2004 in the *Willamette Week*; a single sentence at the end mentions its advocacy of ethno-separatism. Dundas, "The Notorious Michael Moynihan," *Mumblage International*, 2003, https://web.archive.org/web/20030501033031, http://www.mumblage.com/story.php?id=36; Dundas, "tyr: myth, culture, tradition," *Willamette Week*, May 11, 2004, www.wweek.com/portland/article-3194-tyr-myth-culture-tradition.html
181 Gardell, *Gods of the Blood*, pp.302, 318.
182 Ibid, p.302.
183 Ibid, pp.303–4, 318.
184 Ibid, pp.300–302.

15

NAZI-SATANISM

Nikolas Schreck and the Church of Satan

Just as Charles Manson helped bring the Abraxas Clique together, Anton LaVey also became an important common denominator for them. Nonetheless, the role of the Church of Satan in both facilitating the Abraxas Clique's actions and helping contribute to the popularization of *Siege*, especially by Peter Gilmore, has been largely overlooked. More generally, this reflects a larger lack of scholarship on the Nazi–Satanist nexus as a whole. The impact of the Order of Nine Angles (O9A) on the network around the Atomwaffen Division has drawn new attention to this, and recently several reports have been issued there. But there still is not even a single book-length study of either Nazi-Satanism in general or a particular group or individual.

It should be stressed that only a minority of Satanists have ever been neo-Nazis. A 2009 study found that about 10 percent of Satanists felt positively about National Socialism, while 70 percent viewed it negatively.[1]

The Church of Satan

Within the confines of the Nazi-Satanist nexus, neo-Nazis do not seem to have been particularly useful to Satanists, and this is especially true of the Church of Satan. But Satanists have been quite useful to neo-Nazis, and this is especially true of the Church of Satan.

The Church of Satan made its public debut in San Francisco in 1966.[2] This put it at the epicenter of the countercultural explosion of the late 1960s. This multi-faceted movement had a wide-ranging impact, affecting politics, drugs, lifestyle, food—and, of course, spirituality. Part of this included the emergence and expansion of previously marginal or marginal religious

DOI: 10.4324/9780429200090-20

movements, including cults, Eastern religions, paganism, and the occult. Satanism became a visible part of the latter's broadly defined milieu.

What LaVey created was a made-for-media new religion (of sorts). With a salacious emphasis on sexuality and devilish aesthetics, LaVey's best-selling *Satanic Bible* came out in 1969; in it he elucidated his brand of atheistic Satanism based on a philosophy of amoral individualism, influenced by Ragnar Redbeard and Ayn Rand.[3] Satanism blossomed after LaVey, and contemporary Satanists are divided into theists who worship a literal deity and atheists who see Satan as an allegory and literary figure.[4]

However, the Church of Satan was not the only group associated with Nazi-Satanism. While the Church did include members who had those political proclivities, for other groups Nazi-Satanism was central to their beliefs. (And this does not include Satanist groups that embraced other forms of White Supremacy.)

Satanic Policy on National Socialism

Satanism has never been popular with, or even acceptable to, all neo-Nazis; it is a fringe part of an already fringe movement. But some neo-Nazis did embrace this new creed. James Madole—the leader of the fascist National Renaissance Party, which combined occult ideas with National Socialism—had an ongoing relationship with LaVey.

In 1971, despite his general right-wing libertarian approach, LaVey gave public approval for a Satanic fascism. According to *Newsweek*, he sought "the creation of a police state in which the weak are weeded out and the 'achievement-oriented leadership' is permitted to pursue the mysteries of black magic." (Church of Satan member Arthur Lyons claimed that his actual goal was a "benign police state"—a phrase sometimes credited to LaVey himself.) LaVey would repeat this call for a police state explicitly in his last interview.[5]

A few years later, LaVey described Madole's party as "enamored with the Church of Satan." In one account, the occult-fascist leader's apartment had a "satanic altar," and he was known to play LaVey's *The Satanic Mass* album at party meetings.[6] But while LaVey thought he was "a nice chap who is doing his thing," it was another National Renaissance Party member whose actions precipitated an internal discussion about the Church's relationship to National Socialism.

In 1974, Magister Michael Aquino, who was on the Council of Nine, found out that a priest in the Church, Michael Grumboski ("Shai"), had stepped down from that role to join a new Nazi-Satanist group based in Detroit. The Order of the Black Ram was run by Seth Kliphoth (also known as Seth Typhon), who was the Michigan National Renaissance Party organizer—and also a Church of Satan member. (Kliphoth would also spend time in the NSLF.)[7]

In his discussion with Aquino, LaVey dismissed the National Renaissance Party as composed "largely of acned, bucolic types" who

> spend their time getting jeered at in street demonstrations.... I know Madole personally and have been to N.R.P. headquarters. Even have a card. They would do anything for us. So would [the] Klan for that matter. I do not endorse either but acknowledge camaraderie from any source.[8]

However, LaVey added that neo-Nazi groups were actually useful in "drawing off those within our ranks who are unworthy, unstable, or otherwise expendable." These kinds of people, he said, needed only "a symbol and a scapegoat," for which the swastika and pentagram were "interchangeable." But there was no cause for worry because "they will come in handy one day." (In turn, Madole also sought to profit from their relationship by attempting to recruit Church of Satan members to the National Renaissance Party.)[9]

Michael Aquino

Aquino took this opportunity to elucidate the Church's views about National Socialism. According to him, Hitler was a great leader, and "*Mein Kampf* is a political *Satanic Bible*," a kind of how-to guide that showed how to use symbolism and drama to manipulate the masses. (Aquino waved away the role of antisemitism, saying it "was a personal quirk of Hitler's, which...is essentially unimportant," and, furthermore, in the present day it should be "ignored.") But whereas Hitler understood the mood of his day and used that insight to seize power, today's neo-Nazis were buffoons who aped the past and set themselves up to fail. Aquino concluded that "all avowed neo-Nazi groups are pariahs in the eyes of the Church of Satan."[10]

But almost immediately afterward, Aquino left the organization, taking a chunk of the membership with him and forming his own group, the Temple of Set. He was not a National Socialist, but like LaVey, Aquino continued to be interested in the NSDAP. Aquino had already made his fetishization of the SS clear in an essay published while he was in the Church of Satan, but he took this further in October 1982 by going to Heinrich Himmler's Wewelsburg castle to do a magical "working."

His recommended reading also reflected his interests in Nazi Germany, which he split up into "pro" and "anti." Those wanting to learn more from a "neutral" historian were directed toward the works of David Irving. Other books on the list included *Hitler's Secret Conversations 1941–1944*, Alfred Rosenberg's *Race History and Other Essays*, and Madison Grant's *The Passing of the Great Race*.[11]

The Debate Goes On

But the Aquino–LaVey discussion did not end the discussion inside the Church of Satan over Satanism and National Socialism. Gavin Baddeley wrote that in the 1980s it had "polarised into those who embraced sinister Nazi-chic as a confrontational expression of individualism, and those who regarded Nazism as the repellent epitome of conformity."[12]

This continued in *Black Flame* in the 1990s. However, as the inner circle favored the inclusion of neo-Nazis, their opinion prevailed. But that did not mean that the Church of Satan became a neo-Nazi, fascist, or otherwise White Supremacist organization; it has always been based on a right-wing individualist philosophy. So, the Nazi-Satanists existed alongside people of color (Sammy Davis, Jr. had been a member), Jews (LaVey himself was of Jewish descent), and LGBTQ+ people (which LaVey had specifically welcomed in *The Satanic Bible*.) Nonetheless, in an outtake for a Nick Bougas documentary, LaVey for whatever reason denounced the "niggers, kikes, fags, wops, greasers, degenerates that are inferior."[13]

"Zionist Odinist Bolshevik Nazi Imperialist Socialist Fascism"

LaVey continued to make statements sympathetic to fascism through the 1990s. In 1993, he said "If a neo-fascist look—and outlook—makes for men who look like men and women who look like women, I'm all for it."[14] In 1994, repeating popular conservative talking points, LaVey said, "We are already living in an inept and counterproductive fascist state" in the form of "politically correct" liberalism.

> There is nothing inherently wrong with fascism, given the nature of the average citizen.... Now it's not so much a case of avoiding fascism, but of replacing a screwed up, disjointed, fragmented and stupefying kind of fascism with one that is more sensible and truly progressive.[15]

A little later, echoing Aquino's earlier views, LaVey said, "The aesthetics of Satanism are those of National Socialism.... The National Socialists had that drama, coupled with the romance of overcoming such incredible odds." LaVey thought there was "something magical" about the SS taking pride in being evil.[16]

Some of LaVey's essays on Jews also appeared in posthumous collections. "A Plan," in *Satan Speaks*, put his contradictory views on display. LaVey said Satanists "have an affinity for certain elements of both Judaism...and Nazism." He denounced "Holocaust aficionados" while seeing "non-practicing and part-Jews" as "the future of Satanism." Because Jews have historically been associated with Satan by religious antisemites, his line of argument went, they should embrace this association.[17] In addition,

> It will become easier and more convincing for any Satanist to combine a Jewish lineage with a Nazi aesthetic, and with pride rather than with guilt and misgiving. The die is cast with the vast numbers of children of mixed Jewish/Gentile origins. They need a place to go. They need a tough identity. They won't find it in the Christian church, nor will they find it in the synagogue. They certainly won't find acceptance among identity anti-Christian anti-Semites who use noble, rich, and inspirational Norse mythology as an excuse and vehicle to rant about the "ZOG." The only place a rational amalgam of proud, admitted, Zionist Odinist Bolshevik Nazi Imperialist Socialist Fascism will be found—and championed—in the Church of Satan.[18]

Mason and LaVey

Although he has been labeled as such, Mason was never a Satanist. However, in the short period between *Siege*'s publication and the start of his prison term, he made little attempt to dissuade casual observers of this.

Mason's interest in Satanism went back to his youth. In 1968, he bought LaVey's *The Satanic Mass* album from another NSWPP member and used a long excerpt from the album as the epigraph to the September 1983 SIEGE.[19] Another former American Nazi Party member, Kurt Saxon, even joined the Church of Satan.[20]

Others in the party also took note of the new group. In 1970, the original NSLF student group named LaVey as part of a new wave of interest in the occult, which was portrayed with relative nuance. The article argued that interest in the occult was a reaction to social degeneration caused by "cultural and racial aliens." Christian churches were complicit in this, and so white people, in their "panic," turned to the "black arts" to fulfill their needs. But these opinions seemed to be the exception and not the rule. In 1970, Joseph Tommasi attacked one of his comrades by saying, "To put it BLUNTLY…he's a satanist, a devil worshipper."[21]

Mason acknowledged LaVey's Jewish background—not that that had ever stopped him from collaborating with someone before. Jewish or not, Mason would compare him to his lifelong hero, saying "LaVey has showmanship strikingly reminiscent of George Lincoln Rockwell and knows how to use shock and symbolism to defeat the news blackout and to reach people's minds and shatter preconceptions."[22]

In 1988, Boyd Rice told Mason that "I showed him [LaVey] your interview & he was very much impressed & says your views are surprisingly close to his own."[23] Three years later, Michael Moynihan asked LaVey's permission to run an excerpt of his writings. Moynihan told Mason, "I know that he is familiar with you and likes your line—I believe he saw the old video interview with you and said afterwards, 'There needs to be a lot more people like James Mason in the world!'" LaVey replied to Moynihan that he would be "honored" to be included in *Siege*.[24] He also sent Mason an autographed copy of *The Satanic Bible*, inscribing it "To James Mason – a man of courage and reason – a rare combination. Rege Satanas!" A picture of this appeared in the second edition of *Siege*. And LaVey is mentioned three times in the first edition of *Siege*, including being thanked, while an excerpt from *The Satanic Mass*, which had appeared in the newsletter, got a standalone page in the book.[25]

It was around the release of *Siege* that Mason appeared to have the closest association with Satanism. Despite his own lack of self-identification, Mason consented to being billed as a "Neo-Nazi Satanist" for his 1993 appearance on Bob Larson's show. During this period, he was photographed dressing up in a priest's clerical collar for a social event with Satanists.[26] In an interview conducted in October 1994, Mason was queried about his opinion of Satanism. He noted that "LaVey advocates good citizenship," while he sought subversion. Nonetheless, when asked "Do you see a new movement burgeoning from the satanic community and those people who identify with Siege?" Mason replied, "I would hope so." Elsewhere, he also explicitly named Satanism as one of the views that his Universal Order philosophy encompassed.[27]

But after his conversion to Christianity in the mid-1990s, Mason would no longer refer to Satanism in a positive way. In his prison writings, he identified what he called the "Three Faces of Satan." The first were Satanists who followed LaVey's approach, while the second were those engaged in animal torture, child abuse, and murder. But he defined the third, true Satan as another name for Jewish world domination, and denounced the "Satanic Beast System" and "the devil, the Jew."[28] After his rediscovery in the 2010s, Mason turned even further away. In an essay about the Church of Satan, now he said about LaVey, "I neither disown nor do I embrace either the man or his creation."[29]

Nikolas Schreck

Schreck, the fourth member of the Abraxas Foundation and a Satanist who married into the LaVey family, played a brief but important role in the Abraxas Clique.

In 1984, Schreck founded the band Radio Werewolf in Los Angeles. The name had multiple references; Schreck told Tom Metzger that it referred to the NSDAP radio station which tried to rally the regime's supporters in 1945 as the war was coming to a close.[30] As for the name "Schreck" itself, its associations included the German word meaning "fright" or "terror" as well as to Julius Schreck, an important figure in the founding of the SS.

Radio Werewolf was a campy goth band; Schreck wore white face makeup, and drummer Evil Wilhelm sported a monocle. Rice described them as a "novelty Rock Band that did monster Pop songs." Radio Werewolf used numerous Nazi references, some of them obviously tongue-in-cheek; the lyrics for "Triumph of the Will" included "Eva, oh Eva, Come sit on my face / Berlin is burning but we are the master race."[31] Regardless, this would help attract the attention of *real* neo-Nazis. By 1988, despite the clear irony of the early band, Schreck's associations, presentation, and rhetoric implied that the line between irony and belief had been completely blurred—if not crossed entirely.

By 1985, the band was using a werewolf image, made by Robert N. Taylor, as a logo. Like so many others, Schreck also became enamored with Manson, calling him "a sort of shaman, or spiritual spokesmen, for the Western and white consciousness. In the same way that Adolf Hitler was in the '30s, I think that Charles Manson fulfills that same role in our time."[32]

In 1986, Schreck saw *EXIT* and contacted Adam Parfrey, saying he wanted to do benefit shows—which Radio Werewolf called "rallies"—for Manson. Schreck said that he was already thinking about this when, in June 1986, Manson forwarded a letter from him to Rice. And Parfrey was already in contact, independently, with both of them. Schreck described this as "a whole network of interrelations that just came together."[33]

In March 1987, Schreck tried to hold a Friends of Justice concert in Los Angeles, but it was shut down. At the same time, he was collaborating with Parfrey on a publication they hoped to issue.[34]

In 1987, Radio Werewolf appeared twice on *Hot Seat*, the TV show of Wally George, a right-wing shock jock, where they intentionally antagonized both the host and audience. Later asked if he was trolling, Schreck replied, "There's an implication of insincerity in 'trolling' whereas those particular appearances were just slightly caricaturized exaggerations of the general beliefs I espoused at that time."[35]

The same year, he and Evil Wilhelm went on Metzger's *Race and Reason*. (Metzger had attended a performance of theirs around the same time.) The show started with a clip of them playing live, with a swastika flag and the band sieg-heiling—while playing "Triumph of the Will." In the ridiculous interview that followed, they acted the role of superior beings from outer space who were the "true gods of earth." Schreck said their goals were far beyond that of the NSDAP, which "was much too liberal, much too bourgeois." Metzger looked confused at times and was disappointed they did not identify as National Socialists or fascists. Nonetheless, Schreck gave him a button and a membership card in their Radio Werewolf Youth Party.[36]

The Manson File

In 1988, Amok Press released *The Manson File*. Proclaiming Manson as "one of the last true heretics of our time," it was heavy on illustrations and light on text. The contents included Parfrey's *The Revelation of the Sacred Door*, a Rice piece, and several Bougas cartoons. In addition to Manson's kind words for the NSDAP ("I don't believe the Nazis will come back in SS hats and boots; they will probably be people living in peace and harmony"), there were several pages of Mason content: the "Independent Genius" flyer, excerpts from SIEGE, the *National Enquirer* article "Is Charles Manson the New Hitler?," and a picture of Mason with the Manson Family's Sandra Good. And as an apparent attempt to cover "both sides," a piece from another German armed marxist group, the June 2 Movement, was also included.[37]

Early that year, Schreck did a promotional appearance for the book on Maury Povich's *Hard Copy* TV show. He also did a second appearance on Metzger's show, but this time he was much more serious. Unlike Rice's careful attempts to avoid directly using this kind of rhetoric, Schreck described the Abraxas Foundation in explicitly racist terms. Later in the interview, he condemned the "dysgenic ocean of mud that has swept the world."[38]

> we are strictly concerned with the western European tradition .... we have no concern for any other. That's why we maintain a firm alternative to the African culture, the Asian culture, that is dominating the western world. Young people are caught up in a nightmare of racial confusion, and we seek to end that.[39]

Afterward, he and Zeena LaVey spent the night at Metzger's place. Many years later, Schreck was asked about these appearances. Although somewhat ambiguous as to how serious they were, he said there was "tension between the Addams Family and the Manson Family side of Radio Werewolf. By the summer of '87, I felt that the campier, Famous Monsters-inspired aspect... had run its course." But rather than denounce the views he expressed, especially on the second one, Schreck said, "I prefer to let people interpret my work however they want."[40]

Metzger, who was particularly interested in cultural politics, appeared to have taken Schreck at face value. On that same show, he referred to the Abraxas Foundation as "part of the movement"[41] and sold DVDs with Schreck for decades to come.

Schreck was also part of the 8/8/88 performance. In the interviews afterward, he called the Nazi regime "one of the few times in the 20th century that humanity's full potential has been unleashed."[42] Soon after, he married Zeena LaVey, who had also participated in the event. Zeena was a High Priestess in the Church and acted as its official spokesperson from May 1985 to April 1990. Schreck also met her father, Anton LaVey, who made him a Church of Satan member.[43]

The married couple did a variety of talk shows about Satanism, including the by-then obligatory Larson appearance. In addition to espousing his usual Social Darwinism, Schreck condemned homosexuality as unhealthy, unnatural, and unhygienic—although not morally wrong.[44]

Schreck's views on this subject also caused him lasting physical damage. According to Rice, in August 1987 "Schreck was putting up pro-AIDS posters with cartoons of a Gay parade where AIDS victims were marching into an open grave" in an area frequented by gay sex workers. Schreck was spotted and chased to his car, "but before he could shut the door, a guy reached in with a knife and slashed him. His ear was cut off, and it fell into the gutter."[45]

After the success of *The Manson File*, 1989 was a busy year for Schreck. His documentary *Charles Manson Superstar*, based on an interview he did with Manson in San Quentin, was released. Schreck and Zeena LaVey narrated it, and it included comments from Manson which were directed at Mason. The interview was shot by Brian King, who had filmed interviews with Mason, Rice, and Schreck in 1987; footage from the Mason interview ended up in *Charles Manson Superstar*. Schreck also started making a documentary about Anton LaVey, although he abandoned it when the two could not get along.[46] And two Radio Werewolf records were released: *Fiery Summons* and the Savitri Devi–inspired *The Lightning and the Sun*.[47]

Two major breaks happened in 1990. The first was between Schreck and the Abraxas Clique. Rice had already been unhappy with how 8/8/88 went and blamed Schreck, saying he "fucked the whole thing for all of us. Schreck is an incompetent shit. A total fuck up." Moynihan had a different reason. In March 1990, he wrote Mason that a break occurred months before because of Schreck's dishonesty about his background.[48]

Regardless of the burning of that bridge, Schreck hit it off with Death in June's Douglas Pearce after meeting at the London book launch of *The Manson File*. And so both Schreck and Rice wound up on the 1989 Death in June album, *Thè Wäll Öf Säcrificè*.[49]

The second break happened when Zeena LaVey left the Church of Satan at the end of April and denounced her father. After that, the married couple moved to Europe, where they made music under the Radio Werewolf name. (They continued their associations with the Abraxas Circle for a little while, both contributing to *EXIT #5* in 1991.) They also joined Aquino's Temple of Set but later on became Buddhists. In 2015, they divorced amicably.[50]

The Abraxas Clique and the Church of Satan

It wasn't just Schreck with these links, though; all four of the Abraxas Clique had relationships with LaVey. While in prison, Mason wrote that "a number of my closest and best Movement comrades are bona fide high priests in

LaVey's church."[51] *Siege*'s thanks list shows this. Moynihan, himself in the Church of Satan, thanked three who were, or would soon be, in the Church—LaVey, Thorn, and Gilmore's *Black Flame*—plus LaVey's publisher Parfrey. (Rice was noticeably absent, but his influence silently loomed large.)

One reason for this linkage was that LaVey was attuned to the importance of popular culture. He particularly liked to have musicians associated with the Church of Satan and sometimes bestowed membership upon meeting them. LaVey's belief in a hierarchical social world, and in particular his interest in eugenics, also made common ground with the Abraxas Clique.

The publishers of RE/Search cancelled an issue on LaVey after, in Kevin Coogan's words, they "decided LaVey was a reactionary."[52] Former RE/Search collaborator Rice was close to LaVey up until his death and around 1987 had introduced him to Parfrey, who became the beneficiary of the falling out. In 1989, Feral House republished LaVey's *The Satanic Witch* (originally titled *The Compleat Witch*) and in 1992 *The Devil's Notebook*, which included an introduction by Parfrey.[53]

For Mason, the most important thing to come out of the Abraxas Foundation–Church of Satan relationship was Gilmore's interest in, and promotion of, *Siege*. His official Church of Satan publication *Black Flame* ran an advance advertisement with the initial cover design.[54] Upon receiving *Siege*, Gilmore wrote Moynihan,

> My deepest gratitude goes to you for the wonderful and inspiring copy of *SIEGE*. Bravo to you! … I'm truly enjoying my foray into the writings of Mason. He really has learned so many truths on his journey and offers much wisdom to those who will see. This is an important publication, and the time is right for it.… We'll do our best to promote this outstanding effort.[55]

In the same letter, Gilmore said, "the struggle continues in the many theatres of the total war, and the true elite will emerge—as Nature's Law dictates" and ended the letter with "Hail Victory!"[56] In 1993, he gave *Siege* a glowing review in *Black Flame*, calling it a "monumental achievement" and recommending it to Satanists.

> If you are a Satanist and have not gotten a sense of perspective on how your movement fits into American Society, look at this account of the American National Socialist movement and learn. Mason's writing is clear and filled with clarity.[57]

However, Gilmore did not clarify what Mason's truths were or what Satanists had to learn from him—an interesting omission considering that his organization always stressed legality.

In 1994, when Mason and his teenage girlfriend Eva went to New York City for a talk show, Gilmore and Peggy Nadramia (his wife and the Church's future High Priestess) made sure to meet them and take a picture. Afterward, Gilmore told Mason that "It is a rare pleasure to contact others who are fully alive."[58]

Moynihan also played an important role through his connections with the Church of Satan leadership. In 1993, after securing LaVey's consent to use his writings in *Siege*, Moynihan sent his class paper "The Faustian Spirit of Fascism" to Gilmore. Its argument about the relationship between fascism and Satanism fits in well with the ongoing debate inside the Church of Satan over the issue. Gilmore ran it as an article in *Black Flame* in 1994; that same year Moynihan said, "Most of the Satanists I'm in contact with, being realists, are very cognizant of racial issues."[59]

Black Flame also ran full-page ads for the Abraxas Foundation and Storm—both undoubtedly hard-pressed to find places that would do so. The magazine also reviewed numerous publications and records from the Abraxas Circle. These included *Siege, Ohm Clock*, and *Fifth Path* and Electric Hellfire Club, Blood Axis, and Rice albums.

The Abraxas Clique returned Gilmore's interest, although in the end they got more than they gave. A small image of his appeared in the 1991 *EXIT*. In 1992, Rice said Gilmore was on the "same frequency and is also very talented as a composer and musician" and in December used some of his music in a British performance.[60] Moynihan planned to release a Gilmore CD on Storm, *Ragnarok Symphony*, although it never happened.[61]

After Gilmore took the Church's helm, he pontificated on typical right-wing positions that fit comfortably in the mainstream of the Republican Party. For example, in his article "Pervasive Pantywaistism," he wrote that "The minions of 'political correctness' and a new generation of whiner-spawn have attained legislative power to enforce their pusillanimous intolerance for any difference of opinion."[62]

The Abraxas Clique also made sure to promote LaVey during his last years. Moynihan's interviews with LaVey appeared in *Seconds, Black Flame*, and *Lords of Chaos*.[63] In 1997, *Seconds* ran what was billed as LaVey's last interview, which included an introduction by Gilmore. And in 2000, Rice, Parfrey, and Thorn paid their respects to LaVey in a special *Black Flame* memorial issue.[64]

More Satanic Fascism

New Zealand's Kerry Bolton was also involved in this crossover. A prolific writer and editor, he has played an important part in what he has called—in a nod to the Abraxas Foundation—an "international 'occult-fascist axis'." He started the Order of the Left Hand Path in 1982 and the Black Order in

1994. The latter's goals included studying "the esoteric current behind National Socialism, Thule [Society], and the occult tradition from which they are derived."[65] Bolton also published in *Black Flame* and *Ohm Clock* alongside the Abraxas Clique. In the interview that appeared in *Lords of Chaos*, he clearly elucidated the split between cosmopolitan and ethno-nationalist currents in Satanism—the same division that could be found in Heathenism.[66]

Nazi-Satanism also impacted Mason's old group, the National Socialist Movement (NSM), when a 2006 scandal threatened to sink the NSM. Clifford Herrington had now stepped back from leading the NSM but remained its emeritus chairman; he lived in Oklahoma with his wife Maxine Deitrich (née Andrea Herrington). She ran the Joy of Satan, a theistic Satanist group that shared Herrington's local NSM mailing address. The revelation of these ties upset some NSM members, a number of whom were followers of Christian Identity. The NSM's leader, Jeff Schoep, tried to keep all parties happy but was unable to prevent a meltdown and membership exodus, which included Bill White. Schoep ended up having to remove Herrington to keep the ship afloat. Herrington turned around and formed a new group, the National Socialist Freedom Movement, which listed the Joy of Satan as a "comrade organization."[67]

And the Abraxas Clique networks have influenced Satanism well into the 2010s. The popular liberal Satanist group The Satanic Temple ended up mired in controversy at first because of ties to an Alt Right–affiliated lawyer. But the accusations against it took a darker turn when a 2003 radio show, co-hosted by future leader of The Satanic Temple Lucien Greaves, came to light. In it he appeared alongside those in the Abraxas Circle, including Metzger, Gilmore, and George Burdi (formerly Hawthorne). Reflecting themes common in the Circle, Greaves made vicious antisemitic and eugenicist statements.[68]

Order of Nine Angles

Britain's David Myatt is a neo-Nazi who is widely acknowledged as the leading figure in the O9A, which started in the 1970s. This theistic Satanist current has required followers to involve themselves in various extremes as part of their goal of coming in contact with, in scholar Nicholas Goodrick-Clark's words, "sinister forces in the cosmos." These acts can include human sacrifice, and followers are to take on "insight" roles in radical movements, such as Islamism and neo-Nazism. O9A has a decentralized structures based on local "nexions."[69]

Ryan Schuster was interested in Myatt, whose outlook he thought was similar to Mason's. The project was never completed, but while he was working on republishing *Siege*, Schuster also looked into creating an anthology of Myatt's writings and sent Mason two collections of them.[70] However, a theistic Satanism could hardly have been appealing to Mason, who by then was a Christian. There is no evidence of any further link or influence between the O9A and the milieu that facilitated the first two editions of *Siege*.

But O9A *did* have a large impact on the new followers that Mason collected starting in 2015. Members of the Atomwaffen Division were involved in it; like *Siege* itself, the directive to wallow in taboo extremes—such as the fetishization of mass murder and child pornography—fit into the "edgelord" internet culture which fueled the Alt Right. One of the more prominent Atomwaffen members was Joshua Caleb Sutter, the founder the Tempel Ov Blood, which followed O9A doctrines. Martinet Press, which he ran with his wife Jillian Scott Hoy, published material read inside the Atomwaffen network, including his post-apocalyptic novel *Iron Gates*, which was filled with sadistic sexual violence. This was not without internal controversy, and in 2018, it was reported that members were leaving over the fact that others were Satanists.[71]

Even the 2021 revelation that Sutter was an FBI informant did not shake O9A's influence in Atomwaffen circles.[72] After Mason announced that the group had folded, the remnants dutifully started splintering, with O9A being one of the flashpoints. In 2022, after one faction established itself as the National Socialist Order of Nine Angles (NSO9A), the seemingly intrinsic schismatic power of Nazi-Satanism once again came to the fore.

The group issued a new, sixth edition of *Siege* in 2023; it attacked not just Mason but also Manson, LaVey, and, most hallowed of all, Rockwell. In reply, Mason made a video accusing NSO9A of taking money from the federal government to make their expensive edition of *Siege*, which included color printing. Mason was particularly incensed by an animal sacrifice they had reportedly engaged in. He said, "this O9A thing seems to be a prime example of...unbalanced kooks" and "Satanism, it's garbage"—although exempting LaVey from his judgment.[73]

But whether they were linked to security services or not, NSO9A were the ones who channeled Mason's energy from the 1980s. While Mason may have been right in distinguishing O9A and LaVey philosophically, it was Atomwaffen and the NSO9A that continued the legacy of Nazi-Satanism that Mason had abandoned with his Christian turn. This new generation of neo-Nazi youth were all too happy to embrace this particular combination of taboo extremes. And if it infuriated their neo-Nazi elders—just as Mason had done to the adults around him when he joined the American Nazi Party at age 14—perhaps all the better.

Notes

1 Asbjørn Dyrendal, James R Lewis, and Jesper Aagaard Petersen, *The Invention of Satanism* (New York: Oxford University Press, 2016), pp.137, 173.

2 "History of the Church of Satan," *Church of Satan*, www.churchofsatan.com/history. Time is important to the Far Right, and in three different milieus in this study calendar dates are rendered differently than the standard calendar. Moynihan used a system of months taken from Wiligut and based on medieval German. In 1970s NSWPP correspondence, it was common to date years based on Hitler's birth year, 1889. And Gilmore's correspondence was similarly based on 1966—the year the Church of Satan went public. For more on time and the Far Right, see Alexandra Minna Stern, *Proud Boys and the White Ethnostate: How the Alt-Right Is Warping the American Imagination* (Boston: Beacon Press, 2019), chapter 3.

3 Zeena and Nikolas Schreck, compilers, "Anton LaVey: Legend and Reality," February 2, 1998, https://web.archive.org/web/20110716005836, http://satanism central.com/aslv.html. As befitting the insular nature of the reactionary counter-cultural elements in San Francisco, two Manson Family members, Susan Atkins and Bobby Beausoleil, had passing associations with the Church of Satan.

4 Starting in the '00s, academic literature about modern Satanism has proliferated. For general texts, see Chris Mathews, *Modern Satanism*; Jesper Aagaard Petersen, ed., *Contemporary Religious Satanism: A Critical Anthology* (London: Routledge, 2009); and Dyrendal, Lewis, and Petersen, eds., *The Invention of Satanism*.

5 "Evil Anyone?," *Newsweek*, August 16, 1971, p.56; Donald Nugent, "Satan Is a Fascist," [*The Month*, April 1972], p.119. At the end of his life, LaVey said, "I'm all for a police state; no messing around. There should be an armed guard on every street corner. The Israelis have the right idea: school bus drivers and MacDonalds managers carrying Uzis"; Shane & Amy Bugbee, "The Doctor Is in…" (interview with LaVey), *Church of Satan*, www.churchofsatan.com/interview-mf-magazine (originally in *MF Magazine #3* [1997]). Other claims about an affection for Nazi and Klan imagery in the early Church of Satan are cited in Mathews, *Modern Satanism*, p.140.

6 Michael Aquino, *The Church of Satan*, vol. 1, 8th ed. (San Francisco: Michael A. Aquino, 2013), ebook, chapter 32; Goodrick-Clarke, *Black Sun*, p.83; Anton LaVey, *The Satanic Mass* (Murgenstrumm, 1968), www.discogs.com/release/1166426-Anton-LaVey-The-Satanic-Mass

7 Goodrick-Clark, *Black Sun*, p.83. At the time, Aquino did not know that Kliphoth was a member of his organization. Grumboski, who had resigned as a priest, returned in December 1974 as an active Church member; Aquino, *The Church of Satan*, vol. 1, chapter 32.
   In 1977, Kliphoth led the Detroit NSLF. In 1980 he claimed he was Grand Dragon of the Michigan Klan, and worked with the NSM's Bill Russell to get a permit for a rally that August. *National Socialist* 2(1) Fall 1977, p.40; Ken Fireman and Luther Jackson, "Klan and Nazis want to rally in downtown Detroit Aug. 23," *Detroit Free Press*, June 5, 1980, p.19A, www.newspapers.com/image/98503976

8 Aquino, *The Church of Satan*, vol. 1, chapter 32. Rice had written Mason in 1988 that, "Anton was very close to many right wing types in the early '60s—he knew Frankhauser [sic], Burros, Midole [sic] & even claims Robert Shelton wanted the Klan to join forces with the Church of Satan!"; Rice to Mason, [between May 2 and 7], 1988 [Box 9, Folder 20]. Roy Frankhouser and Daniel Burros had both been in the American Nazi Party and the Klan, Madole led the National Renaissance Party, and Shelton was an important Klan leader who opposed the Civil Rights Movement. Other than Madole, who unquestionably knew LaVey, claims about the others should be taken with a grain of salt.

9 Aquino, *The Church of Satan*, vol. 1, chapter 32.

10 Ibid.

11 Aquino, *The Church of Satan*, vol. II, 8th ed. (San Francisco: Michael Aquino, 2013), ebook, Appendix 44; Tim Maroney, "The Nazi Trapezoid," *Temple of the Screaming Electron*, November 11, 1990, https://newtotse.com/oldtotse/en/religion/the_occult/trapezoi.html

12 Baddeley, *Lucifer Rising*, pp.213–14.

13 Anton Szandor LaVey, *The Satanic Bible* (New York: Avon Books, 1969), pp.67–68; *Speak of the Devil: The Canon of Anton LaVey*, dir. Nick Bougas, 1993, www.imdb.com/title/tt0183811. The outtake is at https://queersatanic.tumblr.com/post/667533119913689088/i-enjoy-the-implication-that-the-political-stance

14 Peter Gilmore and Peggy Nadramia, "Interview with Anton LaVey," *Black Flame* 4(3–4) 1993, p.7. Although not nearly to the extent common in the Abraxas Circle, LaVey made other misogynistic statements. This includes a bizarre passage in chapter 3 of *The Satanic Witch*, where he claimed that dominant men and women, as well as lesbians, "prefer sweet dressings, such as French, Russian, Thousand Island." Gay men, and women who are passive and submissive, "prefer Roquefort, bleu cheese, and oil and vinegar". But,

> The taste of sweet dressing, with its minty, tomato, spicy taste (plus the fact that it is most often used when seafood is incorporated in the salad) resembles the odor of a woman's sexual parts and is therefore agreeable to the archetypical male. Conversely, the aroma and taste of the strong, cheesy Roqueforts, blue cheese, oil, and vinegar, etc. is similar to the male scrotal odor and reminiscent of a locker full of well-worn jock straps. This is naturally subliminally appealing to predominantly heterosexual females, passive males and males with homophile tendencies.

Elsewhere, LaVey wrote that "Satanically speaking, I am against abortion. Yet I do consider a problem of overpopulation. Therefore, I advocate compulsory birth control" for parents deemed unfit. (Who was to do the deeming was not specified.) LaVey, "The Third Side: The Uncomfortable Alternative," *Satan Speaks!* (Port Townsend, Washington: Feral House, 1998), p.30.

15 "Anton LaVey" (interview by Michael Moynihan), *Seconds* #27, 1994 (.45 *Dangerous Minds*, p.183).

16 Moynihan and Søderlind, *Lords of Chaos*, pp.233, 236–37; the interviews were conducted between 1994 and 1996. For Aquino's comments, see *The Church of Satan*, vol. II, "Appendix 44: That Other Black Order."

17 LaVey, "A Plan," *Satan Speaks!*, p.20.

18 Ibid, p.22; see also, "The Jewish Question? Or Things My Mother Never Taught Me," pp.69–72. Later in life, some of LaVey's beliefs would be close to, if not cross into, conspiratorial thinking, such as his belief in "secret wars"; Dyrendal, "Hidden Persuaders and Invisible Wars: Anton LaVey and Conspiracy Culture," in Faxneld and Petersen, eds., *The Devil's Party*, pp.123–40.

Moynihan also told another story, true or not, about LaVey and Jews. In an interview, he talked about Hennecke Kardel's *Hitler: Founder of Israel* which, in his summary, "reveals that all of the main Nazi leaders of Germany in the 30s were actually Jews" who "had to commit the Holocaust" in order to establish Israel. (To add to the book's legitimacy, Moynihan ordered it from Metzger.) Moynihan said it was "one of the strangest conspiracy theories I've come across," although "maybe it's even true." Moynihan ordered multiple copies and sent one to LaVey, who was said to have "quite enjoyed it"; White and Moynihan dialogue on *Overthrow.com*

19 Schuster, "Introduction," *Siege*, p.32; "Black Arts Gaining Popularity," *Liberator* #6, April 1970, p.3. The epigraph is in SIEGE 12(9) September 1983, p.1, and is based on lines in *The Satanic Bible*; see "Book of Satan," III–IV, pp.32–34.

20 Most famous as the author of *The Poor Man's James Bond*, Saxon made a special amulet for Zeena LaVey's baptism and dedicated a book to her son Stanton. Blanche Barton, *The Secret Life of a Satanist: The Authorized Biography of Anton Szandor LaVey* (Los Angeles: Feral House, 1992), ebook, chapter Seven; Kurt Saxon, *Classic Ghosts and Vampires* (1978), https://archive.org/details/CLASSICGHOSTSTORIESANDVAMPIRES

21 Tommasi to [Baetter], November [13], 1970 [Box 21, Folder 30]. In 2008, *Conflict*—a British fascist magazine close to the International Third Position—published the booklet *Satanism and Its Allies: The Nationalist Movement Under Attack*. Named and shamed were Madole, Mason, Manson, Myatt, Bolton, the Church of Satan, the Abraxas Clique, and the American Front.

22 Mason interview with AAC (*Articles*, p.243); Burns/Mason, "Three Faces of Satanism." A longer version of the same argument appears as "1-800-HELL-YES" in *Out of the Dust*, vol. 2, pp.60–65 (written May 1996).

23 Rice to Mason, [between May 2 and 7] 1988 [Box 9, Folder 20].

24 Moynihan to Mason, March 8, 1991; Moynihan to Mason, May 1, 1991 [both Folder 11, Folders 1–4].

25 Mason said he received the autographed copy via Moynihan "around 1990." Mason, "Regarding the Church of Satan," *Siegeculture*, [fall 2017?], https://web.archive.org/web/20180104233010, https://www.siegeculture.com/regarding-the-church-of-satan; *Siege*, 2nd ed., p.xxx; *Siege*, 1st. ed., p.362. The third mention was a line that was anonymous in the original SIEGE, but credit was restored in the book; SIEGE 12(9) September 1984, p.4 (*Siege*, pp.488–89).

26 Burns/Mason, "Three Faces of Satanism"; *Articles*, pp.193–94; *Art That Kills*, p.191.

27 Mason interview in *Ohm Clock*, p.9 (*Articles*, pp.92, 97); Mason, "Universal Order," *Rise* (*Articles*, p.84).

28 Burns/Mason, "Three Faces of Satanism"; "Two Definitions of Freedom" and "Prophecy or Physics?," *Out of the Dust* vol. 2, pp.226, 243 (both written March 1997). See also Mason, *Revisiting Revelation*, pp.35, 79, 82.

29 Mason, "Regarding the Church of Satan."

30 "Radio Werewolf 1984–1988," *Nikolas Schreck*, www.nikolasschreck.world/discography/radio-werewolf-1984-1988; Schreck interview with Metzger/*Race and Reason* (video).

31 *Art That Kills*, p.123; "RADIO WEREWOLF - TRIUMPH OF THE WILL (EDIT) | Nikolas Schreck Zeena" (video), uploaded by SonOvBeherit, October 17, 2012, www.youtube.com/watch?v=xnJl60SMWKg

32 *Art That Kills*, pp.150–51; Schreck interview with Metzger/*Race and Reason* (video).

33 Parfrey to Mason, November 3, 1986 [Box 17, Folder 4]; Mason interview with Swezey and King (video).

34 "Radio Werewolf 1984–1988"; Parfrey to Mason, [February] 1987 [Box 17, Folder 4].

35 "Nikolas Schreck & Radio Werewolf's First Wally George's Hot Seat, 1987 (High Quality)" (video), uploaded by The Nikolas Schreck Channel, September 20, 2020, www.youtube.com/watch?v=v8eSWcQY2OE; "'80s 'Sicko, Freako' Goth Band Hilariously Hardtrolls This Kooky Conservative TV Host," *Dangerous Minds*, March 4, 2015, https://dangerousminds.net/comments/80s_sicko_freako_goth_band_hilariously_hardtrolls

36 "Radio Werewolf interviewed by Tom Metzger" (video), [1987], uploaded by Radio Werewolf Unofficial on April 18, 2018, https://altcensored.com/watch?v=SCwYTszhvNs; Metzger to Mason, [July to September] 1987 [Box 7, Folder 21].

37 Schreck, ed., *The Manson File*, pp.13, 29, 32, 33, 59, 90, 139–47.

38 "'80s 'Sicko, Freako' Goth Band"; Schreck interview with Metzger/*Race and Reason* (video).

39 Schreck interview with Metzger/*Race and Reason* (video).

40 Ibid; "Might Is Right 24-Hour Radio Special".

41 Schreck interview with Metzger/*Race and Reason* (video).

42 "8-8-88 Rally plus Interviews" (video).

43 "Interview with Nikolas and Zeena Schreck in *Obsküre Magazine* by Maxime Lachaud, September 2011," *Nikolas Schreck*, https://web.archive.org/web/20111104084231, http://www.nikolasschreck.eu/index.php?option=com_content&view=article&id=88%3Ainterview-with-nikolas-and-zeena-schreck-from-obskuere-magazine-by-maxime-lachaud-september-2011&catid=38&Itemid=57

44 Larson gave the title "First Family of Satanism" to his interview with Schreck and Zeena LaVey; "Bob Larson interviews Nikolas and Zeena Schreck" (video), uploaded by VMFA 312, August 4, 2012, www.youtube.com/watch?v=-BqAz27fx-8

45 @nikolas_schreck_official, Instagram, August 1, 2021, www.instagram.com/p/CSClkNziFsl; *Art That Kills*, p.149.

46 *Charles Manson Superstar* (video); Brian King to author, email, March 16, 2023; Nikolas and Zeena Schreck interview in *Obsküre Magazine*.

47 Radio Werewolf, *The Fiery Summons* (Gymnastic, 1989) and *The Lightning and the Sun* (Unclean Production, 1989), www.discogs.com/Radio-Werewolf-The-Fiery-Summons/master/291456, www.discogs.com/Radio-Werewolf-The-Lightning-And-The-Sun/release/188982

48 Rice interview in *Fifth Path*, p.11; Moynihan to Mason, March 7, 1990 [Box 5, Folder 9].

49 "Death in June: Douglas P. Interview by Robert Ward," *Fifth Path* #1, Spring 1991, p.10; Death in June, *Thè Wäll Öf Säcrificè* (New European Recordings, 1989), www.discogs.com/Dèäth-In-Jünè-Thè-Wäll-Öf-Säcrificè/release/255098

50 *Art That Kills*, p.143; "Radio Werewolf 1984–1988"; "New General Info Page on Zeena's Website," *Zeena*, www.zeenaschreck.com/general-info.html

51 Burns/Mason, "Three Faces of Satanism."

52 Coogan, "How 'Black' Is Black Metal?," p.48n43. For Parfrey's take on what happened between LaVey and RE/Search, see Parfrey, "If We're So Wrong." As he pointed out, LaVey did appear in a later RE/Search publication, however; V. Vale, ed., *Modern Primitives: An Investigation of Contemporary Adornment and Ritual* (San Francisco: RE/Search, 1995).

53 Parfrey interview in *Fifth Path* #4, p.24; Parfrey, "Introduction," LaVey, *Devil's Notebook* (Venice, California: Feral House, 1992). In 1994, LaVey also appeared on the S.W.A.T. album *Deep Inside a Cop's Mind* alongside Parfrey, Rice, Bougas, and Goad; S.W.A.T., *Deep Inside a Cop's Mind* (Amphetamine Reptile, 1994), www.discogs.com/release/818687-SWAT-Deep-Inside-A-Cops-Mind

54 *Black Flame* 3 (1–2) Summer 1991, p.12.

55 Gilmore to Moynihan, May 17, 1993 [Box 11, Folder 2].

56 Ibid.

57 Gilmore, review of *Siege*, *Black Flame* 4 (3–4) 1993, p.27.

58 A group picture of the four appears in *Art That Kills*, although it is incorrectly dated 1992. *Art That Kills*, p.235; Mason to author, January 1, 2023; Gilmore to Mason, March 8, 1994 [Box 18, Folder 34].

59 Gilmore to Moynihan, June 2, 1993 [Box 11, Folder 2]; "The Faustian Spirit of Fascism," *Black Flame*, p.13; Moynihan interview with *Heretic*.

60 *EXIT* #5; Rice interview in *Fifth Path*, p.8; Gilmore to Moynihan, June 2, 1993 [Box 11, Folder 2].

61 Coogan, "How Black," p.48n48.

62 Gilmore, "Pervasive Pantywaistism," *The Satanic Scriptures* (Baltimore: Scapegoat, 2007).

63 LaVey interview with Moynihan in *Seconds*, pp.56–61 (*.45 Dangerous Minds*, pp.178–83); LaVey interview with Moynihan in *Black Flame*, pp.4–7; Moynihan and Søderlind, *Lords of Chaos*, pp.232–40.

64 Gilmore, "LaVey Memorial" and "Anton LaVey: The Dr's Final Interview" (with Rice), *Seconds* #45, 1997, pp.62–71 (*.45 Dangerous Minds*, pp.184–89); Rice, "Remembering LaVey"; Parfrey, "The Tragedy of Anton LaVey"; Thorn, "Diabolical Machinations," *Black Flame* #15, 6(3–4), 2000, pp.6–10, 12–13, 18–19.

65 Goodrick-Clarke, *Black Sun*, pp.226–31; Bolton quote cited in a review of *The Heretic* in *Black Flame* 5 (1–2), 1994, pp.18–19.

66 K.R. Bolton, "Eugenics and Dysgenics," *Black Flame* 4 (3–4), 1993, p.43; "Satanic Dialectics," *Black Flame* 5 (1–2) 1994, pp.31–32; Moynihan and Søderlind, *Lords of Chaos*, p.313.

67 Alexander Zaitchik, "The National Socialist Movement Implodes," SPLC, *Intelligence Report*, Fall 2006, online October 19, 2006, www.splcenter.org/fighting-hate/intelligence-report/2006/national-socialist-movement-implodes; *The National Socialist Freedom Movement: Complete PDF of the Website*, p.47; "Bill White," *SPLC*, www.splcenter.org/fighting-hate/extremist-files/individual/bill-white

68 See Appendix 11, "The Satanic Temple."

69 Goodrick-Clarke, *Black Sun*, pp.216–24, 226.

70 Schuster to Mason, February 10, 2002 [Box 32, Folder 31].

71 Ariel Koch, "The Nazi Satanists Promoting Extreme Violence and Terrorism," *OpenDemocracy*, February 4, 2021, www.opendemocracy.net/en/countering-radical-right/nazi-satanists-promoting-extreme-violence-and-terrorism; Kelly Weill, "Satanism Drama Is Tearing Apart the Murderous Neo-Nazi Group Atomwaffen," *Daily Beast*, March 21, 2018, www.thedailybeast.com/satanism-drama-is-tearing-apart-the-murderous-neo-nazi-group-atomwaffen

72 Matthew Gault, "FBI Bankrolled Publisher of Occult Neo-Nazi Books, Feds Claim," *Vice*, August 25, 2021, www.vice.com/en/article/dyv9zk/fbi-bankrolled-publisher-of-occult-neo-nazi-books-feds-claim

73 Mack Lamoureux, "The Grandfather of Modern Neo-Nazism Is Fighting with Satanic Neo-Nazis Now," *Vice*, July 28, 2023, www.vice.com/en/article/3akvj9/neo-nazis-james-mason-fighting; "Satanic Exposé" (video), posted by SiegeKultur, May 3, 2023, https://odysee.com/@siegekultur:b/Satanic-Expos%C3%A9:6

PART V

Siege the Book (1989–1995)

16

THE BOOK AND THE RECEPTION

The Book

The first edition, bearing the full title of *SIEGE: The Collected Writings of James Mason* and dedicated to Charles Manson, weighed in at 434 pages. Although the copyright date was 1992, it was only released in April 1993. The excerpts from the newsletters were organized into sections by concept, and graphics were added. But it included writings from Joseph Tommasi, George Lincoln Rockwell, and Perry Warthan. This had the effect of emphasizing both guerilla warfare and Mason's American Nazi Party pedigree.

As with any anthology of this type, the arc of Mason's thought was collapsed as materials from different time periods were put together. Although this didn't have a tremendous effect overall, there were two things that it did flatten out. The first was how his views on Christianity changed. The second was the distancing from guerilla warfare, and even praise of mass murderers, as his pessimism grew and he moved away from the attack side and toward the dropping out.

Siege's initial cover design had Hitler, Rockwell, Tommasi, and Manson; it was used in pre-publication ads. But by November 1992, it was swapped out for Mason's original suggestion.[1] The new cover was simple but striking, consisting of the title in red against a black background. The spine and back sported the Storm logo: a black lightning bolt inside a red shield. The interior had a stark but clean minimalist design.

The front matter notes that "The Publisher/Author assume no liability for any use or misuse of the material presented herein" and specifies that the content does not "purport to represent the views of Charles Manson or any of his associates."[2] The text was changed slightly from the newsletters, although mostly to correct phrasing, grammar, typos, and tense. The thanks

DOI: 10.4324/9780429200090-22

list was short. It included Ed Reynolds, Thomas Thorn, Anton LaVey, Peter Gilmore's *Black Flame*, Adam Parfrey, and Robert Ward. The names were removed from all subsequent editions.[3]

Michael Moynihan's introduction, under the name M.M. Jenkins, started with "James Mason is a radical extremist. He has actively dedicated the better part of his life to principles which the average member of society would find terrifying, violent and vicious, if not outright insane." Mason's evolution from "mass strategy" to terrorism was described.[4]

Moynihan recounted Mason's origin story, which the neo-Nazi would repeat many times over the next decades: from a disillusioned student who found the American Nazi Party's address in a book, to joining the party and meeting William Pierce before leaving to navigate a landscape of splinter groups, up through his embrace of Manson and terrorism. Moynihan added his own desires as well in his suggestion that the book could be read either as an overview of a political current or as an advocate of it.

The main part of the book consisted of eight sections totaling 370 pages, as well as five appendix sections running almost 60 pages. The section titles were "The NSLF and the Move towards Armed Struggle," "National Socialism," "Conservatism and the Lost Movement," "The System," "Lone Wolves and Live Wires," "Strength and Spirit," "Leaders," and "Universal Order."

The appendices varied. There were two more Mason pieces: a transcription of his 1985 long-distance address to a Metzger gathering and excerpts from Mason's 1987 video interview with Brian King and Ken Swezey. Additionally, there were several documents from Tommasi's NSLF, including "Strategy for Revolution" and "Building the Revolutionary Party"; Warthan's *Terrorism* and "One Man's Armageddon"; short Rockwell pieces; the NSDAP's 25-point program; and Eric Volmar's "Crazy Men of Destiny" piece with Mason's commentary.

Helped out by the length of the book, Moynihan's editorial choices covered the main themes in SIEGE. The primary political difference was the much stronger focus on guerilla warfare in the book. There were two reasons for this. The creation of the section "The NSLF and the Move Towards Armed Struggle" obviously emphasized it. Second, the inclusion of Tommasi's NSLF writings in the appendix reiterated the theme again at the end of the book.

Additionally, numerous images were included that added greater weight to certain themes and reflected Moynihan's interests. There were, as expected, images of Hitler as well as photos of Mason at various points in his life. The most images—around 20—were related to Tommasi, including pages from the original *Siege*.

Manson had around ten. About 15 others (excluding Tommasi and Manson) highlighted the various killers and armed actors mentioned. NSWPP member-turned-serial killer Joseph Paul Franklin took up about a third of them. And about half a dozen images were directly related to the American Nazi Party.

The rest were scattered in subject, including Pierce (though, strangely, only one photograph—with Mason), the NSLF during both the Duffy and Hand eras, and Warthan. There was also a page of text from LaVey; although there was no direct contact between the two, the connection was clearly stressed. And, of course, Mason's flyers were featured.

Numerous epigraphs were also scattered throughout the book. Many were by Mason's fellow fascists: Hitler, Yockey, Rockwell, Tommasi, Reynolds, and Manson. But many were also leftists, including the anarchist Mikhail Bakunin, Bolshevik intellectual Leon Trotsky, and Chinese Communist leader Mao Zedong. Last, although Mason was still atheist at the time, even a Bible passage found its way in.

Siege could be ordered directly through Storm Books in Denver for $22, including postage.[5]

The Reception

While as a newsletter SIEGE was never popular, the book's first pressing did substantially better. Although it was still overlooked in general, the book garnered more attention from neo-Nazis than the newsletter had. But much more interest was generated from the "alternative culture." *Siege*'s novelty value, because of both Manson and the sheer extremism of Mason's politics, attracted the attention of a number of writers who gave it an unexpected boost.

After the grunge band Nirvana sold millions of copies of their 1991 album *Nevermind*, the underground culture took a commercial turn as it gained a larger audience; significant parts of it morphed into what now was called "alternative culture." One of the central media sources became the "alternative weekly" newspapers, which were the direct heirs of the 1960s underground newspapers, which Mason had so admired. Through Moynihan's connections and publicity work, Mason was featured in seven articles in these between 1993 and 1995—a publicity coup, considering the material.[6]

SIEGE had not attracted much interest between its cessation and Moynihan's resuscitation. There was a one-sentence mention, albeit with the all-important mailing address, of Universal Order in Ivan Stang's *High Weirdness by Mail: A Directory of the Fringe*, which—along with the reprints in *EXIT* and *The Manson File* (and undoubtedly *Apocalypse Culture*)—was, according to Mason, generating "a steady stream of inquiries."[7]

Marketing Plans

Not realizing how long it would take to actually be released, Moynihan started publicizing the book in 1991. Despite Mason's previous approach, which—looked at one way—was a path to complete self-marginalization, he had always hoped to gain more widespread appeal and was very explicit about his admiration for the public relations strategies of Rockwell and LaVey. In May 1991, Mason told Moynihan that one of the old movement's failures was because "one has to have access to the mainstream or else be nothing more than a cult."[8] Unlike the projects created by the typical "born losers" of his movement, neo-Nazi organizations and ideas had to "swim in the mainstream," just as Hitler had done.[9] Mason also said,

> Sensational publicity is a two-way street. We want the exposure and they (the reporters) want a hot scoop. They don't care how they have to twist things in order to scandalize the public and we don't care how badly they portray us as long as, to borrow from Hitler, they say <u>something</u>.[10]

In December 1990, Moynihan floated his plan to market *Siege* to countercultural youth who were not involved in neo-Nazi politics. Specifically, he wanted to court death metal and black metal fans. They were "obsessed with murderers and crime," and he estimated that 90 percent of the members of those bands were white.[11]

In the summer of 1991, Moynihan went over his promotional strategy in greater depth with Mason. The American Front's Bob Heick had offered help, and Moynihan had pitched an interview about *Siege* to George Petros.[12] Moynihan also suggested getting Mason on Bob Larson's show, and soon after Mason made a call-in appearance to the pastor's July 1991 "Manson Maniacs" show.

In 1991, Moynihan had sent out flyers, which generated some premature publicity. *Black Flame* and *Fifth Path* ran advance ads, and the latter a review as well.[13] In December 1992, musician David E. Williams also ran a short review in the Philadelphia alternative weekly *Welcomat*, telling readers they could finally hear "what a real Nazi thinks, unfettered by liberal censorship."[14] (Mason described Williams as "a friend of Michael's," and Moynihan would promote him in the coming years.[15])

Reactions and Reviews

When *Siege* was finally released, the flyer accompanying it led with Metzger's exhortation that "Everyone should read this book!" The book was proclaimed to be the "'bible' of the furthest extremes of radical thought," "The *Mein Kampf* of the '90s," and the "mind fuck of the century."[16]

Accolades from friends rolled in. Parfrey was the first; he called Mason and reportedly "sounded awe-struck." Boyd Rice was also impressed, saying "one can open it at any point and find something good."[17] Nick Bougas and Peter Sotos were likewise enamored. Williams likened it to a carnival with Ferris wheels shaped like swastikas.[18]

One of the more surprising admirers was Martin Kerr, Tommasi's old enemy and an NSWPP stalwart who became a founding member of the New Order. Kerr had also been quietly in touch with Mason for many years, even after the latter quit the party and was attacking its leader Matthias Koehl and had received copies of SIEGE as part of a literature trade. Kerr had previously told Mason that, "Even if you don't come up with the right answers each time, you invariably ask the right questions and raise the right issues." After seeing *Siege*, he described it as "truly a magnificent production: it exceeded my expectations and it is unsurpassed by anything else in book form I have seen in my 27 years in the Movement." Kerr also said he would write a review, although he never got around to it.[19]

While Kerr's perspective must have seemed extremely unlikely considering the source, in another way it made perfect sense. Those in the same political cohort tend to struggle with the issues most prominent in their day. This can lead to a strong agreement over what needs to be addressed, among those who have a strong disagreement over what approach to take. This is because the source of that disagreement stems from having arrived at different answers to the same questions.

But the most important support came from two people: Tom Metzger and Peter Gilmore of the Church of Satan. Both went out of their way to publicize *Siege* and its creators. Gilmore was effusive about the book, and he wrote to both Moynihan and Mason to say so. He also reviewed the book in *Black Flame*, where he recommended it to Satanists.[20]

Neo-Nazi Reactions

Despite their disagreement over Manson, Metzger pulled out the stops for his comrade. The SPLC lawsuit had not stopped the *WAR* newspaper, *Race and Reason*, or Metzger's revolutionary ardor. He distributed *Siege*, getting a box immediately upon its release, which was available for purchase directly through him. It sold well, and in the ensuing months, Metzger received steady shipments of more. A few years later, Mason said that Metzger was "probably" responsible for half of the book's distribution.[21]

In July 1993, he put Mason on the cover of his newspaper and gave him a guest editorial in that issue. At the end of the month, Metzger flew Mason out to California and taped a three-part interview for *Race and Reason*.[22] Metzger called *Siege* "435 pages of hot revolutionary-style White propaganda" and "a terrific book" that was "going to be a high-water mark" for their movement. During the interview, Metzger repeatedly gave out Storm's address so people could get in contact directly.[23]

Metzger also provided Mason with the largest platform he would reach in the 1990s. During a 1993 appearance on the nationally televised show *The McLaughlin Report*, Metzger held up *Siege* and told John McLaughlin to read it in order to "bring yourself up to speed" on the revolutionary mood allegedly brewing in the United States. Metzger's promotional work caused Mason to gush, "Tom is the greatest thing going now."[24]

After *Siege* was out for a while, Moynihan and Mason portrayed it as being blacklisted by the neo-Nazi milieu. Mason went so far as to say it was "banned" and gave two reasons for this. One was jealousy because its design was a "technical masterpiece" (which it most certainly was if one was comparing it with a typical low-production value neo-Nazi publication). The other was that he spoke a "truth" that contradicted "the worlds of fantasy" that other movement leaders lived in. Additionally, Moynihan claimed that while "right wingers and Nazis mostly hated or ignored it...the most enthusiastic responses came from leftists."[25]

But given how little attention the original newsletter had gotten among White Supremacists, the book was a comparative success. (It is also not clear who "banned" it—or what that would have even consisted of.) The lack of attention to the book in 1993 was most likely due to a rejection of the 'Manson as leader' position, the praise of serial killers and mass murderers, the rejection of traditional political organizing, and Mason's personal alienation from and animosity to other movement leaders.[26]

While *Siege* wasn't shouted from every White Supremacist's rooftop, it received more attention than Mason and Moynihan copped to. Reviews, ads, and interviews appeared in a variety of movement periodicals, including Kerry Bolton's *Heretic*; the neo-Nazi journal *Plexus*; two American Front publications, *Greystorm* and *Revolutionary Nationalist*; and several fanzines, including *Ohm Clock*.[27]

Other than Metzger's outreach, the largest White Supremacist platform *Siege* received was in *Resistance*, a glossy music and politics magazine run by George Eric Hawthorne. The magazine was a companion to the record label of the same name; it mainly played to the base readership of Nazi skinheads but also covered other music genres.

During a January 1995 meeting in Denver, Hawthorne discussed the idea of a contribution from Mason, which he sent quickly afterward. Before it appeared, however, Hawthorne wrote about his opinions on Manson, saying "I still don't see the point—it's just too ephemeral, too vague for me." Hawthorne said David Lane of The Order, who by then was also a prisoner, was a much better choice for a leader, and his message was clearer. With Manson, however "we have to sort through hours of bullshit to get one piece of genius." Hawthorne did agree that Manson's popularity among youth could be used as an entry point to racist politics, although casting him as "the Leader of today is very short-sighted and restrictive—he's old, half-insane, in prison, and pretty odd." Nonetheless, Hawthorne admitted, "I could be wrong—best of luck."[28]

In the Spring 1995 *Resistance*, Mason's "Charles Manson: Illusion vs. Reality?" appeared. It elaborated on Mason's claim that Manson was "*the*

Leader today." Mason repeated his previous talking points, including the stress on both the cult leader's anti-system approach and charisma as well as the comparison to Rockwell and Hitler.[29] It was received like a slap in the face to many readers. The next issue ran two articles about it, pro and con. The introduction to them said,

> We were literally flooded with letters and phone calls from irate readers who firmly disagree with this concept, stating that any connection with Manson is pointless and damaging to our credibility. One distributor even clipped out the Manson article before distributing it.[30]

In the end, Mason's attempts to influence the larger neo-Nazi movement had extremely limited success. It seems that other than Metzger and the American Front, both of whom were already prone to violence, only fringe elements bothered to publicly take note of it.

As far as the "leftists" who gave the book "enthusiastic responses," Moynihan gave no examples. Even in the countercultural scene, *Siege* registered as little more than a curio. *NO LONGER A FANzine* appeared to be the only fanzine that was not already politically sympathetic which provided a platform after *Siege's* release; and one anarchist distributor carried it, albeit critically. If anything, the book functioned primarily as irrefutable evidence that Moynihan was directly involved in neo-Nazism.

It would only be much later that *Siege's* real impact would be felt.

Christian Talk

At the end of June 1993, Mason got his own episode on Bob Larson's *Talk Back*. Mason gave an exposition of his views about racism and antisemitism and Christianity—comparing Manson to Jesus. When Larson asked if Mason would kill him to achieve his goals, he replied, "If I thought it would do the job, Bob, I wouldn't hesitate.... But I know it wouldn't, so you can relax." In the room, although not on the air, were three other people: Moynihan, Rice, and a third man who apparently sieg-heiled Larson.[31] The show was billed as "Neo-Nazi Satanism" and released by Larson as a VHS cassette afterward; Moynihan bought copies to sell. About his appearance, Mason said, "He's using us and we're using him."[32]

Alternative Weekly Superstuds

That summer, Mason was on a publicity roll. July was particularly busy. In addition to Metzger promoting Mason in his magazine and on his TV show, two weeklies gave Mason substantial coverage. The *New York Press* ran what was a virtual three-page ad for *Siege*. It rehashed Mason's autobiography: his joining the American Nazi Party, going to the Cincinnati Work House, hooking up with the NSLF, and finally finding Manson. And it ended with Storm's mailing address for interested parties. If the space had been bought as advertising, it is hard to image that it would have read much differently.[33]

But the New York City paper was topped the next week by Denver's *Westword*. At least there was a local tie-in to help justify Alan Prendergast's seven-page cover story. Again, it regurgitated Mason's autobiography, adding some information about his Ohio arrest and his recent Larson appearance. Only if a reader made it to the end would they get to Prendergast's ritual denunciations that Mason's views were "not credible or even rational" and he had a "fairy-tale version of the Holocaust."[34]

Prendergast omitted any reference to his article in 1991 covering Moynihan's run-in with the Secret Service, which whitewashed him of any association with neo-Nazism. That article also claimed Mason wasn't a neo-Nazi, whereas Prendergast's 1993 piece reveled in this. More importantly, the second article acknowledged that Moynihan published *Siege* in Denver—but not that he edited it. Prendergast also failed to mention what must have been obvious: that Moynihan was working on the book at the time of the Secret Service raid he had written about.[35]

The *Westword* piece was another publicity coup for Moynihan and Mason. A picture was even taken at Mason's house of the two of them with Prendergast, and Mason went on a radio show with him.

Afterward, Mason praised Prendergast a second time: "He may be 'anti' but he's anti in a way that makes us look like superstuds or something."[36]

In October 1993, Jim Redden, founder of the Portland, Oregon weekly *PDXS*, wrote an article about Manson's continued popularity; a third of it was focused on Mason. A year later, the same paper would run a piece that included a plug for the Universal Order exhibit in Parfrey's upcoming art show. Steve Schultz interviewed Mason for the article, calling him "smart, articulate, well-read...funny and personable," and *Siege* "one of the better written and more interesting books on political theory that I have read in a long time." What Schultz did not write about was that Extreme Books, an anarchist mail-order book distribution he helped run, sold *Siege*.[37]

But the *piece de resistance* of the publicity wave was in Philadelphia's *Welcomat*. *Siege* had already received a short mention even before its release, but editor Jim Knipfel's "The Other Nazis" was a cover story.[38] Another seven-page feature, it triangulated the neo-Nazi-affiliated underground scene adroitly, profiling Parfrey, Rice, and Moynihan—and correctly positing Mason as a common denominator between them.

On the first page, Knipfel announced his slant by saying what people should be concerned about is not Far Right or neo-Nazi literature but rather new hate crime laws.[39] Knipfel was able to get unusually frank talk out of the

trio, even while repeating their talking points, giving them unchallenged platforms, mocking claims of neo-Nazi involvement, and throwing sand in the
eyes of critics. Parfrey, for example, got to expound on his ideas about hate
crime hoaxes. Knipfel let Rice laugh off accusations of neo-Nazi associations,
even as the musician admitted he had proactively reached out to Mason; the
article similarly let Moynihan off the hook.[40] And like the others, Knipfel
repeated Mason's spoon-fed autobiography, giving him extensive verbatim
quotes to promote his views.

Knipfel himself wrapped up the piece with his own commentary, which
was more sympathetic than the others. While distancing himself from antisemitic conspiracy theories and racial separatism, Knipfel condemned monitoring groups and activists "who are trying to silence those opinions and
viewpoints that they find offensive." In fact,

> so many people in the world seem to be striving for this sameness, this
> homogenization, that it's nice, in a way, to encounter someone so com-
> pletely outside the mindset which loves normality.
>
> We are *not* all created equal, and anyone who tries to force us to try to
> be is a greater danger to us than any Charles Manson or James Mason.[41]

He ends by giving the addresses for Feral House and Storm.[42]

The last piece of publicity of note was the Mason and Moynihan interviews in the summer 1994 *NO LONGER A FANzine* issue. As did other the
interviewers, the editor's commentary denounced Mason's views.[43] While the
interview with Moynihan ended up as the subject of years of discussion, the
Mason one was more prosaic. Mason gave his autobiography once again and
then answered questions about the Holocaust, free speech, American principles, other racist factions, and whether he had mellowed with age.

The *Siege* publicity blitz was nicely book-ended with the September 1994
art show in Seattle that Parfrey curated. Mason's assessment of its impact
was that "we'll be getting ripples off this from now on."[44] In total, Mason
garnered multiple features in weekly papers and fanzines and an appearance
on a national radio show—in addition to Metzger's promotional work and
Parfrey's art show. In July 1994, Moynihan said he'd sold just shy of 300
copies of *Siege*; Mason called this "phenomenal."[45]

Post-1995

Although Mason was in jail, *Siege* continued to draw attention and reviews.
Mason got a two-sentence description (albeit under the pseudonym Alex) in a
new afterword to Vincent Bugliosi's *Helter Skelter*. The genteel fascist magazine the *Scorpion* even ran a very fair-minded review in 1997—a surprise as the
periodical usually distanced itself from more orthodox forms of National

Socialism. In 1998, the music fanzine *Compulsion* did a three-page article on Mason's career. Last, even before the Alt Right, *Siege* also influenced newer White Supremacist activists, including the mystical Third Positionist group The White Order of Thule, who included it on their list of suggested readings.[46]

Notes

1 Mason to Reynolds and Beth, November 1, 1992 [Box 33, Folder 6]; *Siege* advertisement in *Black Flame*, p.12.
2 *Siege*, 1st ed., front matter.
3 The other two were Jo ("for the hospitality in Ohio") and US West Communications, whose office Moynihan had snuck into at night to make copies of the computer discs which were to be used to print it. *Siege*, 1st ed., front matter; Moynihan to Mason, June 17, 1992 [Box 11, Folder 2].
4 Jenkins/Moynihan, "Introduction," *Siege*, 1st ed., p.xi.
5 *Plexus* #13, January 1994, p.vii.
6 Jim Redden, "Manson Is My Co-Pilot," *PDXS* 3 (10) October 25, 1993, pp.3–4 (*Articles*, pp.63–65); Steve Schultz, "Marks of the Beast" pp.3–4 (*Articles*, pp.76–78); Strausbaugh, "Siege Mentality," pp.9–11 (*Articles*, pp.45–48); Prendergast, "Beyond the Pale," pp.23–24, 26–28, 30, 32 (*Articles*, pp.50–58); Knipfel, "The Other Nazis," pp.12–13, 22–26 (*Articles*, pp.68–75); Prendergast, "Double Exposure," pp.13, 15–16, 18, 20, 22 (*Articles*, pp.112–17).
7 Ivan Stang, *High Weirdness by Mail: A Directory of the Fringe—Mad Prophets, Crackpots, Kooks & True Visionaries* (New York: Simon & Schuster, 1988), p.205; Mason to Moynihan, September 20, 1990; Mason to Moynihan October 20, 1990 [both Box 5, Folder 9]; Mason to Rice, September 19, 1988 [Box 9, Folder 20].
8 Mason to Moynihan, May 28, 1991 [Box 11, Folders 1–4].
9 Mason to Moynihan, June 10, 1991[Box 11, Folders 1–4].
10 Mason, "Introduction," *Articles*, p.9.
11 Moynihan to Mason, December 5, 1990 [Box 5, Folder 9]; Moynihan to Mason, September 23, 1991 [Box 11, Folders 1–4]. The author agrees with Moynihan's assessment of the racial composition of the death and black metal fan base.
12 Moynihan to Mason, June 10, 1991 [Box 11, Folders 1–4].
13 *Siege* advertisement, *Black Flame* 3 (1–2), p.12; *Siege* advertisement, *Fifth Path* #2, p.45; *Siege* review, *Fifth Path* #4, pp.72–73.
14 David E. Williams, "Oh Unholy Night," *Welcomat*, December 9, 1992, p.43, reprinted in *Siege* press kit; Moynihan to Mason, January 6, 1993 [both Box 11, Folder 2].
15 Mason to Reynolds/Beth Helen, January 23, 1993 [Box 33, Folder 6]; "David E. Williams - Decadent Priest in the Garden of Earthly Delight" (interview by Moynihan), *Fifth Path* #5, pp.42–44.

   Williams was also one of the first to receive a copy of *Siege*; his copy was signed by both Moynihan and Mason. Although Williams said he wasn't a neo-Nazi—"outside my masturbation fantasies, of course"—nonetheless "in this cowardly chickenshit era--when every shove-food-in-her-cunt feminist is viewed as an 'aesthetic terrorist' and Rush Limbaugh (yawn) is viewed as a 'right-wing lunatic' Mason refreshingly delivers the goods on both counts." Williams also asked if he could rent Moynihan's mailing list; David E. Williams to Moynihan, May 24, 1993 [Box 11, Folder 2].
16 *Siege* promotional flyer, [1992 or 1993] [Box 11, Folders 1–4]; Mason to Moynihan, March 10, 1990 [Box 5, Folder 9].

17 Mason to Moynihan, May 7, 1993; Moynihan to Mason, May 28, 1993 [both Box 11, Folder 2]; Mason to Reynolds and Beth Helen, May 7, 1993 [Box 33, Folder 5].

18 Mason to Reynolds and Beth Helen, May 17, 1993 [Box 33, Folder 5]; Moynihan to Mason, May 28, 1993; David E Williams to Moynihan, May 24, 1993 [both Box 11, Folder 2].

19 Kerr's box in the Kansas archive [Box 10, Folder 7] contains correspondence starting in 1977 (although already ongoing at that point); he also wrote Mason in prison. Today, Kerr has changed his mind about *Siege*, saying that while its "popular in accelerationist circles, it is far outside the mainstream of contemporary NS thought and is irrelevant." Kerr to Mason, August 25, 1992; Kerr to Mason, May 21, 1993; Kerr to author, email, August 14, 2023.

20 See Chapter 15, "Nazi-Satanism."

21 Mason to Reynolds and Beth Helen, July 19, 1993; Mason to Reynolds and Beth Helen, October 19, 1993 [both Box 33, Folder 5]; *WAR* 12(6) July 1993, p.10; Mason interview in *Strength through Joy Productions* (*Articles*, p.146).

22 *WAR* 12(6) [July] 1993, cover, p.2; Knipfel, "The Other Nazis," p.25 (*Articles*, p.74).

23 Mason interview with Metzger/*Race and Reason* (video).

24 Metzger's appearance on *The McLaughlin Report* was included as the introduction to an edited video that Mason made of his *Race and Reason* interview for Denver Community Television in 2003. Mason on Metzger/*Race and Reason* (video); Mason quoted in Knipfel, "The Other Nazis," p.25 (*Articles*, p.74).

25 Mason, "Introduction to the Second Edition," *Siege*, p.16; Mason interview with AAC (*Articles*, p.237); Moynihan interview in *Hit List*, p.52.

26 Just after its release Mason said, "A few 'Movement' types have really crapped out but those were the ones we expected to do that also. Even though we made certain they received copies they've either commented very little or not at all. Green with envy, I'd say." But it's hard to say who would be the "movement types" that he was both on good terms with and ideologically sympathetic to; Robert Miles and, possibly, Harold Covington were the most likely candidates. Mason to Reynolds and Beth Helen, July 19, 1993 [Box 33, Folder 5].

27 *Siege* review, *The Heretic* #5, [1993?], pp.15–16, clipping [Box 11, Folder 2]; *Siege* review, *Plexus* #13, January 1994, pp.5–6 [Box 17, Folder 12]; *Revolutionary Nationalist* [1994], pp.3–4, 19 [Folder D7941]. The fanzines were *Rise, Regal Scroll, Ohm Clock*, and *Warcom Gazette* (*Articles*, pp.83–97, 110).

28 Mason to Hawthorne, January 15, 1995; Hawthorne to Mason, March 20, 1995 [both Box 9, Folder 31].

29 Mason, "Charles Manson: Illusion vs. Reality," *Resistance* #4, Spring 1995, pp.20–22 (*Articles*, pp.101–4).

30 "The ManSon Debate: Two of Our Readers Take Their Sides," *Resistance* #5, Fall 1995, p.31 (*Articles*, p.105). Mason thought the unsigned letters were from Moynihan (pro) and Covington (anti); Mason, "Introduction," *Articles*, p.10. Mason had previously asked Reynolds to submit a response as well; Mason to Reynolds, May 1, 1995 [Box 33, Folder 4].

31 Moynihan, Rice, and Mason interview with Larson/*Talk Back* (video); *Articles*, pp.183, 189.

32 *Articles*, pp.183, 186–89; Mason quoted in Prendergast, "Beyond the Pale," p.32 (*Articles*, p.58).

33 Strausbaugh, "Siege Mentality" (*Articles*, pp.46–48).

34 Prendergast, "Beyond the Pale," p.32 (*Articles*, p.58).

35 Prendergast, "Beyond the Pale," p.24 (*Articles*, p.53).

36 *Articles*, pp.8, 59; Mason to Reynolds/Beth Helen, August 13, 1993 [Box 33, Folder 5].

37 Redden, "Manson Is My Co-Pilot," pp.3–4 (*Articles*, pp.63–65); Steve Schultz, "Marks of the Beast," p.4 (*Articles*, p.78); "Extreme Books Catalog 1994," www. spunk.org/texts/altern/catalog/sp000286.txt. In 1994, Redden also co-authored an article with Parfrey; "Patriot Games," *Village Voice*, October 11, 1994, pp.26–31.
38 Knipfel, "The Other Nazis," cover, pp.12–13, 22–26 (*Articles*, pp.68–75).
39 Ibid, p.12 (*Articles*, p.69).
40 Ibid, pp.13, 23–24 (*Articles*, pp.70, 72–73).
41 Ibid, p.26 (*Articles*, p.75).
42 Ibid.
43 Gervasi introduction to Mason interview in *NO LONGER A FANzine*, p.10.
44 Mason interview in *Ohm Clock*, p.10 (*Articles*, p.98).
45 Prendergast, "Beyond the Pale," p.32 (*Articles*, p.58).
46 Bugliosi, *Helter Skelter*, "Afterword"; Dominic Hampshire, "Siege Mentality" (review), *Scorpion* #18, Spring 1997, pp.34–35 (*Articles*, pp.60–62); "Universal Order," *Compulsion* #3, 1998, pp.49–51 (*Articles*, pp.169–72); "Study List," *Crossing the Abyss* #5, March 1999, p.64.

PART VI

Coda (1995–2017)

17

FROM PRISON TO REVIVAL

With the release of *Siege*, James Mason's life changed. He soon started dating a young teenager, but an incident with a gun ended up with Mason going to prison in 1995. By that time, he had been a neo-Nazi for 30 years. His political philosophy, expounded in SIEGE, had been completed almost a decade before. Mason continued to write in prison and then published a number of books afterward, where he developed his racist UFO-Christian spiritual beliefs. But from then on, his political writings were just footnotes and clarifications to what he had already said. After 2004, he entered a period of minimal activity even of this kind, occasionally reprinting his works, although *Siege* remained a book of interest to White Supremacists. Only in the 2010s with his rediscovery by the new wave of militant neo-Nazis, who published a third edition of *Siege* and then contacted him, did his political work continue—this time, as a mentor to young men.

Teenage Trouble

The book came out in the spring 1993, and throughout the summer Mason was busy doing media. But 41 years old and single, he was lonely and asked Moynihan if he knew "any available females" in the movement. Moynihan did know one, a 15-year-old named Eva who had been previously engaged to Rice. Her age must have only been attractive to Mason, who believed that "underage girls are sheer dynamite."[1] Mason had also known her father through neo-Nazi circles, meeting him in 1977 when he accompanied the NSWWP's Allen Vincent on a visit to Ohio. Eva arrived in Las Animas in December 1993 and proceeded to have a short and chaotic relationship with Mason which ended up changing his life.[2]

DOI: 10.4324/9780429200090-24

Eva corresponded with serial killers; Richard Ramirez, the "Night Stalker," would call their house from prison. She became an object of attention in her own right, and the couple flew to New York City for her appearance on Sally Jessy Raphael's popular talk show.[3] Eva also made two appearances on the Chicago TV talk show *Bertice Berry Show*. (Mason was apparently visible in the audience during one.) In the second episode, "Charles Manson is My Role Model," she appeared alongside her sister as well as Sandra Good, Vincent Bugliosi, and Sharon Tate's sister, Patti.[4]

Mason said he soon tired of the relationship, and Eva went home with her sister after the second show. But in March 1994 she returned to Las Animas, where Mason was spending time with another 15-year-old. Soon the three started hanging out together, and one evening Mason took nude photos of the new girl. By the end of that month, Mason was arrested and charged with "two counts of sexual exploitation of a child and two counts of contributing to the delinquency of a minor."[5]

Mason spent all April in prison, and only made bond in early May. But in the meantime, Eva had already found a new boyfriend, a 19-year-old Latino man. Tensions continued between Eva and Mason—unsurprisingly considering their past relationship and her new love. Things came to a head during an argument during which Mason pulled out a gun and threatened them. Arrested for felony menacing, he was back in jail three weeks after he had been released.[6] By June, he was out again and in August 1994 gave up on small-town life and moved to Denver. Mason originally faced 32 years, but because of problems with prosecuting the case, the original charges were dropped in exchange for him pleading guilty to menacing. Mason was sentenced to three years in prison.[7]

Prison

In early 1995, just before prison, Mason was walking around Denver when he had a spiritual experience that he compared to being in a parallel dimension. Mason had already engaged with a variety of spiritual themes, and despite his avowed atheism, this event set the stage for his turn to Christianity.[8]

In the first part of May 1995, Mason reported to prison. Later that month, Las Animas residents received anonymous letters about a local law enforcement officer and his involvement with the same teenage girls Mason had been associating with. This led, in September 1995, to Alan Prendergast's second *Westword* feature specifically on Mason, which recounted his legal troubles in great detail.[9]

Mason kept his profile up in among readers of White Supremacist publications. The *Resistance* article about Mason's view of Manson appeared in the spring 1995 issue, and the letters about it in the fall. Mason was even able to do a fanzine interview over the phone, which would be one of several new pieces that appeared during his prison years.[10]

As he settled into prison, Mason continued his prolific writing, publishing 24 articles between 1995 and 1997 in Tom Metzger's *WAR*. Metzger had always supported White Supremacist political prisoners, and he dutifully corresponded with Mason during this time.[11] In winter 1996, one of Mason's supporters offered to set up a website for his new writings. Of this, Mason said, "Our mutually formulated strategy for the site was to 'hook' the interest of readers by leading with titles dealing with paranormal phenomena, etc., and injecting along with that a more traditional line of movement thought." The new site, *Universal Order*, was live by summer 1997, at a time when websites were still uncommon. Run by two supporters, Mason wrote short pieces published on the site under the name Robert Burns.[12] His musings focused on Christianity and other spiritual issues, Hitler, UFOs, aliens, Jews, and the pyramids—themes he would continue to explore in his post-prison books. The website also became the primary writing outlet.[13]

The website was especially important for Mason as his new religious turn was alienating many of those who had previously published him. For example, in 2000, Mason said, "I wrote for Metzger solidly for several years but we parted ways once I began to get heavily into the Bible." Nonetheless, the two retained an affinity for each other.[14]

From 1997 to 2001, several recordings were released with either Mason on them or liner notes written by him. He was featured on an album by the band Ethnic Cleansing and two compilations from Warcom Media, and a collection was issued of his appearances on a Canadian radio show. He also wrote liner notes for a Mudoven album and a reissue of a 1966 George Lincoln Rockwell speech.[15]

In late September 1997, Mason was released after serving time in a maximum-security prison under Colorado's mandatory parole for those serving two years.[16] After three weeks, however, he was re-arrested for what he called "a bogus series of parole violations like pornography and association with extremist groups." But this happened just as the Denver streets were filled with racist violence. The city had already been the scene of a murder by The Order in 1985. November 1997 started with two skinheads shooting it out with police, followed by another killing a police officer, after which two other skinheads (one of whom had American Front tattoos) murdered an immigrant.[17]

These events prompted the authorities to move Mason out of the county jail where he was being held and put him in Administrative Segregation in a more secure prison. He did not waste the opportunity, however, and once inside he went back to work; in winter of 1997, wrote a short book about the Bible, *One Verse Charlies*.[18]

Angered that he had been re-arrested, Mason retained legal representation "recommended to me by one friendly reporters on the staff of a Denver paper"—Alan Prendergast.[19] In February 1998, Mason's lawyers were able to get him back out after successfully arguing that his parole was wrongly revoked. Living in Pueblo, Colorado, he edited both volumes of what would later be released as *The Robert Burns Collection*.[20]

But he was arrested a second time for parole violations in October 1998. Tired of fighting with the authorities, Mason "self-revoked" and went back inside to finish his sentence. In the first part of 1999, he said he wrote three separate hundred-page essays. That fall, however, the *Universal Order* website was shut down by its host for its content.[21]

Reflecting on his prison experience, Mason said, "Basically I had a good time because the Colorado prison system is one of the most advanced in the country. You can meet quite a few interesting people." He even appreciated his time spent in solitary confinement, which gave him calm—and his own cell. And he was given the opportunity to have productive political discussions with non-Aryans. Ryan Schuster's biographical essay on Mason even claims that "Muslim Negroes thanked him for educating them about the Jewish Question."[22]

On August 25, 1999, Mason was finally released. He settled down in Denver, where he would stay.[23]

Second Edition *Siege*

Mason was particularly active in the years immediately after his release, culminating in a new edition of *Siege*. In 2000 alone, he self-published five of the books he had written in prison: *One Verse Charlies* in January (and already reissued in June), *The Robert Burns Collection* (the second edition was in May) *The Theocrat* in March, *When We Were All Jews* in April, and *Revisiting Revelation* in July. In 2002, he put out the second volume of *The Robert Burns Collection* and the next year *Articles of* WAR, an anthology of his essays for Metzger, and *Articles and Interviews*, a collection of clippings and publications. Mason also wrote two entries for the *Encyclopedia of White Power*, edited by Jeffrey Kaplan and released on a scholarly press in 2000.[24]

Kaplan wasn't the only scholar interested in Mason, though. Another who found Mason was Greg Johnson—but unlike the others, he was a recent convert to White Supremacy. Finishing his PhD in philosophy at the time he reached out, Johnson had had more traditional right-wing views before meeting Moynihan's collaborator Joshua Buckley in late 1999 or early 2000. After this, Johnson took the plunge into White Supremacist politics, inspired partly by a 2001 meeting with William Pierce, one of the few people in the movement who held a doctorate.[25] (In 2010, Johnson would found the website *Counter-Currents*, which became the premier U.S. website for intellectual fascist thought and an influence on the Alt Right.)

After being given his address by Moynihan, Johnson wrote Mason in May 2001 to ask for help in finding letters from Savitri Devi for a collection he was assembling. Johnson told Mason, "I want to tell you how much I admire both you and your work," especially the "Neo-Nazi Satanism" video with Bob Larson. "I have also read <u>Siege</u> and find myself in complete sympathy with your evaluation of Charles Manson & the world situation in general." Despite his academic background, Johnson did not want to become a professor. Instead, "I and a friend are creating a publishing imprint…. Our aim is to transfuse some of the intellectual energy and vision of the European right to the English-speaking world."[26]

In September 2001, Johnson's friend Ryan Schuster wrote Mason and offered to release a new edition of *Siege*—an offer Mason happily accepted.[27] Schuster told him their new publishing imprint was called Black Sun and was owned by the non-profit organization the Foundation for Human Understanding (FHU). Schuster said it was founded in 1973 but since had "fallen into complete inactivity."[28]

The FHU was run by aging opponents of racial integration who sought to buttress academic arguments for biological racial differences, especially in intelligence. In addition to publishing several books, FHU donated copies to university libraries and even took an ad out in the *New York Times Book Review* to promote its views.[29]

This new FHU imprint took these politics further, however. Black Sun planned on publishing an array of fascists and their precursors: in addition to Savitri Devi, they hoped to release volumes by de Gobineau, Alain de Benoist, and Ernst Jünger.[30]

A proposed mission statement that Schuster sent to Mason described Black Sun Publications as seeking to fight the "Judaic Death Force" by inspiring an "age of pogroms." Unlike the FHU, Black Sun intended to publish books with "a decided National Socialist fervor."[31] Schuster said that they did not agree with all aspects of National Socialism but that, like so many others in Mason's orbit,

> we do recognize the inherent superiority of any spirited system of governance that utilizes a healthy confluence of Nature-based imperatives such as: agrarianism, eugenics, Malthusian doctrine, Social Darwinism, and unilateral opposition to egalitarian fantasies.[32]

(A sanitized version of the mission statement appeared on Black Sun's website, but by then it referred to "Death Forces" which were opposed by a "Vitalist outlook." Apparently, even those promoting neo-Nazi terrorism felt the need to publicly soft-pedal their views.[33])

In November 2001, after going to Denver to meet Mason in person, Schuster sent him an advance of $1,750 for four books. In addition to *Siege, The Theocrat*, and *Revisiting Revelation*, there was also the Rockwell manuscript that Mason had unsuccessfully lobbied Adam Parfrey to publish.[34] But it, too, would meet the same fate.[35]

In May 2002, Schuster returned to Denver. He videotaped a long interview with Mason that became the basis for the new introduction to *Siege*, which has since become Mason's standard biographical account. During the trip, Schuster also recorded a presentation that Mason gave to a class at the University of Phoenix in Denver.[36] (This was one of several classroom talks Mason gave over the years.) After Mason's revival, both videos have continuously been circulated online.

That July, Mason received a big blow when his mentor William Pierce died. Pierce's careful approach of trying to recruit members he considered to be high-caliber, while largely staying clear of attention-grabbing actions, helped him steadily build his organization, with himself as its center. The fame of *The Turner Diaries* didn't hurt either, especially after the 1995 Oklahoma City bombing. The National Alliance had 1,400 dues-paying members, 17 full-time staff, and an annual gross income of $1 million around the time of Pierce's death.[37] But just beforehand, Mason called him after seeing him on TV, and the two old friends made dinner plans. But Pierce was to die the night of the meeting, and Mason would instead give a eulogy at a Denver memorial hosted by the National Alliance. His debt to Pierce was so great that Mason dedicated his anthology *Articles and Interviews*, which he released the next year, to his old mentor.[38]

During the spring of 2003, Mason wrote a new preface and Schuster a new introduction for the edition. Additionally, Parfrey offered to help Schuster with advice for the new edition. In May, Mason gave another talk at the same university. Schuster had since moved to Bozeman, Montana but was planning on making a trip to Denver and come to the talk; Rice had said he would be there as well. However, in the end, neither made it.[39]

According to Mason, Black Sun released the second edition of *Siege* in mid-2003; it had a limited-edition print run of 500. The interior had been reprinted from plates from the first edition, but there were a number of changes.[40] To emphasize the book's argument, the new cover was a photo of the wreckage of the World Trade Center after the 9/11 massacre by Al-Qaeda, which killed almost 3,000 people. Moynihan's introduction was gone, replaced with new pieces by Mason and Schuster, and the only people thanked were "Brian and Sean of World View Productions" in Boston, who had run Mason's website while he was in prison.[41]

In addition to new images, the other main piece added was a new appendix, "Death Throes." It included newspaper clippings and letters from Joseph Tommasi and the various murderers that Mason wrote about. The second edition's reception was far more muted than the first,[42] but it, too, sold out.

Black Sun's ambitious publishing plans did not materialize. The Rockwell book was announced on the Black Sun website, but like *The Theocrat* it never appeared. In fact, the only other title Black Sun would publish was Savitri Devi's *And Time Rolls On*, edited by Johnson, in 2005.[43]

The Quiet In-Between

Mason continued on on his own. In 2003, he released two books. *Articles and Interviews* was a collection of clippings and pictures of both himself and those associated with him, including the National Socialist Liberation Front. His pieces for Metzger's newspapers were anthologized as *Articles of WAR*. That year, he also finished the manuscript of *Out of the Dust*, mostly a collection of writings during his prison period. (A publisher couldn't be found, however, and the manuscript would only be released after his rediscovery.) Mason also started making videos for the cable-access station Denver Community Television (DCTV). Three were about Rockwell and used the materials from Mason's ill-fated book.[44] Another three videos were interviews with Mason himself: by Brian King and Ken Swezey (originally from 1987), Metzger (1993, with additional material added), and Schuster (2002). And Sherif Ali, a black talk show host at the station, had Mason on as a guest in June 2004.[45]

Mason is often seen as having retired from any public work as a National Socialist between this period and his rediscovery. In fact, at least through 2010, he continued to put out new releases. By 2005, he had published several new books: *Race, Religion and Politics*; *The Lost Cause*; and *Horror: Desensitization, Conditioned Reflexes, and Thought Control*. In 2008, he released the third edition of *The Theocrat*.[46] He also made CDs of Rockwell material as well as a reissue of two 7" singles put out in 1964 on Hatenanny, the American Nazi Party's record label.[47] In 2009 and 2010, Mason published *Tyranny of Freedom* and *Harvest of Conspiracy: 1900-2000*.[48] (Additionally, in 2006 the website *Solar General* digitized the second edition of *Siege*, which showed the continuing interest in it while making it freely available online.[49])

Except to insiders, Mason had largely fallen off the map. "Rockwell's Men" were largely retiring from politics or dying. The neo-Nazi movement itself was in the doldrums, too. Overtaken by the militias in the mid-1990s, the last major neo-Nazi event before Charlottesville was a 2002 anti-Israel rally in Washington, DC led by the National Alliance which attracted up to 300 people.[50] The patriotic neoconservatism of George W. Bush's administration, with its wars-turned-occupations in Afghanistan and Iraq, sapped the energy of all of the U.S. Far Right. Even when the liberal Barack Obama was elected the first black president in 2008, it was the militia and Patriot movement which burst forth in reaction, generating new groups and movements like the Oath Keepers and Tea Party. And although there was a spasm of violence in 2009, generally White Supremacists were nonplussed by Obama; many felt the racist ship had long sailed in the United States. For his part, Mason was still in Denver, working as "head of security for several K-Marts."

But things would change for Mason, and in 2015 *Siege*'s time had come. The Alt Right had started its meteoric rise and with it the new wave of aspiring neo-Nazi terrorists on the *Iron March* website. They republished *Siege*, injecting its ideas, and the #ReadSiege hashtag, into a visibility it heretofore had never achieved. The Atomwaffen Division made contact with Mason, and he acted as an advisor to them, while members reissued his books. Mason welcomed acolytes who made pilgrimages to meet him; no doubt, in this, he saw echoes of his youthful journey to the American Nazi Party's headquarters.

Finally, he was now able to attract alienated youth, enamored with National Socialism and mass murderers. Having started as one of its youngest adherents, Mason now took his place as an elder among National Socialists. He could now pass on his decades of experience to eager young men to whom he taught the philosophy of "TOTAL ATTACK or TOTAL DROP OUT!" Granted, this had all taken him decades longer than he had initially hoped. Nonetheless, the plan had finally worked.

In 2019, the local news caught up with Mason. By then, the 67-year-old was living in an apartment for people with low-income housing vouchers and getting free food at a shelter for the elderly.[51] But among a new generation of neo-Nazis, he was a living legend.

Notes

1 Eva's last name has been omitted as she was underage at the time. Mason interview with Schuster (video); *Art That Kills*, p.191.
2 *Art That Kills*, p.191; Prendergast, "Double Exposure," p.16 (*Articles*, p.114).
3 Mason interview with Schuster (video); Prendergast, "Double Exposure," p.18 (*Articles*, p.115).
4 Mason to Moynihan and Thorsten, February 16, 1994 [Box 11, Folder 2]; Reynolds to Mason and Eva, February 10, 1994 [Box 33, Folder 5]; "Charles Manson Betrice Berry Show part1" (video), uploaded by Duchess, September 23, 2011, www.youtube.com/watch?v=B03fnXafIdE&list=PLjTwyDbOmeYtsgJPeT0 DR43YJoO6ovaJ2&index=6; "CHARLES MANSON BETRICE BERRY SHOW part 3" (video), uploaded by Duchess, September 23, 2011, www.youtube.com/watch?v=CSZGkbGGBhM&list=PLjTwyDbOmeYtsgJPeT0DR43YJoO6ovaJ2&index=8
5 Mason interview with Schuster (video); Prendergast, "Double Exposure," pp.13, 16, 18, 20 (*Articles*, pp.112, 114–16).
6 Prendergast, "Double Exposure," pp.20, 22 (*Articles*, p.116); Mason to Reynolds and Beth Helen, May 18, 1994 [Box 33, Folder 3].
7 Mason to Reynolds and Beth Helen, June 26, 1994 [Box 33, Folder 3]; Mason, "Recordings," *Articles*, p.183; Prendergast, "Double Exposure," p.23 (*Articles*, p.117). For Mason's account of this period, see "Early Morning in Copenhagen," *Out of the Dust*, vol. 1, pp.280–89 (written winter 1995–1996).
8 *Revisiting Revelation*, 3rd ed., p.12. See also Appendix 5, "Christianity."
9 Reynolds and Beth Helen to Mason, May 14, 1995 [Box 33, Folder 4]; Prendergast, "Double Exposure."
10 Mason, "Charles Manson: Illusion or Reality?"; Mason interview in *Warcom Gazette* (*Articles*, p.110).
11 For Mason's articles, see clippings in Box 35, Folder 14. For letters Metzger sent to while Mason was in prison, see Box 35, Folder 42 and Box 11, Folder 5.

12 Mason, *One Verse Charlies*, 4th ed., 2018, https://archive.org/details/OneVerse Charlies4thEdition, pp.2, 5; *Universal Order*, https://web.archive.org/ web/19990427113801, http://www.universalorder.com

13 A recommended reading list he made while in prison included *Mein Kampf*, the Bible, Yockey's *Imperium*, Savitri Devi's *Son of the Sun*, Erich Von Daniken's *Chariots of the Gods*, and Bruce Rux's *Architects of the Underworld*; "Required Reading," *Universal Order*, https://web.archive.org/web/19980526141828, http://www.universalorder.com/rr.html

14 Mason, *One Verse Charlies*, p.7; Mason to Joseph Paul Franklin, April 8, 2000 [Box 30, Folder 18]. Mason added in his 2000 letter to Franklin that Metzger "still has all my good wishes and I receive W.A.R. every month." In 2020, Metzger told an interviewer that he continued to recommend *Siege* and its strategy. He added that "Mason's got more brains than most" of the Alt Right and other White Supremacists, whose movement is "gonna be a total failure." Metzger, who had limited influence on that movement, died on November 4, 2020—the day after Donald Trump lost the presidential election to Joseph Biden. "Radio Wehrwolf— Wolfman's Activism & Entertainment: Tom Metzger, 4/30/18," posted on May 1, 2018 by RWW, https://web.archive.org/web/20180922070515, https:// radiowehrwolf.us/2018/05/01/wolfmans-activism-entertainment-tom-metzger

15 *Articles*, pp.200–29.

16 Mason, "Dear Friend" (open letter, prison update), February 16, 1998 [Box 11, Folder 5]; Mason, *One Verse Charlies*, p.2.

17 *Art That Kills*, p.193; "Wave of Skinhead Violence Hits Denver," *SPLC Intelligence Report*, winter 1998, online March 15, 1998, www.splcenter.org/fighting-hate/ intelligence-report/1998/wave-skinhead-violence-hits-denver; "American Front, Criminal Activity," *ADL*, https://web.archive.org/web/20130112013029, http:// www.adl.org/learn/ext_us/american_front/criminal_activity.asp

18 Mason, "Dear Friend"; Mason, *One Verse Charlies*, p.7.

19 Mason to author, November 26, 2022.

20 Mason, "Dear Friend"; "James Mason," *Encyclopedia*, p.198; Mason, *The Robert Burns Collection: Volume 1*, 3rd ed. (November 2001), p.4, http:// siegeculture.org/documents/james/books/RB1.pdf

21 Mason to Metzger, October 24, 1999 [Box 11, Folder 5]; *One Verse Charlies*, p.10. The website was soon moved elsewhere; https://web.archive.org/web/20061 120034312, http://www.geocities.com/orderuniversal

22 *Art That Kills*, p.193; Mason interview with Schuster (video); Schuster, "Introduction to the First Edition," *Siege*, p.33. The incorrect edition that the title identifies (the second is the correct one) has helped obscure the fact that Moynihan had written the original introduction.

23 Schuster, "Introduction," *Siege*, p.33; Mason to Metzger, October 24, 1999 [Box 11, Folder 5].

24 Publication histories are listed in most of the later editions. Mason, *One Verse Charlies*, 4th ed.; *The Robert Burns Collection: Volume 1*, 3rd ed.; *Revisiting Revelation*, 3rd ed.; *The Theocrat*, 4th ed.; *When We Were All Jews*, 1st ed.; *Articles and Interviews*, 3rd. ed.; *Articles of* WAR (2003); *The Robert Burns Collection: Volume 2*, 2nd ed., 2001, http://siegeculture.org/documents/james/ books/RB2.pdf; "National Socialist Liberation Front" and "Universal Order," *Encyclopedia*, pp.221–23, 307–8.

25 Macklin, "Greg Johnson and Counter-Currents," pp.205, 209–10.

26 Greg Johnson to Mason, May 16, 2001; Johnson to Mason, May 16, 2001 [both Box 30, Folder 32]. The Black Sun website would also contain a link to an early version of Johnson's online Savitri Devi archive. "Black Sun Links," *Black Sun Publications*, https://web.archive.org/web/20030409203306, http://www. blacksunpublications.com/sales.htm

27 Schuster to Mason, September 11, 2001. Mason also said some Europeans wanted to reprint it, but the plates from the first edition would not be able to pass through customs; Mason to Schuster, September 15, 2001 [both Box 32, Folder 33].

28 Schuster to Mason, June 18, 2001 [Box 32, Folder 33]. In the meantime, however, Johnson had been able to fundraise $2,000 for the organization. In return for Mason providing pictures from the 1962 WUNS (World Union of National Socialists) conference in Britain, Johnson promised Mason free copies of FHU and Black Sun books; Schuster to Mason, June 10, 2002 [Box 32, Folder 27]; Johnson to Mason, January 2, 2002 [Box 30, Folder 32].

Indeed, the last FHU publishing venture had been almost a decade before. Stanley Burnham's *America's Bimodal Crisis: Black Intelligence in White Society* (Athens, Georgia: Foundation for Human Understanding, 1993) was put out by FHU in a second edition in January 1993 and then a third that September.

29 The FHU was, unsurprisingly, also a recipient of funds from the eugenicist Pioneer Fund; William H. Tucker, *The Science and Politics of Racial Research* (Urbana, Illinois: University of Illinois Press, 1994), pp.252–53.

30 Others included Ludwig Klages, Anthony Ludovici, and Louis-Ferdinand Céline; Johnson to Mason, May 16, 2001 [Box 30, Folder 32]; Schuster to Mason, June 18, 2001 [Box 32, Folder 29].

31 "Mission Statement" for Black Sun Publications, with handwritten note by Schuster [2001 or 2002?] [Box 32, Folder 27].

32 Ibid.

33 "Mission Statement," *Black Sun Publications*, website printout made April 15, 2004, in possession of author (different version than above).

34 The check was for half the full payment: $2,000 for *Siege* and $500 for each of the others. Mason would get the other half the next year, sans $500 for *Revisiting Revelation*, which Black Sun decided not to publish. Schuster to Mason, November 30, 2001 [Box 32, Folder 29]; Schuster to Mason, August 23, 2002 [Box 32, Folder 28].

35 Schuster had become doubtful because of scholarly titles being worked on by other publishers, but Mason convinced him otherwise, saying his would be "non-scholarly" and "pictorial." In June 2002, Mason had submitted a manuscript and Schuster told him, "You really have outdone yourself in constructing this masterpiece!" But what was by-then titled *A Pictorial History of the ANP* would never appear. However, after his rediscovery, Mason digitized and put over 700 photos up on the *Siege Culture* website. Schuster to Mason, October 3, 2001; Mason to Schuster, October 9, 2001 [both Box 32, Folder 33]; Schuster to Mason, June 10, 2002 [Box 32, Folder 27]; "American Nazi Party Photos," *Siege Culture*, https://siegeculture.org/documents/ANP%20Library/ANP%20Photo%20Gallery/ANP%20Photo%20Gallery.pdf

36 Mason interview with Schuster (video); "James Mason Lecture at Phoenix University- 2002" (video), uploaded by R.C. Collier, December 22, 2020, https://worldtruthvideos.website/watch/james-mason-lecture-at-the-university-of-phoenix-2002_TvwkwGLWhl8bOkj.html (video is timestamped May 31, 2002); Schuster to Mason, June 10, 2002 [Box 32, Folder 27].

37 Schuster to Mason, June 10, 2002 [Box 32, Folder 27]; "National Alliance Leader William Pierce Hopes to Acquire Hate Label, Resistance Records," SPLC *Intelligence Report*, Fall 1999, online December 15, 1999, www.splcenter.org/fighting-hate/intelligence-report/1999/national-alliance-leader-william-pierce-hopes-acquire-hate-label-resistance-records

38 "Dedication" and Mason interview in *Iron March* (*Articles*, pp.1, 254).

39 Mason, "Introduction to Second Edition," and Schuster, "Introduction," *Siege*, pp.16, 34; Mason to Schuster, May 13, 2003; Mason to Schuster, June 7, 2003; Schuster to Mason, May 28, 2003 [all three Box 32, Folder 27].

40 Mason to Schuster, August 1, 2003 [Box 32, Folder 27]; *Siege*, 2nd edition, p.vi; Mason, "Introduction to the Third Edition," *Siege*, p.11.

41 Mason to author, January 1, 2023.

42 *Siege*, 2nd ed., pp.435–57. The scant media that appeared included a 2003 interview; Mason interview with AAC (*Articles*, pp.236–47).

43 "Lincoln Rockwell—Books," *Black Sun Publications*, https://web.archive.org/web/20030409223705, http://www.blacksunpublications.com/Rockwell.htm. While the preface was written in October 2002, the book was published "After nearly three years of delays." Schuster is the second person thanked; Savitri Devi, *And Time Rolls On* (Atlanta: Black Sun, 2005), pp.x, xi, https://archive.org/details/DeviSavitriAndTimeRollsOnTheSavitriDeviInterviewsEN1978212S.Scan

44 Mason interview with AAC (*Articles*, p.238); Mason interview in *Iron March* (*Articles*, pp.254–55); Mason to author, November 26, 2022.

In May 2022, a coverless, minimally formatted version of *Out of the Dust* was put on the Internet Archive by a supporter. After an internecine fallout with Mason it was removed, but was later put back up on a different site run by those who took his side. In 2020, three Mason documentaries were put online: "George Lincoln Rockwell: A Retrospective," "George Lincoln Rockwell: Lost Footage," and "George Lincoln Rockwell: Rockwell for Governor!" The three are part of the "George Lincoln Rockwell: The Docu-Series," uploaded by William T. Regad on November 29, 2020, https://archive.org/details/george-lincoln-rockwell-docu-series

45 "James Mason - Interview with Sherif Ali on Breakin' It Down (2004)" (video), uploaded by TheWesternCivilizationLibrary, December 1, 2022, https://worldtruthvideos.website/watch/james-mason-interview-with-sherif-ali-on-breakin-039-it-down-2004-puħ-pų-j-r_W3i4MIJTmCwnNQZ.html (show is dated June 23, 2004).

46 Mason, *Race, Religion and Politics* (2005); Mason, *The Lost Cause* [2005?]; *Horror: Desensitization, Conditioned Reflexes, and Thought Control* (2005), https://ia802302.us.archive.org/8/items/five-books-james-mason/Horror.pdf; *The Theocrat*, April 2008.

47 Odis Cochran with The 3 Bigots, *Ship the Niggers Back* CD (James Mason, 2008) [Box 45, Folder 17]. The original releases were Odis Cochran with The 3 Bigots, "Ship Those Niggers Back!" 7" (Hatenanny, 1964), www.discogs.com/release/4894273-Odis-Cochran-With-The-3-Bigots-Ship-Those-Niggers-Back; G. L. Rockwell and the Coon Hunters, "We Don't Want no Niggers for Neighbors" 7" (Hatenanny, 1964), www.discogs.com/release/5363753-G-L-Rockwell-And-The-Coon-Hunters-We-Dont-Want-No-Niggers-For-Neighbors

48 Mason, *Tyranny of Freedom: Emergence of the Beast*, June 2009; Mason, *Harvest of Conspiracy: 1900-2000*, https://ia802302.us.archive.org/8/items/five-books-james-mason/Harvest%20of%20Conspiracy.pdf

49 "Siege," *Solar General*, published online October 31, 2006.

50 Susan Lantz, Chuck D'Adamo, Howard Ehrlich, and Paul Santomenna, "Fascists Countered in D.C.," *Baltimore IMC*, August 28, 2002, https://web.archive.org/web/20100123022403, http://baltimore.indymedia.org/newswire/display/%201556/index.php

51 Mason interview in *Iron March* (*Articles*, p.254); Jeremy Jojola, "A Prominent Neo-Nazi Lives in an Apartment Not Far from Downtown Denver," *9News*, November 25, 2019, www.9news.com/article/news/investigations/neo-nazi-lives-in-capitol-hill-downtown-denver/73-bb42d1d2-2762-4e60-bf64-3a2e5f739347

18

THE LESSONS OF *SIEGE*

There are many insights and cautionary tales in the story of how James Mason developed his ideas about neo-Nazi revolution and terrorism as well as in how the anthology *Siege* came to be.

Politics

1 Neo-Nazism in specific and the Far Right in general need to be analyzed the same way that other social and movements are. Neo-Nazism comes out of certain social and political conditions; has its origins in prior politics and ideas; has changed over time and will continue to in the future; and has differing levels of support among different classes, locations, ages, and identities. As with other radical political movements, it has revolutionary and reformist wings. The story of James Mason is the story of how the splintering of a singular organization allowed its various parts—including those who embraced terrorism—to pursue their own agenda, in both word and deed.

2 As a corollary of this, terrorism cannot be seen as purely the result of psychological factors such as alienation, lack of critical thinking, and online siloing, which together result in the rejection of diversity and a liberal political framework. This Panglossian approach imagines that the present political mainstream is the standard that all other politics are a wrong-headed rejection of. Furthermore, it looks at the mental state of individuals as the reason for its appeal and dismisses it as, for example, the end result of other failed approaches by a political movement.

3 As in other schools of thought such as Frankfurt School marxism, the ideas developed in SIEGE represent an ideology of *failure*. As Mason

DOI: 10.4324/9780429200090-25

said, "Phase One has phased out"—the American Nazi Party/National Socialist White People's Party (NSWPP) approaches were at a dead end. And he was almost assuredly correct that, in the absence of ground-breaking changes, U.S. society would be united in preventing a neo-Nazi party from coming to power. Mason's turn to guerilla violence, racist mass murder, and dropping out in hopes of a collapse was his answer to a problem he correctly analyzed.

4   Ideas matter. Acts of terrorism do not come out of an intellectual void but are shaped by ideologies that justify and promote them. Past political conclusions get codified in belief systems and therefore have an outsized ability to influence those who come in changed circumstances. While *Siege* comprised Mason's reflections on politics in the 1970s and was written in the '80s, it was reinterpreted for the context of the '00s and beyond. A lone ideologue, even when their initial reception is very small, can end up having an outsized effect.

5   Changes in a movement's orientation need to be carefully watched for signs of success. This can include a change in ideology, strategy, internal culture and organizational forms, and alliances. These can be with elements inside the same political milieu which were previously distant or— of special note— with new political and cultural movements and actors.

William Pierce's National Socialist Liberation Front (NSLF), Joseph Tommasi, and James Mason promoted a neo-Nazism that was open to their contemporary (counter)cultural forms, and they also advocated terrorism in early part of the 1970s. Both of these were new approaches for the postwar U.S. neo-Nazi movement. Organizationally, Tommasi advocated a split overground/underground organizational structure (quite different from the NSWPP), and Mason was an early proponent of the "lone wolf" strategy.

Of special importance was Mason's alliance with the Abraxas Clique, which lead to the creation of *Siege*. This new cultural-political intersection was widely ignored at the time, just as the influence of the Alt Right on the 4chan discussion board and online gaming was overlooked for years.

6   There are parts of radical movements, including White Supremacists, which focus on prisoners. This may include movement members who have gone to prison for political crimes, have become politicized inside, or are potential recruits. Prisoners played an important role for both the NSLF and for Mason. Contact with prisoners isn't a one-way street, however, as it allows for an exchange of ideas. Politicized prisoners often use their time for reflection; Mason created the idea of the National Socialist Movement while imprisoned in the mid-1970s. And his practice of writing prisoners led him to Charles Manson, whose ideas transformed Mason's politics.

7   Mason's organizational and ideological story shows that while there are obvious family relationships, neo-Nazis are not the same as other White Supremacists and cannot be reduced to them. Ideologically, National Socialism does not cleanly fit in with "right-wingism" or a more traditional white nationalism (especially on the question of antisemitism, Aryan mythology, and the need for a one-party state). Organizationally, there has traditionally been a large gulf between neo-Nazis and even their close cousins like the Ku Klux Klan, much less right-wing populists like Trumpists, and this remains the case today.

Culture

The interactions of the Abraxas Clique with Mason and other neo-Nazis offer a different set of insights than those who involve purely political actors. The cultural-political dynamics that the Abraxas Circle engaged in were precursors to those used by the Alt Right, on a much greater scale, in the 2010s.

8   Cultural producers like musicians, writers, and artists—as well as people with certain cultural tastes like counterculturalists—can be drawn to political actors who embrace these cultural forms. The cultural actors will have a different way of doing things and different skill sets as well as a different set of networks, which they can draw on to both produce and disseminate political materials. For example, Michael Moynihan not only had the ability to edit, design, and publish a book, but was able to publicize and distribute *Siege* in totally different places than Mason could have.

The relationship of the larger Abraxas Circle to the core Abraxas Clique and its allied White Supremacists is instructive. Abraxas Clique members, partly facilitated by their relationships to Manson and Anton LaVey, attracted numerous others who participated in the Abraxas Circle. Together, they played on each other's records, published in each other's magazines, and put out each other's books. Within this network, undisguised White Supremacists (Mason, Tom Metzger, Bob Heick, and George Hawthorne) had allies in the Abraxas Clique, who in turn worked with people who were sympathizers—or just didn't care about the racists' presence. This self-enclosed network, which grew over many years, obscured those who had concrete relationships with White Supremacists and also acted as a way that influence was spread to others in the Abraxas Circle. For example, this included Thomas Thorn's inclusion of Mason's ideas in his records. Any time a different kind of network starts to be in close contact with even a small number of fascists, it needs to be looked at carefully, and the core collaborators identified among those who are otherwise merely present.

9 Certain orientations and themes can lead cultural actors into neo-Nazism and similar politics. There are several types of this. First, which the 1980s "extreme culture" was based around, was a wallowing in a cynical nihilism and all types of extremes. These included conspiracy theories, mind control techniques, serial killers, child pornography, and authoritarian regimes—with a special fixation on the Nazis. This drew in those already interested in these ideas, increased interest in them, and led some into adopting these ideas—or, as happened with the Abraxas Clique, at the least collaborating with those who did. If these musicians, writers, and artists don't care if their actions help to hurt or kill others, all the better.

Operating within a cultural milieu based on extremes and irony, authentic neo-Nazis and their collaborators can hide from detection. They may blend in by looking like the others around them so that casual viewers are misled, and the neo-Nazis can also claim that they are not serious about their beliefs: "It's just a joke!"

The second linkage can be made by concepts shared with neo-Nazism. Social Darwinism, eugenics, natural hierarchies, misogyny/anti-feminism, anti-leftism, and opposition to universalism were ideas shared by both neo-Nazis like Mason and the Abraxas Clique and *Might is Right* fans.

10 There are also outside views *of* Nazis and neo-Nazis—though not shared as self-conceptions—that can bring people to National Socialism. Those can include the idea of Hitler as a magician (instead of an inspired leader) and Nazism as evil (they see themselves as the good guys).

11 In the "cultic milieu," ideas which are excluded from mainstream legitimacy mix and match with each other. These often include various conspiracy theories, rejected sciences like eugenics and philosophies like Social Darwinism, and beliefs in UFOs (which Mason would incorporate into his later spiritual thinking). Although the taboo against it still is strong even in these quarters, National Socialism is occasionally included in this mix—something that Adam Parfrey specifically made sure was a part of his assemblage of excluded ideas.

12 Media coverage needs to be handled carefully. *Siege* was able to attract outside attention based on its contents and because it coincided with a wave of interest Manson. Even if this press coverage had not attracted any new readers, it certainly heartened the publisher and author, who reprinted the articles in his own publications. As a rule, coverage of this kind of material should be limited to specialist publications unless there is a pressing reason.

Second, a lot of media coverage did not include any commentary from critics who watch the Far Right. This allowed Mason and Moynihan to set the narrative and propagate falsehoods while simultaneously passing on an opportunity for experts to poke holes in their lies. This was the case even with journalists who were supposedly opposed to their ideas.

Third, while a number of writers were either openly sympathetic to Moynihan or intentionally laundered his reputation, assumedly their parent publications were not. These media platforms should have been confronted about their coverage, especially with backup from experts with mainstream legitimacy, and community pressure used to attempt to force a retraction. Portland, Oregon's *Willamette Week*'s cover article on Moynihan, located in one of the most left-leaning cities in the United States, was a prime example of a missed opportunity to do so.

13 Last, Mason's story shows a dynamic that occurs occasionally if infrequently but is generally nonsensical to outsiders: members of the same groups targeted by neo-Nazis, including but not limited to Jews and LGBTQ+ people, are known to participate in or collaborate with these movements. They may attempt to obscure their background, as Frank Collin did, or may be open about it, as Russell Veh was. As a corollary of this, merely belonging to one of these identities, or having friends or even romantic partners who do, is not a 'get out of jail free' card against criticisms of involvement with neo-Nazism or other kinds of White Supremacist politics.

PART VII

Appendices

APPENDIX 1

The NSM after Mason: Brannen, Herrington, Schoep, and Beyond

The National Socialist Movement (NSM) continued long after James Mason departed, becoming one of the longest-lasting neo-Nazi parties in the United States. Its third leader, Jeff Schoep, grew it to what was at one point was the largest one in the United States. As of 2019, it continued on under a fourth leader.

Along with co-founder Greg Hurles, Mason tried to fuse the NSM with Allen Vincent's National Socialist White Workers' Party (NSWWP) in 1978; however, NSM chairman Robert Brannen rejected this and continued his party.[1] But he lacked both Mason's skill as a propagandist and his connections inside the movement. And the window the group was founded in, when small National Socialist White People's Party (NSWPP) splinter groups were looking to collaborate, had closed. The NSM was now overshadowed by the three larger national groups: the National Socialist Party of America (NSPA), NSWPP, and NSWWP.

But sometimes the tortoise wins the race. At first, the NSM did retain active chapters outside Cincinnati, especially in Detroit. The unit there opened a series of bookstores, attracting local media attention. A split inside it resulted in a second affiliate in the city, the SS Action Group, although it soon went its own way and would also have its turn at becoming a national group.

The Oklahoma City affiliate, Local Group Rockwell, included Clifford Herrington, a prolific publisher who took over the NSM in 1983. The mid-1980s were not good to him, but at the end of the decade, he courted the Nazi skinhead movement and eventually hit gold with Twin Cities teenager Jeff Schoep. Taking over the NSM in 1994, Schoep led the group to national success, although in 2019, he resigned and left the group to a fourth leader, Burt Colucci.

Misinformation About the NSM's Founding

The founding of the NSM is shrouded in misinformation, including from former leaders Clifford Herrington and Jeff Schoep, the party website, and ADL and SPLC. The standard claim is that the NSM was co-founded in 1974 by Brannen and Herrington. Not just is Mason erased from this, but Ryan Schuster's introduction to the second edition of *Siege* even said the group Mason was involved with folded ("the N.S.M. slowly withered and then dissipated entirely"), leading readers to believe the current group is another one entirely.[2] The NSM was actually co-founded in March 1975 by Brannen, Mason, and Hurles. Although Herrington was in contact with three and had a formal affiliation with the group early in its existence, he did not help found it.

The errors about the NSM's founding range across scholarly, monitoring, and movement accounts. The NSM website has consistently given the 1974 date and at one point identified Herrington as Brannen's deputy at the group's founding. Additionally, both were said to have "been long time supporters and Storm Troopers" under George Lincoln Rockwell.[3] Herrington spread similar claims. His history of the NSM, *The Events of 30th June 2006 & its Aftermath: The Thirty Year War Against the NSM*, said that it was founded in 1974 by seven people: four Ohio and Kentucky neo-Nazis (himself, Brannen, Mason, and Steven Love) plus Joseph Tommasi and two others. Herrington said he was "Charter member No.7" as well as a member of "the ANP of Rockwell."[4]

Although he was not around at the time, Schoep has used similar dates. In a 2021 interview, Schoep said that while he has usually given 1974 as the founding date, he also heard that it was 1973 and furthermore had seen publications dated that year.[5]

According to the ADL website, the NSM was "started by two former Rockwell storm troopers, Robert Brannen and Cliff Herrington, in 1974," while an earlier document from the monitoring group said Brannen had been a "Rockwell stalwart." Even further afield has been the SPLC, which said the group was originally named the National Socialist American Workers Freedom Movement and was founded in St. Paul, Minnesota. The SPLC also described Herrington and Brannen as Rockwell's "chief lieutenants" and "officials of the American Nazi Party of the 1960s."[6]

These errors are repeated in the academic literature. Pete Simi and Robert Futrell give the 1974 date, as does George Hawley, who also gave the original name as the National Socialist American Workers Freedom Movement. The NSM is not mentioned at all in Mason's entry in Jeffery Kaplan's *Encyclopedia of White Power*. John George and Laird Wilcox come the closest to being right, giving the 1975 date and both Mason and Brannen as founders, although they still omitted Hurles, said Brannen was in Rockwell's party, and claimed the NSM merged with the National Socialist Liberation

Front (NSLF) in the mid-1980s. Even Martin Kerr's "History of American National Socialism" identified Brannen and Mason as having formed the NSM, albeit in 1976, and that the whole thing merged into the NSWWP. Kerr also claimed that "attempts were made to revive" the NSLF after Tommasi but that these were "unsuccessful."[7]

All early NSM documents contradict these claims. Although Brannen and Herrington were both NSWPP members or supporters, there is no evidence that either one was in the American Nazi Party under Rockwell—much less an important figure.

The 1975 founding date is directly referenced in NSM documents and letters as well as by Mason. In none of these is there a mention of 1974 as a founding date, nor of Herrington as a founding member. For example, in 1977, the NSM periodical said it was founded in March 1975. In 1980, Mason also directly gave the March 1975 date.[8]

In fact, in April 1975, Mason was not even in touch with Herrington and had to write Tommasi in California to get his address. In a short biography of Herrington in the January 1977 NSM's *National Socialist Bulletin*, his actions in 1974 (and directly after) are recounted in some detail—but he is not identified as a founder. Mason himself later made it clear that Herrington's account was not true, calling it "pure imagination," and that "he was in no way part of the founding of the NSM."[9]

Neither is there any evidence pointing to Brannen or Herrington being members of the original American Nazi Party led by Rockwell. According to Herrington's autobiography, he joined the NSWPP in 1969, well after the 1967 name change and assassination of Rockwell. In 1976, Brannen told a reporter that he had participated in the Rudolf Hess rallies since 1968 and also joined the NSWPP that year—again, after Rockwell's death and the name change; still, Brannen claimed to have met Rockwell "a number of times."[10] However, if he had been an official in, or even member of, the American Nazi Party, there was certainly no reason he would have had to downplay it to a local reporter who would have had almost no way to fact-check it.

Mason again refuted the claims of both Brannen and Herrington. Brannen, he pointed out, had not even been granted full membership in the NSWPP. Any claims they made to have met Rockwell or been in the American Nazi Party were "All lies, all fabrications."[11]

One reason the 1974 date might have been given was the typical practice of neo-Nazis of the period to backdate their founding year from when they left the previous project they had worked with. For Mason, that would not have been 1974 and hence he never gave that date—but that was the year the NSWPP expelled Brannen.

Herrington's retroactive declaration of himself as a founder is understandable from the perspective of granting himself more legitimacy inside the organization. But it is possible that he was at least an early member. He obviously fabricated at least one, if not more, of the founding members to pad out the numbers, likely to make sure he could claim to be "Charter member No.7." (In *Mein Kampf*, Hitler claimed he received "a provisional membership card with the number 7" from the group that would become the NSDAP.)[12]

But if Herrington was not the actual seventh charter member, he could have been something similar. In February 1977, the NSM accepted memberships for the first time while noting that "In the beginning we did briefly issue a very limited number of Charter Member applications on a honorary, dues-free basis to some select old comrades." Herrington certainly would have qualified as being one of their "select old comrades." And in his own NSM history, Herrington noted he had been a "NSM Charter Member since 1975"—an odd title and date for someone who supposedly co-founded the party the year prior.[13]

Brannen after Mason (1978–1983)

Just before Mason took his faction of the NSM into Vincent's NSWWP in May 1978, outside monitors said the group had 23 members in the Cincinnati metro area, including Brannen. Afterward, Mason claimed that at the beginning of the year, a "clique of bikers outside Ohio" joined the NSM, which reinvigorated Brannen—though not Mason or Hurles. After the two left, but before the end of the year, the bikers themselves had split and their former leader denounced Brannen.[14] Regardless, he soldiered ahead with the NSM, taking over the *National Socialist Bulletin* and later starting *Social Justice*, a public-facing two-pager. The party also continued their annual Hess rallies in Cincinnati; a newspaper reported that the May 1980 event was attended by 15, including neo-Nazis from Michigan and Oklahoma, which were both states with active NSM units. That year, there were NSM affiliates in New York City, Massachusetts, and Indiana, although the most important were in Rhode Island, Oklahoma City, and Detroit.[15]

Charles Labbe's Ashton, Rhode Island NSM was very active. In 1977 and 1978, it had been a part of Vincent's NSWWP, but, like so many other local neo-Nazi groups, its national affiliations were malleable, and after the 1978 split affiliated with the NSM.[16] In 1980, the group was publishing the *American Herald*, and that June the NSM falsely claimed responsibility for a bombing that happened at the Statue of Liberty, a call that Mason attributed to a Rhode Island member.[17]

Detroit Nazi City

Both Detroit affiliates of the NSM had a local impact. The SS Action Group, which splintered off the Detroit group but remained an NSM affiliate for a while, briefly flourished as a national group during the late 1980s and early 1990s.

Bill Russell's Detroit NSM

Bill Russell led the original Detroit NSM affiliate. In 1972, after three and a half weeks of employment, he was fired from a Ford auto plant because he took a Saturday off to get married. Staging a one-man protest, he drew the attention of the local New Left, who made him a hero; for example, he was featured in *Fifth Estate* newspaper. Between 1972 and 1974, he participated in the city's radical scene, saying of this time, "I went to all the meetings."[18]

Russell got a new job at Chrysler but in 1973 was bitten by a rat. A local paper said that "subsequent rabies shots and rat nightmares made it impossible for him to continue production work." Afterward, he collected a weekly disability check for his psychiatric condition which subsidized his political work.[19]

He switched sides, however, and in 1975, at age 22, drove to Cincinnati to meet with the NSM. By October 1976, the NSM listed Russell's Detroit chapter, and he was soon their most active organizer outside of Ohio.[20] He opened three "bookstores" in quick succession—each evicted amid a flurry of publicity and protests. The first opened in December 1977, and the second in May 1978. Whereas the sign on the first merely had two swastikas and a sign saying "White Power," the second's read "Heil Hitler" and "Jews— There Is an Oven in Your Future."[21]

In January 1978, amidst much local publicity over the bookstores, Mason and Brannen came to Detroit to join Russell for an appearance on a local TV station, but it was cancelled because of the NSM's advocacy of violence. At one of the inevitable demonstrations against the second bookstore in May 1978, police arrested at least 20 out of a crowd of over 150. All of this occurred the same time the NSPA's Skokie ruling was in the news, joining the two in the public mind. One Detroit demonstration in July 1978 was timed to coincide with a counter-demonstration in Chicago against the NSPA's Marquette Park victory march. Both bookstores were quickly closed, leading Russell to declare he was suing for $1,260,000 for violations of his rights.[22]

Brannen was in attendance at the opening of Russell's third bookstore in early September 1978. It lasted 24 days before a judge ruled that as it was rented under false pretenses—Russell had claimed it was a real estate firm—it could not contain political materials, although the space itself did not need to be vacated.[23] Thus ended Detroit's neo-Nazi bookstores.

After Mason and Brannen's split, Russell appeared to go back and forth between aligning with the two, whatever his reasons. Vincent's NSWWP listed the Detroit neo-Nazis as one of theirs in April 1978, and the next year Mason said, "Russell has openly split from Brannen."[24] But if he had, it didn't last long. In 1980, Russell identified as part of the NSM when he applied for a permit to hold a rally in honor of George Lincoln Rockwell; the application drew confrontational protests at the city council hearings. Eventually, it was granted but for an alternative location which Russell refused. At that time, it was estimated his group had less than a dozen people.[25]

Russell popped up again in the news in November 1982 when he and Brannen filed a $3.2 million lawsuit against Carroll County, Tennessee. They claimed their freedom of assembly was violated after some of the NSM's teenage recruits were arrested for vandalism.[26] After that, Russell fell completely out of the public eye—but by then was already eclipsed by his former subordinates, the SS Action Group.

SS Action Group

Like those of other groups, the origins of the SS Action Group are obscured. (The name is a rough translation of *Einsatzgruppen*, the Nazi death squads that executed Jewish civilians en masse as the German army pushed east in World War Two, helping to inaugurate the Holocaust.)

Although there are conflicting accounts of the SS Action group's founding, it appears to have split from Russell's NSM unit in 1979, and its first leader was John Reich (John Moriarity), with Mark Heydrich (Ted Dunn) as his second in command. Previously, while Moriarity/Reich was still in the Detroit NSM, he had taken Mason's place as NSM General Secretary after he left.[27]

The future SS Action Group members had been running security for Russell but after a conflict were expelled in 1979. According to his own account, Russell kicked out seven men who became the SS Action Group because they wouldn't follow his orders.[28] This is consistent with a long section describing a Detroit neo-Nazi group in Raphael S. Ezekiel's 1995 ethnography *The Racist Mind*. While Ezekiel changed both group and individual names, the Detroit group was named the "Death's-Head Strike Group"— clearly a pseudonym for the SS Action Group. The ethnographer reported that the members left because Russell wanted too much "discipline and subordination," didn't like their clothes, didn't appreciate their ideas—and was stealing dues money. At first, the new group did not split away from Brannen, who referred to them as the NSM-SS Action Group at least thru mid-1980, although eventually a parting of ways occurred.[29]

The group had a good nose for publicity and sought out rallies that would devolve into violence. Members appeared in the documentary *Blood in the Face*; the film's poster had a photo of two uniformed members. In the early 1990s, the SS Action Group was also a national organization. In 1990, there were 12 affiliated chapters as far away as New York, California, and Texas; a 1993 handout listed 17.[30] Despite its origins in the NSM, there was no tension with Mason, who listed the group's address in the March 1985 SIEGE. That same month, Reynolds wrote them that, "The SS Action Group has a permanent ally in the Universal Order,"[31] and in 1992, after moving to Alabama, he started working with them. On behalf of the group, both he and his wife Beth Helen Reynolds were interviewed by sociologists Betty Dobratz and Stephanie Shanks-Meile for their book on the White Supremacist movement.[32] In 1993, Mason assured Reynolds that he had a favorable view of the group and later wrote for them. In 1995, Reynolds was publishing an SS Action Group newsletter, *The Future Awaits*.[33]

The 64,000 Vote Nazi: Gerald Carlson

Another former Detroit NSM member who stood out for his later work was Gerald Carlson, briefly a member in early 1978. That October, he registered a new political group, the National Christian Democratic Union, and in late November set up a racist phone hotline, attracting local outrage.[34] In August 1980, he won the Republican Party primary for Michigan's 15th Congressional District, with 53,570 votes (55 percent), and while he lost the general election, he received about the same number of votes (although now it was only 32 percent). Coinciding with Ronald Reagan's 1980 election, Carlson's candidacy was just one of a number of White Supremacists and related Far Right candidates who received unusually high returns.[35]

In March 1981, Carlson ran in a Republican Party special primary election in the Fourth District but received only 701 out of 47,000 votes. But in 1984, he ran again in the 15th District, narrowly winning the primary. In the general election, he did even better than 1980, receiving over 64,000 votes (40 percent).[36]

Herrington: Local Group Rockwell and Second NSM Chairman (1983–1994)

According to Herrington's own online profile, he became a National Socialist in 1962 and joined the NSWPP in 1969. His NSM biography said that future members of the group met him in 1973 at a Cincinnati NSWPP event. At the time, he was in the U.S. Army and stationed at Fort Knox, Kentucky, but would come up to Ohio for events, often with fellow Kentucky neo-Nazi (and future NSLF local leader) Raymond Chaney. In 1974, the year Herrington claimed he co-founded the NSM, he was living in Radcliffe, Kentucky.[37] At the end of 1974, Herrington left the military to work security for the NSWPP in Virginia. Like so many others, he soon had a falling out, and by June 1975 Herrington was, according to Mason, barred from entering party headquarters. Herrington rejoined the Army and was stationed in Europe before returning to the United States.[38]

Oklahoma City Nazis

After he returned, Herrington moved to Oklahoma City and joined the Local Group Rockwell. Originally an NSWPP unit, by January 1976 it was an

NSM affiliate and published a small newsletter, *The Storm*. The Local Group Rockwell also sent its own, separate representative to the October 1976 National Socialist Congress.[39]

Herrington quickly ran into trouble in his new city. Along with fellow Local Group Rockwell member James G. Whittom, he was arrested for literature distribution in April 1977. Here, Herrington's marital problems played a role in his political life, and not for the last time. Making the cover of the local newspaper for being a neo-Nazi, he was evicted from his house, and his wife threatened to divorce him. Herrington resigned from the group and gave control to Whittom, but by August he was back and soon in control of Local Group Rockwell again.[40]

Subsequently, Whittom was thrust into the national spotlight, much to his dismay. By September 1977 Whittom had moved to Mississippi, but he still attended the last National Socialist Congress meeting in March 1978 and considered joining the NSPA. Immediately after John Hinckley, Jr. tried to assassinate President Reagan in 1981, things took a turn when a photo of Whittom—taken at the 1978 meeting when he was dressed in a neo-Nazi uniform—was identified by the press as Hinckley. (Whittom claimed that not never formally joined the NSPA and in fact left the movement soon after.) Nonetheless, the NSPA leadership affirmed that the man in the photo was Hinckley, although it was quickly realized to be a case of mistaken identity. But Whittom, who was deluged with threats, sued the Associated Press for $1.5 million.[41]

Herrington's ambition reached beyond Oklahoma, however. He was the NSM "Chairman Deputy" between 1981 and 1983, during which time the party changed its structure. Starting in January 1983, new recruits had to first join the American Workers Party for a year, after which they could join the NSM.[42] For the next decade, the organization was known as the AWP-NSM.

Herrington took over leadership of the AWP-NSM in 1983 from Brannen, then 56, who was suffering from multiple strokes. (However, as late as August 1984, *Social Justice* was still published out of Cincinnati.[43]) Herrington said he inherited or started numerous NSM publications, including the *National Socialist Bulletin, Social Justice, NS Nationaler, NS Brief,* and the *NSM Magazine.* By the late 1980s, Herrington, aside from running his publishing empire, was meeting with skinheads in Oklahoma. In 1988, he moved to Minneapolis, Minnesota.[44]

Trouble in Bethlehem

Around that time, it appeared that another, younger NSM leader rose to prominence in the group. In October 1988, some skinheads affiliated with the AWP-NSM were arrested after a party where several teenagers were "stabbed, beaten with chains, punched and kicked with steel-tipped boots." Herrington was one of 35 originally named in a lawsuit stemming from the fight, which dragged on for a year. The claims against him were dropped after an $800,000 settlement was reached. Three of the teenagers involved were sent to juvenile prisons, while three adults received sentences of up to six years.[45]

This did not stop the Pennsylvania group, which apparently recruited mostly skinheads. A 1990 article noted that "Commander Bob Scholl" of the Bethlehem AWP-NSM was looking to work with other White Supremacists, and both that year and the next the NSM's *Social Justice* was published out of Bethlehem.[46] But in May 1992, the Bethlehem NSM announced the party was merging with Terry Boyce's Confederate Knights of America, which had established a skinhead division, the SS of America. (At the time, Boyce's group was actively absorbing scattered Klan and Nazi groups.) The NSM also said their two periodicals, *American Skinhead* and *Social Justice*, would continue to be published by the new organization.[47]

Whether this was a repeat of Mason's unauthorized 1978 "merger" of the NSM, or something Herrington went along with it and then changed his mind, is unclear. Back in the Twin Cities, Schoep said that he joined Herrington's organization around 1992. Although it was commonly reported that Schoep was a skinhead at the time, he said he was not and in fact had long hair (although later he did become one). At that point, the NSM was extremely small. Schoep said there were only one or two other units, in addition to a small number of scattered individuals. The group had been cycling through different names, including the National Socialist American Workers Party, the American Workers Movement, and the American Workers Freedom Movement. By the time Schoep joined, it was the National Socialist American Workers Freedom Movement.[48]

In March 1993, Herrington caused a stir by attending a Minnesota legislative hearing on LGBTQ+ rights dressed in a neo-Nazi uniform. A June 1993 newspaper profiled the NSM's organizing work in South St. Paul, saying the party mostly recruited teenagers. Herrington, by then 46, was still the party leader, but now 19-year-old Schoep was his second-in-command.[49]

Schoep Takes the Helm (1994–2019)

In 1994, Herrington moved back to Oklahoma and passed the NSM leadership to Schoep, who changed the name back to simply the NSM and set about reinvigorating the organization. The NSM expanded and became the best-known "uniform and demonstrate" group in the United States. They attempted to marshal some of their old leaders for a National White Unity Meeting in April 1998—which was to feature Brannen, Vincent, and Metzger, along with Schoep—but it was cancelled under pressure.[50] By that time, the party had been so off the radar that one Far Right monitor wrote, "What _has_ the NSM been doing over the years, anyway?" Around the same time, Schoep said that Vincent "became my chief adviser." But this did not last long, as he died the next year, followed in 2004 by Brannen. The NSM kept growing, however, taking advantage of the vacuum left by the collapse of competing groups like the National Alliance. It peaked in 2009 with over 61 chapters in 35 states, becoming the largest neo-Nazi group in the country.[51]

Beforehand, though, it had to weather a 2006 scandal over Herrington's ties to a Satanist group that his wife ran, which ended in Schoep removing his old mentor. Herrington went on to form his own group before briefly rejoining the NSM in 2009, only to leave again soon after.[52]

NSM members became increasingly involved in deadly violence. In June 2006, David Ryan Drake killed a Latino man at a party. In May 2011, Jeff Hall was killed by his 11-year-old son. In May 2012, J.T. Ready, who participated in Arizona vigilante border patrols, killed his girlfriend and her parents and child, before committing suicide. (Ready claimed he had left the party in July 2010, although his next group was mostly NSM members and those close to them.) And in March 2020, at the very beginning of the Covid-19 pandemic, Timothy Wilson was killed in a shoot-out with the FBI while on his way to bomb a hospital.[53]

But the NSM, the cat with nine lives of neo-Nazism, did not drown. A decade later, in a rerun of the White Confederacy, it helped launch a new White Supremacist umbrella group, the Aryan Nationalist Alliance (later renamed the Nationalist Front). It included those the NSM had links to in the 1970s, such as Karl Hand's Racial Nationalist Party of America, the SS Action Group, and Gerhard Lauck's NSDAP/AO. Along with the NSM, a number of Nationalist Front groups would take part in the 2017 Charlottesville demonstration. (These also included Vanguard America, who emerged out of the _Iron March_ forum where Mason was fetishized. Patriot Front, which was to become the largest fascist group in the 2020s, came out of Vanguard America.)[54]

In March 2019, an even more outrageous scandal than Herrington's rocked the NSM: Schoep resigned after it was revealed he had signed legal control of the organization to James Stern, a black activist. Schoep had been named in a civil lawsuit for Charlottesville, _Sines vs Kessler_, and Stern convinced him that if he signed the NSM over to him on paper, Schoep could escape liability. Stern gloated that he had pulled a fast one, but—adding another twist—he died of cancer shortly thereafter. Schoep then declared himself a former White Supremacist and hit the speaker's circuit. However, in November 2021, both Schoep and the NSM were found to be liable and ordered to respectively pay $500,000 and $1 million, although the amount was decreased on appeal.[55]

Defying expectations, the NSM did not collapse, and party stalwart Burt Colucci became the new leader. He was arrested in 2022 after a demonstration, as the NSM continued what it had been doing for decades—the exact opposite of what Mason had intended it to do when he helped found the organization in 1975.[56]

Notes

1 See Chapter 4, "A Tangled Web of Neo-Nazis."
2 Schuster, "Introduction," *Siege*, p.28. Compounding the matter is the existence of other groups with the same name, the most important of which was a British group led by Rockwell's ally Colin Jordan.
3 "The NSM—America's Nazi Party," *National Socialist Movement*, www.nsm88. org/about; "America's Nazi Party," *National Socialist Movement*, http://web. archive.org/web/20070719192640, http://www.nsm88.com/articles/nazi.html
4 The other two were Clarence Brandenburg and "George Zapporalli [sic], Heir apparent, Prince of the House of Lombardy." Brandenburg was an Ohio Klan leader who indeed was associated with Mason and the other local NSWPP members. Brandenburg was involved in a famous Supreme Court case, 1969's *Brandenburg vs Ohio*. Zapporali was the deputy leader of the Western Guard Party in Canada and author of the White Confederacy constitution. C.D. Herrington, *The Events of 30ᵗʰ June 2006 & its aftermath*, pp.3, 18; Barrett, *Is God a Racist? The Right Wing in Canada*; Herrington to Mason, April 19, 1975 [Box 25, Folder 35].
5 Schoep, phone interview with author, February 5, 2021. The publications he referred to may have been copies of Steven Love's 1973 *Southern Ohio Activity Report*, the NSWPP publication which later became Mason's *Ohio National Socialist*.
6 "The National Socialist Movement," *ADL*, www.adl.org/education/resources/ profiles/national-socialist-movement; ADL, *Hate Groups in America*, p.33; "Jeff Schoep," *SPLC*, www.splcenter.org/fighting-hate/extremist-files/individual/jeff-schoep; SPLC, "National Socialist Movement," www.splcenter.org/fighting-hate/ extremist-files/group/national-socialist-movement
7 Pete Simi and Robert Futrell, *American Swastika*, 2nd ed. (Lanham, Maryland: Rowman & Littlefield, 2015), p.17; George Hawley, *The Alt-Right: What Everyone Needs to Know* (New York: Oxford University Press, 2019), p.46; "James Mason," *Encyclopedia*, pp.193–99; John George and Laird Wilcox, *Nazis, Communists, Klansmen, and Others on the Fringe* (Buffalo, New York: Prometheus Books, 1992), p.366; Kerr, "The History of American National Socialism Part 6".
8 "It's Time… for You to Join a Winner!," *National Socialist Bulletin* 6(3) March 1977, p.1; SIEGE 9(8) December 1980, p.4. In 1978, Mason told postal authorities that the NSM name was in use "since very early 1975"; Mason to Biggers, August 26, 1978 [Box 4, Folder 4].
9 Mason to Tommasi, April 2, 1975 [Box 21, Folder 30]; "Oklahoma!," *National Socialist Bulletin* 6(1) January 1977, p.18; Mason to author, November 26, 2022.
10 Herrington, *30 Year War*, p.36; Dave Lyon, "South Lebanon Man Marches to Free Rudolf Hess, Nazi War Criminal," *Western Star*, May 12, 1976, p.10A, reprinted in *National Socialist*, June 1976, p.6.
11 Mason to author, November 26, 2022.
12 Herrington, *30 Year War*, p.3; Hitler, *Mein Kampf*, p.301.
13 "It's Time," *National Socialist Bulletin* 1977, p.1; Herrington, *Thirty Year War*, p.36.

14 The area was specified as reaching to Bethel, Ohio and included Brannen's home in South Lebanon—but this would not have included Mason and Hurles in Chillicothe; Marvin Beard, "The Nazis: Locally, Their Ranks Are Small, Their Influence Smaller," *Cincinnati Enquirer*, April 16, 1978, www.newspapers.com/image/101394100; SIEGE December 1980 9(8), p.5.

15 The first issue of *Social Justice* held by the University of Kansas is January 1983. The name was taken from an antisemitic newspaper run by the infamous as profascist radio priest Father Coughlin in the 1930s. AP, "Nazi group holds march in downtown Cincinnati," *Courier-Journal* (Louisville, Kentucky), May 11, 1980, p.A16, www.newspapers.com/image/109946379; *National Socialist Bulletin* 9(4) April 1980, pp.5–6.

16 In NSWWP's *Stormer* lists Ashton's unit in 1977 and 1978. See *Stormer* 1(1) September 1977, p.14, *Stormer* 1(2) January 1978, p.11 (see also p.21), and *Stormer* 1(3) April 1978, p.30. Mason to Reynolds, August 14, 1978; Reynolds to Mason, August 21, 1978 [both Box 33, Folder 10].

17 "A Nazi Group in R.I. resumes the fight for racism and revolution," *Evening Bulletin* (Providence, Rhode Island), March 20, 1980, clipping reprinted in *National Socialist Bulletin* (5) May 1980, pp.3–4; AP, "Bomb causes $6,000 damage to artifacts at Statue of Liberty," *Dayton Daily News*, June 4, 1980, p.30, www.newspapers.com/image/405835357; SIEGE 9(8) December 1980, p.5.

18 AP, "Detroit Neo-Nazi Began In Politics As Leftist," *Herald-Palladium* (St. Joseph, Michigan), May 30, 1978, p.13, www.newspapers.com/image/365564272

19 "Nazi leader dreams of rats," *Detroit Free Press*, June 7, 1978, www.newspapers.com/image/98598503

20 Robert H. Emmers, "Bill Russell: Portrait of a Nazi," *Detroit Free Press*, August 22, 1980, p.1C, www.newspapers.com/image/98512072; *National Socialist Bulletin* #21, October/November 1976, p.7.

21 Gerald Volgenau, "Religious Groups, Pickets Protest Nazi Bookstore," *Detroit Free Press*, December 29, 1977, p.3A, 5A, www.newspapers.com/image/99062077, www.newspapers.com/image/99062079; "Detroit Nabs More Nazi Protestors," *Petoskey News-Review* (Michigan), May 23, 1978, p.16, www.newspapers.com/image/554766033

22 "Nazis Talk Violence, TV Show Is Cancelled," *Detroit Free Press*, January 11, 1978, www.newspapers.com/image/98927662; "Detroit Nabs More Nazi Protestors," *Petoskey News-Review*; "Anti-Nazi Group Plans Rally," *Petoskey News-Review*, July 3, 1978, p.19, www.newspapers.com/image/554897461; Ishoy, "Nazis again open a bookstore." The NSM eagerly collected and reprinted the newspaper clippings; see *National Socialist Bulletin* 7(1–3) January to March 1978.

23 Ishoy, "Nazis again open a bookstore"; Gerald Volgenau and Tim Kiska, "Judge closes 3d Nazi store," *Detroit Free Press*, September 28, 1978, www.newspapers.com/image/98623733

24 *Stormer* 1(3) April 1978, p.30; Mason to Reynolds, July 26, 1979 [Box 33, Folder 10]; Mason to author, January 1, 2023.

25 Emmers, "Bill Russell." Seth Kliphoth, who had been involved in Nazi-Satanism as well as the NSLF, worked with him to secure the permit; Ken Fireman and Luther Jackson, "Klan and Nazis want to rally in downtown Detroit Aug. 23," *Detroit Free Press*, June 5, 1980, p.A3, www.newspapers.com/image/98504168

26 AP, "Tennessee Town Fights Nazi Group," *Montgomery Advertiser*, November 29, 1982, p.5C, www.newspapers.com/image/257105203

27 "Ill Health Forces Resignation," *National Socialist Bulletin* 7(5) April 1978, p.5.

28 Emmers, "Bill Russell," p.3C; John Steele, "A Brief History of Post-Rockwell National Socialism," *Thoughtcrime*, May 16, 2002, http://hacovington.blogspot.com/2002/05/brief-history-of-post-rockwell-national.html

29 Ezekiel, *The Racist Mind*, pp.xiii, 150 (the chapter on the group is "Part Three: Detroit," pp.147–319). A February 1980 report on their activities, signed by Reich and Heydrich, appeared in the NSM periodical. Another group in Dearborn Heights, SS Action Group II, was also referred to as a part of the NSM. "Activity Report: NSM-SS Action Group, Westland Michigan, Feb 9, 1980," *National Socialist Bulletin* 9(3) March 1980, p.3; "NSM Activity," *National Socialist Bulletin* 9(4) April 1980, p.5.

30 ADL, *Extremism on the Right*, p.62; *Blood in the Face*, dir. Anne Bohlen, Kevin Rafferty, and James Ridgeway, 1991, www.imdb.com/title/tt0101479; "*On Guard*" #5, Summer-Fall 1990, p.5; "SS Action Group, Local Units" (one page sheet), Updated/July 1993 [Box 33, Folder 5]. For a first-person account of a then-Nazi skinhead who took part in a violent melee with the SS Action group, see Arno Michaels, *My Life After Hate* (Milwaukee, Wisconsin: La Prensa de LAH, 2010), chapter 5.

31 SIEGE 14(3) March 1985, p.6; Reynolds to "Comrades of the SS Action Group," March 12, 1985 [Box 33, Folder 7].

32 Reynolds to Mason, December 20, 1993 [Box 33, Folder 5]; Dobratz and Shanks-Meile, *"White Power, White Pride!,"* pp.27, 260.

33 Dobratz and Shanks-Meile, *"White Power, White Pride!,"* p.331; Mason to Reynolds and Beth Helen, June 21, 1993 [Box 33, Folder 5]; Mason to Reynolds and Beth Helen, January 14, 1995 [Box 33, Folder 3].

34 John Castine, "Tapes Spread Racial Hate by Telephone," *Detroit Free Press*, December 2, 1978, pp.A3, 13A, www.newspapers.com/image/98687847, www.newspapers.com/image/98687865

35 "Ex-nazi Trounced in Election Bid," *JTA*, March 26, 1981, www.jta.org/1981/03/26/archive/ex-nazi-trounced-in-election-bid. In addition to Metzger's California primary victory in California, Covington won significant votes in his North Carolina race, while crypto-fascist Lyndon LaRouche qualified for matching funds in his presidential bid.

36 "Ex-nazi Trounced in Election Bid." His primary victory was 5,107 to 4,394; Patricia Montemurri, "Candidate with ties to Nazis, Klan gets 40% of vote in 15th District," *Detroit Free Press*, November 8, 1984, www.newspapers.com/image/99136503

37 Clifford Herrington, *LinkedIn*, www.linkedin.com/in/clifford-herrington-a9161964, accessed March 2022; "Oklahoma!"; Mason to Herrington, April 29, 1974.

38 Mason to Herrington, December 14, 1974 [Box 25, Folder 35]; Mason to Tommasi, June 8, 1975 [Box 21, Folder 30]; "Oklahoma!"; Herrington, *LinkedIn*; Mason to Brannen, June 8, 1975 [Box 4, Folder 4].

39 Herrington to Mason, January 15, 1976 [Box 25, Folder 35]; "NS Congress Meets in Chicago," *NS Report* #7, 1976/1977, p.1.

40 Dennis C. Rupp to NSM, April 30, 1977 [Box 7, Folder 49]; *The Storm* 1(6) May 1977 [Box 28, Folder 36]; "Chairman's Message," *National Socialist Bulletin* 6(10) October 1977, p.6.

41 Whittom to Mason, September 15, 1977 [Box 28, Folder 36]; AP, "Doubts Grow Over Hinckley's Nazi Ties," *Daily Item* (Sunbury, Pennsylvania), April 4, 1981, www.newspapers.com/image/485248563; "Man Mistaken for Reagan Attacker Asserts He Now Fears for His Life," *NYT*, April 9, 1981, www.nytimes.com/1981/04/09/us/man-mistaken-for-reagan-attacker-asserts-he-now-fears-for-his-life.html; UPI, "A news agency was negligent in erroneously identifying James…," April 17, 1981, www.upi.com/Archives/1981/04/17/A-news-agency-was-negligent-in-erroneously-identifying-James/7934356331600

42 Herrington, *LinkedIn*; Questionnaire from the Wilcox Collection, marked September, 1983 [eph 502].

43 "America's Nazi Party," *National Socialist Movement*, http://web.archive.org/web/20070719192640, http://www.nsm88.com/articles/nazi.html; *Social Justice*, February 1–15, 1984 [eph 502].

44 Herrington, *Thirty Year War*, pp.6–8

45 Debbie Garlicki and The Morning Call, "S. Whitehall Teens Sue Skinheads Who Beat Them: 35 Defendants Include Leader of Political Party," *Morning Call* (Allentown, Pennsylvania), October 4, 1990, www.mcall.com/news/mc-xpm-1990-10-04-2777696-story.html; Garlicki and The Morning Call, "$800,000 Settles Suit Over Fight: Gang Stabbed, Kicked, Beat 3 Teens in S. Whitehall," *Morning Call*, July 21, 1993, www.mcall.com/news/mc-xpm-1993-07-21-2937092-story.html; Garlicki, "2 of 3 in Gang-Beating Get Stiffer Sentences," *Morning Call*, August 30, 1991, www.mcall.com/news/mc-xpm-1991-08-30-2810794-story.html

46 A Bethlehem *Social Justice* Q&A included a question which implied such an existing constituency, since it needed be asked: "Is the AWP-NSM solely a Skinhead Movement?" (The answer was "NO. Our organization is open to all White people of European ancestry.") A 1988 newspaper article referred to AWP-NSM member "Tom Scholl." *Social Justice* [1991], published in Bethlehem, Pennsylvania, "Homosexuals Sin" lead story, pp.5–6 [CDR, Box 150]; "National Socialists Seek Unity in PA," *"On Guard,"* #5 Summer-Fall 1990, p.3; Margie Peterson, "'New' Klan claims it will remain non-violent," *Pottsville Republican* (Pennsylvania), July 5, 1988, p.25, www.newspapers.com/image/467571328; *Social Justice* [1991], pp.5–6.

47 Confederate Knights of America, State Office (CKA-PA), Trudie Mest, "Notice, RE: Merger," May 1992 [eph 3232]. In addition to the Bethlehem, Pennsylvania NSM, Boyce's group absorbed Dennis Mahon's WKKK (White Knights of the Ku Klux Klan) in 1990 as an affiliate. Mahon's group was active in Missouri and Oklahoma and was a rival of Herrington, although in 1991 he also advocated for Karl Hand's release. In 1992 Mahon joined Metzger's WAR, but was later sentenced to 40 years for a 2004 mail bombing. D.W. Mahon, "White Knights Merger With Confederate Knights of America," *White Beret*, vol. III, September/October 1990, p.1; "Ku Klux Klan," *Encyclopedia*, p.164; Bill Morlin, "Appeals Court Affirms Conviction of Racist Behind Diversity Office Bombing," *SPLC*, August 7, 2015, www.splcenter.org/hatewatch/2015/08/07/appeals-court-affirms-conviction-racist-behind-diversity-office-bombing

48 Schoep interview with author; Herrington, *30 Year War*, p.9.

49 Dane Smith, "Senate Judiciary Committee easily passes gay rights bill," *Star Tribune*, March 2, 1993, p.5B, www.newspapers.com/image/193015430; Conrad deFiebre, "Nazis take root: South St. Paul keeps watch on neofascists' activities," *Star Tribune*, June 2, 1993, p.1A, 12A, www.newspapers.com/image/193018024, www.newspapers.com/image/193018952

50 According to Herrington, he made Schoep the Commander of the Uniformed Divisions NSM—and so technically was his subordinate. Here there were shades of when Brannen claimed, in 1980, that the NSLF was still part of the NSM and so therefore under his control. Herrington, *30 Year War*, pp.12, 22; "NSM National White Unity Meeting, April 18-19, 1998" (flyer) [CDR, Box 265]; Chris Graves, "Melee erupts at neo-Nazi news conference," *Star Tribune*, April 19, 1998, p.31, www.newspapers.com/image/194274885

51 Lin Collette to Mark Pitcavage, email (printout), April 15, 1998 [CDR, Box 148]; Jeff Schoep, "Commander's Forward," *NSM Magazine*, Spring/Summer 2014, p.2; "National Socialist Movement," *SPLC*. The author confirmed Brannen's death date with a family member.

52 "The National Socialist Movement," *ADL*, www.adl.org/resources/profiles/national-socialist-movement; *The National Socialist Freedom Movement: Complete PDF of the Website*, www.scribd.com/document/371894460/The-Nsfm-PDF. See also Chapter 15, "Nazi-Satanism."

53 "National Socialist Movement," *SPLC*, www.splcenter.org/fighting-hate/extremist-files/group/national-socialist-movement; "National Socialist Movement," *ADL*, www.adl.org/resources/backgrounders/national-socialist-movement; "The National Socialist Movement," *ADL*, www.adl.org/resources/profiles/national-socialist-movement

54 "Historic Alliance formed by U.S. White Nationalists," (press release), April 26, 2016, *NSM*, https://web.archive.org/web/20160502144510, https://www.nsm88.org/press/nsm_pressrelease_historicallianceformedbyuswhitenationalists_april_2016_.htm; "Nationalist Front (formerly known as the Aryan Nationalist Alliance)," *ADL*, February 16, 2021, www.adl.org/resources/backgrounders/nationalist-front-formerly-known-aryan-nationalist-alliance

55 Hatewatch Staff and Brett Barrouquere, "Neo-Nazi Group NSM Faces New Upheaval After James Hart Stern's Death," *SPLC*, November 13, 2019, www.splcenter.org/hatewatch/2019/11/13/neo-nazi-group-nsm-faces-new-upheaval-after-james-hart-sterns-death; "Jeff Schoep," *SPLC*; Ron Kampeas, "Judge slashes Charlottesville penalties by 90%, from $26M awarded by jury to $2.35M," *JTA*, January 4, 2023, www.jta.org/2023/01/04/politics/judge-slashes-charlottesville-penalties-by-90-from-26m-awarded-by-jury-to-2-35m; Kampeas, "Court orders defendants in Charlottesville neo-Nazi lawsuit to pay nearly $5 million for legal costs," *JTA*, March 9, 2023, www.jta.org/2023/03/09/politics/court-orders-defendants-in-charlottesville-neo-nazi-lawsuit-to-pay-nearly-5-million-for-legal-costs

56 Michael Starr, "'The Jew is the devil' Florida Neo-Nazi rally leader arrested, charged," February 7, 2022, *Jerusalem Post*, www.jpost.com/diaspora/antisemitism/article-695770

APPENDIX 2

The Original NSLF and David Duke: Big Nazi on Campus

The National Socialist Liberation Front (NSLF) name originated in 1969 when it was given to the National Socialist White People's Party's (NSWPP's) student group, designed to woo disenchanted radical youth away from the Left. When Joseph Tommasi broke away from the NSWPP in 1974, he borrowed the older group's name. Despite this, there was no genealogical line of descent between the two groups, and their tactics and organizational structure were also completely different. The main similarity was that both groups appropriated New Left rhetoric.

The student group's most famous member, David Ernest Duke, was given control of the NSLF under a new name in 1970, and a number of his subsequent organizations grew directly out of it. He hit pay dirt with his fourth one after the NSLF, the Knights of the Ku Klux Klan (KKKK). Although no longer based on National Socialist ideology, his Klan attracted former American Nazi Party (ANP)/NSWPP members, including second-in-command Karl Hand. But Duke's unscrupulous behavior and comparatively moderate public positions alienated many of them, and resignations and denunciations followed.

Duke would outstrip his peers in fame and influence. In 1989, his strategy seemed to pay off when he became a Louisiana state representative, although this ended up being the pinnacle of his electoral career. It was enough to make Duke a legend among White Supremacists and a boogeyman in the media. Decades later, his name recognition remained high enough to be invoked in both the 2016 and 2020 presidential races as a politician who personified White Supremacy.

Despite having tame politics for his political milieu, Duke has retained some of the influences of the neo-Nazi milieu he originally cut his teeth on. He and James Mason remain living representatives of the NSWPP's militant and moderate wings—a division that has continued among the new generations that have come after them.

NSLF, Beta Version

Mason described the original NSLF as "a political front" created by Pierce in 1969, and was

> intended to compete against the leftist movements on U.S. college campuses. The NSLF was a deliberate takeoff on the National Liberation Front of the Vietnamese, whose struggle was then dominating the news. In this instance, national liberation meant an end to Jewish control of government in a land where Whites are a majority.[1]

Calling itself the "Student Activist Arm of the National Socialist Movement," the NSLF was founded at the NSWPP conference in April 1969. The party triumvirate of Robert Lloyd, William Pierce, and Matthias Koehl all took part in setting it up. Following George Lincoln Rockwell's "Phase" system, the NSLF was to focus on Phase Two—attracting new recruits. The attention-grabbing stunts of Phase One were not to be used, "except in very special circumstances."[2] Duke would rue the day that he chose his special circumstance.

Its main output was the *National Socialist Liberator* newspaper, published between May 1969 and April 1970. (Mason printed it as well as the group's other materials like applications, stationery, and membership cards.) The paper tried to appeal to the rebellious students of the day, addressing topics like the Vietnam War, then at its height. The NSLF condemned the U.S. government as sympathetic to Communism, the proof being that it had not fully committed to the war. Jews were said to both be avoiding military service and running the New Left, in particular the SDS (Students for a Democratic Society).[3] The militant black student movement made for an obvious target, and the *Liberator* ran headlines like "Black Terror Rages in Schools"—although this didn't stop it from also promoting antisemitic comments by Beat poet-turned-black nationalist LeRoi Jones/Amiri Baraka. Presaging the future interest in eco-fascism, the NSLF claimed that environmentalism was "a National Socialist cry" and called for executing "the 1000 most prominent moguls of the carbon monoxide lobby."[4]

The group also issued the flyer "Why does the System hate National Socialism?," written in 1960s revolutionary marxist style, just as the later NSLF would. Hitler was praised for "rejecting bourgeois-capitalist values," freeing Germany from "the international bankers of London and Wall

Street," and rejecting the "materialist interests of Left and Right." It ended by claiming the NSLF had "taken up the struggle for the total replacement of the present decadent, hypocritical, liberal-democratic System with a viable new world order based on social justice and racial idealism."[5] A letter sent to distributors of the *Liberator* emphasized the same talking points, with instructions to "propagandize reds and hippies who are racially sound." It added that after the NSWPP had achieved victory, "the traitors who've wormed their way into our highest offices can be assigned a lamp post."[6] Although unsigned, it was undoubtedly written by William Pierce, whose novel *The Turner Diaries* included just such a scene.

David Duke

The NSLF did not appear very successful on campuses, with one exception: Louisiana State University. There, 19-year-old student David Duke grew the NSLF. The *Liberator* bragged that Duke ordered a thousand copies of each issue to distribute. He also attracted a group of about five acolytes, known as "Dukies." Duke's fiery speeches in the campus's "Free Speech Alley" resulted in controversy, conflict, and attention; he was physically attacked and his newspapers burned. Duke was discussed in the student paper, and he made an antisemitic appearance on a local radio talk show.[7]

But the high point of Duke's college activism was undoubtedly his very Phase One single-man picket in July 1970 against the Jewish left-wing lawyer William Kunstler, one of the lawyers for the Chicago 7. This group of prominent leftists were tried for their part in the 1968 Chicago protests against the Democratic National Convention—the same protests described in Norman Mailer's *Miami and the Siege of Chicago*. Duke was dressed in a stormtrooper outfit with a swastika armband, holding a sign saying "Gas the Chicago 7." A local paper ran a photo of him which, much to his chagrin, followed him around as he tried to make himself palatable to the mainstream.[8]

Duke later denied being an NSLF member, saying he merely spoke on its behalf.[9] But documents from the period directly contradict him. In a letter to the editor of Louisiana State University student paper the *Reveille*, Duke wrote that if an accusation being made against the NSLF was true, "I will quit." The NSWPP's *White Power* newspaper wrote unambiguously about "National Socialist Liberation Front member David Duke" in January 1970. (Martin Kerr has claimed that Duke's involvement goes back even further, that he joined the National Socialist Youth Movement, NSYM, as a high school student and then, at 18, the NSWPP.) In any case, Duke also made an important appearance at the NSWPP congress in September 1970.[10]

The NSWPP's *NS Bulletin* praised Duke as their star college student speaker. During his speech at the conference, he "stressed the importance of 'action, action, action' in reaching new people and building the movement."[11]

He was also given a speaker's slot at a public rally held the next day in Washington, D.C, where he stressed the party's desire to "smash the System." Unlike the New Left, Duke said that the NSWPP's understanding of "the true nature – the Jewish nature – of the System" made the party the only "true revolutionaries."[12]

Police stopped the rally as Duke was pelted with bottles from counter-protestors.[13] While this may have been the highpoint of his time with the NSLF, it was also the end of the student organization. Duke announced to the Congress that the White Student Alliance "will replace" the NSLF and that current members would "automatically have their memberships transferred" to the new student group. (According to Kerr, the NSYM was also rolled into the new group.) A copy of the White Student Alliance publication, *The Racialist*, was included with that issue of the *NS Bulletin*.[14]

The White Student Alliance was also part of Duke's move toward a more broad-based approach. Members no longer had to be National Socialists, only racists—a change making recruitment easier. Nonetheless, the new group's platform closely mirrored the NSWPP's.[15]

By January 1971, there was another name change, and the White Student Alliance became the White Youth Alliance. The NSWPP's paper, *White Power*, downplayed the connection between the party and the new group, writing that the NSLF "has been discontinued to enable its former members to work closely with the new group."[16] The group was apparently put on hiatus when Duke left the country in June 1971 to visit his father and teach English in Laos. One of Duke's biographers, Michael Zatarain, claimed that it was then that Duke's father who convinced him to abandon neo-Nazism.[17]

When Duke returned in November 1971, the organization morphed again. He sent a letter to White Youth Alliance members with a membership form for his new National party, and the old group's paper *The Racialist* was replaced by *The Nationalist*. These changes illustrated Duke's continual tinkering with organizational names and approaches as he sought an optimal political orientation, starting with recruiting neo-Nazis before moving to students and then youths as such. The National party was geared to "young people, high school and college students" and in a month had 600 members.[18] At this point, Duke broke from a straight ideological adherence to National Socialism. Duke wrote to the NSWPP headquarters, telling them that Hitler "is to the racial movement as Inquisition is to Christianity" and that "he was the greatest disaster ever to befall the white race."[19]

Knights of the Ku Klux Klan

The National party disbanded in late 1972, but Duke reappeared in the next year in yet another new organization, the Knights of the Ku Klux Klan (KKKK).[20] Dressed nicely and well spoken, Duke used this new group to give the Klan a facelift. Moving away from a reputation for lynching black people and murdering Civil Rights Movement activists, the KKKK projected a middle-class, educated, mainstream image.

At the same time, and despite his break with the NSWPP and disavowal of Hitler, Duke retained organizational and ideological links with neo-Nazis. The first issue of the KKKK's newspaper, the *Crusader*, had ads for both the NSWPP and National Alliance papers. (In fact, the *Crusader* would carry a dozen articles by Pierce and run a "glowing review" of *The Turner Diaries*, which it also sold.)[21]

Mason asked Hand some questions after he joined up with Duke. Mason said he spoke to Duke on the phone before his Klan days, and at the time Duke "confirmed to me that what he was running, essentially, was a 'kindergarten for National Socialists.'" So why, Mason asked, was Duke's KKKK presenting itself as "anti-NS"—even while they had republished George Lincoln Rockwell's *White Power* "minus the Swastika, any reference to National Socialism, and even the name of the author, Rockwell"? Hand said he shared the concerns about the edition, although "if it wakes up more people to the problem of the Jew, It's alright with me." He also added that he did not see any anti-National Socialist sentiment in the KKKK, and that the presence of, not just Duke and himself, but other former ANP/NSWPP members showed that.[22]

And indeed it was an impressive roster of them. It included not just Hand but Don Black, who like Mason had been in the NSYM; William Grimstad, former editor of *White Power*; and James K. Warner, an early American Nazi Party member.[23] (Black would later become famous for founding *Stormfront*, the most popular White Supremacist website until the Alt Right era.) Later on, Duke would hire another Rockwell veteran, Ralph Forbes, as his 1987 campaign manager. Tom Metzger was also in the KKKK, although he was going in the other direction, heading toward National Socialism. And White Supremacists who favored armed struggle and influenced the neo-Nazi milieu, including Louis Beam and David Lane, were also members.[24]

When Hand left the KKKK in 1979, he denounced Duke for cowardice and backtracking on antisemitism and later accused him of absconding with all the group's valuable parts for his new National Association for the Advancement of White People (NAAWP).[25] Hand also accused Duke of lying when he claimed the new group had 11,000 members; the real number, he said, was 73.[26]

The NSLF had already been targeting Duke. In 1975, the Louisville NSLF accused him of stealing $2,000 in NSWPP seed money earmarked for the White Youth Alliance.[27] A few years later, the Delaware NSLF accused Duke of snitching to police about Hand's whereabouts while he was on the run.[28] And after becoming the NSLF leader, Hand would continue to attack Duke's electoral campaigns; for example, in 1984, he accused him of being "an egomaniac, a liar, a con artist, and a glory hound." These fusillades continued from prison; in 1991, Hand promised to "continue to expose and oppose him" as a "patriot for profit" who had thrown neo-Nazis under the bus.[29]

But the ambitious and savvy Duke had long moved on to bigger things than the tiny world of squabbling neo-Nazis. After running for office several times, he was elected in 1989 as a state representative in Louisiana, serving one term. He tried to build on this by running for higher positions. While Duke did not achieve another victory, he was popular enough to prompt President George H. W. Bush to denounce him during the 1991 Louisiana gubernatorial race; regardless, Duke still finished with 670,000 votes.[30] These electoral forays and their accompanying publicity made Duke the best-known White Supremacist in the United States at the time.

Over the next decades, Duke's profile slowly declined, but he certainly did not disappear. His 1998 autobiography, *My Awakening*, has become something of a White Supremacist classic. He spent the '00s giving talks around the world, including in Ukraine, Russia, and even Iran. This ended in 2002, when he was arrested for tax evasion and defrauding his supporters and spent 15 months in prison. In 2005, he earned a doctorate from a Ukrainian university for his dissertation "Zionism as a Form of Ethnic Supremacism."[31]

In the United States, he has remained visible in the media as a kind of touchstone for White Supremacy. Donald Trump was even challenged during both the 2016 and 2020 elections about his view of Duke.[32] And Duke is not just visible in the media, and he has continued to have a reputation among even younger White Supremacists. He was scheduled to speak at the August 2017 Charlottesville rally. In a replay of the same conflicts as before, the rally took the mass strategy position—while Mason's acolytes shunned the event.

Notes

1 Mason, "National Socialist Liberation Front," *Encyclopedia*, p.221, Kaplan incorrectly said "Tommasi already had, with William Pierce's (well) behind-the-scenes encouragement, founded the NSLF in 1969." Mason has denied this, pointing out that there was no love lost between the two. "Joseph Tommasi," *Encyclopedia*, p.302; Mason to author, November 26, 2022.

2 "NSLF Launched at Arlington Conference," *Liberator* #1, May 1969, p.1. According to Kerr, while Pierce was the "animating spirit of the NSLF, and wrote its literature," Lloyd was the group's "formal leader"; Kerr to author, emails, October 1 and 4, 2023.

3 Mason to author, November 26, 2022 and January 1, 2023; "Vietnam Fiasco Still Big Issue," *Liberator* #2, October 1969, p.1; "Where Are the Jews?," *Liberator* #2, p.2; "Jews for a Democratic Society," *Liberator* #4, January 1970, p.4.

4 "Black Terror Rages in Schools," *Liberator* #4, p.1; "LeRoi Delivers Nugget," *Liberator* #3, December 1969, p.2; "A Modest Proposal," *Liberator* #5, March 1970, p.3.

5 "Why Does the System Hate National Socialism?" (flyer) [Box 47, Folder 31].

6 NSLF Letter, "Dear Racial Comrade," December 7, 1969 [Box 47, Folder 31].

7 "LIBERATOR Burned at LSU," *Liberator* #4, p.4; Zatarain, *David Duke: Evolution of a Klansman*, pp.117–19, 122–26.
8 Zatarain, *David Duke*, pp.115–30; Bridges, *The Rise of David Duke*, pp.14–20. Both books have strong points, but both also have errors in their documentation of Duke's organizational background.
9 Ken Stern, "David Duke: A Nazi in Politics," *Issues in National Affairs* 1(4) 1991, p.3, www.bjpa.org/content/upload/bjpa/issu/ISSUES%204.pdf. See also Bridges, *The Rise of David Duke*, pp.17–18.
10 Letter to the editor, *Reveille*, November 19, 1969, cited in Zatarain, *David Duke*, pp.125–26; Kerr to author, email, October 1, 2023; *White Power*, January-February 1970, p.8, clipping [Bridges; Box 9, Folder 4].
11 "North American Congress Forges New Solidarity," *NS Bulletin* #69, September 1, 1970, p.2 [Bridges; Box 9, Folder 4].
12 "Mall Rally a Smashing Success," *NS Bulletin* #69, September 1, 1970, p.3.
13 Ibid.
14 "White Student Alliance Organized," *NS Bulletin* #69, p.4; "Membership Application for the White Student Alliance," *The Racialist*, special edition, [September 1970], p.4, clipping [Bridges; Box 9, Folder 4]; Kerr to author, email, October 1, 2023.

   Duke's biographies both have errors about this transition. Bridges, in *The Rise of David Duke* (p.19), implied this change only affected Duke's local NSLF, not the national organization, and repeated Duke's false claim that the NSLF was not officially linked to the NSWPP. Zatarain, in a very confused passage, said "the White Student Alliance was a youth arm of the NSLF"; *David Duke*, p.131.
15 "White Student Alliance Organized," *NS Bulletin* #69, p.4; David Ernest Duke, "The White Power Program," *The Racialist*, special edition, pp.1–4 [Bridges; Box 9, Folder 4].
16 Bridges, *The Rise of David Duke*, p.19; "New Organization to Mobilize White Youth," *White Power* [January 1971], clipping [Bridges; Box 9, Folder 4].
17 Bridges, *The Rise of David Duke*, pp.26–30. Zatarain claimed Duke's father convinced him to abandon neo-Nazism by the end of 1970. However, this is contradicted by Duke's links with the NSWPP at that time; *David Duke*, pp.129–30.
18 Bridges, *The Rise of David Duke*, pp.30–31; Zatarain, *David Duke*, p.175.
19 Zatarain, *David Duke*, p.139; "David Duke: In His Own Words," *Texas Observer*, January 17 & 31, 1992, p.10, http://issues.texasobserver.org/pdf/ustxtxb_obs_1992_01_17_issue.pdf
20 Bridges, *The Rise of David Duke*, p.38. The exact circumstance and date of the founding of the KKKK has been, like many other similar groups, a source of disagreement. See "Knights of the Ku Klux Klan," *SPLC*, www.splcenter.org/fighting-hate/extremist-files/group/knights-ku-klux-klan
21 Bridges, *The Rise of David Duke*, pp.39, 43, 44.
22 Mason to Hand, September 5, 1976; Hand to Mason, September 22, 1976 [both Box 25, Folder 23].
23 Bridges, *The Rise of David Duke*, pp.40–41, 132; *NS Bulletin*, August 1, 1970, clipping [Bridges; Box 9, Folder 4]. Hand also mentioned two other ex-NSWPP members, Dave Wydner and Eugene Hough; Hand to Mason, September 22, 1976.
24 "Louis Beam," *SPLC*, www.splcenter.org/fighting-hate/extremist-files/individual/louis-beam; "Knights of the Ku Klux Klan," *SPLC*.
25 Karl Hand, "Letter of Resignation from Karl Hand to David Duke," December 9, 1979, p.2 [Bridges; Box 2, Folder 4]; Hand, "Re: David Duke," press release, [September 1980] [Box 25, Folder 25].

26 Hand to Mason, August 28, 1980 [Box 25, Folder 25]. The NAAWP continued to sell both Rockwell's *White Power* and cassettes of his speeches, as well as Holocaust Denial books; Stern, "David Duke," p.10.

27 "That Old Fiery Cross," *White Liberator* #2, August 1975, p.3.

28 "Money Can't Buy Me Love…," *NSLF Bulletin* [#1, 1980], p.4.

29 Hand, "David Duke for President?," *National Socialist Observer* #8–9, 1985, p.8; Hand to Bridges, October 1, 1991 [Bridges; Box 2, Folder 4].

30 Roberto Suro, "The 1991 Election: Louisiana; Bush Denounces Duke as Racist and Charlatan," *NYT*, November 7, 1991, www.nytimes.com/1991/11/07/us/the-1991-election-louisiana-bush-denounces-duke-as-racist-and-charlatan.html; "Official Election Results, Results for Election Date: 11/16/1991," *Louisiana Secretary of State*, https://voterportal.sos.la.gov/static/1991-11-16/resultsRace/Statewide

31 "David Duke," *SPLC*, www.splcenter.org/fighting-hate/extremist-files/individual/david-duke

32 Amy Sherman, "Biden Wrong When He Says Trump Hasn't Condemned David Duke," *Politifact*, August 27, 2019, www.politifact.com/factchecks/2019/aug/27/joe-biden/biden-wrong-when-he-says-trump-hasnt-condemned-dav

APPENDIX 3

Gary/John Jewell and Perry "Red" Warthan: From Anarchism to National Socialism

Throughout the 1980s, Mason had relationships with Third Position fascists, but almost all of these had spent their entire political careers in the White Supremacist movement. There were two, however, whose trajectory was quite different: John/Gary Jewell and Perry "Red" Warthan. Both of them had been anarchists or syndicalists who were involved in the radical union the Industrial Workers of the World (IWW) in the 1970s. Both fell out with it at near the end of the decade and instead embraced fascism. And both played brief but important roles in SIEGE. Jewell urged Mason to contact Warthan. Warthan in turn acted as Mason's go-between with Manson by visiting him in prison.

John/Gary Jewell

John Jewell (also known as Gary Jewell) was one of the clearest and most public examples in the United States of a leftist moving into Third Positionist politics. He was an important member of the IWW, a revolutionary labor union whose bottom-up structure was close to European syndicalism and which included many anarchists. The IWW sought to organize all workers in all industries and in all countries. It had been of significant importance in the United States between its founding in 1905 through the early 1920s. In the 1970s, it revived, albeit to a much more modest extent, and it was during this period that Jewell and Warthan were members. But Jewell would tire of syndicalism and internationalism and instead became a champion of the *white* working-class and a staff writer for Tom Metzger's *WAR* newspaper.

Jewell started his political career on the Far Right. At the tender age of 13, he organized the National European Party in California and, in the early

1960s, spread racist propaganda both there and in West Germany, where his father was stationed with the U.S. military. However, he changed politics and, after moving to Canada, joined the IWW, in which he was described as being "extremely active" from 1972 to 1978.[1] Jewell ended up on the IWW's General Executive Board (GEB)—the administrative body that oversees matters between the union's conventions—in 1974, 1976, and 1977; additionally, he was the Toronto branch's acting secretary.[2]

While stalwartly defending international workers' solidarity, his statements in the period were consistently concerned with national identities. For example, in October 1976 he said, "I am an Internationalist—although not ashamed that my culture is Anglo-Saxon."[3] He would also later claim that raising dues for Canadian members made them "annexed" by the U.S.-based organization.[4]

In December 1976, Jewell was re-elected to the GEB and became the Canadian representative to the IWW's International Committee. The next year, he was active in the union's General Defense Committee (GDC), which provided help to prisoners, and was the editor of its bulletin.[5] (During this time, he also published in Warthan's *Anarchist Black Hammer*.) However, within the IWW, Jewell became known for his unhinged behavior. For example, one member at the time described Jewell as "a very explosive, angry, divisive character."[6]

According to the Anarchist Black Cross in Britain, "In 1978 Jewell disappeared from the IWW scene only to re-emerge in April 1979 as a 'born again' racist, anti-semite and Strasserite fascist." (Later, Jewell would say that he left the union only after being brought up on "white racism charges."[7])

Now writing as John Jewell, he started the periodical *Direct Action* as well as the "'Black and Red Front' (Revolutionary National Socialists)." In 1982, he told Mason of his admiration for Joseph Tommasi and the NSLF, and described his group as "Aryan Socialists" who stressed Strasserism. In *Direct Action*, Jewell later called on the "White Racial movement" to support three kinds of political movements: "National Separatists," "National Communists," and "Pan-Racist Revolutionaries."[8]

Whereas while in the IWW Jewell had openly defended the claims of Jews to Israeli land,[9] now he became a loquacious antisemite, calling the United States a "Khazar-ruled nigger empire." In his periodical, he said the white race's real enemy were "the Anglo-Israelites"—"the monied Anglo elite, in league with the Zionist Jews." He also specifically named the Left's embrace of LGBTQ+ politics as one of his reasons for embracing the Right. He concluded that "only a blood purge will cleanse it." And in case a reader missed the point, the same issue had several pages of antisemitic passages from Mikhail Bakunin to back up his claims.[10]

Jewell had a much greater influence on Third Position fascism than he did on syndicalism, especially on the circles in and around the National Front.

The Anarchist Black Cross said that he was influential "particularly among the young NF cadre based around Nationalism Today." His fame in Britain spread far enough that the well-known neo-Nazi Colin Jordan denounced him as a "brown Bolshevik." Jewell was reading British fascist periodicals, including *Scorpion* and *Spearhead*, and he influenced Nick Griffin's interest in the Strasser brothers.[11]

Jewell had an important influence on Mason as well, but it was not in the realm of ideas. Instead, it was in the form of a recommendation. In May 1982, Jewell visited Chillicothe, Ohio. Here he suggested that Mason get in touch with the California-based Warthan, who might be willing to act as a go-between with Manson.[12]

The useful recommendation aside, as with most others in their movement, Jewell disagreed with the veneration of Manson. In a 1983 SIEGE, Mason accused Jewell of writing a smear against a "Killer Cult" which included Mason, Warthan, and Manson. Jewell denied he had written anything in public.[13]

Although they did not end up collaborating directly, both Mason and Jewell became regular contributors to Metzger's newspaper. As a *WAR* staff writer, Jewell published numerous articles about (white) labor history, music, and Russia. He was also interviewed by Metzger on *Race and Reason*, where he stressed what, according to him, was the U.S. white working class's struggle against banking interests and opposition to foreign wars.[14]

Perry "Red" Warthan

Other than Manson, the strangest character who crossed Mason's path during this time was undoubtedly Perry "Red" Warthan. Warthan was, in succession, a child-murderer, anarchist, Klan member, neo-Nazi, prison visitor of Manson, the murderer of a teenager, and finally a born-again Christian.

Warthan had a troubled childhood and, at the age of 14, was sent to Napa State Hospital for a 90-day observation period after being caught setting multiple fires.[15] Eighteen days in, with two 12-year-olds keeping watch, Warthan strangled 10-year-old Robert R. Yarak "out of boredom and for sport." Warthan was subsequently kept in the state hospital system until he was an adult, after which he was convicted of voluntary manslaughter in 1964. However, he was declared not guilty by reason of insanity, and finally released in 1966.[16]

He said that, between 1966 and 1973, Warthan held a variety of jobs, including "gas jocky, fuller brush person, cab dispatcher, census taker, dishwasher, carnie, barber, animal rancher, and general laborer." He also joined an outlaw biker gang before federal agents raided his apartment in 1970, seizing an illegal firearm. He said, "This angered me so much, I became an anarchist," and in 1972, Warthan started the Woodstock Anarchist Party, based in Stockton, California, and its *WAP* newsletter.[17]

Despite its silly name—when anarchist Albert Meltzer challenged him on why he formed a "party," he replied "Surely no anarchist would object to an all-night pot party"—the group gained visibility in the small anarchist milieu.[18] In 1974, the Woodstock Anarchist Party reserved a park to be used for a Yippie "smoke-in" during the World's Fair Expo in Spokane, Washington, but ironically, considering Jewell's later politics, they were threatened by a Posse Comitatus group.[19] In 1975 and 1976, the Woodstock Anarchist Party also published the magazine *Anarchist Black Hammer*. It reprinted Emma Goldman, ran articles on black political prisoners and the United Farm Workers (UFW) union, and called for freedom and equal rights for "hetro, a-sexuals, transsexuals."[20]

The Woodstock Anarchist Party attracted a fair amount of attention among anarchists. There was even a short-lived chapter in Australia, which put out a periodical, *The Phantom*. Leigh Kendall, who had been a member, said "Red Warthan sent me a US flag and I and a few of my schoolmates I managed to rope in burnt it outside the US Embassy in Canberra in 1974 in solidarity with the UFW union." Later, after his conversion, Warthan sent the National Socialist White People's Party (NSWPP) newspaper to Kendall—to the latter's disgust.[21]

Warthan also joined the IWW in 1973 and won a position on the GEB at the end of 1976, alongside Jewell.[22] Warthan continued his emphasis on gender equality and put forth a proposal to change the IWW's "macho" art into that with "equal sexual representation." Despite Jewell's support, it failed. Almost immediately afterward, Warthan resigned from the IWW, GEB, GDC, and the Woodstock Anarchist Party, saying that "I still believe in Anarchism and workers self management" and that his departure was "for personal reasons."[23]

He then turned to the White Supremacist movement. He gave two different stories for it. In 1978, he mailed a statement to anarchist groups, saying the catalyst for the change was because his wife had been raped by a group of black men during a robbery. After his imprisonment, however, he said "I had been attacked by a mob of drunk black kids who were searching for a white man to kill"—although the police saved him.[24] Later, Warthan claimed he had never been an anarchist and in fact was just spying on them.[25] But it was more likely that Warthan was trying to cover his track record of, among other things, advocating for feminist and LGBTQ+ politics during his anarchist period.

Warthan was in both a Ku Klux Klan group and the NSWPP for a year before going exclusively with the neo-Nazis. He moved to Oroville, California, where he gathered a small group around his NSWPP unit, which police estimated to be little more than half a dozen, most of whom were young. They leafleted cars and put flyers in school lockers, while Warthan also started a "Dial-A-Nazi" message service.[26]

Not everyone was a teenager, though. One of his unusual associates was Mary Shellhorn; while serving time for armed robbery in federal prison in 1976, she wrote letters threatening to kill President Gerald Ford and signed them with swastikas.[27] According to Warthan, after she was released, she petitioned the Secret Service to remove her from their list of the 400 most potential presidential assassins and instead place her on the 25,000 name "less-likely" list.[28]

Warthan had seen SIEGE and initially wrote Mason in November 1981. Having broken from the NSWPP that year, he told Mason that he was now part of the Chico Area National Socialists (CANS),[29] Aryan Prisoner Association, and the Church of the Natural Order, signing his letter with the title "Reverend."[30] Warthan said he had been expelled from the NSWPP for meeting with Rick Cooper, another activist who had left the party in disgust and became a loud critic of Kerr. Together, they were planning a new group and Cooper had also asked Warthan to get in contact with Mason. (Cooper would go on to form the National Socialist Vanguard in 1983 without Warthan.) Warthan also talked about his teenage following and asked for fifty copies of SIEGE to distribute.[31]

But their relationship changed after Jewell's visit to Mason in March 1982. Mason later told Warthan that he was given "a high recommendation" by Jewell, who had "suggested that I might approach you in one sensitive area that needs attending to." That area was going to San Quentin to visit Manson, who Mason extravagantly claimed "could be holding the key to all the questions.... I need to go myself but can't afford the trip. But we need a good emissary from the NS Movement to go to him and sound him out face-to-face."[32] And so Warthan became Mason's ambassador.

In early July 1982, Warthan made the 100-mile trip to the Vacaville, California state prison for the first of four visits to Manson.[33] Besides helping Mason solidify his relationship with the prisoner, Warthan too benefited from the visits. He said that Manson had given him a letter addressed to the "kids of Oroville," which helped his recruitment efforts and resulted in more young people joining Warthan's group.[34]

Warthan was changing his approach, too. The CANS Bulletin became the NewSletter—"so I'm not controlled by CANS in fact or name." Warthan wrote about his visits to Manson, talking about the cult leader and the NSLF in the same sentence.[35] This angered Karl Hand, who in September 1982 wrote a couple letters to Warthan disavowing Manson while furiously denying that he had any connection with the NSLF—and pointing out that Warthan was not a member, either.[36] Warthan's actions catalyzed the showdown between Mason and Hand.

But Warthan's life was about to change dramatically—again. On October 13, 1982, the remains of 17-year-old Joseph Hoover were found in a remote area outside of Oroville. He had been last seen two weeks before, and his body had eight gunshots to the head.[37] Warthan, now 41 years old, said

Hoover had been a "prospective recruit," but not a member, of his neo-Nazi group. Hoover had also spoken to the police, who wanted to know who was putting neo-Nazi literature in school lockers.[38]

Racial tensions came to a boiling point in the town of less than 10,000 residents. Even though the racist literature had been distributed not just to high school students but also to an elementary school, the students' parents had not been notified, and the local police also ignored complaints.[39] In late October, a two-day school boycott by black students was followed by a call for Oroville's black residents to arm themselves.[40] After weeks of accusations, Warthan was finally arrested in November, along with two accomplices, ages 14 and 17.[41]

In the run-up to Warthan's trial, a December 1982 newspaper article, syndicated by the Associated Press, mentioned the relationship between Warthan, Manson, and Mason. Mason liked it so much he turned it into a Universal Order flyer, and it was reprinted in *Siege*.[42] Warthan was found guilty in May 1983, by which time the two teenagers involved were already serving their time. In June, Warthan received a 27-to-Life sentence; he "flashed a thumb's up sign to reporters as he was led from the courtroom."[43]

Warthan's second murder of a young person caused no concern for Mason. In 1982, he said, "as far as the police informants are concerned, we agree that death is the proper medicine." (A harsh punishment for what would probably have led to a misdemeanor charge.)[44] In fact, Mason jumped on Warthan as a made-to-order martyr, and he became one of the four ex-ANP/NSWPP murderers—alongside Joseph Paul Franklin, Raymond Schultz, and Frank Spisak—that Mason praised.

In September 1983, Warthan's trial statement was issued as the Universal Order flyer "Warthan Indicts the System" and sent to SIEGE subscribers. Using the language of Christian Identity, Warthan claimed he was being prosecuted, just as in the witch trials. Hand's NSLF also reprinted the statement.[45] Another Warthan piece, *One Man's Armageddon*, was serialized in three issues of SIEGE in 1983 and 1984; afterward, it was reprinted as a Universal Order pamphlet and included in *Siege*.[46] It described Warthan's arrest and sentencing as well as some of his broader political views. Among them were the relationship between neo-Nazis and Posse Comitatus—the same group that had threatened the Woodstock Anarchist Party in 1974. Warthan now said, "The Posse Comitatus proclaim 'power to the county,' yet they are generally anti-NS. However even they would allow a county or a number of counties to maintain an NS regime if that is what the population demanded."[47]

Warthan's third publication was *Terrorism*, which was also serialized in SIEGE starting in December 1984 and then also reprinted as a pamphlet and in the anthology. Ranting from his prison cell, Warthan called for a "White Liberation Front" and acts of violence, including lone wolf attacks, which he hoped would ignite a race war.[48] When Rice and Parfrey first wrote Mason, they both asked for a copy of *Terrorism*, although by then it was out-of-print.[49]

Post-1995

In the 1980s and '90s, Warthan unsuccessfully appealed his sentence.[50] According to his 1996 autobiography, he went in to prison as a Christian Identity reverend and once inside started reading the Bible to explore his existing White Supremacist religious beliefs. Instead, he ended up rejecting them as inconsistent with Christian teachings, saying that "In December 1988, I fully accepted the truth, pulled the Nazi stuff off my cell wall, and asked Christ to be my Savior and Friend." Warthan credited his conversion with improving his life, particularly his relationship with his family.[51]

However, this would be Warthan's last reinvention in a life full of them. He died in prison on July 7, 1999.[52]

Notes

1 The *Black Flag* in question—anarchist periodicals frequently use the name—was published in Orkney, Britain by the Anarchist Black Cross, a prisoner support group; "Gary Jewell," *Black Flag* 6(12) June/July 1982, p.11, www.thesparrowsnest.org.uk/collections/public_archive/8510.pdf; John Jewell to Mason, January 29, 1982; John Jewell interview with Metzger/*Race and Reason* (video), [1988?], "John Jewell - Race and Reason,", uploaded AldebaranVideo, November 13, 2020, https://archive.org/details/john-jewell-race-and-reason

2 IWW, *General Organizational Bulletin*, January 1974, p.6, and March–April 1974, p.7 [All issues from the IWW Materials Preservation Project].

3 In the same issue, he said, "I stand for an International, class war IWW"; IWW, *General Organizational Bulletin*, October 1976, pp.10, 12.

4 *General Organizational Bulletin*, February 1978, pp.8–9.

5 Toronto's IWW Defense Local 2 published the GDC's *Industrial Defense Bulletin*. *General Organizational Bulletin*, December 1976, p.3; *General Organizational Bulletin*, February 1977, pp.12–13; *Industrial Defense Bulletin* 4(3) 1978; IWW member, email to author, June 21, 2019 (the member requested to remain anonymous).

6 *Anarchist Black Hammer* #6, 2nd Quarter, 1976, pp.12–20; *Anarchist Black Hammer* #8, 4th Quarter, 1976, pp.1–4; IWW member, email to author, June 21, 2019.

7 "Gary Jewell," *Black Flag*, p.11; Jewell interview with Metzger/*Race and Reason* (video).

8 Jewell to Mason, January 29, 1982; *Direct Action* #70, March 1986, p.1 [both Box 13, Folder 17].

9 *General Organizational Bulletin*, February 1977, p.13.

10 Jewell to Mason, January 29, 1982 [Box 13, Folder 17]; *Direct Action* #71, May 1986, p.2, 6–8; "Gary Jewell," *Black Flag*, p.11.

11 "Gary Jewell," *Black Flag*, p.11; Macklin, *Failed Führers*, p.156n107; *Direct Action* #70, pp.4–5.

12 Mason to Warthan, April 15, 1982 [Box 29, Folder 10].

13 SIEGE 12(11) November 1983, p.6; Jewell to Mason, November 8, 1983; Mason to Jewell, November 14, 1983 [both Box 13, Folder 17].

14 Jewell interview with Metzger/*Race and Reason* (video).

15 Perry Bernard Warthan, "In Crime's Way," *Now What?*, [March 1997], https://nowwhat.cog7.org/in_crimes_way. The publication date was provided by Sherri Langton at *Now What?*; email to author, October 6, 2021.

16 Warthan later said his victim was 13 and that the trial was in 1963. AP, "Napa D.A. reveals '55 slaying by Nazi," *Press Democrat* (Santa Rosa, California), November 10, 1982, p.2B, www.newspapers.com/image/legacy/297016868; Warthan, "In Crime's Way".

17 *General Organizational Bulletin*, October 1976, p.13; Warthan, "In Crime's Way." Later, the Yippies said he claimed to have started it because their movement was "insufficiently pacifist," although it also seemed he wanted to run his own show; "Ex-Anarchist Nazi Nailed," *Overthrow* 4(3) 1982, p.5, www.jstor.org/stable/community.28042346

The Yippies (a nickname for the Youth International Party) became the largest and best known grouping of the 1960s counterculture. Led by Abbie Hoffman and Jerry Rubin, the Yippies were best-known for their humorous political stunts, such as claiming they would levitate the Pentagon during an antiwar protest. Both Hoffman and Rubin would be arrested during the 1968 protests in Chicago at the Democratic National Convention. The Yippies were also known for holding "smoke-in's," a kind of mass, outdoor civil disobedience where people smoked marijuana in defiance of drug laws, usually counting on sheer numbers to prevent mass arrests.

18 Albert Meltzer, *I Couldn't Paint Golden Angels: Sixty Years of Commonplace Life and Anarchist Agitation* (Edinburgh: AK Press, 1996), chapter 18, https://theanarchistlibrary.org/library/albert-meltzer-i-couldn-t-paint-golden-angels

19 "Yippies Plan for Expo '74," *The Signal* (Santa Clarita, California), April 10, 1974, p.31, www.newspapers.com/image/legacy/333370839

20 *Anarchist Black Hammer* #1–8, 1975–1976.

21 Leigh Kendall, emails to author, October 14, October 20, and November 5, 2021.

22 *General Organizational Bulletin*, October 1976, p.13; *General Organizational Bulletin*, December 1976, p.3.

23 *General Organizational Bulletin*, December 1976, p.4. His resignation was announced in *General Organizational Bulletin*, January 1977, p.10.

24 "Ex-Anarchist Nazi Nailed," p.5; Warthan, "In Crime's Way." Albert Meltzer gave a different version of the rape story. In that one, the rape occurred after Warthan joined the Klan. Meltzer also said that Warthan had been in the Klan as a young teenager, around the time of his first murder; Meltzer, *I Couldn't Paint Golden Angels*, chapter 18.

25 Hilary Abramson, "Hate: Nazis Aim for More Publicity," *Sacramento Bee* (California), June 15, 1981, p.1, www.newspapers.com/image/legacy/621391666. Meltzer recounted a very confusing story, from an unnamed source, which claimed Warthan was never an anarchist but infiltrated them on behalf of the Klan, which he apparently rejoined, and then spied on the Klan for James Mason. However, this is not consistent with either Warthan or Mason's words or actions; Meltzer, *I Couldn't Paint Golden Angels*, chapter 18.

26 Warthan, "In Crime's Way"; Abramson, "Hate: Nazis Aim for More Publicity".

27 Abramson, "Hate: Nazis Aim for More Publicity"; UPI, "Swastika packer pleads innocent," *Times News* (Twin Falls, Idaho), August 15, 1976, p.15, www.newspapers.com/image/legacy/567044373; UPI, "Pleads Guilty to Threats," *Lebanon Daily News* (Pennsylvania), October 21, 1976, p.42, www.newspapers.com/image/legacy/518296051

28 Abramson, "Hate: Nazis Aim for More Publicity".

29 Andy Oakley, *88: An Undercover News Reporter's Expose of American Nazis and the Ku Klux Klan* (Skokie, Illinois: P.O. Pub., 1987), p.84.

30 Warthan to Mason, November 9, 1981 [Box 29, Folder 10]; Jim Wood, "Nazis Bring Fear and Loathing to Oroville," *San Francisco Examiner*, October 31, 1982, p.1, www.newspapers.com/image/legacy/462821178. At one point in 1982,

Warthan said he was going to "discontinue the CANS Bulletin as soon as the Church of the Natural Order puts out its first Church Newsletter. The CNO is an anti-miscegenationist church made up of Aryan Christians, Creators, Odinists and others"; Oakley, *88*, p.85.

31 Warthan to Mason, November 9, 1981 [Box 29, Folder 10]. For more on Cooper, see "Rick Cooper," *Encyclopedia*, pp.64–66 and Elinor Langer, *A Hundred Little Hitlers* (New York: Metropolitan Books, 2003).

32 Mason to Warthan, April 15, 1982 [Box 29, Folder 10]. Mason later told Moynihan that Rick Cooper had made the introduction with Warthan. Mason was probably confusing this with the fact that Warthan was working with, and their initial discussions involved, Cooper; Mason to Moynihan, October 20, 1990 [Box 5, Folder 9].

33 Warthan to Mason, [April 19?], 1982; *NewSletter* #31, [1982] [both Box 29, Folder 10].

34 Jennifer Foote, "Nazi's Recruiting Tools: Guns, Uniforms and Video Games" *San Francisco Examiner*, November 8, 1982, p.A18, www.newspapers.com/image/legacy/462806866

35 Warthan to Mason, [April 19?], 1982; *NewSletter* #31 [both Box 29, Folder 10].

36 Hand to Warthan, September 2, 1982; see also Hand to Warthan, September 17, 1982 [both Box 25, Folder 22]. Warthan had clearly identified CANS as closely tied to the NSLF. One of Warthan's "Dial-A-Nazi" messages which called for executing those who engaged in "miscegenation" ended with, "This has been a public service announcement of the National Socialist Liberation Front, brought to you by the Chico Area National Socialists"; Oakley, *88*, p.87.

37 Jennifer Foote, "Oroville Nazi Pleads Innocent; Murder Described in Affidavit," *San Francisco Examiner*, November 9, 1982, p.A7, www.newspapers.com/image/legacy/462809393

38 Wood, "Nazis Bring Fear and Loathing to Oroville".

39 Ibid; Michael Dorgan, "California Town in Web of Racial Hate, Fear—and Murder," *Boston Globe*, November 7, 1982, p.2, www.newspapers.com/image/legacy/437359995. Mason reprinted one clipping from this period in *Siege*, written by Gloria LaRiva of the Workers World Party; "Oroville, Calif., Parents Say: 'Stop the Nazis!'," *Siege*, 1st. ed., p.337.

40 Wood, "Nazis Bring Fear and Loathing to Oroville"; "Suspected of Slaying, Nazi Official Arrested," *Auburn Journal* (California), November 8, 1982, p.A9, www.newspapers.com/image/legacy/379127043

41 Foote, "Oroville Nazi Denies He Killed 17-Year-Old Police Informant," *San Francisco Examiner*, November 8, 1982, pp.A1, A18, www.newspapers.com/image/legacy/462804390, www.newspapers.com/image/462806866; Foote, "Oroville Nazi Pleads Innocent".

42 AP, "Manson Refuses to Help 'Good Friend' Warthan".

43 AP, "Jury Finds Self-Styled Nazi Guilty of Murder," *San Bernardino County Sun* (California), May 27, 1983, p.A6, www.newspapers.com/image/legacy/6460622; UPI, "Nazi Leader Sentenced for Murder," June 16, 1983, www.upi.com/Archives/1983/06/16/Nazi-leader-sentenced-for-murder/8324424584000

44 SIEGE 11(12) December 1982, p.2 (*Siege*, p.411).

45 "Warthan Indicts the System," flyer, Universal Order, dated June 16, 1983, www.publiceyenetwork.us/find/hate/online_85/Aryanbbs-07.html [Box 9, Folder 12]. The flyer was sent with the September 1983 SIEGE, although the statement originally appeared in the *Christian Law Journal*. It was published by Rev. John S. Woods of the Gospel of Christ Kingdom Church in Hayden Lake, Idaho; he had previously worked with Aryan Nations. SIEGE 12(10) October 1983, p.6; *Defiance* #10, p.7; James Aho, *The Politics of Righteousness*, p.132.

46 SIEGE 12(11) November 1983, p.6; SIEGE 12(12) December 1983, p.6; SIEGE 13(1) January 1984, p.6; Warthan, *One Man's Armageddon*, pamphlet, Universal Order, [1984]; *Siege*, pp.523–30.

47 Warthan, "One Man's Armageddon," *Siege*, p.530.

48 SIEGE 13(12) December 1984, p.6; SIEGE 14(1) January 1985 p.6; Warthan, "Terrorism," *Siege*, pp.515–23. Mason also mentioned that an upcoming Warthan autobiography was being prepared, although it was never finished; SIEGE 15(2) February 1986, p.6.

49 Rice to Mason, April 24, 1986[Box 32, Folder 23]; Mason to Rice, April 27, 1986 [Box 9, Folder 20]; Parfrey to Mason, May 27, 1986 [Box 17, Folder 4].

50 "Court Upholds Neo-Nazi's Killing Conviction," *Press-Tribune* (Roseville, California), November 14, 1985, p.6, www.newspapers.com/image/legacy/475255015; "Perry Bernard Warthan, Petitioner-Appellant, v. E. Myers, Superintendent, Respondent-Appellee, 46 F.3d 1149 (9th Cir. 1995)—US Court of Appeals for the Ninth Circuit - 46 F.3d 1149 (9th Cir. 1995) Submitted: Jan. 25, 1995. *Jan. 30, 1995," https://law.justia.com/cases/federal/appellate-courts/F3/46/1149/591440

51 Warthan, "In Crime's Way".

52 "Perry Bernard 'Red' Warthan (1941 – 1999)," *Ancestry.com*, www.ancestry.com/genealogy/records/perry-bernard-red-warthan-24-1y0mfk6. The author confirmed the date with the CDCR California Men's Colony (CMC).

APPENDIX 4

In Praise of Murder Men: Serial Killers, Mass Murderers, and Lone Wolves

Lone Wolves and Leaderless Resistance

As part of the more aggressive half of the "total attack or total dropout" formula, Mason was an early advocate of "lone wolf" attacks and, to a lesser extent, "leaderless resistance." These tactics became popular among White Supremacists after SIEGE, although Louis Beam's 1983 essay "Leaderless Resistance" is generally considered the foundational document. The concepts of the lone wolf and leaderless resistance are sometimes used interchangeably, although there are differences. Far Right monitor Chip Berlet wrote that leaderless resistance refers to "spontaneous, autonomous, unconnected cells seeking to carry out acts of violence, sabotage, or terrorism against a government or occupying military force." Lone wolves, on the other hand, refer to single-actor attacks. (However, the exact meaning of both terms has become fluid over the years, and there are debates over whether they are even useful.[1])

Mason did espouse both these approaches, though infrequently under these names. Greater attention has been called to them when, in the *Siege* anthology, Mason's thoughts were combined in a section heading which Moynihan entitled "Lone Wolves and Live Wires."[2]

Joseph Tommasi's NSLF endorsed a structure that had aspects of leaderless resistance, advocating four-person cells where "No one combat unit knows who constitutes another combat unit." The difference with leaderless resistance was that these units were still part of the NSLF.[3]

Mason advocated single-actor actions both under the label "lone wolf" and without. In the spring of 1980, Mason, while still in Allen Vincent's National Socialist White Workers' Party, praised what he called "secret supporters"—lone wolves in all but name. In the second SIEGE, Mason used the term, saying illegal acts "can and MUST be carried out by INDIVIDUALS and that removes all requirement for talk, the possibility of 'conspiracy' and the danger of a leak! The lone wolf cannot be detected, cannot be prevented, seldom can be traced."[4] He emphasized this as a strategy to avoid federal conspiracy charges, which he was specifically worried about. Mason referred to it again soon after, citing Joseph Paul Franklin's murders as ideal. "No conspiracy there, just the strike of lightning." Instead, Franklin "just DID IT!" Similar calls were repeated in early 1981.[5]

When Karl Hand became the NSLF leader, Mason portrayed him not as the leader of a traditional group but rather running something like a propaganda project. Instead, SIEGE called for individual actions by those unaffiliated with the group, who should "look no further than ourselves for leadership."[6] But as the group became more traditionally structured, Mason dropped this description—although he broke away, SIEGE returned to advocating single-actor actions.[7] (The readers he hoped to inspire could, by Beam's definition, never be classic lone wolves, though, as they were supposed to avoid being on mailing lists!)

Perry "Red" Warthan also endorsed these concepts in his piece "Terrorism," which Mason published. Warthan called the attackers "Lone Eagles" but said that they could band together and become "Wolfpacks."[8]

By the time the first edition of *Siege* came out, the concepts of leaderless resistance and the lone wolf had become widespread amongst White Supremacists. Many of the killers that Mason praised in *Siege* were single actors—including Frederick Cowan, Joseph Paul Franklin, Frank Spisak, James Huberty, and John Hinckley, Jr., while The Order was an example of leaderless resistance. In Mason's publicity rounds after the book came out, he continued to promote these ideas.[9]

In 1995, Mason saw leaderless resistance as having achieved "maturity."

In the 1970s and '80s, the neo-Nazi and other White Supremacist violence he had praised was sporadic, and sometimes he had to scrape the barrel to find examples. But in the decade between The Order and the Oklahoma City bombing, various kinds of violent acts had blossomed. But the latter was the high point, and even then its perpetrators were in the militia movement and were not National Socialists. By Ryan Schuster's interview for the second edition of *Siege*, Mason had a change of mind. The problem, he said, was that while the idea was to "inspire others," it had not happened in practice.[10]

Mason not only advocated general strategies but named specific examples, sometimes giving his critique of their actions. A number of these killers were in the National States Rights Party or American Nazi Party/National Socialist White People's Party (ANP/NSWPP). Cowan was affiliated with the NSRP; Spisak and Warthan had been members of the ANP/NSWPP; and Franklin and Ray Schultz had been in both.

In addition to praising the Manson Family and Warthan, Mason praised many other murderers, sometimes going to great lengths to justify their inclusion. Over time, many of these have drifted into obscurity and in fact might be remembered mostly because of their mention in *Siege*.

Neal Bradley Long (1972–1975)

In 1975, Neal Bradley Long murdered Charles Glatt, a school desegregation planner for Dayton, Ohio. Long was later convicted of killing three black men but claimed to have killed up to 30 more between 1971 and 1975; he was given multiple life sentences.[11]

Mason called him a "proud son of Ohio" as he had killed a Jew and many black men—although he would have preferred if Long had gone out in a gunfight or suicide. In 1976, Mason wrote him in prison (and reprinted the correspondence in a later edition of *Siege*), and Warthan praised him in his "Terrorism" piece.[12]

Long died in prison in 1998.

Michael Pearch (1975)

In April 1975, Michael Pearch shot seven people at random—killing two and wounding five—in Wheaton, Maryland; all of his victims were black. Mason praised that the fact that he did not surrender but was killed by police.[13] Regarding Pearch and others like him, Mason wrote NSLF leader David Rust that "The movement loses nothing in any event but can gain a great deal by offering all these a spiritual shelter."[14]

Frederick Cowan (1977)

Although almost rote today, mass murders by individual neo-Nazis are a relatively new phenomenon in the United States. The first one by a perpetrator connected to a neo-Nazi group was Cowan in 1977. Cowan worked at the Neptune Worldwide Moving Company in New Rochelle, New York, just north of New York City.

After he was suspended by a Jewish supervisor, he returned in February 1977 and went on a rampage. Although he failed to kill his supervisor, he did murder four others, all people of color, followed by a police officer. After a shoot-out with law enforcement, Cowan committed suicide.[15]

Neighbors said Cowan subscribed to the NSRP's newspaper, and his room was filled with Nazi books and photos. However, it's unclear what his actual relationship to the NSRP was, and J.B. Stoner refused to confirm or deny that he was a member. According to Mason, Cowan "supposedly visited NSWPP

HQ at least once and I am told this by John Duffy who was sitting duty officer at the time. Apart from that, he was supposed to be a member of the NSRP."[16]

Mason wanted to see a National Socialist behind every murder, but regardless of Cowan's actual relationship to the NSRP, Mason portrayed him as such and called him a hero.[17] Cowan graced the cover of the National Socialist Movement's (NSM's) *National Socialist Bulletin* in April 1977, and inside an article praised him as one of those who showed the path for others to follow. Nonetheless, Mason said that Cowan's motives and killing of two white people (but not his Jewish boss!) were a failure on his part. Although he should have had a better plan, "Cowan's heart was in the right place," and he played a large role in Mason's "The Case of the Heebie Jeebies," a key early essay which praised various racist murders. Although Pearch had preceded him, Mason said that Cowan "will probably be remembered as the man who fired the Second Shot Heard Round the World."[18]

Joseph Paul Franklin (1977–1980)

Franklin was a former NSWPP member and a notorious serial killer. A sniper, he killed up to 21 people in a three-year period, focusing on mixed-race couples and black men.[19] He later said, "I was actually trying to start a race war. Charlie Manson is also one of my heroes. I got the idea from him."[20] Franklin also admitted to shooting pornographer Larry Flynt.

Mason knew him from their days in the NSWPP, when Franklin was known as James Vaughn. (He would later change his name, inspired in part by Nazi leader Paul Joseph Goebbels.) Franklin had joined the party in 1968[21] and met Mason in early 1969 at the Virginia party headquarters, although Franklin was "not a popular guy" and had a "non-Fascist appearance." But he was brave. Mason often told a story about when, in November 1969, they invaded the offices of the Mobe, the New Mobilization Committee to End the War in Vietnam, which had organized a protest in DC. Franklin was so strongly disliked by the other neo-Nazis that they refused to do the action with him. In the end, however, Mason was able to finally prod some to action, but it was Franklin who forced the headquarters "to be evacuated three times using gas bombs without being caught." Mason was elated, saying "that was my favorite demonstration."[22]

After Franklin left the party, he joined the NSRP in 1973 and then the UKA (United Klans of America) in 1976. The next year he started his killing spree. In March 1978, having already committed a number of murders, Franklin attempted to assassinate Flynt while he was on trial in Lawrenceville, Georgia. The *Hustler* publisher had angered Franklin by running a magazine spread with a black man and white woman.[23] While the attempt failed, Flynt was left paralyzed for the rest of his life.

Although at the time there was no information about who was behind these shootings, in the October 1980 SIEGE Mason praised the May 1979 murder of a federal judge, John Wood, Jr. and the wounding of Urban League president Vernon E. Jordan, Jr. in May 1980; Franklin later admitted to the second shooting. (Wood was killed by Charles Harrelson, the father of actor Woody Harrelson.) Mason counseled that "whoever is responsible will now realize that, henceforth, only head shots are worth risking your ass on."[24]

Mason was ecstatic after Franklin's 1980 arrest, describing him as "a gift from God." What if, Mason mused—just as he did with the Atlanta child murders and Miami riots—what if there were "three, or six, or a DOZEN other 'Joseph Franklins' at work now all over the United States? What would the System do but go crazy?"[25] Mason's local paper, the *Chillicothe Gazette*, quoted him extensively in "They hail those who hate," a piece about Franklin. Mason was so proud of the article that he reprinted it in SIEGE, made a flyer out of it, and included it in the anthology. Mason would also praise Franklin as an example par excellence of the lone-wolf strategy.[26]

Franklin was denounced by all but a few neo-Nazis. The venerable White Supremacist leader Robert Miles held him up as a positive example in 1984. In 1989, William Pierce's novel *Hunter* told the story of a White Supremacist assassin who targeted multi-racial couples; it was dedicated to Franklin.[27] Mason also kept up a correspondence with him in prison between 1996 and 2002, although Franklin mostly asked for financial help.[28]

There was what, at least on the surface, looked like an inconsistency—if not irony—in the support Franklin received. In 1977, the year the killing spree started, Mason had attended a free speech event supporting Flynt. And in 1989, after the shooting, Adam Parfrey wrote his paean to the Nazi skinhead movement in Flynt's *Hustler*.

While awaiting his sentence, Franklin admitted to many more murders than those he was convicted of as well as the attempt on Flynt. In 2013, he was executed.

Raymond Schultz (1977)

The murder committed by Raymond Schultz was perhaps the strangest of those championed. Schultz had been a member of the American Nazi Party and then the Illinois state chairman of the NSRP.[29] In May 1977, he was found unconscious on the floor of the Flossmoor, Illinois suburban home of Sidney Cohen, a Jewish man who helped run a lumber company. Cohen was dead of cyanide poisoning. Schultz was arrested but committed suicide using a cyanide pill in the back of a police car. A search of Schultz's home turned up a hit list of Jews—with Cohen listed first—and a hidden room that contained cyanide and bomb-making parts.[30]

Although the NSRP connection was not known at the time, Mason praised Schultz, and the NSM reprinted news articles about the murder. Not just had he killed a Jewish man, but he also committed suicide rather than be taken alive.[31]

Kenneth Wilson (1977)

In September 1977, Kenneth Wilson was an unwanted guest at a Labor Day church picnic south of Charlotte, North Carolina. The teenager dressed in military clothes with a swastika armband and carried an M-1 rifle. There he shot four black people, killing two, before committing suicide. Harold Covington claimed he was an official supporter of his NSPNC (National Socialist Party of North Carolina), although an investigation found no evidence of that. In his suicide note, addressed to his father, the 17-year-old said he was dating a black woman, which his family disapproved of.[32] Mason praised him as one of the 1977 murderers who had not been taken alive.[33]

Dan White (1978)

Harvey Milk became an icon after the openly gay politician was elected to the San Francisco Board of Supervisors in 1977. In November 1978, Dan White, a former board member, murdered both Milk and Mayor George Moscone. In 1980, Mason praised White at least twice; on one occasion, it was for killing "two vile system creeps," which he hoped would be part of a nation-wide wave of assassinations.[34]

Atlanta Child Murders (1979–1981)

Between 1979 and 1981, there were at least 24 unsolved murders of black children in Atlanta, Georgia.[35] Terror hung over the city as the search for the killer or killers was fruitless; fingers pointed in different directions, including, unsurprisingly, at Klan activity. In 1981, Wayne Williams, a black photographer, was arrested and convicted for two murders. There were lingering questions about his guilt—and, for those sure of it, how many murders he had actually committed. But the killings stopped.

Before Williams's arrest, Mason praised the killings in November 1980, alongside those by Franklin and White. Mason also wrote that the Atlanta murders were "the closest thing yet amounting to what is actually needed in this country." And in April 1981, just before Williams was caught, Mason said, just as with Franklin, that a number of similar events occurring simultaneously could break the System.[36]

Greensboro Massacre (1979)

After months of conflict with local white supremacists, in November 1979 the Communist Workers Party, a Marxist-Leninist group, held a "Death to the Klan" march in Greensboro, North Carolina. It was attacked by a group composed of both Klan members and neo-Nazis, including members of Covington's National Socialist Party of America (NSPA) unit. Five leftists were killed in the attack.[37] Two days later, the NSLF's Ed Reynolds said in a press release, "The Communists deserved it, we think it was wonderful what the Klan did, and our only regret is that all of them weren't killed." Mason told police that it was "the greatest thing to happen in thirty years."[38]

In SIEGE, Mason gave "a special salute to the Men of Greensboro," called them "heroes," and said the action was "a defensive masterpiece."[39] In 1980, Greensboro defendant Wayne Wood received support from the NSLF, by both Duffy and Mason.[40] Mason also encouraged readers to write Frank and Patsy Braswell.[41] In 1983, after two retrials, Frank Braswell was sentenced to five years for plotting a revenge attack in the event that the Greensboro massacre defendants were found guilty. (In a great irony, Braswell's North Carolina unit had started out with the NSWPP and switched to Tommasi's NSLF. After this, Covington took over and made it the NSPNC, which joined the National Socialist Congress and finally fused with Mason's rival, the NSPA).[42]

Bombings and Riots (1980)

Larger events also were mentioned in SIEGE. Mason rarely paid much attention to fascists outside the United States, but he took note of the wave of French and German neo-Nazi terrorism in 1980. This likely referred to bombings at the Munich Oktoberfest and a Paris synagogue. (That year was also the fascist massacre at the Bologna train station in Italy; its fallout led to the spread of Third Positionism among anglophone fascists.) Mason also wrote about riots over racial issues in Miami and other cities.[43]

Joseph Christopher, the .22 Caliber Killer (1980)

In 1980, white spree killer Joseph Christopher murdered at least 11 black men and one dark-skinned Latino man. The first four victims, in Buffalo, New York, were all shot with a .22 rifle, leading to the media dubbing the unknown assailant the ".22-Caliber Killer." Christopher later switched to stabbing as he moved to Manhattan. (In prison, he would later claim that he killed 13 black men.) After his 1981 arrest, he was diagnosed as schizophrenic and said he believed he was fighting in a race war. Christopher died in prison in 1993.[44]

Karl Hand, still in Buffalo at the time, lauded the killings. SIEGE called them an "upbeat note" and praised them again in May 1981.[45]

John Hinckley, Jr. (1981)

In March 1981, John Hinckley, Jr. shot President Ronald Reagan in an assassination attempt. The attack was not driven by politics but rather was an attempt to impress actress Jodie Foster, with whom he had become obsessed. Immediately afterward, incoming NSPA leader Michael Allen told the press that in 1979 Hinckley had been expelled from his group. Two days after the shooting, the Associated Press circulated a photo of a man in a neo-Nazi uniform who was identified as Hinckley. The *New York Times* also reported Hinckley had been in the NSPA. The paper quoted Allen as saying, "He kept talking about going out and shooting people and blowing things up," so he was assumed to be "either a nut or a Federal agent trying to entrap us." The claim was quickly retracted by the news sources, though.[46]

Ironically, the photo turned out to be of James Whittom, Clifford Herrington's former comrade in the NSM-affiliated Local Group Rockwell. Despite the debunking of the photo's identification, the FBI considered it serious enough to investigate whether Hinckley had been a neo-Nazi.[47]

Regardless of the actual truth, Mason embraced the idea of a neo-Nazi Hinckley in the May 1981 SIEGE. While Mason said no president was worth killing, as that would not change the system, "The situation is starved for action, any action, and beggars can't be choosers." Situating Hinckley in the lineage of Greensboro, Franklin, and the .22 Caliber Killer, Mason concluded, "I believe Hinckley is alright and acted in good conscience."[48] By May 1986, Mason admitted that Hinckley was not the neo-Nazi in the photos, but in 1993 Mason flipped back and affirmed that he was.[49]

Hinckley was held in a mental hospital until his release in 2016, after which he became a musician.

Frank Spisak, Jr. (1982)

Frank Spisak, Jr. was one of the handful of murderers that Mason praised who could legitimately be considered neo-Nazis.

Mason had met Spisak around 1970 at the NSWPP bookstore in Cleveland as well as at party functions in Arlington, Virginia, and they had some correspondence in 1971. The NSM paper reported that, in 1975, the White Confederacy condemned Spisak for falsely claiming he was an officer in a neo-Nazi group that he had actually been expelled from.[50]

Spisak transitioned gender, started on hormones, planned to (but didn't) get gender-affirming surgery, and had sex with men and a black female sex worker. But Spisak then reversed course and in 1982 killed three men—two who were black and one whom he thought was Jewish—during what he called "hunting parties." At his trial, Spisak sported a Hitler mustache and gave sieg heils. He was convicted and sentenced to death.[51]

Mason received a letter from death row in January 1984; Spisak said he was already in touch with Warthan and Reynolds. "I don't know what you've seen or heard about my case or me, but I assure you I'm a true **Resistance Fighter** and a **Racial Guerilla Warrior**," Spisak wrote, signing it "A National Socialist P.O.W. in North America."[52]

Mason told Reynolds that he was aware of Spisak's situation but had reservations because of his former gender transition and sexual partners. Mason was able to get over his qualms, sent Spisak literature, and adopted him as a political prisoner. The May 1984 SIEGE reprinted newspaper articles and excerpts from letters focusing on Spisak's politics, with a carefully worded endorsement that stressed that the revolution wouldn't happen "by the book." Mason also listed Spisak's address so supporters could write him, running it in SIEGE several times in 1984. Universal Order even issued one of his writings as the flyer "Frank Spisak on the Racialist Revolutionary Movement."[53]

Spisak would spend years appealing his sentence and transitioned gender once again in prison. An appeal made its way to the Supreme Court, which ruled against it in 2010. After breaking the Ohio state record for time spent on death row, Spisak was executed in February 2011.[54]

Tylenol Poisonings (1982)

In the fall of 1982, panic swept the United States after a rash of cyanide poisonings of bottles of Tylenol, a brand of acetaminophen. This resulted in numerous deaths, and the perpetrator was never caught. The incident led to the current design of many medicine bottles to prevent tampering.

Mason said the poisonings did not seem like the actions of a neo-Nazi. However, the purpose was clearly "to inspire general terror and panic" and so "harsh as it may be, we cannot argue with it."[55]

Gordon Kahl (1983)

Gordon Kahl, a Posse Comitatus member, became a Far Right martyr whose death turned him into a midwestern folk hero. Police attempted to arrest Kahl, who had been jailed for his participation in the Far Right tax resister movement, for parole violations in 1983. This led to a shoot-out in which federal marshals died. Kahl fled and, along with a third law enforcement officer, was killed in a second shoot-out.[56]

Mason was not interested in Patriot movement ideology or activism—with the exception of its violent actions. In August 1983, Mason praised Kahl as an example to be emulated in one of his more ringing declarations.

> Let there no more talk of injustice. Let there only be talk of WAR! In the case of Gordon Kahl, this man took a toll against the Enemy. The shame only is that the toll couldn't have been much, much higher. With a relatively high degree of certainty, those of us who make up the high profile segment of the Movement today may expect to one day face our own similar such test. It is criminal and cowardly to hope to avoid it.... For many of us it will be kill <u>and</u> be killed.[57]

Mason would continue to praise Kahl throughout SIEGE's run.[58]

Bernard Goetz (1984)

Mason paid short shrift to Bernhard Goetz, who committed what was probably the most high-profile shooting of the 1980s with a racial element. In December 1984, Goetz, who was white, shot four black men who he believed were about to mug him in a New York City subway.

Mason addressed the shootings in the March 1985 SIEGE. He mostly dismissed them, saying they were reflective, at best, of "one of the oldest Right Wing theories, to wit, if you push the White Man hard enough, long enough, eventually he'll strike back." To Mason, it was a 'too little, too late' enactment of traditional right-wing politics.[59]

But it is hard to think that Mason's blasé reaction—especially considering his excitement at some of the other killings whose racial motivation was even more dubious—could be separated from the fact that Goetz was from a Jewish background.

James Huberty (1984)

In July 1984, James Huberty walked into a McDonald's restaurant in San Diego, California that was less than half a block from his home in the San Ysidro neighborhood. Armed with a shotgun, a rifle, and a pistol, he proceeded to murder 21 people and injure 19 others before police killed him.[60] Many of the victims were Latino, although this reflected the area's demographics.

As the neo-Nazi murders of the late 1970s had run out, Mason grabbed onto Huberty. In the October 1984 SIEGE, Mason wrote, "Since the killer was white and the victims mainly non-white, it must stand as a stunning victory and a landmark in itself simply by virtue of the LACK of any other really revolutionary action at present."[61]

Although Huberty was not found to have a racial motivation, Mason proclaimed that "this man was definitely one of us." Even though he said the neo-Nazi press did not mention the massacre, in either positive or negative terms, Mason proclaimed that Huberty's massacre "far surpassed" all of the movement's work in the past year.[62]

The Order (1985)

The Order, also known as the Silent Brotherhood and Brüder Schweigen, was the crystallization of a possibility that had long remained in the back of the minds of both White Supremacists and their opponents in the United States: a disciplined underground terrorist group. Its members would go on to become venerated by White Supremacists.

Formed in 1983, The Order included activists associated with Aryan Nations, the National Alliance, and Ku Klux Klan groups. Taking their name from *The Turner Diaries*, they robbed armored trucks—giving significant amounts of the money to White Supremacist leaders—and murdered Alan Berg, a Jewish talk show host in Denver. But the group had a short life span. In December 1984, leader Robert Jay Mathews died after a shoot-out with police, which had ignited a fire which engulfed the building he was in.[63]

Mason and Tom Metzger saw the Order as a reversion to the guerilla strategy of Tommasi, although it was not attached to a party and was closer to leaderless resistance. Unsurprisingly, Mason was excited by them, and the January 1985 SIEGE had The Order on the cover.[64] That May, Mason heaped more praise despite his assumption that "to the best of my knowledge there were absolutely no Nazi affiliates involved." (In fact, Mathews had been in the National Alliance.)[65] Nonetheless, the next month, Mason said that, although he had nothing to do with them, the group had his "one hundred percent" support. "Those few men calling themselves The Order said more in a month of furious action than the rest of us have said in twenty years." Hand's NSLF also praised the group.[66]

Waco, the World Trade Center Bombing, Abortion Doctor David Gunn's Assassination, and the Long Island Railroad Shootings (1993)

In February 1993, several events thrilled Mason. In one, Islamists bombed the garage of the World Trade Center in New York City. (Mason also praised attacks in the Middle East.) In Waco, Texas, federal agents destroyed the compound of the Branch Davidian cult, killing 82 members and making it a cause célèbre for the Far Right. And David Gunn, an abortion doctor, was murdered in Pensacola, Florida. Mason said he was "THRILLED" by these events. "This is what we need a lot more of!"[67] And that December, Colin

Ferguson, who was black, went on a shooting spree on the Long Island Railroad, killing six and wounding 19. Mason said, "This sort of thing is necessary to bring the pot to a boil" and bring white people into a revolutionary racial consciousness.[68]

Oklahoma City Bombing (1995)

In 1995, Timothy McVeigh used a fertilizer bomb on a federal building in Oklahoma City, Oklahoma, killing 168. McVeigh was a participant in the militia movement and at gun shows sold *The Turner Diaries*, which the attack was modeled on.

Mason said, "My morale took a big boost back there in April when the federal building in Oklahoma City got blown. I was walking on cloud nine!" Happening shortly before Mason went to prison, he "considered going to court that day in a Ryder truck." He also said Tommasi would "have admired Oklahoma City. 'Pray for victory and not an end to slaughter.'"[69] In his introduction to the 2002 edition, Schuster said he hoped *Siege* readers would emulate the bombing. And a photo of McVeigh would be displayed in the apartment where two Atomwaffen Division members were murdered by a third in May 2017.[70]

Charles "Chuck" Lawrence (1971)

Although not a murderer, Mason also tried to court Chuck Lawrence, and promoted him in the same fashion as the others in *Siege*. Lawrence was an NSWPP member whom Mason had met in 1969 at party headquarters in Arlington, Virginia, and then hung out with in 1970 at a bookstore he opened in Cuyahoga Falls, Ohio. He was arrested for the February 1971 bombing of the home of Ben Maidenburg, publisher of the *Akron Beacon Journal*.[71] Pleading not guilty by reason of insanity, Lawrence spent several years in a mental institution. Mason wrote him in December 1975 after his release, trying to interest him in the NSLF, but Lawrence declined for fear of being reinstitutionalized. Mason praised him after *Siege* came out, saying he became fed up with "The whole 'Do nothing and send me money' thing" and so took action by himself.[72]

Post-1995

Mason continued to praise events well after 1995. He supported the black metal murderer Varg Vikernes and cheered on the 9/11 attacks. And in 2011, when Anders Breivik's massacred 69 at a socialist youth camp on the Norwegian island of Utøya, plus another eight at the capital in Oslo, Mason said, "The guy was dead on" even if it "won't start anything."[73]

Notes

1 Chip Berlet, "What Is Leaderless Resistance?," *Chip Berlet's Home on the Internet*, September 2017, https://web.archive.org/web/20221129050131, https://www.chipberlet.us/concept/faq-collection/what-is-leaderless-resistance. For a discussion of the changing meanings and conceptions, see Eli Lee, "What Is 'Lone Wolf' Terrorism in the Digital Age?," *Political Research Associates*, November 21, 2015, https://politicalresearch.org/2015/11/21/what-lone-wolf-terrorism-digital-age

2 Mason interview with Schuster (video).

3 Tommasi, "Building the Revolutionary Party," *Siege*, p.510.

4 *White Worker's Bulletin* 9(2) March–April 1980, p.5; SIEGE 9(5) September 1980, pp.3–4 (*Siege*, pp.97–98).

5 SIEGE 9(7) November 1980, p.3 (*Siege*, pp.285–86); SIEGE 10(1) January 1981, pp.5–6 (*Siege*, pp.63–65); SIEGE 10(2) February 1981, pp.4–5 (*Siege*, pp.65–67).

6 SIEGE 10(3) March 1981, pp.3–4.

7 SIEGE 12(10) October 1983, p.5; SIEGE 12(12) December 1983, p.5.

8 Warthan, "Terrorism," *Siege*, pp.515–23.

9 *Siege*, pp.279–318; Prendergast, "Beyond the Pale," p.27 (*Articles*, p.55).

10 Mason interview in *NS Worldview*, p.14; Mason interview with Schuster (video).

11 Josh Sweigart, "Mitchell Slaying Unsolved, but Detective Convinced He Talked to Killer," *Dayton Daily News*, August 30, 2016, www.daytondailynews.com/news/mitchell-slaying-unsolved-but-detective-convinced-talked-killer/Xus9EXxdmKCk5FscxApgBJ

12 Mason, "A Case of the Heebie Jeebies," p.2; *Siege*, 4th ed., pp.602–10; Warthan, "Terrorism," *Siege*, p.517; Sweigart, "Mitchell Slaying Unsolved".

13 "Wheaton Plaza Gunman Had Lived at Friendsville," *Cumberland Evening Times* (Maryland), April 16, 1975, p.39, www.newspapers.com/image/18318048; Mason, "A Case of the Heebie Jeebies," p.2.

14 Mason to Rust, September 29, 1975 [Box 15, Folder 13].

15 James Feron, "Police Link Slayer of Five to a Militant Racist Party," *NYT*, February 16, 1977, www.nytimes.com/1977/02/16/archives/police-link-slayer-of-five-to-a-militant-racist-party.html

16 Ibid; Mason to Moynihan, October 20, 1990 [Box 5, Folder 9]. It should be noted that in his zeal to claim a variety of murderers as neo-Nazis, Mason was sometimes sloppier with his facts than usual.

17 SIEGE 10(4) April 1981, p.4 (*Siege*, p.158).

18 "Revolution under Our Nose," *National Socialist Bulletin* 6(4) April 1977, pp.1–4; Mason, "A Case of the Heebie Jeebies," p.2.

19 Franklin was always coy about how many murders he had committed. He was convicted for six and suspected in at least a dozen more—in addition to those he had only wounded. He killed mixed-race couples, black people, hitchhikers, a Jewish man, and his own girlfriend. Mel Ayton, *Dark Soul of the South: The Life and Crimes of Racist Killer Joseph Paul Franklin* (Washington, DC: Potomac Books, 2011); Paul Vitello, "White Supremacist Convicted of Several Murders Is Put to Death in Missouri," *NYT*, November 20, 2013, www.nytimes.com/2013/11/21/us/joseph-paul-franklin-executed-in-missouri.html

20 Franklin interview in *Gallery*, p.63.

21 Franklin claimed he became a National Socialist in 1963 at age at 13; Ayton, *Dark Soul of the South*, pp.2, 25, 30, 272.

22 SIEGE 9(7) November 1980, p.3 (*Siege*, p.285); SIEGE 10(11) November 1981, p.3 (*Siege*, p.287); Mason interview with Schuster (video).

23 Ayton, *Dark Soul of the South*, pp.34, 36, 64–65.

24 SIEGE 9(6) October 1980, p.1 (*Siege*, p.280); Guillermo Contreras, "Judge Wood's 1979 Slaying by Charles Harrelson Was 'Crime of the Century'," *San Antonio-Express News*, August 26, 2017 (updated May 27, 2021), www. expressnews.com/sa300/article/Wood-Harrelson-1979-slaying-San-Antonio-11962060.php. Jordan later led President Bill Clinton's transition team; Ayton, *Dark Soul of the South*, pp.7–11, 258.

25 SIEGE 9(7) November 1980, pp.2, 3 (*Siege*, p.284, 286); SIEGE 10(4) April 1981, p.4.

26 Frazier, "They hail those who hate." Mason also reprinted it in SIEGE 9(8) December 1980, p.3, and *Siege*, 1st ed., p.58; SIEGE 9(7) November 1980, p.3 (*Siege*, pp.285–86).

27 "Joseph Franklin," *Encyclopedia*, p.114; Durham, *White Rage*, p.100; "William Pierce," *SPLC*, www.splcenter.org/fighting-hate/extremist-files/individual/william-pierce; SIEGE 13(10) October 1984, p.6.

28 Letters between Joseph Paul Franklin and Mason are in Box 30, Folders 18–19.

29 ADL, *Hate Groups in America*, p.35; FBI Report, "National States Rights Party," BH 105–477, April 14, 1965, p.15, part of FBI file, "National States Rights Party," uploaded by Unknown, March 26, 2016, p.334, https://archive.org/details/NationalStatesRightsPartyFBI/NSRP-Chicago-7/page/n333

30 "Checking for Neo-nazi Conspiracy in Two Bizarre Chicago Deaths," *JTA*, June 6, 1977, www.jta.org/archive/checking-for-neo-nazi-conspiracy-in-two-bizarre-chicago-deaths; UPI, "Cohen's Death Puzzles Friends—Hidden Chamber in Basement," *The Herald* (Wheeling, Illinois), June 3, 1977, p.1, www.newspapers.com/image/44594207

31 *National Socialist Bulletin* 6(8) April 1977, p.4.

32 AP, "Sniper at Church Meeting Kept Dates, Nazi Ties from Parents," *Kansas City Times*, September 7, 1977, www.newspapers.com/image/677265946; "Inquiry on North Carolina Sniper Finds No Evidence of Nazi Ties," *NYT*, September 11, 1977, www.nytimes.com/1977/09/11/archives/inquiry-on-north-carolina-sniper-finds-no-evidence-of-nazi-ties.html

33 Mason, "A Case of the Heebie Jeebies," p.2.

34 *White Worker's Bulletin* 9(2) March-April 1980, p.5; SIEGE 9(7) November 1980, p.2 (*Siege*, p.283).

35 Audra DS Burch, "Who Killed Atlanta's Children?," *NYT*, April 30, 2019, www.nytimes.com/2019/04/30/us/atlanta-child-murders.html

36 SIEGE 9(7) November 1980, p.1 (*Siege*, p.281–82); SIEGE 10(4) April 1981, p.2 (*Siege*, p.290).

37 The most comprehensive account of it is Wheaton's *Codename GREENKIL: The 1979 Greensboro Killings*.

38 Reynolds, "To Whoever It May Concern" [press release], November 5, 1979 [Box 33, Folder 9]; *White Worker's Bulletin* 8(6) November-December 1979, p.1.

39 SIEGE 9(8) December 1980, p.6 (*Siege*, p.158); SIEGE 10(4) April 1981, p.4 (*Siege*, p.158); SIEGE 15(5) May 1986, p.4 (*Siege*, p.430).

40 "Hip Shots," *National Headquarters Bulletin* #2, p.5; Wayne Wood, letter to the editor, *National Headquarters Bulletin* #3, p.4; SIEGE 9(6) October 1980, p.6. For more on Wood, see Wheaton, *Codename GREENKIL*, pp.97, 157.

41 SIEGE 13(5) May 1984, p.5.

42 Howard Carr, "Nazis in North Carolina: New Boss to Play by Rules," *Winston-Salem Journal*, July 17, 1977, p.C1, www.newspapers.com/image/938120590; UPI, "A Federal Judge, Astounded by Six American Nazis' Plans...," September 17, 1983, www.upi.com/Archives/1983/09/17/A-federal-judge-astounded-by-six-American-Nazis-plans/5029432619200; "Harold Covington," *Encyclopedia*, pp.79–80.

43 SIEGE 9(7) November 1980, p.4. Mason said there were no fewer than nine racially based riots in the United States in 1980, but of them Miami was the only one to receive significant coverage; SIEGE 10(8) August 1981, p.4.

44 AP, "Buffalo's '.22-Caliber Killer' Dies in Prison," March 4, 1993, https://apnews.com/article/fa1a89e1795b40aa57d668bb81561408

45 "Who Is the .22 Caliber Killer?," *Defiance* #2, 1980; SIEGE 9(7) November 1980, p.1 (*Siege*, p.281); SIEGE 10(5) May 1981, p.6 (*Siege*, p.299). Clippings on the shootings were included in *Siege*, 1st ed., pp.190–91.

46 Leon Daniel, "Reagan Shooting Suspect Has Had Psychiatric Care," UPI, March 31, 1981, www.upi.com/Archives/1981/03/31/Reagan-shooting-suspect-has-had-psychiatric-care/7972124801318; Joseph B. Treaster, "A Life That Started Out with So Much Promise Took Reclusive and Hostile Path," *NYT*, April 1, 1981, www.nytimes.com/1981/04/01/us/a-life-that-started-out-with-much-promise-took-reclusive-and-hostile-path.html; "Associated Press Says a Photo of U.S. Nazi Was Not Hinckley," *NYT*, April 4, 1981, www.nytimes.com/1981/04/04/us/says-a-photo-of-us-nazi-was-not-hinckley.html

47 "Man Mistaken for Reagan Attacker Asserts He Now Fears for His Life," *NYT*, April 9, 1981, www.nytimes.com/1981/04/09/us/man-mistaken-for-reagan-attacker-asserts-he-now-fears-for-his-life.html; Wayne King, "Hinckley Inquiry Studies Alleged Nazi 'Flirtation,'" *NYT*, April 13, 1981, www.nytimes.com/1981/04/13/us/hinckley-inquiry-studies-alleged-nazi-flirtation.html

48 Mason was also hopeful that the idea that a neo-Nazi was Reagan's would-be assassin would convince the public that National Socialists were not allies of the Republicans, since the Left of that time was particularly insistent on calling Reagan a "Nazi"; SIEGE 10(5) May 1981, pp.1, 5–6 (*Siege*, pp.292, 298, 299). Clippings about Hinckley appeared in *Siege*, 1st ed., pp.172, 200–201, 206.

49 SIEGE 15(5) May 1986, p.1 (*Siege*, p.259); Mason interview with Metzger/*Race and Reason* (video).

50 Frank Spisak to Mason, January 23, 1984; for the early correspondence see, for example, Spisak to Mason, May 22, 1971 [both Box 22, Folder 33]. "The White Confederacy Presents: The Official Bi-Centennial 'Rogues Gallery' (of Blacklisted S.O.B.'s)," *Ohio National Socialist* #15, p.6.

51 John Hyduk, "The Long Goodbye," *Cleveland Magazine*, April 23, 2007, https://clevelandmagazine.com/in-the-cle/the-read/articles/the-long-goodbye

52 Spisak to Mason, January 23, 1984 [Box 22, Folder 33].

53 SIEGE 13(5) May 1984, pp.1–4 (*Siege*, pp.305–8); "Frank Spisak on the Racial Revolutionary Movement" [Box 22, Folder 48].

54 Supreme Court of the United States, *Smith, Warden v. Spisak*, No. 08_724, argued October 13, 2009, decided January 12, 2010, www.supremecourt.gov/opinions/09pdf/08-724.pdf; Naimah Jabali-Nash, "Frank Spisak Executed in Ohio for Nazi-Inspired Murders," *CBS News*, February 17, 2011, www.cbsnews.com/news/frank-spisak-executed-in-ohio-for-nazi-inspired-murders

55 SIEGE 12(1) January 1983, p.5 (*Siege*, pp.301–2).

56 George Michael, *Confronting Right-Wing Extremism in the USA* (London: Routledge, 2003), p.46.

57 SIEGE 12(8) August 1983, p.4 (*Siege*, p.346).

58 For example, SIEGE 12(11) November 1983, pp.5–6 (*Siege*, p.90) and SIEGE 13(1) January 1984, p.1 (*Siege*, p.354).

59 SIEGE 14(3) March 1985, pp.5–6 (*Siege*, pp.312–14).

60 Debbi Baker, "Daughter of McDonald's Killer Has Advice for San Bernardino Shooters' Baby," *San Diego Union-Tribune*, August 23, 2016, www.sandiegouniontribune.com/opinion/the-conversation/sdut-daughter-mcdonalds-killer-james-huberty-interview-2015dec15-story.html

61 SIEGE 13(10) October 1984, p.1 (*Siege*, p.310).
62 SIEGE 13(10) October 1984, pp.1–2 (*Siege*, 310–11). Clippings of Huberty were included in *Siege*, 1st ed, pp.216–17.
63 Dobratz and Shanks-Meile, pp.190–99. For a history of The Order, see Kevin Flynn and Gary Gerhardt, *The Silent Brotherhood: Inside America's Racist Underground* (New York: Free Press, 1989).
64 Mason interview with Metzger/*Race and Reason* (video); SIEGE 14(1) January 1985, pp.1, 3.
65 SIEGE 14(5) May 1985, p.1; "David Lane," *SPLC*, www.splcenter.org/fighting-hate/extremist-files/individual/david-lane
66 SIEGE 14(7) July 1985, p.2 (*Siege*, pp.80–82); NSLF, "White Revolution" (flyer), [1985] [Box 25, Folder 24].
67 Mason to Reynolds and Beth Helen, March 17, 1993 [Box 33, Folder 5].
68 Knipfel, "The Other Nazis," p.25 (*Articles*, p.74).
69 Mason interview in *Warcom Gazette* (*Articles*, p.110); "Joseph Tommasi," *Encyclopedia*, p.306; Mason, "My View of the Bombing," *WAR* September 1995, p.4, clipping in Mason, *Articles of WAR* (1993), p.18.
70 Schuster, "Introduction," *Siege*, p.34; "Atomwaffen Division," *SPLC*.
71 Mason to Dorothy F. Lawrence, December 13, 1975, reprinted in *Siege*, 4th ed., p.614; "Neo-Nazi Accused of Placing Bomb at Publisher's Home," *NYT*, March 18, 1971, www.nytimes.com/1971/03/18/archives/neonazi-accused-of-placing-bomb-at-publishers-home.html
72 Ronald D. Clark, "'I'd Just Like to Forget about It'," *Akron Beacon Journal* (Ohio), July 28, 1976, p.D1, www.newspapers.com/image/159203098; *Siege*, 4th ed., pp.611–16; Knipfel, "The Other Nazis," p.25 (*Articles*, p.74).
73 Mason interview in *Iron March* (*Articles*, p.256).

APPENDIX 5

Christianity: Jesus, Hitler, Rockwell, Manson, and UFOs

James Mason had complicated and evolving views about Christianity, which went in several stages. While he was publishing SIEGE, Mason was a staunch atheist. Regardless, in the 1980s and '90s, he compared Charles Manson to Jesus, Adolf Hitler, and George Lincoln Rockwell. Although Mason's exact schema was a little fuzzy, Jesus was portrayed as a spiritual leader; Hitler as both a political and spiritual leader; Rockwell as a political leader; and Manson as a spiritual leader with some political elements.[1] Mason developed these beliefs alongside a varying—though largely negative—view of Christianity, but at the same time he had an increasingly spiritual view of his Universal Order philosophy. However, things took a sudden turn in 1995, when Mason had a spiritual experience just before starting his sentence. While in prison, he embraced a racist-UFO Christianity, developing his beliefs in several post-prison books. But in light of his parallel views about Manson, Jesus, and Hitler, this was not a sudden conversion but rather a trajectory with origins in the beliefs of American Nazi Party/National Socialist White People's Party leaders Rockwell and Matthias Koehl.

Rockwell and Koehl on Jesus and Hitler

Mason's spiritual trajectory started, like so much of his thinking, with the American Nazi Party. And Rockwell's National Socialism started with what he described as, essentially, a spiritual experience. When he first read *Mein Kampf*, it "was like finding part of me." In it, he discovered "abundant 'mental sunshine' which bathed all the gray world suddenly in the clear light of reason and understanding." Hitler's book stabbed into the darkness like lightning bolts of revelation, tearing and ripping away the cobwebs... National Socialism...was the doctrine of scientific, racial idealism, actually, a new "religion" for our times.... Two thousand years ago there had been a similar rise of a new approach or world-view, called a "religion"; a world-view which shook and changed the world forever.[2]

This view was further affected by Rockwell's encounter with Savitri Devi at the 1962 WUNS (World Union of National Socialists) conference. Afterward, both Rockwell and Koehl would become influenced by her doctrine of esoteric Hitlerism.[3] Although Savitri Devi's approach to Hitler's divinity was based on the avatar in Hinduism, the Americans made sure this was adjusted for a largely Christian audience.

Rockwell also encouraged the fusion of National Socialism and Christian Identity. But he went further; according to Jim Saleam, "Rockwell made various allusions to Jesus in reference to Hitler; he once called Hitler 'the greatest man in two thousand years,' but he never went any further than this."[4] Koehl, however, did. In 1972, while Mason was still in the party, Koehl directly compared the two figures, saying the latter could not die as "his immortal spirit transcends the barriers of time and space."[5]

Christianity and Christian Identity

Mason was less prone to this combination, however, and he clearly went through an internal struggle with Christianity for many years. He would have some positive interactions with Christian Identity and promoted Hitler–Jesus comparisons. Mason credited *National Christian News* publisher Oren F. Potito for giving him "my first glimpse of Identity" in 1969. (Potito, who was involved in the National States Rights Party, would also compare Hitler and Jesus.)[6]

In 1970, Mason met Reverend John A. Crites and took part in a recruiting drive at his Christian Identity church the next year. He also was supportive of Pastor Robert Miles; despite a disagreement between them, Mason described him as "a very real hero" and wrote a letter in support of his parole.[7]

In 1975 and 1977, Mason made two National Socialist Movement (NSM) flyers comparing Hitler and Jesus—although he later said they were merely "neat tricks of propaganda."[8] And in 1977, Pastor Glenn Wheeler's Christ's Identity Church sent Mason a minister's certificate, which he reprinted in the NSM's publication along with plugs for the church.[9]

During this time, and separate from his views of Christianity, Mason also started describing his vision of National Socialism in a new way. Although secular on the surface, this vision evoked a spiritual-psychological approach to inner transformation, which had become fairly common in society in the

1970s. For example, in 1978, he said, "We must now begin to undertake a purge of all conservative and reactionary elements INSIDE OURSELVES"; in 1981, he called for "a revolution more total and complete than everything ever before in history." This set the stage for the crypto-spiritual Universal Order philosophy in particular.[10]

Despite his fairly positive views in the 1970s, in July 1981 Mason launched a blistering attack on Christianity in SIEGE. All organized religion was "a terrible and deadly enemy" of the white race, and Christianity in particular was a "noxious and repulsive religion" that was "alien to our blood." The good parts of Christianity were merely those white racial aspects it had absorbed, and after the revolution, the church would go "up against the wall" along with the rest of the "establishment."[11] Mason, following Friedrich Nietzsche, reiterated a few months later that "Christianity is a philosophy of weakness designed in the first place to be popular and catch on amongst slaves in the gutters of the Roman Empire."[12]

He would repeatedly return to wrangling with various questions about Christianity, showing his own struggle with it—even as he upheld atheist answers. In August 1983, he backed away from his line on Christianity, either inspired or pushed by the example of White Supremacist pastors Robert Miles and Richard Butler, both of whom he said he would trust "all the way." Stressing that he was an atheist, as he would several times,[13] he allowed that if comrades were already believers, then Christian Identity was an acceptable path. As with Rockwell, Mason said it "in no way clashes with the National Socialist program," comparing Identity with the Positive Christianity movement promoted in Hitler's Germany. Mason specifically pointed out that he did not "oppose the Identity message within the Movement" and furthermore "that it could easily offer the only best chance the Movement has for working, effective unity."[14]

At this time, Perry "Red" Warthan also emphasized Christianity, such as in his "Warthan Indicts the System" piece which Mason published as a double-sided flyer in summer 1983. Warthan claimed he was being persecuted, just like in the Salem witch trials, by a "Satanic society"—as opposed to being prosecuted for murder.[15]

In February 1984, Mason's progression continued, as he came to terms with religion's hold on White Supremacists, including those he respected. Specifying that he was not "anti-religious"—at least as long as religion was useful to his movement—he still held that Christianity "arose from out of the twisted minds and dirty blood of a dark and lowlife brood of Semites squatting in the Levant."[16] He repeated this assessment in November 1984 but said that while God was not going to save the white race, "To attack religion, any religion, is a foolish waste of time at the best."[17]

In 1986, he returned to thinking about religion. In the March SIEGE, he distinguished between "the one, lost Truth" and organized religion, which took its place. Meanwhile, in June 1986, he noted that he could quote many passages from the Bible and even applied Christian sayings to his circumstances. In 1987, though, he again reaffirmed he was an atheist and that Christianity was an "anti-life force in itself."[18]

In the second half of the 1980s and into the early '90s, Mason's involvement with Satanic priests apparently didn't improve his view of Christianity. He was decidedly caustic in his interviews after *Siege* was released. On Bob Larson's 1993 show, Mason said about Jesus, "His revolution has played itself out" and that, after the National Socialist revolution, Christianity's "propaganda machine" would be dismantled.[19] Around the same time, Mason said, "I am more and more viewing Christian Identity as a complete waste of time. However, I have seen it perform a useful function as a conveyer belt for new people into the true movement."[20]

But Mason would soon have a change of heart. In early 1995, Ed Reynolds was ordained as a pastor in two mail-order ministries, and he sent Mason copies of these certificates along with hand-written Bible verses. Looking back, Mason said he, "first began earnestly to look into the Bible" when he first started his prison sentence in 1995.[21]

And Manson Makes Three

In 1981, Mason started developing his succession argument about Manson, which would connect him to Jesus, Hitler, and Rockwell. In the September 1981 SIEGE, Mason quoted a Family member who compared Rockwell and Manson. The next fall, he described U.S. neo-Nazism as "thirteen years in the wilderness"—that is, between the 1969 Tate–LaBianca murders and Mason crowning Manson the new leader in 1982.[22] In 1983, Mason elaborated on this:

> Two years after the assassination of Commander Rockwell and the end of that phase and that strategy there appeared on the world scene the man who would extend the content and definition of the Idea itself in order to fit perfectly the situation in the world today as we have it. That new threshold was and is represented by Charles Manson.[23]

Just as the various NSWPP splinter groups proclaimed themselves to be the true heirs of Rockwell, in 1984 Mason said the "RACIALLY AND POLITICALLY CONSCIOUS FAMILY" he was promoting was "the actual melding of the George Lincoln Rockwell Idea and the Charles Manson Idea." In 1987, Mason would prop up the Universal Order philosophy by claiming it was consistent with Rockwell's notion of the "golden mean."[24]

As SIEGE progressed, Mason also started making comparisons between Jesus, Hitler, and Manson. In fall 1981, Mason was already saying Hitler and

Manson's philosophies were different names for each other.[25] In July 1982, Mason wrote that Manson was the next neo-Nazi leader after Hitler—but also compared Manson to Jesus.[26]

That September and October, Mason printed pieces from Eric Volmar calling for a "spiritual-mystical" fascism. In "Crazy Men of Destiny," Volmar called for a coming prophet and elsewhere said this person would "come on like Charles Manson."[27] In August 1983, even as Mason reaffirmed his atheism again, he wrote about the need for National Socialism to have a spiritual component.

> A well-balanced movement containing all elements of human existence would seem to be the only thing capable of filling the vacuum that is yawning before us as alienation continues to grow from the plastic crap, cheap "imitation of life" that the System offers. Every angle from the most personal to the political and the religious, if that is what people still claim to want.[28]

At this point, Mason was citing Savitri Devi as well as developing his Universal Order philosophy, which had a spiritual component and which Mason explicitly said was compatible with religious traditions. Furthermore, according to Mason, Manson was a "holy man" who had the power to save his followers from this corrupt System. In the mid-1990s, Mason would continue to refer to the idea that Manson was a holy man.[29]

In the November 1984 SIEGE, Mason started referring to Jesus, Hitler, and Manson in the same breath, comparing how they were all treated before their greatness was acknowledged. In May 1986, Mason again compared Manson to Jesus, saying today's racist Christians would probably look down on Jesus for his clothes, hair, and lifestyle—just as they were doing with Manson.[30]

In June 1993, Mason made the Manson–Hitler–Jesus connection more explicit during his appearance on the Larson show:

> There have been more than one re-appearances of Christ-types on earth since Jesus. Hitler was one, Manson's another one. That doesn't mean they're the same person, it means they're the same personality type.[31]

Prodded by Larson, Mason made one distinction between them: Hitler was "probably greater" than Jesus. The next month, Mason also distinguished Hitler and Manson, saying that whereas Manson was a holy man, Hitler was the "last man of Western Civilization."[32]

Post-1995

By 1996, scholars communicating with Mason observed that he now had "come to realize the religiosity of his own commitment to National Socialism."[33] The Jesus he came to know in prison was certainly one of his own making. In 1998, Mason corresponded with the widow of Christian Identity minister Wesley Swift. And in a letter to the Heathen racist Katja Lane, he said that "many old comrades of mine are dismayed these days over my seeming 'conversion.'"[34]

His post-release books were fixated on his newfound religiosity, such as his comparison between *Mein Kampf* and the Bible in *The Theocrat* as well as his *Revisiting Revelation*. Mason's new beliefs combined his existing racism and antisemitism with Christianity, the divinity of Hitler, time travel, Atlantis, and parallel universes. Mason now held that God "was a colonizing race of extraterrestrials who came here 500,000 years ago" and fused their DNA with apes; whites were superior because they had the most of this alien element. Mason's views about aliens and the Bible were influenced by Erich von Däniken's *Chariots of the Gods?* For example, Mason borrowed von Däniken's argument that parts of the Bible were actually describing alien spaceships. Aliens were also part of the belief systems of other White Supremacists, including Swift's belief system.[35]

After Mason's revival, his followers republished a number of these works.[36]

Notes

1 Mason specifically points out Hitler's dual nature in SIEGE 12(3) March 1983, p.2 (*Siege*, p.393).

2 Rockwell, *This Time the World*, chapter 7, pp.128–29.

3 Goodrick-Clarke, *Hitler's Priestess*, pp.196-203, 213–14, 223–24.

4 Jim Saleam, "American Nazism," chapter 3.

5 Saleam also noted that these views became pronounced in the NSWPP by 1974, possibly as a reaction to the party's splintering. Koehl, "The Future Calls: Transcript of a Radio Broadcast by Matt Koehl on April 16, 1972," *New Order*, www.theneworder.org/fc-website.html; Saleam, "American Nazism," chapter 3. By 1983, this tendency became dominant and Koehl transformed the party into the New Order, an inward-looking Hitler-worshipping cult. Goodrick-Clarke noted the extent that Koehl, especially after the party became the New Order, developed his style of Hitler worship, including its tie to Christianity; *Black Sun*, pp.16–18.

6 Mason to Moynihan, October 7, 1992 [Box 11, Folder 12]; Mason, *One Verse Charlies*, p.13, see also pp.3, 4; Newton, *The National States Rights Party*, pp.45, 87–88.

7 Newton, *The National States Rights Party*, p.13; SIEGE 13(2) February 1984, pp.1–3; Mason to Rust, February 25, 1976; Mason to Rust, April 28, 1976 [both Box 15, Folder 13].

8 Mason, *One Verse Charlies*, p.14.

9 *National Socialist Bulletin* 6(4) April 1977, pp.12–13; *National Socialist Bulletin* 6(6) June 1977, p.18.

10 *Special Bulletin*, p.2; SIEGE 10(12) December 1981, p.4.

11 SIEGE 10(7) July 1981, pp.1, 4, 6 (*Siege*, pp.328–40).

12 SIEGE 10(11) November 1981, p.5.

13 Mason reaffirms this a number of times, including in SIEGE 12(8) August 1983, p.4 (*Siege*, p.468), SIEGE 13(11) November 1984, p.2 (*Siege*, p.382), and SIEGE 15(6) June 1986, p.2 (*Siege*, p.386).

14 SIEGE 12(8) August 1983, p.5.

15 Warthan, "Warthan Indicts the System".
16 SIEGE 13(2) February 1984, p.1.
17 SIEGE 13(11) November 1984, p.1 (*Siege*, pp.380–83).
18 SIEGE 15(3) March 1986, p.5 (*Siege*, p.379); SIEGE 15(6) June 1986, pp.2–3; Mason interview with Swezey and King (video).
19 Mason interview with Larson/*Talk Back* (video).
20 Mason interview in *NO LONGER A FANzine*, p.16; Mason, "Universal Order," *Rise* #2 (*Articles*, p.84).
21 Reynolds to Mason, May 12, 1995 [Box 33, Folder 4]; Mason, *Revisiting Revelation*, p.95; Mason interview in *Warcom Gazette* (*Articles*, p.110).
22 SIEGE 10(9) September 1981, p.5 (*Siege*, p.406); SIEGE 11(11) November 1982, p.4 (*Siege*, p.442).
23 SIEGE 12(7) July 1983, p.3 (*Siege*, p.419); Mason interview in *Regal Scroll* (*Articles*, pp.86–87).
24 SIEGE 13(3) March 1984, p.2 (*Siege*, p.472); Mason interview with Swezey and King (video); *Siege*, p.559.
25 SIEGE 10(9) September 1981, p.5 (*Siege*, p.405, but note that the text in the anthology is slightly different).
26 SIEGE 11(7) July 1982, p.2.
27 SIEGE 11(9) September 1982, pp.2–5 (*Siege*, pp.542–50); SIEGE 11(10) October 1982, p.6 (*Siege*, p.549).
28 SIEGE 13(8) August 1983, pp.4–5 (*Siege*, pp.468–69).
29 Ibid; Strausbaugh, "Siege Mentality," p.11 (*Articles*, p.48); Redden, "Manson Is My Co-Pilot," p.3 (*Articles*, p.64).
30 SIEGE 13(11) November 1984, p.5 (*Siege*, p.428); SIEGE 15(5) May 1986, pp.4–5 (*Siege*, pp.430–33).
31 Mason interview with Larson/*Talk Back* (1993).
32 This also reflected Mason's use of Savitri Devi's language about Hitler being the "last man against time." Mason interview with Larson/*Talk Back* (1993); Strausbaugh, "Siege Mentality," p.11 (*Articles*, p.48); SIEGE 11(10), October 1982, p.4 (Siege, p.414).
33 Kaplan, "Religiosity and the Radical Right," in Kaplan and Tore Bjørgo, eds., *Nation and Race: The Developing Euro-American Racist Subculture* (Boston: Northeastern University Press, 1998), p.121n20.
34 Mason to Susan, May 8, 1998 [Box 33, Folder 1]; Mason to Katja Lane, May 26, 1998 [Box 7, Folder 2].
35 Erich von Däniken, *Chariots of the Gods?* (Toronto: Bantan, 1968/1972), pp.34–44; *One Verse Charlies*, p.13; Mason to Betty A. Dobratz, May 13, 2000 [Box 2, Folder 28]. For more on the crossover between White Supremacists, anti-semitism, and UFOs, see Michael Barkun, *A Culture of Conspiracy* (Berkeley: University of California Press, 2003).
36 These included *The Theocrat*, *Revisiting Revelation*, and *One-Verse Charlies*. For Mason's post-2016 views, see "Christian Identity," *Siegeculture*, https://web.archive.org/web/20190802235742, https://siegekultur.info/christian-identity

APPENDIX 6

Women, Gay Men, and Extreme Pornography

The story of *Siege* involves very few women who participated directly—although James Mason scrupulously kept references to personal relationships out of his correspondence, which may have obscured part of this. Regardless, for Mason and the 1970s and early '80s neo-Nazi groups that he was a member of, women as the subject of discussion was far more common, and the role they were assigned in Mason's political world shifted as his associations changed. He was undoubtedly forward-thinking during his time in the neo-Nazi splinter groups, and the National Socialist Liberation Front (NSLF) actively encouraged women's political participation. Later, he relegated them to a more traditional role after he became influenced by the Manson Family. As he moved into the orbit of the Abraxas Clique, the mood turned into an ugly misogyny, something that would also become a pillar of the Alt Right.[1]

Gay men were also discussed in these neo-Nazi groups. Contrary to the standard public statements from these groups, neo-Nazis like George Lincoln Rockwell, Mason, and the NSLF's David Rust all tolerated the presence of gay men in their groups under certain conditions. At times, they even expressed that they had no issues on the personal level.

Pornography—especially child pornography but also bestiality—played a role in the story of *Siege*. It appears to have facilitated social bonding and fed into the fascination with extremes.

Scarce Women

"Women should be trained like dogs"

The NSLF's position on women was a repudiation of the American Nazi Party's. According to James K. Warner, Rockwell didn't want women as members at all but changed his mind because he wasn't in a position to turn down dues money. Warner also said that Rockwell believed that women "have no place in politics and should be trained like dogs," that in his future neo-Nazi regime they "will be reduced to serfdom with no rights at all," and even those who are party members will be "dismissed."[2] A 1965 FBI file also stressed the lack of women activists in the party.

> At one time, Rockwell indicated that he was going to establish a "Naziette's Branch" to be called the "Shower Troopers," but nothing ever came of it. Although a few females have been listed as members, they have never been appointed to positions of importance in the Party. The only woman known to work on ANP premises is Rockwell's personal "secretary."[3]

According to a 1971 FBI report on the National Socialist White People's Party (NSWPP), women could be "official supporters" but not "storm troopers, executives, or achieve any administrative status which would involve giving orders to men." This later changed, however. Around 1974, the NSWPP established the National Socialist Women's Organization, but it was disbanded when the party became the New Order. Today, the group has no prohibitions on women's participation, including in leadership roles.[4]

Women as the Vanguard

The NSLF took a position in direct contradiction to this, probably inspired by the visible presence of women in leftist groups like the Weather Underground. They said, "We recognize that women have played a vanguard role in most revolutionary efforts and involve them in every aspect of NSLF." (Mason would later praise the role women played in the Left, especially after the Brinks robbery.)[5]

And there were a number of women in the NSLF at different points in time. In the Joseph Tommasi-era *Siege* #1, NSLF Membership Secretary Kathy Andre was pictured with a rifle and credited with "three combat missions." In their other periodical the NSLF said, "Our women are allowed participation in all areas of NSLF activities, limited only by their abilities and talents."[6]

A number of other women, including Tommasi's wife, Rose, were involved in the group. She participated in the NSLF from the start and continuing into Rust's tenure until it was clear she was pregnant. According to Rust, "there were 5–10 women at any given time working with us or for us," including male members' wives and girlfriends who supported the NSLF's approach. As with Tommasi, Rust said, "We were open to women in any capacity they were able to fulfill—but I was careful not to alienate women who identified as wives and mothers first and foremost."[7]

Women were even more visible in Allen Vincent's National Socialist White Workers' Party (NSWWP). Numerous women appeared in *The California Reich*, though in domestic settings, and the *New York Times* profiled a woman who was in the group. The cover of the first *Stormer* had a picture of a line of armband-clad neo-Nazis; the two closest to the camera were women, albeit not in combat helmets like the men. Charlotte Reich was listed as part of the editorial staff from 1977 on, and there was an advice column, "White Women Ask," in several issues. While in many NSWWP representations women appeared in traditional, conservative gender roles, the party stood out by ensuring that it did not project the image of a macho, all-male organization. Rather, it was one that women were not (just) passive supporters of but could play an active role in.[8]

In the January 1981 SIEGE, Mason praised both "White Men and Women as Comrades-in-Arms in the Revolution!" In 1981, Reynolds's NSLF unit had at least two women involved in the group. He told Mason and John Duffy they were both bisexual, a point he brought up to refute accusations that they were lesbians![9] In 1982, Mason was eager to promote two women prisoners he was in contact with and who he believed were politically aligned. He ran their addresses in SIEGE, telling Reynolds, "How many times in Right Wing shit have you seen <u>WOMEN</u> in prison to write to??"[10] In 1984 and 1985, Mason printed Perry "Red" Warthan's writings which welcomed women to take "an active role in terrorism against the System" though warning that they "cannot afford to have dependent children."[11] And in the last iteration of the NSLF, Mary Sue Hand ran the prisoner outreach program.

"The problem in every case lies with the man"

Mason criticized the ANP/NSWPP approach and sought to forge something new. Seeking to recruit and involve women, he condemned the old party's "unreal and unhealthy 'stag' atmosphere."[12] But he did not stop there, saying "Maybe the deadliest built-in source of destruction the U.S. Right has is its attitudes toward women." Addressing how common it was for movement members to be in unhappy marriages, "The problem in every case lies with the man." He concluded,

> The U.S. Right is made up of frustrated men, men who are afraid of this or that or the other and seek the company of others who are similarly frustrated and frightened, in order to be able to ease their angst and perhaps

work out some of their fantasies. What woman on earth would respond to that? Women don't respond to the false macho of the phony paramilitary of the U.S. Right nor are they turned on by the secretiveness of it all.[13]

Mason also noted the failure of other groups' attempts at involving women by placing "them into uniforms and under the same kind of discipline as the men a la American Legion, etc. It doesn't work."[14]

Women Questions, Family Answers

The Manson Family provided Mason his answer regarding the appropriate way for women to take part in political work. The majority of the (all-white) group were women—including those who took part in the murders at Sharon Tate's house.[15] And Mason was impressed, not just by the militancy of the Manson Family women, but by their presence; he described them as having

> a religious, "apart" quality. They are in fact very moral, quaint in many ways, naive in some ways, polite, soft-spoken, but more fiercely dedicated than most I've known calling themselves National Socialist. They are scrupulously honest. They bewilder me at times. They are very, very slick.[16]

But these soft-spoken women were beholden to a misogynist who exerted total control over them. Vincent Bugliosi painted a picture of sexual and physical abuse. When confronted with a 16-year-old who was not obedient enough, Charles Manson "punched her in the mouth; kicked her across a room; hit her over the head with a chair leg; and whipped her with an electrical cord." She stayed in the group. In another instance, a 13-year-old girl was initiated into the group by being sodomized by Manson while Family members watched. (To prove he was being even-handed, Manson also performed oral sex on a "young boy."[17])

As Mason's apocalyptic pessimism deepened, and despite not having a family himself, he wrote in 1983 that the Manson Family's Death Valley base needed to be copied "in hundreds of thousands of locations across the country."

> Hand-in-hand with revolution, with survival, is the elemental component of the Family. It is really the only way the System can be destroyed, really the only way we can survive. TRIBES of White Warriors, bands of White Men with their Women and Children who have drawn together and then pulled away from the System to allow it to fall without taking them with it.[18]

In March 1984, he claimed his ideas were found in both Manson and Rockwell's views. He advocated that couples with children would affiliate into tribes and then communities until a new racial nation arose.[19]

This was two steps back from praising women's roles as Manson Family killers. While women's place in this new racial family was part of very traditional conservative gender norms, the male's role was also downplayed (from warrior to household head). It was also far removed from Rockwell's desire for a male-dominated society where women were literally reduced to a position of "serfdom."[20]

Nonetheless, as Mason encountered the misogynistic views of the Abraxas Circle, he made no attempt to push back against them. Both Boyd Rice and Jim Goad would be arrested for domestic abuse, Thomas Thorn openly described himself as a misogynist, and Adam Parfrey went to war against feminism. Much later, even Michael Moynihan, one of the least misogynistic, would make it clear that part of his seven-point program was "A harmonious relationship between men and women versus the 'war between the sexes.'"[21]

Nazis and Gays, Gay Nazis

Casual observers often assume that neo-Nazis are viciously anti-gay at all times.[22] However, this is not always the case, and Mason's attitudes were no exception to this.

Mason would repeat over many years that the presence of gay men was a constant issue for neo-Nazis, especially as their movement perpetually lacked sufficient numbers. A specific issue which occupied him, and others in the NSWPP diaspora, was how they defined themselves in relation to Russell Veh's National Socialist League, an openly gay neo-Nazi group which had access to various hard-to-find books and films. Tommasi's NSLF denounced this group by name; the second issue of *Siege* said gays were not allowed in their organization and labeled homosexuality part of "an expanding degenerate democratic society." Below it was a cartoon about a family killing their gay son.[23]

From the end of 1975 through early 1976, Mason and Rust had hoped to find evidence proving the rumor that NSWPP leader Matthias Koehl was gay, in order to oust him. (Ironically, both the National Socialist Movement and NSLF worked with the National Socialist Party of America's Frank Collin, who would be arrested for sexually assaulting boys.)

Despite this, Rust and Mason's letters reveal the more complicated attitudes that some neo-Nazis held in private. Rust wrote that the NSLF would accept help from anyone, regardless of their sexual orientation, as long as they were "dedicated, make worthwhile contributions, and do not conduct themselves in any way that will embarrass the movement." He even went so far as to say, "I admire their honesty and courage to bear both crosses, National Socialism and homosexuality."[24]

Mason agreed, though emphasizing that a masculine gender performance was required, and he cited Rockwell as a precedent. "About half of Rockwell's best men, including officers, were queer and he <u>knew</u> it"—although they were tolerated only as long as "A man conducted himself as a man." And so both Rust and Mason agreed to tolerate Veh and his group, particularly because they had access to scarce copies of Rockwell's *White Power*.[25]

But gay men did not occupy much space in the thinking of Mason's various projects; inveighing against them was not common. In one of the few mentions in the 1970s, the NSM opposed Christian Right activist Anita Bryant's successes in overturning newly established gay rights ordinances. In 1977 they wrote, "The attitude of the revolutionary is to cheer on all ills which best the society we are sworn to destroy and replace. Let the queers run wild and rampant!"—the idea being that if straight men were propositioned sexually, they would embrace homophobia.[26]

After Mason left both the NSM and NSLF, both groups adopted more homophobic positions. SIEGE had the obligatory denunciations of gays in passing, but Mason's attitude towards Veh became increasingly warm. In August 1983, Mason wrote that while he had hated the personal ads in the National Socialist League's magazine, "Outside of that—and as long as it doesn't bring grief to the Movement—it's none of my damn business and I frankly couldn't care less." Noting that at that time the ads were gone, he started to promote Veh's World Service (and later World Service Film League) book and video distribution. These were advertised for years on SIEGE's page six, where Mason listed friendly contacts. In fact, in April 1985, Mason announced that he was collaborating with Veh to distribute videocassettes and that a list would be mailed to SIEGE subscribers, although this did not seem to have occurred.[27]

Extreme Pornography

Mason had an ongoing interest in 15- and 16-year-old girls and especially liked to photograph them. His penchant for this caused him no end of legal trouble, culminating in his 1994 arrest and subsequent sentence. Additionally, Ed Reynolds's letters to Mason included first-person (assumedly fantasy) descriptions of father–daughter incest, and Moynihan sent material about bestiality.

Even in the 1970s, Mason made his taste for porn publicly known by writing an article about the NSM's attendance at an event for *Hustler*'s Larry Flynt. "Outraged" comrades wrote in, but Mason defended the NSM position, saying that porn was better in the past and that it would not be going away.[28]

Mason did not just share politics with Reynolds; the two had similar sexual interests as well. In 1989, Reynolds sent several letters to Mason that were written in child-like cursive handwriting and from the perspective of a pre-adolescent girl, which contained detailed descriptions of incest with her father. The writer's identity was not made explicit, nor was the intended recipient—although obviously Reynolds received them before passing them on. In one response, Mason said he was glad that neither his additional pictures nor his diary were seized during the police raids in Ohio.[29] In January 1991, Reynolds shared a letter, which his girlfriend addressed to him, which expressed a desire to role-play being a 13-year-old; the language used in the letter was similar to the others. A few months later, Reynolds asked Mason, "Do you like pictures of pregnant women with milky tits? I hope so because I'll have plenty of them"—because his partner was pregnant.[30]

In 1990, Reynolds sent newspaper clippings on court rulings about child pornography; Mason asked if there were any states near Reynolds that did not have these laws. In 1991, Mason told him about a photo shoot with two 13-year-old girls and that he wished he had "'pushed' things a little further" with them.[31] And in 1992, Mason wrote Reynolds that

> I've noticed a lot of "Abuse" and "Incest" type themes on shows like Sally and Phil, etc. What they need to produce are a few father-daughter teams where both parties just swear by it and love it all the way (and you know there have to be as many of those as there are of the other kind they like to parade on TV.)

> I can't see anything wrong with producing a healthy White child regardless of how its gets produced. (And there are some really aggressive twelve-year-olds out here... and younger).[32]

To a lesser extent, Mason's correspondence with Moynihan also included discussion of sexual matters, such as whether child pornography was legal in Colorado, and Moynihan also sent material about bestiality. Moynihan handwrote, on a printout of an article about an actress who did bestiality films, a note: "Jim—here's some utterly degenerate entertainment I'm sure you'll enjoy perusing."[33] Another mailing included a guide with a detailed description of how to have sex with dogs, goats, sheep, pigs, cows, and horses.[34]

Just as the combination of Satanism and neo-Nazi terrorist ideology reappeared in the Alt Right, so did Mason's predilection for extreme pornography. It was prominent in the image board 4Chan, one of the main breeding grounds for the movement. Even in the Proud Boys, who otherwise had unexceptional Far Right views, some members traded extreme pornography.[35]

The Order of Nine Angles also promoted pedophilia as part of its wallowing in extremes, and this was picked up by the Atomwaffen Division network. One-time Atomwaffen leader John Cameron Denton (aka Rape) said that "Mason lists his favorite types of porn and recommends the best types of beastiality … He even gives tips on how to fuck certain animals"—possibly from the same guide Moynihan sent. (Unsurprisingly, Denton himself was accused by other Atomwaffen members of trading child pornography.)[36] Members of the British group Sonnenkrieg Division "expressed adoration of and calls for the weaponization of sexual violence and pedophilia." In 2019, Jacek Tchorzewski, who was linked to the group, was convicted of possessing pornography involving children as young as five as well as other extreme pornography, including necrophilia.[37]

Notes

1 A strong misogyny pervaded almost all quarters of the Alt Right, including in Siege Culture. One study found that women deemed enemies were subjected to rape threats, and that these types of threats were valorized in movement graphics. The Alt Right also had a deep crossover with the online subculture known collectively as the "manosphere" or male supremacist movement. The most famous part of it, the "incels"—involuntary celibates—have been tied to a number of murders. Bethan Johnson and Matthew Feldman, "Siege Culture after *Siege*: Anatomy of a Neo-Nazi Terrorist Doctrine," *International Centre for Counter-Terrorism*, ICCT Research Paper, July 21, 2021, p.11, https://icct.nl/publication/siege-culture-anatomy-of-a-neo-nazi-terrorist-doctrine; Spencer Sunshine, "Three Pillars of the Alt Right," *Political Research Associates*, December 4, 2017, https://politicalresearch.org/2017/12/04/three-pillars-of-the-alt-right-white-nationalism-antisemitism-and-misogyny; Emily K. Carian, Alex DiBranco, and Chelsea Ebin, eds., *Male Supremacism in the United States: From Patriarchal Traditionalism to Misogynist Incels and the Alt-Right* (London: Routledge, 2022).
2 Warner, *Swastika Smearbund*.
3 FBI report, "American Nazi Party," June 1965, p.36, in "FBI Monograph American Nazi Party," uploaded August 16, 2106 by ernie1241, p.57, https://archive.org/details/FBIMonographAmericanNaziParty
4 FBI report from SAC, St. Louis (157-27), January 8, 1971, in Tommasi FBI report; Kerr, "The History of American National Socialism, Part 7"; Kerr to author, email, September 14, 2023.
5 Tommasi, "Strategy for Revolution," *Siege*, p.509; SIEGE 12(3), March 1983, p.5 (*Siege*, pp.461–63).
6 *Siege* #1, p.5; *National Socialist Review* #4, p.4.
7 Rust to author, July 13, 2022.
8 Issues consulted were from September 1977 to January 1980. Reich is listed as an editor in all these issues, and "White Women Ask—Letters to Erika Reich" appears in 2(2–4), 1979–1980. (Assumedly, after Mason's departure Reich continued as editor, and the women's column continued.) For a profile of Sandra Silva, a woman in Allen's NSWPP chapter just before it left the party, see Lacey Fosburgh, "Lonely and Full of Hate, She Joined the Nazi Party—She's Less Lonely Now," *NYT*, June 6, 1974, www.nytimes.com/1974/06/06/archives/lonely-and-full-of-hate-she-joined-the-nazi-partyshes-lonely-now-an.html
9 SIEGE 10 (1) January 1981, p.6 (*Siege*, p.65); Reynolds to Mason and Duffy, January 26, 1981 [Box 33, Folder 10].
10 SIEGE 11(1) January 1982, pp.5–6; Mason to Reynolds and Rita, December 16, 1981. However, Mason quickly found out that they were not actually interested in the cause; Mason to Reynolds and Rita, May 14, 1982 [Box 33, Folder 9].
11 Warthan, "Terrorism," *Siege*, p.520.

12 SIEGE 13(3) March 1984, p.2 (*Siege*, p.472). Mason also wrote, "There is something very wrong with any organization that doesn't have its share of women. What is called for today is a strong Movement— normal and natural—to do the job, and not anything weird or introverted"; SIEGE 12(3) March 1983, p.5 (*Siege*, p.463).

13 SIEGE 12(3) March 1983, p.5 (*Siege*, p.463).

14 Ibid; "Women in the N.S.L.F.," *National Socialist Review* #4, p.4.

15 SIEGE 12(3) March 1983, p.5 (*Siege*, pp.461–62).

16 SIEGE 10(9) September 1981, p.5 (*Siege*, p.407).

17 Bugliosi, *Helter Skelter*, Part 3, "The Investigation—Phase Two"; "Part 4: The Search for the Motive".

18 SIEGE 12(1) January 1983, p.5 (*Siege*, p.448).

19 SIEGE 14(3) March 1984, p.2 (*Siege*, p.472); SIEGE 14(3) March 1984, pp.1–2 (*Siege*, pp.469–71).

20 Warner's term describing Rockwell's views, cited in Simonelli, *American Fuehrer*, p.80.

21 Thorn interview in *Black Flame*, p.19; *TYR* #1, p.9.

22 The term "gay" is used rather than contemporary labels like LGBTQ+ for two reasons. One, it is the least-derogatory term used by the neo-Nazis themselves, and all instances of named individuals were cis-men. Additionally, it should not be assumed that neo-Nazi attitudes towards gay men were identical to their views toward people who identified as lesbian, bisexual, trans, etc.

23 *Siege* #2, p.7.

24 Rust to Mason, January 5, 1976 [Box 15, Folder 13].

25 Mason to Rust, March 5, 1976; Rust to Mason, March 3, 1976 [both Box 15, Folder 13]. Despite Rockwell admitting that, "there is a tendency for queers to come here," he said he would gas "queer traitors" even before "Jew Communist traitors." Simonelli, *American Fuehrer*, p.77; see also Schmaltz, *Hate*, pp.222–23.

26 "A Hint of Mint," *National Socialist Bulletin* 6(4) April 1977, p.9.

27 Like many other neo-Nazis, Veh was inspired in his choice of names by the NSDAP; the World Service was a German news agency in the 1930s which spread antisemitic propaganda internationally. SIEGE 12(8) August 1983, p.6; SIEGE 14(4) April 1985, pp.5–6; Mason to author, January 1, 2023.

28 "N.S.M. Gets 'HUSTLED'," *National Socialist Bulletin* 6(2) February 1977, p.12; "Mason on Pornography," *National Socialist Bulletin* 6(5) May 1977.

29 Several of these "letters" were sent from Reynolds to Mason, apparently in October and November 1989; Mason to Reynolds, October 28, 1989 [both Box 33, Folder 8].

30 Beth Helen to Reynolds, January 22, 1991; Reynolds to Mason, March 20, 1991 [both Box 33, Folder 6].

31 Reynolds to Mason, April 26, 1990 [Box 33, Folder 8]; Mason to Reynolds, April 15, 1991 [Box 33, Folder 6].

32 Mason to Reynolds and Beth, February 15, 1992 [Box 33, Folder 6].

33 Mason to Moynihan, November 25, 1992; Moynihan to Mason, clippings and printout, [November] 1992 [both in Box 11, Folder 12].

34 BeastBoy, "A Guide to Selecting a Female Animal for Fun and Friendship," [June or July] 1993 [Box 11, Folder 2].

35 Will Carless, "They Joined the Wisconsin Proud Boys Looking for Brotherhood. They Found Racism, Bullying and Antisemitism," *USA Today*, June 21, 2021, www.usatoday.com/story/news/nation/2021/06/21/proud-boys-recruitment-targets-men-looking-community/7452805002

36 Joshua Fisher-Birch, cited in Mack Lamoureux, "What You Need to Know about the Obscure Occult Group Linked to Toronto Murder," *Vice*, September 28, 2020, www.vice.com/en/article/xg8bmj/the-order-of-nine-angles-the-obscure-occult-group-linked-to-toronto-murder-of-mohamed-aslim-zafis; Nate Thayer,

"Treasure Trove of User Data Released by Anti-Fascist Hackers Lead to Identities of Scores of Clandestine Domestic Terrorists," *Nate Thayer - Journalist*, December 5, 2019, https://web.archive.org/web/20210211111631, https://www.nate-thayer. com/secret-identities-of-u-s-nazi-terror-group-revealed; Rachel Weiner, "Accused former Atomwaffen Division Leader Shared Child Pornography, Prosecutors Allege in Va. Court," *Washington Post*, March 13, 2020, www.washingtonpost. com/local/public-safety/alleged-former-atomwaffen-division-leader-shared-child-pornography-prosecutors-allege-in-va-court/2020/03/13/ea6ced0c-6544-11ea-acca-80c22bbee96f_story.html

37 Alex Newhouse, "The Threat Is the Network: The Multi-Node Structure of Neo-Fascist Accelerationism," *CTC Sentinel* 14(5), June 2021, https://ctc.usma.edu/ the-threat-is-the-network-the-multi-node-structure-of-neo-fascist-accelerat ionism; Lizzie Dearden, "Neo-Nazi Terror Offender Jailed over Indecent Images of Children and Extreme Pornography," *The Independent*, July 22, 2020, www. independent.co.uk/news/uk/crime/neo-nazi-child-abuse-prison-sentence-porn-sonnenkrieg-division-a9632636.html

APPENDIX 7

Against Capitalism and the Liberal State: The Left, Third Positionism, Islamists, and Racial Separatism

The Left was often on James Mason's mind. Over time, his position about it changed, however. Early on, Mason engaged in physical attacks against leftists while holding that the Left as a whole had taken over the U.S. government. But he would move to cheering on its attempts at destroying the System and expressing admiration for its armed struggle faction. He even suggested pursuing an alliance—a testament to how far his thought had changed from the days of the American Nazi Party accusing white Jewish Communists of being the puppet masters of black Civil Rights Movement activists.

Like some other fascists, Mason appreciated the original Bolsheviks' ruthless use of violence to seize power as well as Joseph Stalin's nationalism.[1] In 1979, Mason had already analyzed the Soviet leadership as Communist in name but Russian nationalist in action.[2]

He also admired the New Left of the 1960s: its will and solidarity, the complexity and appeal of its affiliated newspapers, the presence of women as committed activists—and, especially, its popularity. Mason's interest was noticed by others, too. "I was told at party headquarters in the 60s, when everything was so ultra-right and ultra-conservative, that I would've made a beautiful Communist."[3]

Mason knew that the New Left, in particular, was doing something right that National Socialists were doing wrong. And the answer that William Pierce initially suggested, and Joseph Tommasi ran with, was to borrow many of the slogans, looks, and tactics of the New Left militants—not the least of which was the name SIEGE itself.

In doing so, Mason's politics came close to those of Third Position fascism. This anti-capitalist minority tendency embraced racial separatism rather than supremacy, and often included ecological politics. In the United

States, the Third Positionists often called for an alliance (or at least tactical coordination) with radical leftists who were trying to destroy the System, as well as other racial separatists, especially the Nation of Islam. They also embraced Islamist groups in the Middle East who attacked Israel and the United States. However, despite the similarities on several of these points, Mason's views differed from Third Positionists on others, and he never identified as such. Despite this, he worked closely with a number of them and received their support in turn.

Hippies and Communists

The American Nazi Party hated Communists. Rockwell claimed "Marxist-Zionist traitors" controlled not just the Civil Rights Movement but the U.S. government itself. But he still saw the police as protectors if not allies, and the staunchly anti-Communist FBI head J. Edgar Hoover as on his side. Reflecting on this, in 1985 Mason said that Rockwell's approach, "Rings crazy as hell today... It involved depending upon and even HELPING the Pigs against the urban revolutionaries!!"[4]

At a meeting arranged by Tom Metzger, Mason regaled his listeners with the exploits of NSWPP members, including "after-hours and 'unofficial', out-of-uniform 'night rides' when we numbered from four to six, during which we disrupted our share of communist and assorted Left Wing gatherings." The most infamous incident occurred during November 1969, when Joseph Paul Franklin and Mason took part in an invasion of an anti-war group's headquarters, and later Mason made trouble for anti-war protestors in his home town.[5] In 1972, NSWPP members also disrupted the leftist counter-protest at the Republican National Convention in Miami.[6]

Simultaneously, the NSWPP tried to recruit disenchanted radical youth, including Communists and counterculturalists, through its student group, the original NSLF. It used language borrowed from New Left rhetoric, albeit with a strong antisemitic bent and National Socialist endgame. Tommasi's NSLF would do the same.[7]

Many sayings appeared in *Siege* which were either coined or popularized by 1960s radicals and countercultural figures like Malcolm X, Bob Dylan, Jerry Rubin, and different Black Panther leaders. These included "Political Power Stems from the Barrel of a Gun"; "by any means necessary"; "That's what we call SEIZING THE TIME!"; "Do It!"; "Those not busy being born are busy dying"; "heighten the contradictions"; "Our most eloquent statements will not be made in courtrooms, but in the streets"; and "The weapon of criticism will never equal the criticism of weapons. NSLF prefers a paralyzed enemy to a well-criticized one."[8] To these, Mason added slogans like "Smashing the Pig System."[9] *Siege* also included numerous quotes from leftists like Bakunin, Lenin, Trotsky, Mao, and Rubin.[10]

Nonetheless, the NSLF under Tommasi and Rust made a point to attack socialist bookstores. One claim of responsibility included "We don't want to harass the socialists, we want to exterminate them."[11] When Mason joined the NSLF, Rust told him to infiltrate leftist groups in order to destroy them—but, before doing so, to be sure and get hold of their books on guerilla war.[12]

This approach was noted by the NSWPP's Matthias Koehl, who claimed the NSLF was made up of "<u>Marxist Apers</u> and <u>National Bolshevists</u>." The NSLF in turn thought this would actually help them try to recruit those neo-Nazis who had such an influence![13]

Brinks

Even before his change of approach in 1981, there were elements of the Left that Mason admired. In 1976, he told Rust that neo-Nazis should Americanize their politics, the same way that U.S. Communists dropped references to "Mother Russia." To Michael Moynihan, he said that he admired the 1960s underground newspapers, which were "alive" (and had "very good porn") compared with their "bone dry and dull" neo-Nazi competitors.[14]

Mason's opinions shifted even during the period that SIEGE was still part of the NSLF. At first, he stuck to the traditional position that Communists controlled the U.S. government. He claimed that the New Left, Yippies, and black radicals had won their war and that their ideas were now those of the System.[15]

The October 1981 robbery of a Brinks armored truck in Nyack, New York, which resulted in the deaths of a guard and two police, changed Mason's thinking. It had been carried off as a joint action between the Black Liberation Army and the May 19th Communist Organization.[16] The December 1981 SIEGE was a paean to them. Mason said that while Communist militants and non-white racial nationalists were deluded into thinking the United States was a racist country—whereas neo-Nazis knew it was "a Jew/Nigger/Liberal cesspool"—nonetheless "SOMEBODY HIT THE SYSTEM! And <u>that</u> is all that counts." Emphasizing an antisemitic reading of the actions, he wrote,

> If a bunch of Black Nationalists rob a Brinks truck, if they kill some System Pigs, WHO CARES??!! Jew money is the lifeblood of the Jew System so let the niggers or anyone else who cares to open a damned artery![17]

He would stick to his new outlook, even adding Jews to his pool of potential revolutionaries. In June 1984, he wrote that, "As for what any Black or group of Blacks may do—likewise with Jews or any non-Whites" shouldn't be concerning. Their actions disrupt the System's stability, and "anything that contributes to friction, chaos and anarchy can only help us in the long run."[18]

In September 1985, he made his most comprehensive statement about this. He added that a civil war would most likely take place in the cities where the "extreme Left" and "Black and colored nationalists" were "primed and 'psyched up' for it already, armed to the very teeth, and suffer no shortage of expendable manpower." Mason advised White Supremacists to avoid becoming the target of said revolutionaries, instead letting them "take the brunt of the first, strongest System counter-attacks" while inflicting damage in return. Once things collapsed into chaos, Mason's comrades would have the possibility of mobilizing white people to take over towns and small cities.[19]

In May 1985, Philadelphia police ended a standoff with the black nationalist group MOVE by bombing their building, which ended up killing almost a dozen members and burning down two blocks of residential housing. After the event, Mason pushed his claims even further. While in the past neo-Nazis would have supported the bombing, from his new revolutionary perspective, "WE MUST WISH THEM WELL IN ANY FUTURE CLASHES THEY MAY HAVE AGAINST THE SYSTEM!" Emphasizing that "the best revolutionaries in the United States are non-White," he made a suggestion that did cross the line into Third Positionism.

> We may not picture ourselves as "allied" to these colored and Leftist groups but we must see that they too are being attacked by the common enemy, the System. Perhaps a dialogue couldn't hurt. Could there be a greater nightmare for the System and its Pigs than the two widely divergent revolutionary elements in coordination?[20]

Third Position Fascism

Many of Mason's closest allies in the 1980s and '90s were Third Position fascists. This strain of fascism is distinguishable primarily by its anti-capitalist politics, although today it typically also stresses racial separatism, environmentalism, and sometimes animal rights. Third Positionists support all types of racial separatist movements as well as anti-American and anti-Western forces in the world. These include authoritarian governments, both nationalist and Communist (such as North Korea, Bashar al-Assad's Syria, and Muammar Gaddafi's Libya), and Islamists that operate outside of the West. But one of the most visible features of Third Positionism is that they often seek to ally with, or cross-recruit members from, the Left. This sometimes gives rise to them calling for the "Left and Right to Unite and Smash the System."

Third Positionism is a logical endnote for the parts of National Socialist ideology that reject capitalist modernity. In fact, the NSDAP had a more pronounced anti-capitalist faction during its early years, although Hitler excised these elements by expelling Otto Strasser and then murdering his brother during the Night of the Long Knives in 1934. Nonetheless, at least on a philosophical level, National Socialism has always remained hostile to the atomizing, alienating, and disenchanting effects of capitalist society, regardless of actual practice. Third Positionism is just those impulses made concrete.

Although Third Positionism emerged under that name in Italy in the 1970s, various influences informed it and new ones are constantly added. Preceding it was not just the NSDAP's Strasserite faction, but also Yockey; de Benoist and the French New Right; the early period of Mussolini; and even nationalist factions on the Left like the prewar National Bolsheviks in Germany. It is more popular in Eastern Europe—Eduard Limonov's National Bolshevik Party in Russia was the best-known example—and is itself a larger trend of Red/Brown politics which pull from both the Left and Far Right.

Third Positionism is often overlooked by observers of the Far Right. When they do note it, it's often dismissed as either an oddity or something without greater meaning in terms of ideas, strategies, and tactics. And while it's true that Third Positionism has mostly been a fringe player, it has an outsized influence. It opens new directions for fascism to develop in, is a welcoming home for intellectuals, and is far more open to cross-pollination with other unorthodox forms of fascism and non-fascist movements such as revolutionary nationalism, various separatisms, Marxist-Leninism, and anarchism.

Mason has sometimes been referred to as a Third Positionist. Even Ryan Schuster, who reissued *Siege*, described it as "the best exposition of Third Positionist theory emerging from the wreckage of Western Civilization."[21] However, this was not the case. Despite Mason's tactics, he always believed the goal was an orthodox National Socialist state. On rare occasions, he also emphasized the "socialist" part of his philosophy and at one point even promoted Povl H. Riis-Knudsen's "National Socialism: A Left-Wing Movement."[22]

Nonetheless, he worked with a number of Third Positionists, including Gary/John Jewell, Metzger, and the American Front. And Mason believed, especially as time went on, in a kind of separatism. Mason's claim to be beyond "right-wingism" also pointed toward the Third Position. (Sometimes, Third Positionists claim to be "Neither Left nor Right," although most on the Left consider them to be on the extreme end of the Right.) But the greatest similarity with the political current was Mason's embrace—catalyzed by the Brinks robbery and reinforced by the MOVE bombing—of attacks against the System by Communists, black nationalists, and Islamists.

Arab Radicals and Islamists

Like a number of U.S. White Supremacists, Mason looked at Islamists favorably. In addition to praising 9/11, Mason and his comrades also paid attention to a variety of Middle Eastern anti-U.S. and anti-Zionist actors.

The NSLF under Rust had had a strong anti-Zionist focus, and Mason later followed this. In 1979, he praised the Iranian Revolution. Noting that the Palestine Liberation Organization (PLO) had moved into the former Israeli embassy in Tehran, Mason declared that "The Arabian-Moslem community of the world is our natural political ally." Far from being African or Chinese, Mason (following an existing strain of National Socialist thinking) argued that "Most of their cultural roots are ancient Aryan and in their Koran it is flatly stated that the Jew is the Devil." Indeed, PLO leader Yasser Arafat was "doing a historic, monumental job of uniting and inspiring the Moslem world against Zionism and the bandit state of Israel."[23]

After Egyptian leader Anwar Sadat was assassinated by Islamists in 1981 for making a peace treaty with Israel, Mason said, "That was the most utterly brave and heroic thing I've ever witnessed." He appreciated that they had "an aggressive philosophy that tolerates no compromise" and was openly antisemitic. Therefore, "We 100% support Moslem fundamentalism among the Arabs." In 1983, he praised the suicide bombing of a U.S. Marine base which killed 241—"The key ingredient, of course, being raw guts."[24] Mason and Ed Reynolds were also excited by the 1985 hijacking of a TWA 847, allegedly by Hezbollah.[25]

Later on, Mason was also inspired by the bombing of the World Trade Center in 1993 as well as Al-Qaeda's destruction of the World Trade Center and damage to the Pentagon on 9/11. In this he was not alone, as some other White Supremacists felt the same way.[26]

Rejecting a conspiracy theory popular on both the Left and Right, Mason said 9/11 was "a genuine act on the part of these Muslim fanatics"—as opposed to a false-flag operation by the U.S. government. Asked about a White Supremacist–Islamist alliance, Mason said that as long as there was honesty and respect, it was a possibility. The cover of Schuster's edition of *Siege* was a picture of the ruins of the World Trade Center after the attack. Mason continued to praise 9/11 in his post-prison *Revisiting Revelation*.[27]

Mason also cast Manson as someone who "bridges the gap between Left and Right." Manson himself praised Libya's Gaddafi for his antisemitism. According to him, the Libyan leader was "called evil because he's not hooked up in that same dream that runs the U.S.-and-U.S.S.R.-Jews' money control."[28] And Moynihan would sell Gaddafi's short work outlining his political philosophy, *The Green Book*, through the Storm distro.[29]

White Separatism

White Supremacists have taken different stances about their racial end goal. These have included subjecting people of color to second-class citizenship, returning to Jim Crow segregation, confining groups to reservations, re-enslavement, or mass expulsions.

Rockwell had publicly called for repatriation of black Americans to Africa, although he also praised black nationalists who sought a separate state within current U.S. borders. Tommasi, however, rejected white separatism when specifically asked about it.[30]

In the 1980s, separatism became a popular demand among U.S. White Supremacists, part and parcel with a rejection of the federal government and a turn to revolutionary politics. This version advocated breaking up the country into separate racial states—or at least breaking a white state off. The most popular idea was the Pacific Northwest Territorial Imperative, which hoped to found this state in the majority white Pacific Northwest. Unlike Metzger, Mason never directly endorsed this plan. But other areas had also been proposed, and in 1981, Mason denounced this strategy as a trap by "Big Brother," naming Harold Covington's proposed Carolina Free State specifically.[31]

In the mid-1990s through the '00s, Mason would waver on his position. As part of Mason's interest in emulating the Family's Death Valley hideaway, he called Manson "the original racial separatist."[32] In 1993, Mason repeated Rockwell's call to send black Americans "to other continents, to other parts of the earth" by giving them a "free one-way ticket" and "a very large cash subsidy"—specifying this as a form of separatism. (In 1994, Mason repeated Rockwell's plans to create reservations for those who wouldn't leave.)[33] In 1995, Mason said he wanted "true racial separatism, NOT 'White supremacy' or segregation as in the past." That year, he also appeared to endorse the classical U.S. separatist position, saying it had a chance—as sending people of color away voluntarily would not happen. Mason also drew on his experiences in the racially segregated prison system, offering it as a model for the outside.[34] In 1998, Mason referred to "what we espouse in the Separatist Movement." But in 2000, he wrote that the End-Time must come because "there now is no longer any place for any remnant to retreat,"[35] and elsewhere that year he said, "Certainly there is the so-called 'Northwest Imperative' but I don't think that is the answer." In a 2004 interview, however, he again directly rejected supremacy in favor of separatism.[36]

Notes

1 SIEGE 12(11) November 1983, pp.3–4; SIEGE 13(10) October 1984, p.5; SIEGE 13(2) February 1984, p.2.
2 *White Worker's Bulletin* 8(2) March–April 1979, p.7 [Box 47, Folder 29]. Mason was not unique in this perspective, and nor was Yockey the only rightist to adopt this position. As far back as the 1920s, Russia monarchists like the Smenovekhovtsy made similar arguments; see Christopher Gilley, *The 'Change of Signposts' in the Ukrainian Emigration: A Contribution to the History of Sovietophilism in the 1920s* (Hannover: Ibidem Press, 2009).
3 Strausbaugh, "Siege Mentality," p.9 (*Articles*, p.46).
4 Simonelli, *American Fuehrer*, pp.33–34; SIEGE 14(9) September 1985, p.3.

5 *Siege*, pp.495, 497; SIEGE 10(7) July 1981, p.4 (*Siege*, p.334).
6 Bill Boyarsky, "Republicans Ready to Acclaim Nixon," *Los Angeles Times*, August 21, 1972, p.21, www.newspapers.com/image/386089529
7 See Chapter 3, "Joseph Tommasi" and Appendix 2, "The Original NSLF and David Duke".
8 *Siege*, pp.442, 466, 508–515; see also 509.
9 SIEGE 10(12) December 1981, p.1 (*Siege*, p.248). The term "pig system" appeared almost a dozen times in *Siege*.
10 *Siege*, pp.36, 74, 156, 173, 202, 319, 337.
11 Cordova, "Socialist Workers Party Bombed," clipping reprinted in *National Socialist Review* #2, 1975, p.3.
12 Rust to Mason, February 4, 1976 [Box 15, Folder 13].
13 Rust to Mason, December 16, 1975 [Box 15, Folder 13].
14 Rust to Mason, December 10, 1976; Mason to Rust, December 20, 1977 [both Box 15, Folder 13]; Mason to Moynihan, October 22, 1992 [Box 11, Folder 12].
15 SIEGE 9(7) November 1980, p.5; SIEGE 9(4) August 1980, p.2 (*Siege*, p.57).
16 The Brinks robbery in Nyack, New York was undertaken as a joint operation by two groups which came from the armed wing of the New Left. The white members were in the May 19th Communist Organization (M19CO), which had emerged from the Weather Underground, while the Black Liberation Army had its origins in the Black Panther Party. For an overview, see William Rosenau, *Tonight We Bombed the Capitol: The Explosive Story of M19, America's First Female Terrorist Group* (New York: Atria Books, 2019). Metzger would also be supportive of the BLA prisoners from the robbery; "Black Separatist Faces Trial," *WAR* 5(2), 1986.
17 SIEGE 10(12), December 1981, pp.1–2 (*Siege*, pp.248–51; slight changes in the text).
18 SIEGE 13(6) June 1984, p.3 (*Siege*, pp.179–80; here "Jews or any Non-Whites" was changed to "alien congregations").
19 SIEGE 14(9) September 1985, pp.3–4 (*Siege*, pp.82–84).
20 SIEGE 14(6) June 1985, p.5 (*Siege*, pp.317–18).
21 "James Mason, SIEGE," *Black Sun*, https://web.archive.org/web/20030410023425, http://www.blacksunpublications.com/siege.html
22 SIEGE 9(6) October 1980, p.4 (*Siege*, p.147); SIEGE 14(6) June 1985, p.6.
23 *White Worker's Bulletin* 8(2) March–April 1979, p.7.
24 SIEGE 10(11) November 1981, pp.4, 5; SIEGE 12(12) December 1983, p.4.
25 SIEGE 14(8) August 1985, p.4 (*Siege*, p.236); Reynolds to Mason, June 16, 1985 [Box 33, Folder 7].
26 Mason interview with AAC (*Articles*, p.240). For an analysis of both the rhetoric and reality of White Supremacist–Islamist connections, see Aaron Winter, "My Enemies Must Be Friends: The American Extreme Right, Conspiracy Theory, Islam and the Middle East," in Michael Butter and Marcus Reinkowski, eds., *Conspiracy Theories in the Middle East and the United States: A Comparative Approach* (Berlin: de Gruyter, 2014), pp.35–58.
27 Mason interview with Schuster (video); Mason, *Revisiting Revelation*, p.66.
28 Strausbaugh, "Siege Mentality," p.10 (*Articles*, p.47); Schreck, ed., *The Manson File*, p.142; Schreck interview with Metzger/*Race and Reason* (video).
29 "Storm Catalog Summer 1993" [Box 11, Folders 1–4].
30 Nonetheless, privately Rockwell said that masses of black people needed to be killed to facilitate an exodus to Africa. Simonelli, *American Fuehrer*, pp.34, 74; Cordova, "Joseph Tommasi: His Last Interview," p.18.
31 SIEGE 10(1) January 1981, p.5.
32 Mason, "The Prophet," *Out of the Dust*, vol.1, p.253; see also SIEGE 12(1) January 1983, p.5 (*Siege*, p.448).

33 Mason interview with Larson (video); Knipfel, "The Other Nazis," p.25 (*Articles*, p.74).
34 Mason interview in *NO LONGER A FANzine*, p.17; Mason interview in *Ohm Clock*, p.8 (*Articles*, p.96); Mason, "Well-Directed Hate," *Out of the Dust*, vol.2, p.167.
35 Mason to Katja Lane, May 26, 1998 [Box 7, Folder2]; Mason, *Revisiting Revelation*, p.22.
36 Mason to Dobratz, May 13, 2000 [Box 2, Folder 28]; Mason interview with Sherif Ali (video).

APPENDIX 8

Robert N. Taylor and Thomas Thorn

Two Abraxas Circle members who played a limited role in James Mason's development, but are worthy of attention on their own, are the musicians Robert N. Taylor and Thomas Thorn. Taylor was a folk musician in the 1960s, influenced Michael Moynihan's heathen interests, and become part of the foundation for the fascist counterculture that the Abraxas Clique wished to build. Thorn, a musician who achieved more commercial success than the others in the 1990s, was involved with both Moynihan and Mason.

Robert N. Taylor and Changes

Taylor's history is intertwined with the history of where the U.S. Far Right overlaps with racist Heathenism. In the United States, this religion started out as part of the wave of new spiritual movements in the 1960s.

But before this, Taylor was a member of the Minutemen, a 1960s armed, anti-Communist Far Right group that was a precursor to the militia movement. He joined the organization at 14 and remained in it for 12 years, becoming the national spokesman, a member of its executive council, and editor of its magazine, *On Target*.[1] (In 1978, Mason had a friendly meeting with the Minutemen's leader, Robert DePugh, and they took pictures together.[2])

In 1969, Taylor formed Changes, a Far Right folk duo. They would play at a coffeehouse run by the Process Church, a religious group sometimes wrongly seen as Satanist, and that was also falsely rumored to have a connection with Manson. Taylor contributed to one issue of the group's magazine.[3]

In 1976, Taylor formed a pagan group called Northernway, which went on to split into two factions: one Wiccan and the other Asatrú. His Asatrú group became the Wulfing Kindred. The same year, Stephen McNallen's Viking Brotherhood would also become the Asatrú Free Assembly.[4]

But the Asatrú scene also ended up fracturing. Like the vast majority of pagans, the "universalists" had no ethnic basis for membership. However, the other two factions did. McNallen was one of the most prominent figures of the soft version, called "ethnic Asatrú." They held that all religions have a biological basis, and so Asatrú was only for Northern Europeans. However, the third faction—sometimes called "racial Odinism"—was openly White Supremacist and tied to that political movement.[5]

Taylor and Michael Murray, a former member of the American Nazi Party, were both in the Asatrú Free Assembly.[6] When it folded in 1987, they continued the soft ethnic strain by founding the Asatrú Alliance the next year. *Vor Tru*, which had been founded in 1977, became the group's paper, under their joint editorial control.[7]

Like Moynihan, Taylor was quite prolific. Periodicals he contributed to included Stephen McNallen's *Runestone*, Robert Ward's *Fifth Path*, and George Petros's *EXIT*.[8] Taylor also was an editor at *Vor Trú* and *Othala*, the Asatrú Alliance's "family-oriented magazine."[9] In 1992 or 1993, Taylor's Wulfings Kindred transitioned into being the Tribe of Wulfings.[10] In 1993, Taylor met Moynihan, who would join the group. When *Fifth Path* closed up shop in 1994, Ward went to *Vor Trú*, where he became the managing editor, while Moynihan and Taylor helped out with editorial duties.[11]

In 1994, Taylor appeared at the Parfrey-organized "Cult Rapture" art show in Seattle. Along with Moynihan and Manson, Taylor was featured in the show's poster and at the event he distributed his pamphlet *Cult of Revolution*. The first half could have passed as a revolutionary anarchist tract and included writings by Pierre-Joseph Proudhon and Sergei Nechayev. The second half was militia movement–style coded antisemitism which denounced "hidden puppet masters" controlling the world banking system and ended with a plea to break up the United States into separate racial states. Moynihan was thanked for continuing "to bear the torch."[12]

That year, Taylor also started writing for *Seconds*, sometimes sharing a byline with Moynihan. His most standout piece was an interview with Lyndon LaRouche, a former Trotskyist who went on to lead his own crypto-fascist political cult. In either that year or the next, Taylor was in Denver and met Mason.[13]

In 1996, Moynihan would revive Taylor's music career by remastering old Changes recordings and issuing them on Storm, followed by many new albums.[14] (As a racist folk group, Changes has been promoted as a forerunner to neofolk.) By 1999, Moynihan and Taylor were no longer editors at *Vor Trú*, and the Tribe of Wulfings left the Asatrú Alliance that year as well.[15]

Taylor continued to make music, releasing many albums as part of Changes. But he did not forget politics, and he both spoke and played a set at Richard Spencer's National Policy Institute conference in 2015.[16] And in 2016, *Remnants of a Season: The Collected Poems of Robert N. Taylor*, edited by Moynihan and Joshua Buckley, was released as a joint publication on their respective presses, Ultra! and Dominion.

Thomas Thorn and the Electric Hellfire Club

Thomas Thorn is best known for playing with the popular 1990s group My Life With The Thrill Kill Kult. But he also played a role in the Satanist–Nazi nexus that promoted Mason. A close friend of Moynihan's, Thorn played the 1988 Belgium show with him that influenced NON's Japanese tour. The Abraxas Circle also introduced Thorn to influential people. Through Rice, he met Anton LaVey and became a Church of Satan priest, while Moynihan introduced him to Mason, whose influence could be seen on Electric Hellfire Club records.

In 1986, Thorn played with the Boston band Sleep Chamber, at one point alongside Moynihan.[17] After he left the east coast to go to college in Wisconsin, Thorn formed the industrial noise duo Slave State with Boris Dragos in 1987.[18] Thorn described their music as

> Shouted vocals and shrieking atonal synthesizers over echoed drum machine rhythms. The songs dealt with themes of power and domination: political, social, sexual. The image we projected was decidedly totalitarian with our black jumpsuits and shaved heads.[19]

Moynihan simply dubbed them a "techno Skinhead band." They released two cassettes in 1988, *Age of Man* and *White Land, White Rule*; the latter, whatever Slave State's intentions, would come across to a normal observer as a straight-up White Supremacist release.[20] Nonetheless, as with the others in the Abraxas Circle, Thorn accused liberals of being the real fascists.

> I think that one of the things we set out to do was to prove the inherent fascism in left-wing activism. We were always the ones accused of being fascist and I always said, sure, we have those interests and fascinations.[21]

(He added that the band were primarily "libertines," however.) Thorn later said, "Slave State was a satanic band, there was no question about that" and that "Satanism and fascism are basically inseparable elements, and Slave State was definitely interested in presenting it that way."[22] During the summer of 1988, Thorn was in Europe, where he and Moynihan performed their fascist-themed Belgium event, also billed as Slave State.[23]

Shortly thereafter, Thorn moved to Chicago to try and make it in the music scene. Slave State shifted to playing industrial dance (which he dubbed "brutal authoritarian disco") and attempted to get a contract with Wax Trax!, a leading label in that genre. Instead, Thorn—then going by Buck Ryder—ended up playing keyboards with one of the label's acts, My Life With The Thrill Kill Kult, between April 1989 and December 1990.[24] Meanwhile, Dragos had gone to California, where he committed suicide in 1989, thereby ending the possibility Thorn nourished of reviving Slave State.[25]

After My Life With The Thrill Kill Kult, Thorn formed his own group, the commercially oriented Electric Hellfire Club. In an interview where Buckley described Slave State as "rife with fascist imagery," Thorn agreed and added, "Conceptually, Slave State and Electric Hellfire Club are very much the same, they just deal with issues in different way."[26] The new group started releasing material in 1991 and soon signed with Cleopatra Records, the most popular goth label in the United States at the time.

Moynihan also connected Thorn with Mason. In late summer of 1992, the band visited Las Animas, Colorado, which Mason described as the first "by anyone remotely movement." Thorn was even thanked in the first edition of *Siege*, which he described as "a very worthwhile book which contains a wealth of valuable ideas."[27]

In August 1994, Mason would see a Denver show by the group, where he was photographed wearing a minister's suit and collar.[28] The two clearly got along well, as Thorn visited Mason twice in November 1995.[29]

Mason's handiwork also was seen on the Electric Hellfire Club's 1994 EP, *Satan's Little Helpers*. The liner notes included a long excerpt from Manson's Universal Order pamphlet, and one track was named after Mason's phrase "Night of the Buck Knives."[30] What Thorn did, that even Moynihan hadn't, was to give Mason's work an appearance on what was at least a moderately commercially successful album.

Nonetheless, Thorn would later separate himself from Mason's politics—although not on the basis of racism, antisemitism, or the like. In 1997, he said, "As for Mason's fascism, it probably *is* anti-individual, and that's why no one in the Electric Hellfire Club is especially interested in joining any sort of political movement. Political movements *in general* are anti-individual."[31]

In the meantime, Thorn did the Abraxas Clique's circuit: he went on Bob Larson's show, joined the Church of Satan, played music with Clique members, and was interviewed in their publications. He also contributed a small piece to the unreleased *EXIT* issue, and Moynihan interviewed him for *Fifth Path*. In 1993, the first of three interviews with Thorn appeared in *Seconds*.[32]

In 1996, the Electric Hellfire Club album *Calling Dr. Luv* included a number of people from the Abraxas Circle. On the recording itself were Rice, Moynihan, and Diabolos Rex; Bob Heick even made an appearance, while lyrics were taken from *The Satanic Bible*.[33]

That year, the Electric Hellfire Club toured with NON; while in San Francisco, Rice brought Thorn to meet LaVey, who made him a priest. (It was the only time the two would meet.[34]) Blood Axis had previously contributed a short, minute-and-a-half song to Electric Hellfire Club's 1995 album *Kiss the Goat*, and Thorn would also play with Blood Axis, under the pseudonym Alfred Thomas.[35]

The Electric Hellfire Club would release a couple more albums in 2000 and 2001. Citing declining sales in the record industry, they stopped putting out new releases but remained active sporadically into the mid-2010s. But Thorn and his bandmates would never recapture their (modest) success of the mid-1990s.

Notes

1 J Harry Jones, Jr., *The Minutemen* (New York: Doubleday, 1968); Jack Dash, "American Psychos: Fascist Hippies Coming to Town," *Who Makes the Nazis?*, July 17, 2013, https://web.archive.org/web/20210418004124, www.whomakesthe nazis.com/2013/07/american-psychos-fascist-hippies-coming.html (originally from *Stigma*, 2005); Robert H Collins, "Anti-Red Unit Gets Top Rating," *St. Louis Post-Dispatch*, November 10, 1970, p.4C, www.newspapers.com/image/139882155

2 For example, in one letter he thanks Mason for sending photos to him. Robert DePugh to Mason, September 30, 1978; Mason to de Pugh, October 21, 1978 [both in Box 14, Folder 12].

3 Taylor, "The Process: A Personal Reminiscence," in Parfrey, ed., *Apocalypse Culture, Expanded & Revised*.

4 Gardell, *Gods of the Blood*, pp.260, 264–65.

5 Ibid, p.153; Coogan, "How Black," p.45.

6 In 1994, McNallen created a new group, the Asatrú Folk Assembly, which continues to this day. In 1998 the SPLC reported that one of its members, Ronald "Ragnar" Schuett, was a former organizer of both the SS Action Group in Colorado and the Hammerskins, a national racist skinhead group with a reputation for violence—no small feat for Nazi skinheads; "New Brand of Racist Odinism on the March," SPLC *Intelligence Report*, Winter 1998, online March 15, 1998, www.splcenter.org/fighting-hate/intelligence-report/1998/new-brand-racist-odinist-religion-march

7 Gardell, *Gods of the Blood*, pp.260, 262.

8 "Fifth Path Contributors Page," *Fifth Path* #5, 1994, p.5. For an example of his contributions, see "The Swastika, Sacred and Profane" in *EXIT* #5.

9 "Fifth Path Contributors Page," *Fifth Path* #5, p.5.

10 Gardell, *Gods of the Blood*, p.265.

11 Ibid, pp.298, 300; "A Final Note to Our Readers," *Fifth Path* #5, p.2. According to Wolff, who also joined the Tribe of Wulfings, Ward ran the magazine between issues forty-nine and fifty-nine; Markus Wolff, introduction to "Were Valkyries Real?," *Hex Magazine* #2, Fall/Winter 2007, online introduction online, https://hexmagazine.com/harvest/issue-2

12 R Nicholas Taylor, *The Cult of Revolution* (Underworld Amusements, 1994/2018); Parfrey, *Cult Rapture*, p.6.

13 "Lyndon LaRouche" (interview by Robert N Taylor), *Seconds* #40, 1996, pp.60ff (.*45 Dangerous Minds*, pp.168–77); Mason to author, January 1, 2023.

14 Changes would go on to release over a dozen records between 1995 and 2019 for various labels; "Changes," www.discogs.com/artist/82126-Changes

15 Gardell, *Gods of the Blood*, p.386n14.
16 Claus Brinker, "The National Policy Institute's 2015 Conference," *Counter-Currents*, November 2, 2015, https://counter-currents.com/2015/11/the-national-policy-institutes-2015-conference
17 For example, he played on Sleep Chamber, *Babylon* 12" (Inner-X-Music, 1986) and *Live On WZBC 11/5/86* cassette (Inner-X-Music, 1986), www.discogs.com/master/329116-Sleep-Chamber-Babylon, www.discogs.com/release/258038-Sleep-Chamber-Live-On-WZBC-11586
18 Thorn claimed he was barred from two classes at the University of Wisconsin in Madison because of the band; @RevThomasThorn (Reverend Thomas Thorn), April 10, 2018, www.facebook.com/RevThomasThorn/posts/1921939111209552
19 @RevThomasThorn (Reverend Thomas Thorn), November 5, 2015, www.facebook.com/489342694469208/posts/slave-statei-came-into-the-genre-referred-to-as-industrial-dance-music-through-t/952138094856330
20 Moynihan interview in *Esoterra*; Slave State, *Age of Man* cassette (Arbeit Group, 1988), www.discogs.com/release/224797-Slave-State-Age-Of-Man; Slave State, *White Land White Rule* cassette (AWB Recording, 1988), www.discogs.com/master/1702476-Slave-State-White-Land-White-Rule

   According to Discogs, the Arbeit Group label was run by Slave State; they released cassettes by several other bands in addition to the Slave State publication *Im Bau* and five issues of the *U-Bahn* fanzine in 1987 and 1988; "Arbeit Group," www.discogs.com/label/18037-Arbeit-Group. For U-Bahn, see "Coup De Grace Booklets & Writings," https://bloodaxisarchives.wordpress.com/coup-de-grace/coup-de-grace-booklets-writings
21 In the same interview, he said he could "take or leave Hitler," although he was much more interested in Himmler; "The Electric Hellfire Club: Burn, Baby, Burn" (Thomas Thorn interviewed by Moynihan), *Fifth Path* #4, Winter 1992, pp.34, 35.
22 Ibid, p.34; Thorn interview in *Black Flame*, p.18.
23 Moynihan interview in *Esoterra*.
24 Thorn did not appear on any albums, however. @RevThomasThorn, Facebook, November 5, 2015, www.facebook.com/489342694469208/posts/slave-statei-came-into-the-genre-referred-to-as-industrial-dance-music-through-t/952138094856330; Buzz McCoy, cited in Tracy George, email to author, October 2, 2022.
25 @RevThomasThorn (Reverend Thomas Thorn), Facebook, April 10, 2018, www.facebook.com/RevThomasThorn/posts/1921939111209552
26 Thorn interview in *Black Flame*, p.18.
27 Mason to Reynolds and Beth, August 8, 1992 [Box 33, Folder 6]; *Siege*, 1st ed., title page; Thorn interview in *Black Flame*, p.18.
28 *Articles*, pp.69, 193–94.
29 Moynihan to Mason, December 1, 1995 [Box 11, Folder 2].
30 The EP thanked "Jim Mason (For the quote & song title)," and a different mix of the same song also appeared on their next album, *Kiss the Goat*. Electric Hellfire Club, "Night of the Buck Knives (Altamont Mix)," *Satan's Little Helpers* EP (Cleopatra, 1994), www.discogs.com/release/764254-The-Electric-Hellfire-Club-Satans-Little-Helpers
31 Thorn interview in *Black Flame*, p.18.
32 Thorn interview in *Fifth Path*, pp.32–37; *EXIT* #6; "Electric Hellfire Club" (interview), *Seconds*, #24, 1993, pp.24–26. See also *Seconds* #43 (1997) and #51 (2000).
33 Diabolos Rex was one of the Satanists in the Abraxas Circle. His name is rendered different ways in different places, including as Rex Diabolos and Diabolos Rex Church. Electric Hellfire Club, *Calling Dr. Luv* (Cleopatra, 1996), www.discogs.com/release/161159-The-Electric-Hellfire-Club-Calling-Dr-Luv

34 Justin Norton, "Satan's Little Helpers: An Oral History of the Electric Hellfire Club," *Decibel*, October 31, 2016, www.decibelmagazine.com/2016/10/31/satan-s-little-helpers-an-oral-history-of-the-electric-hellfire-club; "Diabolical Machinations: My First and Last Meeting with Anton Szandor LaVey," *Black Flame* 6(3–4) 2000, p.19.

35 Blood Axis, "The Abattoir Eternal" on Electric Hellfire Club, *Kiss the Goat* (Cleopatra, 1995), www.discogs.com/master/29679-The-Electric-Hellfire-Club-Kiss-The-Goat; Moynihan interview in *Occidental Congress*. Thorn played on the Blood Axis tracks on the compilation *Im Blutfeuer* (Cthulhu, 1995), www.discogs.com/release/184376-Various-Im-Blutfeuer

APPENDIX 9

Michael Merritt and Keith Stimely

Two characters who played bit roles in James Mason's post-SIEGE life and the Abraxas Clique were, respectively, Michael Merritt and Keith Stimely. Neither has received much attention. Merritt was a neo-Nazi who was thinking along similar lines as Mason in the mid-1980s and would play a role after SIEGE ended. Stimely was one of the connections between Holocaust denial networks and Adam Parfrey, Boyd Rice, and others.

Michael Merritt

Michael Merritt was an obscure but prolific publisher, primarily of his own writings on a new kind of National Socialist philosophy with a strong spiritual element, similar to Mason's Universal Order. Mason held him in high enough regard that Merritt received the list of SIEGE subscribers when it ended.

In 1982 in Torrance, California, Merritt was publishing *White Struggle* as part of the American Workers Party (not to be confused with the name associated with the post-Mason National Socialist Movement). He opposed National Socialist groups that acted in secret, and he stressed the need for an Americanized version of the movement. From 1982 to 1984, Merritt published *The People's Observer*, where he wrote about movement building. Merritt's focus was now stopping immigration and instituting a nationalized economy, as he addresses economic issues to a greater extent than other neo-Nazis.[1]

Merritt also had international connections. In 1983, an Australian White Supremacist, Jack van Tongeren, visited Los Angeles. He claimed that Merritt, his tour guide, had been "in an elite combat unit in South Vietnam." At the American Workers Party's Third Party Congress in October 1984, Merritt's group decided to fuse with another one, the Teutonic Order, and after doing so *The People's Observer* became *The New Dawn*.[2] The number of activists involved in this congress was undoubtedly underwhelming, even by neo-Nazi standards.

In 1982, Merritt said the American Workers Party was for "one hundred percent Christian patriotic Americans." By 1985, he had turned his back on Christianity as "an alien religion" and self-published *A New Philosophy for the 21st Century*. Merritt's paper became focused on promoting this new approach, as "The traditional philosophy of the movement is bankrupt." This "New Philosophy" had a prophetic, self-consciously Nietzschean influence.[3] It tread the same ground as Mason's Universal Order so much that when SIEGE folded in 1986, not only was *The New Dawn* one of the two publications that inherited the subscription list, but Mason also started writing for it as well.[4] In December 1987, Mason told his comrade Ed Reynolds that he was working with only four people, of which "Metzger and Merritt more or less represent the traditional style of the movement but they are among the best and most sincere." In the late 1980s, Merritt also published other periodicals, such as *The Perilous Times*, which Mason also contributed to, as well as *Speaking Out*.[5]

One of the last times Merritt's name popped up was in 1988, when *Speaking Out* reprinted, without permission, a list of Asatrú Alliance kindreds. This prompted protests from Mike Murray—himself a former American Nazi Party member—because the Heathen group, though ethno-nationalists, did not want to be visibly associated with the politics as extreme as Merritt's. Murray went so far as to publish a letter in *Vor Trú* denouncing Merritt and demanding that the list not be reprinted in future issues.[6]

Keith Stimely

Keith Stimely edited the premier Holocaust denial publication in the United States, worked as a journalist, and became close to the Abraxas Clique toward the end of his short life.

Curiously, Stimely showed up the first time in (what would become) the Abraxas Circle in 1978, when Mason was still editing *The Stormer* for Allen Vincent. The magazine reprinted Stimely's review of *The California Reich*, which included his description of attending a meeting of Vincent's NSWWP.[7]

Stimely worked as assistant director of Willis Carto's Institute for Historical Review (IHR) from June 1982 to November 1983 and as the *Journal of Historical Review*'s editor from February 1983 to February 1985.[8] The IHR published short works of his, like the *1981 Revisionist Bibliography* and *$50,000 Auschwitz Reward Unclaimed: 'Gas Chambers' Myth Continues to Crumble* in 1983.[9]

During this time, his public statements included calling the Holocaust a hoax because, "No Jews died as a result of an extermination program." (He did grant that "Perhaps up to one million Jews perished from all causes, including malnutrition, typhus, old age, and acts of war.")[10] But like so many others in these circles, he had a quarrelsome nature and was infuriated at Carto's infamous manipulations, which lead to Stimely's exit from the IHR. It was accompanied by an open letter denouncing Carto which was widely circulated to those around the journal.[11]

In September 1987, fellow denier William Grimstad asked if he could give Stimely's addresses to Parfrey. Stimely, by then in a master's program at Portland State University, met with Parfrey and the two became friends.[12] In 1990, Rice and Moynihan received a visit from Stimely in Denver. He was about to publish a book he had helped write on how to use a graphic design program and offered to help with the mechanicals of *WAKE*. (When *WAKE* finally appeared in 1992, Stimely was listed as "production consultant."[13])

Stimely wrote the Halloween 1991 cover story for the Portland alternative newspaper *Willamette Week*, profiling Diabolos Rex, a local Satanist. Stimely made sure to point out that he was a misogynistic misanthrope who supported eugenics and was allied with the "neo-Nazi" Abraxas Foundation. (In the same city the next year, Stimely was listed as a pianist for a "Total War" performance which included Rice, Moynihan, and Rex.[14])

Stimely also started the KS Agency, which was a publicity agency. In November 1991, he put out a press release to announce that he had signed Parfrey and Feral House. In March 1992, he wrote a puff piece in another local alternative paper, *PDXS*, promoting an upcoming Parfrey talk at Powell's Books.[15] It was met by a feminist protest, and years later Parfrey blamed him for it—now claiming Stimely was never his publicist and had acted as such without approval.[16]

Just before his death, Stimely was working on another profile for *PDXS*, this time about the American Front leader Bob Heick, who was living in Portland.[17] But it would never be completed, as Stimely died at 35 in December 1992.[18]

Notes

1   *White Struggle*, [Fall 1982], pp.1–2; *White Struggle*, Winter 1982–83, pp.1–2. The name of *The People's Observer* is the English translation of the NSDAP paper *Völkischer Beobachter*, and six issues were published between 1982 and 1984; *People's Observer* #1, October 1982, pp.1–3 [all D2444].

2   Jack van Tongeren, *The ANM Story: The Pre-Revolutionary Years, 1970–1989*, 2004, p.50, https://archive.org/details/theanmstory; Teutonic Order (Deutscher Ritterorden), *Bulletin*, October 15, 1984 [eph 502]. Despite being convicted for firebombing Asian-owned restaurants, van Tongeren himself was not white; Crispian Chan, "Confronting a terrorist," *Australian Broadcasting Corporation*, September 29, 2023, www.abc.net.au/news/2023-09-30/unravel-firebomb-crispian-chan-neo-nazis/102868544. For more on the phenomenon of non-white National Socialists, see Sunshine and Isaac, "Nazis of Color," *Unicorn Riot*, July 12, 2023, https://unicornriot.ninja/2023/nazis-of-color

3 *People's Observer* #3, December 1982, p.4; *The New Dawn* 2(2) December 1985, pp.2, 3, 5.

4 Mason to Merritt, May 5, 1986 [Box 22, Folder 1]; Mason, "It Seems to Me," *The New Dawn* 3(5) November 1986, pp.3–4; Mason, "Were We Dreaming?," *The New Dawn* 4(1) January 1987, pp.3–5.

5 Mason to Reynolds, December 25, 1987 [Box 33, Folder 8]; ADL, *Extremism on the Right*, p.48.

6 Kaplan, *Radical Religion in America: Millenarian Movements from the Far Right to the Children of Noah* (Syracuse, New York: Syracuse University Press, 1997), pp.20–21.

7 Stimely, "Fourth Reich in California," clipping from unknown source, reprinted in *Stormer* #3, p.15.

8 "Selected IHR Author Biographies," *Institute for Historical Review*, www.ihr.org/other/authorbios.html; "Keith Stimely on Willis Carto; Prefatory Note," [1985], *Willis Carto archive*, https://wac.monkey-factory.com/others/1985-----stimely

9 Stimely, *Revisionist Bibliography—1981*, *Institute for Historical Review*, www.ihr.org/books/stimely/stimely.shtml; Stimely, *$50,000 Auschwitz Reward Unclaimed: 'Gas Chambers' Myth Continues to Crumble*, IHR Special Report (Torrance, California: Institute for Historical Review, [1983]).
  The IHR's reward was claimed by Holocaust survivor Mel Mermelstein, although he was forced to go to court to collect. He was awarded $90,000 and the IHR was ordered to make an apology; Sam Roberts, "Mel Mermelstein, Holocaust Survivor Who Sued Deniers, Dies at 95," *NYT*, February 1, 2022, www.nytimes.com/2022/02/01/us/mel-mermelstein-dead.html

10 "Historians laugh down massacre 'hoax' claims," *Edmonton Journal* (Alberta, Canada), April 30, 1983, p.B3, www.newspapers.com/image/472193647

11 "Prefatory Note" and "The Problem of Willis A. Carto, or: Goodbye to All That" (open letter), February 25, 1985 [Stimely collection; Box 2, Folder 2]. The prefatory note is online; "Keith Stimely on Willis Carto," [1985], *Willis Carto archive*, https://wac.monkey-factory.com/others/1985-----stimely

12 Grimstad to Stimely, September 7, 1987 [Stimely collection]; Linda Maizels, "The Universal Nature of Hatred," pp.55, 64.

13 Monyihan to Mason, June 1, 1990; *WAKE*, p.1. The graphic design book was released in 1991; Stimely with David Blatner and Stephen F. Roth, *The Quark Xpress Book* (Berkeley, California: Peachpit Press, 1991).

14 Stimely, "Satan's Storm Trooper," *Willamette Week*, October 31–November 6, 1991, p.13; Coogan, *Dreamer of the Day* (Brooklyn: Autonomedia, 1999), p.530n24.

15 "Adam Parfrey and 'Feral House' Sign with KS Agency," press release, November 21, 1991 [Stimely collection]; Stimely, "Meet the Apocalypse Man: Can Portland Handle Him?," *PDXS* (Portland, Oregon) 1(25) March 2–15, 1992, p.4.

16 Parfrey, "If We're So Wrong," p.5.

17 Maizels, "The Universal Nature of Hatred," p.73.

18 Coogan, *Dreamer of the Day*, p.526. Stimely, once the up-and-coming young man of Holocaust denial, was not forgotten however. In 1998, with Carto gone, Stimely's overview of Oswald Spengler appeared in the *Journal of Historical Review*, and his piece on Lawrence Dennis appeared in the first issue of *The Occidental Quarterly* in 2001. "Oswald Spengler: An Introduction to His Life and Ideas," *Journal of Historical Review* 17(2) March/April 1998, pp.2ff, www.ihr.org/jhr/v17/v17n2p-2_Stimely.html; "Lawrence Dennis and a 'Frontier Thesis' for American Capitalism," *Occidental Quarterly*, Fall 2001, pp.47–76, www.unz.com/print/OccidentalQuarterly-2001q3-00047

APPENDIX 10

Varg Vikernes and the Heathen Front

Amongst the secondary literature, one of the less common claims is that James Mason was the leader of the U.S branch of the Heathen Front. Related to this is his contact with the Norwegian black metal musician Varg Vikernes, the purported founder of the group.

Vikernes recorded as Burzum in the early 1990s and became one of the most influential black metal acts. At the same time, he also participated in numerous church burnings, which had become a trend in Norway. He also played in Mayhem until 1993, when he murdered their guitarist, Euronymous, after which he was in prison until 2009.

Vikernes is not just known for his music and crimes but also his political-spiritual views. Before his arrest he espoused Nazi-Satanism and afterward became a racist Odinist. (While in some statements he was explicit that he had been a Satanist, in others he denied ever having been one.[1])

Familiar Thoughts

In 1996, Adam Parfrey's Feral House Audio co-released the Burzum album *Filosofem*.[2] Vikernes was also the focus of the 1998 Feral House book *Lords of Chaos*, and he was later the central figure in the movie of the same name. In 1995, Mason praised Vikernes, saying "killing any number of people and blowing up any number of buildings" is "ultimate heroism"—although there needed to be many actions like this "simultaneously." According to Schuster, while in prison Mason wrote an essay about Vikernes called "Move to the Light"; the record label and publisher Cymophane asked if it could be used as a preface to the English-language edition of Vikernes's manifesto *Vargsmal*.[3] In 1997, the musician wrote Mason, saying that he had become a "great admirer of SEIGE," which Michael Moynihan had sent him in prison. "The book shocked me...the thoughts portrayed in it was very familiar.... If I had read SIEGE, let us say one or two years earlier than I did, it would have been a great help to me—really."[4] (In 2003, Mason told an interviewer that Vikernes "epitomizes the Man of Action, which the West is in dire need of.... I wish him the best."[5])

Heathen Front

According to *Lords of Chaos*, Vikernes, while in prison, said he both formed and was "chieftain" of the Norwegian Heathen Front. The second edition of the book made additional claims, including that Vikernes also founded the international parent group, the Allgermanische Heidnische Front (Pan-Germanic Heathen Front). Despite the fact that the early Norwegian Heathen Front had the same address as Vikernes's prison address, the organization denied he was its founder—even though he wrote its program.[6]

Regardless of Vikernes's exact role, the international group spread, and affiliates in other countries formed. A website run on behalf of Mason while he was in prison included a link to the Allgermanische Heidnische Front.[7] In 1999, a monitoring group's report on White Supremacist music claimed that Mason led the Vinland Heathen Front in the United States; the SPLC repeated this claim.[8]

However, the claim that Mason led the Vinland Heathen Front is implausible for four reasons. First, Mason never showed any interest in any kind of Heathen or pagan beliefs. Second, in Mason's voluminous papers at the University of Kansas, there is no documentation about the Heathen Front. Third, Mason was an atheist until just before his time in prison, during which he created his own brand of Christianity. And fourth, forming—and certainly leading—an organization would be counter to Mason's dictums which he had carefully elaborated in SIEGE. When asked about the Heathen Front, he said "I was never any sort of 'leader' with any of them."[9]

Notes

1 In *Lords of Chaos*, Vikernes was cited as saying Satanists will often become Asatrú practitioners. "We can see that again and again. We see it with Bathory, I see it in myself. I was interested in Satanism to where I advocated it....with the whole Black Metal community...but now there's a growing interest in pan-Germanic heathenism." In a 1995 interview, Vikernes gave contradictory statements about being a neo-Nazi and Satanist. Kaplan said that in his letters to him in 1995 and 1996, Vikernes repeatedly denied he was ever a Satanist. Moynihan and Søderlind, *Lords of Chaos*, p.153; "Into the Lion's Cage Interview with Varg Vikernes 'Sounds of Death' Magazine (#5, 1995), by Stephen O'Malley," www.burzum.org/eng/library/1995_interview_sounds_of_death.shtml; Kaplan, "Religiosity and the Radical Right," in Kaplan and Bjørgo, eds., *Nation and Race*, p.122n29.

2 Burzum, *Filosofem* (Misanthropy Records/Cymophane Productions/Feral House Audio, 1996), www.discogs.com/release/1327160-Burzum-Filosofem

3 Joe Conason, "Hitler Youth?," *Salon*, May 4, 1999, www.salon.com/1999/05/04/ nazis; Schuster to Mason, July 1, 2002 [Box 32, Folder 29].

4 Varg Vikernes to Mason, September 10, 1997 [Box 16, Folder 22].

5 Mason interview with AAC (*Articles*, pp.243–44).

6 Moynihan and Søderlind, *Lords of Chaos*, p.166; Moynihan and Søderlind, *Lords of Chaos*, 2nd ed., ebook, chapter 8.

7 "Links," *Universal Order*, https://web.archive.org/web/19990508160318, http:// www.universalorder.com/wizzf.html. The link in question went to www. heathenfront.org

8 Devin Burghart, ed., *Soundtracks to the White Revolution: White Supremacist Assaults on Youth Music Subcultures* (Chicago: Center for New Community/ Northwest Coalition for Human Dignity, 1999), p.62; Ward, Lunsford, and Massa, "Black Metal Spreads a Neo-Nazi Hate Message."

9 The author could not find any documents related to the Heathen Front or similar subjects in his archival collection. "Papers of James N. Mason," *University of Kansas, Kenneth Spencer Research Library Archival Collection*, https://archives. lib.ku.edu/repositories/3/resources/5069; Mason to author, January 1, 2023.

APPENDIX 11

The Satanic Temple: The Lasting Influence of the Abraxas Circle

After its launch in 2013, The Satanic Temple (TST) quickly expanded into a national organization and became the most important Satanist organization of its day. It created a radical transformation in Satanism by carving out a significant space that was feminist and left of center. But despite this, and just as with Satanist groups before it, TST would be dogged by associations with the Far Right—a number of which were directly tied to the Abraxas Circle.

The fact that these connections remain the object of discussion many years later shows the influence of the reactionary counterculture the Abraxas Clique helped launch. Part of this is because circles would go on to function in the absence of direct participation by Michael Moynihan, Boyd Rice, or James Mason. Even the cult of Manson wasn't necessary. But they continued to knit together a milieu that didn't just wallow in extremes but was inclusive of open White Supremacists.

A New Kind of Satanism

TST gained significant media coverage when, in an attempt to enforce Church/State separation, it challenged U.S. local and state governments that promoted Christianity. For example, this included suing over a monument depicting the Ten Commandments in the Arkansas state capitol, to either force their hand to remove it or allow a Satanist statue to be placed there as well. But what was probably the most popular appeal among the TST base was their challenge to state-level restrictions on abortion by claiming religious exemptions. (TST fell on the atheist side of Satanism while still claiming legal rights as a religious organization.) Alongside this were standard

Satanic events such as black masses. The organization quickly gained a very left-leaning following, including many feminists—although the leadership's ideology was politically liberal and not leftist.

TST drew in a range of people from different backgrounds: Satanists disaffected with the Church of Satan, participants in other non-monotheistic religious milieus, atheists, leftists, feminists, various counterculturalists (especially goths), connoisseur of agit-prop theater, and a large LGBTQ+ contingent. This new approach to Satanism showed that it could be playful but politically involved and repudiated the past associations of Satanism with the Far Right. But soon after TST's founding, the truth of that repudiation was challenged from inside the organization itself.

According to Joseph Laycock's account of the group, the foundational essay laying out the future TST was completed in December 2012. The inaugural event, in January 2013, was not the launch of a new organization, however, but rather a filmed publicity stunt. After several other events that garnered sympathetic media coverage, the first TST chapter was formed in the summer of 2014 and was quickly followed by others.[1]

TST and the Far Right

However, there was an internal rebellion after it became known that TST's leader, Lucien Greaves (né Doug Misicko and also known as Doug Mesner), had a less-than-liberal past. The flashpoint was the TST's use of a lawyer with connections to the Alt Right, but other things came to light as well. Coming in the middle of the Trump administration, this unsurprisingly angered many in the group's LGBTQ+ and feminist base.

Lawyer Marc Randazza was representing TST in a legal complaint; he was known for defending numerous Far Right clients, including Alt Right neo-Nazi Andrew Anglin, editor of the *Daily Stormer*. The TST leadership justified the choice of representation because Randazza was working pro bono; furthermore, as a First Amendment lawyer, Randazza had clients with different political perspectives. But it was public knowledge that he had done more than that, including attending Far Right political events and making personal political statements reflecting those politics—as well as previously being fined for unethical professional behavior.[2]

In the best of cases, it was not a good look for an organization committed to reproductive and LGBTQ+ rights. In the summer of 2018, TST chapters started to split or leave the organization. For example, in their statement upon withdrawing from the organization, the former Los Angeles chapter said Randazza was "not a neutral actor" but rather "an ally to Nazis and to alt-right provocateurs."[3]

At that point, Greaves's past came under much more scrutiny.

Is Might Right?

As disenchant spread, members started to dig up details of Greaves's past associations with the Far Right. The most damning was a 2003 episode of Shane Bugbee's internet radio show which Greaves had co-hosted. (Bugbee would be involved in the founding of TST but soon after had a falling out.)

Bugbee was a transgressive artist and publisher who was a Church of Satan priest as well as part of the extended Abraxas Circle. Bugbee had a particular interest in serial killers but also had ties to White Supremacists. Although he was not part of that movement, Bugbee, like others in the Church of Satan, was willing to work with those who were. (However, neither he nor Greaves had contact with Mason.[4])

Around 1995, Bugbee had been hired by George Hawthorne to promote RAHOWA as they tried to break into the mainstream music industry. Among other things, Bugbee accepted a RAHOWA ad for the magazine of the Milwaukee Metal Fest, which he helped organize, and included the band on two associated compilations.[5]

Bugbee was also an energetic promoter of *Might is Right*, which he first saw when Hawthorne sent him a copy. Already familiar with its arguments because of *The Satanic Bible*, Bugbee was so taken by Ragnar Redbeard's book that he reprinted it several times, including editions with a foreword that he had personally solicited from Anton LaVey. Hawthorne also wrote the afterward to Bugbee's editions and introduced him to Katja Lane, the wife of imprisoned The Order member David Lane and a prominent White Supremacist publisher in her own right. She contributed an editor's note to Bugbee's printings.[6] (Later editions also included an afterword by the Church of Satan's Peter Gilmore.)

After the release of the 1997 edition, which included LaVey's contribution, Bugbee went to San Francisco and met him; according to Bugbee, he was the last priest christened directly by LaVey, and he did his last interview (via fax) in order to promote the release of *Might is Right*.[7] Bugbee also was an associate of *EXIT* and *Seconds* editor George Petros, who included a profile of him in the *Art That Kills* anthology. And Bugbee also worked with Jim Goad, reprinting *ANSWER ME!* #4 while Goad was in prison; after his release, Bugbee also included him on the Angry White Male Tour in 2001.[8]

Antisemitism on the Air

That same year, Bugbee met Greaves (then still going by Mesner) when Greaves was looking for a copy of *Might is Right*. They remained close for years, and Greaves provided art for Bugbee's 2003 edition of the book.[9] But it was a September 11, 2003, episode of Bugbee's internet radio show of the same name, which celebrated the release of the new edition, which would dog both of them for years. The guests on the 24-hour special, which Greaves co-hosted, included Metzger, Gilmore, and Hawthorne (who by then had changed his name to Burdi after leaving RAHOWA). There was no shortage of bigotry from the hosts. Like others in the Abraxas Circle, Bugbee and Greaves's comments appeared to be a mix of a tongue-in-cheek approach and extremism for its own sake—but it also appeared to represent views they held, sometimes exaggerated (as Nikolas Schreck described his own) and sometimes not. None of it, however, came across as things they were actively opposed to.

Bugbee threatened to "get six big niggers" to rape the "fucking fag" Thomas Thorn, while Greaves referred to "nigger sodomites" and declared himself "an Aryan king." He also waxed on about the necessity of eugenics, bemoaning the fact that the Nazis had delegitimized the field, and he and Bugbee discussed which Jews should be the object of hatred. When one guest espoused Holocaust denial, Bugbee interjected that, "I hate the Jews" (although he later made exemptions for LaVey and the Three Stooges) and declared Hitler "a great man." [10]

After Bugbee played racist speeches given by Burdi while he was still in the White Supremacist movement, Greaves interviewed him. Burdi specified that he no longer held those politics, although he denounced antifascists and said his departure was not because he thought his ideas were wrong but because he "was out of energy" and felt that taking part in the movement resulted in a "loss of individuality."

In Greaves's interview with Metzger, they again discussed how to define Jews and then argued about supposed intelligence differences between black and white people. Metzger unsurprisingly held that black people had lower intelligence. Greaves built off this assumption by trying to convince him that there was no need "to enact racial laws, you just have to enact intelligence laws" because a "good segment of the population would have to drop off, you could still do it on an equal level around the board." Similarly, when Greaves interviewed Gilmore later in the show, they also spoke about their shared interest in eugenics. [11] In regard to implementing a eugenics program, Gilmore said, "I think that that is definitely something that that needs to be done... it's the only way to actually evolve our species."

2011 Emails and Salem Art Show

But Greaves's interest in these ideas was apparently not just an artifact of the early '00s. Internal emails which Bugbee introduced into a court case involving TST show that he and Greaves talked about making a new version of *Might is Right* in 2011. Greaves said it could incorporate "current science regarding altruism, collectivism, and general behavior"—but then use it to show how others can be manipulated into violence. "A manual for coercion and manipulation. More evil than the first book by orders of magnitude." [12]

Similar was an email exchange posted on a website critical of TST. Dated June 2013—after TST was already off and running—it referred to the earlier discussion about updating *Might is Right*. Although now the selling points of coercion and manipulation were absent, both Greaves and Bugbee downplayed the book's antisemitic elements (according to Greaves, it merely talked about "Jews in an ambiguous fashion that I took to mean religious practitioners") while arguing for a "TST version of this book." (Almost a decade later, Greaves said the new version was intended to be a repudiation of the arguments in the original.)[13]

Another link to the Abraxas Clique was an October 2015 art show, which was the first event at the TST headquarters in Salem, Massachusetts. (However, it had not formally opened yet.) The event celebrated a new Feral House release about William Mortensen, a photographer who influenced LaVey. The book itself was co-edited by Moynihan, and the show was curated by Adam Parfrey, who spoke at the opening.[14] While Moynihan didn't attend, former American Front leader James Porrazzo did. Parfrey made sure to openly brag on the Feral House website about the presence of both the former Nazi skinhead leader and his wife, with whom he posed for photographs.[15]

Greaves had previously met Parfrey and provided some assistance with a Feral House book on the Process Church, a 1960s religious group. Greaves also said he was at the Salem show either before or after Parfrey's talk, although he was not present for it. After Parfrey's death in 2018, Greaves tweeted that he was "Honored to have known him." Later, he said that at the time he was unfamiliar with Parfrey's more racist statements.[16]

Anti-Antifa, But Free Speech for Fascists

Greaves had always positioned himself and TST as supporters of free speech. But after the new revelations, his comments on the Alt Right and antifascists took on a new light, especially since they matched Far Right talking points about free speech for themselves, while simultaneously attacking antifascists.

Even before the Randazza scandal, Greaves's conduct regarding the 2016 Left Hand Path Consortium had already made antifascists distrustful. Bowing to community pressure, the fascist Augustus Invictus was removed from the event's speaker list. (Invictus had previously acted as a lawyer for arrested American Front members who were in the anti-Porrazzo faction. At the time of the Consortium, Invictus was scheduled to speak at a National Socialist Movement event, and the next year he was also slated to speak at the Charlottesville rally.) In turn, Greaves, who was also booked for the event, publicly withdrew because of what he described as "a harmful message in support of censorship." He further argued that fascism was a legitimate subject of debate because of its ongoing presence in Satanist and related circles—although he held that this was a way to counter it.[17]

In June 2017, just two months before Charlottesville, Greaves condemned what he described as a "screaming mob of mindless fascistic 'anti-fascists'" who were "ignorant little assholes." Conversely, he defended the "free speech" of Milo Yiannopoulos—a key figure in popularizing the White Supremacist wing of the Alt Right and bringing it into an alliance with mainstream Trumpism—without any such negative language. He even went so far as to dismiss the content of Yiannopoulos's views entirely ("I still don't give a shit about what he's saying") rather than challenging them, as he had previously advocated.[18]

Although he later admitted his information was incorrect, in June 2019 Greaves repeated the false claim that Far Right disinformation peddler Andy Ngo was the victim of a concrete milkshake thrown at him at a demonstration; Greaves used it as yet another opportunity to take a swipe at antifascists. Again, he did not say negative things about the Far Right actor in question. Later, Greaves said that the reason for attacking the antifascist Left for violating free speech was because his audience was left-leaning; he also said he defended the free speech of leftists and antifascists.[19]

Apologies

Both Greaves and Bugbee have since publicly apologized for their words and actions in the '00s and specifically for the 2003 radio show. Bugbee said he was particularly taken aback when Alt Right members contacted him to tell him how *Might is Right* inspired them. He has also admitted that working with Hawthorne was a mistake and made clear that he is neither a White Supremacist nor adjacent to those politics anymore.[20]

Greaves has apologized for the broadcast and renounced the views he had expressed on the 2003 show. Calling his younger self "an ignorant kid with a lot of outrage and a big idiot mouth," he said TST itself was a "refutation" of those views and the organization "will always be for anybody, of any background, who identifies with the values we espouse." A comprehensive critique of eugenics was also put on the TST website.[21]

Nonetheless, alongside continuing accusations against TST for its internal structure, financial dealings, and lawsuits against its critics, Greaves's appearance on the *Might is Right* show has continued to be brought up by critics. This shows very clearly how the toxic hangover of the Abraxas Circle has not yet subsided.[22]

While TST caused a sea change in modern Satanism, one of the ironies of the fights within the organization is that it also helped propel an explicitly left-wing and antifascist Satanism among the breakaway factions. They, in turn, have helped push forward a critical examination of Nazi-Satanism. This has not just included struggling with Satanism's past, but also identifying individuals, especially in the Church of Satan, linked to those politics in the present. This has included Moynihan's friend David E. Williams as well as Jack Donovan, an important figure during the early period of the Alt Right.[23]

And so the battle over the politics of modern Satanism rages on.

Notes

1 Joseph P. Laycock, *Speak of the Devil: How the Satanic Temple Is Changing the Way We Talk About Religion* (New York: Oxford University Press, 2020), ebook, chapter 2.

2 Luke O'Brien, "Alex Jones' Lawyer Violated Legal Ethics By Soliciting Porn Bribes. Just How Dirty Is Marc Randazza?," *HuffPost*, December 27, 2018, www.huffpost.com/entry/alex-jones-lawyer-marc-randazza_n_5c1c283ae4b08aaf7a86b9e4.

3 Anna Merlan, "The Satanic Temple Is Engulfed in a Civil War Over a Decision to Hire an Attorney With a Stable of Alt-Right Clients," *Jezebel*, August 7, 2018, https://jezebel.com/the-satanic-temple-is-engulfed-in-a-civil-war-over-a-de-1828130997; Joe Mullin, "Bribery, Gay Porn, and Copyright Trolls: The Rise and Fall of Lawyer Marc Randazza: Arbiter Says Randazza 'Negotiated' a Bribe, Lied to Employer, and Must Pay $600k," *Ars Technica*, November 5, 2015, https://arstechnica.com/tech-policy/2015/11/how-copyright-lawyer-marc-randazza-got-famous-lost-friends-and-went-broke.

4 Shane Bugbee, phone interview with author, September 13, 2021; Lucien Greaves, phone interview with author, January 24, 2022.

5 Bugbee interview with author; RAHOWA, "The Snow Fell" on the *Milwaukee Metal Music Mania 1995* and "Might is Right," *Milwaukee's Metal Music Mania #3* (Mike Hunt Music, n.d.). www.discogs.com/release/8179798-Various-Milwaukee-Metal-Music-Mania-1995, www.discogs.com/release/14177279-Various-Milwaukees-Metal-Music-Mania-3.

6 Bugbee interview with author; Redbeard, *Might is Right* (Chicago: M.H.P. & Co., 1996/1997).

7 Bugbee interview with author; LaVey interview with Shane & Amy Bugbee.

8 *Art That Kills*, pp. 206–65; Bugbee interview with author. The tour also included performers who did not have these political ties; Amy Benfer, "I Offend, Therefore I Am," *Salon*, June 14, 2001, www.salon.com/2001/06/14/angry_males.

9 Anna Merlan, "Trolling Hell: Is the Satanic Temple a Prank, the Start of a New Religious Movement—or Both?," *Village Voice*, www.villagevoice.com/2014/07/22/trolling-hell-is-the-satanic-temple-a-prank-the-start-of-a-new-religious-movement-or-both; Shane Bugbee, "Unmasking Lucien Greaves, Leader of the Satanic Temple," *Vice*, July 30, 2013, www.vice.com/en/article/4w7adn/unmasking-lucien-greaves-aka-doug-mesner-leader-of-the-satanic-temple.

10 For all quotes from the show, see "Might Is Right 24-Hour Radio Special," https://the.satanic.wiki/index.php/Might_Is_Right_24-Hour_Radio_Special.

11 Greaves became interested in eugenics around 2001. His URL for his blog *Dysgenics* was registered in 2001 and was updated through 2018, although its content was not centrally based on the title. Greaves interview with author; *Whois Domain Lookup*, www.whois.com/whois/dysgenics.com; Dysgenics.com on Internet Archive, https://web.archive.org/web/20080130090812, http://www.goldstem.com/dysgenics/cgi-bin/blosxom.cgi, https://web.archive.org/web/20181020192351, http://www.dysgenics.com.

12 Doug Mesner to Shane Bugbee, email, November 9, 2011, reproduced in "Cave v. Thurston Exhibit 2 - Declaration of Shane Bugbee — Document #188, Attachment #2, District Court, E.D. Arkansas Docket Number: 4:18-cv-00342 Date Filed: November 16th, 2021, Uploaded: November 19th, 2021," Exhibit F, p.32 in PDF, www.courtlistener.com/docket/7274697/188/2/cave-v-thurston.

13 Douglas Mesner to Cevin Soling and Shane Bugbee, email, June 13, 2013; reproduced at "The Satanic Temple's Lucien Greaves: 'I'm an Aryan king!'," *Evergreen Memes for Queer Satanic Fiends*, October 25, 2021, https://queersatanic.tumblr. com/post/666056014876098560/the-satanic-temple-crowdsources-effort-to; Greaves interview with author.

14 Greaves interview with author; Larry Lytle, and Moynihan, eds., *American Grotesque: The Life and Art of William Mortensen* (Port Townsend, Washington: Feral House, 2014); "Salem Art Gallery Presents William Mortensen and Ritual America," *Facebook Event*, Sunday, October 11, 2015, www.facebook.com/events/1485820981747402. Moynihan also contributed to a related Feral House book published the same year; William Mortensen, and George Dunham, *The Command to Look: A Master Photographer's Method for Controlling the Human Gaze*.

15 Parfrey, "Against the Modern World," *Feral House*, October 16, 2015, https://web. archive.org/web/20190815063657, https://feralhouse.com/against-the-modern-world. The photos were posted October 12, 2015 in the New Resistance closed Facebook group; screenshots in possession of author.

16 The Tweet's thread includes an argument with the author. @LucienGreaves, Twitter, May 11, 2018, https://twitter.com/LucienGreaves/status/9948558613 09902848; Greaves interview with author.

17 "Fascist Lawyer Augustus Invictus Dropped from International Left Hand Path Consortium Event in Atlanta," *Atlanta Antifascists*, March 14, 2016, https:// atlantaantifa.org/2016/03/14/fascist-lawyer-augustus-invictus-dropped-from-international-left-hand-path-consortium-event-in-atlanta; @lucien.greaves (Lucien Greaves), *Facebook*, March 14, 2016, www.facebook.com/permalink.php?story_ fbid=1175397379161206&id=865376096830004, https://web.archive.org/ web/20190924005737, https://www.facebook.com/lucien.greaves/posts/i-regret-to-announce-that-i-have-withdrawn-from-my-role-as-a-scheduled-speaker-a/1175397379161206.

18 Keegan Hankes, "Whose Alt-Right Is It Anyway?," *SPLC*, August 25, 2016, www. splcenter.org/hatewatch/2016/08/25/whose-alt-right-it-anyway; "Never Let Your Activism Be Artless: An Interview With Lucien Greaves of The Satanic Temple," *Haute Macabre*, June 28, 2017, https://web.archive.org/web/20171001061537, http://hautemacabre.com/2017/06/never-let-your-activism-be-artless-an-interview-with-lucien-greaves-of-the-satanic-temple.

19 @LucienGreaves, June 30, 2019, Twitter, https://twitter.com/LucienGreaves/ status/1145416498049093632; Greaves interview with author.

20 Bugbee interview with author.

21 Cited in Stephen Bradford Long, "Why I Haven't Left the Satanic Temple," May 21, 2020, https://stephenbradfordlong.com/2020/05/21/why-i-havent-left-the-satanic-temple; "Church of Satan vs Satanic Temple," *The Satanic Temple*, https://thesatanictemple.com/pages/church-of-satan-vs-satanic-temple.

22 See, for example, posts at *Evergreen Memes for Queer Satanic Fiends*, https:// queersatanic.tumblr.com.

23 "Meet a Church of Satan Nazi," five part series, *Trident Antifascism*, https:// tridentantifascism.blackblogs.org; "Into the Devil's Den: Carl Abrahamsson and the whitewashing of the Church of Satan," *Aleph's Heretical Domain*, December 17, 2019, https://mythoughtsbornfromfire.wordpress.com/2019/12/17/into-the-devils-den-by-carl-abrahamssonand-the-whitewashing-of-the-church-of-satan.

PART VIII
End Matter

PERIODICAL LIST

James Mason's Books

Siege (1993)
One Verse Charlies (2000)
Robert Burns Collection, vol. 1 (2000); vol. 2 (2002)
The Theocrat (2000)
When We Were All Jews (2000)
Revisiting Revelation (2000)
Articles of WAR (2003)
Articles and Interviews (2003)
Race, Religion and Politics (2005)
The Lost Cause [2005?]
Horror: Desensitization, Conditioned Reflexes, and Thought Control (2005)
Tyranny of Freedom (2009)
Harvest of Conspiracy: 1900-2000 (2010)
Out of the Dust, vols. 1 and 2 (2022)
National Socialist Liberation Front (Compiled by Mason with V.S. Snyder, [2022])
Note: *Original publication dates are given; many have been reissued, some several times.*

Periodicals Edited by Mason, plus Selected Others

The following publications were consulted for the book.

A note on Mason's numbering: The periodical numbering sequence started with the Cincinnati's NSWPP's *Local Activity Report* (#1–6, 1972), which retroactively became volume one, and then was continued by the *Southern Ohio Activity Report* (#7–13, 1973), which was edited by party member Steven Love. This second publication was taken over by the NSM and became the *Ohio National Socialist* (#14–16, 1975–76) and then the George Dietz–funded *National Socialist* (#17–19, 1976). (Two post-Dietz issues of this periodical were not included in the numbering sequence.)

After the falling out with Dietz, the NSM started the *National Socialist Bulletin* (#20 to 7[4], 1976–1978)—although Mason only included in the numbering schema the issues he edited, before his break with Robert Brannen. (There were no issues 5 and 6 that year; Mason kept those numbers in his system to maintain continuity.) The sequence continued with his NSWWP side publication the *White Worker's Bulletin*, which ran from 7(7) to 9(3) in 1978 to 1980. It is with 9(4) that SIEGE started in 1980 and ran through 15(6) in 1986, which is the end of the sequence.

Local Activity Report, *Cincinnati NSWPP (Love, editor)*

#2, March 1972
#5–6, June & July 1972
* *becomes* Southern Ohio Activity Report

Southern Ohio Activity Report, *Cincinnati NSWPP (Love, editor)*
#7, February 1973
#8, March 1973
#9, April 1973
#10, May 1973
#11, June 1973
#12, July 1973
#13, August 1973
* *becomes* Ohio National Socialist

Ohio National Socialist, *NSM (Mason, editor)*
#14, Autumn 1975
#15, Winter 1975/76
#16, Spring 1976
* *becomes* National Socialist

National Socialist, *NSM and NSLF (Mason, editor)*
#17, June 1976
#18, July 1976
#19, August 1976
* *numbering sequence does not include the two 1977 and 1978* National Socialist *issues but instead continues with* National Socialist Bulletin

NSM only

2(1) Fall 1977
2(2) Winter 1977/78

National Socialist Bulletin, *NSM (Mason, editor)*

#20, September–October 1976
#21, October–November 1976
#22, November 1976
#23, December 1976
6(1) January 1977
6(2) February 1977
6(3) March 1977
6(4) April 1977
6(5) May 1977
6(6) June 1977
6(7) July 1977
6(8) August 1977
6(9) September 1977
6(10) October 1977
6(11) November 1977
6(12) December 1977
7(1) January 1978
7(2) Feb 1978
7(3) March 1978
7(4) April 1978

Special Bulletin—To All Members of the NSM, NSLF, & NSWPP—
Announcement of Merger, May-June 1978
* *Mason leaves the NSM and Brannen takes over as publication editor (see*
  below).

Stormer, *NSWWP (Mason, editorial staff; editor-in-chief starting with 1[4])*

1(1) September 1977
1(2) January 1978
1(3) April 1978
1(4) Summer 1978
2(1) Winter 1979
2(2) [1979]
2(3) [1979]
2(4) January 1980

White Worker's Bulletin, *NSWWP (Mason, editor)*

7(7) July 1978
7(8) August 1978
7(9) September 1978
7(10) October–November 1978
8(1) January–February 1979
8(2) March–April 1979
8(3) May–June 1979
8(4) July–August 1979
8(5) September–October 1979
8(6) November–December 1979
9(1) January–February 1980
9(2) March–April 1980
9(3) May–June 1980

SIEGE, *NSLF under Duffy (Mason, editor)*

9(4) August 1980
9(5) September 1980
9(6) October 1980
9(7) November 1980
9(8) December 1980
10(1) January 1981
10(2) February 1981
10(3) March 1981

NSLF under Hand

10(4) April 1981
10(5) May 1981
10(6) June 1981
10(7) July 1981
10(8) August 1981
10(9) September 1981
10(10) October 1981
10(11) November 1981
10(12) December 1981
11(1) January 1982
11(2) February 1982
11(3) March 1982
11(4) April 1982
11(5) May 1982

11(6) June 1982
11(7) July 1982
11(8) August 1982
11(9) September 1982
11(10) October 1982

SIEGE, *Universal Order (Mason, editor)*

11(11) November 1982
11(12) December 1982
12(1) January 1983
12(2) February 1983
12(3) March 1983
12(4) April 1983
12(5) May 1983
12(6) June 1983
12(7) July 1983
12(8) August 1983
12(9) September 1983
12(10) October 1983
12(11) November 1983
12(12) December 1983
13(1) January 1984
13(2) February 1984
13(3) March 1984
13(4) April 1984
13(5) May 1984
13(6) June 1984
13(7) July 1984
13(8) August 1984
13(9) September 1984
13(10) October 1984
13(11) November 1984
13(12) December 1984
14(1) January 1985
14(2) February 1985
14(3) March 1985
14(4) April 1985
14(5) May 1985
14(6) June 1985
14(7) July 1985
14(8) August 1985
14(9) September 1985

14(10) October 1985
14(11) November 1985
14(12) December 1985
15(1) January 1986
15(2) February 1986
15(3) March 1986
15(4) April 1986
15(5) May 1986
15(6) June 1986

Related NSLF and NSM Publications

Liberator, *original NSLF as NSWPP student group*

#1, May 1969
#2, October 1969
#3, December 1969
#4, January 1970
#5, March 1970
#6, April 1970

The Racialist, *White Student Alliance*

special edition, 1970

Siege, *NSLF under Tommasi*

#1, Third Quarter, 1974
#2, Fourth Quarter, [November] 1974

National Socialist Review, *NSLF under Tommasi*

#1, January 1975
#2, February 1975
#3, March 1975

NSLF under Rust

[#4, December 1975]
#5, February 1976
#6, April 1976
#7, July 1976

NSLF under Duffy

#8, 2(1) Fall 1979
* *unpublished until 2003 in* Articles & Interviews

White Liberator, *Louisville NSLF under Chaney*

#1, July 25, 1975
#2, August 1, 1975
#3, August 8, 1975
#5, [May 1976]
* *folds into the* National Socialist, *but restarts after the Dietz affair*

NSLF Enforcement Bulletin, *Louisville NSLF under Chaney*

October [1976]

The Eagle News, *UWPP/White Confederacy*

#1 [early 1976]

Eastern Front, *Wilmington, Delaware NSLF under Duffy*

[#1] [January 1977?]

Jailbreak, *Wilmington, Delaware NSLF under Duffy*

[#1] [1977]

National Headquarters Bulletin, *Wilmington, Delaware NSLF under Duffy*

[#1] [September 1980?]
[#2] [October 1980]
#3 [December 1980?]
* *cover only says "National Socialist Liberation Front"*

The Storm, *Local Group Rockwell, NSM affiliate*

#2, December 1976
#3, January 1977
#4, February 1977
#5, March 1977
#6, May 1977

#7, June 1977
#8, July 1977

National Socialist Bulletin, *NSM (Brannen, editor)*

7(5) April 1978 *(date should be May 1978, as 7[4] was already issued as April)*
8(6) June 1979
9(1) January 1980
9(2) February 1980
9(3) March 1980
9(4) April 1980
9(5) May 1980
9(6) June 1980
9(7) July 1980
10(7) July 1981
12(8) August 1983

Defiance, *National Guard Party (Hand, editor)*

January 1975

Defiance *(Hand, editor), NSPA*

#1, 1980
#2, 1980

NSLF

#3, [February 1981]
#4, [late February or early March 1981]
#5, 1982
#6, 1982
#7, 1982
#8, 1982
#9, 1983
#10, January 1984
sample issue, 1985
* *In addition to the National Guard Party and NSLF, Hand also used the name* Defiance *for KKKK publications.*

National Socialist Observer, *NSLF under Hand*

1(4) December 1984
2(1) January 1985
2(2–3) February–March 1985
2(4) April 1985
2(5–6) May/June 19852(7) July-August 1985
#8–9 September–December 1985
#10 June 1986

Combat Report, *Waverly, New York NSLF*

Spring 1984
Summer 1984
Fall-Winter 1985

National Socialist Report, *[Corning, New York NSLF?]*

2(3) July–Sept 1985

INTERVIEWS

Shane Bugbee
Joseph A. Gervasi
Lucien Greaves
Karl Hand
Leigh Kendall
Martin Kerr
Brian King
Gerhard Lauck
Luma/United Front Against Fascism
James Mason
David Rust
Jeff Schoep

Selected Secondary Bibliography

Anti-Defamation League of B'nai B'rith, *Hate Groups in America: A Record of Bigotry and Violence* (New York: ADL, 1982).
———, *Extremism on the Right: A Handbook* (New York: ADL, 1988).
Ayton, Mel, *Dark Soul of the South: The Life and Crimes of Racist Killer Joseph Paul Franklin* (Washington, DC: Potomac Books, 2011).
Baddeley, Gavin, *Lucifer Rising: Sin, Devil Worship & Rock'n'Roll* (London: Plexus, 1999).
Barkun, Michael, *A Culture of Conspiracy: Apocalyptic Visions in Contemporary America* (Berkeley: University of California Press, 2003).
———, *Religion and the Racist Right: The Origins of the Christian Identity Movement* (Chapel Hill: University of North Carolina Press, 1994).

Berlet, Chip and Matthew N. Lyons, *Right-Wing Populism in America: Too Close for Comfort* (New York: Guilford Press, 2000).

Bornstein, Jerry, *The Neo-Nazis: The Threat of the Hitler Cult* (New York: Julian Messner, 1986).

Bridges, Tyler, *The Rise of David Duke* (Jackson: University Press of Mississippi, 1994).

Clark, Brian M., *Boyd Rice: A Biography* (Discriminate Media, 2015).

Dobratz, Betty A., and Stephanie L. Shanks-Meile's *"White Power, White Pride!" The White Separatist Movement in the United States* (New York: Twayne Publishers, 1997).

Durham, Martin, *White Rage: The Extreme Right and American Politics* (Abingdon: Routledge, 2007).

Ellerin, Milton, *The American Nazis: Some Recent Developments* (New York: American Jewish Committee, 1974).

———, *American Nazis -- Myth or Menace?* (New York: American Jewish Committee, 1977).

Ford, Simon, *Wreckers of Civilisation: The Story of COUM Transmission and Throbbing Gristle* (London: Black Dog Publishing, 1999).

Gardell, Mattias, *Gods of the Blood: The Pagan Revival and White Separatism* (Durham, North Carolina: Duke University Press, 2003).

Goodrick-Clarke, Nicholas, *Black Sun: Aryan Cults, Esoteric Nazism and the Politics of Identity* (New York: NYU Press, 2002).

———, *Hitler's Priestess: Savitri Devi, the Hindu-Aryan Myth, and Neo-Nazism* (New York: NYU Press, 1998).

———, *The Occult Roots of Nazism: Secret Aryan Cults and Their Influence on Nazi Ideology* (New York: NYU Press, 1985/1992).

Kaplan, Jeffrey, ed., *Encyclopedia of White Power: A Sourcebook on the Radical Racist Right* (Walnut Creek, California: Altamira Press/Roman & Littlefield, 2000).

Kerr, Martin, *The History of American National Socialism, New Order* (n.d.), www.theneworder.org/NS-History.html

Macklin, Graham, *Failed Führers: A History of Britain's Extreme Right* (London: Routledge, 2020).

Mathews, Chris, *Modern Satanism: Anatomy of a Radical Subculture* (Westport, Connecticut: Praeger, 2009).

Michael, George, *Willis Carto and the American Far Right* (Gainesville: University Press of Florida, 2008).

Newton, Michael, *The National States Rights Party: A History* (Jefferson, North Carolina: McFarland, 2017).

Ridgeway, James, *Blood in the Face: The Ku Klux Klan, Aryan Nations, Nazi Skinheads, and the Rise of a New White Culture*, 2nd ed. (New York: Thunder Mouth Press, 1990/1995).

Saleam, Jim, "American Nazism in the Context of the American Extreme Right: 1960–1978," M.A. thesis, University of Sydney, 1985.

Schmaltz, William H., *Hate: George Lincoln Rockwell and the American Nazi Party* (Washington, DC: Brassey's, 1999).

Simonelli, Frederick J., *American Fuehrer: George Lincoln Rockwell and the American Nazi Party* (Urbana: University of Illinois Press, 1999).

Wheaton, Elizabeth, *Codename GREENKIL: The 1979 Greensboro Killings* (Athens: University of Georgia Press, 1987).

Zatarain, Michael, *David Duke: Evolution of a Klansman: An Unauthorized Biography* (Gretna, Louisiana: Pelican, 1990).

Zeskind, Leonard, *Blood and Politics: The History of the White Nationalist Movement from the Margins to the Mainstream* (New York: Farrar Straus Giroux, 2009).

INDEX

Pages followed by "n" refer to notes.

For Product Safety Concerns and Information please contact our EU
representative GPSR@taylorandfrancis.com
Taylor & Francis Verlag GmbH, Kaufingerstraße 24, 80331 München, Germany

www.ingramcontent.com/pod-product-compliance
Lightning Source LLC
Chambersburg PA
CBHW051946270326
41929CB00015B/2553

9 780367 190606